The Fourth Genre

The Fourth Genre

Contemporary Writers of/on Creative Nonfiction

SECOND EDITION

Robert L. Root, Jr.
Central Michigan University

Michael Steinberg
Michigan State University

Longman

New York   San Francisco   Boston
London   Toronto   Sydney   Tokyo   Singapore   Madrid
Mexico City   Munich   Paris   Cape Town   Hong Kong   Montreal

Vice President and Editor-in-Chief: Joseph Opiela
Vice President: Eben W. Ludlow
Marketing Manager: Melanie Craig
Supplements Editor: Donna Campion
Full Service Production Manager: Mark Naccarelli
Project Coordination, Text Design, and Electronic Page Makeup: Nesbitt Graphics, Inc.
Cover Design Manager: Wendy Ann Fredericks
Cover Designer: Kay Petronio
Cover Photos: Locket: Kay Petronio; Leaf © Jeff Venier/Artville
Manufacturing Buyer: Al Dorsey
Printer and Binder: Hamilton Printing Company
Cover Printer: The Lehigh Press, Inc.

For permission to use copyrighted material, grateful acknowledgement is made to the copyright holders on pp. 435–438, which are hereby made part of this copyright page.

Library of Congress Cataloging-in-Publication Data

The fourth genre : contemporary writers of/on creative nonfiction/[compiled by] Robert L. Root, Jr., Michael Steinberg.—2nd ed.
    p. cm
    Includes bibliographical references and index.
    ISBN 0-205-33715-5 (alk. paper)
      1. Essays.   2. Essay—Authorship. I. Root, Robert L. II. Steinberg, Michael, 1940–

PN6142.F68   2001
808.4—dc21   2001029783

Please visit our website at http://www.ablongman.com

ISBN 0-205-33715-5

   5 6 7 8 9 10—HT—04 03

The essay is a notoriously flexible and adaptable form. It possesses the freedom to move anywhere, in all directions. It acts as if all objects were equally near the center and as if "all subjects are linked to one another" (Montaigne) by free association. This freedom can be daunting, not only for the novice essayist confronting such latitude but for the critic attempting to pin down its formal properties.

—*Phillip Lopate*

Admirers of nailed-down definitions and tidy categories may not like to hear it, but all writers and readers are full-time imaginers, all prose is imaginative, and fiction and nonfiction are just two anarchic shades of ink swirling around the same mysterious well. Those of us who would tell a story can only dip in our pens. We can never claim full certainty as to which shade of ink we're using.

—*David James Duncan*

The boundaries of creative nonfiction will always be as fluid as water.

—*Mary Clearman Blew*

Don't spread it around, but it's a sweet time to be an essayist.

—*Joseph Epstein*

Contents

PART **2** *Talking about Creative Nonfiction*   *223*

PART 3 *Composing Creative Nonfiction* 369

Alternative Contents

Subgenres of Creative Nonfiction

Personal Essay

Segmented Essay

Critical Essay

Literary Journalism

PARTS 2 AND 3   *Processes and Criticism of Creative Nonfiction*

Memoir

Writing

Essay

Genre Issues

Academic Writing

Preface

Beginning the Conversation

Rationale and Overview

The Fourth Genre, Second Edition, is an anthology devoted to contemporary works of creative nonfiction. The readings in all three sections encompass the genre's full spectrum: personal essays and memoirs, literary journalism, and academic/ cultural criticism. Creative nonfiction is the kind of literary writing that regularly appears in small magazines, reviews, and journals, such as *The Georgia Review, Shenandoah,* and *The American Voice;* in trade magazines, such as *Harper's, Double-take,* and *The New Yorker;* and in book-length essay and memoir collections. One of the hallmarks of this form is that the boundaries between subgenres are quite expansive. That's because its writers often braid narrative telling with fictional and poetic techniques and combine portraiture and self-reflection with reportage and critical analysis. In that regard *The Fourth Genre* highlights the elasticity and versatility of this still-evolving genre.

We also see creative nonfiction as the subject that binds together the three disparate strands in most English departments: literature, creative writing, and composition. Traditionally, the study of literature has been centered on analysis and interpretation in three genres—poetry, fiction, and drama; the study of creative writing has also focused on those genres; and composition has become the domain of nonfiction. We believe that this unnatural separation can be bridged by acknowledging creative nonfiction as the fourth genre. That is, we think of creative nonfiction simultaneously as a form of literature, as a goal of creative writing, and as the aesthetic impulse in composition.

This book, then, attempts to present creative nonfiction in a framework that emphasizes its keystone status:

- It is a reader for writers of creative nonfiction, providing a range of samples of the forms and strategies practiced by many contemporary writers.
- It is an anthology for students of nonfiction literature, providing not only examples of its variety but also theoretical and critical responses to the form by critics, teachers, and the writers themselves.

- It is a collection for students of composing practices, providing reflections on the forms and strategies by the essayists, memoirists, literary journalists, cultural critics, poets, and novelists who write creative nonfiction.

These specifications make *The Fourth Genre* most suitable for courses in composition, creative writing, and genre literature. And not coincidentally, these are the courses in which we used the book in its classroom testing stages.

The fact that each of us was simultaneously asked to develop courses in creative nonfiction at different universities also says something about the fourth genre's emergence in the past decade or so. Anthologies and collections of personal essays, nature writing, literary journalism, cultural criticism, travel writing, and memoirs have proliferated in recent years, and literary magazines have begun to include creative nonfiction and the essay among the forms they regularly publish. Workshops in creative nonfiction have also been featured at writers' conferences and writers' workshops, and individual conferences have been organized solely around "writing the self," "environmental writing," and "travel writing." *The Fourth Genre* therefore represents our attempt to compile a contemporary anthology that approaches creative nonfiction from a number of perspectives, trying not to let our efforts prescribe its boundaries or place limits on its possibilities.

Creative nonfiction encompasses a variety of styles, sensibilities, and forms. Its writers share a common desire to speak in a singular voice as active participants in their own experience. This impulse often overlaps the writer's need to mediate that experience by serving as a witness/correspondent, thus creating a unique synergy. As a result, creative nonfictionists may write to establish or define an identity, to explore and chronicle personal discoveries and changes, to examine personal conflicts, to interrogate their opinions, or to connect themselves to a larger heritage and community. Given this context, the style, focus, and structure of each work may vary. Any given piece can be lyrical, expository, meditative, informational, reflective, self-interrogative, exploratory, analytical, and/or whimsical. Moreover, a work's structure might be a traditional "linear" narrative or it may create its own disjunctive and segmented form.

To take advantage of the genre's flexibility and emphasis on the writer's presence and voice, we have chosen readings that are representative, accessible, and challenging to students in advanced composition and creative writing workshops, as well as to those in genre-specific literature courses. We assume that student readers will be asked to write their own creative nonfiction and that, at the same time, they will be developing a personal/ critical theory that reflects the genre's possibilities.

Perhaps our most vital concern is to initiate a writer-to-reader conversation on and about creative nonfiction. Therefore, we've designed the book to be interactive by dividing it into three separate yet interconnected sections: a representative anthology of personal essays, memoirs, works of literary journalism, and personal cultural criticism as currently practiced by recognized and emerging writers; a gathering of essays and articles that centers on more general matters of craft, definition, and theory; and a section in which four writers discuss how their accompanying works of creative nonfiction were composed.

This organization encourages student writers to learn their craft the way most successful writers have learned theirs: by reading what other writers have written, by picking up tips and ideas from writers about the way they write, and by applying specific strategies culled from the readings to their own writing.

Selections and Organization

The Fourth Genre's most distinctive features are the range and scope of the readings and the interconnectedness of the three sections. In selecting these particular works, we have tried to maintain a balance between writing that is serious and informal, rigorous and pleasurable. In all instances, our criteria were that the writings be stimulating and that they have literary worth; that they be wide-ranging in subject and form, familiar at times and challenging at others; and that they be strong examples of the kind of thought-provoking and authentic writing that is being done in the genre today.

In addition, several other considerations guided our choices, perhaps the most compelling of which was our desire to counterbalance the recent creative nonfiction anthologies and manuals that identify the genre as equivalent to literary journalism. Such books tend to place little emphasis on the personal, autobiographical, and "literary" impulses (discovery, exploration, reflection) that generate much of the writing we call creative nonfiction. While we think of this genre as broad and inclusive, we feel that creative nonfiction's identity is more closely connected to the spirit of Montaigne's work than it is to matters of subject, reportage, and research. That is to say, Montaigne's essays were first and foremost intimate and *personal,* and he actively cultivated self-exploration and self-discovery. As such, his writings express the digressions, meanderings, meditations, ruminations, and speculations that characterize a singular, idiosyncratic mind at work. As Montaigne himself says, "It is myself I portray."

This point of view is not meant to duck the issue of self-examination as it extends to larger connections and broader subjects. Quite the contrary. In fact, we believe along with cultural critic Marianna Torgovnick that "All writing about self and culture is personal in that writers and critics find some of their richest material in experience. . . . Often our search for personal meaning is precisely what generates our passion and curiosity for the subjects we research and write about." It is this kind of curiosity and self-exploration that mark the majority of selections in this book—be they personal essays, memoirs, reportage, academic criticism, or a commingling of more than one of these subgenres.

Other concerns that guided our choices are:

- to interest aspiring writers and curious readers who come to this genre from an assortment of academic disciplines;

- to spotlight representative, accessible writers from a variety of fields—literature, science, nature writing, women's studies, journalism, rhetoric and composition, and cultural studies among them; and
- to offer readings that remind us of the breadth and possibilities of this continually evolving genre.

To these ends, we present the reader with a broad range of published samples. In addition, we provide essays and articles by writers and teachers about the forms in which they work. Along with pieces by established writers, we've tried to select works that are less frequently taught and anthologized—provocative writing that we think will stimulate fresh and enthusiastic responses from students and teachers. In choosing these particular readings, we're hoping that *The Fourth Genre* will generate numerous alternatives for using creative nonfiction in the classroom.

Part One, Writing Creative Nonfiction, is an anthology/sampler of contemporary creative nonfiction. It is intended to showcase the variety of voices and personas, the flexibility and expansiveness, and the range of subject matter and structures that creative nonfiction is able to embrace. Part One is also a representative mix of thematic explorations, self-portraitures, investigations into subject matter and ideas, and personal discoveries and disclosures. Not only do the specific subjects change as they are taken up by different writers, but also the techniques each writer uses to explore his or her subject can vary widely. Some writers use straightforward narrative and reportage; others blend narrative telling with fictional techniques such as scenes, characters, and dialogue; and still others explore their subjects in more lyrical, discursive, or poetic ways.

However diverse these approaches might be, the individual pieces are marked by the distinctiveness of the author's presence, no matter whether he or she is the center of the piece or an observer-reporter. Therefore, in all the writings in this section we witness the mind of the writer as he or she attempts to examine what Marianna Torgovnick describes as "some strongly felt experience, deeply held conviction, long-term interest, or problem that has irritated the mind."

In Part Two, Talking about Creative Nonfiction, we have chosen essays by working writers and teachers who are as passionate about discussing matters of craft as they are articulate in explaining their theories about the nature of creative nonfiction. Because several of these authors have also written pieces that appear in Part One, we invite the reader to pair selections to see what strategies, theories, and perspectives the writers have developed. In addition, we suggest that teachers and students explore how the essays in Part One serve as examples of the kinds of theoretical stances that the writers and teachers in Part Two advocate.

Another way to approach the writing in Part Two is to view it as a writer's conversation about the possibilities and boundaries of the genre. Consider, for example, the differing views on literal and invented truth in memoir as proposed by Mary Clearman Blew, Patricia Hampl, Fern Kupfer, and Annie Dillard; compare Phillip Lopate's idea of the personal essay as a "self-interrogative form" with Scott Russell Sander's notion of the essayist as "the singular first-person"; or examine passionate yet differing approaches by Marianna Torgovnick and Jane Tompkins to using the personal voice in academic writing.

You can also use this section of the book to probe more deeply into the assortment of composing strategies—that is, the use of differing narrative stances and personas; the employment of disjunctive and segmented mosaics; and the pointedly fictional and poetical techniques that memoirists, personal essayists, literary journalists, and cultural critics adopt in their writings.

All of these perspectives, then, anchor the genre in the notions, theories, and designs of working writers, many of whom are also writing teachers. As such, they give the reader an "inside" and personal look at the various ways the genre is evolving, and at the same time they provide a broader, more inclusive view of how contemporary creative nonfiction is being written and defined.

In Part Three, Composing Creative Nonfiction, four writers add their voices to the conversation in an attempt to help the student (and teacher) bridge the gap between experienced and emergent writers. In addition to the pieces themselves, Maureen Stanton, Simone Poirier-Bures, Mary Elizabeth Pope, and Emily Chase discuss their composing processes, sharing decisions on the drafts and revisions that their works-in-progress have undergone. In so doing, they focus our attention on the writing process itself.

We created this section not only to give aspiring student writers an inside look at how these pieces evolved, but also to demonstrate the many possibilities that characterize this genre. We also think that student writers will benefit greatly from paying attention to the disclosures from emerging writers, especially as these writers supplement and reinforce the readings in Parts One and Two. In addition, the cross references between all three sections open up the conversation further by revealing additional aspects of its texts and authors. And finally, by pairing the emerging writers' works with their own comments about their work, we are encouraging and reinforcing the kind of dialogue established in Parts One and Two.

Essentially then, Part One is an anthology *of* creative nonfiction, Part Two is an anthology *on* creative nonfiction, and Part Three is a shorter collection *of and about* the writing of creative nonfiction.

The readings in all three sections and the book's interactive organization, therefore, express why we think that creative nonfiction is the most accessible and personal of all four literary genres, as well as why we believe that the time is ripe for extending this dialogue to curious and interested students.

Apparatus

In keeping with the spirit of the genre's flexibility, we have provided a minimum of editorial apparatus. We assume that teachers will mix and match whichever readings suit their inclinations and teaching designs. And rather than impose a thematic, historical, or subgeneric interpretation on its users, or lock the book into a pattern based on our course designs, we prefer to emphasize the genre's multiple dimensions and possibilities. Moreover, in keeping with our intent to acquaint students (and teachers) with the rich body of work that's being produced in creative nonfiction today, we've tried to make this anthology as flexible and user-friendly as possible. We want to give students permission to think of themselves as apprentice/fellow writers, to urge them to experience their writing as an inside out activity, and finally to guide them in learning to read in more "writerly" ways.

That said, along with this preface we have provided guidelines and rationales for using this book. The introduction, for example, offers an expanded discussion of why creative nonfiction is the fourth genre. It also contains a detailed explanation of what we think are the five main elements of creative nonfiction. In the section on Writers, Readers, and the Fourth Genre, we talk about the personal connections between writer and reader while offering specific examples of why we think of creative nonfiction as both a literary and transactional genre. Here we also discuss creative nonfiction as a genre that pushes at boundaries, as well as a genre whose practitioners write primarily to connect themselves in more intimate, expressive, and personal ways with their readers. In the section entitled Joining the Conversation, we expand on the notion of why we designed *The Fourth Genre* as an inclusive, ongoing conversation about the art and craft of writing creative nonfiction. Moreover, in the introductions to all three sections—Part One's anthology, Part Two's readings about the genre, and Part Three's dialogue on composing processes—we offer overviews of each section, as well as suggestions for using the book interactively.

Another apparatus is contained in the book's three tables of contents, all of which suggest alternative ways to read and teach *The Fourth Genre.* The table of contents at the front of the book is organized alphabetically to give teachers and students the option of deciding which readings they will match up or pair with one another. Subgenres of Creative Nonfiction, the first alternative table of contents, cross-references the readings from Parts One and Three according to Forms of Creative Nonfiction, and categorizes the Part Two and Part Three readings under the heading Processes and Criticism of Creative Nonfiction. Approaches to Writing and Discussing Creative Nonfiction, the second alternative table of contents, also categorizes the readings according to subgenres. Under each subgenre (memoir, personal essay, etc.), we offer readers three approaches for examining creative nonfiction: Writers on Their Work, Further Examples of the Form, and Further Discussion of the Form. All of these, of course, are meant to be suggestive rather than prescriptive.

In addition to the guidelines within the text, we have written a comprehensive and detailed instructor's manual. It gives specific teaching suggestions and explanations for using the text in three different classroom settings. More specifically, it provides an assortment of options for organizing the materials in composition, creative writing, and literary genre courses. In all instances we've included brief discussions of the readings as creative nonfiction, as well as suggestions for pairing or clustering selections according to subgenres, compatible themes, and issues of craft. We've also designed questions that offer different perspectives on the readings and address matters of composing. Finally, we have provided a variety of writing prompts and suggestions for dealing with students' writing in all three classroom settings.

Acknowledgments

The paths by which the two of us have come to creative nonfiction are familiar to many writers and teachers. Writing has played an important role in both of our lives. It has been the subject of college courses and post-college workshops in poetry, fiction, drama, essay, environmental writing, film writing, and professional writing. It has been the preoccupation that has produced both published and unpublished work in a variety of forms—creative nonfiction, of course, but also poetry, fiction, drama, sports journalism, and radio commentary. As it does for so many other writers, the habit of writing colors the way we approach almost everything we do in life.

We also have been teachers for most of our adult lives, particularly of writing courses and courses on the teaching of composition. Happily, the center of our teaching and our scholarship alike has been the study of and immersion in the activity that energizes our nonacademic lives.

In recent years, we have initiated courses in creative nonfiction in Western Michigan University's MFA/Ph.D. program, in Michigan State University's American Studies graduate program, and in Central Michigan University's Composition and Communication master's program. As we designed these courses and consulted with one another, we agreed to encourage our students to write essays that covered a range of contemporary creative nonfiction and to give them a range of strategies through which to do that. Moreover, we invited them into the genre by asking them to consider not only what contemporary writers were publishing but also what those same writers were saying about the kind of work they do. As an ongoing activity, we continued to share our own work-in-progress with our students and to "publish" anthologies of student writing within the classes.

And so we have come to this book attempting to center creative nonfiction, to keep centered on it as writers and teachers and students of the fourth genre ourselves, and to invite further speculation about it by readers, writers, and teachers interested in how we write, think about, and teach creative nonfiction now.

Along the way we have been aided in our growth as writers and development as teachers of creative nonfiction by an array of colleagues, students, and teachers, as well by both our partners. In particular, we want to acknowledge the following:

From Michael Steinberg: The students in English 631 at Western Michigan University and Shirley Clay Scott, former English chair at Western, who gave me the opportunity to develop the MFA/Ph.D. program's first creative nonfiction workshop; the students in American Studies 891 at Michigan State University, and Peter Levine, the program's director, and David Cooper, the current acting director, for allowing me free rein in designing my course; Donald Murray, whose writing and teaching has continued to inspire me; Skip Renker, who provided valuable input and advice when I needed it; Doug Noverr, my department chair, and Pat McConeghy, associate dean of Arts and Letters, both of whom granted me release time from teaching to complete this book; Lee Hope, the director of the Stonecoast Writer's Conference, who over the course of three summers gave me the opportunity to develop a creative nonfiction workshop in conjunction with five wonderful colleagues: Phyllis Barber, David Bradley, Stephen Dunn, David Huddle, and Syd Lea. My special thanks to them for showing me how it's done. Thanks as well to Dr. Sam Plyler, who kept the faith throughout this project. And finally to Carole Berk Steinberg, my gratitude, as always, for her unconditional support and unflagging encouragement.

From Robert Root: The students in English 601 and English 593 at Central Michigan University, who first responded to these readings and wrote so many memorable essays themselves, in particular Carol Sanford, Mary Beth Pope, Sandra Smith, Emily Chase, and Amy Hough; the clerical staff in the Department of English at CMU, headed by Carol Swan and Carole Pasche, particularly the student assistants who worked on this manuscript, Jennifer Baars, Kelli S. Fedewa, Star Ittu, and Gretchen M. Morley; Becky Wildfong, Tom Root, and Caroline Root, good writers all; and Susan Root, whose understanding and support make all burdens lighter.

We are grateful for the recommendations and advice of the reviewers of the first edition of the anthology, including Charles Anderson, University of Arkansas at Little Rock, and Doug Hesse, Illinois State University, and reviewers who recommended changes for the second edition, including Kim Barnes, University of Idaho, John Boe, University of California, Davis, Megan Fulwiler, University of New Hampshire, Toby Fulwiler, University of Vermont, Brenda Mann Hammack, Roanoke College, Frederick S. Lapisardi, California University of Pennsylvania, Simone Poirer-Bures, Virginia Polytechnic Institute and State University, Dale Rigby, Western Kentucky University, Mimi Schwartz, Richard Stockton College of New Jersey, and Maureen Stanton, Ohio State University. We are also grateful for the assistance of Grace Trudo and the expert guidance of Eben Ludlow.

Robert L. Root, Jr. and Michael Steinberg

Introduction

Creative Nonfiction, the Fourth Genre

Creative nonfiction is the fourth genre. This assumption, declared in the title of this book, needs a little explaining. Usually literature has been divided into three major genres or types: poetry, drama, and fiction. Poets, dramatists, and novelists might arrange this trio in a different order, but the idea of three literary genres has, until very recently, dominated introductory courses in literature, generic divisions in literature textbooks, and categories of literature in bookstores. Everything that couldn't be classified in one of these genres or some subgenre belonging to them (epic poetry, horror novels) was classified as "nonfiction," even though, as Jocelyn Bartkevicius points out elsewhere in this collection, they could be classified as "nonpoetry" just as well. Unfortunately, this classification system suggests that everything that is nonfiction should also be considered nonliterature, a suggestion that is, well, nonsense.

We refer to creative or literary nonfiction as the fourth genre as a way of reminding readers that literary genres are not limited to three; we certainly do not intend the term to indicate ranking of the genres but rather to indicate their equality. It would be better to have a more succinct, exclusive term for the genre. Writers have been composing literary forms of nonfiction for centuries, even if only recently have they begun to use the terms *creative nonfiction* or *literary nonfiction* to separate it from the nonliterary forms of nonfiction. And, after all, although it is creative or imaginative or literary, its being nonfiction is still what distinguishes it from the other literary genres.

The shape of creative nonfiction is, in Robert Atwan's phrase, "malleable" and, in O. B. Hardison's, "Protean." Perhaps we can picture its throbbing, pulsing, mercurial existence as locations on a series of intersecting lines connecting the poles of the personal and the public, the diary and the report, the informal and the formal, the marginalia and the academic article, the imaginative and the expository. Creative nonfiction essays would be located on these lines somewhere within the boundaries set by neighboring genres, not only "the three creative genres" of fiction, poetry, and drama but also the "expressive" genres of diary, journal, and autobiography and the "objective" genres of traditional (as opposed to literary) journalism, criticism, and polemic and technical writing. It may be fair to say that creative nonfiction centers in the essay but continually strains against the boundaries of other genres, endeavoring to push them back and to expand its own space without altering its own identity.

The Elements of Creative Nonfiction

Yet despite all the elusiveness and malleability of the genre and the variety of its shapes, structures, and attitudes, works of creative nonfiction share a number of common elements, although they may not all be present all the time in uniform proportions. The most pronounced common elements of creative nonfiction are *personal presence, self-discovery and self-exploration, veracity, flexibility of form*, and *literary approaches to nonfiction*.

Personal Presence

Writers of creative nonfiction tend to make their personal presence felt in the writing. Whatever the subject matter may be—and it can be almost anything— most creative nonfiction writing, as Rosellen Brown says of the essay, "presents itself, if not as precisely true, then as an emanation of an identifiable speaking voice making statements for which it takes responsibility" (5). In such writing the reader encounters "a persona through whose unique vision experience or information will be filtered, perhaps distorted, perhaps questioned"; the writer's voice creates an identity that "will cast a shadow as dense and ambiguous as that of an imaginary protagonist. The self is surely a created character" (5).

Throughout the various forms of creative nonfiction, whether the subject is the writer's self (as perhaps in personal essays and memoirs) or an objective, observed reality outside the self (as perhaps in nature essays and personal cultural criticism), the reader is taken on a journey into the mind and personality of the writer. Some writers directly engage in interrogations of the self by unequivocally examining and confronting their own memories, prejudices, fears, even weaknesses. Others are more meditative and speculative, using the occasion of remembered or observed experience to connect to issues that extend beyond the self and to celebrate or question those connections. Still others establish greater distance from their subjects, taking more of an observer's role than a participant's role. Yet even as they stand along the sidelines we are aware of their presence, because their voice is personal, individual, not omniscient.

This sense of the author's presence is a familiar element of essays and memoirs, of course. These center on the author's private reflections and experiences. As essayist Phillip Lopate writes,

> The hallmark of the personal essay is its intimacy. The writer seems to be speaking directly into your ear, confiding everything from gossip to wisdom. Through sharing thoughts, memories, desires, complaints, and whimsies, the personal essayist sets up a relationship with the reader, a dialogue—a friend-

ship, if you will, based on identification, understanding, testiness, and companionship. (xxiii)

But personal presence can also pull subject-oriented writing (principally journalistic and academic writing) into the realm of creative nonfiction. Arguing a need for "writerly models for writing about culture," Marianna Torgovnick insists, "Writing about culture is personal. Writers find their material in experience as well as books, and they leave a personal imprint on their subjects. They must feel free to explore the autobiographical motivation for their work, for often this motivation is precisely what generates writers' interests in their topics" (3). Including this personal voice in cultural criticism surrenders some of the authority—or the pretense of authority—generally found in academic writing, but substitutes for it the authority of apparent candor or personal honesty. What Rosellen Brown writes of the personal essayist is applicable to all creative nonfiction writers: "the complex delight of the essayist's voice is that it can admit to bewilderment without losing its authority" (7). This sense of personal presence is one of the most forceful elements of creative nonfiction.

Self-Discovery and Self-Exploration

As many writers in this book suggest—either directly or indirectly—this genre encourages self-discovery, self-exploration, and surprise. Often, the writer "is on a journey of discovery, often unasked for and unplanned," Rosellen Brown writes. "The essayist is an explorer, whereas the fiction writer is a landed inhabitant" (7). Phillip Lopate speaks of self-discovery that takes place in essays as writing that "not only monitors the self but helps it gel. The essay is an enactment of the creation of the self" (xliv). This genre grants writers permission to explore without knowing where they will end up, to be tentative, speculative, reflective. Because writing creative nonfiction so often reveals and expresses the writer's mind at work and play, the genre permits us to chart the more whimsical, nonrational twists and turns of our own imaginations and psyches. More frequently than not, the subject matter becomes the catalyst or trigger for some personal journey or inquiry or self-interrogation. Writers who seem most at home with this genre are those who like to delve and to inquire, to question, to explore, probe, meditate, analyze, turn things over, brood, worry—all of which creative nonfiction allows, even encourages.

Such interests may seem at first glance appropriate only to a narrow range of "confessional writing," but in much of the best creative nonfiction, writers use self-disclosure as a way of opening their writing to a more expansive exploration. This genre, then, is a good choice for writers who like to reach for connections that extend beyond the purely personal. As W. Scott Olson writes, "As the world becomes more problematic, it is in the little excursions and small observations that we can discover ourselves, that we can make an honest connection with others, that we can remind each other of what it means to belong to one another" (viii).

Flexibility of Form

One of the most exciting elements of creative nonfiction is the way in which contemporary writers "stretch the limits of the form" and "are developing a [nonfiction] prose that lives along the borders of fiction and poetry" (Atwan x). Contemporary creative nonfiction uses the full range of style and structure available to other literary and nonliterary forms. Most often, readers have noticed the use of fictional devices in creative nonfiction, particularly in what is termed *the nonfiction novel* or in certain examples of literary journalism, which Mark Kramer has defined as "extended digressive narrative nonfiction" (21). Rosellen Brown, who refers to the personal essay as a "nonfiction narrative," believes it is "every bit as much an imaginative construction as a short story" and that "it must use some, if not all, of the techniques of fiction: plot, characterization, physical atmosphere, thematic complexity, stylistic appropriateness, psychological open-endedness" (5).

And yet, while narrative elements may frequently play a part in creative nonfiction, the genre often works with lyrical, dramatic, meditative, expository, and argumentative elements as well. As Annie Dillard says, "The essay can do everything a poem can do, and everything a short story can do—everything but fake it" (xvii). It can also do everything a diary, a journal, a critical article, an editorial, a feature, and a report can do.

Moreover, perhaps more frequently than in other genres, creative nonfiction writers are likely to innovate and experiment with structure. They draw not only on narrative chronology and linear presentation but also on nonlinear, "disjunctive," or associative strategies. They use different angles and perspectives to illuminate a point or explore an idea, drawing on visual and cinematic techniques such as collages, mosaics, montages, and jump cuts. They can leap backward and forward in time, ignoring chronology of event to emphasize nonsequential connections and parallels; they can structure the essay around rooms in a house or cards in a tarot deck; they can interrupt exposition or narrative with passages from journals and letters or scenes from home movies. Part of the excitement of the genre is its openness to creative forms as well as to creative contents, its invitation to experiment and push at boundaries between genres, and its ability to draw on an unlimited range of literary techniques.

Veracity

Because it sometimes draws on the material of autobiography, history, journalism, biology, ecology, travel writing, medicine, and any number of other subjects, creative nonfiction is reliably factual, firmly anchored in real experience, whether the author has lived it or observed and recorded it. As essayist and memoirist Annie Dillard writes, "The elements in any nonfiction should be true not only artistically—the connects must hold at base and must be veracious, for that is the convention and the covenant between the nonfiction writer and his reader" ("Introduction" xvii). Like the rest of us, the nonfiction writer, she says, "thinks about actual things. He can make sense of them analytically or artistically. In either case he renders the real world coherent and meaningful, even if only bits of it, and even if that coherence and meaning reside only inside small texts" (xvii). For critic Barbara Lounsbery, who is principally speaking of literary journalism, factuality is central, by which she means: "Documentable subject matter chosen from the real world as opposed to 'invented' from the writer's mind"; she adds that "anything in the natural world is game for the nonfiction artist's attention" (xiii).

But factuality or veracity is a trickier element than it seems. As David James Duncan observes,

> We see into our memories in much the way that we see across the floor of a sunbaked desert: everything we conjure, every object, creature, or event we perceive in there, is distorted, before it reaches us, by mirages created by subjectivity, time, and distance. . . . The best that a would-be nonfiction writer can do is use imperfect language to invoke imperfectly remembered events based on imperfect perceptions. (55)

Artistry needs some latitude; self-disclosure may be too risky to be total, particularly when it involves disclosure of others. Just as Thoreau compressed two years at Walden Pond into one to get the focus he needed for his great book, creative nonfiction writers sometimes alter the accuracy of events in order to achieve the accuracy of interpretation. Some of this is inadvertent—the great challenge of memoir writing is knowing how much we remember is reliable and accepting the likelihood that we are "inventing the truth." "You can't put together a memoir without cannibalizing your own life for parts," Annie Dillard writes in "To Fashion a Text." "The work battens on your memories. And it replaces them" (70). Memories blur over time and edit themselves into different forms that others who had the same experience might not recognize. Finding the language to describe experience sometimes alters it, and your description of the experience becomes the memory, the way a photograph does. At the least we may feel a need to omit the irrelevant detail or protect the privacy of others not as committed to our self-disclosure as we are. The truth may not necessarily be veracious enough to take into court or into a laboratory; it need only be veracious enough to satisfy the writer's purpose and the art of the writing.

Literary Approaches to Nonfiction

The language of creative nonfiction is as literary, as imaginative, as that of other literary genres and is similarly used for lyrical, narrative, and dramatic effects. What separates creative nonfiction from "noncreative nonfiction" (if we can be forgiven the use of that term for a moment to categorize all nonfiction outside this genre) is not only "the unique and subjective focus, concept, context and point of view in which the information is presented and defined" (Gutkind v–vi) but also the ways in which language serves the subject. This is partly what Chris

Anderson is alluding to when he writes that certain essays and journalism are not literary (x), and what Barbara Lounsbery means by claiming that, no matter how well the other elements of a nonfiction work are achieved, "it may still fail the standards of literary nonfiction if its language is dull or diffuse" (xv). When Annie Dillard turned from writing poetry to writing literary nonfiction, she

> was delighted to find that nonfiction prose can also carry meaning in its structures and, like poetry, can tolerate all sorts of figurative language, as well as alliteration and even rhyme. The range of rhythms in prose is larger and grander than it is in poetry, and it can handle discursive ideas and plain information as well as character and story. It can do everything. I felt as though I had switched from a single reed instrument to a full orchestra. ("To Fashion" 74–75)

When writers of poetry or fiction turn to creative nonfiction, as poet Mary Karr does in her memoir, *The Liar's Club,* or poet Garrett Hongo does in his memoir, *Volcano,* they bring with them the literary language possible in those other genres and are able to use it.

Poets and novelists aren't the only ones drawing on literary techniques in nonfiction. Some journalists have taken so literary an approach to their reportage that they have created a writing form that straddles literature and journalism, and often can be identified as a form of creative nonfiction. In addition, a number of primarily academic writers have sought a more personal perspective in the cultural criticism they write. They have made the language of their academic discourse more expansive, more intimate, more literary, allowing the reader to share their subjective reactions to the ideas and experiences they discuss. Like Thoreau, they retain rather than omit "the *I,* or first person," acknowledging, as he did, that we "commonly do not remember that it is, after all, always the first person that is speaking" (3). By doing so they do not simply present their information or opinions but also extend *themselves* toward the reader and draw the reader closer. In essence, they move the written work beyond presentation into conversation.

The writer in creative nonfiction is often the reader's guide, pointing out the sights along the way, the places of interest where special attention is required. In such writing the reader is treated like a spectator or an audience. But often the writer is the reader's surrogate, inviting her to share the author's space in imagination and to respond to the experience as if she is living it. In such writing the reader is treated like a participant. In creative nonfiction, then, in addition to exploring the information being presented—the ways in which various ideas, events, or scenes connect to one another and relate to some overarching theme or concept or premise—the reader also has to examine the role the writer takes in the work. The writer's role and the structure of the writing are not as predictable in creative nonfiction as they are in other forms, such as the news article or the academic research paper, the sermon or the lecture. The structure of the essay or article may be experimental or unexpected, an attempt to generate literary form out of subject matter instead of trying to wedge subject matter into an all-purpose literary form. When it departs from linear, tightly unified forms to achieve its purpose, contemporary creative nonfiction does not simply meander or ramble like the traditional essay ("My Style and my mind alike go roaming," Montaigne said [761]); instead, it moves in jump cuts, flashbacks, flash-forwards, concentric or parallel or tangential strands. Readers sometimes have to let the works themselves tell them how they should be read.

Writers, Readers, and the Fourth Genre

The interaction between the writer and the genre in which the writer works influences the outcome of the work. Writers of other nonfiction forms such as criticism, journalism, scholarship, or technical and professional writing tend to leave themselves out of the work and to view the work as a means to an end; they want to explain, report, inform, or propose. For them the text they produce is a vehicle, a container or package, to transport information and ideas to someone else, the intended readers. Some people have referred to these forms as *transactional writing*. Writers of other literary forms such as poetry, fiction, and drama tend to put themselves in the work and to view the work as an end in itself; they want to reflect, explore, speculate, imagine, and discover, and the text they create is a structure, an anchored shape like a sculpture or a monument or a building, to which interested readers are drawn. The result is often called *poetic* or *creative writing*. Writers of creative nonfiction by definition share the qualities of both groups of writers, and the work they create reflects varying measures of both kinds of writing.

Many creative nonfiction writers whose works are found in this book joined this conversation from the direction of their writing in other literary genres. Experienced poets or fictionists, they came to the fourth genre by way of personal essays and memoirs, nonfiction forms compatible with the desire for lyric and narrative expression, the desire to give voice to memory and meditation and acts of emotional and intellectual discovery. They came to it not only because of a need to write nonfiction but also because of a desire for creative expression. Similarly, creative nonfiction is also written by critics, journalists, and scholars who approach their writing in the way that essayists and memoirists do—that is, by inhabiting the work and by approaching it from a literary perspective more than (or as much as) from a critical, reportorial, or scholarly perspective.

We do not necessarily see sharply definable boundaries here, whose coordinates we can map precisely—neighboring nonfiction forms often share the same terrain for a long distance on either side of their common border. Yet, just as when you are traveling you don't need precise knowledge of geography or topography to sense that you're not in Kansas (or Vermont or California) anymore, so in reading you can also sense when a text is a work of "literary" nonfiction and not the "transactional" forms usual to journalism, scholarship, or criticism.

Because nonfiction in general has sometimes, mistakenly, been regarded as if it were an arid, barren wasteland of nonliterature surrounding lush, fertile oases of literature, it is important to make this clear: a great deal of nonfiction has always been literary, and it is the contemporary writers of literary or creative forms of nonfiction who are the focus of this book. The nonliterary forms of nonfiction are not our focus, but in some of those forms it is frequently difficult to notice when a writer slips over the border into the literary form. To make it easier to talk about creative nonfiction, then, we urge you to see it centered in the approaches taken by the essayist and memoirist and spiraling outward toward aesthetically oriented critics and literary journalists.

Readers come to creative nonfiction with different expectations from those they bring to the other genres. At the core of those expectations may be, in a sense, the hope of becoming engaged in a conversation. Much fiction, drama, poetry, and film is presented as performance, as entertainment essentially enclosed within itself—we are usually expected to appreciate or admire its creators' artistry whether we are encouraged to acknowledge their intensity or insight. Much nonliterary nonfiction (various forms of journalism and academic writing, for example) is presented as a transaction delivering information, sometimes objective, sometimes argumentative—we are usually expected to receive or accept their creators' knowledge or data the way we would a lecture or a news broadcast. Creative nonfiction, which is simultaneously literary and transactional, integrates these discourse aims: it brings artistry to information and actuality to imagination, and it draws on the expressive aim that lies below the surface in all writing. Expressive writing breaks the surface most notably in personal writing such as journals, diaries, and letters, but it has connected with the reader most prominently in the personal or familiar essay. Other forms of writing have at center the personal impulse, the need for expression, but the essay has traditionally been the outlet by which that impulse finds public voice.

Readers turn to creative nonfiction to find a place to connect to the personal voice, to connect not to art or knowledge alone but to another mind. This means that writers too have a place to connect, a genre that gives them permission to speak in the first person singular, not only about their knowledge and their beliefs but also about their uncertainties and their passions, not only about where they stand but also about the ways they arrived there, not only about the worlds they have either imagined or documented but also about the worlds they have experienced or inhabit now. Creative nonfiction may be the genre in which both reader and writer feel most connected to one another.

Joining the Conversation

We think of *The Fourth Genre* as an inclusive, ongoing conversation about the art and craft of writing creative nonfiction. We want to exemplify and describe this evolving genre, allow it to define itself and preserve its vital elasticity, and avoid arbitrary and imprecise subcategorizing and classifying. Unlike conversations in real life, a conversation in an anthology allows only one speaker at a time to speak and no one is interrupted by anyone else. The reader is the one who has to make the individual speakers connect. We've tried to make the conversation a little easier to follow by putting the speakers in different rooms. The people who simply share their own examples of creative nonfiction have the largest room, at the front of the anthology, where the writing more or less speaks for itself. The people who have ideas and opinions about the nature of this genre, the kinds of writing it contains and the kinds of writers who produce it, have another room, where both those who write creative nonfiction and those who study or examine it have their opportunities to speak. In the final room are those who attempt to explain how they wrote their own specific examples of creative nonfiction—the circumstances of composition and the tribulations of drafting and revising—where the conversation focuses on the composing processes of working writers.

In real life you would not be able to hear all the speakers in this conversation, but in an anthology you can, because the speakers wait until you get to them before they speak. In spite of the layout of the place, you should feel free to wander back and forth among the rooms, following someone else's recommendations or your own inclinations and intuitions. Naturally, we encourage you to join the conversation, provide your own examples, discuss your own ideas of genre, theory, and technique, share your own composing processes.

Read selections in Part One, Writing Creative Nonfiction, to get a sense of the range of contemporary creative nonfiction. The writers here reveal the variety of voices and personas, the flexibility and expansiveness, and the breadth of subject matter and structures creative nonfiction may adopt. It is a representative blend. It includes examples of the personal essay, the memoir, the travel essay, the nature essay, literary journalism, and personal cultural criticism. (See the Alternative Contents: Subgenres of Creative Nonfiction for further subdivisions and categories.) These selections also present a range of forms and structures, from the narrative and the lyrical to the discursive and the reportorial, from the traditional (chronology or argument) to the individual and unconventional (unique arrangements of segments or organization around a pattern of tarot cards).

Many of these works demonstrate the futility of labels, qualifying easily under the genre heading of creative nonfiction for personal presence, literary language, and other defining elements but straddling the boundaries of two or more subgenres, perhaps simultaneously literary journalism and personal essay, travel narrative and environmental reporting, or memoir and cultural criticism. Instead they model the intimate relationship between form and content in creative nonfiction. Perhaps they will also suggest to you ways to invent forms that serve your own ends as a writer.

Read selections in Part Two, Talking about Creative Nonfiction, to get a sense of what writers, critics, and scholars have to say about the nature of creative nonfiction and its various subgenres. Many of the authors in this section have also written selections in Part One. They take the form personally, sometimes discussing their own personal motives and composing strategies, sometimes the elements of the form in which they work. As some of them point out, the tradition of essayist goes back centuries, to the work of Montaigne, Addison and Steele, Lamb and Hazlitt, and as this genre reemerges, it is contemporary practitioners, for the most part—the people who write and teach creative nonfiction—who are setting the terms of this conversation. This section mixes thoughts, opinions, speculations, critiques, theories, and assertions by working writers about the art and craft of their genre.

Many of the Part Two pieces can be paired with essays in Part One. Writing in Part One often serves as examples of the more theoretical positions in Part Two; writing in Part Two often gives new perspective on writing in Part One. So you can compare memoirs with the memoirists' discussion of the form, essays with the essayists' reflections on being essayists, cultural criticism with the critics' justifications for personal academic writing.

Other authors also give us insight into the forms and issues of creative nonfiction—the art of the memoir or of literary journalism, the elements of the disjunctive form or the question of truthfulness in nonfiction texts. Such essays attempt to give a personal perspective to a critical speculation on the forms in which the writers are working. They ground the genre in the behaviors and motives of working writers rather than in disembodied theories of literature or composing. They give the reader the opportunity to step back from the individual readings and take a longer view of process and text.

Read selections in Part Three, Composing Creative Nonfiction, for a sense of the work habits, craft techniques, and serendipity used to create a work of creative nonfiction. Here a group of writers discuss their composing processes for specific works, also reproduced in this section. They share drafts, explain revisions, and map the motives for changes in their works-in-progress. They focus our attention in this conversation on the most fundamental aspect of the work, the composing itself, and bring us to the place where the reader can continue the conversation as a writer. If Part One gives us examples of the variety of creative nonfiction and Part Two gives us a lively discussion of the practices and products of the genre, Part Three gives us a chance to sit at the shoulder of the writer herself and follow her through the twists and turns of creation. These writers reflect in their practices the ways writers in other parts of the book created their own selections. By example they suggest ideas and strategies that we can use in our own composing processes.

We think the fourth genre is the most accessible and urgent genre. It may not be necessary to read all three parts of this book or to read all selections in the parts you do read to get a sense of what creative nonfiction is about. We hope the book is flexible enough that readers can get what they want from it by coming at it from a number of different directions. Yet readers who do read in all three parts will get a fuller understanding of the breadth and power of this genre. And because the time is particularly right for other writers to join this conversation, we hope that wide reading in this book will help spur your writing of creative nonfiction and give you a writer's perspective on the art and craft of the fourth genre.

Robert L. Root, Jr. and Michael Steinberg

Works Cited

Anderson, Chris. "Introduction: Literary Nonfiction and Composition." *Literary Nonfiction: Theory, Criticism, Pedagogy.* Ed. Chris Anderson. Carbondale: Southern Illinois UP, 1989. ix–xxvi.

Atwan, Robert. "Foreword." *The Best American Essays 1988.* Boston: Ticknor and Fields, 1988. ix–xi.

Brown, Rosellen. "Introduction." *Ploughshares* 20:2/3 (Fall 1994): 5–8.

Dillard, Annie. "Introduction." *The Best American Essays 1988.* Boston: Ticknor and Fields, 1988. xiii–xxii.

———. "To Fashion a Text." *Inventing the Truth: The Art and Craft of Memoir.* Ed. William Zinsser. Boston: Houghton-Mifflin, 1987. 53–76.

Duncan, David James. "Nonfiction = Fiction." *Orion* 15:3 (Summer 1996): 55–57.

Gutkind, Lee. "From the Editor." *Creative Nonfiction* 1:1 (1993): v–vi.

Hongo, Garrett. *Volcano: A Memoir of Hawai'i.* New York: Knopf, 1995.

Karr, Mary. *The Liar's Club: A Memoir.* New York: Viking Penguin, 1995.

Kramer, Mark. "Breakable Rules for Literary Journalists." *Literary Journalism.* Ed. Norman Sims and Mark Kramer. New York: Ballantine, 1995. 21–34.

Lopate, Phillip. "Introduction." *The Art of the Personal Essay: An Anthology from the Classical Era to the Present.* New York: Anchor/Doubleday, 1994. xxiii–liv.

Lounsbery, Barbara. *The Art of Fact: Contemporary Artists of Nonfiction.* Contributions to the Study of World Literature, No. 35. New York: Greenwood Press, 1990.

Montaigne, Michel de. *The Complete Works.* Trans. Donald M. Frame. Stanford: Stanford UP, 1957. 761.

Olson, W. Scott. "Introduction." *Old Friends, New Neighbors: A Celebration of the American Essay.* Ed. W. Scott Olson. *American Literary Review* 5:2 (Fall 1994): v–viii.

Thoreau, Henry. *Walden.* Ed. J. Lyndon Shanley. Princeton: Princeton UP, 1973. 3.

Torgovnick, Marianna. "Introduction." *Eloquent Obsessions: Writing Cultural Criticism.* Ed. Marianna Torgovnick. Durham: Duke UP, 1994.

The Fourth Genre

Part 1

Writing Creative Nonfiction

Contemporary creative nonfiction, like any other literary genre, offers a great deal of latitude to writers in terms of what they are able to do in the form. "There are as many kinds of essays as there are human attitudes or poses," the great American essayist E. B. White once observed. "The essayist rises in the morning and, if he has work to do, selects his garb from an unusually extensive wardrobe: he can pull on any sort of shirt, be any sort of person, according to his mood or his subject matter—philosopher, scold, jester, raconteur, confidant, devil's advocate, enthusiast" (vii). In general the observation is appropriate for the whole range of creative nonfiction.

This section of the book samples widely from the range of contemporary creative nonfiction. Its selections reveal the variety of voices and personas, the flexibility and expansiveness, and the range of subject matter and structures creative nonfiction may adopt. It is a representative blend, demonstrating the malleability of the genre. Some pieces are fairly straightforward examples of the traditional personal essay, such as Kathleen Norris exploring the paradoxical theme of celibate passions and Phillip Lopate rambling discursively over the subject of his own body. Others center on nature or environmental or ecological topics but vary their approaches; Linda Hogan centers on a single flower discovered while walking, Annie Dillard makes an intimate experience of an encounter with a weasel, and Gretel Ehrlich gives us a journal-like essay on sheepherding. Some examples of literary journalism center on different approaches to examining place, as Pico Iyer does with Los Angeles International Airport, John McPhee with Scotland, and André Aciman with Illiers-Combray. The personal approach to cultural criticism allows Vicki Hearne to explore the intelligence of primates and Jane Tompkins to ponder the significance of a museum commemorating Buffalo Bill Cody.

The range of approaches within a subgrouping suggests the flexibility of the form, the ways writers use creative nonfiction not as a vessel to be filled with meaning but rather as a way of constructing a shape appropriate to the meaning they create by writing. The ways that Mary Clearman Blew, Judith Ortiz Cofer, and Patricia Hampl present their remembrances of parents and of childhood vary

1

as much as did their experiences growing up. The techniques with which other memoirists present the past vary as well. For example, Phyllis Barber uses a highly fictional technique of development for her childhood visit to the atomic bomb site, Frank Conroy presents his memoir of shooting pool almost as an instruction manual, and Naomi Shihab Nye conducts her piece as a lyrical essay rather than a personal narrative. These readings suggest that the writer's feeling about the subject has more to do with the way the final version reads than any arbitrary set of generic guidelines. Even as we hint at the variety of pieces in this part of the book, we have to acknowledge the futility of labels. Most of the selections can be classified in a number of ways. For example, Brenda Peterson's "Animal Allies" can be treated as an example of American nature writing and set beside the other writing on that subject, but it is set in a classroom with such detail that it simultaneously can be regarded as a personal essay on child psychology and as an article on teaching. Here, as in so many of these readings, we discover again that it is not a uniform structure or organization that links these selections but the common thread of the writer's personal presence, sometimes at considerable remove in essays not obviously about personal experience yet nevertheless there, examining subject matter in the light of personal inquiry.

A number of these pieces are what we term *segmented essays,* selections that try out nonlinear patterns or structures. Mary Clearman Blew's essay weaves among different family members and different times and events to piece together elements of family history; Nancy Willard builds her essay about friendship around an arrangement of tarot cards; Naomi Shihab Nye collects three miniature memoirs under one collective heading. Such structures let us see how intimately form and content are connected in creative nonfiction and how they can be invented to serve the ends of the author. Moreover, they help extend our understanding of the range of writing that creative nonfictionists do.

"What happened to the writer is not what matters; what matters is the large sense that the writer is able to *make* of what happened," Vivian Gornick once observed, writing about the author's presence in memoirs. "The narrator in a memoir is an instrument of illumination, but it's the writing itself that provides revelation" (5). These selections suggest to us the possibilities of form, structure, voice, persona, approach, presentation, ways of describing what happened, and ways of making sense of what happened. Reading widely in Part One will not only give you a solid sense of what we write when we write creative nonfiction but will also open up your own possibilities for subject matter and design. Reading other writers triggers our own memories and our own speculations. We do not so much imitate others' subjects and structures as use them as a bridge to our resources and inventions.

Part One, Writing Creative Nonfiction, is in effect a minianthology of contemporary writing. As such it is complemented by the other two parts of the book, and we invite you to explore those other sections in connection with your reading in this part. For example, when reading the memoirs by Mary Clearman Blew and Patricia Hampl in Part One, you may want to read their essays about the memoir in Part Two, a section in which writers talk about creative nonfiction, and Simone Poirier-Bures's selections about memoir in Part Three, which pairs writers' essays with articles explaining how they wrote them. Or you might follow up Jane Tompkins's essay on the Buffalo Bill museum in Part One with readings by Tompkins and Marianna Torgovnick about personal academic writing in Part Two and Emily Chase's pair of readings in Part Three, a literary essay and an account of writing the literary essay. There are many possibilities for interaction among these three sections of the book.

Writers always find it helpful to see what other writers are doing, to hear them talk about how they are doing it, and to free-associate with their own memories and reflections from the ideas and stories that others share. Those who read these selections with a writer's eye will discover insights and perspectives that will serve their own writing well.

Works Cited

Gornick, Vivian. "The Memoir Boom." *Women's Review of Books* 13: 10–11 (July 1996): 5.
White, E. B. "Foreword." *Essays of E. B. White.* New York: HarperCollins, 1997.

In Search of Proust

André Aciman

It was by train that I had always imagined arriving in Illiers-Combray—not just any train but one of those drafty, pre–World War, rattling wagons which I like to think still leave Paris early every morning and, after hours of swaying through the countryside, squeak their way into a station that is as old and weather-beaten as all of yesteryear's provincial stops in France. The picture in my mind was always the same: the train would come to a wheezing halt and release a sudden loud chuff of steam; a door would slam open; someone would call out "Illiers-Combray"; and, finally, like the young Marcel Proust arriving for his Easter vacation just over a century ago, I would step down nervously into the small, turn-of-the-century town in Eure-et-Loir which he described so lovingly in *À la Recherche du Temps Perdu*.

Instead, when I finally made my way to Illiers-Combray, late last year, I arrived by car with Anne Borrel, the curator of the Proust Museum there, who had offered to pick me up at my Paris hotel that morning. In my pocket was a cheap and tattered Livre de Poche edition of *Swann's Way*, which I had brought in the hope that I'd find a moment to read some of my favorite passages on holy ground. That was to be my way of closing the loop, of coming home to a book I had first opened more than thirty years before.

I had bought it with my father, when I was fifteen, one summer evening in Paris. We were taking a long walk, and as we passed a small restaurant I told him that the overpowering smell of refried food reminded me of the tanneries along the coast road outside Alexandria, in Egypt, where we had once lived. He said he hadn't thought of it that way, but, yes, I was right, the restaurant did smell like a tannery. And as we began working our way back through strands of shared memories—the tanneries, the beaches, the ruined Roman temple west of Alexandria, our summer beach house—all this suddenly made him think of Proust. Had I read Proust? he asked. No, I hadn't. Well, perhaps I should. My father said this with a sense of urgency, so unlike him that he immediately tempered it, for fear I'd resist the suggestion simply because it was a parent's.

The next day, sitting in the sun on a metal chair in Lamartine Square, I read Proust for the first time. That evening, when my father asked how I had liked what I'd read, I feigned indifference, not really knowing whether I intended to spite a father who wanted me to love the author he loved most or to spite an author who had come uncomfortably close. For in the eighty-odd pages I had read that day I had rediscovered my entire childhood in Alexandria: the impassive cook, my bad-tempered aunts and skittish friends, the buzz of flies on sunny afternoons spent reading indoors when it was too hot outside, dinners in the garden with scant lights to keep mosquitoes away, the "ferruginous, interminable" peal of the garden bell announcing the occasional night guest who, like Charles Swann, came uninvited but whom everyone had nevertheless been expecting.

Every year, thousands of Prousto-tourists come to the former Illiers, which extended its name in honor of Proust's fictional town, Combray, in 1971, on the centennial of his birth. The town knows it, proclaims it, milks it. Today, Illiers-Combray sells around two thousand madeleine pastries a month. The shell-shaped cakes are displayed in the windows of pastry shops like propitiatory offerings to an unseen god and are sold by the dozen—in case one wants to take some home to friends or relatives, the way pilgrims take back holy water from the Jordan or an olive twig from Gethsemane.

For the reader on a Proustian pilgrimage, tasting a madeleine is the supreme tribute to Proust. (As no pâtisserie fails to remind the tourists, it was on tasting a madeleine, now the most famous sponge cake in the history of world literature, that the adult narrator of Proust's novel was transported to his boyhood days in Combray.) It is also a gesture of communion through which readers hope, like Proust, to come home to something bigger, more solid, and ultimately, perhaps, truer than fiction itself. Anne Borrel often tells these Proust groupies that the cult of the madeleine is blasphemous, as are the claims made by one of the *pâtissiers* that members of the *famille* Proust used to purchase their madeleines on his premises. (In earlier drafts of the novel, Proust's madeleines may have been slices of melba toast, which evolved into toasted bread, only later to metamorphose into the sponge cakes.) But no one listens. Besides, going to Illiers-Combray and not tasting a madeleine would be like going to Jerusalem and not seeing the Wailing Wall or to Greenwich and not checking your watch. Luckily, I was able to resist temptation: during my visit, on a Sunday just a few days before Christmas, all the pastry shops were closed.

Before going to the Proust Museum, Anne Borrel and I had lunch at a tiny restaurant called Le Samovar. Plump and middle-aged, Borrel is the author of a cookbook and culinary history titled *Dining with Proust*. She told me that some of the tourists come from so far away and have waited so long to make the trip that as soon as they step into Proust's house they burst into tears. I pictured refugees getting off a ship and kneeling to kiss the beachhead.

I asked about Proust's suddenly increasing popularity. "Proust," Borrel replied, "is a must." (She repeated these four words, like a verdict, several times during the day.) She reminded me that there were currently six French editions of *À la Recherche du Temps Perdu* in print. I told her that a fourth English-language edition was due to appear in 2001. And that wasn't all: trade books on Proust and coffee-table iconographies were everywhere; in Paris, I had seen at least half a dozen new books that bore Proust's name or drew on Proustian characters occupying precious space on the display tables of bookstores and department stores. Even Proust's notes, manuscripts, and publishing history had been deemed complicated enough to warrant a book of their own, called *Remembrance of Publishers Past*. Add to that T-shirts, watches, CDs, concerts, videos, scarves, posters, books on tape, newsletters, and a comic-strip version, entitled "Combray," whose first printing, of twelve thousand copies, sold out in three weeks. Not to mention the 1997–98 convention in Liège celebrating the seventy-fifth anniversary of Proust's death, with sessions on music and Proust, eating and Proust, a writing competition (on the subject of "Time Lost and Time Regained"), and a colloquium on asthma and allergies.

This kaleidoscope of Proustophernalia is matched by as many testimonials and tributes to Proust, in which he takes many forms. There is Proust the élitist and high-society snob; Proust the son of a Jewish mother; Proust the loner; Proust the dandy; Proust the analytical aesthete; Proust the soulful lovelorn boy; Proust the tart, the dissembling coquette; the Belle Époque Proust; the professional whiner; the prankster; the subversive classicist; the eternal procrastinator; and the asthmatic, hypochondriac Proust.

But the figure who lies at the heart of today's Proust revival is the intimate Proust, the Proust who perfected the studied unveiling of spontaneous feelings. Proust invented a language, a style, a rhythm, and a vision that gave memory and introspection an aesthetic scope and magnitude no author had conferred on either before. He allowed intimacy itself to become an art form. This is not to say that the vertiginous spate of memoirs that have appeared recently, with their de-rigueur regimens of child, spouse, and substance abuse, owe their existence, their voice, or their sensibility to Proust—clearly, they owe far more to Freud. But it does help to explain why Proust is more popular today, in the age of the memoir, than he has been at any other time in the century.

Like every great memoirist who has had a dizzying social life and a profoundly lonely one, Proust wrote because writing was his way of both reaching for an ever elusive world and securing his distance from it. He was among the first writers in this century to disapprove of the critics' tendency to seek correspondences between an artist's work and his private life. The slow, solitary metamorphosis of what truly happened into what, after many years, finally emerges in prose is the hallmark of Proust's labor of love.

Proust is at once the most canonical and the most uncanonical author, the most solemnly classical and the most subversive, the author in whom farce and lyricism, arrogance and humility, beauty and revulsion are indissolubly fused, and whose ultimate contradiction reflects an irreducible fact about all of us: we are driven by something as simple and as obvious as the desire to be happy, and, if that fails, by the belief that we once have been.

My conversation with Anne Borrel was interrupted by the arrival of customers outside Le Samovar. "Take a look at those four," Borrel said, pointing to the two couples dawdling at the entrance. "I'll bet you anything they're *proustiens*." She referred to all tourists as *proustiens*—meaning not Proust scholars but individuals whom the French like to call *les amis de Proust*, Proustologues, Proustolaters, Proustocentrics, Proustomaniacs, Proustophiles, Proustophiliacs, Proustoholics . . . or *fidèles* (to use a term dear to Proust's malevolent arch-snob, Mme. Verdurin).

One of the four opened the door of the restaurant and asked in a thick Spanish accent whether lunch was still being served. "*Pintades*"—Guinea hens—"are all that's left," snapped the owner of Le Samovar. Borrel and I exchanged a complicitous glance, because talk of fowl immediately brought to mind a discussion we'd had in the car about Proust's servant, Françoise, who in *Swann's Way* butchers a chicken and then curses it for not dying fast enough.

The four tourists were shown to a table. One asked the proprietor what time the Proust Museum would open that afternoon, and he regretfully informed them that the museum was closed for the holidays. They were crestfallen. "What a pity! And we've come all the way from Argentina."

Anne Borrel had heard every word of the exchange. She reminded me of a teacher who with her back turned to the class while she's writing on the blackboard knows exactly who's whispering what to whom. She leaned over and told one of the Argentines, "You may have come to the right place."

Overjoyed, the Argentine blurted out, "You mean Marcel Proust used to eat here, in this restaurant?"

"No," Borrel answered, smiling indulgently. She told them that an improvised tour of the house could be arranged after coffee, and the Argentines went back to talking softly about Proust, staring every once in a while at our table with the thrilled and wary gaze of people who have been promised a miracle.

By the time our coffee was served, we had also acquired two English and three French *proustiens*, and a warm, festive mood permeated Le Samovar. It was like the gathering of pilgrims in Chaucer's Tabard Inn. Introductions were unnecessary. We knew why we were there, and we all had a tale to tell. By then, some of us would have liked nothing more than a fireplace, a large cognac, and a little prodding to induce us to recount how we had first come to read Proust, to love Proust, how Proust had changed our lives. I was, it dawned on me, among my own.

After dessert, Borrel put on her coat. "*On y va?*" she asked, rattling a giant key chain that bore a bunch of old keys with long shafts and large, hollowed oval heads. She led us down the Rue du Docteur Proust, named after Proust's father, who by the turn of the century had helped to halt the spread of cholera in Europe. The sidewalks and streets were empty. Everyone seemed to be away for the holidays. Franco-jazz Muzak emanated from loudspeakers, mounted on various lampposts, that were apparently intended to convey a festive yule spirit, but otherwise Illiers-Combray was deserted and gray—a dull, cloying, humdrum, wintry, ashen town, where the soul could easily choke. Small wonder that Marcel developed asthma, or that he had the heebie-jeebies on returning home after long evening walks with his parents, knowing that by the time dinner was served life would hold no surprises—only the inevitable walk up the creepy staircase and that frightful drama called bedtime.

Borrel stopped at one of many nondescript doors along the empty street. She stared at it for a moment, almost as though she were trying to remember whether this was indeed the right address, then took out her keys, inserted one into the lock, and suddenly gave it a vigorous turn, yanking the door open.

"*C'est ici que tout commence*," she said.

One by one, we filed into Proust's garden. Fortunately, no one cried. Borrel pointed to a little bell at the top of the gate. I couldn't contain myself. "Could this be the ferruginous bell?" I asked. It was a question she'd heard before. She took a breath. "You mean not the large and noisy rattle which deafened with its ferruginous, interminable, frozen sound any member of the household who set it off by coming in 'without ringing,' but the double peal, 'timid, oval, gilded,' of the visitor's bell, whereupon everyone would exclaim, 'A visitor! Who on earth could it be?'" (She was quoting from memory, and every time one of us asked a question after that she would recite the answer.)

Next she led us into the restored, relatively humble middle-class house—by no means the large villa I'd always imagined. The kitchen, where I'd envisaged Françoise cooking the chicken she had viciously butchered, was a sunless alcove. The dining room, with a small round table and dark wood panelling, was a depressing melee of browns. Then we came to Marcel's bedroom, with its tiny Empire-style bed, the magic lantern that kept him company at night when he dreaded sleep, and nearby the George Sand novel bound in red. In another room was the sofa that Proust had given to his maid, Céleste Albaret, and which her daughter had donated to the museum—and which was perhaps the inspiration for the fictional sofa that Marcel inherited from his Tante Léonie, made love on, and eventually passed along to the owner of a brothel.

When Borrel indicated another room, on the second floor, I interrupted her to suggest that it must surely be the room where, under lock and key, Marcel discovered the secret pleasures of onanism. Borrel neither confirmed nor denied my allegation. She said only, "The little room that smelt of orris-root . . . [where] I explored, across the bounds of my own experience, an untrodden path which I thought was deadly." In this way, I was summarily put in my place—for presuming to show off and for implying that I could make obvious what Proust's oblique words had made explicit enough.

Back in the garden, I told her that the way she had opened the main door had reminded me of the moment in the novel when, after a long, moonlit family walk, Marcel's father pretends to be lost. Everyone in our group suddenly remembered the episode, and, excited, one of the Englishmen described it to his friend, explaining that it was only after making everyone else panic in the dark that Marcel's father had finally taken a key out of his pocket and quietly inserted it in what the others until then had failed to see was the back gate to their very own house. According to the Englishman, Marcel's admiring mother, stunned by her husband's ability to save the day, had exclaimed, *"Tu es fantastique!"*

"Tu es extraordinaire!" Borrel corrected him.

I had always liked that scene: the family wandering in the moonlight, the boy and his mother convinced that they're lost, the father teasing them. It reminded me of the way Proust's sentences roam and stray through a labyrinth of words and clauses, only to turn around—just when you are about to give up—and show you something you had always suspected but had never put into words. The sentences tell you that you haven't really drifted far at all, and that real answers may not always be obvious but aren't really hidden, either. Things, he reminds us, are never as scary as we thought they were, nor are we ever as stranded or as helpless as we feared.

Borrel left us for a moment to check on something inside the museum, and we spent some time discussing our favorite Proust passages. We all wondered which gate Swann's prototype would come through in the evenings, and where the aunts had been sitting when they refused to thank him for his gift but finally consented to say something so indirect that Swann failed to realize that they actually were thanking him.

"It all seems so small," said the Englishman, who was visibly disappointed by the house.

My thoughts drifted to a corner of the garden. The weather was growing colder, and yet I was thinking of Marcel's summer days, and of my own summer days as well, and of the garden where, deaf to the world, I had found myself doing what Proust described in his essay "On Reading":

> giving more attention and tenderness to characters in books than to people in real life, not always daring to admit how much I loved them . . . those people, for whom I had panted and sobbed, and whom, at the close of the book, I would never see again, and no longer know anything about. . . . I would have wanted so much for these books to continue, and if that were impossible, to have other information on all those characters, to learn now something about their lives, to devote mine to things that might not be entirely foreign to the love they had inspired in me and whose object I was suddenly missing . . . beings who tomorrow would be but names on a forgotten page, in a book having no connection with life.

The guided tour took more than two hours. It ended, as all guided tours do, in the gift shop. The guests were kindly reminded that, despite the impromptu nature of today's visit, they shouldn't forget to pay for their tickets. Everyone dutifully scrambled to buy Proust memorabilia. I toyed with the idea of buying a Proust watch on whose dial were inscribed the opening words of *À la Recherche du Temps Perdu*: *"Longtemps, je me suis couché de bonne heure."* But I knew I'd never wear it.

The visitors began talking of heading back to Paris. I was almost tempted to hitch a ride with one of them, but Borrel had promised to take me for a night walk through the streets of Illiers-Combray and then accompany me to the train station. The others stood idly about in the evening air, obviously reluctant to put Illiers-Combray behind them. They exchanged addresses and telephone numbers. "Proust is a must," I heard the Argentine say, an infatuated giggle in his voice. When Borrel left the shop to lock the back door, I was suddenly alone.

As I looked out the window at the garden where the Proust family had dined on warm summer evenings, I was seized with a strange premonition of asthma. How could Marcel have ever loved such a place? Or had he never loved it? Had he loved only the act of returning to it on paper, because that was how he lived his life—first by wanting to live it, and later by remembering having wanted to, and ultimately by writing about the two? The part in between—the actual living—was what had been lost.

Proust's garden was little more than a place where he had once yearned to be elsewhere—never the primal scene or the ground zero. Illiers itself was simply a place where the young Proust dreamed of a better life to come. But, because the dream never came true, he had learned to love instead the place where the dream was born. That life did happen, and happened so intensely, to someone who seemed so reluctant to live it is part of the Proustian miracle.

This is the irony that greets all Proust pilgrims: they go in search of things that Proust remembered far better than he had ever really known them, and which he yearned to recover more than he had ever loved them. In the end, like the boy mentioned by Freud who liked to lose things because he enjoyed finding them, Proust realized that he couldn't write about anything unless he thought he had lost it first. Perhaps I, too, had come here in order to lose Combray, if only to rediscover it in the pages I knew I would read on the way home.

My train wasn't due for an hour and a half, and Anne Borrel invited me to have a cup of tea at her house before our walk. We closed the door to the museum and set off down dark and deserted alleys.

"Illiers gets so empty," she said, sighing.

"It must be lonely," I said.

"It has its plusses."

Her house was bigger than Proust's and had a far larger garden and orchard. This seemed odd to me—like finding that the gatekeeper owns a faster car and has better central heating than the owner of the palace.

As we headed back to the train station after our tea, I walked quickly. Borrel tried to stop long enough to show me the spot where the Prousts had returned from their Sunday promenades, but I didn't want to miss my connection to Paris. It seemed a shame that, after so many years, this longed-for moonlit walk, so near at hand, should be the very thing I'd forfeit. But the last thing I needed was to be sentenced to a sleepless night in Proust's boyhood town. I alluded to a possible next time. Borrel mentioned spring, when Proust's favorite flower, the hawthorn, would be in bloom. But I knew, and perhaps she knew, too, that I had no plan to return.

On my way to Paris, I skimmed through the pages of "Combray," the first chapter of *In Search of Lost Time*. As I read about the steeples of Martinville or Tante Léonie, eternally perched in her bedroom, on the first floor, overlooking Rue Saint-Jacques, it occurred to me that I had rushed back to the book not to verify the existence of what I had just seen but to make certain that those places I remembered and loved as though my own childhood had been spent among them had not been altered by the reality of the dull, tile-roofed town shown to me by Anne Borrel.

I wanted to return to my first reading of Proust—the way, after seeing a film based on a novel, we struggle to resurrect our private portrait of its characters and their world, only to find that the images we've treasured for so long have vanished, like ancient frescoes exposed to daylight by a thoughtless archeologist. Would my original image of a stone villa with a spacious dining room and a wide staircase leading to the child's solitary bedroom be able to withstand the newly discovered little house with its squeaky wooden stairwell and drab, sunless rooms? And could this tawdry garden really be the glorious place where Marcel read away entire afternoons on a wicker chair under a chestnut tree, lost to the voices of those calling him inside and to the hourly chime of the church of Saint-Hilaire—whose real name, as I had found out that day, was not Saint-Hilaire but Saint Jacques, which, moreover, was not really the name of the street watched over by Tante Léonie, who, it turned out, was herself more likely to have been an uncle.

Inside the sepia cover of *Swann's Way* I searched also for the sense of wonder I had brought to it that summer evening more than thirty years before, when I'd had the good fortune to be with a man who was the first person to mention Proust to me and who, because he was unable to give me so many things then, had only this to give me, and gave it tentatively, self-consciously, as though he were giving part of himself, as he told me about Proust—how Proust remembered things that everyone else seemed to forget, how he saw through people though they still managed to fool him, and how he did all those things in sentences that were ever so long—and steered me, as we rushed to buy the first volume before the stores closed, to a writer I have since loved above all others, not just because of who he was and what he wrote, or because of who I became the more I read him, but because on that late-summer evening I already knew I had just received, perhaps without my father's knowing it, his dearest, most enduring gift of love.

Oh, Say Can You See?

Phyllis Barber

Over a radio microphone, into the nation's and FDR's ears, Grandma sang "The Star-Spangled Banner." "Oh, say can you see," she sang, my grandma who ironed for nickels and scrubbed for dimes, "by the dawn's early light, what so proudly we hailed?" Everybody in Boulder City recommended her for the program because they'd heard her at lots of funerals.

A big black open car full of VIPs delivered her home from the dedication ceremony. She waved good-bye. That's what my daddy told me.

I think she sang by the memorial, in between the statues—broad-chested men flanked by tall stiff wings pointing skyward. I hope those ninety-six men who died building the dam got fluffier wings, or else they probably never will fly out of their graves.

More than anything, I remember the dam and that story about Grandma. But there was an atom bomb test too—a rip in the sky, a gash that showed the sky's insides for a minute. I remember thinking about my Band-Aid box. I never could have unwrapped enough Band-Aids even if I had pulled the red string exactly down the side crease without tearing into the flat side of the paper where the red letters are printed. After that minute passed, the sky's blood and the earth's dust made a big cloud, a busy one. It drifts over my mind sometimes.

I got my first chance at swearing because of Hoover Dam—"I went to the dam to get some dam water. I asked the dam man for some of his dam water and the dam man said no."

Damns were frowned on at my house. So I chanted the forbidden whenever I could, with a flourish, making sure Mama and Daddy heard.

Actually, we called it Boulder Dam. At one time or another, everybody talked about jumping off or sliding down the curving concrete, but nobody did it except one time a man from New York did. His note said he lost his money gambling in Las Vegas and that nothing mattered anyway.

"He looked like a mass of jelly," said Uncle Tommy, an electrician at the dam.
"Could you see his face at all?" I asked.

"It was like a leaky puzzle, liquid in the cracks."

I wanted to ask more, but my Aunt Grace changed the subject.

Whenever anybody came to visit we always took them to see the dam. Down to Black Canyon, down to 120 degrees in the shade where heat ricocheted off sizzling boulders.

Every time, even now, I stop at the memorial on the Nevada side. The two bronzed angels stand guard over a message: "It is fitting that the flag of our country should fly in honor of those men . . . inspired by a vision of lonely lands made fruitful." My sister Elaine used to say that some of them fell off scaffolds into wet, pouring cement. Concrete soup. I always looked to see if a hand or a foot stuck out anywhere in the dam and checked for bumps on the surface.

The cloud had bumps, swollen and bulging. I've seen many shapes of clouds in my life—lambs, potatoes, even alligators, but I saw only one like that lumpy mushroom. Its cap reminded me of the North Wind, the puffy-cheeked one who bets with the Sun and blows fiercely to get coats off people's backs. Instead of sky and trees, it blew into the earth and got everything back in its face—sand, splintered tumbleweeds, thousands of years of rocks battering their own kind, crashing, colliding against each other, the dry desert silt, jaggedly rising from ribboned gullies and rain patterns on the sand, rising into a cloud that looked like a mushroom capped by the swollen-cheeked North Wind.

My father was proud of Hoover Dam. He helped build it, drove trucks hauling fill. He also loved the desert. Mama never thought much of it, not much at all.

"Herman, it's so hot here, so dusty. No creeks, no greenery. It's not human to live here."

My daddy always smiled when she started in. I liked his smile when she seemed unhappy.

"Herman, can't we move before it's too late?"

Daddy never argued this subject. He just reminded Mama of his mother, the grandma who sang, and how she saved her family with a letter to her relative: "Can't find work. We've tried everything in the Great Basin—farming in Idaho, mining in Nevada, selling shoes in Utah. Thought you might have a place for my husband and sons helping on that big new dam."

"It seemed like we were heading for Mecca, it did," he used to say. "All those mirages on the highway and our tires never getting wet. Sunshine, wide open-armed skies, and promises."

"Promises? Of what?" Mama asked. "How can you cultivate rocks in Black Canyon, Hoover Dam cement, the sand, the sage, the yucca?"

"I have a job, a wife, three children, and an address," he said.

"God bless the government."

The one time Mama did leave the desert and the dam, the time when my father put on his navy uniform with the brass buttons to go sailing in the Pacific, she wasn't treated as she should have been. Daddy always reminded her. Mother thought her relatives would help out with me and Elaine when she moved to

Idaho Falls, Idaho, but all extra hands were needed for milking, haying, harvesting potatoes.

"I'm sorry, but—" they all said.

Mama taught school—six grades in one room. She was tired at night when she picked me up from the scratch-and-bite nursery school for war orphans. She didn't talk much then, so I looked for Daddy under the covers, under the bed, and in the bathtub.

"Why did Daddy go away? Is he coming back?"

Mama read letters to us, words like China, Okinawa, kamikaze, Battleship *Missouri*, destroyers, phrases like "I miss you," "When the war is over," and "When we get back home to Boulder City, I'll roll down Administration Hill with Elaine and Phyllis."

Rolling. Me rolling, repeating my face to the green grass. The cloud rolling, repeating itself to the open sky. And deep inside the busy cloud topped by the North Wind puffing in the wrong direction, a fire burned. Not a bonfire, but a tall fire hedged by a column of jumbled whites, browns, and grays. A thick fire mostly hidden but not quite. Black smoke twisted away from the red fire, sometimes losing itself in the confusion, sometimes slithering out into the blue. The cloud burned, scarring its belly, melting its insides with red and yellow while it rolled over and over in the same place.

We still pass Administration Hill every time we drive to the dam to go on the world's longest elevator ride, dropping down deep into the stomach, the belly of Hoover, to the hum of big red generators with white round lights on top.

The guide always talks about kilowatts, power to southern California, and spillover precautions. I used to watch the ant tractors and drivers circling the generators stories below while he explained.

"Now if you'll follow me, we'll go directly into the Nevada diversion tunnel," a voice from a bullhorn said. Our feet echoed through a dripping cave, man-blasted, the voice said.

Water roared through a giant gray penstock (the guide called it) under the square observation room. I barely heard his speech. He pointed to yellow, red, blue, and green lines on a painted chart under a green metal lampshade. Outside the glassed, chicken-wired window, a man balanced on a catwalk to check bolts twice his size. The room trembled. The water rushed. I was glad I didn't have to tightrope catwalks and check pipes as big as the world.

"If you'll step this way, I'll lead you now to the base of the dam. Watch your step, ladies and gentlemen."

Outside, we looked up, up, everywhere up. Big cables stretched across, miles overhead—cables that lowered tons of railroad cars onto the tracks where we stood. I moved my toe quickly at the thought. Over the edge of the wall, the Colorado whirled green pools into white foam.

One time I told my mother the river must be mad.

"Rivers don't get angry, Phyllis," she said.

"This one does. It doesn't like going through all those tunnels and generators. It would suck me down forever if I fell in."

"You won't fall in. Mother's here to protect you."

Reassured, I ran from the wall to the center point where I could spread-eagle across two states.

"Ma'am," blared the bullhorn, "will you kindly keep your child with the tour group?"

My mother jerked me back into Arizona, told me to stop wandering off, to stay with the group.

Once when I was about six, Uncle Tommy scooped me into his arms. The temperature must have been 128 degrees that day.

"See, Phyllis honey. See the steepest, longest slide on earth." He not only held me up, but leaned me over the edge to see better.

"Uncle Tommy. Put me down." I kicked and squirmed.

"Not yet, honey. Look at the big river down there. We stopped that river. We did it. Look. We harnessed it. That's where you were a few minutes ago on the tour. See the railroad tracks?" He held me with only one arm as he pointed.

"Uncle Tommy. Put me down. Please. I don't like to look there." My head buried into his gray uniform but got stopped at the metal numbers on his badge.

"Ah, come on honey. Uncle Tommy wouldn't let anything happen to you." He still held me so I could see over the edge.

"Let me down. Let me down."

"Gee, why are you so upset. I wouldn't—"

I ran away from his words, away to the car that boiled the closest two feet of air around its metal surface. The door handle was untouchable, unopenable. I couldn't hide away to cry. I had to do it in the air, on top of that dam, in front of people from Manila, Cheyenne, and Pittsburgh.

I used to wonder if there had been devils in that redfire cloud. My mother always talked about how devils like fire and red and gambling, even how the world would end by fire because of them. I imagined horns balancing on top of their red caps that buttoned tight, holding all that cunning close between their ears while they rolled and tumbled in the churning clouds, while the fire burned yellow and red at the center and in my eyes when I think about it.

One night after Uncle Tommy leaned me out over the edge of the dam, he and my mother balanced a bed on the overhead cables, thousands of feet above concrete and water.

"You have disobeyed again," Mama said. "Always running off."

"I'm sorry."

"You'll have to sleep out there tonight, Phyllis. Maybe you'll learn to listen."

"Please, Mother, not at the dam. I'll be good. I'll listen. I won't go away without telling you ever again."

"Just climb up the ladder, honey," said Uncle Tommy. "Nothing to worry about."

"Please no," I said as I climbed the ladder, up, up, high above the scenic viewpoint where tourists said "ooh" and "aahhh." The wind blew, the cables rose and fell and twirled jump rope. I wore my blue furry Donald Duck slippers and my rosy chenille bathrobe, and I put one and then another foot ahead, in front.

For a minute I walked on the wind and wasn't afraid. Then I got to the creaking bed, leaning downside at every shift in weight.

"Rock-a-bye baby," Mama sang from the cliff's edge. "Hush-a-bye." Uncle Tommy accompanied her on his trumpet.

The bed started to slip. The bedsprings scraped over the cables, fingernails on a blackboard, slipping one by one.

"Mama," I screamed.

Mama leaned as far out over the edge as she could while Uncle Tommy held her knees. We stretched for each other. Like long, rubbery, airless balloons we stretched and stretched, arching, reaching, trying to connect.

"Hold me, Mama."

Our fingertips only pointed at each other as I passed.

I tried to make a sail out of the quilt. I stood up to catch the wind with it but couldn't keep my balance. One Donald Duck slipper, followed by the other, followed by me in rosy chenille, sailed through the night toward the dam to get some dam water from the dam man.

After it mushroomed, the cloud started to break apart and dot the sky, and I thought of the time I climbed a leafless tree. Instead of watching where I was going, I talked to Rocky, my dog, who jumped and yelped at the bottom. Someone else had broken the twig that raked my cheek, that beaded the slash with red. A necklace of red pearls, almost. Dot dash dot. A design that stared at me in the mirror until it got better and faded away just like the cloud did.

Everybody wants to see the dam. It's famous. One day when I was about ten, another big black car, open and full of important men, drove through Boulder City. Flags stuck out on both sides of the windshield, rippling. I tried every possible angle to see Ike, running around legs, pushing through to openings but finding none. I was missing everything. Everybody who had closed shop and home for the afternoon was crowding to see Ike, too.

"Daddy, hold me up so I can see."

His dark blue uniformed arms full of baby brother, he pointed to the sill of Central Market's picture window. Stacks of returnable glass bottles towered behind the pane and wiggled every time a reflected parade watcher moved.

I climbed to the ledge as the fire engine and two police cars sirened past. Even standing there, I could see only flashing red lights, the backs of heads, and an occasional helium balloon drifting, ownerless.

"Daddy, I can't see."

Somehow he managed to pick me up in time. Ike, his uniform dotted with brass and ribbons, looked just like the *Newsreel* pictures at the Boulder Theatre. He smiled and waved just like on *Newsreel,* too. I didn't need to see him after all. I already knew.

I liked the high school band best. The flags and the band.

"Children," my daddy said at the dinner table that night, "you are lucky to live in America." His blue eyes moistened as they always did when he talked about God and country. We all knelt by our chairs, and Daddy said, "We thank thee for such men as General Eisenhower to lead our great country. Bless our friends and relatives. Help us to live in peace. In the name of Jesus Christ, amen."

I saw Ike again on *Newsreel* several weeks later. He was still waving and smiling, framed by the granite-like building blocks of the dam. He didn't look too big next to the dam. Neither did his friends.

One morning, about five o'clock, our gray Plymouth drove in the opposite direction from the dam, toward Las Vegas, out by Railroad Pass where Uncle Tommy played trumpet on Saturday night. Elaine and I kept warm under a friendship quilt and read the embroidered names of Mama's old friends, waiting.

"It's time," Daddy said. "Watch. Don't miss this. We should be able to see everything, even if it is seventy-five miles away."

We waited some more, eating apples and crackers.

"It's got to be time," he said.

My neck cramped. I looked at the sunrise.

"There it is, there it is," he yelled.

I saw the flash, but mostly my father's face and his brass buttons that seemed to glow red for one instant.

"That's how I came home to you, everybody. Just look at that power."

The cloud flowered, mushroomed, turned itself inside out, and poured into the sky. Red fire burned in the middle of browns and grays, colors that hid the red almost. But it was there—the fire burning at the center, the red fire that charred the North Wind's puffed cheeks and squeezed eyes until it blew itself away, trailing black smoke and its pride. It was there in the middle of the rising columns of earth and clouds boiling over, clouds bursting into clouds, whipping themselves inside out, changing colors over and over. Red, yellow, and black, colors from the fire. Gray, brown, and beige, sand from the desert floor, Daddy said.

And then the picture blurred at its edges, unfocused itself into other shapes—smoke arches, long floating strings, dots and dashes. In no time at all, everything floated away, on the jet stream, Daddy told us.

"I thought it would last longer," I said. "Won't they do it again?"

Daddy laughed, "It's time to go home now and get some hot breakfast. Wasn't that amazing, kids?"

Everyone who had gotten up to watch the blast talked about it in school that day. "Did you see it?" Our desert land had been chosen once again for an important government project.

The front page of that night's newspaper had pictures of the before and after—frame houses before, no frame houses after; dummied soldiers before, no recognizable dummies after. Surprised cattle lay flat out in the dead grass on their sides, their hair singed white on the up side. Yucca Flats. Frenchman Flats. Mercury Test Site. Household words.

"Nobody can get us now," my daddy said.

I don't think about it much, but sometimes when I punch my pillow for more fluff, ready to settle into sleep, the cloud mists into long red airy fingers over everything, reaching across the stark blue.

The Unwanted Child

Mary Clearman Blew

December 1958. I lie on my back on an examination table in a Missoula clinic while the middle-aged doctor whose name I found in the Yellow Pages inserts his speculum and takes a look. He turns to the sink and washes his hands.

"Yes, you're pregnant," he says. "Congratulations, Mommy."

His confirmation settles over me like a fog that won't lift. Myself I can manage for, but for myself and *it?*

After I get dressed, he says, "I'll want to see you again in a month, Mommy."

If he calls me Mommy again, I will break his glasses and grind them in his face, grind them until he has no face. I will kick him right in his obscene fat paunch. I will bury my foot in his disgusting flesh.

I walk through the glass doors and between the shoveled banks of snow to the parking lot where my young husband waits in the car.

"You're not, are you?" he says.

"Yes."

"Yes, you're not?"

"Yes, I am! Jeez!"

His feelings are hurt. But he persists: "I just don't think you are. I just don't see how you could be."

He has a theory on the correct use of condoms, a theory considerably more flexible than the one outlined by the doctor I visited just before our marriage three months ago, and which he has been arguing with increasing anxiety ever since I missed my second period. I stare out the car window at the back of the clinic while he expounds on his theory for the zillionth time. What difference does it make now? Why can't he shut up? If I have to listen to him much longer, I will kill him, too.

At last, even his arguments wear thin against the irrefutable fact. As he turns the key in the ignition his eyes are deep with fear.

"But I'll stand by you," he promises.

Why get married at eighteen?

When you get married, you can move into married student housing. It's a shambles, it's a complex of converted World War II barracks known as the Strips, it's so sorry the wind blows through the cracks around the windows and it lacks hot-water heaters and electric stoves, but at least it's not the dormitory, which is otherwise the required residence of all women at the University of Montana. Although no such regulations apply to male students, single women must be signed in and ready for bed check by ten o'clock on weeknights and one on weekends. No alcohol, no phones in rooms. Women must not be reported on campus in slacks or shorts (unless they can prove they are on their way to a physical education class), and on Sundays they may not appear except in heels, hose, and hat. A curious side effect of marriage, however, is that the responsibility for one's virtue is automatically transferred from the dean of women to one's husband. Miss Maurine Clow never does bed checks or beer checks in the Strips.

When you get married, you can quit making out in the back seat of a parked car and go to bed in a bed. All young women in 1958 like sex. Maybe their mothers had headaches or hang-ups, but *they* are normal, healthy women with normal, healthy desires, and they know the joy they will find in their husbands' arms will—well, be better than making out, which, though none of us will admit it, is getting to be boring. We spend hours shivering with our clothes off in cars parked in Pattee Canyon in subzero weather, groping and being groped and feeling embarrassed when other cars crunch by in the snow, full of onlookers with craning necks, and worrying about the classes we're not attending because making out takes so much time. We are normal, healthy women with normal, healthy desires if we have to die to prove it. Nobody has ever said out loud that she would like to go to bed and *get it over with* and get on with something else.

There's another reason for getting married at eighteen, but it's more complicated.

By getting married I have eluded Dean Maurine Clow only to fall into the hands of in-laws.

"We have to tell the folks," my husband insists. "They'll want to know."

His letter elicits the predictable long-distance phone call from them. I make him answer it. While he talks to them I rattle dishes in the kitchen, knowing exactly how they look, his momma and his daddy in their suffocating Helena living room hung with mounted elk antlers and religious calendars, their heads together over the phone, their faces wreathed in big grins at his news.

"They want to talk to you," he says finally. Then, "Come on!"

I take the phone with fear and hatred. "Hello?"

"Well!!!" My mother-in-law's voice carols over the miles. "I guess this is finally the end of college for you!"

A week after Christmas I lean against the sink in my mother's kitchen at the ranch and watch her wash clothes.

She uses a Maytag washing machine with a wringer and a monotonous, daylong chugging motor which, she often says, is a damn sight better than a washboard. She starts by filling the tub with boiling water and soap flakes. Then she agitates her whites for twenty minutes, fishes them out with her big fork, and feeds them sheet by sheet into the wringer. After she rinses them by hand, she reverses the wringer, and feeds them back through, creased and steaming hot, and carries them out to the clothesline to freeze dry. By this time the water in the tub has cooled off enough for the coloreds. She'll keep running through her loads until she's down to the blue jeans and the water is thick and greasy. My mother has spent twenty-five years of Mondays on the washing.

I know I have to tell her I'm pregnant.

She's talking about college, she's quoting my grandmother, who believes that every woman should be self-sufficient. Even though I'm married now, even though I had finished only one year at the University of Montana before I got married, my grandmother has agreed to go on lending me what I need for tuition and books. Unlike my in-laws, who have not hesitated to tell me I should go to work as a typist or a waitress to support my husband through college (after all, he will be supporting me for the rest of my life), my grandmother believes I should get my own credentials.

My mother and grandmother talk about a teaching certificate as if it were a gold ring which, if I could just grab it, would entitle the two of them to draw a long breath of relief. Normally I hate to listen to their talk. They don't even know you can't get a two-year teaching certificate now, you have to go the full four years.

But beyond the certificate question, college has become something that I never expected and cannot explain: not something to grab and have done with but a door opening, a glimpse of an endless passage and professors who occasionally beckon from far ahead—like lovely, elderly Marguerite Ephron, who lately has been leading four or five of us through the *Aeneid*. Latin class has been my sanctuary for the past few months; Latin has been my solace from conflict that otherwise has left me as steamed and agitated as my mother's whites, now churning away in the Maytag; Latin in part because it is taught by Mrs. Ephron, always serene, endlessly patient, mercilessly thorough, who teaches at the university while Mr. Ephron works at home, in a basement full of typewriters with special keyboards, on the translations of obscure clay tablets.

So I've been accepting my grandmother's money under false pretenses. I'm not going to spend my life teaching around Fergus County the way she did, the way my mother would have if she hadn't married my father. I've married my husband under false pretenses, too; he's a good fly-fishing Helena boy who has no idea in the world of becoming a Mr. Ephron. But, subversive as a foundling in a fairy tale, I have tried to explain none of my new aspirations to my mother or grandmother or, least of all, my husband and his parents, who are mightily distressed as it is by my borrowing money for my own education.

"—and it's all got to be paid back, you'll be starting your lives in *debt!*"

"—the important thing is to get *him* through, *he's* the one who's got to go out and face the world!"

"—what on earth do you think you'll do with your education?"

And now all the argument is pointless, the question of teaching certificate over quest for identity, the importance of my husband's future over mine, the relentless struggle with the in-laws over what is most mine, my self. I'm done for, knocked out of the running by the application of a faulty condom theory.

"Mom," I blurt, "I'm pregnant."

She gasps. And before she can let out that breath, a frame of memory freezes with her in it, poised over her rinse tub, looking at me through the rising steam and the grinding wringer. Right now I'm much too miserable to wonder what she sees when she looks at me: her oldest daughter, her bookish child, the daydreamer, the one she usually can't stand, the one who takes everything too seriously, who will never learn to take no for an answer. Thin and strong and blue-jeaned, bespectacled and crop-haired, this girl could pass for fifteen right now and won't be able to buy beer in grocery stores for years without showing her driver's license. This girl who is too miserable to look her mother in the face, who otherwise might see in her mother's eyes the years of blight and disappointment. She does hear what her mother says:

"Oh, Mary, no!"

My mother was an unwanted child. The fourth daughter of a homesteading family racked by drought and debt, she was only a year old when the sister nearest her in age died of a cancerous tumor. She was only two years old when the fifth and last child, the cherished boy, was born. She was never studious like her older sisters nor, of course, was she a boy, and she was never able to find her own ground to stand on until she married.

Growing up, I heard her version often, for my mother was given to a kind of continuous oral interpretation of herself and her situation. Standing over the sink or stove, hoeing the garden, running her sewing machine with the permanent angry line deepening between her eyes, she talked. Unlike the stories our grandmothers told, which, like fairy tales, narrated the events of the past but avoided psychological speculation ("Great-great-aunt Somebody-or-other was home alone making soap when the Indians came, so she waited until they got close enough, and then she threw a ladle of lye on them . . ."), my mother's dwelt on the motives behind the darkest family impulses.

"Ma never should have had me. It was her own fault. She never should have had me if she didn't want me."

"But then you wouldn't have been born!" I interrupted, horrified at the thought of not being.

"Wouldn't have mattered to me," she said. "I'd never have known the difference."

What I cannot remember today is whom my mother was telling her story to. Our grandmothers told their stories to my little sisters and me, to entertain us, but my mother's bitter words flowed past us like a river current past small, ignored onlookers who eavesdropped from its shores. I remember her words, compulsive, repetitious, spilling out over her work—for she was always working—and I was awed by her courage. What could be less comprehensible than not wanting to be? More fearsome than annihilation?

Nor can I remember enough about the circumstances of my mother's life during the late 1940s and the early 1950s to know why she was so angry, why she was so compelled to deconstruct her childhood. Her lot was not easy. She had married into a close-knit family that kept to itself. She had her husband's mother on her hands all her life, and on top of the normal isolation and hard work of a ranch wife of those years, she had to provide home schooling for her children.

And my father's health was precarious, and the ranch was failing. The reality of that closed life along the river bottom became more and more attenuated by the outward reality of banks and interest rates and the shifting course of agribusiness. She was touchy with money worries. She saw the circumstances of her sisters' lives grow easier as her own grew harder. Perhaps these were reasons enough for rage.

I recall my mother in her middle thirties through the telescoped eye of the child which distorts the intentions of parents and enlarges them to giants. Of course she was larger than life. Unlike my father, with his spectrum of ailments, she was never sick. She was never hospitalized in her life for any reason but childbirth, never came down with anything worse than a cold. She lugged the armloads of wood and buckets of water and slops and ashes that came with cooking and washing and ironing in a kitchen with a wood range and no plumbing; she provided the endless starchy meals of roast meat and potatoes and gravy; she kept salads on her table and fresh or home-canned vegetables at a time when iceberg lettuce was a town affectation.

She was clear-skinned, with large gray eyes that often seemed fixed on some point far beyond our familiar slopes and cutbanks. And even allowing for the child's telescoped eye, she was a tall woman who thought of herself as oversized. She was the tallest of her sisters. "*As big as Doris* is what they used to say about me!"

Bigness to her was a curse. "You big ox!" she would fling at me over some altercation with my little sister. True to the imperative that is handed down through the generations, I in turn bought my clothes two sizes too large for years.

All adult ranch women were fat. I remember hardly a woman out of her teens in those years who was not fat. The few exceptions were the women who had, virtually, become a third sex by taking on men's work in the fields and corrals; they might stay as skinny and tough in their Levis as hired hands.

But women who remained women baked cakes and cream pies and breads and sweet rolls with the eggs from their own chickens and the milk and butter and cream from the cows they milked, and they ate heavily from appetite and from fatigue and from the monotony of their isolation. They wore starched cotton print dresses and starched aprons and walked ponderously beside their whiplash husbands. My mother, unless she was going to be riding or helping in the hayfields, always wore those shapeless, starched dresses she sewed herself, always cut from the same pattern, always layered over with an apron.

What was she so angry about? Why was her forehead kneaded permanently into a frown? It was a revelation for me one afternoon when she answered a knock at the screen door, and she smiled, and her voice lifted to greet an old friend of hers and my father's from their single days. Color rose in her face, and she looked pretty as she told him where he could find my father. Was that how outsiders always saw her?

Other ranch women seemed cheerful enough on the rare occasions when they came in out of the gumbo. Spying on them as they sat on benches in the shade outside the horticulture house at the county fair or visited in the cabs of trucks at rodeos, I wondered if these women, too, were angry when they were alone with only their children to observe them. What secrets lay behind those vast placid, smiling faces, and what stories could their children tell?

My mother believed that her mother had loved her brother best and her older sisters next best. "He was always The Boy and they were The Girls, and Ma was proud of how well they did in school," she explained again and again to the walls, the stove, the floor she was mopping, "and I was just Doris. I was average."

Knowing how my grandmother had misjudged my mother, I felt guilty about how much I longed for her visits. I loved my grandmother and her fresh supply of stories about the children who went to the schools she taught, the games they played, and the books they read. School for me was an emblem of the world outside our creek-bottom meadows and fenced mountain slopes. At eight, I was still being taught at home; our gumbo road was impassable for most of the school months, and my father preferred that we be kept safe from contact with "them damn town kids," as he called them. Subversively I begged my grandmother to repeat her stories again and again, and I tried to imagine what it must be like to see other children every day and to have a real desk and real lessons. Other than my little sister, my playmates were mostly cats. But my grandmother brought with her the breath of elsewhere.

My mother's resentment whitened in intensity during the weeks before a visit from my grandmother, smoldered during the visit itself, and flared up again as soon as my grandmother was safely down the road to her next school. "I wonder if she ever realizes she wouldn't even have any grandchildren if I hadn't got married and had some kids! *The Girls* never had any kids! Some people should never have kids! Some people should never get married!"

With a child's logic, I thought she was talking about me. I thought I was responsible for her anger. I was preoccupied for a long time with a story I had read about a fisherman who was granted three wishes; he had used his wishes badly, but I was sure I could do better, given the chance. I thought a lot about how I would use three wishes, how I would use their potential for lifting me out of the present.

"What would you wish for, if you had three wishes?" I prodded my mother.

She turned her faraway gray eyes on me, as though she had not been ranting about The Girls the moment before. "I'd wish you'd be good," she said.

That was what she always said, no matter how often I asked her. With everything under the sun to wish for, that unfailing answer was a perplexity and a worry.

I was my grandmother's namesake, and I was a bookworm like my mother's older sisters. Nobody could pry my nose out of a book to do my chores, even though I was marked to be the outdoor-working child, even though I was supposed to be my father's boy.

Other signs that I was not a boy arose to trouble us both and account, I thought, for my mother's one wish.

"Mary's getting a butt on her just like a girl," she remarked one night as I climbed out of the tub. Alarmed, I craned my neck to see what had changed about my eight-year-old buttocks.

"Next thing, you'll be mooning in the mirror and wanting to pluck your eyebrows like the rest of 'em," she said.

"I will not," I said doubtfully.

I could find no way through the contradiction. On the one hand, I was a boy (except that I also was a bookworm), and my chores were always in the barns and corrals, never the kitchen. *You don't know how to cook on a wood stove?* my mother-in-law was to cry in disbelief. *And you grew up on a ranch?*

To act like a boy was approved; to cry or show fear was to invite ridicule. *Sissy! Big bellercalf!* On the other hand, I was scolded for hanging around the men, the way ranch boys did. I was not a boy (my buttocks, my vanity). What was I?

"Your dad's boy," my mother answered comfortingly when I asked her. She named a woman I knew. "Just like Hazel. Her dad can't get along without her."

Hazel was a tough, shy woman who rode fences and pulled calves and took no interest in the country dances or the "running around" her sisters did on weekends. Hazel never used lipstick or permed her hair; she wore it cut almost like a man's. Seen at the occasional rodeo or bull sale in her decently pressed pearl-button shirt and new Levis, she stuck close to her dad. Like me, Hazel apparently was not permitted to hang around the men.

What Hazel did not seem interested in was any kind of fun, and a great resolve arose in me that, whatever I was, I was going to have . . . whatever it was. I would get married, even if I wasn't supposed to.

But my mother had another, darker reason to be angry with me, and I knew it. The reason had broken over me suddenly the summer I was seven and had been playing, on warm afternoons, in a rain barrel full of water. Splashing around, elbows and knees knocking against the side of the barrel, I enjoyed the rare sensation of being wet all over. My little sister, four, came and stood on tiptoe to watch. It occurred to me to boost her into the barrel with me.

My mother burst out of the kitchen door and snatched her back.

"What are you trying to do, kill her?" she shouted.

I stared back at her, wet, dumbfounded.

Her eyes blazed over me, her brows knotted at their worst. "And after you'd drowned her, I suppose you'd have slunk off to hide somewhere until it was all over!"

It had never crossed my mind to kill my sister, or that my mother might think I wanted to. (Although I had, once, drowned a setting of baby chicks in a rain barrel.) But that afternoon, dripping in my underpants, goose-bumped and ashamed, I watched her carry my sister into the house and then I did go off to hide until it was, somehow, all over, for she never mentioned it at dinner.

The chicks had been balls of yellow fuzz, and I had been three. I wanted them to swim. I can just remember catching a chick and holding it in the water until it stopped squirming and then laying it down to catch a fresh one. I didn't stop until I had drowned the whole dozen and laid them out in a sodden yellow row.

What the mind refuses to allow to surface is characterized by a suspicious absence. Of detail, of associations. Memories skirt the edge of nothing. There is for me about this incident that suspicious absence. What is being withheld?

Had I, for instance, given my mother cause to believe I might harm my sister? Children have done such harm, and worse. What can be submerged deeper, denied more vehemently, than the murderous impulse? At four, my sister was a tender, trusting little girl with my mother's wide gray eyes and brows. A younger sister of an older sister. A good girl. Mommy's girl.

What do I really know about my mother's feelings toward her own dead sister? Kathryn's dolls had been put away; my mother was never allowed to touch them.

"I'll never, never love one of my kids more than another!" she screamed at my father in one of her afternoons of white rage. The context is missing.

During the good years, when cattle prices were high enough to pay the year's bills and a little extra, my mother bought wallpaper out of a catalog and stuck it to her lumpy walls. She enameled her kitchen white, and she sewed narrow strips of cloth she called "drapes" to hang at the sides of her windows. She bought a stiff tight cylinder of linoleum at Sears, Roebuck in town and hauled it home in the back of the pickup and unrolled it in a shiny flowered oblong in the middle of her splintery front room floor.

Occasionally I would find her sitting in her front room on her "davenport," which she had saved for and bought used, her lap full of sewing and her forehead relaxed out of its knot. For a moment there was her room around her as she wanted it to look: the clutter subdued, the new linoleum mopped and quivering under the chair legs that held down its corners, the tension of the opposing floral patterns of wallpaper, drapes, and slipcovers held in brief, illusory harmony by the force of her vision.

How hard she tried for her daughters! Over the slow thirty miles of gumbo and gravel we drove to town every summer for dentist appointments at a time when pulling teeth was still a more common remedy than filling them, when our own father and his mother wore false teeth before they were forty.

During the good years, we drove the thirty miles for piano lessons. An upright Kimball was purchased and hauled home in the back of the pickup. Its carved oak leaves and ivories dominated the front room, where she found time to "sit with us" every day as we practiced. With a pencil she pointed out the notes she had learned to read during her five scant quarters in normal school, and made us read them aloud. "F sharp!" she would scream over the throb of the Maytag in the kitchen as one of us pounded away.

She carped about bookworms, but she located the dim old Carnegie library in town and got library cards for us even though, as country kids, we weren't strictly entitled to them. After that, trips home from town with sacks of groceries included armloads of library books. Against certain strictures, she could be counted on. When, in my teens, I came home with my account of the new book the librarian kept in her desk drawer and refused to check out to me, my mother straightened her back as I knew she would. "She thinks she can tell one of my kids what she can read and what she can't read?"

On our next visit to the library, she marched up the stone steps and into the mote-filled sanctum with me.

The white-haired librarian glanced up inquiringly.

"You got *From Here to Eternity?*"

The librarian looked at me, then at my mother. Without a word she reached into her drawer and took out a heavy volume. She stamped it and handed it to my mother, who handed it to me.

How did she determine that books and dentistry and piano lessons were necessities for her daughters, and what battles did she fight for them as slipping cattle prices put even a gallon of white enamel paint or a sheet of new linoleum beyond her reach?

Disaster followed disaster on the ranch. An entire season's hay crop lost to a combination of ancient machinery that would not hold together and heavy rains that would not let up. A whole year's calf crop lost because the cows had been pastured in timber that had been logged, and when they ate the pine needles from the downed tops, they spontaneously aborted. As my father grew less and less able to face the reality of the downward spiral, what could she hope to hold together with her pathetic floral drapes and floral slipcovers?

Bundled in coats and overshoes in the premature February dark, our white breaths as one, my mother and I huddle in the shadow of the chicken house. By moonlight we watch the white-tailed deer that have slipped down out of the timber to feed from the haystack a scant fifty yards away. Cautiously I raise my father's rifle to my shoulder. I'm not all that good a marksman, I hate the inevitable explosive crack, but I brace myself on the corner of the chicken house and sight carefully and remember to squeeze. Ka-crack!

Eight taupe shapes shoot up their heads and spring for cover. A single mound remains in the snow near the haystack. By the time my mother and I have climbed through the fence and trudged up to the haystack, all movement from the doe is reflexive. "Nice and fat," says my mother.

Working together with our butcher knives, we lop off her scent glands and slit her and gut her and save the heart and liver in a bucket for breakfast. Then, each taking a leg, we drag her down the field, under the fence, around the chicken house and into the kitchen, where we will skin her out and butcher her.

We are two mid-twentieth-century women putting meat on the table for the next few weeks. Neither of us has ever had a hunting license, and if we did, hunting season is long closed, but we're serene about what we're doing. "Eating our hay, aren't they?" says my mother. "We're entitled to a little venison. The main thing is not to tell anybody what we're doing."

And the pregnant eighteen-year-old? What about her?

In June of 1959 she sits up in the hospital bed, holding in her arms a small warm scrap whose temples are deeply dented from the forceps. She cannot remember birthing him, only the long hours alone before the anesthetic took over. She feels little this morning, only a dull worry about the money, money, money for college in the fall.

The in-laws are a steady, insistent, increasingly frantic chorus of disapproval over her plans. *But, Mary! Tiny babies have to be kept warm!* her mother-in-law keeps repeating, pathetically, ever since she was told about Mary's plans for fall quarter.

But, Mary! How can you expect to go to college and take good care of a husband and a baby?

Finally, *We're going to put our foot down!*

She knows that somehow she has got to extricate herself from these sappy folks. About the baby, she feels only a mild curiosity. Life where there was none before. The rise and fall of his tiny chest. She has him on her hands now. She must take care of him.

Why not an abortion?

Because the thought never crossed her mind. Another suspicious absence, another void for memory to skirt. What she knew about abortion was passed around the midnight parties in the girls' dormitory: *You drink one part turpentine with two parts sugar.* Or was it the other way around? . . . *two parts turpentine to one part sugar. You drink gin in a hot bath . . .*

She has always hated the smell of gin. It reminds her of the pine needles her father's cattle ate, and how their calves were born shallow-breathed and shriveled, and how they died. She knows a young married woman who begged her husband to hit her in the stomach and abort their fourth child.

Once, in her eighth month, the doctor had shot her a look across his table. "If you don't want this baby," he said, "I know plenty of people who do."

"I want it," she lied.

No, but really. What is to become of this eighteen-year-old and her baby?

Well, she's read all the sentimental literature they shove on the high school girls. She knows how the plot is supposed to turn out.

Basically, she has two choices.

One, she can invest all her hopes for her own future in this sleeping scrap. *Son, it was always my dream to climb to the stars. Now the tears of joy spring at the sight of you with your college diploma . . .*

Even at eighteen, this lilylicking is enough to make her sick.

Or two, she can abandon the baby and the husband and become really successful and really evil. This is the more attractive version of the plot, but she doesn't really believe in it. Nobody she knows has tried it. It seems as out of reach from ordinary daylight Montana as Joan Crawford or the Duchess of Windsor or the moon. As she lies propped up in bed with the sleeping scrap in her arms, looking out over the dusty downtown rooftops settling into noon in the waning Eisenhower years, she knows very well that Joan Crawford will never play the story of her life.

What, then? What choice is left to her?

What outcome could possibly be worth all this uproar? Her husband is on the verge of tears these days; he's only twenty himself, and he had no idea what trouble he was marrying into, his parents pleading and arguing and threatening, even his brothers and their wives chiming in with their opinions, even the minister getting into it, even the neighbors; and meanwhile his wife's grandmother firing off red-hot letters from her side, meanwhile his wife's mother refusing to budge an inch—united, those two women are as formidable as a pair of rhinoceroses, though of course he has no idea in the world what it took to unite them.

All this widening emotional vortex over whether or not one Montana girl will finish college. What kind of genius would she have to be to justify it all? Will it be enough that, thirty years later, she will have read approximately 16,250 freshman English essays out of an estimated lifetime total of 32,000?

Will it be enough, over the years, that she remembers the frozen frame of her mother's face over the rinse tub that day after Christmas in 1958 and wonders whether she can do as much for her son as was done for her? Or that she often wonders whether she really lied when she said, *I want it?*

Will it be enough? What else is there?

Independence Day, Manley Hot Springs, Alaska

Lisa D. Chavez

Independence Day, 1975. I was twelve. A little more than a month before, my mother had withdrawn me from school early, loaded up our car—a flashy but impractical Camaro with dual side-pipes—and headed north for Alaska. She brought with her everything she thought essential: daughter; dog; photos of the family she was leaving behind; a haphazard scattering of household goods; and two army surplus sleeping bags, purchased especially for the trip. What she was traveling toward was uncertain but full of promise—a mysterious box, beguilingly wrapped.

What she was leaving behind was certain; perhaps that is why she was so eager to go. A narrow rented house in southern California; a steady, if boring, secretarial job; a marriage proposal from a man she didn't love. What she was leaving behind were her everyday fears: her route to work through Watts, a place blighted and dangerous even then. The muggings in the company parking lot. The fear of being a young woman alone with her child in a decaying neighborhood, a derelict factory looming across the street. The fear, perhaps, of succumbing to a loveless marriage for the security it offered.

I was too young to really understand my mother's concerns, but I felt her tension. My mother and her women friends wore their fears like perfume, like the lingering scent of smoke from the erupting fires of those violent days. I remember the things my mother's friends talked about: the Manson murders; the serial killer who left body parts scattered on the freeway in trash bags; the man in our own town who killed five people in a movie theater. And the more personal terrors, the ones they alluded to less directly: fear of the arm slipping around the neck from behind, fear of the window breaking in the house in the middle of the night.

Fear for their children in a place gone crazy. Or just the fear of being alone. And while my world was a child's world, full of long imaginative games in the park near our house, or afternoons watching Disney movies at the mall, I also heard my mother and her friends talking about getting out, moving to someplace safe. My mother was looking for sanctuary, and for a new start. She picked Alaska, as far north as she could drive.

Independence Day, 1975. We've been in Alaska less than a month and are still exploring. Now we have driven as far north as the road will take us, landed here, on the banks of the Tanana River. Manley Hot Springs. A town with no function really, except for the raw springs: two pools of hot water bubbling up out of the ground. There's a lodge with a few desultory cabins ringing it. A combination gas station/store. That is all. Down the river a half a dozen miles lies Minto, an Athabascan Indian village. Fairbanks, the biggest city in the interior, swollen to a population of 60,000 by pipeline construction, lies less than a hundred miles south, far enough away—along these rough gravel roads—to be totally insignificant.

And I am twelve. Everything new astounds me, and everything is new. My mother parks near the river and goes to find a place to stay. Instantly I am occupied, walking our dog, wetting the toes of my canvas tennis shoes in the silty current, kicking sprays of gravel into the air. Under my breath a constant stream of conversation. I narrate the scene to myself, add it to the elaborate and constant story I whisper of my adventures in Alaska. Drunk on the stories of Jack London, the poems of Robert Service, I imagine myself a lone adventurer, a sled dog driver, a saloon girl. I do not see what is in front of me: a shabby small town where people stare openly at that frivolous car—bright orange and marked by its out-of-state plates—and the young woman in white, high-heeled sandals and her daughter that have emerged from it. I do not see the men swigging out of a bottle at the picnic table by the river. I do not see the people getting out of a banged up riverboat, or the beer cans they toss in the current. No. I am in my own Alaska, and it is beautiful. I erase the people, and I am alone in my fantasy of wilderness, only graceful paper birch and the sun turning the river to tinfoil. Even when two men pull a rifle out of the boat, aim it at the sky and shoot, I am unsurprised. Only when my mother hurries me into the car do I understand I should be afraid.

There is only one place to stay, in the hulking log building that serves as a lodge. And there is only one room left, above the bar. We take it, noting the sagging double bed and rust-stained sink. The bathroom is down the hall.

Manley holds few attractions. The hot springs itself—housed in another log structure, this one with steamy windows that gaze at the road like rheumy eyes—is booked out by the hour, and we discover it is rented for the entire evening. We go for a walk with our German shepherd, but we quickly run out of road to walk on. We circle the gas station yet again.

"When does it get dark?" I ask my mother; even though I already know that it does not get dark at night in Fairbanks, I cannot be sure the rules are not different here.

"In August," my mother replies, an answer she has learned from the locals. She looks nervous, walks fast. Finally, I manage to really see around me, to note the people drinking at picnic tables, the hairy-faced men entering the store with guns in holsters. She hustles us back to our little room.

And I continue to ponder the light. If it never gets dark, I wonder, when do kids get to shoot off their fireworks? This year I have no fireworks, no magical cones of cardboard with their heady black smell of powder, cones with names like "Showers of Falling Stars" and "Golden Peacock" that spray the summer night with shivering sparks of sheer delight. Fireworks are illegal here, my mother tells me, and I feel sorely cheated.

All through the sunlit night we hear voices shout and slur from the bar, and outside gunfire and laughter. Years later I will discover that Alaska is not the only place where people discharge guns on holidays, but then I knew only my mother's fear which passed to me like a virus. I lay still on the double bed beside her, pretending to sleep. At 5:00 A.M. a shot in the bar and a shuddering silence. From the car, distant and insistent, our dog's furious barking.

Time passes. I pretend to sleep. The dog barks. My mother nudges me. "Someone needs to walk the dog." That someone is me.

Years later I recount the story. People question me. Why did she send you, a child? What they are asking, what they are telling me, is that my mother was a bad mother. Perhaps. But maybe she thought it was safe; how could she know? And she was tired, and scared herself, and perhaps she thought my childishness would protect me in a way her youth and gender might not protect her.

Perhaps it was a mark of my mother's blind innocence. I like to think that she had some of the indomitable optimism of those who made the same trek before: the stampeders to the gold rush of '98, or the others that came, like we did, lured north by the pipeline boom of '74 and '75. She wanted to believe—like so many did—that Alaska was a land of golden opportunity. Think of what she had done: left a good-paying job and man who wanted to marry her to journey to a place where she knew no one, where she had no prospects at all. For her, I think Alaska represented the possibility of the undiscovered, while California was a territory already mapped with freeways and shopping malls, mile upon mile of housing developments, and the barbed wire threat of barrio and ghetto.

That summer, we were still caught up in the romance of Alaska. We sang Johnny Horton songs on the Alcan Highway: "North to Alaska," and "When It's Springtime in Alaska It's Forty Below." I wrote "Alaska or Bust" with my finger in the dust that caked the car, and my mother smiled and let it stay. She told me that we would have our own house in the country, and I believed her, even though when we got to Fairbanks we lived in a campground next to the fairgrounds, and I stayed there all day exploring muskeg woods behind the camp while my mother worked at Dairy Queen. There were none of the expected high-paying jobs, none of the dream houses that we could afford. We knew no one. But my mother, like me, was lost in her own dream of Alaska, and she refused to be discouraged. So now, when I think back to that time, I try not to judge her too harshly. Alaska was her sanctuary, and she could not imagine, then, that anything could go wrong.

I am a child; I do what she asks. Put on my worn jean jacket. Push my straight dark hair behind my ears, then tie it back with a blue bandana. This is the look I have adopted since I arrived, Indian chic. I do not know what it means, exactly, to dress like this, but I have seen young men and women outfitted in this way—people my mother told me were Indian—and I decide I will dress that way too, because Indians are cool, aren't they? And as I am a bit Indian—a mixture of Chicana and Southwestern Indian and Norwegian that I will much later learn to call Mestiza—I am determined to dress appropriately. My attire adjusted, I move toward the door. Look pleadingly at my mother's blanketed back. I really don't want to go out. Then, in imitation of my mother, I sigh loudly, pick up the keys. Step out into the hall.

Creep down the narrow stairs. Afraid, in my childish way, of strangers, of being where I think I am not supposed to be, up late in a room above a bar. And I see a man on the landing. His back to me. And he whips around and raises a shotgun and aims it at my face. "I told all you goddamn Indians to get the fuck out of my bar."

I am twelve, and I have never seen a gun before. I am twelve, and I come from California, where night follows day in an orderly fashion, where on the Fourth of July I whirl like a comet with sparklers clutched tight in two hands. Where I place black pellets on the pavement to watch them transform into sooty snakes. I am twelve, and I am frozen on the landing of a strange staircase, with a shotgun staring in my face with its one, unblinking eye.

I am usually a silent child, but my fear makes me speak. My mouth opens and out rush words, tumbling over one another like frightened animals. My mother. California. The dog in the car, maybe already peeing on the seat. The dog is like a ship I swim to, desperately. He lowers the gun and I skitter past, fly to the door. Which I cannot open; it is locked. The man raises the latch, shoves me outside.

I stand outside on the cool grass, the early morning bright and exotic around me. I close my eyes for a moment and wish hard for home. Then open them to see revelers sway aimlessly by, laughing, cursing, swigging from bottles. I move toward the safety of the car.

And I am twelve, and I don't know what to do, can't think about what happened to me in any coherent fashion. I do not understand. I know racism exists—though I do not know what it is called—but not like this. I thought it was something else, people who called black people bad names, people who snickered when they heard my last name. Mexican, they'd sneer. I knew that. Knew shame, about my last name, which I claimed was Spanish, not Mexican, knowing that to be less shameful, although I didn't know why. But nothing more. Not then. And Indian, what was that to me? An exotic people with feathers, that had some slight relation to my father, to me. But I was not Indian. Nor Mexican. Nor Norwegian. Not really. I am just myself, a quiet girl who liked to read, to write, a girl who had always loved the Fourth of July, the night's rich promise broken by the sizzle and spark of fire.

And now I have been shaken into a world I don't understand, a cold, foreign world, where men I don't know can hate me for the way I look. I don't know what to do, so I take the dog for a walk. She sniffs desultorily, squats on the lawn to pee. I look at the new grass stains on my jeans, souvenirs from the fall I took from the man's push. Two young men pass by, say hello. They have witnessed my ejection from the lodge.

"Did he hurt you?" one asks. They are both Indian; their glossy black hair is tied back with bandanas. They wear T-shirts, jean jackets.

I am afraid to answer, but I shake my head.

"He's an asshole," the other young man says. His words are slow and strangely accented; I will soon learn to recognize this as a village accent. "Fucking white man." He shakes a fist at the lodge.

I try to smile to show my gratefulness, and watch them with head bowed as they walk away. They are drunk; I know that even then, but their words redeem me nonetheless. Later I will understand those words as my introduction into a place I will dwell for all my time in Alaska, those words which delineate me as one of them, as a Native person. For in Alaska, as I would learn, the complexity of my ethnicity was irrelevant; I looked Native, therefore I was.

For a long time I crouch beside the car with my arms around the dog's neck. What will I do? I could sleep in the car, but my mother will be mad. But can I go back in? What if the man won't let me? What if he . . . my thoughts veer away from certain subjects. The dog pulls away, shakes herself. I must go back.

I stand at the door. Through the window I can see the man watching, see the slim shadow of the gun. I am afraid. My legs shake; my hand is weak, but I push the door open.

And the man grabs my shoulder hard. Twists me toward him. Peers down into my face. He is bearded and the hair on his face makes him as frightening as a fierce animal. "All right," he says, though I have no idea what he means. For me, nothing is right. He pushes me toward the stairs and I run up them, breathless, heart somersaulting. I imagine too clearly a sudden crack, a searing pain in my spine. In our room I collapse on the bed as if shot. Tears first, then the story.

My mother waits until the next morning to confront the lodge owner. She gets the story while I mop a pancake around my plate, too scared and shamed to eat. The bearded man is the man who owns the lodge, and he tells his side calmly, reasonably, as if there is nothing unusual about pointing shotguns at twelve-year-olds. Some Indians from Minto were partying in the bar, he tells us, and wouldn't leave at closing time. So he fired a shot of tear gas, cleared the place out. As for me, "she looks like a goddamn Native," he says, and shrugs. And the other guests eating breakfast look at me, nod. There is nothing more to say, no apologies necessary. And my mother's angry words are just irritations, like BBs fired at a grizzly bear.

We left soon after that, and my mother drove as fast as she dared on that gravel road, gripping the steering wheel tight, her hands like fists clenched. I was quiet. I didn't know I should be angry. Didn't know, really, why I felt so ashamed. Even my mother's anger couldn't take that shame away, for under her anger I sensed her own fear of this place she'd brought me to, of these people. Her confusion. She repeated that the man had thought I was Indian, as if somehow that should explain it. But that confused me. Because I *was* Indian, though not Alaskan Indian, and not all Indian. Did that make what the man did excusable? My mother did not explain.

What did it mean to be Indian? Did I put it on with the clothes I wore? Why was my appearance read one way in California and another way in Alaska? In California, where everyone aimed for a tan, my skin color was something to be envied, when it could be separated from the stigma of my Mexican last name. I had grown vain of it, in a childish way. Proud that I often had the best "tan." I secretly looked down on lighter-skinned children, was sure their pink and white skin was ugly, undesirable. Otherwise why would my mother and so many others spend hours roasting themselves brown on the beach? I got it naturally; I must be superior. In Alaska, far from beaches, where the long dark winters bleached skin as pale as the long months of snow, brown skin did not mean beach and health, but it meant something else, something I would understand some people thought shameful. Native. That's what it meant, and I would discover how that word could be spit out with as much disgust as any racial slur.

Manley Hot Springs was a defining moment of my life in Alaska. It was the first time someone mistook me for an Alaskan Native—and one of the most frightening—but it would not be the last. My entire life in Alaska has been shaped by the fact that people—both white and Native—think I am Athabascan or Yupik, Tlingit or Inupiat. I reaped the benefits of that: smiles and conversation from old Yupik women on the bus, an unquestioned acceptance in villages and at Native cultural events. When I taught at the university, I connected easily with Native students. But I also reaped the pain.

When I tell this story to people, there is a coda I usually include. A few years after our trip up to Manley, a similar thing happened; again the lodge owner tried to throw some people out of the bar; again he waved a shotgun. But this time it was not at a child who looked Native. It was at a man—and while I don't know if he was white or Native, I do know he was armed, and he shot first and killed the lodge owner. As vengeful as it sounds, my mother and I were pleased by this, and when I retell it as the logical end to my own story, I smile. He infected me with his hatred, and I was—am—glad he is dead. I like this end because it is satisfying; it gives the story a sort of rough justice. It gives life—so messy and vague—an aesthetically pleasing shape, as neat as fiction. I also like the way I appear in this version: invulnerable, a tough person who can speak of death coolly. Perhaps my liking for this end is left over from my turbulent adolescence, a time so fraught with pain that my only tool of survival was the tough facade I adopted and my insistence that nothing could hurt me. Perhaps the story, ended this way, is proof of that.

The real end of the story is more complicated. Because of course I was not untouched. I learned to be afraid, learned that Alaska—as beloved as it would become—was not the sanctuary my mother had hoped for. My mother was able to close her eyes and keep hoping. For me, any possibility of sanctuary was shattered. On the drive back to Fairbanks, I had asked my mother if we could go home. She knew I didn't mean the campground. We live here now, was what she told me, and I remember crying when she said that. I think even then I wondered how I would survive.

In a few years, my mother would have what she dreamed of—the high-paying construction job, her own house. In a few years she would also slam into prejudice and violence on the job, but by then, Alaska was home, so she never seriously considered leaving.

In a few years, I would hear things and learn more: hear the smug tone of the high-school counselor as he tried to steer me into the vocational track—despite my good grades; hear, more than once, the anxiety in a white boyfriend's voice as he asked for assurance that I wasn't really Native; hear the nervous laughter at a party when a white man told how he raped "a squaw" in the back of a truck. Hear the silence that followed that laughter. I was spit at in small towns, refused service in bars. In just a few years, I could recite the litany of insults so many people of color know. But I would also learn to put a name to what was happening to me, and learn to be angry. I would learn that what happened to me was not my fault, nor was it unique to Alaska. Even later, I would learn to mold my anger into something I could use.

But I didn't know any of that then. I only knew fear, and shame.

I never wore the bandana or jean jacket again.

History as Fiction, Fiction as History

Michelle Cliff

I am reading *The New York Times* on Sunday, January 4, 1994. There is the following headline: RECOMPENSE BEING SOUGHT FOR MASSACRE. The article underneath the headline describes events of seventy-one years ago when a white mob terrorized a black town in Florida. The town was named Rosewood. During the rampage of the white mob at least eight people were killed; every house, every place of business, church, school, was burned to the ground. Today, the town consists of a single house and a sign bearing the town's name.

Rosewood is an American ghost town. Not born of the romantic, mythic violence of the Old West, but created of something else—banal, commonplace.

American history has been tamed. The books record no evidence of Rosewood or what happened there, or elsewhere.

How do we capture the history that remains only to be imagined? That which has gone to bush, lies under the sea, is buried in the vacant lots of big cities.

In my mind I erect a scaffolding; I attempt to describe what has not been described. I try to build a story on the most delicate of remains.

I traverse the American landscape as someone foreign-born, as a writer, a novelist, as a woman who has fallen in love with this country—certain that this love demands accountability. This love impels my search into America's past.

Some months ago I was driving to the University of Virginia. There was to be a panel on women and multiculturalism. I am weary of the shorthand which passes for cultural commentary, political awareness in these times. Why can't we use more words? Why can't we take the time to say what we mean? Why do we settle for a term like multiculturalism, as if it means the same to us all? Why must the complexity of America always be reduced to simplicity?

On my way to the university I cross the Hudson River at the Fishkill Correctional Facility, which I mistake for Sing Sing. When you drive this country you become aware of places where people are kept, you begin to tell them by sight, from a distance, the state-of-the-art and the ancient.

Huge rolls of razor wire, like baled hay, like the kind strung on the fences in Johannesburg's suburbs. One of these places reminds me of another.

I remember when I saw San Quentin by night. A wrong turn on the way to the Pacific Ocean, and then the lit-up Oz, but yellow, not green like the Emerald City. It was a Friday night; scores of dressed-up women were leaving the prison. I parked and went inside to ask directions, and noticed a sign saying San Quentin Gift Shop hanging above the guard's head. The entire prison was washed in yellow light. I thought about George Jackson and his life and death.

I thought about his prison letters as a testament to his intellectual survival. About all of us communicating from what may seem like prison. Where the guards wear the uniform of what will be released as American history.

I am driving past the coal mines of eastern Pennsylvania. Like the salt mines of Detroit, the refineries of New Jersey, there are small houses, gardens, clotheslines hung with laundry bang up against them.

Slag heaps stand like monuments.

From the height of the Alleghenies I descend into the terrain of farmland, battlefield. I am preparing to write a book about the black-centered struggle for emancipation, a struggle which for the most part has been excised from the official record, and from the volumes which cascade from library shelves, the various miniseries and Hollywood movies smitten with the period of enslavement and the Civil War. Whenever I mention the heroine of my novel—the entrepreneur and radical Mary Ellen Pleasant—to scholars of this period, they say they have never heard of her, or they ask me, in a non-questioning way, "Didn't she run whorehouses in San Francisco?"

I have done research in libraries in search of Mary Ellen Pleasant. I have read an interview she gave to an African-American newspaper, *The San Francisco Elevator*. I am getting a picture of her in my mind, this woman who funded what we know as John Brown's raid on Harpers Ferry, who went south with a wagonload of guns to arm the slaves. Now, on this journey across the American landscape, I am also in search of the past she inhabited. And it is all around me. The past coexists with the present in this amnesiac country in this forgetful century. It is as Toni Morrison says in *Beloved*. "Everything is now. It is all now."

If eyes can be inherited, dimples, tendencies, why not memories; why can't our DNA contain inklings of the past?

I am nearing Antietam battlefield. On the car radio they are playing gospel music from our nation's capital. Blessed Assurance, Jesus is mine! Oh, what a foretaste of glory divine! The D.J. cuts in, apologizes for playing Pat Boone, saying she wanted to give the boy a chance, but "enough is enough."

I drive through the battlefield. It is early morning. A mist hangs over the cornfield. Cows are grazing. The same farmhouses, barns that were witnesses in

1862. I pick up a stone, also a witness. The past closes in. I have seen photos of that day and recognize the ditch where the bodies were piled like cordwood when the day was over. I walk through the ditch. Blackbirds pick over last year's cornstalks. Pick through the ground. There is the sound of a mockingbird calling for its mate. An old sound. And behind that plaint the hum of cars in the early morning, Saturday, on a secondary road in the Maryland countryside.

I drive on to Sharpsburg where the graves lie. Row upon row of tiny white stones. The word *unknown* repeats and repeats. So many times that to read it may become meaningless. The stones resemble nothing so much as babies' teeth. I store this image away, to use later. Everything is grist for the mill of the imagination. I recall a play by the African-American playwright May Miller, *The Straggler*. A one-act play which dwells on the ironic thought: What if the Unknown Soldier were black?

I drive through the gorge which is Harpers Ferry. John Brown is noted here and there. What did I expect? I hold nothing against John Brown. He cannot help what history has made of him.

I arrive at the University of Virginia where I am informed by the graduate student who is my escort that Thomas Jefferson didn't own slaves, which is news to me. Villagers, as they're officially known, built the university, Monticello, every rotunda the great man dreamed of. They liked him so much they just pitched in. She tells me this with a straight face.

She continues my orientation: Sally Hemings, the slavewoman who bore Jefferson several children, either didn't exist or she was white.

I ask her if she's ever met a white person named Jefferson, or Washington, for that matter.

I suggest that she read Barbara Chase-Riboud's novel *Sally Hemings*, which, like my proposed book, like Maryse Conde's *Tituba* and Morrison's *Beloved*, attempts to rescue an African-American woman from the myth of American history.

She does not seem interested.

It is through fiction that some of us rescue the American past. As artists, Morrison has said, it is our job to imagine the unimaginable. The interior of the slave ship, for example. The rush to suicide of the cargo, for example. But also: the resisters, female and male. Those who organized and armed themselves and fought back. The history of armed and organized African-American resistance has been made unimaginable by the official histories of this country. One or two incidents are allowed in these sanctioned pages, but these more often than not end with the hanging of the hero. The extraordinary extent of ordinary people involved in a centuries' long struggle goes unacknowledged.

I am driving along a secondary road beside Lake Erie on a Sunday afternoon in early summer. There are high soft clouds on the horizon. My eye catches a sign, hand-painted, in earth colors, by the side of the road. WELCOME TO TOUSSAINT COUNTRY. Nothing else. Or does it say TOUSSAINT COUNTY?

Either way my heart jumps. Did some of the Black Jacobins, as C. L. R. James called them, end up here? Why would many people consider this a bizarre thought, and me some sort of extremist for having it?

Jamaican slaves, recalcitrant and troublesome, ended up in Nova Scotia. Why not Haitians in Ohio? The state of *Beloved*. Stop on the Underground Railroad. Why not use our historical imaginations, envisioning the armed and organized network as extending throughout the Western Hemisphere? Wherever the institution of slavery thrived.

I am thrilled by these unimaginable thoughts.

A few days later, I am in Omaha, in an old brick building on the black side of town. Around the building are small tidy houses, vegetable and flower gardens, lilacs are in bud, rhubarb stalks are beginning to redden, tulips are just about over. It is early afternoon. There are housedresses, work clothes, undershirts, and nightgowns flapping in the breezes of the Great Plains, off the Missouri River. On the street are debris of rusting cars, and a beat-up place with the "best barbecue in Omaha" has ceased to exist.

A woman, disheveled, crack-skinny, runs in front of my car screaming, "Bitch!"

She is a casualty of our forgetfulness.

Here again the present collides with the past in this Midwestern city, as it does everywhere in this American landscape. The brick building is the Great Plains Black Museum, in this town where Malcolm X was born.

The rooms of the museum are packed. A son's graduation portrait from West Point. Buffalo soldiers on duty at Fort Robinson. Did they witness the death of Crazy Horse?

A woman in a high-neck collar, her hair upswept with tortoiseshell combs. A man in a high-neck collar with a watch fob across his vest. Named and unnamed, these faces are the past. Tuskeegee airmen. A woman named Liza Suggs who wrote her family's story of their escape from slavery. Records of towns named Brownlee and Brownville, all-black towns in Nebraska: the legend explains why such settlements were necessary, and suggests that towns with the words "free" or "brown" in their names, dotting the American landscape, were African-American communities.

I find here the epitaph of Ben Hodges:

SELF-STYLED
DESPERADO
A COLORFUL PIONEER
1856–1929

Upstairs a pioneer dwelling has been recreated. Quilts, canned goods, recipes, home remedies, iron bedstead. I find myself imagining the families who put this food by, who passed through the phases of human life on this bedstead, under this quilt. I pass my hand across the label on a Mason jar holding strawberry jam, imagining another hand. This, too, is history.

In the basement a figure in an Olympic warm-up suit raises a black-gloved fist. In the basement are newspapers from 1919. They lie on a table next to the black Olympian.

Headlines—

LYNCHING   RIOTS   RACE
RED SUMMER (bold in red ink)
RIOTING
RACE
LYNCHING ELUDED
RIOTING   RACE   RACE
RACE   WAR HERO
LYNCHING

The head-and-shoulders mannequin from the window of a black beauty salon stands to one side. On one bare shoulder is inscribed:

LADY DAY
1915–1959

At the end they chained her to her hospital bed. They said they'd found a white powder around her nostrils. I think back to the woman on the street in the bright sunlight. I think of "Strange Fruit."

My book is coming together in my head.

I make notes and drive on to Grand Island, which promises something called a pioneer museum. I ask the woman at the desk if she has any information on black American homesteaders in Nebraska.

"Oh, there were no black people in Nebraska," she says.

This is comic and tragic at the same time.

I wonder for a moment where her own people came from. Were they among the Irish who fled the great famines? I remember reading a letter written by Frederick Douglass on a visit to Ireland, witnessing the consequences of British racism, recognizing the need to make common cause. I remember reading that when Douglass spoke in Boston, scores of Boston Irish came to listen and to cheer him.

I end my journey in the California wine country in the town of Napa. I am visiting the grave of Mary Ellen Pleasant. At one side of the plot is a huge white oleander bush, at the other a huge blackberry bush. The petals of the oleander and the juice of the blackberries meet on the ground. On the marble slab between is the epitaph she insisted on.

SHE WAS A FRIEND OF JOHN BROWN

Behind those seven words lies an extraordinary life.

Silent Dancing

Judith Ortiz Cofer

We have a home movie of this party. Several times my mother and I have watched it to-gether, and I have asked questions about the silent revelers coming in and out of focus. It is grainy and of short duration, but it's a great visual aid to my memory of life at that time. And it is in color—the only complete scene in color I can recall from those years.

We lived in Puerto Rico until my brother was born in 1954. Soon after, because of economic pressures on our growing family, my father joined the United States Navy. He was assigned to duty on a ship in Brooklyn Yard—a place of cement and steel that was to be his home base in the States until his retirement more than twenty years later. He left the Island first, alone, going to New York City and tracking down his uncle who lived with his family across the Hudson River in Paterson, New Jersey. There my father found a tiny apartment in a huge tenement that had once housed Jewish families but was just being taken over and trans-formed by Puerto Ricans, overflowing from New York City. In 1955 he sent for us. My mother was only twenty years old, I was not quite three, and my brother was a toddler when we arrived at El Building, as the place had been christened by its newest residents.

My memories of life in Paterson during those first few years are all in shades of gray. Maybe I was too young to absorb vivid colors and details, or to discrimi-nate between the slate blue of the winter sky and the darker hues of the snow-bearing clouds, but that single color washes over the whole period. The building we lived in was gray, as were the streets, filled with slush the first few months of my life there. The coat my father had bought for me was similar in color and too big; it sat heavily on my thin frame.

I do remember the way the heater pipes banged and rattled, startling all of us out of sleep until we got so used to the sound that we automatically shut it out or raised our voices above the racket. The hiss from the valve punctuated my sleep (which has always been fitful) like a nonhuman presence in the room—a dragon sleeping at the entrance of my childhood. But the pipes were also a connection to all the other lives being lived around us. Having come from a house designed for a single family back in Puerto Rico—my mother's extended-family home—it was curious to know that strangers lived under our floor and above our heads, and that the heater pipe went through everyone's apartment. (My first spanking in Paterson came as a result of playing tunes on the pipes in my room to see if there would be an answer.) My mother was as new to this concept of beehive life as I was, but she had been given strict orders by my father to keep the doors locked, the noise down, ourselves to ourselves.

It seems that Father had learned some painful lessons about prejudice while searching for an apartment in Paterson. Not until years later did I hear how much resistance he had encountered with landlords who were panicking at the influx of Latinos into a neighborhood that had been Jewish for a couple of generations. It made no difference that it was the American phenomenon of ethnic turnover which was changing the urban core of Paterson, and that the human flood could not be held back with an accusing finger.

"You Cuban?" one man had asked my father, pointing at his name tag on the navy uniform—even though my father had the fair skin and light brown hair of his northern Spanish background, and the name Ortiz is as common in Puerto Rico as Johnson is in the United States.

"No," my father had answered, looking past the finger into his adversary's angry eyes. "I'm Puerto Rican."

"Same shit." And the door closed.

My father could have passed as European, but we couldn't. My brother and I both have our mother's black hair and olive skin, and so we lived in El Building and visited our great-uncle and his fair children on the next block. It was their private joke that they were the German branch of the family. Not many years later that area too would be mainly Puerto Rican. It was as if the heart of the city map were being gradually colored brown—*café con leche* brown. Our color.

The movie opens with a sweep of the living room. It is "typical" immigrant Puerto Rican decor for the time: the sofa and chairs are square and hard-looking, upholstered in bright colors (blue and yellow in this instance) and covered with the transparent plastic that furniture salesmen then were so adept at convincing women to buy. The linoleum on the floor is light blue; where it had been subjected to spike heels, as it was in most places, there were dime-size indentations all over it that cannot be seen in this movie. The room is full of people dressed up: dark suits for the men, red dresses for the women. When I have asked my mother why most of the women are in red that night, she has shrugged and said, "I don't remember. Just a coincidence." She doesn't have my obsession for assigning symbolism to everything.

The three women in red sitting on the couch are my mother, my eighteen-year-old cousin, and her brother's girlfriend. The novia is just up from the Island, which is apparent in her body language. She sits up formally, her dress pulled over her knees. She is a pretty girl, but her posture makes her look insecure, lost in her full-skirted dress, which she has carefully tucked around her to make room for my gorgeous cousin, her future sister-in-law. My cousin has grown up in Paterson and is in her last year of high school. She doesn't have a trace of what Puerto Ricans call la mancha *(literally, the stain: the mark of the new immigrant—something about the posture, the voice, or the humble demeanor that makes it obvious to everyone the person has just arrived on the mainland). My cousin is wearing a light, sequined, cocktail dress. Her brown hair has been lightened with peroxide around the bangs, and she is holding a cigarette expertly between her fingers, bringing it up to her mouth in a sensuous arc of her arm as she talks animatedly. My mother, who has come up to sit between the two women, both only a few years younger than herself, is somewhere between the poles they represent in our culture.*

It became my father's obsession to get out of the barrio, and thus we were never permitted to form bonds with the place or with the people who lived there. Yet El Building was a comfort to my mother, who never got over yearning for *la isla.* She felt surrounded by her language: the walls were thin, and voices speaking and arguing in Spanish could be heard all day. *Salsas* blasted out of radios, turned on early in the morning and left on for company. Women seemed to cook rice and beans perpetually—the strong aroma of boiling red kidney beans permeated the hallways.

Though Father preferred that we do our grocery shopping at the supermarket when he came home on weekend leaves, my mother insisted that she could cook only with products whose labels she could read. Consequently, during the week I accompanied her and my little brother to La Bodega—a hole-in-the-wall grocery store across the street from El Building. There we squeezed down three narrow aisles jammed with various products. Goya and Libby's—those were the trademarks that were trusted by her *mamá,* so my mother bought many cans of Goya beans, soups, and condiments, as well as little cans of Libby's fruit juices for us. And she also bought Colgate toothpaste and Palmolive soap. (The final *e* is pronounced in both these products in Spanish, so for many years I believed that they were manufactured on the Island. I remember my surprise at first hearing a commercial on television in which "Colgate" rhymed with "ate.") We always lingered at La Bodega, for it was there that Mother breathed best, taking in the familiar aromas of the foods she knew from Mamá's kitchen. It was also there that she got to speak to the other women of El Building without violating outright Father's dictates against fraternizing with our neighbors.

Yet Father did his best to make our "assimilation" painless. I can still see him carrying a real Christmas tree up several flights of stairs to our apartment, leaving a trail of aromatic pine. He carried it formally, as if it were a flag in a parade. We were the only ones in El Building that I knew of who got presents on both Christmas and *día de Reyes,* the day when the Three Kings brought gifts to Christ and to Hispanic children.

Our supreme luxury in El Building was having our own television set. It must have been a result of Father's guilt feelings over the isolation he had imposed on us, but we were among the first in the barrio to have one. My brother quickly became an avid watcher of Captain Kangaroo and Jungle Jim, while I loved all the series showing families. By the time I started first grade, I could have drawn a map of Middle America as exemplified by the lives of characters in *Father Knows Best, The Donna Reed Show, Leave It to Beaver, My Three Sons,* and (my favorite) *Bachelor Father,* where John Forsythe treated his adopted teenage daughter like a princess because he was rich and had a Chinese houseboy to do everything for him. In truth, compared to our neighbors in El Building, we were rich. My father's navy check provided us with financial security and a standard of living that the factory workers envied. The only thing his money could not buy us was a place to live away from the barrio—his greatest wish, Mother's greatest fear.

In the home movie the men are shown next, sitting around a card table set up in one corner of the living room, playing dominoes. The clack of the ivory pieces was a familiar sound. I heard it in many houses on the Island and in many apartments in Paterson. In Leave It to Beaver, *the Cleavers played bridge in every other episode; in my childhood, the men started every social occasion with a hotly debated round of dominoes. The women would sit around and watch, but they never participated in the games.*

Here and there you can see a small child. Children were always brought to parties and, whenever they got sleepy, were put to bed in the host's bedroom. Babysitting was a concept unrecognized by the Puerto Rican women I knew: a responsible mother did not leave her children with any stranger. And in a culture where children are not considered intrusive, there was no need to leave the children at home. We went where our mother went.

Of my preschool years I have only impressions: the sharp bite of the wind in December as we walked with our parents toward the brightly lit stores downtown; how I felt like a stuffed doll in my heavy coat, boots, and mittens; how good it was to walk into the five-and-dime and sit at the counter drinking hot chocolate. On Saturdays our whole family would walk downtown to shop at the big department stores on Broadway. Mother bought all our clothes at Penney's and Sears, and she liked to buy her dresses at the women's specialty shops like Lerner's and Diana's. At some point we'd go into Woolworth's and sit at the soda fountain to eat.

We never ran into other Latinos at these stores or when eating out, and it became clear to me only years later that the women from El Building shopped mainly in other places—stores owned by other Puerto Ricans or by Jewish merchants who had philosophically accepted our presence in the city and decided to make us their good customers, if not real neighbors and friends. These establishments were located not downtown but in the blocks around our street, and they were referred to generically as La Tienda, El Bazar, La Bodega, La Botánica. Everyone knew what was meant. These were the stores where your face did not turn a clerk to stone, where your money was as green as anyone else's.

One New Year's Eve we were dressed up like child models in the Sears catalogue: my brother in a miniature man's suit and bow tie, and I in black patent-leather shoes and a frilly dress with several layers of crinoline underneath. My mother wore a bright red dress that night, I remember, and spike heels; her long black hair hung to her waist. Father, who usually wore his navy uniform during his short visits home, had put on a dark civilian suit for the occasion: we had been invited to his uncle's house for a big celebration. Everyone was excited because my mother's brother Hernan—a bachelor who could indulge himself with luxuries—had bought a home movie camera, which he would be trying out that night.

Even the home movie cannot fill in the sensory details such a gathering left imprinted in a child's brain. The thick sweetness of women's perfumes mixing with the ever-present smells of food cooking in the kitchen: meat and plantain *pasteles,* as well as the ubiquitous rice dish made special with pigeon peas—*gandules*—and seasoned with precious *sofrito* sent up from the Island by somebody's mother or smuggled in by a recent traveler. *Sofrito* was one of the items that women hoarded, since it was hardly ever in stock at La Bodega. It was the flavor of Puerto Rico.

The men drank Palo Viejo rum, and some of the younger ones got weepy. The first time I saw a grown man cry was at a New Year's Eve party: he had been reminded of his mother by the smells in the kitchen. But what I remember most were the boiled *pasteles,* plantain or yucca rectangles stuffed with corned beef or other meats, olives, and many other savory ingredients, all wrapped in banana leaves. Everybody had to fish one out with a fork. There was always a "trick" *pastel*—one without stuffing—and whoever got that one was the "New Year's Fool."

There was also the music. Long-playing albums were treated like precious china in these homes. Mexican recordings were popular, but the songs that brought tears to my mother's eyes were sung by the melancholy Daniel Santos, whose life as a drug addict was the stuff of legend. Felipe Rodríguez was a particular favorite of couples, since he sang about faithless women and brokenhearted men. There is a snatch of one lyric that has stuck in my mind like a needle on a worn groove: *De piedra ha de ser mi cama, de piedra la cabezera . . . la mujer que a mi me quiera . . . ha de quererme de veras. Ay, Ay, Ay, corazón, porque no amas . . .* I must have heard it a thousand times since the idea of a bed made of stone, and its connection to love, first troubled me with its disturbing images.

The five-minute home movie ends with people dancing in a circle—the creative filmmaker must have set it up, so that all of them could file past him. It is both comical and sad to watch silent dancing. Since there is no justification for the absurd movements that music provides for some of us, people appear frantic, their faces embarrassingly intense. It's as if you were watching sex. Yet for years, I've had dreams in the form of this home movie. In a recurring scene, familiar faces push themselves forward into my mind's eye, plastering their features into distorted close-ups. And I'm asking them: "Who is *she?* Who is the old woman I don't recognize? Is she an aunt? Somebody's wife? Tell me who she is."

"See the beauty mark on her cheek as big as a hill on the lunar landscape of her face—well, that runs in the family. The women on your father's side of the family wrinkle early; it's the price they pay for that fair skin. The young girl with the green stain on her wedding dress is *la novia*—just up from the

Island. See, she lowers her eyes when she approaches the camera, as she's supposed to. Decent girls never look at you directly in the face. *Humilde,* humble, a girl should express humility in all her actions. She will make a good wife for your cousin. He should consider himself lucky to have met her only weeks after she arrived here. If he marries her quickly, she will make him a good Puerto Rican–style wife; but if he waits too long, she will be corrupted by the city, just like your cousin there."

"She means me. I do what I want. This is not some primitive island I live on. Do they expect me to wear a black mantilla on my head and go to mass every day? Not me. I'm an American woman, and I will do as I please. I can type faster than anyone in my senior class at Central High, and I'm going to be a secretary to a lawyer when I graduate. I can pass for an American girl anywhere—I've tried it. At least for Italian, anyway—I never speak Spanish in public. I hate these parties, but I wanted the dress. I look better than any of these *humildes* here. *My* life is going to be different. I have an American boyfriend. He is older and has a car. My parents don't know it, but I sneak out of the house late at night sometimes to be with him. If I marry him, even my name will be American. I hate rice and beans—that's what makes these women fat."

"Your *prima* is pregnant by that man she's been sneaking around with. Would I lie to you? I'm your *tía política,* your great-uncle's common-law wife—the one he abandoned on the Island to go marry your cousin's mother. *I* was not invited to this party, of course, but I came anyway. I came to tell you that story about your cousin that you've always wanted to hear. Do you remember the comment your mother made to a neighbor that has always haunted you? The only thing you heard was your cousin's name, and then you saw your mother pick up your doll from the couch and say: 'It was as big as this doll when they flushed it down the toilet.' This image has bothered you for years, hasn't it? You had nightmares about babies being flushed down the toilet, and you wondered why anyone would do such a horrible thing. You didn't dare ask your mother about it. She would only tell you that you had not heard her right, and yell at you for listening to adult conversations. But later, when you were old enough to know about abortions, you suspected.
    "I am here to tell you that you were right. Your cousin was growing an *americanito* in her belly when this movie was made. Soon after, she put something long and pointy into her pretty self, thinking maybe she could get rid of the problem before breakfast and still make it to her first class at the high school. Well, *niña,* her screams could be heard downtown. Your aunt, her *mamá,* who had been a midwife on the Island, managed to pull the little thing out. Yes, they probably flushed it down the toilet. What else could they do with it—give it a Christian burial in a little white casket with blue bows and ribbons? Nobody wanted that baby—least of all the father, a teacher at her school with a house in West Paterson that he was filling with real children, and a wife who was a natural blonde.
    "Girl, the scandal sent your uncle back to the bottle. And guess where your cousin ended up? Irony of ironies. She was sent to a village in Puerto Rico

to live with a relative on her mother's side: a place so far away from civilization that you have to ride a mule to reach it. A real change in scenery. She
found a man there—women like that cannot live without male company—but
believe me, the men in Puerto Rico know how to put a saddle on a woman like
her. *La gringa,* they call her. Ha, ha, ha. *La gringa* is what she always wanted to
be. . . ."

The old woman's mouth becomes a cavernous black hole I fall into. And as I fall, I
can feel the reverberations of her laughter. I hear the echoes of her last mocking
words: *la gringa, la gringa!* And the conga line keeps moving silently past me.
There is no music in my dream for the dancers.

When Odysseus visits Hades to see the spirit of his mother, he makes an offering of sacrificial blood, but since all the souls crave an audience with the living,
he has to listen to many of them before he can ask questions. I, too, have to hear
the dead and the forgotten speak in my dream. Those who are still part of my life
remain silent, going around and around in their dance. The others keep pressing
their faces forward to say things about the past.

My father's uncle is last in line. He is dying of alcoholism, shrunken and
shriveled like a monkey, his face a mass of wrinkles and broken arteries. As he
comes closer I realize that in his features I can see my whole family. If you were to
stretch that rubbery flesh, you could find my father's face, and deep within *that*
face—my own. I don't want to look into those eyes ringed in purple. In a few
years he will retreat into silence, and take a long, long time to die. *Move back, Tío,* I
tell him. *I don't want to hear what you have to say. Give the dancers room to move. Soon
it will be midnight. Who is the New Year's Fool this time?*

Running the Table

Frank Conroy

When I was fifteen and living in New York City, I was supposed to be going to Stuyvesant High School and in fact I did actually show up three or four times a week, full of gloom, anger and adolescent narcissism. The world was a dark place for me in those days. I lived in a kind of tunnel of melancholy, constantly in trouble at home, in school and occasionally with the police. (Pitching pennies, sneaking into movies, jumping the turnstile in the subway, stealing paperback books— fairly serious stuff in that earlier, more innocent time.) I was haunted by a sense of chaos, chaos within and chaos without. Which is perhaps why the orderliness of pool, the Euclidean cleanness of it, so appealed to me. The formality of pool struck me as soothing and reassuring, a sort of oasis of coolness, utterly rational and yet not without its elegant little mysteries. But I'm getting ahead of myself.

One day, meandering around 14th Street, I stepped through the open doors on an impulse and mounted the long, broad stairway. Halfway up I heard the click of the balls. What a marvelous sound! Precise, sharp, crisp, and yet somehow mellow. There was an intimacy to the sound that thrilled me. At the top of the stairs I pushed through saloon-style swinging doors and entered a vast, hushed, dim hall. Rows of pool tables stretched away in every direction, almost all of them empty at this early hour, but here and there in the distance, a pool of light, figures in silhouette circling, bending, taking shots. Nearby, two old men were playing a game I would later learn to be billiards on a large table without pockets. The click of the three balls, two white, one red, was what I had heard on the stairs. The men played unhurriedly, pausing now and then with their cues held like walking sticks to stare down at the street below. Cigar smoke swirled in the air.

I had walked into Julian's, little knowing that it was one of the most important pool halls on the East Coast. I was impressed by the stark functionality of the place—the absence of decoration of any kind. It seemed almost institutional in its atmosphere, right down to the large poster hung on the cashier's cage setting out

49

the rules and regulations. No drinking, no eating, no sitting on the edges of the tables, no spitting except in the cuspidors, no massé shots, etc. Tables were twenty-five cents an hour. Cue sticks were to be found on racks against the walls. Balls available from the cashier as he clocked you in.

"How do you play?" I asked.

The cashier was bald and overweight. He wore, for some reason, a green eyeshade. "You from Stuyvesant?"

I nodded, and he grunted, reached down to some hidden shelf and gave me a small paper pamphlet, pushing it forward across the worn wooden counter. I scanned it quickly. Basic information about straight pool, eight ball, nine ball, billiards, snooker, and a few other games. "Start with straight pool," he said. "Go over there and watch those guys on twenty-two for a while. Sit still, don't talk, and don't move around."

I did as I was told, sitting on a kind of mini-bleachers against the wall, my chin in my hands. The two men playing were in their twenties, an Abbott-and-Costello duo, thin Bud wearing a vest and smoking constantly, pudgy Lou moving delicately around the table, using the bridge now and then because of his short arms. They paid no attention to me and played with concentration, silent except for calling combinations.

"Six off the thirteen," Lou said.

Bud nodded. They only called combinations. All straight shots, no matter how difficult, were presumably obvious. After a while, with a few discreet glances at my pamphlet, I began to get the hang of it. All the balls, striped and solid, were fair game. You simply kept shooting until you missed, and then it was the other guy's turn. After each run, you moved some beads on a wire overhead with the tip of your cue, marking up the number of balls you'd sunk. So much for the rules. What was amazing was the shooting.

Object balls clipped so fine they moved sideways. Bank shots off the cushion into a pocket. Long combinations. Breakout shots in which a whole cluster of balls would explode in all directions while one from the middle would limp into a nearby pocket. And it didn't take long to realize that making a given shot was only part of what was going on. Controlling the position of the cue ball after the shot was equally important, so as to have a makable next shot. I could see that strategy was involved, although how they made the cue ball behave so differently in similar situations seemed nothing short of magical. Lou completed a run of nine or ten balls and reached fifty on the wire overhead. He had won, apparently.

"Double or nothing?"

Bud shook his head. Money changed hands. Lou put the balls in a tray, turned out the light over the table, and both men checked out at the cashier's. I sat for a while, thinking over what I had seen, reading the pamphlet again. I didn't have enough money to play that day, but I knew I was coming back.

Sometime in the late sixties, as an adult, I went to the Botanic Garden in Brooklyn to visit the recently completed Zen rock garden. It was a meticulous re-creation of a particular installation from a particular Japanese monastery. No one else was there. I sat on the bench gazing at the spiral patterns in the sand, looking at the black rocks set like volcanic islands in a white sea. Peace. Tranquility. As absurd as it may sound, I was reminded of my childhood experience of Julian's on a quiet afternoon—a sense of harmony, of an entirely disinterested material world entirely unaffected by one's perception of it.

For me, at fifteen, Julian's was a sort of retreat, a withdrawal from the world. I would shoot for hours at a time, racking up, breaking, shooting, racking up, breaking, shooting, in a solitary trance. Or I would surrender to the ritual of practice—setting up long shots over the length of the table again and again, trying to sink a shot with the same configuration ten times in a row, and then twenty, and then a more difficult configuration to a different pocket three times in a row, and then five, etc. I did not get bored with the repetition. Every time a ball went in the pocket I felt satisfaction. When I missed I simply ignored the fact, reset the shot and tried again. This went on for several weeks at a remote table in a far corner of the hall—table nineteen—which nobody else ever seemed to want. Once in a while I'd play with another kid, usually also from Stuyvesant, and split the time. After a couple of months I would sometimes play for the time—loser pays—against opponents who looked even weaker than myself. But most of the time I played alone.

Late one afternoon, racking up on table nineteen for perhaps the tenth time, I noticed a man sitting in the gloom up against the wall. He was extremely thin, with a narrow face and a protruding brow. He wore a double-breasted suit and two-tone shoes, one leg dangling languidly over the other. He gave me an almost imperceptible nod. I chalked the tip of my cue, went to the head of the table and stroked a clean break. Aware that I was being watched, I studied the lie of the balls for a moment and proceeded to sink seven in a row, everything going according to plan, until I scratched. I pulled up the cue ball and the object ball, recreated the shot and scratched again.

"Why don't you use English?" he asked quietly.

I stared at the table. "What's English?"

A moment's pause. "Set it up again," he said.

I did so.

"Aim, but don't hit. Pretend you're going to shoot."

I made a bridge with my left hand, aimed at the object ball and held the tip of my stick right behind the center of the cue ball.

"All right. All lined up?"

"Yes," I said, almost flat on the table.

"Do not change the line. Are you aiming at the center of the cue ball?"

"Yes."

"Aim a quarter of an inch higher."

"You mean I should. . . ." For some reason what he was suggesting seemed almost sacrilegious.

"Yes, yes. Don't hit the cue ball in the center. Strike a quarter of an inch above. Now go ahead. Shoot."

I made my stroke, watched the object ball go in, and watched the cue ball take a different path after impact than it had before. It didn't scratch this time, but missed the pocket, bounced smartly off the cushion and rolled to a stop near the center of the table for an easy next shot.

"Hey. That's terrific!" I said.

"That's English." He unfolded his legs and stood up. He came over and took the pool cue from my hands. "If a person pays attention," he said, "a person can learn about ninety-five percent of what he needs to know in about ten minutes. Ten minutes for the principles, then who knows how many years for the practice." His dark, deep-set eyes gave his face a vaguely ominous cast. "You want to learn?"

"Absolutely," I said without hesitation. "Yes."

As it turned out, it took about half an hour. The man teaching me was called Smilin' Jack, after the comic-strip character and presumably because of his glum demeanor. He was a Julian's regular, and it was my good luck to have caught him when somebody had stood him up for what was to have been a money game. I could sense that he enjoyed going through the drill—articulate, methodical, explicating on cause and effect with quiet relish, moving the balls around the table with no wasted motion whatsoever, executing the demo shots with a stroke as smooth as powdered silk—it was an elegant dance, with commentary. A sort of offering to the gods of pool.

I cannot possibly recount here what I learned. Follow, draw, left and right English and how they affect the movement of the cue ball after impact. The object ball picking up opposite English from the cue ball. The effectiveness of different kinds of English as a function of distance (between cue ball and object ball) and of speed. *Sliding* the cue ball. Playing the diamond points. Shooting a ball frozen on the cushion. How to read combinations, and on and on. I paid very close attention and jotted down what notes I could. (*Over*shoot bank shots to the side pockets. *Under*shoot bank shots to the corner pockets.) At the end of the half hour my head ached. In addition to trying to grasp the principles, I'd been trying to film the whole thing, to superimpose an eidetic memory on the cells of my brain, so I could retrieve what I'd seen at will. I was exhausted.

He handed me the stick, shot his cuffs and adjusted the front of his jacket with a slight forward movement of his shoulders. "That should keep you busy for a while." Then he simply walked away.

"Thanks," I called after him.

Without looking back, he raised his hand and gave a laconic little wave.

Practice, practice. Months of practice. It was a delicate business, English, affected by things like the relative roughness of the cue tip and its ability to hold chalk, or the condition of the felt, or infinitesimal degrees of table lean. But it worked. There was no doubt about it, when you got the feel of it you greatly increased your power over the all-important position of the cue ball. There was a word for it—the "leave," as in "good shot, but a tough leave." And of course the more you could control the leave, the more deeply involved was the strategy—planning out how to sink twelve balls in a row, rather than just five or six. Progress was slow, but it was tangible, and very, very satisfying. I began to beat people. I moved off table nineteen up toward the middle of the hall and began to beat almost everybody from Stuyvesant.

The most important hurdle for a straight-pool player involves being able to run into the second rack. You have to sink fourteen balls and leave the fifteenth ball and the cue ball positioned in such a way as to be able to sink the last ball (breaking open the new rack at the same time) and have a good enough leave to start all over again. I achieved this shortly before my sixteenth birthday, with a run of twenty-three.

The owners of Julian's recognized the accomplishment as a significant rite of passage and awarded certain privileges to those who had achieved it. During my last year of high school a cue of my own selection, with my name taped to the handle, was kept in a special rack behind the cashier's cage. No one else could use that particular cue stick. It was reserved, along with thirty or forty others for young players who had distinguished themselves.

I was a nonentity at school, but I could walk up to the cage at Julian's and the cashier would reach back for my stick and say, "Hey, Frank. How's it going?"

What a splendid place it was.

There's a lot to feel in pool, a physical aspect to the game, which means you have to play all the time to stay good. I've lost most of my chops (to borrow a word from jazz), but I still drop down to my local bar, the Foxhead, every now and then to play on the undersize table. It's a challenge arrangement. Put your name on the chalkboard, slip two quarters in the slot when it's your turn, and try to win.

There's a good deal more chance in eight ball, your basic bar game, than in straight pool, but it's fun. We've got some regulars. Jerry, a middle-aged man with a gorgeous stroke (a nationally ranked player in his youth), can beat anybody who walks into the place if he isn't furious at having to play doubles, at kids slopping beer onto the felt, or some other infraction of civilized behavior. There's Doug, a graduate student who always looks as if he'd spent the previous night in a cardboard box in an alley and who hits every shot as hard as he can, leaving the question of where the cue ball is going to end up more or less to the gods, in the hope that they will thus tangibly express the favor in which they hold him. (He is a poet.) We have George, an engineer, who exhausts our patience by approaching each situation with extreme care, circling the table several times, leaning over to stare down at a cluster of balls in what appears to be a hypnotic trance, chalking up with the care of Vermeer at the easel and running through a complicated series of various facial and physical tics before committing himself. There's Henry, who programs the jukebox to play "Brown Sugar" ten times in a row before he racks up. We've got students, working people, teachers, nurses (Yes. Women! Smilin' Jack would be scandalized) and barflies. We've got everybody at the Foxhead.

There are nights when I can hold the table for a couple of hours, but not very often. My touch is mostly gone, and bifocals make things difficult. Still, a bit of Julian's is still with me and, at the very least, I talk a good game.

Living Like Weasels

Annie Dillard

A weasel is wild. Who knows what he thinks? He sleeps in his underground den, his tail draped over his nose. Sometimes he lives in his den for two days without leaving. Outside, he stalks rabbits, mice, muskrats, and birds, killing more bodies than he can eat warm, and often dragging the carcasses home. Obedient to instinct, he bites his prey at the neck, either splitting the jugular vein at the throat or crunching the brain at the base of the skull, and he does not let go. One naturalist refused to kill a weasel who was socketed into his hand deeply as a rattlesnake. The man could in no way pry the tiny weasel off, and he had to walk half a mile to water, the weasel dangling from his palm, and soak him off like a stubborn label.

And once, says Ernest Thompson Seton—once, a man shot an eagle out of the sky. He examined the eagle and found the dry skull of a weasel fixed by the jaws to his throat. The supposition is that the eagle had pounced on the weasel and the weasel swiveled and bit as instinct taught him, tooth to neck, and nearly won. I would like to have seen that eagle from the air a few weeks or months before he was shot: was the whole weasel still attached to his feathered throat, a fur pendant? Or did the eagle eat what he could reach, gutting the living weasel with his talons before his breast, bending his beak, cleaning the beautiful airborne bones?

I have been reading about weasels because I saw one last week. I startled a weasel who startled me, and we exchanged a long glance.

Twenty minutes from my house, through the woods by the quarry and across the highway, is Hollins Pond, a remarkable piece of shallowness, where I like to go at sunset and sit on a tree trunk. Hollins Pond is also called Murray's Pond; it covers two acres of bottomland near Tinker Creek with six inches of water and six thousand lily pads. In winter, brown-and-white steers stand in the middle of it, merely dampening their hooves; from the distant shore they look like miracle itself, complete with miracle's nonchalance. Now, in summer, the steers are gone. The water lilies have blossomed and spread to a green horizontal plane that is terra firma to plodding blackbirds, and tremulous ceiling to black leeches, crayfish, and carp.

This is, mind you, suburbia. It is a five-minute walk in three directions to rows of houses, though none is visible here. There's a 55 mph highway at one end of the pond, and a nesting pair of wood ducks at the other. Under every bush is a muskrat hole or a beer can. The far end is an alternating series of fields and woods, fields and woods, threaded everywhere with motorcycle tracks—in whose bare clay wild turtles lay eggs.

So. I had crossed the highway, stepped over two low barbed-wire fences, and traced the motorcycle path in all gratitude through the wild rose and poison ivy of the pond's shoreline up into high grassy fields. Then I cut down through the woods to the mossy fallen tree where I sit. This tree is excellent. It makes a dry, upholstered bench at the upper, marshy end of the pond, a plush jetty raised from the thorny shore between a shallow blue body of water and a deep blue body of sky. The sun had just set. I was relaxed on the tree trunk, ensconced in the lap of lichen, watching the lily pads at my feet tremble and part dreamily over the thrusting path of a carp. A yellow bird appeared to my right and flew behind me. It caught my eye; I swiveled around—and the next instant, inexplicably, I was looking down at a weasel, who was looking up at me.

Weasel! I'd never seen one wild before. He was ten inches long, thin as a curve, a muscled ribbon, brown as fruitwood, soft-furred, alert. His face was fierce, small and pointed as a lizard's; he would have made a good arrowhead. There was just a dot of chin, maybe two brown hairs' worth, and then the pure white fur began that spread down his underside. He had two black eyes I didn't see, any more than you see a window.

The weasel was stunned into stillness as he was emerging from beneath an enormous shaggy wild rose bush four feet away. I was stunned into stillness twisted backward on the tree trunk. Our eyes locked, and someone threw away the key.

Our look was as if two lovers, or deadly enemies, met unexpectedly on an overgrown path when each had been thinking of something else: a clearing blow to the gut. It was also a bright blow to the brain, or a sudden beating of brains, with all the charge and intimate grate of rubbed balloons. It emptied our lungs. It felled the forest, moved the fields, and drained the pond; the world dismantled and tumbled into that black hole of eyes. If you and I looked at each other that way, our skulls would split and drop to our shoulders. But we don't. We keep our skulls. So.

He disappeared. This was only last week, and already I don't remember what shattered the enchantment. I think I blinked, I think I retrieved my brain from the weasel's brain, and tried to memorize what I was seeing, and the weasel felt the yank of separation, the careening splashdown into real life and the urgent current of instinct. He vanished under the wild rose. I waited motionless, my mind suddenly full of data and my spirit with pleadings, but he didn't return.

Please do not tell me about "approach-avoidance conflicts." I tell you I've been in that weasel's brain for sixty seconds, and he was in mine. Brains are private places, muttering through unique and secret tapes—but the weasel and I both plugged into another tape simultaneously, for a sweet and shocking time. Can I help it if it was a blank?

What goes on in his brain the rest of the time? What does a weasel think about? He won't say. His journal is tracks in clay, a spray of feathers, mouse blood and bone: uncollected, unconnected, loose-leaf, and blown.

I would like to learn, or remember, how to live. I come to Hollins Pond not so much to learn how to live as, frankly, to forget about it. That is, I don't think I can learn from a wild animal how to live in particular—shall I suck warm blood, hold my tail high, walk with my footprints precisely over the prints of my hands?—but I might learn something of mindlessness, something of the purity of living in the physical senses and the dignity of living without bias or motive. The weasel lives in necessity and we live in choice, hating necessity and dying at the last ignobly in its talons. I would like to live as I should, as the weasel lives as he should. And I suspect that for me the way is like the weasel's: open to time and death painlessly, noticing everything, remembering nothing, choosing the given with a fierce and pointed will.

I missed my chance. I should have gone for the throat. I should have lunged for that streak of white under the weasel's chin and held on, held on through mud and into the wild rose, held on for a dearer life. We could live under the wild rose wild as weasels, mute and uncomprehending. I could very calmly go wild. I could live two days in the den, curled, leaning on mouse fur, sniffing bird bones, blinking, licking, breathing musk, my hair tangled in the roots of grasses. Down is a good place to go, where the mind is single. Down is out, out of your ever-loving mind and back to your careless senses. I remember muteness as a prolonged and giddy fast, where every moment is a feast of utterance received. Time and events are merely poured, unremarked, and ingested directly, like blood pulsed into my gut through a jugular vein. Could two live that way? Could two live under the wild rose, and explore by the pond, so that the smooth mind of each is as everywhere present to the other, and as received and as unchallenged, as falling snow?

We could, you know. We can live any way we want. People take vows of poverty, chastity, and obedience—even of silence—by choice. The thing is to stalk your calling in a certain skilled and supple way, to locate the most tender and live spot and plug into that pulse. This is yielding, not fighting. A weasel doesn't "attack" anything; a weasel lives as he's meant to, yielding at every moment to the perfect freedom of single necessity.

I think it would be well, and proper, and obedient, and pure, to grasp your one necessity and not let it go, to dangle from it limp wherever it takes you. Then even death, where you're going no matter how you live, cannot you part. Seize it and let it seize you up aloft even, till your eyes burn out and drop; let your musky flesh fall off in shreds, and let your very bones unhinge and scatter, loosened over fields, over fields and woods, lightly, thoughtless, from any height at all, from as high as eagles.

From a Sheepherder's Notebook: Three Days

Gretel Ehrlich

When the phone rang, it was John: "Maurice just upped and quit and there ain't nobody else around, so you better get packed. I'm taking you out to herd sheep." I walked to his trailerhouse. He smoked impatiently while I gathered my belongings. "Do you know *anything* about herding sheep after all this time?" he asked playfully. "No, not really." I was serious. "Well, it's too late now. You'll just have to figure it out. And there ain't no phones up there either!"

He left me off on a ridge at five in the morning with a mare and a border collie. "Last I saw the sheep, they was headed for them hills," he said, pointing up toward a dry ruffle of badlands. "I'll pull your wagon up ahead about two miles. You'll see it. Just go up that ridge, turn left at the pink rock, then keep agoing. And don't forget to bring the damned sheep."

Morning. Sagesmell, sunsquint, birdsong, cool wind. I have no idea where I am, how to get to the nearest paved road, or how to find the sheep. There are tracks going everywhere so I follow what appear to be the most definite ones. The horse picks a path through sagebrush. I watch the dog. We walk for several miles. Nothing. Then both sets of ears prick up. The dog looks at me imploringly. The sheep are in the draw ahead.

Move them slow or fast? Which crossing at the river? Which pink rock? It's like being a first-time mother, but mother now to two thousand sheep who give me the kind of disdainful look a teenager would his parent and, with my back turned, can get into as much trouble. I control the urge to keep them neatly arranged, bunched up by the dog, and, instead, let them spread out and fill up. Grass being scarce on spring range, they scatter.

Up the valley, I encounter a slalom course of oil rigs and fenced spills I hadn't been warned about. The lambs, predictably mischievous, emerge dripping black. Freed from those obstacles, I ride ahead to find the wagon which, I admit, I'm afraid I'll never see, leaving the sheep on the good faith that they'll stay on their uphill drift toward me.

"Where are my boundaries?" I'd asked John.

"Boundaries?" He looked puzzled for a minute. "Hell, Gretel, it's all the outfit's land, thirty or forty miles in any direction. Take them anywhere they want to go."

On the next ridge I find my wagon. It's a traditional sheepherder's wagon, rounded top, tiny wood cookstove, bed across the back, built-in benches and drawers. The rubber wheels and long tongue make it portable. The camp tender pulls it (now with a pickup, earlier with teams) from camp to camp as the feed is consumed, every two weeks or so. Sheep begin appearing and graze toward me. I picket my horse. The dog runs for shade to lick his sore feet. The view from the dutch doors of the wagon is to the southeast, down the long slit of a valley. If I rode north, I'd be in Montana within the day, and next week I'll begin the fifty-mile trail cast to the Big Horns.

Three days before summer solstice; except to cook and sleep I spend every waking hour outside. Tides of weather bring the days and take them away. Every night a bobcat visits, perched at a discreet distance on a rock, facing me. A full moon, helium-filled, cruises through clouds and is lost behind rimrock. No paper cutout, this moon, but ripe and splendid. Then Venus, then the North Star. Time for bed. Are the sheep bedded down? Should I ride back to check them?

Morning. Blue air comes ringed with coyotes. The ewes wake clearing their communal throats like old men. Lambs shake their flop-eared heads at leaves of grass, negotiating the blade. People have asked in the past, "What do you do out there? Don't you get bored?" The problem seems to be something else. There's too much of everything here. I can't pace myself to it.

Down the valley the sheep move in a frontline phalanx, then turn suddenly in a card-stacked sequential falling, as though they had turned themselves inside out, and resume feeding again in whimsical processions. I think of town, of John's trailerhouse, the clean-bitten lawn, his fanatical obsession with neatness and work, his small talk with hired hands, my eyesore stacks of books and notes covering an empty bed, John smoking in the dark of early morning, drinking coffee, waiting for daylight to stream in.

After eating I return to the sheep, full of queasy fears that they will have vanished and I'll be pulled off the range to face those firing-squad looks of John's as he says, "I knew you'd screw up. Just like you screw up everything." But the sheep are there. I can't stop looking at them. They're there, paralyzing the hillside with thousands of mincing feet, their bodies pressed together as they move, saucerlike, scanning the earth for a landing.

Thunderstorm. Sheep feed far up a ridge I don't want them to go over, so the dog, horse, and I hotfoot it to the top and ambush them, yelling and hooting them back down. Cleverly, the horse uses me as a windbreak when the front moves in. Lightning fades and blooms. As we descend quickly, my rein-holding arm looks to me like a blank stick. I feel numb. Numb in all this vividness. I don't seem to occupy my life fully.

Down in the valley again I send the dog "way around" to turn the sheep, but he takes the law into his own hands and chases a lamb off a cliff. She's wedged upside down in a draw on the other side of the creek. It will take twenty minutes to reach her, and the rest of the sheep have already trailed ahead. This numbness is a wrist twisting inside my throat. A lone pine tree whistles, its needles are novocaine. "In nature there are neither rewards nor punishments; there are only consequences." I can't remember who said that. I ride on.

One dead. Will she be reborn? And as what? The dog that nips lambs' heels into butchering chutes? I look back. The "dead" lamb convulses into action and scrambles up the ledge to find his mother.

Twin terrors: to be awake; to be asleep.

All day clouds hang over the Beartooth Mountains. Looking for a place out of the wind, I follow a dry streambed to a sheltered inlet. In front of me, there's something sticking straight up. It's the shell of a dead frog propped up against a rock with its legs crossed at the ankles. A cartoonist's idea of a frog relaxing, but this one's skin is paper-thin, mouth opened as if to scream. I lean close. "It's too late, you're already dead!"

Because I forgot to bring hand cream or a hat, sun targets in on me like frostbite. The dog, horse, and I move through sagebrush in unison, a fortress against wind. Sheep ticks ride my peeling skin. The dog pees, then baptizes himself at the water hole—full immersion—lapping at spitting rain. Afterward, he rolls in dust and reappears with sage twigs and rabbit brush strung up in his coat, as though in disguise—a Shakespearian dog. Above me, oil wells are ridge-top jewelry adorning the skyline with ludicrous sexual pumps. Hump, hump go the wells. Hump, hump go the drones who gather that black soup, insatiable.

We walk the fuselage of the valley. A rattlesnake passes going the other way; plenty of warning but so close to my feet I hop the rest of the day. I come upon the tin-bright litter of a former sheep camp: Spam cans flattened to the ground, their keys sticking up as if ready to open my grave.

Sun is in and out after the storm. In a long gully, the lambs gambol, charging in small brigades up one side, then the other. Ewes look on bored. When the lamb-fun peters out, the whole band comes apart in a generous spread the way sheep ranchers like them. Here and there lambs, almost as big as their mothers, kneel with a contagiously enthusiastic wiggle, bumping the bag with a goatlike butt to take a long draw of milk.

Night. Nighthawks whir. Meadowlarks throw their heads back in one ecstatic song after another. In the wagon I find a piece of broken mirror big enough to see my face: blood drizzles from cracked lips, gnats have eaten away at my ears.

To herd sheep is to discover a new human gear somewhere between second and reverse—a slow, steady trot of keenness with no speed. There is no flab in these days. But the constant movement of sheep from water hole to water hole, from camp to camp, becomes a form of longing. But for what?

The ten other herders who work for this ranch begin to trail their sheep toward summer range in the Big Horns. They're ahead of me, though I can't see them for the curve of the earth. One-armed Red, Grady, and Ed; Bob, who always bakes a pie when he sees me riding toward his camp; Fred, wearer of rags; "Amorous Albert"; Rudy, Bertha, and Ed; and, finally, Doug, who travels circus-like with a menagerie of goats, roosters, colts, and dogs and keeps warm in the winter by sleeping with one of the nannies. A peaceful army, of which I am the tail end, moving in ragtag unison across the prairie.

A day goes by. Every shiver of grass counts. The shallows and dapples in air that give grass life are like water. The bobcat returns nightly. During easy jags of sleep the dog's dreampaws chase coyotes. I ride to the sheep. Empty sky, an absolute blue. Empty heart. Sunburned face blotches brown. Another layer of skin to peel, to meet myself again in the mirror. A plane passes overhead—probably the government trapper. I'm waving hello, but he speeds away.

Now it's tomorrow. I can hear John's truck, the stock racks speak before I can actually see him, and it's a long time shortening the distance between us.

"Hello."

"Hello."

He turns away because something tender he doesn't want me to see registers in his face.

"I'm moving you up on the bench. Take the sheep right out the tail end of this valley, then take them to water. It's where the tree is. I'll set your wagon by that road."

"What road?" I ask timidly.

Then he does look at me. He's trying to suppress a smile but speaks impatiently.

"You can see to hell and back up there, Gretel."

I ride to the sheep, but the heat of the day has already come on sizzling. It's too late to get them moving; they shade up defiantly, their heads knitted together into a wool umbrella. From the ridge there's whooping and yelling and rocks being thrown. It's John trying to get the sheep moving again. In a dust blizzard we squeeze them up the road, over a sharp lip onto the bench.

Here, there's wide-open country. A view. Sheep string out excitedly. I can see a hundred miles in every direction. When I catch up with John I get off my horse. We stand facing each other, then embrace quickly. He holds me close, then pulls away briskly and scuffles the sandy dirt with his boot.

"I've got to get back to town. Need anything?"

"Naw . . . I'm fine. Maybe a hat. . . ."

He turns and walks his long-legged walk across the benchland. In the distance, at the pickup, an empty beer can falls on the ground when he gets in. I can hear his radio as he bumps toward town. Dust rises like an evening gown behind his truck. It flies free for a moment, then returns, leisurely, to the habitual road—that bruised string which leads to and from my heart.

Northeast Direct

Dagoberto Gilb

I'm on board Amtrak's number 175 to Penn Station. I've traveled by train a couple of times in the past year, but last time I discovered that each car had one electrical outlet. Besides lots of room, besides that comforting, rolling motion, it's what I think about now when I think about the train. My Powerbook has a weak battery, and I can plug in and type as long as I want.

The car is empty. Maybe three of us new passengers, two previously seated. So I do feel a little awkward taking the seat right behind this guy who I saw hustle on several minutes before I did. He'd already reclined his aisle seat, thrown his day bag and warm coat on the one by the window. He was settled. I'm sure he was more than wondering why, with so many empty seats all around, I had to go and sit directly behind him. But I felt something too. Why did *he* have to pick a seat a row in front of the electrical outlet? And if he grumbled when I bumped the back of his seat to get by, I grumbled because I had to squeeze past to get over to the window seat behind him.

I'm over it quickly because I've got my machine on and I'm working. And he seems to be into his world too. He's taken a daily planner out, and he's checking a few things. I see this because, his seat reclined, I'm given a wedge view of his face looking forward and to the side. I see his left eye and the profile of his nose when he turns toward his window. When the conductor comes by for our tickets, he asks if there's a phone, then gets up to use it. I get immersed and barely notice him return.

I pause, and my eyes float up. He's holding a thick new book. I'm sort of looking it over with him. The way the cover feels, the way the chapters are set out. It seems like an attractively produced history book, and I bet he just bought it. He puts it down, then reaches over to the seat in front of me and brings up another.

The other book is the paperback of my novel! I *cannot* believe it! He stares at the cover for a moment, then he opens it. He's reading the acknowledgments page! When he's done he turns back to the title page for a moment, then puts the book down. He gets up and goes to a forward car, where the conductor said he'd find a phone.

How improbable is this? I mean, mine is definitely not a Danielle Steel, not a John Grisham. If it is this much shy of miraculous that I would be on a train with someone who had heard of my books at all, how much more miraculous that, because of an electrical outlet on a train, I'd be sitting inches from a person who just purchased the book and is opening it before my eyes? And look at it this way: of the possible combinations of seating arrangements in the train car, how many could give me this angle? And what if he hadn't put his seat back?

I know what you're thinking. That I should lean over and say, Hey man, you will *never* guess who's sitting behind you! No, that's not me. I don't want to do that. I won't. I want him to be my anonymous reader. How many opportunities does a writer have to learn a truthful reaction, really truthful, to his writing? How absorbed will he be? Will he smile at parts, groan at others? How about his facial expressions? Will his eyes light up or go dull?

As he's walking back, he's staring at me a little too strongly—but he can't know who I am. I'm feeling, naturally enough, self-conscious. He can't possibly know he's in the eyes of the author himself—to think it would be even *more* ridiculous than that it's true. It could be the bright yellow shirt I have on, which is a banner really, a United Farm Workers T-shirt celebrating Cesar Chávez. It reads *Cada trajabador es un organizador*. People are always looking at it and I practically can't wear it because they do. But he's not paying attention to my shirt. It's that I'm the dude sitting behind him, typing into his ear, breathing on his neck while we're on this empty train, with so much room, so many seats, with so much possible spacing. I think he probably doesn't like me. He's probably got names for me.

He sits down. He's picked up the book! He's gone to page one and he's *reading!* Somehow I just can't believe it, and I'm typing frantically about him and this phenomenon. He's a big guy, six-two. Wire glasses, blue, unplayful eyes. Grayish hair, indicating he's most likely not an undergrad, and beneath a Brown University cap, which, because he's wearing the cap, indicates he's probably not a professor. Grad student in English? Or he's into reading about the Southwest? Or maybe the cover has drawn him to the purchase. He's turned to page two! He's going! I have this huge smile as I'm typing. Bottom page two, and yes, his eyes shift to page three!

Suddenly he stops there. He gets up again. The phone is my bet. I'm taking the opportunity. I'm dying to know the name of the bookstore he's gone to, and I kind of arch upwards, over the back of the seat in front of me, to see a glossy store bag, when just as suddenly he's on his way back and he's eyeing me again. I squirm under the psychic weight of these circumstances, though now also from the guilty fact that I'm being so nosy. I pretend I am stretching, looking this way and that, rotating my neck—such uncomfortable seats, wouldn't you say?

He's reading the novel *again*. Page four, page five, page six! A woman walks by and he doesn't even glance up, isn't even curious whether she is attractive or not. He's so engrossed! He's *totally* reading now. No, wait. He stops, eyes to the window where it's New England, beautifully composed and framed by this snowy winter. Those tall, boxy two- and three-story board-and-batten houses painted colonial gray and colonial blue, two windows per floor, hip and gable roof, nubs of chimney poking up. Oh no, he's putting the book down. Closes it, mixes it into his other belongings on the seat next to him. It's because he's moving. He must hear my manic typing and he feels crowded and so he's picking up his stuff and going up an aisle. What an astute, serious, intelligent reader I have to feel so cramped! My reader wants to read in silence, be alone with his book and the thoughts generated by it and his reaction to it and he doesn't like some dude behind him jamming up his reading time and space with this muttering keyboard sound—it just makes me *smile* thinking how keen my reader's psychic synapses are to be responding to what his conscious mind cannot know is occurring. It must be a raging psychic heat, a dizzying psychic pheromone. When he has settled comfortably into his new seat, he pulls the novel back up. He's reading again! Reading and reading! When that young woman passes through on her return, no, again, he does not look up. He's dedicated, fully concentrating. He's really reading, one page after another.

New England: white snow, silver water, leafless branches and limbs. Lumber and boat and junk yards. The bare behind of industry, its dirty underwear, so beautifully disguised by winter.

My reader has fallen asleep. We haven't been on the train an hour and my writing has made him succumb to a nap? Nah, I don't find it a bad thing. Not in the slightest. It's really a compliment. How many books do you fall asleep with? The conductor wakes him up, though. He's sorry but he found that daily planner on the seat behind him and wanted to make sure it belonged to him. But my reader goes right back to sleep. He's dead asleep now. A goner. I pass him on my way to buy myself a drink, and he's got his left thumb locked inside the book, his index finger caressing the spine, pinching. You see, my reader does not want to lose his place.

We both wake up at New Haven. Probably getting a little carried away. I thought he might get off here—walking the book into Yale. He reopens it. He's at the beginning of chapter two. He does read slowly. He's lazy? I say he's thoughtful, a careful, considerate reader, complementing precisely the manner in which I wrote the novel. It's not meant to be read quickly. He's absolutely correct to read it the way he does.

Forty-five minutes outside Penn Station, many passengers have boarded, cutting my reader and me off. He is still up there reading, but with the passage of time, and our physical distance blunted more by a clutter of other minds sitting between and around us, the shock and mystery have lessened in me. I have adjusted, accepted it. By now I am behaving as though it were ordinary that a stranger two aisles above is reading my work. Like every other miracle that happens in life, I am taking the event for granted already, letting it fade into the everyday of people filling trains, going home from work, going. He is reading the novel, and I am certain, by the steady force and duration of his commitment, that he fully intends to read unto the end. He and I both can look around, inside the car and out the window, and then we go back, him to the book, me to the computer keyboard, no longer writing about this.

So when the moment comes, ask what, how? Tap him on the shoulder, say excuse me, but you know I couldn't help but notice that book you're reading, and it's such an amazing coincidence, it *really* is *so* amazing how this can happen, but I was just talking with a friend about that very novel this morning—change that—I was talking to two friends, and one thought it was just great, while the other— change that—and one thought it was just great, and I wondered what you felt about it, and how did you hear of it anyway?

After the conductor announces Penn Station, we stand and get our coats on, and, the train still swaying, move down the aisle and toward the door with our bags. I'm waiting right behind him. Can easily tap him on the shoulder. But nobody else is talking. No one, not a word. So I can't either, especially when I'd be making fake conversation. Train stops, door opens, people in front of him move forward, and a woman in an aisle steps in between me and him with her large, too-heavy-for-her suitcase. He's shot out quickly ahead of me now, up an escalator, several more people between us. When I reach the main floor of the station, get beneath the flapping electronic board that posts trains and times and departure tracks, I have caught up with him. He has stopped to get his bearings. Just as I am at his shoulder, he takes off in the same direction I'm going.

So we're walking briskly side by side in cold Penn Station. You know what? He doesn't want to talk. I am sure he has no desire to speak with me. Would definitely not want to have that conversation I'd planned. No time for me to fumble around and, maybe, eventually, tell him how I am the writer. This is New York City, no less. He's in a hurry. He'd grimace and shake his head, brush me off. He already thinks I am one of those irritating people you encounter on a trip, the one always at the edge of your sight, the one you can never seem to shake. And so as I begin a ride up the escalator toward the taxi lines, I watch him go straight ahead, both of us covered with anonymity like New England snow.

Oval

Gail Griffin

Silly Putty

It came in a plastic egg that fit in your palm, split lengthwise. Inside, it lay proto-plasmic, fetal pink. It didn't harden or pull apart like clay. When you bit into it, your eyetooth sank and then popped through, as through a rubber lip. We pulled it like taffy, rolled it into worms or into balls we bounced off the floor or desktop. We pressed it down onto newspaper and then peeled it away, drawing up the faces of Nancy and Sluggo, Snoopy, Archie and Veronica, a bold headline letter, a scrap of news. Then we'd stretch it, distorting the faces, elongating the story into parody. Finally we'd fold it into a mouth that chewed and swallowed letters and colors, working them back into the pink, graying it to beige. Putty took it all in, even the funnies we didn't understand, the news we wouldn't hear for years.

Fractured Skull

If there were a film it would show Mary's head ricocheting back off the tree and hitting mine, the back ridge of her skull slamming into my broad, flat forehead. The big kids got blamed for letting us go down on the toboggan without one of them. How new we were, to have hung on as the tree rushed toward us, to have been too frightened, too rapt in speed simply to fall off, roll away into the snow. I had a big lump, navy blue and green. Mary had a fractured skull. She hadn't yet shed her cloudy baby tongue, so she said it was *fwack-shode*. She disappeared from kindergarten for long weeks, and we felt her absence like a small ghost. When she came back, wearing a soft pink-and-white wool hat, it was as if she were an angel returned from some edge we hadn't known about, where her head, now fuzzy bald like a new chick's, had cracked and some of her pale lisping life had seeped out.

Rabbit Egg

The book was large and thin, shiny dark green, and it had no words. A baby rabbit, small and brown, curled inside an egg, fast asleep. Outside, in the world, a duck studied the egg lovingly. The duck pecked and kicked at it, jumped on it, rolled it down a hill, but the shell held and the rabbit slept, curled into itself, bigger and bigger for every page. Finally the rabbit was full-grown, still cramped inside the now-huge egg, quiet, four feet pressing against the inside of the shell like a giant pushing against the pearly shell of a sky, having outgrown a perfect, fragile world. The egg cracked, finally, and rabbit woke to duck, to this weird love waiting as if it were meant to be.

Parish Streets

Patricia Hampl

Lexington, Oxford, Chatsworth, continuing down Grand Avenue to Milton and Avon, as far as St. Albans—the streets of our neighborhood had an English, even an Anglican, ring to them. But we were Catholic, and the parishes of the diocese, unmarked and ghostly as they were, posted borders more decisive than the street signs we passed on our way to St. Luke's grade school or, later, walking in the other direction to Visitation Convent for high school.

We were like people with dual citizenship. I *lived* on Linwood Avenue, but I *belonged* to St. Luke's. That was the lingo. Mothers spoke of daughters who were going to the junior-senior prom with boys "from Nativity" or "from St. Mark's," as if from fiefdoms across the sea.

"Where you from?" a boy livid with acne asked when we startled each other lurking behind a pillar in the St. Thomas Academy gym at a Friday night freshman mixer.

"Ladies' choice!" one of the mothers cried from a dim corner where a portable hi-fi was set up. She rasped the needle over the vinyl, and Fats Domino came on, insinuating a heavier pleasure than I yet knew: *I found my thrill . . . on Blueberry Hill.*

"I'm from Holy Spirit," the boy said, as if he'd been beamed in to stand by the tepid Cokes and tuna sandwiches and the bowls of sweating potato chips on the refreshments table.

Parish members did not blush to describe themselves as being "from Immaculate Conception." Somewhere north, near the city line, there was even a parish frankly named Maternity of Mary. But then, in those years, the 1950s and early 1960s, breeding was a low-grade fever pulsing amongst us unmentioned, like a buzz or hum you get used to and cease to hear. The white noise of matrimonial sex.

On Sundays the gray stone nave of St. Luke's church, big as a warehouse, was packed with families of eight or ten sitting in the honey-colored pews. The fathers wore brown suits. In memory they appear spectrally thin, wraithlike and spent, like trees hollowed of their pulp. The wives were petite and cheerful with helmet-like haircuts. Perkiness was their main trait. But what did they say, these small women, how did they talk? Mrs. Healy, mother of fourteen ("They can afford them," my mother said, as if to excuse her paltry two. "He's a doctor."), never uttered a word, as far as I remember. Even pregnant, she was somehow wiry, as if poised for a tennis match. Maybe these women only wore a *look* of perkiness, and like their lean husbands, they were sapped of personal strength. Maybe they were simply tense.

Not everyone around us was Catholic. Mr. Kirby, a widower who was our next door neighbor, was Methodist—whatever that was. The Nugents across the street behind their cement retaining wall and double row of giant salvia, were Lutheran, more or less. The Williams family, who subscribed to the *New Yorker* and had a living room outfitted with spare Danish furniture, were Episcopalian. They referred to their minister as a priest—a plagiarism that embarrassed me for them because I liked them and their light, airy ways.

As for the Bertrams, our nearest neighbors to the west, it could only be said that Mrs. Bertram, dressed in a narrow suit with a peplum jacket and a hat made of the same heathery wool, went *somewhere* via taxi on Sunday mornings. Mr. Bertram went nowhere—on Sunday or on any other day. He was understood, during my entire girlhood, to be indoors, resting.

Weekdays, Mrs. Bertram took the bus to her job downtown. Mr. Bertram stayed home behind their birchwood Venetian blinds in an aquarium half-light, not an invalid (we never thought of him that way), but a man whose occupation it was to rest. Sometimes in the summer he ventured forth with a large wrench-like gadget to root out the masses of dandelions that gave the Bertram lawn a temporary brilliance in June.

I associated him with the Wizard of Oz. He was small and mild-looking, going bald. He gave the impression of extreme pallor except for small, very dark eyes.

It was a firm neighborhood rumor that Mr. Bertram had been a screenwriter in Hollywood. Yes, that pallor was a writer's pallor; those small dark eyes were a writer's eyes. They saw, they noted.

He allowed me to assist him in the rooting-out of his dandelions. I wanted to ask him about Hollywood—had he met Audrey Hepburn? I couldn't bring myself to manœuvre for information on such an important subject. But I did feel something serious was called for here. I introduced religion while he plunged the dandelion gadget deep into the lawn.

No, he said, he did not go to church. "But you do believe in God?" I asked, hardly daring to hope he did not. I longed for novelty.

He paused for a moment and looked up at the sky where big, spreading clouds streamed by. "God isn't the problem," he said.

Some ancient fissure split open, a fine crack in reality: so there *was* a problem. Just as I'd always felt. Beneath the family solidity, the claustrophobia of mother-father-brother-me, past the emphatic certainties of St. Luke's catechism class, there was a problem that would never go away. Mr. Bertram stood amid his dandelions, resigned as a Buddha, looking up at the sky which gave back nothing but drifting white shapes on the blue.

What alarmed me was my feeling of recognition. Of course there was a problem. It wasn't God. Life itself was a problem. Something was not right, would never be right. I'd sensed it all along, some kind of fishy vestigial quiver in the spine. It was bred in the bone, way past thought. Life, deep down, lacked the substantiality that it *seemed* to display. The physical world, full of detail and interest, was a parched topsoil that could be blown away.

This lack, this blankness akin to chronic disappointment, was everywhere, under the perkiness, lurking even within my own happiness. "What are you going to do today?" my father said when he saw me digging in the backyard on his way to work at the greenhouse.

"I'm digging to China," I said.

"Well, I'll see you at lunch," he said, "if you're still here."

I wouldn't bite. I frowned and went back to work with the bent tablespoon my mother had given me. It wasn't a game. I wanted out. I was on a desperate journey that only looked like play. I couldn't explain.

The blank disappointment, masked as weariness, played on the faces of people on the St. Clair bus. They looked out the windows, coming home from downtown, unseeing: clearly nothing interested them. What were they thinking of? The passing scene was not beautiful enough—was that it?—to catch their eye. Like the empty clouds Mr. Bertram turned to, their blank looks gave back nothing. There was an unshivered shiver in each of us, a shudder we managed to hold back.

We got off the bus at Oxford where, one spring, in the lime green house behind the catalpa tree on the corner, Mr. Lenart (whom we didn't know well) had slung a pair of tire chains over a rafter in the basement and hanged himself. Such things happened. Only the tight clutch of family life ("The family that prays together stays together.") could keep things rolling along. Step out of the tight, bright circle, and you might find yourself dragging your chains down to the basement.

The perverse insubstantiality of the material world was the problem: reality refused to be real enough. Nothing could keep you steadfastly happy. That was clear. Some people blamed God. But I sensed that Mr. Bertram was right not to take that tack. *God is not the problem.* The clouds passing in the big sky kept dissipating, changing form. That was the problem—but so what? Such worries resolved nothing, and were best left unworried—the unshivered shiver.

There was no one to blame. You could only retire, like Mr. Bertram, stay indoors behind your birchwood blinds, and contemplate the impossibility of things, allowing the Hollywood glitter of reality to fade away and become a vague local rumor.

There were other ways of coping. Mrs. Krueger, several houses down with a big garden rolling with hydrangea bushes, held as her faith a passionate belief in knowledge. She sold *World Book* encyclopedias. After trying Christian Science and a stint with the Unitarians, she had settled down as an agnostic. There seemed to be a lot of reading involved with being an agnostic, pamphlets and books, long citations on cultural anthropology in the *World Book*. It was an abstruse religion, and Mrs. Krueger seemed to belong to some ladies' auxiliary of disbelief.

But it didn't really matter what Mrs. Krueger decided about "the deity-idea," as she called God. No matter what they believed, our neighbors lived not just on Linwood Avenue; they were in St. Luke's parish too, whether they knew it or not. We claimed the territory. And we claimed them—even as we dismissed them. They were all non-Catholics, the term that disposed nicely of all spiritual otherness.

Let the Protestants go their schismatic ways; the Lutherans could splice themselves into synods any which way. Believers, non-believers, even Jews (the Kroners on the corner) or a breed as rare as the Greek Orthodox whose church was across the street from St. Luke's—they were all non-Catholics, just so much extraneous spiritual matter orbiting the nethersphere.

Or maybe it was more intimate than that, and we dismissed the rest of the world as we would our own serfs. We saw the Lutherans and Presbyterians, even those snobbish Episcopalians, as rude colonials, non-Catholics all, doing the best they could out there in the bush to imitate the ways of the homeland. *We* were the homeland.

Jimmy Guiliani was a bully. He pulled my hair when he ran by me on Oxford as we all walked home from St. Luke's, the girls like a midget army in navy jumpers and white blouses, the boys with the greater authority of free civilians without uniforms. They all wore pretty much the same thing anyway: corduroy pants worn smooth at the knees and flannel shirts, usually plaid.

I wasn't the only one Jimmy picked on. He pulled Moira Murphy's hair, he punched Tommy Hague. He struck without reason, indiscriminately, so full of violence it may have been pent-up enthusiasm released at random after the long day leashed in school. Catholic kids were alleged, by public school kids, to be mean fighters, dirty fighters.

Jimmy Guiliani was the worst, a terror, hated and feared by Sister Julia's entire third grade class.

So, it came as a surprise when, after many weeks of his tyranny, I managed to land a sure kick to his groin and he collapsed in a heap and cried real tears. "You shouldn't *do* that to a boy," he said, whimpering. He was almost primly admonishing. "Do you know how that feels?"

It's not correct to say that it was a sure kick. I just kicked. I took no aim and had no idea I'd hit paydirt—or why. Even when the tears started to his eyes and he doubled over clutching himself, I didn't understand.

But I liked it when he asked if I knew how it felt. For a brief, hopeful moment I thought he would tell me, that he would explain. Yes, tell me: how *does* it feel? And what's *there*, anyway? It was the first time the male body imposed itself.

I felt an odd satisfaction. I'd made contact. I wasn't glad I had hurt him, I wasn't even pleased to have taken the group's revenge on the class bully. I hadn't planned to kick him. It all just *happened*—as most physical encounters do. I was more astonished than he that I had succeeded in wounding him, I think. In a simple way, I wanted to say I was sorry. But I liked being taken seriously, and could not forfeit that rare pleasure by making an apology.

For a few weeks after I kicked him, I had a crush on Jimmy Guiliani. Not because I'd hurt him. But because he had paused, looked right at me, and implored me to see things from his point of view. *Do you know how it feels?*

I didn't know—and yet I did. As soon as he asked, I realized obscurely that I did know how it felt. I knew what was there between his legs where he hurt. I ceased to be ignorant at that moment. And sex began—with a blow.

The surprise of knowing what I hadn't realized I knew seemed beautifully private, but also illicit. That was a problem. I had no desire to be an outlaw. The way I saw it, you were supposed to know what you had been *taught*. This involved being given segments of knowledge by someone (usually a nun) designated to dole out information in measured drams, like strong medicine.

Children were clean slates others were meant to write on.

But here was evidence I was not a blank slate at all. I was scribbled all over with intuitions, premonitions, vague resonances clamoring to give their signals. I had caught Mr. Bertram's skyward look and its implicit promise: life will be tough. There was no point in blaming God—the Catholic habit. Or even more Catholic, blaming the nuns, which allowed you to blame Mother and God all in one package.

And here was Jimmy Guiliani drawing out of me this other knowledge, bred of empathy and a swift kick to his privates. *Yes, I know how it feels.*

The hierarchy we lived in, a great linked chain of religious being, seemed set to control every entrance and exit to and from the mind and heart. The buff-colored *Baltimore Catechism*, small and square, read like an owner's manual for a very complicated vehicle. There was something pleasant, lulling and rhythmic, like heavily rhymed poetry, about the sing-song Q-and-A format. Who would not give over heart, if not mind, to the brisk nannyish assurance of the Baltimore prose:

> Who made you?
> *God made me.*
> Why did God make you?
> *God made me to know, love and serve Him in this world, in order to*
> *be happy with Him forever in the next.*

What pleasant lines to commit to memory. And how harmless our Jesuitical discussions about what, exactly, constituted a meatless spaghetti sauce on Friday. Strict constructionists said no meat of any kind should ever, at any time, have made its way into the tomato sauce; easy liberals held with the notion that meatballs could be lurking around in the sauce, as long as you didn't eat them. My brother lobbied valiantly for the meatball *intactus* but present. My mother said nothing doing. They raged for years.

Father Flannery, who owned his own airplane and drove a sports car, had given Peter some ammunition when he'd been asked to rule on the meatball question in the confessional. My mother would hear none of it. "I don't want to know what goes on between you and your confessor," she said, taking the high road.

"A priest, Ma, a *priest*," my brother cried. "This is an ordained priest saying right there in the sanctity of the confessional that meatballs are OK."

But we were going to heaven my mother's way.

Life was like that—crazy. Full of hair-splitting, and odd rituals. We got our throats blessed on St. Blaise day in February, with the priest holding oversized beeswax candles in an X around our necks, to ward off death by choking on fishbones. There were smudged foreheads on Ash Wednesday, and home May altars with plaster statuettes of the Virgin festooned with lilacs. Advent wreaths and nightly family rosary vigils during October (Rosary Month), the entire family on their knees in the living room.

There were snatches of stories about nuns who beat kids with rulers in the coat room; the priest who had a twenty-year affair with a member of the Altar and Rosary Society; the other priest in love with an altar boy—they'd had to send him away. Not St. Luke's stories—oh no, certainly not—but stories, floating, as stories do, from inner ear to inner ear, respecting no parish boundaries. Part of the ether.

And with it all, a relentless xenophobia about other religions. "It's going to be a mixed marriage, I understand," one of my aunts murmured about a friend's daughter who was marrying an Episcopalian. So what if he called himself High Church? What did that change? He was a non-Catholic.

And now, educated out of it all, well climbed into the professions, the Catholics find each other at cocktail parties and get going. The nun stories, the first confession traumas—and a tone of rage and dismay that seems to bewilder even the tellers of these tales.

Nobody says, when asked, "I'm Catholic." It's always, "Yes, I was brought up Catholic." Anything to put it at a distance, to diminish the presence of that grabby heritage that is not racial but acts as if it were. "You never get over it, you know," a fortyish lawyer told me a while ago at a party where we found ourselves huddled by the chips and dip, as if we were at a St. Thomas mixer once again.

He seemed to feel he was speaking to someone with the same hopeless congenital condition. "It's different now, of course," he said. "But when we were growing up back there. . . ." Ah yes, the past isn't a time. It's a place. And it's always there.

He had a very Jimmy Guiliani look to him. A chastened rascal. "I'm divorced," he said. We both smiled: there's no going to hell anymore. "Do they still have mortal sin?" he asked wistfully.

The love-hate lurch of a Catholic upbringing, like having an extra set of parents to contend with. Or an added national allegiance—not to the Vatican, as we were warned that the Baptists thought during John Kennedy's campaign for president. The allegiance was to a different realm. It was the implacable loyalty of faith, that flawless relation between self and existence which we were born into. A strange country where people prayed and believed impossible things.

The nuns who taught us, rigged up in their bold black habits with the big round wimples stiff as frisbees, walked our parish streets; they moved from convent to church in twos or threes, dipping in the side door of the huge church "for a little adoration," as they would say. The roly-poly Irish-born monsignor told us to stand straight and proud when he met us slouching along Summit toward class. And fashionable Father Flannery who, every night, took a gentle, companionable walk with the old Irish pastor, the two of them taking out white handkerchiefs, waving them for safety, as they crossed the busy avenue on the way home in the dark, swallowed in their black suits and cassocks, invisible in the gloom.

But the one I would like to summon up most and to have pass me on Oxford as I head off to St. Luke's in the early morning mist, one of those mid-May weekdays, the lilacs just starting to spill, that one I want most to materialize from "back there"—I don't know her name, where, exactly, she lived, or who she was. We never spoke, in fact. We just passed each other, she coming home from six o'clock daily Mass, I going early to school to practice the piano for an hour before class began.

She was a "parish lady," part of the anonymous population that thickened our world, people who were always there, who were solidly part of us, part of what we were, but who never emerged beyond the bounds of being parishioners to become persons.

We met every morning, just past the Healy's low brick wall. She wore a librarian's cardigan sweater. She must have been about forty-five, and I sensed she was not married. Unlike Dr. and Mrs. Harrigan who walked smartly along Summit holding hands, their bright Irish setter accompanying them as far as the church door where he waited till Mass was over, the lady in the cardigan was always alone.

I saw her coming all the way from Grand where she had to pause for the traffic. She never rushed across the street, zipping past a truck, but waited until the coast was completely clear, and passed across keeping her slow, almost floating pace. A lovely, peaceful gait, no rush to it.

When finally we were close enough to make eye contact, she looked up, straight into my face, and smiled. It was such a *complete* smile, so entire, that it startled me every time, as if I'd heard my name called out on the street of a foreign city.

She was a homely woman, plain and pale, unnoticeable. But I felt—how to put it— that she shed light. The mornings were often frail with mist, the light uncertain and tender. The smile was a brief flood of light. She loved me, I felt.

I knew what it was about. She was praying. Her hand, stuck in her cardigan pocket, held one of the crystal beads of her rosary. I knew this. I'd once seen her take it out of the left pocket and quickly replace it after she had found the handkerchief she needed.

If I had seen a nun mumbling the rosary along Summit (and that did happen), it would not have meant much to me. But here on Oxford, the side street we used as a sleepy corridor to St. Luke's, it was a different thing. The parish lady was not a nun. She was a person who prayed, who prayed alone, for no reason that I understood. But there was no question that she prayed without ceasing, as the strange scriptural line instructed.

She didn't look up to the blank clouds for a response, as Mr. Bertram did in his stoic way. Her head was bowed, quite unconsciously. And when she raised it, keeping her hand in her pocket where the clear beads were, she looked straight into the eyes of the person passing by. It was not an invasive look, but one brimming with a secret which, if only she had words, it was clear she would like to tell.

Can an Ape Tell a Joke?

Vicki Hearne

W.H. Auden wrote that poetry survives in those places where "executives would never want to tamper." Similarly, the knowledge of animals survives in places where academics would never want to tamper, even now that many of them have added their voices to the babble that presently obscures the reality of animals. It survives in the circus, eerily revealed by Mark Twain as a place where truth is guarded by scams—by what most would consider tawdry but which Huckleberry Finn embraced as "gaudy." It lives in the shabbier parts of public parks where dog obedience classes are conducted. And it lives at the racetrack, where the beauty of the horses, glowing as though each were the darling of the infinite god of detail, stands in sharp contrast to the gray faces of the gamblers.

But perhaps the least likely place one would expect to find deep knowledge about animals is in a trained-orangutan act on a Las Vegas stage—specifically, in the act performed for many years by Bobby Berosini and his five orangutans at the Stardust Hotel and Casino. I first saw Bobby Berosini's Vegas act three years ago, shortly after he received an unwelcome dose of national celebrity. Now that I've spent a week with him and his orangutans, and watched a dozen of his performances, I'm convinced that he deserves his celebrity, though not for the reasons he has come by it.

I would not ordinarily have ventured to Las Vegas to watch a trained-orangutan show, but Bobby Berosini, who immigrated to the United States from his native Czechoslovakia in 1964, is no ordinary animal trainer. I had heard he'd won numerous comedy awards for his act, and that he had probably done more with orangutans—famously difficult animals to train—than any trainer ever has. But this was not the reason for his sudden notoriety. He had been accused in 1989 of abusing his orangutans by, among others, People for the Ethical Treatment of Animals. This in itself was not unusual: these days animal trainers are regularly attacked by animal-rights activists. What was unusual in this case was that the trainer had fought back, suing PETA for defamation and invasion of privacy. And, most unusual of all, he had won his case: after a five-week trial in which Berosini brought his orangutans into court, a jury found PETA, along with several individual activists, guilty of "reckless disregard of the truth" and awarded Berosini $3.1 million in damages. (The judgment is currently on appeal.)

Berosini did not sue for harassment, but while I was in Las Vegas his Australian-born wife, Joan, described to me the harrowing experience of receiving repeated death threats against themselves and their animals in the middle of the night; of spending six months living with armed security guards twenty-four hours a day; and of being forced to shop at a different supermarket each day, since some of the threats had detailed plans to poison the orangs' food. (Many animal-rights activists believe that wild animals are better off dead than confined in any way by humans.) Even today, the harassment continues: when Berosini recently moved his act to the Five Star Theatre in Branson, Missouri, the PETA picketers followed.

Mad as some of these tactics were, the charges against Bobby Berosini were not ones that could be summarily dismissed. PETA had circulated a videotape, made surreptitiously backstage by a Stardust dancer, that purported to document the abuse. The tape, which was broadcast on *Entertainment Tonight,* is of extremely poor quality, but it appears to show Berosini and his assistants on about a half-dozen occasions preparing the animals to go onstage. In each instance one of the orangutans—it's hard to tell, but it looks like the same orang each time—seems to act up and is then threatened, shaken, or struck by Berosini with a wand or baton of some kind.

Jeanne Roush, then PETA's director of research and investigations, and one of the losing defendants, charged that the orangs were routinely beaten into submission right before going onstage. Berosini said that, on each of the occasions videotaped, he had had to correct the orangutan backstage because a dancer was making sounds of distressed animals to rile the orangutans. Before I got to Las Vegas, it was impossible to sort out who was telling the truth, so I decided not to pay too much attention to what was being said on either side.

What I would pay attention to, I decided, was what I saw myself—and what, as an animal trainer, I know about animals. I know, for example, that the "correction" of an animal in training is an intricate and poorly understood subject. Properly applied at the right moment, a correction will cause the animal to stop aggressive behavior and perform happily and well. But a correction that expresses the trainer's anger, impatience, or fear, or that is applied when the animal is honestly confused rather than disobedient, will leave the animal unable to perform. Since no one had said that the orangs muffed their performances after the corrections we see on the tape, I can only assume that Berosini was using good judgment.

I assume this also from the uncontested fact that the animals were performing live, twice a night, six nights a week, at liberty—that is, without any physical restraint on an unguarded stage. Roger Fouts, a primatologist who testified in another performing-ape case, has said that "you can get anyone to do anything if you beat them," but, in fact, this is not so. You can perhaps accomplish a fair amount by beating an animal or person who cannot escape (though you can't thereby engage the victim's higher faculties), but not if you beat an animal or person you then leave at liberty.

These thoughts occurred to me before I had had a chance to watch Berosini work, so I came to Las Vegas prepared to doubt PETA's charges. And after spending a week with Berosini, watching twelve performances and joining him backstage before several of them, I saw nothing to make me think he was a cruel or phony trainer—no thumps, no fists. (Could Berosini have acted differently while I was around? Possibly, but any trainer who behaves differently in public than in private will soon lose the respect of his animals.)

What I did see, there amid the Vegas glitz and against the ugly backdrop of this furious animal-rights battle, was mastery, and even a kind of miracle. Berosini and his orangs are, to be sure, masters of much that is gaudy—his act is a half hour of animal slapstick and off-color skits sandwiched between the usual Vegas dancing girls and boys; the orangs wear shorts and funny hats and make obscene gestures to the audience. But Bobby Berosini and his orangs are masters of something else as well—of the miracle that was unavailable to Job, who, as the voice in the whirlwind thunderously reminded him, could not engage the wild animals in any fruitful, cooperative enterprise. Bobby Berosini can.

As well as being a gifted trainer, Berosini is a gifted comedian, though by his reckoning he is not the only comedian on the Stardust stage. When I asked him, between shows in the Stardust's coffee shop, what motivates his orangs to work, he said to me, passionately, "*We* are comedians. *We* are comedians. Do you understand me?"

Comedians? Orangutans? This is not a reasonable remark, from the point of view of either popular or institutionally sanctioned knowledge about animals. If, as many human-rights activists and academics believe, animals are capable of feeling and suffering but not of elaborate intentions and creative thought, then Berosini's orangs *must* be beaten into submission, since food rewards would not be powerful enough to motivate their complex actions. Besides, animals could not possibly know the mood or muse of comedy. They lack the conceptual apparatus to handle the mischievous shifts in meaning required for jokes.

When Berosini told me that his orangutans are comedians, I nodded my head vigorously; the enchantment of the act had not worn off. But what does it mean to say of an animal that he or she is a comedian? This question leads back onstage, to the act itself, and to the sorts of questions Berosini and his orangs toss about, invert, capsize, and rescue, only to turn them on their head, time and time again.

The running theme of the act is "How I Train Them." Berosini keeps saying to the audience, "People ask me how I get them to do things," or "People ask me how I train them," and then he supplies different "answers." At one point the answer is, "You have to show them who is boss." He brings Rusty out to show him who is boss, and Rusty not only refuses to jump onto the stool provided for the purpose but tricks his trainer into doing so by pretending incomprehension until Berosini finally demonstrates, jumping onto the stool himself. Once Berosini has dutifully jumped, Rusty invites the audience to applaud.

Berosini goes on to mock much scientific and popular wisdom about operant conditioning—training that relies more on the carrot than on the stick—by demonstrating how he doesn't need to train the orangutans at all because "I have magic orang cookies." A fast and lively slapstick round results from his failed attempts to get Bo to eat a cookie; the cookie is juggled, spit into the audience, hidden, fed to Berosini, but never eaten by the orangutan.

Then there is yet another variation on the theme: "People ask me how I train them. The truth is, I do not have to train them, because I just mesmerize them." Bo is then asked to come forward and be a hypnotic subject. There is much crooning of "You are getting very, very sleepy." Bo drops her shoulders, stands more and more still, and—wonder of wonders—closes her eyes. Pleased with the trance, the "trainer" whispers, "Are you asleep?" All of a sudden Bo grins outrageously, nods her head vigorously, and then immediately droops back into her "mesmerized" posture. The joke, again, is on Berosini—or, rather, on the Berosini character, who, of course, stands for the audience and for our overblown ideas about our superior intelligence and ability to control the world.

As Berosini explains when he is offstage, the way he trains is not "traditional," in that he does not teach his animals "tricks" but rather teaches them through the flow of their intelligence interacting with his. He explains that whereas a suggestion for a move or gesture or gag often originates with him, it is just as likely to come from the orangutan; the trainer must be as adept at picking up cues from the animals as they are at picking up cues from him. And orangutans demand this kind of handling. "I do not train them to do what I know how to do," he told me, "because you just cannot do that. It doesn't work!" According to Berosini, orangutans are the hardest of all the apes to teach a trick to because they are so self-contained, so mentally poised. The same idea is expressed in scholarly literature on orangs with reference to their marked lack of social interaction in the wild. Unlike most other apes, they are not dependent on social support and approval, which vastly complicates the training relationship. An orangutan is irredeemably his or her own person—"the most poetic of the apes," as primate researcher Lyn Miles once told me.

Miles had in mind the difference between orangutans and chimps. Chimps are much admired for their use of tools and their problem-solving relationship with things as they find them. A chimp looks inferential, ingenious, and ever so active while taking the various IQ tests that science presents him with—a hexagonal peg, say, and several holes of different shapes, only one of them hexagonal. Here, the chimp shows his tremendous initiative right away, holding the peg this way and that, trying out this, that, and the other hole; this, that, and the other angle. He *experiments*, he is filled with the inventor's work ethic; he tries, essays, tests, probes, he is full of the integrity of logic, or if not logic then at least something very American: he is so enterprising, so resourceful.

Give your orangutan the hexagonal peg and the several different holes, hide behind the two-way mirror, and watch how he engages the problem. And watch and watch and watch—because he will not engage the problem. He uses the peg to scratch his back, has a look-see at his right wrist, makes a halfhearted and soon abandoned attempt to use his fur for a macramé project, stares dreamily out the window if there is one and at nothing in particular if there is not, and the sun begins to set. (The sun will also set if you are observing a chimp, but the chimp is a lot busier, so you are less likely to mark the moment in your notes. An orangutan observer has plenty of time to be a student of the varieties of sunset.) You watch, and the orang dreams, and your notes perhaps consist of nothing more than memoranda on the behavior of the clock, when casually, and as if thinking of something else, the orangutan slips the hexagonal peg into the hexagonal hole. And continues staring off dreamily.

Professor Miles says that this sort of behavior contradicts the traditional finding that orangs are dumber than chimps. It is rather, she says, that chimps are problem-oriented whereas orangs are insight-oriented, the dreamers and visionaries of the world of the great apes. Which is all well and good, but how do you entertain five hundred people for half an hour twice a night, every night, six nights a week, for seven years, with animals whose forte is meditation, animals who do not do tricks? It's like trying to entertain a Las Vegas audience with five performing poets.

In the wild, too, orangs have not provided ethologists with the glamorous behaviors that, say, Jane Goodall's chimps have given her. I found no reports of orangs doing anything like the equivalent of fashioning special sticks to fish for termites, for instance. Orang observers instead report such exciting phenomena as the "fruit stare," which some people say is a function of the difficulty orangutans have foraging for food in the wild. Orangutans need to develop the fruit stare because trees can be coy about when, where, and how much they fruit, and the fruit is often hidden in the canopy of leaves. The fruit stare is an expression of reverie, but it is a reverie directed outward rather than inward—"like thinking with your eyes," naturalist Sy Montgomery has said. "That's why they are so spaced out."

But all this only explains why there are not many orangutan acts in the world and not how Bobby Berosini manages to put on an orangutan act night after night.

What Berosini says, again and again, is, "We are comedians. Do you understand me? Do you realize what I am telling you? We are comedians, my orangs and I." His voice is urgent now, but not frantic the way it is when PETA and the charges of abuse and the harassment are the topic. The act, he explains, is a collaboration: "Rusty will have an idea for a gag, and maybe I don't like his idea, but often I do, so I leave my gag aside and accept his idea, or maybe I sometimes insist that we still do it the other way. Or maybe Tiga insists that the old way was funnier, and then I have to laugh at myself and accept what she says. She has as many ideas as I do. She is an old campaigner, Tiga, she knows what she is doing."

I find the act screamingly funny, not only because the timing is so good but because the content is so intelligent, even if the orang humor can be a bit coarse. There are, for instance, the many sardonic jokes about "monkeys" and "monkey business." These are jokes about the audience, about humanity's ignorance about its fellow primates, because, of course, orangs are not monkeys—they are, along with chimps, gorillas, and humans, great apes. But this is the sort of detail people consistently get wrong. One witness in another performing-ape controversy told me a story about a zookeeper and an animal he referred to as "some sort of monkey." I pressed to discover what sort, and he said, "It doesn't matter. They're all monkeys, aren't they?"

Well, no, they are not, and it does matter, especially when you are claiming to speak with authority about the animals in question. I've listened to anthropologist Daniel Povinelli hold forth passionately about the importance of understanding the differences not only between monkeys and apes but also between different species of ape and different species of monkey. He says that there are pronounced morphological differences between monkeys and apes, and also pronounced psychological differences: "The apes are doing something different." For Povinelli, it is almost as radical a mistake to confuse monkeys with apes as it would be to confuse elephants with pigs or wolves with golden retrievers. "Evolution would be impossible without difference," Povinelli points out. "There can hardly be anything more fundamental than recognizing, studying, and appreciating the enormous differences, especially the psychological differences, among different animals."

Povinelli and Berosini are very different people, with very different relationships to animals, but they have in common a passionate belief that the details about an animal, whether psychological or morphological, are not merely pedantic decorations but should compel our respect. Berosini is a performer and Povinelli is a scientist, so they would probably disagree about what counts as a violation of this code, but they meet in insisting that there is such a code and that it matters. Indeed, when I told Povinelli that in his act Berosini calls his animals "monkeys" and makes no attempt to correct himself, he was somewhat shocked and not entirely reassured by my explanation of the dark comic irony of the usage.

Berosini, however, is nothing if not canny; it means something when he monkeys around. When Bo nods her head vigorously or applauds his "wit" when he makes a "monkey" joke, there is a sophisticated edge here, as if a physicist were joking around by blurring the difference between an atom and a molecule.

You have to know a great deal more than the bulk of the audience knows, or cares to know, about animals and the politics of animals in order to hear the sardonic implications in the reiteration of the "just monkeys" bit. These darker jibes ride on the back of traditional slapstick, but the jokes are, as perhaps true slapstick always is, constructed both from and about our intellectual ineptitude and hubris; every time one of the orangs makes a "monkey" out of Berosini, the joke is on us. Our brutishness and our intellectual incompetence are one.

But the act is comedy, true comedy, and not merely a collection of dark and sardonic jokes. The orangs and the audience and humanity itself, as represented by the character Berosini portrays, are redeemed in the end, in part by the sheer quicksilver beauty of the timing. When the audience laughs, at times with true joy, a joy free of malice, it is, after all, humanity that is being celebrated, since the ability to laugh without malice at one's own failings—and to see in those failings one's connection with everyone else in the room, a connection made through laughter—is no mean ethical feat.

If Berosini's act can be said to have one overriding theme, it is training— obedience—itself. "Obedience" comes from an old French word that means "to hear" or "to heed," "to pay attention to." The great trainers of every kind of animal, from parakeet to dog to elephant, have said for millennia that you cannot get an animal to heed you unless you heed the animal; obedience in this sense is a symmetrical relationship. In a given instance it may start with the human, who perhaps says to the dog, "Joe, sit!" Soon, however, the dog will take the command and turn it, use it to respond, to say something back. The dog might, for example, take to sitting in a sprightly fashion when one gets out a dumbbell, as if to say: "Yes, that's it, let's go!" It is at this moment that true training with any species, in- cluding humans, either begins or fails. If the human obeys, hears, heeds, responds to what the animal is now saying, then training begins. If the human "drops" the animal at this point, not realizing that the task has only begun, then the dog or orangutan will disobey.

Animals, like people, are motivated in many ways. Berosini's orangs are motivated offstage in the same way they appear to be motivated onstage: when they make a gesture, they get a response. Their trainer obeys them, unless they are committing mayhem. The intelligent responsiveness of animals is for us one of the most deeply attractive things about them, not only because we are a lone- some and threatened tribe but because intelligent responsiveness is a central, abiding good. The intelligent responsiveness of trainers, which some of them call respect, is what makes trainers attractive to animals, and may be the whole of the secret of "having a way with animals."

In the comic mismatch between the Berosini character's ideas about the orangs and the nature of the orangs themselves as they triumph continually over the would-be lordly "trainer," our fond hopes are mocked, but not cruelly. The world, which is to say the human project, is in trouble, but within the tiny world of Berosini's act a way is found, even if it is a stumbling, awkward way, to true re- sponsiveness between ourselves and animals. Even the audience gets a response, as when Rusty invites us to applaud Berosini or when Tiga gives an audience member one of her "magic orang cookies," and does so gently, though without a hint of subservience.

Berosini also gets laughs by mocking the character of the orangs—Tiga's on- stage character has a drinking problem and loose morals—but the "How I Train Them" series of gags is the most intellectually satisfying part of the act. Interest- ingly, Bo's simulation of the hypnotic trance is a play on the sort of spacy con- sciousness ethologists have observed in orangutans. There is the same dreami- ness, the trance that frames the unpredictable moment of alert intelligence. Bo's eyes are closed, but otherwise she seems to be imitating the fruit stare in much the same way that a dressage horse—one so highly educated that we say he or she "dances"—imitates, with some variations, the postures and gestures of a horse in "nature."

The radical claim being made here is that the animals are "referring to," or at least imitating, these gestures deliberately, with some sense—if not precisely our sense—of the meaning of what they are doing. Berosini says that Bo is in on the joke, or at least on *some* joke, and that it is her interest and pleasure in such monkeying around that make it possible for him to work with her as he does. This is speculative, of course, but it could be argued that Berosini's is a more parsimonious explanation than an explanation based on conditioning would be. Indeed, it's questionable whether any model of conditioning, however elaborate, can explain behavior this complex, particularly since every performance the act changes, with both Berosini and the orangs offering improvisations. Talk of conditioned responses may be helpful in understanding part of a trained animal's development (or, for that matter, a dancer's or a poet's or an actor's or a philosopher's), but animal performance at this level makes more sense when viewed as rudimentary expressions of at least one primeval artistic impulse—the impulse to play with meaning.

Bo's trance-breaking grin is wonderfully timed, a case of high slapstick, if there can be such a thing; it is also, for me at least, an eerie instant of revelation in which I see something fairly exact in Berosini's claim that his orangs are comedians. But how might such an animal joke come about? Let's say that you are teaching the animal to be "mesmerized," and the animal spontaneously adds the mischievous nodding grin. This is a joke about who's in control, though not necessarily a joke about hypnosis. You accept the move and ask for it on purpose next time, and it becomes part of the routine. The animal offers it spontaneously at first, and then continues with it, perhaps for the same reason we repeat a phrase or a joke—because it felt so delicious the first time.

Berosini's act gives the orangs a point of view, one that I find credible as an animal point of view, and it gives their intelligence pride of place, as do other clever disobedience acts in the tradition—an ancient tradition going back to the Greeks, in which the *eiron,* or apparently lowly character, triumphs over the apparently noble character through wit, awareness, quickness of perception. (The word *eiron* gives us our word "irony.") In circus and movie tradition, the most familiar form of such comedy is the disobedient-dog act, in which the trainer character attempts to induce the dogs to display loyalty, nobility, and willing service; instead, they trip the trainer, disgrace the legacy of Rin Tin Tin by stealing a purse from an audience member, "bite" the trainer, and so on.

It is not Lassie and Rin Tin Tin themselves who are mocked by the disobedient-dog act but rather our own self-serving ideas of the selflessness of dogs, such as the pious notion that dogs "want to please" and work "for love of the handler." Berosini's orangs work with this sort of material wonderfully, displaying their intelligence against the backdrop of our ideas of their debasement.

If Berosini's comedy is somewhat dark and sharp-edged when you take a close look at it, that may be in part because of the tradition of comedy he inherits as a Czech, a tradition that has had to learn, over and over again, how to ensure the survival of intelligence in forms that escape the more violent scrutiny of various regimes. At any rate, the act I saw is one kind of shield for the mind, one kind of comic courage by means of which sanity survives amid social and political darkness.

One of Berosini's most famous monkey jokes occurred in court. During my stay in Las Vegas shortly after the 1990 trial, I heard it at least two dozen times. At one point during Berosini's testimony, PETA's lawyer asked him to tell the audience how he taught Bo to give the finger. He replied, "I'll give you a demonstration of how to give the finger if you want." This is just the way his orangs perform in his act, ragging him, continually foiling him with impudence, back talk, irreverence, impiety. And they give him the finger. In one way or another, most animals do give their trainers the finger—a great deal of animal humor is coarse, to put it mildly. I have long suspected that the real reason it was for so long heresy, an excommunicable offense, to say that animals have souls is that if you say they have souls, then their jokes and comments have meaning, and no bureaucratic or ecclesiastical or philanthropic dignity can survive animal vaudeville.

Joan Berosini told me that one juror, who asked to remain anonymous, said after the case was over, "It would be abuse to take the orangs away from Bobby." Is there anything to this, anything that can be understood without elevating Berosini to Patron Saint of Apes—a position that would destroy his comic art and that is, in any case, already held by Jane Goodall? Or, to turn the question around, what is the source of the improbable idea that the act's flow and liveliness and energy could possibly be achieved by beatings?

I do not think that the orangs mean their antics the way the audience interprets them. But I do think they mean *something* by them, and that they are motivated to stay onstage, rather than run loose in the audience, not by terror—which is a poor motivator—but by an interest in what they are doing.

So what *do* they mean, what are they doing? I am convinced that some animals—quite a few Airedales, for example, and also Border collies—are interested, and take pleasure, in something like the grammar of gesture itself, much as a dancer does. A bird dog in the field intends to retrieve the bird; the same dog cantering gaily after a dumbbell in an obedience ring "means" only that movement—not the retrieving of a bird, but the glorious gestures of retrieving. A Lippizaner means not to display himself before mares (which is what his movements would mean in "nature") but to call attention to the grandeur and intricacy of the display. These gestures are all metaphors, second inheritances of nature, in the same way poetry is a second inheritance of language. To call any of this—or poetry or dance, for that matter—"play," as some are wont to do, misses the point; it is work that is as serious as play, to borrow a phrase from the poet John Hollander. Such work is the highest use and pleasure of the mind, and orangutans plainly do have minds. The mind may remain satisfied in the wild, where the primitive problems of survival overwhelm other impulses, but if the other great apes are as close to us psychologically as some people claim and have minds, then it is good for those minds to develop.

And yet training in and of itself, apart from questions of abuse, makes people uneasy. In medieval times ecclesiasts believed that trained animals had devils in them—that dancing dogs were dancing satanically. In our time the idea of the "unnatural" has replaced the idea of the demonic, and for some it does not matter whether or not animals are abused, since keeping and training them is itself "unnatural" or "ethologically inappropriate," as though it were unnatural to develop the mind. These days the contemporary horror of the "unnatural" infects visions of life with domestic animals as well, but the possibility of the hearth—by which I mean a place where the human and animal may sit side by side—is much more likely to be denied when wild animals are in question.

Certainly you cannot have the same relationship with a wolf as with a dog, yet it does not follow from this that there can be *no* relationship. Today, at a time when the habitats of wild animals are rapidly disappearing, the terms of this relationship need to be reinvented, not abjured. We need to learn what we can from Berosini and other trainers—but particularly the wild-animal trainers—about how this might be done. A dog and her trainer, or a horse and his trainer, do not have to "meet each other halfway," because they already share the same social space. An orangutan and his trainer, however, must travel some conceptual distance to meet each other and work together. That this is possible, what it means that it is possible, what implications it has for the possibilities of mutual respect between wild animals and humans—this strikes me as a matter of urgent importance.

That is, I believe not only that the training of wild animals is acceptable but that the knowledge trainers have, which has been eschewed by science and philosophy and the church for millennia, may contain clues to imaginative and enlightened ways we might escape our age's violence and sentimentality toward the nonhuman world, and thereby genuinely take up the burden of our responsibility toward animals. In the Book of Job, the voice in the whirlwind points out that the wild goat and the unicorn and the ostrich and the warhorse are beyond Job. But the orangutan is not beyond Bobby Berosini, and it behooves us to understand why, to know that there is something to understand, and that the prurient contemplation of abuse, so popular in a self-servingly sentimental climate, will not open understanding here. Furthermore, the mongering of irresponsible images of abuse only obscures our views of the real cruelties that do exist.

James Thurber, who defended the intelligence of animals and animal wit as vigorously as anyone ever has, once wrote this about human wit: "The perfect tribute to perfection in comedy is not immediate laughter, but a curious and instantaneous tendency of the eyes to fill." This, I keep thinking, and not weepy displays of ignorant outrage and pity, is the tribute owed to Berosini's orangs. But be careful your vision does not mist too much. Bo and Rusty and Tiga and Niki and Benny are quite clear-eyed. Trainers speak often of how uncannily good animals are at "reading" people, and of training as a humbling activity. That's because when you train an animal you teach yourself and the animal a "language" by means of which the animal can tell you more than you may have wanted to know about what he or she sees in looking at you. If there is a moral to the act that the orangs are in on, it is this: be sure that when Tiga looks into your eyes she finds a clarity and amused intelligence fit to answer her own, lest she turn from you, leaving you in the foolish darkness yet again.

Walking

Linda Hogan

It began in dark and underground weather, a slow hunger moving toward light. It grew in a dry gulley beside the road where I live, a place where entire hillsides are sometimes yellow, windblown tides of sunflower plants. But this plant was different. It was alone, and larger than the countless others that had established their lives farther up the hill. This one was a traveler, a settler, and like a dream beginning in conflict, it grew where the land had been disturbed.

I saw it first in early summer. It was a green and sleeping bud, raising itself toward the sun. Ants worked around the unopened bloom, gathering aphids and sap. A few days later, it was a tender young flower, soft and new, with a pale green center and a troop of silver-gray insects climbing up and down the stalk. Over the summer this sunflower grew into a plant of incredible beauty, turning its face daily toward the sun in the most subtle of ways, the black center of it dark and alive with a deep blue light, as if flint had sparked an elemental fire there, in community with rain, mineral, mountain air, and sand.

As summer changed from green to yellow there were new visitors daily, the lace-winged insects, the bees whose legs were fat with pollen, and grasshoppers with their clattering wings and desperate hunger. There were other lives I missed, those too small or hidden to see. It was as if this plant with its host of lives was a society, one in which moment by moment, depending on light and moisture, there was great and diverse change.

There were changes in the next larger world around the plant as well. One day I rounded a bend in the road to find the disturbing sight of a dead horse, black and still against a hillside, eyes rolled back. Another day I was nearly lifted by a wind and sandstorm so fierce and hot that I had to wait for it to pass before I could return home. On this day the faded dry petals of the sunflower were swept across the land. That was when the birds arrived to carry the new seeds to another future.

In this one plant, in one summer season, a drama of need and survival took place. Hungers were filled. Insects coupled. There was escape, exhaustion, and death. Lives touched down a moment and were gone.

I was an outsider. I only watched. I never learned the sunflower's golden language or the tongues of its citizens. I had a small understanding, nothing more than a shallow observation of the flower, insects, and birds. But they knew what to do, how to live. An old voice from somewhere, gene or cell, told the plant how to evade the pull of gravity and find its way upward, how to open. It was instinct, intuition, necessity. A certain knowing directed the seed-bearing birds on paths to ancestral homelands they had never seen. They believed it. They followed.

There are other summons and calls, some even more mysterious than those commandments to birds or those survival journeys of insects. In bamboo plants, for instance, with their thin green canopy of light and golden stalks that creak in the wind. Once a century, all of a certain kind of bamboo flower on the same day. Neither the plants' location, in Malaysia or in a greenhouse in Minnesota, nor their age or size make a difference. They flower. Some current of an inner language passes among them, through space and separation, in ways we cannot explain in our language. They are all, somehow, one plant, each with a share of communal knowledge.

John Hay, in *The Immortal Wilderness*, has written: "There are occasions when you can hear the mysterious language of the Earth, in water, or coming through the trees, emanating from the mosses, seeping through the undercurrents of the soil, but you have to be willing to wait and receive."

Sometimes I hear it talking. The light of the sunflower was one language, but there are others, more audible. Once, in the redwood forest, I heard a beat, something like a drum or heart coming from the ground and trees and wind. That underground current stirred a kind of knowing inside me, a kinship and longing, a dream barely remembered that disappeared back to the body. Another time, there was the booming voice of an ocean storm thundering from far out at sea, telling about what lived in the distance, about the rough water that would arrive, wave after wave revealing the disturbance at center.

Tonight I walk. I am watching the sky. I think of the people who came before me and how they knew the placement of stars in the sky, watched the moving sun long and hard enough to witness how a certain angle of light touched a stone only once a year. Without written records, they knew the gods of every night, the small, fine details of the world around them and of immensity above them.

Walking, I can almost hear the redwoods beating. And the oceans are above me here, rolling clouds, heavy and dark, considering snow. On the dry, red road, I pass the place of the sunflower, that dark and secret location where creation took place. I wonder if it will return this summer, if it will multiply and move up to the other stand of flowers in a territorial struggle.

It's winter and there is smoke from the fires. The square, lighted windows of houses are fogging over. It is a world of elemental attention, of all things working together, listening to what speaks in the blood. Whichever road I follow, I walk in the land of many gods, and they love and eat one another. Walking, I am listening to a deeper way. Suddenly all my ancestors are behind me. Be still, they say. Watch and listen. You are the result of the love of thousands.

Where Worlds Collide

Pico Iyer

They come out, blinking, into the bleached, forgetful sunshine, in Dodgers caps and Rodeo Drive T-shirts, with the maps their cousins have drawn for them and the images they've brought over from *Cops* and *Terminator 2;* they come out, dazed, disoriented, heads still partly in the clouds, bodies still several time zones—or centuries—away, and they step into the Promised Land.

In front of them is a Van Stop, a Bus Stop, a Courtesy Tram Stop, and a Shuttle Bus Stop (the shuttles themselves tracing circuits A, B, and C). At the Shuttle Bus Stop, they see the All American Shuttle, the Apollo Shuttle, Celebrity Airport Livery, the Great American Stageline, the Movie Shuttle, the Transport, Ride-4-You, and forty-two other magic buses waiting to whisk them everywhere from Bakersfield to Disneyland. They see Koreans piling into the Taeguk Airport Shuttle and the Seoul Shuttle, which will take them to Koreatown without their ever feeling they've left home; they see newcomers from the Middle East disappearing under the Arabic script of the Sahara Shuttle. They see fast-talking, finger-snapping, palm-slapping jive artists straight from their TV screens shouting incomprehensible slogans about deals, destinations, and drugs. Over there is a block-long white limo, a Lincoln Continental, and, over there, a black Chevy Blazer with Mexican stickers all over its windows, being towed. They have arrived in the Land of Opportunity, and the opportunities are swirling dizzily, promiscuously, around them.

They have already braved the ranks of Asian officials, the criminal-looking security men in jackets that say "Elsinore Airport Services," the men shaking tins that say "Helping America's Hopeless." They have already seen the tilting mugs that say "California: a new slant on life" and the portable fruit machines in the gift shop. They have already, perhaps, visited the rest room where someone has written, "Yes on Proposition 187. Mexicans go home," the snack bar where a slice of pizza costs $3.19 (18 quetzals, they think in horror, or 35,000 dong), and the sign that urges them to try the Cockatoo Inn Grand Hotel. The latest arrivals at Los Angeles International Airport are ready now to claim their new lives.

Above them in the terminal, voices are repeating, over and over, in Japanese, Spanish, and unintelligible English, "Maintain visual contact with your personal property at all times." Out on the sidewalk, a man's voice and a woman's voice are alternating an unending refrain: "The white zone is for loading and unloading of passengers only. No parking." There are "Do Not Cross" yellow lines cordoning off parts of the sidewalk and "Wells Fargo Alarm Services" stickers on the windows; there are "Aviation Safeguard" signs on the baggage carts and "Beware of Solicitors" signs on the columns; there are even special phones "To Report Trouble." More male and female voices are intoning, continuously, "Do not leave your car unattended" and "Unattended cars are subject to immediate towaway." There are no military planes on the tarmac here, the newcomers notice, no khaki soldiers in fatigues, no instructions not to take photographs, as at home; but there are civilian restrictions every bit as strict as in many a police state.

"This Terminal Is in a Medfly Quarantine Area," says the sign between the terminals. "Stop the Spread of Medfly!" If, by chance, the new Americans have to enter a parking lot on their way out, they will be faced with "Cars left over 30 days may be impounded at Owner's Expense" and "Do not enter without a ticket." It will cost them $16 if they lose their parking ticket, they read, and $56 if they park in the wrong zone. Around them is an unending cacophony of antitheft devices, sirens, beepers, and car-door openers; lights are flashing everywhere, and the man who fines them $16 for losing their parking ticket has the tribal scars of Tigre across his forehead.

The blue skies and palm trees they saw on TV are scarcely visible from here: just an undifferentiated smoggy haze, billboards advertising Nissan and Panasonic and Canon, and beyond those an endlessly receding mess of gray streets. Overhead, they can see the all-too-familiar signs of Hilton and Hyatt and Holiday Inn; in the distance, a sea of tract houses, mini-malls, and high-rises. The City of Angels awaits them.

It is a commonplace nowadays to say that cities look more and more like airports, cross-cultural spaces that are a gathering of tribes and races and variegated tongues; and it has always been true that airports are in many ways like miniature cities, whole, self-sufficient communities, with their own chapels and museums and gymnasiums. Not only have airports colored our speech (teaching us about being upgraded, bumped, and put on standby, coaching us in the ways of fly-by-night operations, holding patterns, and the Mile High Club); they have also taught us their own rules, their own codes, their own customs. We eat and sleep and shower in airports; we pray and weep and kiss there. Some people stay for days at a time in these perfectly convenient, hermetically sealed, climate-controlled duty-free zones, which offer a kind of caesura from the obligations of daily life.

Airports are also, of course, the new epicenters and paradigms of our dawning post-national age—not just the bus terminals of the global village but the prototypes, in some sense, for our polyglot, multicolored, user-friendly future. And in their very universality—like the mall, the motel, or the McDonald's outlet—

they advance the notion of a future in which all the world's a multiculture. If you believe that more and more of the world is a kind of mongrel hybrid in which many cities (Sydney, Toronto, Singapore) are simply suburbs of a single universal order, then Los Angeles's LAX, London's Heathrow, and Hong Kong's Kai Tak are merely stages on some great global Circle Line, shuttling variations on a common global theme. Mass travel has made L.A. contiguous to Seoul and adjacent to São Paulo, and has made all of them now feel a little like bedroom communities for Tokyo.

And as with most social trends, especially the ones involving tomorrow, what is true of the world is doubly true of America, and what is doubly true of America is quadruply true of Los Angeles. L.A., legendarily, has more Thais than any city but Bangkok, more Koreans than any city but Seoul, more El Salvadorans than any city outside of San Salvador, more Druze than anywhere but Beirut; it is, at the very least, the easternmost outpost of Asia and the northernmost province of Mexico. When I stopped at a Traveler's Aid desk at LAX recently, I was told I could request help in Khamu, Mien, Tigrinya, Tajiki, Pashto, Dari, Pangasinan, Pampangan, Waray-Waray, Bambara, Twi, and Bicolano (as well, of course, as French, German, and eleven languages from India). LAX is as clear an image as exists today of the world we are about to enter, and of the world that's entering us.

For me, though, LAX has always had a more personal resonance: it was in LAX that I arrived myself as a new immigrant, in 1966; and from the time I was in the fourth grade, it was to LAX that I would go three times a year, as an "unaccompanied minor," to fly to school in London—and to LAX that I returned three times a year for my holidays. Sometimes it seems as if I have spent half my life in LAX. For me, it is the site of my liberation (from school, from the Old World, from home) and the place where I came to design my own new future.

Often when I have set off from L.A. to some distant place—Havana, say, or Hanoi, or Pyongyang—I have felt that the multicultural drama on display in LAX, the interaction of exoticism and familiarity, was just as bizarre as anything I would find when I arrived at my foreign destination. The airport is an Amy Tan novel, a short story by Bharati Mukherjee, a Henry James sketch set to an MTV beat; it is a cross-generational saga about Chang Hsieng meeting his daughter Cindy and finding that she's wearing a nose ring now and is shacked up with a surfer from Berlin. The very best kind of airport reading to be found in LAX these days is the triple-decker melodrama being played out all around one—a complex tragicomedy of love and war and exile, about people fleeing centuries-old rivalries and thirteenth-century mullahs and stepping out into a fresh, forgetful, born-again city that is rewriting its script every moment.

Not long ago I went to spend a week in LAX. I haunted the airport by day and by night, I joined the gloomy drinkers listening to air-control-tower instructions on earphones at the Proud Bird bar. I listened each morning to Airport Radio (530 AM), and I slept each night at the Airport Sheraton or the Airport Hilton. I lived off cellophaned crackers and Styrofoam cups of tea, browsed for hours among Best Actor statuettes and Beverly Hills magnets, and tried to see what kinds of America the city presents to the new Americans, who are remaking America each day.

It is almost too easy to say that LAX is a perfect metaphor for L.A., a flat, spaced-out desert kind of place, highly automotive, not deeply hospitable, with little reading matter and no organizing principle. (There are eight satellites without a center here, many international arrivals are shunted out into the bleak basement of Terminal 2, and there is no airline that serves to dominate LAX as Pan Am once did JFK.) Whereas "SIN" is a famously ironical airline code for Singapore, cathedral of puritanical rectitude, "LAX" has always seemed perilously well chosen for a city whose main industries were traditionally thought to be laxity and relaxation. LAX is at once a vacuum waiting to be colonized and a joyless theme park—Tomorrowland, Adventureland, and Fantasyland all at once.

The postcards on sale here (made in Korea) dutifully call the airport "one of the busiest and most beautiful air facilities in the world," and it is certainly true that LAX, with thirty thousand international arrivals each day—roughly the same number of tourists that have visited the Himalayan country of Bhutan in its entire history—is not uncrowded. But bigger is less and less related to better: in a recent survey of travel facilities, *Business Traveller* placed LAX among the five worst airports in the world for customs, luggage retrieval, and passport processing.

LAX is, in fact, a surprisingly shabby and hollowed-out kind of place, certainly not adorned with the amenities one might expect of the world's strongest and richest power. When you come out into the Arrivals area in the International Terminal, you will find exactly one tiny snack bar, which serves nine items; of them, five are identified as Cheese Dog, Chili Dog, Chili Cheese Dog, Nachos with Cheese, and Chili Cheese Nachos. There is a large panel on the wall offering rental-car services and hotels, and the newly deplaned American dreamer can choose between the Cadillac Hotel, the Banana Bungalow (which offers a Basketball Court, "Free Toast," "Free Bed Sheets," and "Free Movies and Parties"), and the Backpacker's Paradise (with "Free Afternoon Tea and Crumpets" and "Free Evening Party Including Food and Champagne").

Around one in the terminal is a swirl of priests rattling cans, Iranians in suits brandishing pictures of torture victims, and Japanese girls in Goofy hats. "I'm looking for something called Clearasil," a distinguished-looking Indian man diffidently tells a cashier. "Clearasil?" shouts the girl. "For your face?"

Upstairs, in the Terrace Restaurant, passengers are gulping down "Dutch Chocolate" and "Japanese Coffee" while students translate back and forth between English and American, explaining that "soliciting" loses something of its cachet when you go across the Atlantic. A fat man is nuzzling the neck of his outrageously pretty Filipina companion, and a few Brits are staring doubtfully at the sign that assures them that seafood is "cheerfully served at your table!" Only in America, they are doubtless thinking. A man goes from table to table, plunking down on each one a key chain attached to a globe. As soon as an unsuspecting customer picks one up, touched by the largesse of the New World and convinced now that there is such a thing as a free lunch in America, the man appears again, flashes a sign that says "I Am a Deaf," and requests a dollar for the gift.

At a bank of phones, a saffron-robed monk gingerly inserts a credit card, while schoolkids page Jesse Jackson at the nearest "white courtesy telephone." One notable feature of the modern airport is that it is wired, with a vengeance: even in a tiny, two-urinal men's room, I found two telephones on offer; LAX bars rent out cellular phones; and in the Arrivals area, as you come out into the land of plenty, you face a bank of forty-six phones of every kind, with screens and buttons and translations, from which newcomers are calling direct to Bangalore or Baghdad. Airports are places for connections of all kinds and *loci classici*, perhaps, for a world ruled by IDD and MCI, DOS and JAL.

Yet for all these grounding reminders of the world outside, everywhere I went in the airport I felt myself in an odd kind of twilight zone of consciousness, that weightless limbo of a world in which people are between lives and between selves, almost sleepwalking, not really sure of who or where they are. Light-headed from the trips they've taken, ears popping and eyes about to do so, under a potent foreign influence, people are at the far edge of themselves in airports, ready to break down or through. You see strangers pouring out their life stories to strangers here, or making new life stories with other strangers. Everything is at once intensified and slightly unreal. One L.A. psychiatrist advises shy women to practice their flirting here, and religious groups circle in the hope of catching unattached souls.

Airports, which often have a kind of perpetual morning-after feeling (the end of the holiday, the end of the affair), are places where everyone is ruled by the clock, but all the clocks show different times. These days, after all, we fly not only into yesterday or this morning when we go across the world but into different decades, often, of the world's life and our own: in ten or fifteen hours, we are taken back into the twelfth century or into worlds we haven't seen since childhood. And in the process we are subjected to transitions more jolting than any imagined by Oscar Wilde or Sigmund Freud: if the average individual today sees as many images in a day as a Victorian saw in a lifetime, the average person today also has to negotiate switches between continents inconceivable only fifty years ago. Frequent fliers like Ted Turner have actually become ill from touching down and taking off so often; but, in less diagnosable ways, all of us are being asked to handle difficult suspensions of the laws of Nature and Society when moving between competing worlds.

This helps to compound the strange statelessness of airports, where all bets are off and all laws are annulled—modern equivalents, perhaps, to the hundred yards of no-man's-land between two frontier crossings. In airports we are often in dreamy, floating, out-of-body states, as ready to be claimed as that suitcase on Carousel C. Even I, not traveling, didn't know sometimes if I was awake or asleep in LAX, as I heard an announcer intone, "John Cheever, John Cheever, please contact a Northwest representative in the Baggage Claim area. John Cheever, please contact a service representative at the Northwest Baggage Claim area."

As I started to sink into this odd, amphibious, bipolar state, I could begin to see why a place like LAX is a particular zone of fear, more terrifying to many people than anywhere but the dentist's office. Though dying in a plane is, notoriously, twenty times less likely than dying in a car, every single airline crash is front-page news and so dramatic—not a single death but three hundred—that airports are for many people killing grounds. Their runways are associated in the mind's (televisual) eye with hostages and hijackings; with bodies on the tarmac or antiterrorist squads storming the plane.

That general sense of unsettledness is doubtless intensified by all the people in uniform in LAX. There are ten different security agencies working the Tom Bradley Terminal alone, and the streets outside are jam-packed with Airport Police cars, FBI men, and black-clad airport policemen on bicycles. All of them do as much, I suspect, to instill fear as to still it. "People are scared here," a gloomy Pakistani security guard told me, "because undercover are working. Police are working. You could be undercover, I could be undercover. Who knows?"

And just as L.A. is a province of the future in part because so many people take it to be the future, so it is a danger zone precisely because it is imagined to be dangerous. In Osaka's new $16 billion airport recently, I cross-examined the Skynet computer (in the Departures area) about what to expect when arriving at LAX or any other foreign airport. "Guard against theft in the arrival hall," it told me (and, presumably, even warier Japanese). "A thief is waiting for a chance to take advantage of you." Elsewhere it added, "Do not dress too touristy," and, "Be on your guard when approached by a group of suspicious-looking children, such as girls wearing bright-colored shirts and scarves." True to such dark prognostications, the side doors of the Airport Sheraton at LAX are locked every day from 8:00 P.M. to 6:00 A.M., and you cannot even activate the elevators without a room key. "Be extra careful in parking garages and stairwells," the hotel advises visitors. "Always try to use the main entrance to your hotel, particularly late in the evening. Never answer your hotel room door without verifying who is there."

One reason airports enjoy such central status in our imaginations is that they play such a large part in forming our first (which is sometimes our last) impression of a place; this is the reason that poor countries often throw all their resources into making their airports sleek, with beautifully landscaped roads leading out of them into town. L.A., by contrast, has the bareness of arrogance, or simple inhospitality. Usually what you see as you approach the city is a grim penitential haze through which is visible nothing but rows of gray buildings, a few dun-hued warehouses, and ribbons of dirty freeway: a no-colored blur without even the comforting lapis ornaments of the swimming pools that dot New York or Johannesburg. (Ideally, in fact, one should enter L.A. by night, when the whole city pulses like an electric grid of lights—or the back of a transistor radio, in Thomas Pynchon's inspired metaphor. While I was staying in LAX, Jackie Collins actually told *Los Angeles* magazine that "Flying in [to LAX] at night is just an orgasmic thrill.") You land, with a bump, on a mess of gray runways with no signs of welcome, a hangar that says "T ans W rld Airlines," another broken sign that announces "Tom Bradl y International Ai port," and an air-control tower under scaffolding.

The first thing that greeted me on a recent arrival was a row of Asians sitting on the floor of the terminal, under a sign that told them of a $25,000 fine for bringing in the wrong kinds of food. As I passed through endless corridors, I was faced with almost nothing except long escalators (a surprisingly high percentage of the accidents recorded at airports comes from escalators, bewildering to new-comers) and bare hallways. The other surprise, for many of my fellow travelers, no doubt, was that almost no one we saw looked like Robert Redford or Julia Roberts or, indeed, like anyone belonging to the race we'd been celebrating in our in-flight movies. As we passed into the huge, bare assembly hall that is the Customs and Immigration Center here, I was directed into one of the chaotic lines by a Noriko and formally admitted to the country by a C. Chen. The man waiting to transfer my baggage (as a beagle sniffed around us in a coat that said "Agriculture's Beagle Brigade" on one side and "Protecting American Agriculture" on the other) was named Yoji Yosaka. And the first sign I saw, when I stepped into America, was a big board being waved by the "Executive Sedan Service" for one "Mr. T. Ego."

For many immigrants, in fact, LAX is quietly offering them a view of their own near futures: the woman at the Host Coffee Shop is themselves, in a sense, two years from now, and the man sweeping up the refuse is the American dream in practice. The staff at the airport seems to be made up almost entirely of recent immigrants: on my very first afternoon there, I was served by a Hoa, an Ephraim, and a Glinda; the waitpeople at a coffee shop in Terminal 5 were called Ignacio, Ever, Aura, and Erick. Even at the Airport Sheraton (where the employees all wear nameplates), I was checked in by Viera (from "Bratislavia") and ran into Hasmik and Yovik (from Ethiopia), Faye (from Vietnam), Ingrid (from Guatemala City), Khrystyne (from Long Beach, by way of Phnom Penh, I think), and Moe (from West L.A., she said). Many of the bright-eyed dreamers who arrive at LAX so full of hope never actually leave the place.

The deeper drama of any airport is that it features a kind of interaction almost unique in our lives, wherein many of us do not know whom we are going to meet or whom others are going to meet in us. You see people standing at the barriers outside the Customs area looking into their pasts, while wide-open newcomers drift out, searching for their futures. Lovers do not know if they will see the same person who kissed them good-bye a month ago; grandparents wonder what the baby they last saw twenty years ago will look like now.

In L.A. all of this has an added charge, because unlike many cities, it is not a hub but a terminus: a place where people come to arrive. Thus many of the meetings you witness are between the haves and the hope-to-haves, between those who are affecting a new ease in their new home and those who are here in search of that ease. Both parties, especially if they are un-American by birth, are eager to stress their Americanness or their fitness for America; and both, as they look at each other's made-up self, see themselves either before or after a stay in L.A.'s theater of transformation. And so they stream in, wearing running shoes or cow-boy hats or 49ers jackets, anxious to make a good first impression; and the people who wait for them, under a halfhearted mural of Desertland, are often American enough not to try to look the part. Juan and Esperanza both have ponytails now, and Kimmie is wearing a Harley-Davidson cap backward and necking with a

Japanese guy; the uncle from Delhi arrives to find that Rajiv not only has grown darker but has lost weight, so that he looks more like a peasant from back home than ever.

And the newcomers pour in in astonishing numbers. A typical Sunday evening, in a single hour, sees flights arriving from England, Taiwan, the Philippines, Indonesia, Mexico, Austria, Germany, Spain, Costa Rica, and Guatemala; and each new group colors and transforms the airport: an explosion of tropical shades from Hawaiian Air, a rash of blue blazers and white shirts around the early flight from Tokyo. Red-haired Thais bearing pirated Schwarzenegger videos, lonely Africans in Aerial Assault sneakers, farmers from changeless Confucian cultures peering into the smiles of a Prozac city, children whose parents can't pronounce their names. Many of them are returning, like Odysseus, with the spoils of war: young brides from Luzon, business cards from Shanghai, boxes of macadamia nuts from Oahu. And for many of them the whole wild carnival will feature sights they have never seen before: Japanese look anxiously at the first El Salvadorans they've ever seen, and El Salvadorans ogle sleek girls from Bangkok in thigh-high boots. All of them, moreover, may not be pleased to realize that the America they've dreamed of is, in fact, a land of tacos and pita and pad thai—full, indeed, of the very Third World cultures that other Third Worlders look down upon.

One day over lunch I asked my Ethiopian waitress about her life here. She liked it well enough, she said, but still she missed her home. And yet, she added, she couldn't go back. "Why not?" I asked, still smiling. "Because they killed my family," she said. "Two years back. They killed my father. They killed my brother." "They," I realized, referred to the Tigreans—many of them working just down the corridor in other parts of the hotel. So, too, Tibetans who have finally managed to flee their Chinese-occupied homeland arrive at LAX to find Chinese faces everywhere; those who fled the Sandinistas find themselves standing next to Sandinistas fleeing their successors. And all these people from ancient cultures find themselves in a country as amnesiac as the morning, where World War II is just a rumor and the Gulf War a distant memory. Their pasts are escaped, yes, but by the same token they are unlikely to be honored.

It is dangerously tempting to start formulating socioeconomic principles in the midst of LAX: people from rich countries (Germany and Japan, say) travel light, if only because they are sure that they can return any time; those from poor countries come with their whole lives in cardboard boxes imperfectly tied with string. People from poor countries are often met by huge crowds—for them each arrival is a special occasion—and stagger through customs with string bags and Gold Digger apple crates, their addresses handwritten on them in pencil; the Okinawan honeymooners, by contrast, in the color-coordinated outfits they will change every day, somehow have packed all their needs into a tiny case.

If airports have some of the excitement of bars, because so many people are composing (and decomposing) selves there, they also have some of the sadness of bars, the poignancy of people sitting unclaimed while everyone around them has paired off. A pretty girl dressed in next to nothing sits alone in an empty Baggage Claim area, waiting for a date who never comes; a Vietnamese man, lost, tells an official that he has friends in Orange County who can help him, but when the friends are contacted, they say they know no one from Vietnam. I hear of a woman who got off and asked for "San Mateo," only to learn that she was meant to disembark in San Francisco; and a woman from Nigeria who came out expecting to see her husband in Monroe, Louisiana, only to learn that someone in Lagos had mistaken "La." on her itinerary for "L.A."

The greetings I saw in the Arrivals area were much more tentative than I had expected, less passionate—as ritualized in their way as the kisses placed on Bob Barker's cheek—and much of that may be because so many people are meeting strangers, even if they are meeting people they once knew. Places like LAX— places like L.A.—perpetuate the sense that everyone is a stranger in our new floating world. I spent one afternoon in the airport with a Californian blonde, and I saw her complimented on her English by a sweet Korean woman and asked by an Iranian if she was Indian. Airports have some of the unsteady brashness of singles bars, where no one knows quite what is expected of them. "Mike, is that you?" "Oh, I didn't recognize you." "I'd have known you anywhere." "It's so kind of you to come and pick me up." And already at a loss, a young Japanese girl and a broad, lonely-looking man head off toward the parking lot, not knowing, in any sense, who is going to be in the driver's seat.

The driving takes place, of course, in what many of the newcomers, primed by video screenings of *L.A. Law* and *Speed,* regard as the ultimate heart of darkness, a place at least as forbidding and dangerous as Africa must have seemed to the Victorians. They have heard about how America is the murder capital of the world; they have seen Rodney King get pummeled by L.A.'s finest; they know of the city as the site of drive-by shootings and freeway snipers, of riots and celebrity murders. The "homeless" and the "tempest-tost" that the Statue of Liberty invites are arriving, increasingly, in a city that is itself famous for its homeless population and its fires, floods, and earthquakes.

In that context, the ideal symbol of LAX is, perhaps, the great object that for thirty years has been the distinctive image of the place: the ugly white quadruped that sits in the middle of the airport like a beached white whale or a jet-age beetle, featuring a 360-degree circular restaurant that does not revolve and an observation deck from which the main view is of twenty-three thousand parking places. The Theme Building, at 201 World Way, is a sad image of a future that never arrived, a monument to Kennedy-era idealism and the thrusting modernity of the American empire when it was in its prime; it now has the poignancy of an abandoned present with its price tag stuck to it. When you go there (and almost nobody does) you are greeted by photos of Saturn's rings and Jupiter and its moons, by a plaque laid down by L.B.J. and a whole set of symbols from the time when NASA was shooting for the heavens. Now the "landmark" building, with its "gourmet-type restaurant," looks like a relic from a time long past, when it must have looked like the face of the future.

Upstairs, a few desperately merry waiters are serving nonalcoholic drinks and cheeseburgers to sallow diners who look as if they've arrived at the end of the world; on the tarmac outside, speedbirds inch ahead like cars in a traffic jam. "Hello All the New People of LAX—Welcome," says the graffiti on the elevator.

The Theme Restaurant comes to us from an era when L.A. was leading the world. Nowadays, of course, L.A. is being formed and reformed and led by the world around it. And as I got ready to leave LAX, I could not help but feel that the Theme Building stands, more and more, for a city left behind by our accelerating planet. LAX, I was coming to realize, was a good deal scruffier than the airports even of Bangkok or Jakarta, more chaotic, more suggestive of Third World lawlessness. And the city around it is no more golden than Seoul, no more sunny than Taipei, and no more laid-back than Moscow. Beverly Hills, after all, is largely speaking Farsi now. Hollywood Boulevard is sleazier than 42nd Street. And Malibu is falling into the sea.

Yet just as I was about to give up on L.A. as yesterday's piece of modernity, I got on the shuttle bus that moves between the terminals in a never-ending loop. The seats next to me were taken by two tough-looking dudes from nearby South Central, who were riding the free buses and helping people on and off with their cases (acting, I presumed, on the safe assumption that the Japanese, say, new to the country and bewildered, had been warned beforehand to tip often and handsomely for every service they received). In between terminals, as a terrified-looking Miss Kudo and her friend guarded their luggage, en route from Nagoya to Las Vegas, the two gold-plated sharks talked about the Raiders' last game and the Lakers' next season. Then one of them, without warning, announced, "The bottom line is the spirit is with you. When you work out, you chill out and, like, you meditate in your spirit. You know what I mean? Meditation is recreation. Learn math, follow your path. That's all I do, man, that's all I live for: learnin' about God, learnin' about Jesus. I am *possessed* by that spirit. You know, I used to have all these problems, with the flute and all, but when I heard about God, I learned about the body, the mind, and the flesh. People forget, they don't know, that the Bible isn't talkin' about the flesh, it's talkin' about the spirit. And I was reborn again in the spirit."

His friend nodded. "When you recreate, you meditate. Recreation is a spiritually uplifting experience."

"Yeah. When you do that, you allow the spirit to breathe."

"Because you're gettin' into the physical world. You're lettin' the spirit flow. You're helpin' the secretion of the endorphins in the brain."

Nearby, the Soldiers of the Cross of Christ Church stood by the escalators, taking donations, and a man in a dog collar approached another stranger.

I watched the hustlers allowing the spirit to breathe, I heard the Hare Krishna devotees plying their wares, I spotted some Farrakhan flunkies collecting a dollar for a copy of their newspaper, *The Final Call*—redemption and corruption all around us in the air—and I thought: welcome to America, Miss Kudo, welcome to L.A.

Life in Motion

Nicole Lamy

1

Three years ago I took pictures of all the houses I've lived in. The houses impress not in beauty but in number—twelve houses before I turned thirteen. For me the moves had always resisted coherent explanation—no military reassignments or evasion of the law. I wanted to gather the photos as charms against fallible memory, like the list of lost things I used to keep: a plastic purse filled with silver dollars, a mole-colored beret, a strip of negatives from my brother's first day of kindergarten. I planned to bind the photos in an album and give them to my mother. Maybe then, I thought, we could read our lives like straightforward narratives. Wise readers know that all stories follow one of two paths: The Stranger Comes to Town or The Journey. My life in motion suggested both.

2

When idea turned to plan, I asked my father for a list of the addresses I couldn't remember. Instead, as I had hoped, he offered to drive me through Maine, New Hampshire, and Massachusetts himself. My father, too, took photographs, and I wanted to draw him into my life a little, remind him of the times during car trips when, as dusk deepened, he would switch on the light inside the car, without prompting, so that I could continue to read.

3

I photographed the houses and the apartments and the surprising number of duplexes (so often did we live in the left half of a house that I wonder if I've developed a right-hemisphere problem—I imagine the right side of my brain paler and more shriveled than its better half, as atrophied and bleached as an arm that has been in a cast all summer), though I never asked to be let inside. I remembered the flow of rooms in most houses and I could imagine walking through them in a sort of Ciceronian memory system for childhood.

4

The photographs pretend no artistic merit. I centered most of the houses in my viewfinder as I stood on opposite sidewalks. Occasionally a branch or a piece of the neighboring house appears at the edge of the frame. Otherwise the book is a collection of residential mug shots. I wasn't accustomed to snapping pictures of whole buildings without people cluttering the frames, and as I focused before each shot I thought of the pictures my father had taken during his early twenties: ducks and snowdrifts and weathered cottages. Looking through my father's pictures, my mother would squint with mock earnestness at yet another image of a dilapidated barn and ask, "Where were we, behind the barn?"

5

At the first house—125 Wood Street, a gray three-family at the edge of the campus where my father had been a sophomore—I toyed with perspective. I held my camera at my hip; I crouched by the mailboxes, trying to imagine a toddler's vantage point. No pre-school impressions came flooding back; I gained nothing but stares from the neighbors. I thought of the family lore about the short time we lived on Wood Street. By 1972, the sixties still hadn't retreated from Lewiston, Maine. The perennial students who shared our building kept the house reeking pleasantly of weed, and our downstairs neighbor wandered up to our apartment now and again to shower, since her bathtub was occupied by her pet duck. Her thesis, my mother insisted, had something to do with roller skates, and she decorated her apartment with black lights and mini-marshmallows, dipped in fluorescent paint, which she stuck to branches that hung from her ceiling. At night, when the lights came on, visitors were treated to an electrifying set of unlikely constellations.

6

From Maine we moved south to New Hampshire. Rooting out the apartments in the freshly overdeveloped landscape of New Hampshire was a trickier prospect; some of the photos of these houses show unfamiliar additions, self-installed skylights. Some had new, paved-over driveways, others aluminum siding. One apartment complex in southern New Hampshire remained intact, though the surrounding woods had been leveled to receive three new strip malls. When we wandered closer to the Massachusetts border, images reversed themselves and I found myself remembering the houses' odd absences: an oval of yellowed grass showed where an above-ground pool had sat; a chimney stopped abruptly with no fireplace attached.

During each move, after the boxes had been unpacked, my father would turn their openings to the ground and use a pocketknife to cut windows and doors. The refrigerator boxes were best, skyscrapers with grass floors. In my cardboard house I would read cross-legged into the evening, ignoring my parents' invitations to take-out dinners in our new yard until my father lifted the box off me and walked away, bearing my cardboard home, leaving me blinking in the dusk.

7

Now when I leave my apartment for vacation, no matter how anticipated the trip, I experience numbing panic—will I ever see home again? I'm sympathetic to Rilke's Eurydice: What did she care about Orpheus and his willpower? Sure, she had her reasons: hell living had filled her with death and isolated her from human touch. No doubt she could have grown accustomed to the rocks and rivers of Hades. Who among us can get our mind around a move that drastic? From one side of the eternal duplex to the other. Each time I return home from vacation, rooms don't appear the same as I left them. Walls seem to meet floors at subtly altered angles. Careful inspections—heel-toe, heel-toe around each of the rooms—reveal no evidence of the perceived.

8

After my parents split, I kept most of my assorted five-year-old's treasures at the white three-family where I lived with my mother, watched over by a grim, disapproving landlady. My father's wall-to-wall-carpeted bachelor apartment always smelled faintly of hops; he and his two roommates all owned water beds and motorcycles. My personal inventory at my father's new home was limited to a Holly Hobbie nightgown, *The Little Princess*, and Milton Bradley's Sorry!, a game that requires players to apologize without sincerity after forcing their competitors to start again.

9

I found the post-divorce houses on my own. At one address, the brown-stained house I had known in early grade school wasn't there at all. Developers had knocked it down, then paved over the spot to provide parking for the neighboring convenience store and candy shop. On the winter afternoon when I visited, I snapped a photo of a stray shopping cart that had rolled away from the convenience store to the spot where the kitchen had been. The shot, of the lonely shopping cart illuminated by a hazy beam of light, has a Hallmark devotional-card quality. I have no sentimental feelings about the house, though. I even felt satisfaction when I saw the smoothly paved parking lot; it was as though I had willed the destruction of the site of many childhood disappointments (new stepfather! mid-first-grade school switch! dog runs away from home!).

The edges of the photograph give more away. At the top of the frame I can spot a sliver of the foundation of the house that backed up to ours. My friend Annette lived there, an only child whose mother cut women's hair in the pink room adjacent to their dining room and whose father cured meat, hung in strips—dark and pale, meat and fat—in their cellar.

At the left edge of the frame, the tail of an *a* is visible, part of a glowing sign advertising "Gina—Psychic," the fortune-teller who set up shop next door.

10

In a decorative gesture, I planned to hand-color the photographs as if they were pre-Kodachrome portraits of children with blossom-pink cheeks and lips. Armed with the oils and pencils, however, I only touched up a piece of every home—a chimney, a storm door, a front gate. If stacked, they'd make a flip-book composite of a home.

Red shutters and verdant bushes decorate the house after the last fold in the book. There, the three of us—mother, sister, and new brother, aged three—began living alone together for the first time. The stepfather had come and gone, leaving the three of us to find balance in our uneasy triumvirate. Neighbors and shopkeepers looked at us, curious. I could tell that the age gaps perplexed them—too few years between a mother and daughter who chatted like girlfriends and too many between a sister and brother who looked almost like mother and son. Their confusion was compounded by my mother's youth and beauty and by the way at age thirteen I seemed to have passed directly to thirty-five.

The red-shuttered house was home the longest, and it is the only house my brother remembers. When I handed the coloring pencils over to him to spruce up the image of the old house, he colored the whole thing. He and my mother still live in that duplex, formerly the parish house for the Congregational church across the street. We haven't been the only ones comfortable there. Pets and pests flourish: a dog, rabbits, guinea pigs, escaped reptiles, moths and silverfish, hollow shells of worms in macaroni boxes, squirrels in the attic.

The parish house has walls that slant toward the middle and floorboards that creak too frequently and too loudly to be creepy. During the first year, while discovering the rules and limits of our new family, we cleared the dining room table each night after dinner and began to play.

The three of us played games from my mother's childhood—tiddledywinks, pick-up-sticks, PIT. And after my brother fell asleep, my mother and I drank tea and played Password, Boggle, and Scrabble, stopping only when the board was almost filled and our wooden racks held two or three impossible consonants. A few years ago, chasing a marble that had slipped through a wrought iron heating grate, my brother lifted the panel by one of its iron curls and found, caught in the black cloth, game pieces of all kinds: dice, tiddledywinks, cribbage pegs, smooth wooden squares with black letters—pieces we had barely missed from games we had continued to play.

11

When the photo project was complete, I felt a historian's satisfaction. I had gathered the proof of my life and given it a shape. To create the album I cut a long strip of black paper and folded and flipped it as if to cut paper dolls. I printed the images small and pasted them in the accordion book. Held from the top, the book tumbles open to reveal twelve homes logically connected.

My mother saw the book as evidence of a life hastily lived. When she unknotted the ribbon around the tidy package and allowed it to unfold, I watched her face seize up.

"Ha, ha," she pushed the sounds out with effort. "All my failures," she said as she held the book away from her in an exaggerated gesture. I had tried to piece a story out of a life that I saw as largely unplanned. For my mother, this life led by reaction had eventually settled into a kind of choice. I was ashamed I thought it was mine to figure out.

12

One night, a few weeks before I moved out of the parish house duplex into my own apartment, I returned home and wheeled my bike around to the back of the house. Glancing up at the brightly lit windows, I was afforded an unusual glimpse of the daily theater of my family. From my spot in the yard I saw a woman in the kitchen chopping vegetables and talking on the phone, while a couple of rooms over, a gangly teenage boy sat in a chair by the television. Startled to be given a chance to see the house as a stranger might, I watched for a few moments and tried to imagine the lives of those inside.

Portrait of My Body

Phillip Lopate

I am a man who tilts. When I am sitting, my head slants to the right; when walking, the upper part of my body reaches forward to catch a sneak preview of the street. One way or another, I seem to be off-center—or "uncentered," to use the jargon of holism. My lousy posture, a tendency to slump or put myself into lazy, contorted misalignments, undoubtedly contributes to lower back pain. For a while I correct my bad habits, do morning exercises, sit straight, breathe deeply, but always an inner demon that insists on approaching the world askew resists perpendicularity.

I think if I had broader shoulders I would be more squarely anchored. But my shoulders are narrow, barely wider than my hips. This has always made shopping for suits an embarrassing business. (Françoise Gilot's *Life with Picasso* tells how Picasso was so touchy about his disproportionate body—in his case all shoulders, no legs—that he insisted the tailor fit him at home.)

When I was growing up in Brooklyn, my hero was Sandy Koufax, the Dodgers' Jewish pitcher. In the doldrums of Hebrew choir practice at Feigenbaum's Mansion & Catering Hall, I would fantasize striking out the side, even whiffing twenty-seven batters in a row. Lack of shoulder development put an end to this identification; I became a writer instead of a Koufax.

It occurs to me that the restless angling of my head is an attempt to distract viewers' attention from its paltry base. I want people to look at my head, partly because I live in my head most of the time. My sister, a trained masseuse, often warns me of the penalties, like neck tension, that may arise from failing to integrate body and mind. Once, about ten years ago, she and I were at the beach and she was scrutinizing my body with a sister's critical eye. "You're getting flabby," she said. "You should exercise every day. I do—look at me, not an ounce of fat." She pulled at her midriff, celebrating (as is her wont) her physical attributes with the third-person enthusiasm of a carnival barker.

"But"—she threw me a bone—"you do have a powerful head. There's an intensity. . . ." A graduate student of mine (who was slightly loony) told someone that she regularly saw an aura around my head in class. One reason I like to teach is that it focuses fifteen or so dependent gazes on me with such paranoiac intensity as cannot help but generate an aura in my behalf.

I also have a commanding stare, large sad brown eyes that can be read as either gentle or severe. Once I watched several hours of myself on videotape. I discovered to my horror that my face moved at different rates: sometimes my mouth would be laughing, eyebrows circumflexed in mirth, while my eyes coolly gauged the interviewer to see what effect I was making. I am something of an actor. And, as with many performers, the mood I sense most in myself is that of energy-conserving watchfulness; but this expression is often mistaken (perhaps because of the way brown eyes are read in our culture) for sympathy. I see myself as determined to the point of stubbornness, selfish, even a bit cruel—in any case, I am all too aware of the limits of my compassion, so that it puzzles me when people report a first impression of me as gentle, kind, solicitous. In my youth I felt obliged to come across as dynamic, arrogant, intimidating, the life of the party; now, surer of myself, I hold back some energy, thereby winning time to gather information and make better judgments. This results sometimes in a misimpression of my being mildly depressed. Of course, the simple truth is that I have less energy than I once did, and that accumulated experiences have made me, almost against my will, kinder and sadder.

Sometimes I can feel my mouth arching downward in an ironic smile, which, at its best, reassures others that we need not take everything so seriously—because we are all in the same comedy together—and, at its worst, expresses a superior skepticism. This smile, which can be charming when not supercilious, has elements of the bashful that mesh with the worldly—the shyness, let us say, of a cultivated man who is often embarrassed for others by their willful shallowness or self-deception. Many times, however, my ironic smile is nothing more than a neutral stall among people who do not seem to appreciate my "contribution." I hate that pain-in-the-ass half-smile of mine; I want to jump in, participate, be loud, thoughtless, vulgar.

Often I give off a sort of psychic stench to myself, I do not like myself at all, but out of stubborn pride I act like a man who does. I appear for all the world poised, contented, sanguine when inside I may be feeling self-revulsion bordering on the suicidal. What a wonder to be so misread! Of course, if in the beginning I had thought I was coming across accurately, I never would have bothered to become a writer. And the truth is I am not misread, because another part of me is never less than fully contented with myself.

I am vain about these parts of my body: my eyes, my fingers, my legs. It is true that my legs are long and not unshapely, but my vanity about them has less to do with their comeliness than with their contribution to my height. Montaigne, a man who was himself on the short side, wrote that "the beauty of stature is the only beauty of men." But even if Montaigne had never said it, I would continue to attribute a good deal of my self-worth and benevolent liberalism to being tall. When I go out into the street, I feel well-disposed toward the (mostly shorter) swarms of humanity; crowds not only do not dismay, they enliven me; and I am tempted to think that my passion for urbanism is linked to my height. By no means am I suggesting that only tall people love cities; merely that, in my case, part of the pleasure I derive from walking in crowded streets issues from a confidence that I can see above the heads of others, and cut a fairly impressive, elevated figure as I saunter along the sidewalk.

Some of my best friends have been—short. Brilliant men, brimming with poetic and worldly ideas, they deserved all of my and the world's respect. Yet at times I have had to master an impulse to rumple their heads; and I suspect they have developed manners of a more formal, *noli me tangere* nature, largely in response to this petting impulse of taller others.

The accident of my tallness has inclined me to both a seemingly egalitarian informality and a desire to lead. Had I not been a writer, I would surely have become a politician; I was even headed in that direction in my teens. Ever since I shot up to a little over six feet, I have had at my command what feels like a natural, Gregory Peck authority when addressing an audience. Far from experiencing stage fright, I have actually sought out situations in which I could make speeches, give readings, sit on panel discussions, and generally tower over everyone else onstage. To be tall is to look down on the world and meet its eyes on your terms. But this topic, the noblesse oblige of tall men, is a dangerously provoking one, and so let us say no more about it.

The mental image of one's body changes slower than one's body. Mine was for a long while arrested in my early twenties, when I was tall and thin (165 pounds) and gobbled down whatever I felt like. I ate food that was cheap and filling, cheeseburgers, pizza, without any thought to putting on weight. But a young person's metabolism is more dietetically forgiving. To compound the problem, the older you get, the more cultivated your palate grows—and the more life's setbacks make you inclined to fill the hollowness of disappointment with the pleasures of the table.

Between the age of thirty and forty I put on ten pounds, mostly around the midsection. Since then my gut has suffered another expansion, and I tip the scales at over 180. That I took a while to notice the change may be shown by my continuing to purchase clothes at my primordial adult size (33 waist, 15½ collar), until a girlfriend started pointing out that all my clothes were too tight. I rationalized this circumstance as the result of changing fashions (thinking myself still subconsciously loyal to the sixties' penchant for skintight fits) and laundry shrinkage rather than anything to do with my own body. She began buying me larger replacements for birthdays or holidays, and I found I enjoyed this "baggier" style, which allowed me to button my trousers comfortably, or to wear a tie and, for the first time in years, close my top shirt button. But it took even longer before I was able to enter a clothing store myself and give the salesman realistically enlarged size numbers.

Clothes can disguise the defects of one's body, up to a point. I get dressed with great optimism, adding one color to another, mixing my favorite Japanese and Italian designers, matching the patterns and textures, selecting ties, then proceed to the bathroom mirror to judge the result. There is an ideal in my mind of the effect I am essaying by wearing a particular choice of garments, based, no doubt, on male models in fashion ads—and I fall so far short of this insouciant gigolo handsomeness that I cannot help but be a little disappointed when I turn up so depressingly myself, narrow-shouldered, Talmudic, that grim, set mouth, that long, narrow face, those appraising eyes, the Semitic hooked nose, all of which express both the strain of intellectual overachieving and the tabula rasa of immaturity . . . for it is still, underneath, a boy in the mirror. A boy with a rapidly receding hairline.

How is it that I've remained a boy all this time, into my late forties? I remember, at seventeen, drawing a self-portrait of myself as I looked in the mirror. I was so appalled at the weak chin and pleading eyes that I ended up focusing on the neckline of the cotton T-shirt. Ever since then I have tried to toughen myself up, but I still encounter in the glass that haunted uncertainty—shielded by a bluffing shell of cynicism, perhaps, but untouched by wisdom. So I approach the mirror warily, without lighting up as much as I would for the least of my acquaintances; I go one-on-one with that frowning schmuck.

And yet, it would be insulting to those who labor under the burden of true ugliness to palm myself off as an unattractive man. I'm at times almost handsome, if you squinted your eyes and rounded me off to the nearest *beau idéal*. I lack even a shred of cowboy virility, true, but I believe I fall into a category of adorable nerd or absentminded professor that awakens the amorous curiosity of some women. "Cute" is a word often applied to me by those I've been fortunate enough to attract. Then again, I attract only women of a certain lopsided prettiness: the head-turning, professional beauties never fall for me. They seem to look right through me, in fact. Their utter lack of interest in my appeal has always fascinated me. Can it be so simple an explanation as that beauty calls to beauty, as wealth to wealth?

I think of poor (though not in his writing gifts) Cesare Pavese, who kept chasing after starlets, models, and ballerinas—exquisite lovelies who couldn't appreciate his morose coffeehouse charm. Before he killed himself, he wrote a poem addressed to one of them, "Death Will Come Bearing Your Eyes"—thereby unfairly promoting her from rejecting lover to unwitting executioner. Perhaps he believed that only beautiful women (not literary critics, who kept awarding him prestigious prizes) saw him clearly, with twenty-twenty vision, and had the right to judge him. Had I been more headstrong, if masochistic, I might have followed his path and chased some beauty until she was forced to tell me, like an oracle, what it was about me, physically, that so failed to excite her. Then I might know something crucial about my body, before I passed into my next reincarnation.

Jung says somewhere that we pay dearly over many years to learn about ourselves what a stranger can see at a glance. This is the way I feel about my back.

Fitting rooms aside, we none of us know what we look like from the back. It is the area of ourselves whose presentation we can least control, and which therefore may be the most honest part of us.

I divide backs into two kinds: my own and everyone else's. The others' backs are often mysterious, exquisite, and uncannily sympathetic. I have always loved backs. To walk behind a pretty woman in a backless dress and savor how a good pair of shoulder blades, heightened by shadow, has the same power to pierce the heart as chiseled cheekbones! . . . I wonder what it says about me that I worship a part of the body that signals a turning away. Does it mean I'm a glutton for being abandoned, or a timid voyeur who prefers a surreptitious gaze that will not be met and challenged? I only know I have often felt the deepest love at just that moment when the beloved turns her back to me to get some sleep.

I have no autoerotic feelings about my own back. I cannot even picture it; visually it is a stranger to me. I know it only as an annoyance, which came into my consciousness twenty years ago, when I started getting lower back pain. Yes, we all know that homo sapiens is constructed incorrectly; our erect posture puts too much pressure on the base of the spine; more workdays are lost because of lower back pain than any other cause. Being a writer, I sit all day, compounding the problem. My back is the enemy of my writing life: if I don't do exercises daily, I immediately ache; and if I do, I am still not spared. I could say more, but there is nothing duller than lower back pain. So common, mundane an ailment brings no credit to the sufferer. One has to dramatize it somehow, as in the phrase "I threw my back out."

Here is a gossip column about my body: My eyebrows grow quite bushy across my forehead, and whenever I get my hair cut, the barber asks me diplomatically if I want them trimmed or not. (I generally say no, associating bushy eyebrows with Balzackian virility, *élan vital;* but sometimes I acquiesce, to soothe his fastidiousness.) . . . My belly button is a modest, embedded slit, not a jaunty swirl like my father's. Still, I like to sniff the odor that comes from jabbing my finger in it: a very ripe, underground smell, impossible to describe, but let us say a combination of old gym socks and stuffed derma (the Yiddish word for this oniony dish of ground intestines is, fittingly, *kish-kas*). . . . I have a scar on my tongue from childhood, which I can only surmise I received by landing it on a sharp object, somehow. Or perhaps I bit it hard. I have the habit of sticking my tongue out like a dog when exerting myself physically, as though to urge my muscles on; and maybe I accidentally chomped into it at such a moment. . . . I gnash my teeth, sleeping or waking. Awake, the sensation makes me feel alert and in contact with the world when I start to drift off in a daydream. Another way of grounding myself is to pinch my cheek—drawing a pocket of flesh downward and squeezing it—as I once saw JFK do in a filmed motorcade. I do this cheek-pinching especially when I am trying to keep mentally focused during teaching or other public situations. I also scratch the nape of my neck under public stress, so much so that I raise welts or sores which then eventually grow scabs; and I take great delight in secretly picking the scabs off. . . . My nose itches whenever I think about it, and I scratch it often, especially lying in bed trying to fall asleep (maybe because I am conscious of my breathing then). I also pick my nose with formidable thoroughness when no one, I hope, is looking. . . . There is a white scar about the size of a quarter on the juicy part of my knee; I got it as a boy running into a car fender, and I can still remember staring with detached calm at the blood that gushed from it like a pretty, half-eaten peach. Otherwise, the sight of my own blood makes me awfully nervous. I used to faint dead away when a blood sample was taken, and now I can control the impulse to do so only by biting the insides of my cheeks while steadfastly looking away from the needle's action. . . . I like to clean out my ear wax as often as possible (the smell is curiously sulfurous; I associate it with the bodies of dead insects). I refuse to listen to warnings that it is dangerous to stick cleaning objects into your ears. I love Q-Tips immoderately; I buy them in huge quantities and store them the way a former refugee will stock canned foodstuffs. . . . My toes are long and apelike; I have very little fellow feeling for them; they are so far away, they may as well belong to someone else. . . . My flattish buttocks are not offensively large, but neither do they have the "dream" configuration one sees in jeans ads. Perhaps for this reason, it disturbed me puritanically when asses started to be treated by Madison Avenue, around the seventies, as crucial sexual equipment, and I began to receive compositions from teenage girl students declaring that they liked some boy because he had "a cute butt." It confused me; I had thought the action was elsewhere.

About my penis there is nothing, I think, unusual. It has a brown stem, and a pink mushroom head where the foreskin is pulled back. Like most heterosexual males, I have little comparative knowledge to go by, so that I always feel like an outsider when I am around women or gay men who talk zestfully about differences in penises. I am afraid that they might judge me harshly, ridicule me like the boys who stripped me of my bathing suit in summer camp when I was ten. But perhaps they would simply declare it an ordinary penis, which changes size with the stimulus or weather or time of day. Actually, my penis does have a peculiarity: it has two peeing holes. They are very close to each other, so that usually only one stream of urine issues, but sometimes a hair gets caught across them, or some such contretemps, and they squirt out in two directions at once.

This part of me, which is so synecdochically identified with the male body (as the term "male member" indicates), has given me both too little, and too much, information about what it means to be a man. It has a personality like a cat's. I have prayed to it to behave better, to be less frisky, or more; I have followed its nose in matters of love, ignoring good sense, and paid the price; but I have also come to appreciate that it has its own specialized form of intelligence which must be listened to, or another price will be extracted.

Even to say the word "impotence" aloud makes me nervous. I used to tremble when I saw it in print, and its close relation, "importance," if hastily scanned, had the same effect, as if they were publishing a secret about me. But why should it be *my* secret, when my penis has regularly given me erections lo these many years—except for about a dozen times, mostly when I was younger? Because, even if it has not been that big a problem for me, it has dominated my thinking as an adult male. I've no sooner to go to bed with a woman than I'm in suspense. The power of the flaccid penis's statement, "I don't want you," is so stark, so cruelly direct, that it continues to exert a fascination out of all proportion to its actual incidence. Those few times when I was unable to function were like a wall forcing me to take another path—just as, after I tried to kill myself at seventeen, I was obliged to give up pessimism for a time. Each had instructed me by its too painful manner that I could not handle the world as I had previously construed it, that my confusion and rage were being found out. I would have to get more wily or else grow up.

Yet for the very reason that I was compelled to leave them behind, these two options of my youth, impotence and suicide, continue to command an underground loyalty, as though they were more "honest" than the devious strategies of potency and survival which I adopted. Put it this way: sometimes we encounter a person who has had a nervous breakdown years before and who seems cemented over sloppily, his vulnerability ruthlessly guarded against as dangerous; we sense he left a crucial part of himself back in the chaos of breakdown, and has since grown rigidly jovial. So suicide and impotence became for me "the roads not taken," the paths I had repressed.

Whenever I hear an anecdote about impotence—a woman who successfully coaxed an ex-priest who had been celibate and unable to make love, first by lying next to him for six months without any touching, then by cuddling for six more months, then by easing him slowly into a sexual embrace—I think they are talking about me. I identify completely: this, in spite of the fact, which I promise not to repeat again, that I have generally been able to do it whenever called upon. Believe it or not, I am not boasting when I say that: a part of me is contemptuous of this virility, as though it were merely a mechanical trick that violated my true nature, that of an impotent man absolutely frightened of women, absolutely secluded, cut off.

I now see the way I have idealized impotence: I've connected it with pushing the world away, as a kind of integrity, as in Molière's *The Misanthrope*—connected it with that part of me which, gregarious socializer that I am, continues to insist that I am a recluse, too good for this life. Of course, it is not true that I am terrified of women. I exaggerate my terror of them for dramatic effect, or for the purposes of a good scare.

My final word about impotence: Once, in a period when I was going out with many women, as though purposely trying to ignore my hypersensitive side and force it to grow callous by thrusting myself into foreign situations (not only sexual) and seeing if I was able to "rise to the occasion," I dated a woman who was attractive, tall and blond, named Susan. She had something to do with the pop music business, was a follower of the visionary religious futurist Teilhard de Chardin, and considered herself a religious pacifist. In fact, she told me her telephone number in the form of the anagram, N-O-T-O-W-A-R. I thought she was joking and laughed aloud, but she gave me a solemn look. In passing, I should say that all the women with whom I was impotent or close to it had solemn natures.

The sex act has always seemed to me in many ways ridiculous, and I am most comfortable when a woman who enters the sheets with me shares that sense of the comic pomposity behind such a grandiloquently rhetorical use of the flesh. It is as though the prose of the body were being drastically squeezed into metrical verse. I would not have known how to stop guffawing had I been D.H. Lawrence's lover, and I am sure he would have been pretty annoyed at me. But a smile saying "All this will pass" has an erotic effect on me like nothing else.

They claim that men who have long, long fingers also have lengthy penises. I can tell you with a surety that my fingers are long and sensitive, the most perfect, elegant, handsome part of my anatomy. They are not entirely perfect—the last knuckle of my right middle finger is twisted permanently, broken in a softball game when I was trying to block the plate—but even this slight disfigurement, harbinger of mortality, adds to the pleasure I take in my hands' rugged beauty. My penis does not excite in me nearly the same contemplative delight when I look at it as do my fingers. Pianists' hands, I have been told often; and though I do not play the piano, I derive an aesthetic satisfaction from them that is as pure and Apollonian as any I am capable of. I can stare at my fingers for hours. No wonder I have them so often in my mouth, biting my fingernails to bring them closer. When I write, I almost feel that they, and not my intellect, are the clever progenitors of the text. Whatever narcissism, fetishism, and proud sense of masculinity I possess about my body must begin and end with my fingers.

Brothers

Bret Lott

This much is fact: There is a home movie of the two of us sitting on the edge of the swimming pool at our grandma and grandpa's old apartment building in Culver City. The movie, taken sometime in early 1960, is in color, though the color has faded, leaving my brother Brad and me milk white and harmless children, me a year and a half old, Brad almost four, our brown hair faded to only the thought of brown hair. Our mother, impossibly young, sits next to me on the right of the screen. Her hair, for all the fading of the film, is coal black, shoulder length, and parted in the middle, curled up on the sides. She has on a bathing suit covered in purple and blue flowers, the color in them nearly gone. Next to me on the left of the screen is Brad, in his white swimming trunks. I am in the center, my fat arms up, bent at the elbows, fingers curled into fists, my legs kicking away at the water, splashing and splashing. I am smiling, the baby of the family, the center of the world at that very instant, though my little brother, Tim, is only some six or seven months off, and my little sister, Leslie, the last child, just three years distant. The pool water before us is only a thin sky blue, the bushes behind us a dull and lifeless light green. There is no sound.

My mother speaks to me, points at the water, then looks up. She lifts a hand to block the sun, says something to the camera. Her skin is the same white as ours, but her lips are red, a sharp cut of lipstick moving as she speaks. I am still kicking. Brad is looking to his right, off the screen, his feet in the water, too, but moving slowly. His hands are on the edge of the pool, and he leans forward a little, looks down into the water. My mother still speaks to the camera, and I give an extra-hard kick, splash up shards of white water.

Brad flinches at the water, squints his eyes, while my mother laughs, puts a hand to her face. She looks back to the camera, keeps talking, a hand low to the water to keep more from hitting her. I still kick hard, still send up bits of water, and I am laughing a baby's laugh, mouth open and eyes nearly closed, arms still up, fingers still curled into fists.

More water splashes at Brad, who leans over to me, says something. Nothing about me changes: I only kick, laugh. He says something again, his face leans a little closer to mine. Still I kick.

This is when he lifts his left hand from the edge of the pool, places it on my right thigh, and pinches hard. It's not a simple pinch, not two fingers on a fraction of skin, but his whole hand, all his fingers grabbing the flesh just above my knee and squeezing down hard. He grimaces, his eyes on his hand, on my leg.

My expression changes, of course: In an instant I go from a laughing baby to a shocked one, my mouth a perfect O, my body shivering so that my legs kick even harder, even quicker, but just this one last time. They stop, and I cry, my mouth open even more, my eyes all the way closed. My hands are still in fists.

Then Brad's hand is away, and my mother turns from speaking to the camera to me. She leans in close, asking, I am certain, what's wrong. The movie cuts then to my grandma, white skin and silver hair, seated on a patio chair by the pool, above her a green-and-white-striped umbrella. She has a cigarette in one hand, waves off the camera with the other. Though she died eight years ago, and though she, too, loses color with each viewing, she is still alive up there, still waves, annoyed, at my grandpa and his camera, the moment my brother pinched hell out of me already gone.

This much is fact, too: Thumbtacked to the wall of my office is a photograph of Brad and me taken by my wife in November 1980, the date printed on the border. In it we stand together, me a good six inches taller than him, my arm around his shoulder. The photograph is black and white, as though the home movie and its sinking colors were a prophecy pointing to this day twenty years later: We are at the tidepools at Portuguese Bend, out on the Palos Verdes Peninsula; in the background are the stone-gray bluffs, to the left of us the beginning of the black rocks of the pools, above us the perfect white of an overcast sky.

Brad has on a white Panama hat, a collarless shirt beneath a gray hooded sweatshirt. His face is smooth shaven, and he is grinning, lips together, eyes squinted nearly shut beneath the brim of the hat. It is a goofy smile, but a real one.

I have on a cardigan with an alpine design around the shoulders, the rest of it white, the shawl collar on it black here, though I know it to have been navy blue. I have on a buttondown Oxford shirt, sideburns almost to my earlobes. I have a mustache, a pair of glasses too large for my face; and I am smiling, my mouth open to reveal my big teeth. It isn't my goofy smile, but it's a real one too.

These are the facts of my brother: the four-year-old pinching me, the twenty-four-year-old leaning into me, grinning.

But between the fact of these two images lie twenty years of the play of memory, the dark and bright pictures my mind has retained, embroidered upon, made into things they are and things they are not. There are twenty years of things that happened between my brother and me, from the fistfight we had in high school over who got the honey bun for breakfast, to his phone call to me from a tattoo parlor in Hong Kong where he'd just gotten a Chinese junk stitched beneath the skin of his right shoulder blade; from his showing me one summer day how to do a death drop from the jungle gym at Elizabeth Dickerson Elementary, to him watching while his best friend and our next-door neighbor, Lynn Tinton, beat me up on the driveway of our home in a fight over whether I'd fouled Lynn or not at basketball. I remember—no true picture, necessarily, but what I have made the truth by holding tight to it, playing it back in my head at will and in the direction I wish it to go—I remember lying on my back, Lynn's knees pinning my shoulders to the driveway while he hit my chest, and looking up at Brad, the basketball there at his hip, him watching.

I have two children now. Both boys, born two and a half years apart. I showed the older one, Zeb—almost eight—the photograph, asked him who those two people were. He held it in his hands a long while.

We were in the kitchen. The bus comes at seven-twenty each morning, and I have to have lunches made and breakfasts set out—all before that bus comes and before Melanie takes off for work, Jacob in tow, to be dropped off at the Montessori school on her way in to her office.

I waited, and waited, finally turned from him to get going on his lunch.

"It's you," he said. "You have a lot of hair," he said.

"Who's the other guy?" I said. I looked back at him, saw the concentration on his face, the way he brought the photograph close, my son's eyes taking in his uncle as best he could.

He said, "I don't know."

"That's your uncle Brad," I said. "Your mom took that picture ten years ago, long before you were ever born."

He still looked at the picture. He said, "He has a beard now."

I turned from him, finished with the peanut butter, and spread jelly on the other piece of bread. This is the only kind of sandwich he will eat at school. He said from behind me, "Only three years before I was born. That's not a long time." I stopped, turned again to him. He touched the picture with a finger. He said, "Three years isn't a long time, Dad."

But I was thinking of my question: *Who's the other guy?* and of the truth of his answer: *I don't know.*

Zeb and Jake fight. Melanie and I were upstairs wrapping Christmas presents in my office, a room kept locked the entire month of December for the gifts piled up in there. We heard Jake wailing, dropped the bucket of Legos and the red-and-green HO! HO! HO! paper, ran for the hall and down the stairs.

There in the kitchen stood my two sons, Jacob's eyes wet, him whimpering now, a hand to his bottom lip. I made it first, yelled, "What happened?"

"I didn't do it," Zeb said, and backed away from me, there with my hand to Jacob's jaw.

Melanie stroked Jacob's hair, whispered, "What's wrong?"

Jacob opened his mouth then, showed us the thick wash of blood between his bottom lip and his tongue, a single tooth, horribly white, swimming up from it. "We were playing Karate Kid," Zeb said, and now he was crying. "I didn't do it," he said, and backed away even farther.

One late afternoon a month or so ago, Melanie backed the van into the driveway to make it easier to unload all the plastic bags of groceries. When we'd finished we let the boys play outside, glad for them to be out of the kitchen while we sorted through the bags heaped on the counter, put everything away. Melanie's last words to the two of them, her leaning out the front door into the near-dark: "Don't play in the van!"

Not ten minutes later Jacob came into the house, slammed shut the front door like he always does. He walked into the kitchen, his hands behind him. He said, "Zeb's locked in the van." His face takes on the cast of the guilty when he knows he's done something wrong: His mouth gets pursed, his eyebrows go up, his eyes look right into mine. He doesn't know enough yet to look away. "He told me to come get you." He turned, headed for the door, and I followed him out onto the porch, where, before I could even see the van in the dark, I heard Zeb screaming.

I went to the van, tried one of the doors. It was locked, and Zeb was still screaming.

"Get the keys!" he was saying. "Get the keys!" I pressed my face to the glass of the back window, saw Zeb inside jumping up and down. "My hand's caught," he cried.

I ran into the house, got the keys from the hook beneath the cupboard, only enough time for me to say to Melanie, "Zeb's hand's closed in the back door," and turn, run back out. I made it to the van, unlocked the big back door, and pushed it up as quick as I could, Melanie already beside me.

Zeb stood holding the hand that'd been closed in the door. Melanie and I both took his hand, gently examined the skin, wiggled the fingers, and in the dull glow of the dome light we saw that nothing'd been broken, no skin torn. The black foam lining the door had cushioned his fingers, so that they'd only been smashed a little, but a little enough to scare him, and to make blue bruises there the next day. Beneath the dome light there was the sound of his weeping, then the choked words, "Jacob pulled the door down on me."

From the darkness just past the line of light from inside the van came my second son's voice: "I didn't do it."

I have no memory of the pinch Brad gave me on the edge of that apartment-complex pool, no memory of my mother's black hair—now it's a sort of brown—nor even any memory of the pool itself. There is only that bit of film.

But I can remember putting my arm around his shoulder in 1980, leaning into him, the awkward and alien comfort of that touch. In the photograph we are both smiling, me a newlywed with a full head of hair, him only a month or so back from working a drilling platform in the Gulf of Mexico. He'd missed my wedding six months before, stranded on the rig, he'd told us, because of a storm.

What I believe is this: That pinch was entry into our childhood; my arm around him, our smiling, is the proof of us two surfacing, alive but not unscathed.

And here are my own two boys, already embarked.

From Birnam Wood to Dunsinane

John McPhee

In most families, a generation or two is time enough to erase even a major infamy, but centuries upon centuries have not in this respect been kind to the Macbeths, as anyone knows who knows one. I've known several Macbeths, and I particularly remember the moments in which I met them, because in most instances a faint shadow seemed to cross their faces when their surname was exposed to yet another stranger. The latest of these is R.C. Macbeth, of Scarsdale. We were introduced—as travellers, as strangers, in a small town in New England—by a motel-keeper who was serving our breakfast, and who in her friendly way seemed to think that we would have much to say to each other simply because our names were derivationally Scottish. This Macbeth was a big, broad-shouldered man with bright eyes and an engagingly unprepossessing manner. As it happened, he did have a lot to say. He had scarcely sat down before he was well into a mild harangue about the injuries that had been done to his family through poetic license and dramatic journalism—manipulations of the pen. He said that his collateral ancestor Macbeth, King of Scotland, was a good king and is buried with other Scottish kings on the island Iona in a sanctuary where only authentic and duly entitled kings are at rest; that no one who had poached the throne of Scotland would ever have been buried, or at least would have long remained buried, on Iona; that Macbeth, in 1040, killed King Duncan not in bed but in battle; that Macbeth's claim to rule the Scots was as legitimate as Duncan's, each, through his mother, being a great-grandson of King Kenneth I; and that Macbeth settled the claim, as was the custom in his time, with his sword in fair and open fight. His reign lasted seventeen years. I could be well assured that something quite different from tyranny or depravity was the atmosphere that generally emanated from his fortress on the summit of Dunsinane Hill.

I said to Mr. Macbeth, "I'm sorry you have this cross to bear."

Macbeth lifted his coffee cup, indicating that he would drink to that. He drank. Then he said, "I've never been to Scotland. In a year or two, though, I'm going to go."

I said, "Let me give you a name and address. Donald Sinclair, Balbeggie, Perthshire. I'll write it down. He's a farmer. He's the cousin of a friend of mine. I don't know Sinclair very well, but I don't think he would mind if you were to seek him out, which is what I did once. I was in Scotland with my family, and one day—just for the experience—we went by the most direct way we could find from Birnam Wood to Dunsinane. It's a ten-mile trip. Sinclair calls himself a tenant farmer. Technically, that's what he is, but his father-in-law happens to be his landlord, and the family owns a very handsome piece of Perthshire—five thousand acres. Their estate is called Dunsinnan, and more or less in the middle of it is Dunsinane Hill."

Macbeth slowly set down his plastic coffee cup on the Formica surface of the table. I told him the details of the pilgrimage as I had made it.

Birnam Wood, on the edge of the Craigvinean Forest, stands across the River Tay from a medieval town, Dunkeld, and has been replaced to some extent by Birnam, a village that developed in the late nineteenth century. Birnam Wood now is deep and thick, dark green, with an understory of gorse and bracken, and white slashes of birch angling upward among larches and pines. In all likelihood, the boughs of such trees could not have been the boughs that went to Dunsinane. Apparently the forest was once predominantly oak. The present Birnam Wood, cut who knows how many times, seems to be merely a collateral descendant of the forest that once was there, for the presence of a number of slim oaks among the pines suggests what must have been, in the virgin stand, the climax tree. The army assembled by Siward, Malcolm, and Macduff would have marched under oak leaves. By the river is one immensely impressive piece of evidence suggesting that this was so. One tree, an oak, remains from—according to local testimony—the time of Macbeth. It stands in a riparian grove of grasses, weeds, and rusting junk. Nothing much is made of it. I used up half a morning finding it. A postman on the principal street of Birnam had told me about it. "The old trees are away now, unfortunately. But there is still one left. It is propped up." We picked our way downhill—my four small daughters, my wife, and I—along dirt pathways strewn with discarded plastic bottles and fragments of broken glass. The groundscape was somewhat cleaner and more inviting closer to the river, where another path ran along parallel to the current and passed under the high canopies of trees at least a century old. These were whips, seedlings, saplings by comparison with the tree we finally found. There it was, standing without fence or fanfare, its trunk outmassing the Heidelberg tun, its roemerian canopy all but stopping the sunlight: the last tree of Birnam Wood, a living monument to the value of staying put.

My wife and children and I joined hands, and we wrapped ourselves to the tree with arms extended. The six of us reached less than halfway around. The big oak was so gnarled that it appeared to be covered with highly magnified warts. Each of ten principal limbs had the diameter of a major oak in itself, and the lower ones, jutting out almost horizontally, were supported in six places by columns set in the ground. One great limb was dead. In the base of the trunk were cavelike holes. Lichen grew on the bark as if the tree were already down and moldering. But despite all that, the tree was green throughout its canopy—leafy and alive. This big oak alone could have camouflaged an army.

We sat down on the riverbank and had lunch. The Tay was fast, clear, and shallow, and about two hundred yards downstream was a small rip, a touch of white water. The flow was southerly, in the general direction of Dunsinane, so the army would have moved for some distance along the river on its way to the hill. We ate cold roast beef, white chocolate, and Islay Mini-Dunlop cheese. I reached up and took a leaf from the great oak, and we began the journey.

First, we stopped in at the Esso Autodiesel & Petrol Agency in Birnam and had the tank of our car filled, for five shillings sixpence halfpenny the gallon. The attendant gave the children Esso tiger tails. Below Birnam the riverine country-side was lush with wheat fields, haycocks, oats, barley. Multicolored lupines and wild foxgloves grew in meadows where herds of Aberdeen Angus were sleeping, all draped together with their necks across the necks of the cows beside them. It was a clear day, warm but not hot. A tractor plowing a field was followed by flights of seagulls. The gulls were eating the worms that the tractor turned up. We moved through a grove of seventy-foot cedars, copper beeches, and hemlocks on a dark lane running among standing stones, through weirdly overgrown formal gardens, and past an Italianate castle no more than a century old, now boarded shut and falling to ruin. We later found in a book on Dunkeld and Birnam that this (Murthly Castle) had been the home of an exotic peer who had once ornamented the grounds with herds of buffalo from Wyoming. In his milieu, he may not have been eccentric. Even today, we know someone in the same part of Perthshire who keeps a considerable herd of pet red deer, and when he goes off in summer to the far north—to Caithness—he takes his red deer with him in chartered freight cars.

Murthly Hospital, for mental patients, came soon after Murthly Castle and was about a third of the way from Birnam Wood to Dunsinane. Like the decaying structure upriver, the main buildings of the hospital, amorphous and ugly, must have been about a century old, and in their setting among woods and fields by the Tay they did not seem as forbidding in the sunlight as they must in the gloom of rain. The place belied itself, if it ever could, this day. Women sat on benches in brightly colored straw hats. Men in coveralls bowled on a lawn. Others gardened. Distress was invisible, but nonetheless my children were unnaturally quiet. Doctors crossed the grounds in white jackets. A big nurse, whose size was a kind of manifesto of control, carried a fragile and extremely old woman in her arms. Rows of stone cottages had names over their doors like Tuke, Robertson, Bruce. Among them, a giant and rusting television aerial was planted in the earth like a tree. One of the men on the bowling court left the game and ran toward us, smiling and waving his arms. I did not for a moment know what I wanted to do. He was running hard. Was I going to avoid him and renew, in one more way, his hurt; or was I going to become enskeined in a dialogue that could, in the end, be even less successful in the breaking? I left him behind, standing by the road, without expression, watching us go.

The country opened out again beyond the hospital, and the river made an erratic series of turns to the north, the east, the southeast, and, finally, the southwest, forming an irregular loop about two miles broad. Anybody moving overland from Birnam Wood to Dunsinane would cross this loop, and so did we, first going through the Haugh of Kercock, a low-lying meadow by the river. In a fank in the meadow, men were shearing sheep. Lambs were bleating wildly. Shorn ewes stood around looking silly and naked. One man had the head of a ewe in his arms, and was wrestling with her desperately, rolling on the ground. Moving on, we skirted a marshland called the Bloody Inches. Beautiful farm country followed toward Kinclaven, a village by the Tay, on the far side of the loop. In the fields, huge strawstacks had been constructed like houses—rectangular, with vertical walls, and tops sloping up to ridgelines. Moving along an unpaved lane, we came to a church that was black with age, and among the tombstones beside it a man was digging a grave. We stopped to ask him the way to Dunsinane. He said he had been digging graves there forty-four years and had been born and raised in Kinclaven but had no idea how to get to Dunsinane. He said, "It's not far. It's a small place, I can tell you that." His shovel struck something in the ground. He explained that when he digs graves he often encounters the foundations of churches that, one after another, had been on the site before this one. A church must have been there when Macbeth's castle stood on Dunsinane Hill. According to the Scottish historian R. L. Mackie, Macbeth was so religious that he once made a pilgrimage to Rome. All the way to the Vatican and back, he flung money at the poor. Since he lived less than five miles away from Kinclaven, he and Lady Macbeth must have gone to church here from time to time.

We crossed the river, made a right, went through a railway embankment, made a left at Cargill Smithy, and began a long upgrade toward Gallowhill, Wolfhill, and Dunsinnan, through villages of strawstacks, and more wheat, oats, and barley in dark-red earth. We found Donald Sinclair among his steadings, some two miles from Dunsinane Hill.

Sinclair seemed amused that we wanted to climb his hill, and not at all put out. I had thought that people must come in battalions to Dunsinane, and that Sinclair probably spent a lot of his time protecting his land. He said that was not the case. A busload of Boy Scouts from Perth might turn up once in a rare while, but that was about all. Few people seem to realize that there really is a Dunsinane Hill. Shakespeare, he said, took an "n" out of Dunsinnan and added an "e," but did not create the hill. "The name in Gaelic means 'hill of the ants.' Streams of little men went up and down the hill when the castle was being built. Shall we go?"

We drove with him through fields and in woodland, made a few turns, and all at once saw a high green hill fringed with rowan trees and mountain ash in blossom. Dunsinane is at the southwestern end of the serrated line of the Sidlaw Hills. The other Sidlaws, reaching away to the northeast, were all mauve-brown with heather, and Dunsinane stood out among them because it was bright green. Heather apparently will not grow where man has ever performed his constructions. Even from the foot of Dunsinane, we could see that its summit was flat—absolutely truncated, as if it had been sliced level with a knife. We started up its

grassy, southern slope. Sinclair's Herefords were grazing there. "I raise beef cattle," he said. "They summer on the hill. When a busload of Boy Scouts comes, it is
much to my horror, because I've got a bull amongst the cows here." Sinclair was
wearing wide-wale corduroy trousers, a threadbare baggy sweater, a shirt, a wool
tie. Still in his forties, a tall man, he looked weathered, as if he had always been
there. He seemed to be at one with his land and his hill, and nothing about his
loose-postured walk suggested that he was a graduate of Sandhurst, which he
was—a career military man, born off a wheat farm in Manitoba, raised in England, an Army officer from the Second World War until the early nineteen-sixties,
when he became the tenant farmer of Dunsinane Hill. We went around a shoulder
of the terrain. "There he is," Sinclair said. We passed close by a congenial-looking
Hereford bull. He was rust-red, almost top-heavy, the kind of animal that appears
to consist of about nine tons of solid steak, and, with his white-rug face, to be as
fierce as Ferdinand. "We call him Old Joe."

The slopes of the hill rose and converged with an almost volcanic symmetry,
so the climb became quite steep. We passed a spring. "This is where Macbeth got
his water," Sinclair said. "The sort of outer fortifications must have reached this
far." We kept moving up, breathing hard and not talking for a while, until Sinclair
paused for a moment, tilted his head back, looked up at the summit, and said,
"It's pretty impregnable, I should think. I shouldn't like to climb up here and
have people pouring boiling oil on me."

The summit was flat and oval, and Macbeth's floor plan was evident there,
for the foundation protruded in lumpy ridges under the turf. The castle was no
cramped little broch. It was a hundred and twenty feet wide and two hundred
and twenty-five feet long—just slightly larger than the Parthenon. Hill of the ants,
indeed: Macbeth apparently did not do things by halves. The view from the summit over the patchwork Scottish countryside was extraordinary. It is a virtual certainty that Shakespeare never set eyes on Dunsinane. If he had, he would have
described it. In fact, his entire description of Dunsinane Hill comes in two words,
"high" and "great."

> Macbeth shall never vanquished be until
> Great Birnam Wood to high Dunsinane Hill
> Shall come against him.

> Great Dunsinane he strongly fortifies:
> Some say he's mad.

Curlews and oyster catchers cried overhead. This was June, and we could
see the Grampians, far in the distance, with snow still on them. We could see,
three hundred and sixty degrees around us, a fifth of Scotland—to Fife, to
Dundee—and out over the North Sea. It would be hard to imagine a more apt or
beautiful setting for a fortress home. Sinclair said that the Picts had chosen the
spot centuries before Macbeth, and that Dunsinane had been only one of a whole
line of Pictish forts in the Sidlaws—"a sort of defense effort against the Vikings."

We sat down on the base of a rampart. A cool, erratic wind was blowing. Sinclair told us, offhandedly, that the supposed Stone of Scone now in Westminster Abbey is actually a worthless rock from Dunsinane Hill. He said that the real Stone of Scone had been buried in Dunsinane Hill long ago, when the substitute was chosen, and that the real one had been dug up in the nineteenth century only to be reburied after a short time, and that despite all the more recent flurries about the (fake) Stone of Scone in Westminster Abbey, the real one was still there in the hill. Sinclair pointed out Scone, over toward Perth, and added that that was the dullest direction to look in, for, with the dubious exceptions of Scone and Perth, "you can't see anything madly exciting." Closer in and on a more northerly line, he called attention to a small stone house trimmed in red, and he said, "That is where Macbeth settled his three wise women." Moving his hand, pointing, he said, "That farm down there is called Balmalcolm. The next one is Fairy Green, where they found a Pictish stone called the Spunky Dell. The trees down here on the north slope were planted by my father-in-law. He's reforesting. They are five-year-old Scotch pines and some larch."

Macbeth did not die at Dunsinane. Birnam Wood moved, and so forth, according to Holinshed's questionable *Chronicles*, but Macbeth was ignominiously driven away, a fugitive king humbled before his people, and he lived three more years before he was killed, by Malcolm Canmore (Big-Headed Malcolm), on some undramatic moor in Aberdeen. I had been reading W.C. Mackenzie's history of the Highlands only a few days before this, and there on the summit of Dunsinane I found that I could almost remember verbatim Mackenzie's summary line: "By the irony of circumstances, Macbeth, branded as long as literature lasts with the stain of blood, was the friend of the poor, the protector of the monks, and the first Scottish king whose name appears in ecclesiastical records as the benefactor of the Church." It simply was not in him to shout at an enemy here on these ramparts in the hour of his death:

> I will not yield,
> To kiss the ground before young Malcolm's feet
> And to be baited with the rabble's curse.
> Though Birnam Wood be come to Dunsinane,
> And thou oppos'd, being of no woman born,
> Yet I will try the last. Before my body
> I throw my warlike shield. Lay on, Macduff,
> And damn'd be him that first cries "Hold, enough!"

The race being what it is, we prefer him the second way, and Shakespeare knew what we wanted. I had been twirling by its stem the leaf from the Birnam oak, and I dropped it on the top of the hill. We went down to Sinclair's farmhouse for tea, and tea included, among other things, banana sandwiches and Nesquik chocolate milk shakes.

Mr. Macbeth, after a struggle over the check, paid for my breakfast. As we parted, he told me that he had once been a salesman of advertising space for a magazine, and that he had spent half his days in reception foyers waiting to get in to see various kinds of executives. On arrival, he would give his name routinely to the receptionist, then sit down, pick up a magazine, and wait. During this interval, slow, obscure, primordial stirrings would apparently go on in the receptionist's mind, for time and again—and never, he thought, with conscious intent—the receptionist would eventually say to him, "You may go in now, Mr. Macduff."

The Queimada

Michele Morano

And later, after the mussels, after the pulpo a la gallega, the swirling bits of octopus flesh in a sauce of garlic and tomatoes, after the glasses of wine and loaves of bread broken and passed hand to hand, after the strong local blue cheese spread thick on thin crackers and the apples drizzled with honey, after we have all eaten as much as we can and then picked the remains from one another's plates, tucking into our mouths one more bite, one more spoonful, one more tangy or sweet or salty fingertip, then we turn, lights dimmed and candles aflame, to the Queimada.

In the kitchen Chus shows me the brown ceramic bottle, the label handwritten: Aguardiente. I say it aloud. The other words I cannot pronounce because they are in the dialect of Galicia, the province where Chus was born. He is the only Gallego among us, the only person with roots in the land of magic and spirits, of incantations. Chus opens the bottle, holds it out for me to smell, explains that this is liquor made from the skins of grapes, not quite wine, not quite whiskey, and stronger than either. May I taste it, I ask, and Chus smiles, not yet, not until we tame it with fire.

His smile is full, expectant. In this apartment, which is not where he lives but where he spends his extra time with a dozen other artists, painting, sculpting, developing photographs, Chus is more himself than anywhere else. I have seen him in bars, at the homes of mutual friends, on the street as he heads off to work, and nowhere else does he look quite so full, quite so content. And above all tonight, a night on which he has brought this group together—his coworkers from the newspaper, their partners and friends—to share food and drink and the experience of calling spirits to us.

Around the table there is silence and arms resting on stomachs. Rays of moonlight outline the window shades, outline Chus positioning the large clay bowl in the middle of the table. I say that the moon is full on the winter solstice, imagine, and the others sigh yes, how amazing. I arrived with a full moon, I do not say, and I will see six more, perhaps seven, and then I will leave. I am already nostalgic, already sad for the day I arrived here, so impressionable and with so much faith. And sad for this night, too, which I am already imagining as memory, the night of my first Queimada in a cold apartment on Calle Independencia, Oviedo, Spain.

And then we begin. Chus says to me, the foreigner, the person for whom every ritual is new: Pretend we're on a beach. The waves are rolling into the shore, the sand is moving under our feet. We can feel the spirits rushing on the wind to listen to our pleas. His eyes move around the table, to Lola, to Begoña and Pascual, to Isabel and her eight-year-old daughter Virginia, to Alberto, to Pilar, to me. He waits until we are all focused intently on him. And then he smiles and shrugs and begins.

The wooden ladle brims at the level of our eyes. Pilar lights a match, and we inhale as the fire erupts, pulsing over the ladle, dripping down and across the surface of the sugared Aguardiente in the bowl. Chus stirs carefully before scooping again, lifting and holding and releasing a long blue stream of liquid fire. Over and over, the motion in his wrist hypnotic, he stirs and lifts and spills, finding a rhythm that the words begin to ride.

Three months ago, I did not understand the language here. I listened to the words and sometimes understood them but not the language, not at all. Spanish. Castellano. And then early one morning in a lighted bar when I was tired from a long day, a day of taking Spanish classes and teaching English classes and making my way through the unfamiliar streets, Lola and Pilar talked and I listened to the sounds like short, lapping waves. The table was round, I remember, and small. They smoked Ducados, lighting and exhaling, waving their hands, and I drifted off as in a dream. In this dream I could hear their words and the words came not singly but in pairs or triangles and then in long lines that slipped by inseparable. The lines floated around me, background noises circling closer and closer, until words draped themselves in sentences upon and around and within my mind and there, in a lighted bar at 5:00 A.M. with Lola and Pilar laughing, the dialogue sprang alive and I understood.

Now I listen and the words float through me in phrases that will never make sense. Now I look around at the faces, the slight smiles, closed eyes, the full-stomached belief in the power of rituals even though not one of us understands what is happening here. Even Chus does not understand, or remember, all of what he says. This is a poem, a prayer to the dark spirits, a rhyme he tries to call back from the depths of memory. In place of certain lines, he hums, the rhythm held deep within his throat, within the motion of his arm and shoulder. Our faces are beginning to glisten, and I am memorizing the movements, listening to the almost familiar sounds, like Castellano but not quite, like the language of my sleeping dreams, on the verge always of being remembered. The sounds swirl and lift and pour and burn, and I am so open, so thankful for the warmth and the transport back into the part of my mind where language rises and falls like fire dancing on liquid, that I don't notice Chus is humming and humming, dissolving with the last line, the final word, into laughter.

And later, after the fire has calmed itself, after our faces have turned red and we have dabbed them with napkins, after we have pushed back our chairs and Isabel's eight-year-old daughter Virginia has come to stand beside me, beside the only other person as amazed as she is, Chus covers the bowl with a white cloth and in a moment there is only the liquid, warm and sweet.

And familiar. I drink from a ceramic cup with no handle, and nod to Chus. Yes, I like it. Yes, it's strong. I rub my stomach, where the heat pools. Alberto puts his hand on my shoulder, jostling me in the rough way he jostles everyone. You'll be a Spaniard soon, his mustache smiles, and everyone smiles, at me, at each other, at the middle of the table. And yes, it seems possible that I may become a Spaniard. That I may be transformed so entirely by this place and these people, whose goal one Friday night each month is to gather together, to eat and drink and introduce the American roommate of Lola to some specialty of this land. Last month it was cheese, ten kinds of cheese from the region of Asturias, and sidra, hard cider poured from a bottle held over the head into a glass held below the hip. Everyone marveled at how much I love sidra, and I couldn't tell them that it wasn't the taste at all, that the taste was neither here nor there, something one gets accustomed to, but rather it was the feeling. Drinking sidra, every time, my body turns into a sponge. Even before the alcohol can take hold, my shoulders broaden, my hips relax, I expand.

Or the month before, paella. Gazpacho. Red wines from Andalucia. Hard green olives stuffed with anchovies, fried sardines. And in months to come, Spanish tortillas, Spanish crepes, sangria. Deep-fried onions which Lola and I will spend an entire day stuffing with tuna fish. We will skip the month of January because Chus and Begoña and Pascual will be skiing in France, but as the spring moves on we will rearrange our schedules, plan and cajole and set aside the time because the time will be moving more quickly and this will be our way of marking it. Our way of making sure it doesn't get ahead of us, of measuring the months by the stacks of dishes in the sink, by the number of people we squeeze around the dining room table.

As the liquid cools, it thickens. I sip and kiss, drawing my lips together and slowly apart. Syrup builds on the rim of my cup, on all the cups and on all the mouths glistening in the candlelight. Begoña rests an arm on Pascual's knees, Lola strokes Virginia's hair, Chus leans back, legs extended beneath the table, hands clasped across his chest. We are full.

My thoughts rise and fall, bobbing through months and moments, coming to rest finally at the darkening end of a cold day last week. I was walking the northern edge of the Parque de San Francisco where the kiosks selling Christmas wares made me homesick for something I couldn't identify, something I've never even had. The bag on my shoulder was heavy, my coat was heavy as well, though not particularly warm, and I felt small within my skin, aware that with each step I took things rattled loose inside me. And then, miraculously, a new kiosk appeared up ahead, on the corner of the park. An older woman dressed in a blue coat gestured toward the setting sun, toward the mountains where she'd collected the chestnuts, and I nodded as she rolled a piece of newspaper into a cone, filled it, took the 150 pesetas I handed her. Chestnuts! I nearly burst out laughing, walking slowly and then more quickly, with no destination in mind. One by one I extracted them, pulled away the hulls, held the warm flesh on my tongue. I walked for a long time, delighting in the texture and the taste, in the practicality of the newspaper and my good fortune.

Now, as I settle into the fullness, I think it is for this that I travel, for this that I sold all my belongings and took off for a place I didn't know. These moments, walking through a park eating chestnuts, sitting at this table where by now no one is speaking, are why I have liked myself in Spain more than I have ever liked myself before. I am less encumbered here, more receptive to experience. And more appreciative of the texture of daily life. Which includes these people. My God, look how beautiful they are, how generous and happy. And this room, with the artwork, the photographs and paintings made by Chus and all of his artist friends. And the table itself. Look at this table! Plates and glasses and cups and candles and crumbs and rings of wine, the stains of consummation. My eyes close. I see my own blood, pressing against my skin, pulsing.

And later, after the second cupful, after the flush has receded, after Virginia has become bored with watching and begun to draw pictures of Papa Noël on a sketch pad belonging to Chus, after Pilar and Alberto have located the full moon over the city from the windows of the front room and described it to the rest of us who cannot move, I turn to Lola.

Years later, when I have not heard from Lola for a long, long time, I will have periodic dreams about her, wild, grief-stricken dreams from which I will wake sobbing. In my subconscious she will become an emblem of loss, of what we give up when we travel, what we leave behind. But now, half-way through my year of living in her apartment, Lola simply *is*, every day.

She is thirty-three. She is beautiful. She is quiet, graceful, present. When something delights her she smiles with her whole body, and when something makes her angry or sad she speaks more quickly than I can follow. She is the connective tissue here, the person most responsible for this particular group of people coming together. From the day I moved in, after answering Lola's advertisement for a bedroom to rent—to a foreign graduate student, preferably—she has shared her friends with me.

We are shy with each other sometimes, polite and careful about the intertwining of our lives in such a small space. But at other times, after an evening with friends, Lola's friends from the newspaper or my friends from the English department, after some beer and then whiskey and then cognac, we walk along the cobbled streets of the old section of town, past the lighted cathedral, through the empty fish market, arm in arm the way Spanish women do.

Lola's best friend is also named Lola, so that I've taken to distinguishing them as "my Lola" and "the other Lola." When I see Pilar or Begoña on the street they sometimes say, Lola was here just minutes ago—*your* Lola.

One day months ago I came home and found my Lola sitting on the couch, pale. This was before the language got inside me, before I stopped wrestling with individual words, and although I knew that what she was telling me was very serious, I didn't understand exactly what it was. She said, someone called you today, a man with a very unusual name. She said, placing her hand in the middle of her chest: *hearing that name affected me.*

Now, her eyes are focused on the table, but she is listening to Isabel, nodding in agreement about the problem of Papa Noël, the increasing commercialization of Christmas in this country. She sees me watching, smiles and flushes. What I understand now, now that I understand, is this: four years ago, the love of Lola's life, a man with a very unusual name, died in a helicopter crash in the mountains east of Oviedo. He was a rescue worker, searching for a young boy who had wandered off a trail on a very cold day. I have heard the story in bits and pieces, from various people on various occasions, and mostly I force myself not to think about it because when I think about it I can't breathe.

I have seen photographs, heard details. They were magic together. The first time he saw her, in the psychology department office where she was a student worker, he walked right up and kissed her full on the lips, then left without saying a word. A week later he came back and a week after that he showed up at her apartment with a pan of chicken he had baked. He was married, and by then Lola knew it and refused to let him in. So he walked across the street to a pay phone, called her up and said, "You don't have to become involved with me, but you do have to eat this chicken because I made it for you. And you will love it." And she did. And shortly after, he left his wife and moved in with Lola in the kind of move that rarely happens in these situations, and for four years they were magic until he fell out of the sky and died.

I want to ask Chus to light the fire again, to stir the names and repeat the incantation. I want to drink again from the first cup and feel its magic, its hope, its eternal buoyancy eternally veering toward loss.

And later, after Isabel leaves with the sleepy Virginia, after the circle shrinks and we have each put on a sweater or wrapped a blanket around our shoulders in this ancient, heatless building, after the conversation has turned to work and the clock moves toward two, Chus ladles out a third helping to each of us. We clutch our cups, lukewarm now, in both hands and raise them toward we know not what. May the evil spirits be banished, says Chus, humming again to mock his priestly self.

It is December 21, the beginning of winter, the night of a full moon. I know that in seven days I will ride a bus to Madrid to meet the man I love, the man who is coming to visit me from New York. I know that in seven days I will hold my breath waiting to see him, and that when he leaves two weeks later I will hold my breath again, against the riskiness of this long separation. But I do not know that months later, after a series of angry phone calls and pleading letters, I will sit heartbroken in a crowded movie theater with Lola by my side. When a man on screen dies in a car accident, Lola will begin to cry and will lean over to whisper harshly that at least the man I love is alive, at least I can see him again if I choose to. And she will be right about the simplicity of things, and also wrong, and I will hold her hand until the lights come on.

In the spring that is yet to come, on a night that will be hotter than it should be, Lola and I will ride down Calle Argüelles and see Chus leaning against a dark building, pleading with a small blond woman who sobs and slaps her palms against the stone wall. Lola will slow the car until Chus looks toward us and then she will speed up and say, "Poor Chus. Life is hard," and we will never mention it again. I will think then and always after of his face tonight, of the smile and the secrets and the way his throat moves as he hums, begging in the wordless way we all must for the spirits to be kind.

Celibate Passion

Kathleen Norris

> *The Cherub was stationed at the gate of the earthly paradise with his flaming sword to teach us that no one will enter the heavenly paradise who is not pierced with the sword of love.*
>
> —St. Francis de Sales, *Treatise on the Love of God*

Celibacy is a field day for ideologues. Conservative Catholics, particularly those who were raised in the pre-Vatican II church, tend to speak of celibacy as if it were an idealized, angelic state, while feminist theologians such as Uta Ranke-Heinemann say, angrily, that "celibate hatred of sex is hatred of women." That celibacy constitutes the hatred of sex seems to be a given in the popular mythology of contemporary America, and we need only look at newspaper accounts of sex abuse by priests to see evidence of celibacy that isn't working. One could well assume that this is celibacy, impure and simple. And this is unfortunate, because celibacy practiced rightly is not at all a hatred of sex; in fact it has the potential to address the sexual idolatry of our culture in a most helpful way.

One benefit of the nearly ten years that I've been a Benedictine oblate has been the development of deep friendships with celibate men and women. This has led me to ponder celibacy that works, practiced by people who are fully aware of themselves as sexual beings but who express their sexuality in a celibate way. That is, they manage to sublimate their sexual energies toward another purpose than sexual intercourse and procreation. Are they perverse, their lives necessarily stunted? Cultural prejudice would say yes, but I have my doubts. I've seen too many wise old monks and nuns whose lengthy formation in celibate practice has allowed them to incarnate hospitality in the deepest sense. In them, the constraints of celibacy have somehow been transformed into an openness that attracts people of all ages, all social classes. They exude a sense of freedom. They also genderbend, at least in my dreams. Sister Jeremy will appear as a warrior on horseback, Father Robert as a wise old woman tending a fire.

The younger celibates of my acquaintance are more edgy. Still contending mightily with what one friend calls "the raging orchestra of my hormones," they are more obviously struggling to contain their desires for intimacy, for physical touch, within the bounds of celibacy. Often they find their loneliness intensified by the incomprehension of others. In a culture that denies the value of their striving, they are made to feel like fools, or worse.

Americans are remarkably tone-deaf when it comes to the expression of sexuality. The sexual formation that many of us receive is like the refrain of an old Fugs' song: "Why do ya like boobs a lot—ya gotta like boobs a lot." The jiggle of tits and ass, penis and pectorals, assault us everywhere—billboards, magazines, television, movies. Orgasm becomes just another goal; we undress for success. It's no wonder that in all this powerful noise, the quiet tones of celibacy are lost; that we have such trouble comprehending what it could mean to dedicate one's sexual drives in such a way that genital activity and procreation are precluded. But celibate people have taught me that celibacy, practiced rightly, does indeed have something valuable to say to the rest of us. Specifically, they have helped me better appreciate both the nature of friendship, and what it means to be married.

They have also helped me recognize that celibacy, like monogamy, is not a matter of the will disdaining and conquering the desires of the flesh but a discipline requiring what many people think of as undesirable, if not impossible—a conscious form of sublimation. Like many people who came into adulthood during the sexually permissive 1960s, I've tended to equate sublimation with repression. But my celibate friends have made me see the light; accepting sublimation as a normal part of adulthood makes me more realistic about human sexual capacities and expression. It helps me to respect the bonds and boundaries of marriage.

Any marriage has times of separation, ill-health, or just plain crankiness, in which sexual intercourse is ill-advised. And it is precisely the skills of celibate friendship—fostering intimacy through letters, conversation, performing mundane tasks together (thus rendering them pleasurable), savoring the holy simplicity of a shared meal, or a walk together at dusk—that can help a marriage survive the rough spots. When you can't make love physically, you figure out other ways to do it.

Monastic people are celibate for a very practical reason: the kind of community life to which they aspire can't be sustained if people are pairing off. Even in churches in which the clergy are often married—Episcopal and Russian Orthodox, for example—their monks and nuns are celibate. And while monastic novices may be carried along for a time on the swells of communal spirit, when that blissful period inevitably comes to an end, the loneliness is profound. One gregarious monk in his early thirties told me that just as he thought he'd settled into the monastery, he woke up in a panic one morning, wondering if he'd wake up lonely every morning for the rest of his life.

Another monk I know regards celibacy as an expression of the essential human loneliness, a perspective that helps him as a hospital chaplain, when he is called upon to minister to the dying. I knew him when he was still resisting his celibate call—it usually came out as anger directed toward his abbot and community, more rarely as misogyny—and I was fascinated to observe the process by which he came to accept the sacrifices that a celibate, monastic life requires. He's easier to be with now; he's a better friend.

This is not irony so much as grace, that in learning to be faithful to his vow of celibacy, the monk developed his talent for relationship. It's a common occurrence. I've seen the demands of Benedictine hospitality—that they receive all visitors as Christ—convert shy young men who fear women into monks who can enjoy their company. I've witnessed this process of transformation at work in older monks as well. One friend, who had entered the monastery very young, was, when I first met him, still suffering acutely from an inadequate and harmful sexual formation. Taught that as a monk he should avoid women, he faced a crisis when he encountered women as students and colleagues on a college faculty. Fear of his own sexual desires translated all too easily into misogyny. As a good Benedictine, however, he recognized, prayed over, and explored the possibilities for conversion in this situation. Simply put, he's over it now. I'm one of many women who count him as a dear friend, including several who became serious scholars because he urged them on.

One reason I enjoy celibates is that they tend to value friendship very highly. And my friendships with celibate men, both gay and straight, give me some hope that men and women don't live in alternate universes. In 1990s America, this sometimes feels like a countercultural perspective. Male celibacy, in particular, can become radically countercultural if it is perceived as a rejection of the consumerist model of sexuality, a model that reduces women to the sum of her parts. I have never had a monk friend make an insinuating remark along the lines of, "You have beautiful eyes" (or legs, breasts, knees, elbows, nostrils), the usual catalogue of remarks that women grow accustomed to deflecting. A monk is supposed to give up the idea of possessing anything and, in this culture, that includes women.

Ideally, in giving up the sexual pursuit of women (whether as demons or as idealized vessels of purity), the male celibate learns to relate to them as human beings. That many fail to do so, that the power structures of the Catholic church all but dictate failure in this regard, comes as no surprise. What is a surprise is what happens when it works. Once, after I'd spent a week in a monastery, I boarded a crowded Greyhound bus and took the first available seat. My seatmate, a man, soon engaged me in conversation, and it took me a while to realize that he wasn't simply being friendly, he was coming on to me. I remember feeling foolish for being so slow to catch on. I remember thinking, "No wonder this guy is acting so strange; he didn't take a vow of celibacy."

When it works, when men have truly given up the idea of possessing women, healing can occur. I once met a woman in a monastery guest house who had come there because she was pulling herself together after being raped, and said she needed to feel safe around men again. I've seen young monks astonish an obese and homely college student by listening to her with as much interest and respect as to her conventionally pretty roommate. On my fortieth birthday, as I happily blew out four candles on a cupcake ("one for each decade," a monk in his twenties cheerfully proclaimed), I realized that I could enjoy growing old with these guys. They were helping me to blow away my fears of middle age.

As celibacy takes hold in a person, over the years, as monastic values supersede the values of the culture outside the monastery, celibates become people who can radically affect those of us out "in the world," if only because they've learned how to listen without possessiveness, without imposing themselves. With someone who is practicing celibacy well, we may sense that we're being listened to in a refreshingly deep way. And this is the purpose of celibacy, not to attain some impossibly cerebral goal mistakenly conceived as "holiness" but to make oneself available to others, body *and* soul. Celibacy, simply put, is a form of ministry—not an achievement one can put on a résumé but a subtle form of service to others. In theological terms, one dedicates one's sexuality to God through Jesus Christ, a concept and a terminology I find extremely hard to grasp. All I can do is to catch a glimpse of people who are doing it, incarnating celibacy in a mysterious, pleasing, and gracious way.

The attractiveness of the celibate is that he or she can make us feel appreciated, enlarged, no matter who we are. I have two nun friends who invariably have that effect on me, whatever the circumstances of our lives on the infrequent occasions when we meet. The thoughtful way in which they converse, listening and responding with complete attention, seems always a marvel. And when I first met a man I'll call Tom, he had much the same effect on me. I wrote in my notebook, "such tenderness in a man . . . and a surprising, gentle, kindly grasp of who I am." (Poets aren't used to being listened to, let alone understood, by theologians.) As our friendship deepened, I found that even brief, casual conversations with him would often inspire me to dive into old, half-finished poems in an attempt to bring them to fruition.

I realized, of course, that I had found a remarkable friend, a Muse. I was also aware that Tom and I were fast approaching the rocky shoals of infatuation, a man and a woman, both decidedly heterosexual, responding to each other in unmistakably sexual ways. We laughed; we had playful conversations as well as serious ones; we took delight in each other. At times we were alarmingly responsive to one another, and it was all too easy to fantasize about expressing that responsiveness in physical ways.

The danger was real, but not insurmountable; I sensed that if our infatuation were to develop into love, that is, to ground itself in grace rather than utility, our respect for each other's commitments—his to celibacy, mine to monogamy—would make the boundaries of behavior very clear. We had few regrets, and yet for both of us there was an underlying sadness, the pain of something incomplete. Suddenly, the difference between celibate friendship and celibate passion had become all too clear to me; at times the pain was excruciating.

Tom and I each faced a crisis the year we met—his mother died, I suffered a disastrous betrayal—and it was the intensity of these unexpected, unwelcome experiences that helped me to understand that in the realm of the sacred, what seems incomplete or unattainable may be abundance, after all. Human relationships are by their nature incomplete—after twenty-one years, my husband remains a mystery to me, and I to him, and that is as it should be. Only hope allows us to know and enjoy the depth of our intimacy.

Appreciating Tom's presence in my life as a miraculous, unmerited gift helped me to place our relationship in its proper, religious context, and also to understand why it was that when I'd seek him out to pray with me, I'd always leave feeling so much better than when I came. This was celibacy at its best, a man's sexual energies so devoted to the care of others that a few words could lift me out of despair, give me the strength to reclaim my life. Abundance indeed. Celibate love was at the heart of it, although I can't fully comprehend the mystery of why this should be so. Celibate passion—elusive, tensile, holy.

Three Pokes of a Thistle

Naomi Shihab Nye

Hiding Inside the Good Girl

"She has the devil inside her," said my first report card from first grade. I walked home slowly, holding it out from my body, a thistle, a thorn, to my mother, who read the inside, then the note on the back. She cried mightily, heaves of underground rivers, we stood looking deep into the earth as water rushed by.

I didn't know who he was.

One day I'd smashed John's nose on the pencil sharpener and broken it. Stood in the cloakroom smelling the rust of coats. I said No. No thank you. I already read that and it's not a very good story. Jane doesn't do much. I want the spider who talks. The family of little women and their thousand days. No. What I had for breakfast is a secret. I didn't want to tell them I ate dried apricots. I listened to their lineage of eggs. I listened to the bacon crackle in everyone else's pail. Thank you.

What shall we do, what shall we do? Please, I beg you. Our pajamas were flying from the line, waists pinned, their legs fat with fabulous air. My mother peeled beets, her fingers stained deep red. She was bleeding dinner for us. She was getting up and lying down.

Once I came home from school in the middle of the day in a taxi. School gave me a stomachache. I rode in the front passenger seat. It would be expensive. My mother stood at the screen door peering out, my baby brother perched on her hip. She wore an apron. The taxi pulled up in front of the blue mailbox I viewed as an animal across from our house—his opening mouth. Right before I climbed out, another car hit the taxi hard from behind so my mother saw me fly from the front seat to the back. Her mouth wide open, the baby dangling from her like fringe. She came toward us running. I climbed up onto the ledge inside the back window to examine the wreckage. The taxi driver's visored cap had blown out the window. He was shaking his head side to side as if he had water in his ears.

You, you, look what a stomachache gets you. Whiplash.

The doctor felt my neck.

Later I sat on the front steps staring at the spot where it had happened. What about that other driver? He cried when the policeman arrived. He was an old man coming to mail a letter. I was incidental to the scene, but it couldn't have happened without me. *If you had just stayed where you belonged. . . .* My classmates sealed into their desks laboring over pages of subtraction, while out in the world, cars were banging together. Yellow roses opened slowly on a bush beside my step. I was thinking how everything looked from far away.

Then I was old. A hundred years before I found it, Mark Twain inscribed the front of his first-edition leatherbound book, "BE GOOD—AND YOU WILL BE LONE-SOME." In black ink, with a flourish. He signed his name. My friend had the book in a box in her attic and did not know. It was from her mother's collection. I carried it down the stairs, trembling. My friend said, "Do you think it is valuable?"

Language Barrier

Basically our father spoke English perfectly, though he still got his *b*s and *p*s mixed up. He had a gentle, deliberate way of choosing words. I could feel him reaching up into the air to find them. At night, he told us whimsical, curling "Joha" stories which hypnotized us to sleep. I especially liked the big cooking pan that gave birth to the little pan. My friend Marcia's father who grew up in the United States hardly talked. He built airplanes. I didn't think I would want to fly in anything he made. When Marcia asked him a question, he grunted a kind of pig sound. He sank his face into the paper. My father spilled out musical lines, a horizon of graceful buildings standing beside one another in a distant city. You could imagine people living inside one of my father's words.

He said a few things to us in Arabic—fragrant syllables after we ate, blessings when he hugged us. He hugged us all the time. He said, "I love you" all the time. But I didn't learn how to say "Thank you" in Arabic till I was fourteen, which struck me, even then, as a preposterous omission.

Marcia's father seemed tired. He had seven children because he was a Catholic, Marcia said. I didn't get it. Marcia's mother threw away the leftovers from their table after dinner. My mother carefully wrapped the last little mound of mashed potato inside waxed paper. We'd eat it later.

I felt comfortable in the world of so many different people. Their voices floated around the neighborhood like pollen. On the next block, French-Canadians made blueberry pie. I wanted a slice. It is true that a girl knocked on our door one day and asked to "see the Arab," but I was not insulted. I was mystified. Who?

Sometimes Marcia and I slept together on our screened-in back porch, or in a big green tent in her yard. She was easy to scare. I said the giant harvest moon was coming to eat her and she hid under her pillow. She told me spider stories. We had fun trading little terrors.

When I was almost ready to move away, Marcia and I stood in Dade Park together one last time. I said good-bye to the swings and benches and wooden seesaws with chipped red paint. Two bigger boys rode up on bicycles and circled us. We'd never seen them before. One of them asked if we knew how to do the F-word. I had no idea what they were talking about. Marcia said she knew, but wouldn't tell me. The boys circled the basketball courts, eyeing us strangely. Walking home with Marcia, I felt almost glad to be moving away from her. She stuck her chest out. She said, "Did you ever wish someone would touch you in a private place?"

I looked in the big dictionary at home. Hundreds of F-words I didn't know reached their hands out so it took a long time. And I asked my mother, whose face was so smooth and beautiful and filled with sadness because nothing was quite as good as it could be.

She didn't know either.

Bra Strap

It felt like a taunt, the elastic strap of Karen's bra visible beneath her white blouse in front of me in fifth grade. I saw it even before Douglas snapped it. Who did she think she was, growing older without me?

I spent the night with her one Saturday. In the bathtub together, we splashed and soaped, jingling our talk of teachers, boys, and holidays. But my eyes were on her chest, the great pale fruits growing there. Already they mounded toward stems.

She caught me looking and said, "So?" Sighing, as if she were already tired. Said, "In my family they grow early." Downstairs her bosomy mother stacked cups in a high old cabinet that smelled of grandmother's hair. I could hear her clinking. In my family they barely grew at all. I had been proud of my mother's boyishness, her lithe trunk and straight legs.

Now I couldn't stop thinking about it: what was there, what wasn't there. The mounds on the fronts of certain dolls with candy-coated names. One by one, watching the backs of my friends' blouses, I saw them all fall under the spell. I begged my mother, who said, "For what? Just to be like everybody else?"

Pausing near the underwear displays at Famous and Barr, I asked to be measured, sizing up boxes. "Training Bra"—what were we in training for?

When Louise fell off her front porch and a stake went all the way through her, I heard teachers whispering, "Hope this doesn't ruin her for the future." We discussed the word "impaled." What future? The mysteries of ovaries had not yet been explained. Little factories for eggs. Little secret nests. On the day we saw the film, I didn't like it. If that was what the future meant, I didn't want it anymore.

As I was staring out the window afterwards, my mouth tasted like pennies, my throat closed up. The leaves on the trees blurred together so they could carry me.

I sat on a swivel chair practicing handwritings. The backwards slant, the loopy up-and-down. Who would I ever be? My mother was inside the lawyer's office signing papers about the business. That waiting room, with its dull wooden side tables and gloomy magazines, had absolutely nothing to do with me. Never for a second was I drawn toward the world of the dreary professional. I would be a violinist with the Zurich symphony. I would play percussion in a traveling band. I would bake zucchini muffins in Yarmouth, Nova Scotia.

In the car traveling slowly home under a thick gray sky, I worked up courage. Rain, rain, the intimacy of cars. At a stoplight, staring hard at my mother, I asked, "What really happens between men and women to make babies?"

She jumped as if I'd thrown ice at her.

"Not *that!* Not *now!*" From red to green, the light, the light. "There is *oh so much you do not know.*"

It was all she ever told me. The weight of my ignorance pressed upon us both.

Later she slipped me a book, *Little Me, Big Me.* One of the more incomprehensible documents of any childhood: "When a man and a woman love one another enough, he puts his arms around her and part of him goes into part of her and the greatness of their love for one another causes this to feel pleasurable."

On my twelfth birthday, my father came home with our first tape recorder. My mother produced a bouquet of shiny boxes, including a long, slim one. My Lutheran grandparents sat neatly on the couch as the heavy reels wound up our words. "Do you like it? Is it just what you've been waiting for?"

They wanted me to hold it up to my body, the way I would when I put it on. My mother shushing, "Oh, I guess it's private!"

Later the tape would play someone's giggles in the background. My brother? Or the gangs of little girl angels that congregate around our heads, chanting, "Don't grow up, don't grow up!"

I never liked wearing it as much as I did thinking about it.

When the Body Begins to Fall Apart on the Academic Stage

Lucia Perillo

I used to teach at a college attached to a Benedictine monastery, and though I never quite understood how anyone could find happiness in the monastic life (bad food, no sex), my religious colleagues inspired my envy for one reason: They could wear robes to work. Black robes, under which they wore old jeans or sweatpants or even their pajamas—I gauged this from the two inches of leg exposed below the hem. While the rest of us were sized up via our clothing and hairstyles, our wearing of makeup or going without, the monks were able to impart knowledge in a manner that seemed pure. They seemed to be almost blank slates. From neck to ankle, at least, the monks were liberated from the scrutiny of their audience.

In lieu of wearing a robe, I have often thought about teaching with a paper bag over my head. It would have to be a big bag, though, because I'd want it to cover my entire body. My teaching life has coincided with a period during which I have grown increasingly disabled, and as I grow older—and my body becomes more decrepit—I find myself intimidated by the degree to which teaching is measured in terms of its performance quality, the body being the prime instrument of performance.

Actually, I was once a good performer. In my former career, as a park ranger, I did an impersonation of the first woman to climb Mount Rainier that brought standing ovations from the campfire crowd. The first symptom of the disease that I later found out I had—it turned out to be multiple sclerosis—showed up at my first faculty meeting on my first academic job, shortly after my last ranger summer, when I stood to introduce myself and went into a swoon. The rest of the faculty members no doubt wondered what kind of nut they'd just hired. Afterward, a theater professor offered to help me overcome my stage fright.

It's bad enough to have to cope, privately, with one's body falling apart; there's something grotesque about having to display that disintegration on a public stage. With real actors, the hook comes from the wings as soon as the body starts to falter, even if that faltering comes from mere age (and especially if the body in question belongs to a woman). Multiple sclerosis, though extremely variable in effect, sometimes can be a not particularly pleasant sight to behold in its latter stages. The comedian Richard Pryor—perhaps the most famous performer to become affected by M.S.—has not been much in public view since his disease became visibly apparent.

I was thinking about those concerns—and my own presentation of my body— while watching the recent remake of Hitchcock's *Rear Window*. In this version, the Jimmy Stewart character was played by Christopher Reeve, who (as the whole world knows) has been a quadriplegic since a riding accident some years back. It was not a particularly good remake (I don't know why anyone bothers trying to remake Hitchcock), but I was relieved to see that the reasons it didn't work had little to do with Reeve's being in a wheelchair. The technology that is now essential to him pretty much faded into invisibility when the suspense kicked in. (If anything, the movie failed because the suspense was not cultivated to its fullest effect.)

While teaching does not require the level of physical dexterity that acting does, it does require a demanding schedule of public display, often in front of hundreds of people, many times a week.

In the first stages of my illness, I found myself annoyed that my students were so blankly oblivious to the fact that there was anything wrong with me. I remember struggling to return some papers and hearing grumbling and groans when I finally gave up and asked the students to come to me. On the other hand, I was paranoid when students began noticing that something indeed was wrong: "Why are you walking funny?" they asked. My response was a puzzled glower: "Who says I'm walking funny?"

Now the jig is up—okay, I do walk funny. The progress of the disease, fortunately, has been slower than the speed at which students go through my classes, and those who know me now have always known me as disabled, which relieves me from having to provide explanations. For the most part, students have been gracious and kind and truly helpful, to the point of packing up boxes to help me move. But it makes me feel strange, this intimacy into which I am forced with my students, who will see my symptoms wax (and wane—but mostly wax, unfortunately). For most professors, the functioning of their bodies is not something they have to share with their students. And though it seems a violation of professional "distance" to allude to my physical troubles, it also seems disingenuous to pretend that nothing's wrong.

Disability can transform self-presentation in all manner of peculiar ways: One new chapter in the continuing saga of my illness is that wearing pantyhose (a loathsome word) now makes my legs feel as though they've been tightly wound with bandages. A minor impairment, I thought—easily shed by switching from skirts to pants—until I read a recent article in *The Chronicle* about the signals sent by professional attire: Several people made the comment that job interviewees should wear skirts instead of pants (that is, so long as they are women). If there are to be no skirts for me, then no new jobs for me, I guess.

Similarly, I remember years ago, when I was tending the job booth at a major academic convention, being lectured by one of my co-volunteers (obviously a higher-status member of the pack than I) about the hellish schedule to which the English department liked to subject job candidates. "We want to see whether they've got the stamina," she said, as if applying for an academic job were a try-out for the football team. My disability not yet visible, I didn't say what I thought: that this practice might unjustly eliminate many fine candidates whose bodies would not be able to tolerate the 48 hours of grilling.

While I'm wary of blanket statements about the so-called "disability experience," or even about M.S. in particular, I will say that, for me, being caught in the maelstrom of this illness has been like riding a hot-air balloon that's losing altitude: I've had to jettison whatever drags me down. My self-therapeutic process has mostly meant consciously cutting the number of things that I worry about—if the people interviewing me for a job are so superficial that all they see when they look at me is a pair of pants, then I don't want to work with them. Sometimes my face goes numb and I drool out of one side of my mouth (not very flattering to one's self-image). But, hey, I tell myself, I've got more important things to worry about than a little spittle.

Probably the biggest blow to my self-esteem as a public figure came last year, when I was invited to another college as a visiting poet. I gave my talk standing up, though I preceded it with the disclaimer that I might very well fall down and that if I did, the audience could do me a favor by pretending not to notice. But I made it through the hour on my feet, and so was feeling pretty good about myself—until, while walking away from the podium, I tripped and rolled across the carpet.

Of course, the people in the audience were trapped in a state of cognitive dissonance, confused about what they ought to do. Seeing them variously displaying sympathetic mortification and fright, while remembering that they were supposed to pretend this had not happened, caused me to burst out laughing. There I was, the visiting poet, lying on the auditorium floor in hysterics. It was a situation in which neither robe nor bag, I suppose, would have done me any good.

Animal Allies

Brenda Peterson

"My imaginary friend really lived once," the teenage girl began, head bent, her fingers twisting her long red hair. She stood in the circle of other adolescents gathered in my Seattle Arts and Lectures storytelling class at the summer Seattle Academy. Here were kids from all over the city—every color and class, all strangers one to another. Over the next two weeks we would become a fierce tribe, telling our own and our tribe's story. Our first assignment was to introduce our imaginary friends from childhood. This shy fourteen-year-old girl, Sarah, had struck me on the first day because she always sat next to me, as if under my wing, and though her freckles and stylish clothes suggested she was a popular girl, her demeanor showed the detachment of someone deeply preoccupied. She never met my eye, nor did she join in the first few days of storytelling when the ten boys and four girls were regaling one another with futuristic characters called Shiva and Darshon, Masters of the Universe. So far the story lines we'd imagined were more Pac-Man than drama. After the first two days I counted a legion of characters killed off in intergalactic battle. The settings for all these stories portrayed the earth as an environmental wasteland, a ruined shell hardly shelter to anything animal or human. One of the girls called herself Nero the White Wolf and wandered the blackened tundra howling her powerful despair; another girl was a unicorn whose horn always told the truth. All the stories were full of plagues and nuclear wars—even though this is the generation that has witnessed the fall of the Berlin Wall, the end of the Cold War. Their imaginations have been shaped by a childhood story line that anticipates the end of this world.

After three days of stories set on an earth besieged by disease and barren of nature, I made a rule: No more characters or animals could die this first week. I asked if someone might imagine a living world, one that survives even our species.

It was on this third day of group storytelling that Sarah jumped into the circle and told her story:

"My imaginary friend is called Angel now because she's in heaven, but her real name was Katie," Sarah began. "She was my best friend from fourth to tenth grade. She had freckles like me and brown hair and more boyfriends—sometimes five at a time—because Katie said, 'I *like* to be confused!' She was a real sister too and we used to say we'd be friends for life. . . ." Sarah stopped, gave me a furtive glance and then gulped in a great breath of air like someone drowning, about to go down. Her eyes fixed inward, her voice dropped to a monotone. "Then one day last year, Katie and I were walking home from school and a red sports car came up behind us. Someone yelled, 'Hey, Katie!' She turned . . . and he blew her head off. A bullet grazed my skull, too, and I blacked out. When I woke up, Katie was gone, dead forever." Sarah stopped, stared down at her feet and murmured in that same terrible monotone, "Cops never found her murderer, case is closed."

All the kids shifted and took a deep breath, although Sarah herself was barely breathing at all. "Let's take some time to write," I told the kids and put on a cello concerto for them to listen to while they wrote. As they did their assignment, the kids glanced over surreptitiously at Sarah, who sat staring at her hands in her lap.

I did not know what to do with her story; she had offered it to a group of kids she had known but three days. It explained her self-imposed exile during lunch hours and while waiting for the bus. All I knew was that she'd brought this most important story of her life into the circle of storytellers and it could not be ignored as if *she* were a case to be closed. This story lived in her, would define and shape her young life. Because she had given it to us, we needed to witness and receive—and perhaps tell it back to her in the ancient tradition of tribal call and response.

"Listen," I told the group as the cello faded and they looked up from their work. "We're going to talk story the way they used to long ago when people sat around at night in circles just like this one. That was a time when we still listened to animals and trees and didn't think ourselves so alone in this world. Now we're going to carry out jungle justice and find Katie's killer. We'll call him before our tribe. All right? Who wants to begin the story?"

All the Shivas and Darshons and Masters of the Universe volunteered to be heroes on this quest. Nero the White Wolf asked to be a scout. Unicorn, with her truth-saving horn, was declared judge. Another character joined the hunt: Fish, whose translucent belly was a shining "soul mirror" that could reveal one's true nature to anyone who looked into it.

A fierce commander of this hunt was Rat, whose army of computerized comrades could read brain waves and call down lightning lasers as weapons. Rat began the questioning and performed the early detective work. Katie, speaking from beyond the earth, as Sarah put it, gave us other facts. We learned that two weeks before Katie's murder, one of her boyfriends was shot outside a restaurant by a man in the same red car—another drive-by death. So Sarah had not only seen her best friend killed at her side, but she had also walked out into a parking lot to find Katie leaning over her boyfriend's body. For Sarah, it had been two murders by age thirteen.

With the help of our myriad computer-character legions we determined that the murderer was a man named Carlos, a drug lord who used local gangs to deal cocaine. At a party Carlos has misinterpreted Katie's videotaping her friends dancing as witnessing a big drug deal. For that, Rat said, "This dude decides Katie's got to go down. So yo, man, he offs her without a second thought."

Bad dude, indeed, this Carlos. And who was going to play Carlos now that all the tribe knew his crime? I took on the role, and as I told my story I felt my face hardening into a contempt that carried me far away from these young pursuers, deep into the Amazon jungle where Rat and his own computer armies couldn't follow, where all their space-age equipment had to be shed until there was only hand-to-hand simple fate.

In the Amazon, the kids changed without effort, in an easy shape-shifting to their animal selves. Suddenly there were no more Masters of the Universe with intergalactic weapons—there was instead Jaguar and Snake, Fish and Pink Dolphin. There was powerful claw and all-knowing serpent, there was Fish who could grow big and small, and a dolphin whose sonar saw past the skin. We were now a tribe of animals, pawing, running, invisible in our jungle, eyes shining in the night, seeing Carlos as he canoed the mighty river, laughing because he did not know he had animals tracking him.

All through the story I'd kept my eye on Sarah who played the role of her dead friend. The detachment I'd first seen in her was in fact the deadness Sarah carried, the violence that had hollowed her out inside, the friend who haunted her imagination. But now her face was alive, responding to each animal's report of tracking Carlos. She hung on the words, looking suddenly very young, like a small girl eagerly awaiting her turn to enter the circling jump rope.

"I'm getting away from you," I said, snarling as I'd imagined Carlos would. I paddled my canoe and gave a harsh laugh, "I'll escape, easy!"

"No!" Sarah shouted. "Let *me* tell it!"

"Tell it!" her tribe shouted.

"Well, Carlos only thinks he's escaping," Sarah smiled, waving her hands. "He's escaped from so many he's harmed before. But I call out 'FISH!' And Fish comes. He swims alongside the canoe and grows bigger, bigger until at last Carlos turns and sees this HUGE river monster swimming right alongside him and that man is afraid because suddenly Fish turns his belly up to Carlos's face. Fish forces him to look into that soul mirror. Carlos sees everyone he's ever killed and all the people who loved them and got left behind. And Carlos sees Katie and me and what he's done to us. He sees everything and he knows his soul is black. And he really doesn't want to die now because he knows then he'll stare into his soul mirror forever. But Fish makes him keep looking until Carlos starts screaming he's sorry, he's so sorry. Then . . . Fish *eats* him!"

The animals roared and cawed and congratulated Sarah for calling Fish to mirror a murderer's soul before taking jungle justice. Class had ended, but no one wanted to leave. We wanted to stay in our jungle, stay within our animals—and so we did. I asked them to close their eyes and call their animals to accompany them home. I told them that some South American tribes believe that when you are born, an animal is born with you. This animal protects and lives alongside you even if it's far away in an Amazon jungle—it came into the world at the same time you did. And, I told them, it dies with you to guide you back into the spirit world.

The kids decided to go home and make animal masks, returning the next day wearing the faces of their chosen animal. When they came into class the next day it was as if we never left the Amazon. Someone dimmed the lights, there were drawings everywhere of jaguars and chimps and snakes. Elaborate masks had replaced the Masters of the Universe who began this tribal journey. We sat behind our masks in a circle with the lights low and there was an acute, alert energy running between us, as eyes met behind animal faces.

I realize that I, who grew up in the forest wild, who first memorized the earth with my hands, have every reason to feel this familiar animal resonance. But many of these teenagers have barely been in the woods; in fact, many inner-city kids are *afraid* of nature. They would not willingly sign up for an Outward Bound program or backpacking trek; they don't think about recycling in a world they believe already ruined and in their imaginations abandoned for intergalactic nomad futures. These kids are not environmentalists who worry about saving nature. And yet, when imagining an Amazon forest too thick for weapons to penetrate, too primitive for their futuristic Pac-Man battles, they return instinctively to their animal selves. These are animals they have only seen in zoos or on television, yet there is a profound identification, an ease of inhabiting another species that portends great hope for our own species's survival. Not because nature is "out there" to be saved or sanctioned, but because nature is *in* them. The ancient, green world has never left us though we have long ago left the forest.

What happens when we call upon our inner landscape to connect with the living rainforests still left in the natural world? I believe our imagination can be as mutually nurturing as an umbilical cord between our bodies and the planet. As we told our Amazon stories over the next week of class, gathered in a circle of animal masks, we could feel the rainforest growing in that sterile classroom. Lights low, surrounded by serpents, the jaguar clan, the elephants, I'd as often hear growls, hisses, and howls as words. Between this little classroom and the vast Amazon rainforest stretched a fine thread of story that grew thicker each day, capable of carrying our jungle meditations.

When Elephant stood in the circle and said simply, "My kind are dying out," there was outrage from the other animals.

"We'll stop those poachers!" cried Rat and Chimp. "We'll call Jaguar clan to protect you." And they did.

This protection is of a kind that reaches the other side of the world. Children's imagination is a primal force, just as strong as lobbying efforts and boycotts and endangered species acts. When children claim another species as not only their imaginary friend, but also as the animal within them—their ally—doesn't that change the outer world?

This class believes it to be so. They may be young, but their memories and alliances with the animals are very old. By telling their own animal stories they are practicing ecology at its most profound and healing level. Story as ecology—

it's so simple, something we've forgotten. In our environmental wars the emphasis has been on saving species, not *becoming* them. We've fallen into an environmental fundamentalism that calls down hellfire and brimstone on the evil polluters and self-righteously struts about protecting other species as if we are gods who can save their souls.

But the animals' souls are not in our hands. Only our own souls are within our ken. It is our own spiritual relationship to animals that must evolve. Any change begins with imagining ourselves in a new way. And who has preserved their imaginations as a natural resource most deeply? Not adults, who so often have strip-mined their dreams and imagination for material dross. Those who sit behind the wheel of a Jaguar have probably forgotten the wild, black cat that first ran with them as children. Imagination is relegated to nighttime dreams, which are then dismissed in favor of "the real world." But children, like some adults, know that the real world stretches farther than what we can see—that's why they shift easily between visions of our tribal past and our future worlds. The limits of the adult world are there for these teenagers, but they still have a foot in the vast inner magic of childhood. It is this magical connection I called upon when I asked the kids to do the Dance of the Animals.

The day of the big dance I awoke with a sharp pain at my right eye. Seems my Siamese, who has always slept draped around my head, had stretched and his claw caught the corner of my eye. In the mirror I saw a two-inch scratch streaking from my eye like jungle make-up or a primitive face-painting. "The mark of the wildcat," the kids pronounced it when I walked into the dimly lit room to be met by a circle of familiar creatures. Never in ten years had my Siamese scratched my face. I took it as a sign that the dance began in his animal dream.

I put on my cobra mask and hissed a greeting to Chimp, Rat, Jaguar, and Unicorn. Keen eyes tracked me from behind colorful masks. I held up my rain stick which was also our talking stick and called the creatures one by one into the circle. "Sister Snake!" I called. "Begin the dance!"

Slowly, in rhythm to the deep, bell-like beat of my Northwest Native drum, each animal entered the circle and soon the dance sounded like this: Boom, step, twirl, and slither and stalk and snarl and chirp and caw, caw. Glide, glow, growl, and whistle and howl and shriek and trill and hiss, hiss. Each dance was distinct—from the undulating serpent on his belly, to the dainty high hoofing of Unicorn, from the syncopated stomps of Chimp on all-fours to Rat's covert jitterbug behind the stalking half-dark Jaguar. We danced, and the humid, lush jungle filled this room.

In that story line stretching between us and the Amazon, we connected with those animals and their spirits. And in return, we were complete—with animals as soul mirrors. We remembered who we were, by allowing the animals inside us to survive.

The dance is not over as long as we have our animal partners. When the kids left our last class, they still wore their masks fiercely. I was told that even on the bus they stayed deep in their animal character. I like to imagine those strong, young animals out there now in this wider jungle. I believe that Rat will survive the inner-city gangs; that Chimp will find his characteristic comedy even as his parents deal with divorce; I hope that Unicorn will always remember her mystical truth-telling horn. And as for Sarah who joined the Jaguar clan, elected as the first girl-leader over much mutinous boy-growling—Sarah knows the darkness she stalks and the nightmares that stalk her. She has animal eyes to see, to find even a murderer. Taking her catlike, graceful leave, she handed me a poem she'd written; it said "Now I can see in the dark" and was signed "Jaguar—Future Poet."

Celebrating Creation

Chet Raymo

Even the sparrow finds a home, and the swallow a nest, where she rears her brood beside thy altars.

Psalm 84:3

Late last summer, in the west of Ireland, I spent a night in the Gallarus Oratory, a tiny seventh-century church of unmortared stone. It is the oldest intact building in Ireland, and one of the oldest in Europe. The oratory is about the size of a one-car garage, in the shape of an overturned boat. It has a narrow entrance at the front and a single tiny window at the rear, both open to the elements. Even during the day one needs a flashlight to explore the interior.

I can't say exactly why I was there, or why I intended to sit up all night, sleeplessly, in that dark space. I had been thinking about skepticism and prayer, and I wanted to experience something of whatever it was that inspired Irish monks to seek out these rough hermitages perched on the edge of Europe, or—as they imagined—the edge of eternity. They were pilgrims of the Absolute, seeking their God in a raw, ecstatic encounter with stone, wind, sea, and sky.

The Gallarus Oratory is something of a tourist mecca, but at night the place is isolated and dark, far from human habitation. From the door of the oratory, one looks down a sloping mile of fields to the twinkling lights of the village of Ballydavid on Smerwick Harbor.

The sun had long set when I arrived, although at that latitude in summer the twilight never quite fades from the northern horizon. It was a moonless night, ablaze with stars, Jupiter brightest of all. Meteors occasionally streaked the sky, and satellites cruised more stately orbits. Inside, I snuggled into a back corner of the oratory, tucked my knees under my chin, and waited. I could see nothing but

148

the starlit outline of the door, not even my hand in front of my face. The silence was broken only by the low swish of my own breath.

As the hours passed, I began to feel a presence, a powerful sensation of something or someone sharing that empty darkness. I am not a mystical person, but I knew that I was not alone, and I could imagine those hermit monks of the seventh century sharing the same intense conviction of "someone in the room." At last, I was spooked to the point that I abandoned my interior corner and went outside.

A night of exceptional clarity! Stars spilling into the sea. And in the north, as if as a reward for my lonely vigil, the aurora borealis danced toward the zenith. How can I describe what I saw? Rays of silver light streaming up from the sea, as if from some enchanted Oz just over the horizon, shimmering columns of fairy radiance. As I watched from the doorway of oratory, I remembered something the nineteenth-century explorer Charles Francis Hall wrote about watching the aurora from the Arctic: "My first thought was, 'Among the gods there is none like unto Thee, O Lord; neither are there any works like unto thy works!' . . . We looked, we SAW, we TREMBLED."

Hall knew he was watching a natural physical phenomenon, not a miracle, but his reaction suggests the power of the aurora even on a mind trained in the methods of science. What then did the monks of Gallarus think of the aurora, 1,300 years ago, at a time when the supernatural was the explanation of choice for exceptional phenomena? Stepping out from the inky darkness of their stone chapel, they must surely have felt that the shimmering columns of light were somehow meant for them alone, a sign or a revelation, an answer to their prayers.

We have left the age of miracles behind, but not, I trust, our sense of wonder. Our quest for encounter with the Absolute goes arm in arm with our search for answers. We are pilgrim scientists, perched on the edge of eternity, curious and attentive. The Gallarus Oratory was built for prayer, at a time when the world was universally thought to be charged with the active spirit of a personal God: Every stone might be moved by incantation, every zephyr blew good or ill; springs flowed or dried up at the deity's whim; lights danced in a predawn sky as a blessing or portent. Today, we know the lights are caused by electrons crashing down from the sun, igniting luminescence. But our response to the lights might still be one of prayerful attention, and they lead us, if we let them, into encounter with the Absolute.

Traditional religious faiths have three components: a shared cosmology (a story of the universe and our place in it), spirituality (personal response to the numinous), and liturgy (public expressions of celebration and gratitude, including rites of passage). The apparent antagonism of science and religion centers almost entirely on cosmology: What is the universe? Where did it come from? How does it work? What is the human self? What is our fate? Humans have always had answers to these questions. The answers have been embodied in stories—tribal myths, scriptures, church traditions. All of these stories derived from a raw experience of the creation, such as my experiences inside and outside of the Gallarus Oratory. All of them contain enduring wisdom. But as a reliable cosmological component of religious faith they have been superseded by what cultural historian and Roman Catholic priest Thomas Berry calls the New Story—the scientific story of the world.

The New Story is the product of thousands of years of human curiosity, observation, experimentation, and creativity. It is an evolving story, not yet finished. Perhaps it will never be finished. It is a story that begins with an explosion from a seed of infinite energy. The seed expands and cools. Particles form, then atoms of hydrogen and helium. Stars and galaxies coalesce from swirling gas. Stars burn and explode, forging heavy elements—carbon, nitrogen, oxygen—and hurl them into space. New stars are born, with planets made of heavy elements. On one planet near a typical star in a typical galaxy life appears in the form of microscopic self-replicating ensembles of atoms. Life evolves, over billions of years, resulting in ever more complex organisms. Continents move. Seas rise and fall. The atmosphere changes. Millions of species of life appear and become extinct. Others adapt, survive, and spill out progeny. At last, human consciousness appears. One species experiences the ineffable and wonders what it means, and makes up stories—of invisible spirits who harbor in darkness, of gods who light up the sky in answer to our prayers—eventually making up the New Story.

The New Story has important advantages over all the stories that have gone before:

It works. It works so well that it has become the irreplaceable basis of technological civilization. We test the New Story in every way we can, in its particulars and in its totality. We build giant particle accelerating machines to see what happened in the first hot moments of the Big Bang. We put telescopes into space to look for the radiation of the primeval explosion. With spectroscopes and radiation detectors we analyze the composition of stars and galaxies and compare them to our theories for the origin of the world. Always and in every way we try to prove the story wrong. When the story fails, we change it.

It is a universal story. Although originally a product of Western culture, it has become the story of all educated peoples throughout the world; scientists of all cultures, religions, and political persuasions exchange ideas freely and apply the same criteria of verification and falsification. Like most children, I was taught that my story—Adam and Eve, angels, miracles, incarnation, heaven, hell, and all the rest—was the "true story," and that all others were false. Sometimes our so-called "true" stories gave us permission to hurt those who lived by other stories. The New Story, by its universality, helps put the old animosities behind us.

It is a story that emphasizes the connectedness of all people and all things. Some of the old stories, such as the one I was taught as a child, placed humankind outside of space and time, gifted us with unworldly spirit, and gave us dominion over the millions of Earth's other creatures. The New Story places us squarely in a cosmic unfolding of space and time, and teaches our biological affinity to all humanity. We are ephemeral beings, inextricably related to all of life, to the planet itself, and even to the lives of stars.

It is a story that asserts our responsibility for our own lives and the future of the planet. In the New Story, no omniscient deity intervenes at will in the creation, answers prayers, or leads all things to a predetermined end. We are on our own, in the immensity of creation, with an awesome responsibility to use our talents wisely.

It is a story that reveals a universe of unanticipated complexity, beauty, and dimension. The God revealed by the New Story is not the paltry personal projection of ourselves who attracted and bedeviled our ancestors. It is, in the words of the Jesuit theologian David Toolan, "the Unnamable One/Ancient of the Days of the mystics, of whom we can only speak negatively (not this, not that), a 'wholly other' hidden God of Glory," or in the felicitous phrase of novelist Nikos Kazantzakis, "the dread essence beyond logic."

We should treasure the ancient stories for the wisdom and values they contain. We should celebrate the creation in whatever poetic languages and rituals our traditional cultures have taught us. But only the New Story has the global authority to help us navigate the future. It is not the "true" story, but it is certainly the truest. Of all the stories that might provide the cosmological basis of contemporary religious feeling, it is the only one that has had its feet held to the fire of exacting experience.

The New Story informed my response to the dancing lights in the night sky at Gallarus. What I saw was not a portent or miracle, but rather nature's exquisite signature of the magnetic and material entanglement of Earth and sun.

As the sun brightened the eastern horizon and the last shreds of aurora faded, I was suddenly startled by a pair of swallows that began to dart in and out of the Gallarus Oratory, hunting insects on the wing. I followed them inside and discovered a nest with three chicks perched on a protruding stone just above the place I had been sitting. The mysterious presence I had felt so strongly in the darkness was not a god, nor spirit, nor succubus, nor demon, but the respirations and featherings of swallows.

Cloud Crossing

Scott Russell Sanders

Clouds are temporary creatures. So is the Milky Way, for that matter, if you take the long entropic view of things. I awake on a Saturday in mid-October with the ache of nightmares in my brain, as if I have strained a muscle in my head. Just a week before I turn thirty-three, just a month before my son turns one, I do not need physics or nightmares to remind me that we also are temporary creatures.

Baby Jesse is changing cloud-fast before my eyes. His perky voice begins pinning labels on dogs and bathtubs and sun. When I say, "Want to go for a walk?" on this morning that began with nightmares of entropy, he does not crawl towards me as he would have done only a few days ago. He tugs himself upright with the help of a chair, then staggers toward me like a refugee crossing the border, arms outstretched, crowing, "Wa! Wa!"

So I pack baby and water and graham crackers into the car, and drive thirty miles southeast of Eugene, Oregon, to a trailhead on Hardesty Mountain. There are several hiking paths to the top, ranging in length from one mile to six. I choose the shortest, because I will be carrying Jesse's twenty-two pounds on my back. I have not come here to labor, to be reminded of my hustling heart. I have come to watch clouds.

Markers on the logging road tell us when we drive up past 2,500 feet, then 2,750 and 3,000. Around 3,250 the Fiat noses through the first vapors, great wrinkled slabs of clouds that thicken on the windshield. In the back seat Jesse strains against his safety harness, his hands fisted on the window, hungry to get out there into that white stuff. I drive the last few hundred yards to the trailhead with lights on, in case we meet a car groping its way down the mountain.

Beside a wooden sign carved to announce HARDESTY MOUNTAIN TRAIL, I park the Fiat with its muzzle downhill, so we can coast back to the highway after our walk in case the weary machine refuses to start. I lean the backpack against the bumper and guide Jesse's excited feet through the leg-holes, one of his calves in each of my hands. "Wa! Wa!" he cries, and almost tips the pack over into the sorrel dust of the logging road. Shouldering the pack requires acrobatic balancing, to keep him from tumbling out while I snake my arms through the straps. Once safely aloft, assured of a ride, he jounces so hard in the seat that I stagger a few paces with the same drunken uncertainty he shows in his own walking.

Clouds embrace us. Far overhead, between the fretted crowns of the Douglas fir, I see hints of blue. Down here among the roots and matted needles, the air is mist. My beard soon grows damp; beads glisten on my eyelashes. A few yards along the trail a Forest Service board, with miniature roof to protect its messages, informs us we are at 3,600 feet and must hike to 4,237 in order to reach the top of Hardesty. Since I came to see the clouds, not to swim in them, I hope we are able to climb above them into that tantalizing blue.

On my back Jesse carries on a fierce indecipherable oration concerning the wonders of this ghostly forest. Giddy with being outside and aloft, he drums on my head, yanks fistfuls of my hair. Every trunk we pass tempts him more strongly than the apple tree could ever have tempted Eve and Adam. He lurches from side to side, outstretched fingers desperate to feel the bark. I pause at a mammoth stump to let him touch. Viewed up close, the bark looks like a contour map of the Badlands, an eroded landscape where you might expect to uncover fossils. While Jesse traces the awesome ridges and fissures, I squint to read another Forest Service sign. No motorized vehicles, it warns, and no pack animals.

I surely qualify as a pack animal. For long spells in my adult life, while moving house or humping rucksacks onto trains or hauling firewood, I have felt more like a donkey than anything else. I have felt most like a beast of burden when hauling my two children, first Eva and now Jesse. My neck and shoulders never forget their weight from one portage to another. And I realize that carrying Jesse up the mountain to see clouds is a penance as well as a pleasure—penance for the hours I have sat glaring at my typewriter while he scrabbled mewing outside my door, penance for the thousands of things my wife has not been able to do on account of my word mania, penance for all the countless times I have told daughter Eva "no, I can't; I am writing." I know the rangers did not have human beasts in mind when they posted their sign, yet I am content to be a pack animal, saddled with my crowing son.

As I resume walking, I feel a tug. Jesse snaps a chunk of bark from the stump and carries it with him, to examine at leisure. Beneath one of the rare cottonwoods I pick up a leathery golden leaf, which I hand over my shoulder to the baby, who clutches it by the stem and turns it slowly around, tickling his nose with the starpoints. The leaf is a wonder to him, and therefore also to me. Everything he notices, every pebble, every layered slab of bark, is renewed for me. Once I carried Eva outside, in the first spring of her life, and a gust of wind caught her full in the face. She blinked, and then gazed at the invisible breath as if it were a flight of angels streaming past. Holding her in the crook of my arm that day, I rediscovered wind.

Fascinated by his leaf, Jesse snuggles down in the pack and rides quietly. My heart begins to dance faster as the trail zigzags up the mountain through a series of switchbacks. Autumn has been dry in Oregon, so the dirt underfoot is powdery.

Someone has been along here inspecting mushrooms. The discarded ones litter the trail like blackening pancakes. Except for the path, worn raw by deer and hikers, the floor of the woods is covered with moss. Fallen wood is soon hidden by the creeping emerald carpet, the land burying its own dead. Limegreen moss clings fuzzily to the upright trunks and dangles in fluffy hanks from limbs, like freshly dyed wool hung out to dry. A wad of it caught in the fist squeezes down to nothing.

A lurch from the backpack tells me that Jesse has spied some new tempta-tion in the forest. Craning around, I see his spidery little hands reaching for the sky. Then I also look up, and notice the shafts of light slanting down through the treetops. The light seems substantial, as if made of glass, like the rays of search-lights that carve up the night sky to celebrate a store's opening or a war's end. "Light," I say to Jesse. "Sunlight. We're almost above the clouds." Wherever the beams strike, they turn cobwebs into jeweled diagrams, bracelet limbs with rhine-stones of dew. Cloud vapors turn to smoke.

The blue glimpsed between trees gradually thickens, turns solid, and we emerge onto a treeless stony ridge. Clear sky above, flotillas of clouds below, mountains humping their dark green backs as far as I can see. The sight of so many slick backs arching above the clouds reminds me of watching porpoises from a ship in the Gulf of Mexico. Vapors spiral up and down between cloud lay-ers as if on escalators. Entire continents and hemispheres and galaxies of mist drift by. I sit on the trail with backpack propped against a stone ledge, to watch this migration.

No peace for meditation with an eleven-month-old on your back. An ache in my shoulders signals that Jesse, so near the ground, is leaning out of the pack to capture something. A pebble or beetle to swallow? A stick to gnaw? Moss, it turns out, an emerald hunk of it ripped from the rockface. "Moss," I tell him, as he rotates this treasure about three inches in front of his eyes. "Here, feel," and I stroke one of his palms across the velvety clump. He tugs the hand free and re-sumes his private exploration. This independence grows on him these days faster than his hair.

"Clouds," I tell him, pointing out into the gulf of air. Jesse glances up, sees only vagueness where I see a ballet of shapes, and so he resumes his scrutiny of the moss. "Not to eat," I warn him. When I check on him again half a minute later, the moss is half its former size and his lips are powdered with green. Nothing to do but hoist him out of the pack, dig what I can from his mouth, then plop him back in, meanwhile risking spilling both of us down the mountainside. A glance down the dizzying slope reminds me of my wife's warning, that I have no busi-ness climbing this mountain alone with a baby. She's right, of course. But guilt, like the grace of God, works in strange ways, and guilt drives me up here among the skittery rocks to watch clouds with my son.

"Let Daddy have it," I say, teasing the hunk of moss from his hand. "Have a stick, pretty stick." While he imprints the stick with the marks of his teeth, four above and two below, I spit on the underside of the moss and glue it back down to the rock. Grow, I urge it. Looking more closely at the rockface, I see that it is crumbling beneath roots and weather, sloughing away like old skin. The entire mountain is migrating, not so swiftly as the clouds, but just as surely, heading grain by grain to the sea.

Jesse seems to have acquired some of the mountain's mass as I stand upright again and hoist his full weight. With the stick he idly swats me on the ear.

The trail carries us through woods again, then up along a ridge to the clearing at the top of Hardesty Mountain. There is no dramatic feeling of expansiveness, as there is on some peaks, because here the view is divvied up into modest sweeps by Douglas firs, cottonwoods, great gangling heaps of briars. The forest has laid siege to the rocky crest, and will abolish the view altogether before Jesse is old enough to carry his own baby up here. For now, by moving from spot to spot on the summit, I can see in all directions. What I see mostly are a few thousand square miles of humpbacked mountains looming through the clouds. Once in Ohio I lived in a valley which the Army Corps of Engineers thought would make a convenient bed for a reservoir. So the Mahoning River was dammed, and as the waters backed up in that valley, covering everything but the highest ridges, drowning my childhood, they looked very much like these clouds poured among the mountains.

"Ba! Ba!" Jesse suddenly bellows, leaping in his saddle like a bronco rider.

Bath, I wonder? Bed? Bottle? Ball? He has been prolific of B-words lately, and their tail-ends are hard to tell apart. Ball, I finally decide, for there at the end of the arrow made by his arm is the moon, a chalky peachpit hanging down near the horizon. "Moon," I say.

"Ba! Ba!" he insists.

Let it stay a ball for a while, something to play catch with, roll across the linoleum. His sister's first sentence was, "There's the moon." Her second was, "Want it, Daddy." So began her astronomical yearnings, my astronomical failures. She has the itch for space flight in her, my daughter does. Jesse is still too much of a pup for me to say whether he has caught it.

We explore the mountaintop while the ocean of cloud gradually rises. There are charred rings from old campfires. In a sandy patch, red-painted bricks are laid in the shape of a letter A. Not large enough to be visible from airplanes. If Hardesty Mountain were in a story by Hawthorne, of course, I could use the scarlet A to accuse it of some vast geological harlotry. If this were a folklore mountain, I could explain the letter as an alphabetical inscription left by giants. But since this is no literary landscape, I decide that the bricks formed the foundation for some telescope or radio transmitter or other gizmo back in the days when this summit had a lookout tower.

Nearby is another remnant from those days, a square plank cover for a cistern. The boards are weathered to a silvery sheen, with rows of rustblackened nailheads marking the joints. Through a square opening at the center of the planks I catch a glint. Water? Still gathering here after all these years? Leaning over the hole, one boot on the brittle planks, I see that the glint is from a tin can. The cistern is choked with trash.

At the very peak, amid a jumble of rocks, we find nine concrete piers that once supported the fire tower. By squatting down beside one of those piers I can rest Jesse's weight on the concrete, and relieve the throb in my neck. I imagine the effort of hauling enough materials up this mountain to build a tower. Surely they used horses, or mules. Not men with backpacks. So what became of the tower when the Forest Service, graduated to spotter planes, no longer needed it? Did they pry out every nail and carry the boards back down again? A glance at the ground between my feet supplies the answer. Wedged among the rocks, where rains cannot wash them away, are chunks of glass, some of them an inch thick. I pick up one that resembles a tongue, about the size for a cocker spaniel. Another one, a wad of convolutions, might be a crystalline brain. Peering up through it at the sun, I see fracture lines and tiny bubbles. Frozen in the seams where one molten layer lapped onto another there are ashes. Of course they didn't dismantle the tower and lug its skeleton down the mountain. They waited for a windless day after a drenching rain and they burned it.

The spectacle fills me: the mountain peak like a great torch, a volcano, the tower heaving on its nine legs, the windows bursting from the heat, tumbling among the rocks, fusing into molten blobs, the glass taking on whatever shape it cooled against.

There should be nails. Looking closer I find them among the shards of glass, sixteen-penny nails mostly, what we called spikes when I was building houses. Each one is somber with rust, but perfectly straight, never having been pried from wood. I think of the men who drove those nails—the way sweat stung in their eyes, the way their forearms clenched with every stroke of the hammer—and I wonder if any of them were still around when the tower burned. The Geological Survey marker, a round lead disk driven into a rock beside one of the piers, is dated 1916. Most likely the tower already stood atop the mountain in that year. Most likely the builders are all dead by now.

So on its last day the Hardesty fire tower became a fire tower in earnest. Yesterday I read that two American physicists shared the Nobel Prize for discovering the background radiation left over from the Big Bang, which set our universe in motion some fifteen billion years ago. Some things last—not forever, of course, but for a long time—things like radiation, like bits of glass. I gather a few of the nails, some lumps of glass, a screw. Stuffing these shreds of evidence in my pocket, I discover the graham cracker in its wrapping of cellophane, and I realize I have not thought of Jesse for some minutes, have forgotten that he is riding me. That can mean only one thing. Sure enough, he is asleep, head scrunched down into the pack. Even while I peek at him over my shoulder he is changing, neurons hooking up secret connections in his brain, calcium swelling his bones as mud gathers in river deltas.

Smell warns me that the clouds have reached us. Looking out, the only peaks I can see are the Three Sisters, each of them a shade over 10,000 feet. Except for those peaks and the rocks where I stand, everything is cotton. There are no more clouds to watch, only Cloud, unanimous whiteness, an utter absence of shape. A panic seizes me—the same panic I used to feel as a child crossing the street when approaching cars seemed to have my name written on their grills.

Suddenly the morning's nightmare comes back to me: everything I know is chalked upon a blackboard, and, while I watch, a hand erases every last mark.

Terror drives me down the Hardesty trail, down through vapors that leach color from the ferns, past trees that are dissolving. Stumps and downed logs lose their shape, merge into the clouds. The last hundred yards of the trail I jog. Yet Jesse never wakes until I haul him out of the pack and wrestle him into the car harness. His bellowing defies the clouds, the creeping emptiness. I bribe him with sips of water, a graham cracker, a song. But nothing comforts him, or comforts me, as we drive down the seven graveled miles of logging road to the highway. There we sink into open space again. The clouds are a featureless gray overhead.

As soon as the wheels are ringing beneath us on the blacktop, Jesse's internal weather shifts, and he begins one of his calm babbling orations, contentedly munching his cracker. The thread of his voice slowly draws me out of the annihilating ocean of whiteness. "Moon," he is piping from the back seat, "moon, moon!"

Pliny and the Mountain Mouse

Reg Saner

Dim though his brain may be, the marmot feels winter will come soon. And long. Longer than any of his previous twelve. From each of these, gaunt after seven or more months of hibernation in a rocky burrow, he has wakened; to at once waddle forth, to rummage spring snow for juicy alpine tundra plants, to mate, to sun, now and then to frolic with others in his chummy colony, and—properly fattened—to reenter the burrow: again to sleep away winter.

His "language" of gesture and squeaks is enormously older than words; but no European language names even the continent this particular marmot lives on. His region of high rocks hasn't yet been discovered by Old World tongues, though one day it will be called "colorado" by men speaking a version of Latin. That his home among granite chunks sits twelve thousand feet in the air, with superb mountain views on three sides, the marmot-brain translates to *always,* and *always* to *is.*

Even for this marmot, whose sense of history isn't wider than body fat and the sun's present height, today's rise and set of sky is numbered: August 24, A.D. 79.

You and I aren't here yet. At such altitude, nobody is. In A.D. 79, "nobody" is still only Indians. "Somebody" is only a marmot. Cool wind, blowing lightly out of late summer, licks his pelt. Opulent tufts of cinnamon fur lift along the plump back, slur a moment, subside. Because in the warmish afternoon, his ridgeline is only just dappled by the fast blue shadows of cloud-faces that mythologies copy, this marmot suns. He lies full-stretch on a rock slab. To stir himself overmuch would burn off precious fat his busy incisors have nibbled all the brief tundra summer to acquire, so he moves only his head, in those quick, darting glances small animals learn from their instructors the foxes, the coyotes, the eagles.

Close cousin to groundhogs and woodchucks, the high-country *Marmota flaviventris,* or yellow-bellied kind, often relies on talus-piles of granite to provide fortresslike burrows only a bear or wolverine could dilapidate. Such hideaways protect the numerous offspring, five or six to a litter, which by summer's end are full grown.

Does the marmot breed to defeat predators, or do they prey on his colony to defeat his fast breeding? The answer is part of that circle whose opposites create each other; the molecular keys in the blood, the living shapes taken by time. A ravenous hawk; a slightly ludicrous bag of fat fur. Appetites that have learned how to repeat themselves. To what end? None that any living creature—now or to come—ever will know. To be. Each to do its kind.

Seven thousand miles to the east, in the Roman resort town of Herculaneum, guests leaving a dinner party find their way home through moonlit, sultry, sea-level air; air that thickens to an indigo blur across the Neapolitan bay toward the naval base at Misenum. There, sweating out the dog days of August—even at night—sits Pliny the Elder, a science writer whose tireless goose quill nibbles away at the creamy blankness on a fresh vellum. Pliny is himself fat as butter, and sweats as if he were melting, but he is as usual hard at it well before dawn, an omnivore of other men's books, which—he frankly admits—his own writing feeds on, just as his compulsive quill-nib feeds on blank vellum like a tiny animal storing up fame.

Among stones of a continent Pliny never heard of, the marmot has eaten back his lost bulk hardly a day too soon, and has almost finished lining his burrow with tundra grasses gathered for stuffing into the sleeping chamber as insulation and nest. Food will be body fat, however much his summer's nibbling has managed to accrue. And high-country autumn comes early. He knows it not as a name but a time when his world begins entering more into shadow. *If* the oncoming winter is neither too deep nor too long, his body fat will suffice.

During hard winters, however, dormancy proves a risky survival device. One marmot in five either freezes outright or starves. Among the small mercies of nature, on this twenty-fourth day of Augustus, is this particular marmot's blindness to his future. Breeze tousling his glossy pelt doesn't tell what it hears: that the oncoming season is coming to kill him, turn him to stone. And to quench the others sharing the family burrow.

Heat haze of southern Italy, moon-silvered. Pliny sweats, dips his quill into an inkhorn, and shares the same ignorance.

Just now, however, his scientific compulsion spurs him to update earlier pages of his already voluminous *Natural History*. Pliny is inserting some new facts about marmots, which he calls Alpine mice; "Some people say they form a chain and let themselves down into their cave that way, male and female alternately holding the next creature's tail by the teeth. One, lying on its back, hugs a bundle of grass and is hauled in by the others. Consequently at this season their backs show marks of rubbing."

Pliny's view of human life is rather gloomy; mankind as he knows it staggers along from misery to fresh misery, ruin to ruin. But the natural world! As inexhaustible as fascinating. "Some people say" may sound, he is fully aware, hardly better than gossip; yet nature is so prodigal of oddities that one's wildest guess may prove too tame. Like the haymaking marmot his pen has just described, Pliny's habit of reaping truth from old books and storing it up in his own year-upon-year scribbling, book after book, rules his waking hours so compulsively he hardly spares time to bathe, much less to ask himself, "Why?" Nor will he ever.

He never will, because what neither Pliny-the-nature-writer nor his friends across the bay in Herculaneum and Stabiae foresee is, simply, "Nature": in a few hours the trim, vineyarded summit of Vesuvius will blow sky high. In a few hours, Pliny's concern for those friends and his scientific curiosity will combine to strangle him. Soon, on the undiscovered continent of which Pliny knows nothing, a particular "Alpine mouse" will waddle into his burrow, plug the entrance with small stones and hay, then begin a winter trance no summer can waken.

The same incurable yen that draws Pliny unaware toward his suffocation saves his nephew. Before setting sail across the Bay of Naples for his fatal lesson in volcanology, the uncle invites Pliny the Younger—an eighteen-year-old—to come along if he wants. In aftertimes, by then an author himself, the nephew will recall, "To this invitation I answered that I'd rather continue studying. Besides, as it happened, my uncle had assigned me an essay to write." Writer's itch runs in the family.

At twelve thousand feet along an unknown continental divide, the night of twenty-fourth Augustus opens with snow crystals flying past; ice migrations of white flies that sting like salt. Meanwhile, along the Vesuvian shores it is finally morning. All night a hailstorm of pumice has scorched the roofs of Stabiae, piling up, drifting. A cinder snow that smokes. Roof beams crack and collapse, house walls totter.

By the seashore Pliny the Elder gulps at the air, supported between two slaves who lay him down on a scrap of sailcloth. He calls for cold water, drinks it, flops back. By now volcanic ash has begun its steady, floating fall. It descends soundlessly. Panicked Romans scatter the stuff as they run, stumble, collapse. Lightly, the ash begins to clothe each fallen body. In a few days it will smother the town. Years hence, in a reminiscent mood Pliny the Younger will sit—obese as his uncle—pushing a quill across vellum: "Three mornings later his body was found on the spot, intact . . . more like a man asleep than dead."

Three mornings later it is evening in another country, whose mountain sun has just set. Lofty ridgelines looking down into their own lakes see that sunset dismantled. Summer-plump, backside ruddied by alpenglow, the marmot stands hindlegged atop his rock, forepaws snugged against chest-fur, nose whiskers twitching, brown eyes staring east. He gives a reedy squeak. Answered by another . . . then another. A marmot "harem" and colony, a dozen in all, talking to themselves. They've harvested tundra plants, almost enough. How hard they've worked their worn pelts show: the narrow squeeze to and fro since midsummer, carrying cut grasses past snug entrance rocks and deep into the burrow, has scraped their back-fur haggard.

A trained and patient ear, or a marmot's, could identify as many as six distinctive variants on the shrill calls that led ancient Alpine people to nickname these animals "whistlers": Calls of "Eaglehawk!" Calls of "My rock, not yours!" Calls of "Fox!" Calls of "Love *me*! Love *me*! Love *me*!" Calls of "Wingflown! Foxgone!" No wonder their silly, piping squeaks this evening are almost musical. After a gestation of about a month, the summer's young have reached full size of six to ten pounds in just weeks. Only the last of the haymaking remains. Abruptly the east-squinting marmot, boss male of the harem, falls silent. Up out of the distant, alluvial, proto-Coloradan plain floats a great fullness, a moon pale as winter; pale as a sun made of snow.

We can be here now. It's our turn . . . to be, and be curious. We know all about Pompeii, Stabiae; know Herculaneum too was buried. Oh yes, volcanic detritus enclosed many of the dead so perfectly that—in modern times, once Pliny's contemporaries had, as it were, evaporated—plaster casts could be made of their living absences. Lime-white, like snowmen. Startlingly "us," therefore touching. Theoretically. Anyhow, we ourselves avoid erupting volcanoes.

And, yes, it is poignant—in theory—to think of a marmot family in its burrow, like a banked fire; each furry curl asleep, nose between hind paws, like so many embers ashed over. Winter sets in: the marmot body temperature dips to about ten degrees above freezing. From pulsing twice every second the hibernating heart slows to half that. Then slower. Finally, as much as a full quarter-minute or more goes by . . . between beats.

During hibernation marmots rouse, stir somewhat, then sleep again—unless their body fat runs out, or winter cold runs too long too deep, and the tiny heart ceases. As when a lit match, held upright, weakens till its shrunken flame seeps back into the matchhead; a glow, a red cinder—suddenly black.

But the small, distant deaths of animals common as wind don't sadden anyone. No more than we're saddened by all the once-upon-a-time crickets and dormice ashed over at Pompeii. Besides, those life-like but plaster agonies recovered from Pompeiian dailyness are of folks who would have died ages ago, even if Vesuvius's summit hadn't smithereened. Centuries *are* distance, aren't they?

Of his unswerving industry, how much did Pliny expect would survive? Apart from his considerable military service, he wrote a work twenty "books" long on Rome's wars with Germany, wrote an eight-book text on rhetoric, penned a lengthy chronicle of his own times in thirty-one books, and crowned his literary achievement with that eccentric museum, his *Natural History*, gleaned from authors and treatises innumerable. Time, which called Pliny out of the dust into sunlight, and which lent him his encyclopaedic curiosity, has ground nearly all that to powder. He knew well how "Nature" begets and devours us, just as Chronos ate his own children. Of Pliny's written mind, only the *Natural History* has made it all the way to now.

As for his year upon year of curious labor, might some lost remnants exist as an undetectable nuance in what the European mind has become? Surely so. However, such consolation feels cheerless as a cubic meter of interstellar medium: one or two floating atoms, the rest a black vacuum.

Which makes Pliny's compulsive curiosity, despite his patchwork and pack-rat science, all the more touching. Laborious days and nights belied his own glum estimate of the human situation. We survive by not believing what we know. Is that because our unconscious knows something truer than fact? Maybe it knows that what we most admire can't die, including the best of ourselves—which we don't invent, merely inherit or borrow. And which, like the world, is nobody's possession. Is wave-lengths, passing through us.

And passing through those wilderness creatures that cold will freeze solid this winter? A gnat is the weight of astonishing centuries, surely as a finch wing has been shaped by however old the sky is. But our emotions require of objects a certain size to help bridge the gap between them and ourselves. Where's the line to be drawn? At bugs on a windshield? By no means even then. So says reason. Reason says the line must be a circle wide as our minds.

So when it comes to the spark in all animal hardihood—meaning ours—I often see an outcrop on Colorado's continental divide. To think mountains "majestic" we mustn't inhale overlong their bone-barren summits and crazed smash-ups of rock. A few hours, or days; then clear out. Nothing has been here since the beginning, but great crags pretend they have. They pretend we living things aren't here at all; or if so, mere passing fancies of the sun. Even in midsummer their petrified light can chill, so winter near their summits can be—in the root sense of the word—terrific. To look at ice cliffs long, and in storm, and alone . . . kills the heart. Nonetheless, atop one uppermost slab near the Corona trail suns a lone marmot; sluggish, dim-witted, inconsiderable, heroic.

Straight overhead the sky is an ultraviolet blue so intense it verges on purple. Late August sun drills down. Light breeze pours over the divide, ruffling the marmot's pelt, glossy as a chestnut. Moment to moment his head winks north, winks west in quick, circumspicuous caution. The sunning torso, plump as a loaf, doesn't stir. He sees me, and sees me keeping my distance. He has no idea.

He knows nothing, really, of the success of his own species, doesn't know that his ancestors reached North America from Asia, across the land bridge spanning what is now the Bering Strait, and were at home here, just like this, when Pliny the Elder wrote and Vesuvius erupted. Now found all over the globe, he has gone where not even the map can go, hearing rivers that had never been heard. He has been snared, trapped, poisoned, and shot: for his fur in Mongolia, for his oil in lands diverse as Switzerland and Siberia. Under the guise of woodchuck he is thought a mere varmint and thus—in much of the United States—an appropriate focus for gunsights. His avatars waddled about and snoozed beneath Pleistocene skies of the Ice Age. He is content to live where little else can. He endures.

How could he know that I, the biped who under a backpack leans slightly forward and stares, admire his stamina entirely? How could either of us foresee that his serio-comic, jawless profile, his buck teeth, twitchy nose whiskers and sluff of a tail, his wide-eyed blinkings and lookouts for predators will combine with the twelve thousand foot altitude to make his silly bump of a figure not only wholeheartedly dear to me but—long as I live—half immortal?

When did humans first find the marmot amusing? Pliny's account seems to have been written with a smile. Certainly the mountain mouse—as the French tongue still names him—once delighted Europeans visiting the fairs and markets where animal trainers entertained; among the camels and tame bears, spectators could see many a humble marmot "dancing" to flute notes played by its keeper, often a child from the Tyrol.

Amusement, however, did not prevent Alpine dwellers in modern times from hunting the slow creature almost to extinction, both for its fat—reputed to cure rheumatism, among other ills—and for its pelt. As late as 1944 an estimated sixteen thousand marmots were killed in Switzerland alone, till naturalists persuaded pharmaceutical dealers that marmot-annihilation would benefit no one. Though belief in the curative powers of marmot fat still persists among folk of the European Alps, the animals have dodged the threat of extinction. In contrast, Mongolia's Bobac marmot breeds so fast no such threat exists—despite the millions of furs annually harvested there, and the many hundreds of tons of marmot fat. And despite the fact that Mongolian marmots often carry plague.

As for me, before and since, I've seen marmots by the hundreds, seen their low profiles flow over or peer out of rock piles from here to the end of the world. In Alaska's Brooks Range I made my first acquaintance with his species by way of a raided food cache the critters gnawed into. In Switzerland's sole national park I've watched marmot youngsters wrestle each other repeatedly, as we did when kids, for the sheer fun of it, toppling, flopping, grappling each other and rolling together downhill. That Swiss pair didn't behave *like* human kids. Their play-wrestling seemed *identical*.

On a frosty mid-July night high in Colorado's Gore Range the weird roar that woke me was marmot incisors munching a hole in my empty Nalgene water-bottle. One twilight evening just below the 14,200-foot summit of Longs Peak, bright marmot-whistles seemed to match the first few stars like question and answer. A mile from the crest of Arapahoe Pass there's a particularly untimid marmot who, as I approach, rises hindlegged to his full height of some eighteen inches and, in exactly the same spot, tries to stare me down. Amid that shattered labyrinth of stone chaos, his world and home, what a bold fellow he is! Since marmots live but a dozen years or thereabouts, his annual defiance feels huge. We gaze at each other. In our silence much seems possible, though nothing much happens: two creatures, looking a little farther than themselves.

But that *other* marmot surviving miles away on the Corona Trail—why should he, a dozen years after my glimpse of him, continue to seem so special? There where the left hand slopes away as alpine tundra, half meadow, and the right hand is sheer fall, hundreds of feet down to rockscapes ugly as slag, down toward acres of grit-littered, permanent snow, my emblematic marmot at first seemed no different from hundreds. It's just that, to remember what sheer courage looks like, my mind's eye often invokes him.

There, under a sky barely fly-specked with ravens, and atop a jut of flat granite, he suns. Wind ruffles his fur. He blinks, peers around him at nothing. At what there is. His instincts and eyes, his nut-brown pelt, his nose and paws, all seem shapes taken by a design whose true name I don't know—any more than that dim creature knew his. Which I see, now, given his Old World origins, might as well have been Pliny.

My Father Always Said

Mimi Schwartz

For years I heard the same line: "In Rindheim,[1] you didn't do such things!" It was repeated whenever the American world of his daughters took my father by surprise. Sometimes it came out softly, in amusement, as when I was a Pilgrim turkey in the P.S. 3 Thanksgiving play. But usually, it was a red-faced, high-blood-pressure shout—especially when my sister, Ruth, became "pinned" to Mel from Brooklyn or I wanted to go with friends whose families he didn't know.

"But they're Jewish," I'd say, since much of our side of Forest Hills was. The eight lanes of Queens Boulevard divided the Jews, Irish, and Italians pushing out of Brooklyn, the Bronx, and Manhattan from the old guard WASPs of Forest Hills Gardens. No Jews or Catholics over there—except for a few blocks near the Forest Hills Tennis Stadium where, from fifth grade on, we kids all went to watch what is now the U.S. Tennis Open, our end-of-summer ritual before school.

"You're not going," my father would announce before all such rituals.

"But everybody's going."

It was the wrong argument to make to a man who fled Hitler's Germany because of everybody. But I couldn't know that because he rarely talked about *that* Germany, only about his idyllic Rindheim where everybody (as opposed to the everybody I knew) did everything right. If my friends didn't have an aunt, grandmother, or great grandfather originally from Rindheim or vicinity, they were suspect. They could be anybody, which is exactly why I liked them—not like the Weil kids whose mother was "a born Tannhauser," as if that were a plus.

"I don't care about everybody!" my father would shout (that was his second favorite line); but it was a losing battle for him. My sister smoked at fifteen, I wore lipstick at twelve; we hung out at Penn Drug after Friday night basketball games

---

[1]I've changed the name, but all else is true.

with friends who were third-generation Brooklyn and Rumania—and didn't give a hoot that "In Rindheim, you didn't do such things!"

The irony of those words was inchoate—even to him, I realize now—until we went back to his village to visit the family graves. I was thirteen; it was eight years after World War II ended, and my father wanted to show me where his family had lived for generations, trading cattle. He wanted me, the first American-born in the family, to understand that "Forest Hills, Queens is not the world" (his third favorite line). A hard task to tackle, but my father was tough, a survivor who had led his whole clan, like Moses, out of Nazi Germany and into Queens, New York. He was ready for an American teen-age me.

"So Mimi-a-la, this is Rindheim!" my father boomed as the forest opened upon a cluster of fifty or so red-peaked houses set into the hillside of a tiny, green valley. We had driven for hours through what looked like Hansel and Gretel country, filled with foreboding evergreens that leaned over the narrow, winding roads of the *Schwarzwald*. Even the name, *Schwarzwald*, which meant Black Forest, gave me the creeps after being weaned on Nazi movies at the Midway Theater on 71st Avenue; but I was optimistic. Life here did look prettier than in Queens.

We drove up a rutted main street and stopped before a crumbling stone house with cow dung in the yard. "This was *our* house!" my father announced, as I watched horse flies attacking the dung, not just in *our* yard but in every yard on Eelinger Weg. And there were cows and chickens walking in front of our rented car. What a bust! My mother at least came from a place with sidewalks (we had driven by her old house in Stuttgart, sixty kilometers north, before coming here). My father, I decided at once, was a hick. All his country hero adventures about herding cows with a book hidden in one pocket and his mother's home-baked raspberry *linzertorte* in the other were discounted by two cows chewing away in stalls where I expected a car to be.

A stooped, old man with thick jowls and a feathered leather cap came out of the house with a big smile and a vigorous handshake for my dad who, looking squeezed in his pin-striped suit, nodded now and then and looked polite, but did not smile back.

"Sind Sie nicht ein Loewengart, vielleicht Julius oder Artur?" The man jabbered on, and my mother translated. He was Herr Schmidt, the blacksmith, and recognized my dad at once. "Aren't you a Loewengart, maybe Julius or Arthur?" This man had bought the family house in 1935 from Uncle Julius, the last of my family to leave Rindheim, and was remembering how my father and his brothers, Sol and Julius, used to play in his shop—with all his tools. *"Eine nette Familie, sehr nette,"* ("A fine family, very fine") he kept saying.

I understood nothing because I had learned no German in our house in Queens. When my father reached Ellis Island, he announced that our family would not speak the language of those who drove them out of Germany. Which was fine with me. It was embarrassing enough in those days to have parents who, for all my coaching, couldn't stop saying *'fader'* and *'moder'* to my American-born friends.

The man beckoned us towards my dad's old house, but my father shook his head, *"Nein, Danke!"* and backed us quickly away. I wanted to go in and see his old room; but my father did not. It would be forty years before I'd follow Frau Hummel, the blacksmith's daughter, up the narrow, dark stairs to a loft with two windows like cannon holes and search the heavy low beams for my dad's initials—A. L.—carved in the worn, smooth wood.

"And here's my downtown! No Penn Drugstore to hang around here!" my Dad said cheerfully, as we drove past four buildings leaning together like town drunks. "And here's where Grunwald had his kosher butcher shop and Zundorfer, his dry goods. And here's the *Gasthaus Kaiser*! We Jews had wonderful *Purim* and *Shuvuott* dances here—with green branches and ferns and pink flowers, like marbles in the candlelight. . . ." I could picture Mr. Grundwald—he sold sausages in Queens—but I couldn't picture my big-bellied, bald-headed Dad dancing, a kid like me.

We turned into an alley and stopped next to a gray building with stone columns in the doorway and corners decorated with what looked like railroad ties set into stone. I wouldn't have noticed it tucked among the houses.

"Here's where we spent every Friday night," my father said, getting us out of the car to look at the old synagogue. He pointed to a Hebrew inscription carved onto a stone plaque above the doorway: "How great is God's house and the doorway to Heaven," he translated haltingly in his rusty Hebrew. Right below the stone plaque was a wooden beam with another inscription, this one in German. It said the same thing, my father said, but it was new. He'd never seen it before.

I found out later that the German inscription had been added in 1952, the year before we came. That's when the Jewish synagogue was converted into the Protestant Evangelical Church to accommodate Eastern Germans who, fleeing the Russian troops late in World War II, resettled into the empty Jewish houses of this Catholics/Jewish village. Keeping the same words on the doorway inscription was meant as a tribute of respect: that this building was still God's house. But the 250 Rindheim Jews who had fled to America and Israel were never grateful. Their beautiful synagogue was no more; that's what counted.

"Well, at least it didn't become a gymnasium or a horse stable, like in other villages," the mayor's wife told me huffily in 1993 when I returned to Rindheim on my own. Two other villagers nodded vigorously, but a lively woman, who said she used to live next door to my great uncle, said, *"Na Ja,* I wouldn't be so happy if our Catholic church became a mosque—and believe me, we have plenty of Turks here . . ."

" . . . They are our new Jews," someone interjected.

" . . . *Na Ja,"* the lively woman shrugged and continued, "and I wouldn't feel good just because the Moslems said our church was still God's house."

They pointed out "the Moslems," four men squatting around a table and sipping Turkish coffee in a terraced yard below the synagogue. Many came, according to the lively woman, in the the 1960s as guest workers from Turkey and Afghanistan and now made up twenty percent of Rindheim. These men lived in the old *Gasthaus Kaiser*, where my father danced at *Purim* Festivals and where my

Aunt Hilda and family once lived above the restaurant. This village is more like Forest Hills than you thought, Dad, I told myself, wishing he were around to discuss these ironies of migration. (The Forest Hills Gardens of my childhood is now owned by wealthy Asians and our block on 110th Street is now filled with Iranians.)

My father loosened his tie and wiped beads of sweat from his forehead with a checkered handkerchief. "And if you weren't in your synagogue by sundown on Friday, and not a minute later, *and* all day on Saturday, you were fined, a disgrace to your family. Three stars had to shine in the evening sky before *Shabbat* (the Sabbath) was over and you could go home."

I thought of his fury whenever I wanted to go bowling on Saturday at Foxy's Alley where all the boys hung out. Not that my father went to synagogue in Queens. The most religious he got, as far as I could see, was to play his record of Jan Pierce singing the *Kol Nidre* on *Yom Kippur*, the day of repentance. And he fasted—which I tried once or twice but got hungry when my mother ate a bagel. She never fasted.

The sun was high, the car seat sticky on my thighs, so I happily sat in the shade of four tall, arched windows which someone had been fixing. But my mother was heading for the car, saying she didn't like standing in the open where everyone could see us. We should go. In fact, she would have skipped Germany altogether and stayed in Belgium with my sister who had married a Belgian Jew (instead of Mel from Brooklyn); but my father insisted that we make this pilgrimage.

"Aren't we going inside?" I asked when my father started to follow my mother. He was usually the leader on everything, the man who, in 1933, as soon as Hitler came to power, convinced his brothers, sister, cousins, and parents-in-law, forty people in all, to leave Germany as quickly as possible; the man who figured out schemes for smuggling money taped to toilets on night trains to Switzerland—it took two years—so that they'd have enough cash for America to let them in. (Jews without a bank account or sponsor had no country willing to take them from Hitler's Germany.)

"No reason to go in. The building is just a shell. Everything was gutted by fire during *Kristallnacht*."

"What's that?"

I imagined some Jewish festival with candles out of control. In 1953 there was no *Schindler's List*, no Holocaust Museum, so I never heard about one night in 1938, when the Nazis systematically burned all the synagogues in Germany to destroy the Jewish life. All I knew was good Americans, who looked like Jimmy Stewart and Gregory Peck, fighting mean-looking men in black uniforms who clicked their heels a lot and shouted, "Heil Hitler." And we won.

"*Kristallnacht* was when the Jews finally realized they had to leave—and fast—even from Rindheim where it wasn't so bad. Jews felt safe here, too safe—until the synagogue was torched, everything in flames."

He stopped talking. "Go on!" I urged, but he held back, tentative. Not at all like him.

"My cousin Fritz . . . Do you remember him?" I shook my head, no. "He lived over there once," my father pointed down the alley, "and when he smelled smoke, he raced over. He was part of the Fire Brigade and began shouting to others in the Brigade, 'Why don't we do something? Get the hoses!' Men he knew all his life were standing around, silent. 'Against orders!' snapped a Nazi brownshirt, a stranger. 'Except if Christian houses start to burn!' He pointed his rifle at Fritz. So everything inside was lost—the Torah, the Ark. . . ."

I thought about the old blacksmith who lived in our house. Was he there? Was he one of those firemen? Why was he so friendly if he hated the Jews?

"But these people weren't from Rindheim," my father said quickly. "They were thugs from outside, brought in trucks by the Nazis to do their dirty work."

My father, already in America by then, had heard this from many Rindheim Jews who, like Fritz, left as soon after *Kristallnacht* as they could get exit visas. "The Rindheimers we grew up with didn't take part. They wouldn't do such a thing!" my father had been assured by those who resettled in America.

He opened the car door. "In fact many Non-Jews helped the Jews fix the store and house windows that were also smashed that night. But for that the Non-Jews got in trouble. Everyone who helped was sent to the Front as cannon fodder."

"What's that?" I asked.

"It's what you feed into big guns so they will shoot."

I imagined a young man being stuffed into a cannon, like at the circus, and aimed at American guns, his mother in the red doorway of the house we just passed, getting a telegram, crying like in the movies. But I wasn't going to feel sorry, not when they let the synagogue burn.

Later I would hear this term, cannon fodder, used again and again by Rindheim Jews—and always with the same "broken window" story. It was as if they had decided collectively on this tale and how it illustrated that their Non-Jewish neighbors meant well. "It wasn't their fault. They were afraid, too," they'd say with more sympathy than anger. But, like my parents, the Jews who returned to Rindheim to visit the family graves did so quickly, never wanting to stand and talk in the open or re-enter old rooms of memory.

I was hungry, but my father stopped again, this time in front of a shabby building with three tiers of windows. This was his school, he said, and it looked like mine, but P.S. 3 had a paved playground and good swings. This just had dirt.

"We Jews had the first floor and one teacher, Herr Spatz, who taught everybody, in all eight grades, everything. The Christians had the other two floors."

"How come?" I asked, for I'd never heard of dividing kids by anything but age.

My father looked surprised. "That's how it was done. We learned Torah and they didn't. They went to school on Saturdays and we didn't. But to high school, we went together, six kilometers to Horb, those who went."

"And did you talk to each other—and play games?" I thought of Tommy Molloy in the schoolyard, saying that I killed Christ, but then he asked me to play stickball on his team, and I said okay.

"Of course. We all got along. Rindheim was not so big."

I wouldn't argue about that! The schoolyard was deserted and, looking for movement in a meadow on the far hill, I saw a giant white cross ringed by menacing forest that kept its distance, like dark green bodyguards. The cross was also new, my father said. It wasn't even there when he was a child or even when he came home for a *Shabbat*, after moving to the city of Frankfurt in 1921 to work and later to marry.

"Remember how we had to park the car two kilometers away and walk to my father's?" He nudged my mother. "No Jew dared to drive here on *Shabbat*! Am I right?"

"Absolutely not. You'd be run out of town." My mother laughed for the first time all day and turned to tell me about how she, a big city girl from Stuttgart, first came to this village for her cousin Max's wedding. She wore a red, lace dress. "Very shocking!" she said with delight. "Everyone was whispering but your father. He came up and asked for every dance!" Her shoulders eased with nostalgia, wisps of black hair loosened from her chignon, and I leaned forward, close to her neck that always smelled of almond soap, to hear more about my parents having fun.

My father made a sharp left turn up a dirt road that zigzagged up a hill and stopped in front of a run-down stone farmhouse with half a roof. We needed a key for the Jewish cemetery and it was hanging on the peg "where it has always been," my father said. This was the Brenner family house; they were the gravediggers, who had been burying the Rindheim Jews for generations. Before Hitler, of course. A quarter of a mile farther, a giant stone portal emerged from nowhere—the kind that led to castles—and the fat key opened the heavy gate that led us deep into woods.

I still remember the sunlight on that day, how it streamed on the gravestones, a thousand of them tipped but all standing, in an enchanted forest light. It was a place to whisper and walk on tiptoe, even if you were an American thirteen. I remember the softness of the ground, a carpet of moss and leaves, and the stillness, as if the trees were holding their breath until we found everyone: my grandmother, Anna, born Tannhauser (1872–1915), and my grandfather, Rubin (1866–1925), both marked by sleek, dark marble gravestones that looked new despite the underbrush. And Rubin's father, Raphael (1821–1889), and his father, Rubin Feit (1787–1861), their pale sandstone gravestones carved with elaborate vines and scrolls eroded by time.

I tried to imagine faces: a grandfather who enforced strict rules about work, manners, and Torah; a grandmother who, in the faded photo over my parents' bed, laughed with my father's twinkle, when life pleased him. She had died when my father was not much older than I was, of infection, not Hitler, my father said. So had his dad, who refused to go to the hospital two hours away.

But all I could picture were the grandparents I knew: the *Omi* and *Opa* who lived three blocks away in Queens and "babysat," against my loudest objections that I was too old for that. This grandfather walked my dog so I didn't have to and wove yards of intricately patterned shawls and slipcovers on his loom in our attic. This grandmother made delicious, heart-shaped butter cookies and told stories of how they escaped in a little boat from Denmark to Sweden, and then to a chicken farm on Long Island where she, a city woman from Stuttgart, sang to her hens every morning—until my grandfather's heart attack made them move three blocks from us.

"Do you want to put down stones?" my father asked, placing small ones on his father's grave, his lips moving as in prayer, and then on his mother's grave—and on the others. He had found the stones under the wet leaves, and my mother, wobbling in high heels, was searching for more, enough for both of us.

"What for?" I asked, not wanting to take what she was offering. I would find my own.

"It's how you pay tribute to the dead," my father said, looking strangely gaunt despite his bulk. "The dead souls need the weight of remembrance, and then they rise up to God more easily . . . If we lived nearby, there'd be many stones," he said softly to his father's grave.

In later years, there would be more stones, as more Rindheim Jews came to visit the graves of their ancestors, but eight years after the war there were no others. I placed a smooth, speckled white with mica on Anna's grave and rougher grey ones on the men's. My father nodded. Some connection had been made, he knew, the one he had run from and returned to, the one I resisted even as I lay stones.

There were Loewengarts all over the place, mixed in with Pressburgers and Froehlichs and Grunwalds and Landauers, the same names again and again for they all married each other—or someone Jewish from a nearby village. There were four or five with Jews. My father said he had been daring to marry a woman from so far away—sixty kilometers! But when my mother found a gravestone that might be her second cousin on her mother's side, I thought: not *so* daring!

We were next to a wire fence in the far end of the cemetery where the weeds were high. My mother had disappeared, so it was just my father and I among rows of tiny graves no higher than my kneecaps, their writing almost rubbed off.

We were among the children's graves, my father said, slipping on wet leaves, but catching himself as I reached for his hand. I wanted him standing, especially with my mother gone. Above me, I heard the warble of a single bird and shivered. My father pointed out a headstone carved like a tree trunk but with its limbs cut off. It meant the person died young, in the prime of life, he said, and I thought of my sister Hannah who died soon after they arrived in America—before I was born. I didn't know the details then—how their doctor, also a German refugee, didn't know about the new antibiotics on the market—only that the sweet face with green eyes who hung over my parents' bed was buried in New Jersey somewhere.

I was glad to move back among the larger stones, worn and substantial like adults. I saw one dated 1703. You could tell the older stones, my father said, because all the writing—what little was left—was in Hebrew. The newer gravestones were mostly in German because by 1900, Jews no longer had to pay extra taxes as Jews, so they had started to feel very German, as if they really belonged.

"Did all the Rindheim Jews move to New York?" I was thinking about how many came to our house in Queens and pinched my cheeks over the years.

"Many, yes," he lectured, "but some moved to Palestine as a group. Others went to Chicago, Paris, even Buenos Aires . . ." We were now before a headstone carved with a broken flower, its stem snapped in two. He touched it. "And some stayed," he said quietly. "There were many, especially old people, who were like my *Tante* Rosa and thought no one would bother her. 'I'll be fine,' she kept saying. Later . . . we tried to send her money, but then . . ." His voice trailed off.

"Is she buried here?"

He shook his head. "She was deported." I asked no more, for I knew what deported meant, had seen the pictures of Auschwitz in *Life* magazine. I'd always been relieved that my Dad was smart and had gotten the whole family out in time—except for this *Tante* Rosa. I imagined a handful of old people getting into a wagon, but no one I knew, so it didn't seem so bad.

The sun rays had faded, the forest turned gray and dank, and we were near the entrance again, standing before a large monument in black stone, with the inscription, "Erected to honor the victims of the persecution of the Jews—1933–1945." No individual names were listed, so I kept imagining only a handful of old people and walked on, stopping at a memorial that had a face: Joseph Zundorfer, his features carved in bronze above his name. He had been a Jewish fighter pilot in World War I with many medals. "Shot down," my father said, placing a stone on the grave, and I pictured a hero like Gregory Peck.

Eighty-seven Jews, not a handful, were deported from my father's village during 1941 and 1942, I found out forty years later. They died in the concentration camps of Lublin, Riga, Theresienstadt; but with no names engraved in stone and no faces to admire, they remained anonymous to me that day. What registered to an American teenager who lost no one she really knew was the sunlight on my family's graves, and how a thousand Jews, related to me, were buried, safe and secure for centuries in these high woods.

"In Rindheim, we didn't do such things!" suddenly carried more weight, giving me a history and legitimacy that would have made me not mind, as much, if my father continued to say that line. But he didn't. When we came home from that trip, he took up golf and played every weekend with American friends who never heard of Rindheim. Their world of congeniality became ours and I was expected to enter its promise. "Smile, smile! You are a lucky girl to be here!" is what I remember after that as my father's favorite line. His magical village of memory had disappeared among the graves that weren't there and the weightless souls with no stones of remembrance.

The Masked Marvel's Last Toehold

Richard Selzer

MORNING ROUNDS.

On the fifth floor of the hospital, in the west wing, I know that a man is sitting up in his bed, waiting for me. Elihu Koontz is seventy-five, and he is diabetic. It is two weeks since I amputated his left leg just below the knee. I walk down the corridor, but I do not go straight into his room. Instead, I pause in the doorway. He is not yet aware of my presence, but gazes down at the place in the bed where his leg used to be, and where now there is the collapsed leg of his pajamas. He is totally absorbed, like an athlete appraising the details of his body. What is he thinking, I wonder. Is he dreaming the outline of his toes? Does he see there his foot's incandescent ghost? Could he be angry? Feel that I have taken from him something for which he yearns now with all his heart? Has he forgotten so soon the pain? It was a pain so great as to set him apart from all other men, in a red-hot place where he had no kith or kin. What of those black gorilla toes and the soupy mess that was his heel? I watch him from the doorway. It is a kind of spying, I know.

Save for a white fringe open at the front, Elihu Koontz is bald. The hair has grown too long and is wilted. He wears it as one would wear a day-old laurel wreath. He is naked to the waist, so that I can see his breasts. They are the breasts of Buddha, inverted triangles from which the nipples swing, dark as garnets.

I have seen enough. I step into the room, and he sees that I am there.

"How did the night go, Elihu?"

He looks at me for a long moment. "Shut the door," he says.

I do, and move to the side of the bed. He takes my left hand in both of his, gazes at it, turns it over, then back, fondling, at last holding it up to his cheek. I do not withdraw from this loving. After a while he relinquishes my hand, and looks up at me.

"How is the pain?" I ask.

He does not answer, but continues to look at me in silence. I know at once that he has made a decision.

"Ever hear of The Masked Marvel?" He says this in a low voice, almost a whisper.

"What?"

"The Masked Marvel," he says. "You never heard of him?"

"No."

He clucks his tongue. He is exasperated.

All at once there is a recollection. It is dim, distant, but coming near.

"Do you mean the wrestler?"

Eagerly, he nods, and the breasts bob. How gnomish he looks, oval as the huge helpless egg of some outlandish lizard. He has very long arms, which, now and then, he unfurls to reach for things—a carafe of water, a get-well card. He gazes up at me, urging. He *wants* me to remember.

"Well . . . yes," I say. I am straining backward in time.

"I saw him wrestle in Toronto long ago."

"Ha!" He smiles. "You saw *me*." And his index finger, held rigid and up-right, bounces in the air.

The man has said something shocking, unacceptable. It must be challenged.

"You?" I am trying to smile.

Again that jab of the finger. "You saw *me*."

"No," I say. But even then, something about Elihu Koontz, those prolonged arms, the shape of his head, the sudden agility with which he leans from his bed to get a large brown envelope from his nightstand, something is forcing me to-ward a memory. He rummages through his papers, old newspaper clippings, photographs, and I remember. . . .

It is almost forty years ago. I am ten years old. I have been sent to Toronto to spend the summer with relatives. Uncle Max has bought two tickets to the wrestling match. He is taking me that night.

"He isn't allowed," says Aunt Sarah to me. Uncle Max has angina.

"He gets too excited," she says.

"I wish you wouldn't go, Max," she says.

"You mind your own business," he says.

And we go. Out into the warm Canadian evening. I am not only abroad, I am abroad in the *evening!* I have never been taken out in the evening. I am terribly excited. The trolleys, the lights, the horns. It is a bazaar. At the Maple Leaf Gardens, we sit high and near the center. The vast arena is dark except for the brilliance of the ring at the bottom.

It begins.

The wrestlers circle. They grapple. They are all haunch and paunch. I am shocked by their ugliness, but I do not show it. Uncle Max is exhilarated. He leans forward, his eyes unblinking, on his face a look of enormous happiness. One after the other, a pair of wrestlers enter the ring. The two men join, twist, jerk, tug, bend, yank, and throw. Then they leave and are replaced by another pair. At last it is the main event. "The Angel vs. The Masked Marvel."

On the cover of the program notes, there is a picture of The Angel hanging from the limb of a tree, a noose of thick rope around his neck. The Angel hangs just so for an hour every day, it is explained, to strengthen his neck. The Masked Marvel's trademark is a black stocking cap with holes for the eyes and mouth. He is never seen without it, states the program. No one knows who The Masked Marvel really is!

"Good," says Uncle Max. "Now you'll see something." He is fidgeting, waiting for them to appear. They come down separate aisles, climb into the ring from opposite sides. I have never seen anything like them. It is The Angel's neck that first captures the eye. The shaved nape rises in twin columns to puff into the white hood of a sloped and bosselated skull that is too small. As though, strangled by the sinews of that neck, the skull had long since withered and shrunk. The thing about The Angel is the absence of any mystery in his body. It is simply *there.* A monosyllabic announcement. A grunt. One looks and knows everything at once, the fat thighs, the gigantic buttocks, the great spine from which hang knotted ropes and pale aprons of beef. And that prehistoric head. He is all of a single hideous piece, The Angel is. No detachables.

The Masked Marvel seems dwarfish. His fingers dangle kneeward. His short legs are slightly bowed as if under the weight of the cask they are forced to heft about. He has breasts that swing when he moves! I have never seen such breasts on a man before.

There is a sudden ungraceful movement, and they close upon one another. The Angel stoops and hugs The Marvel about the waist, locking his hands behind The Marvel's back. Now he straightens and lifts The Marvel as though he were uprooting a tree. Thus he holds him, then stoops again, thrusts one hand through The Marvel's crotch, and with the other grabs him by the neck. He rears and . . . The Marvel is aloft! For a long moment, The Angel stands as though deciding where to make the toss. Then throws. Was that board or bone that splintered there? Again and again, The Angel hurls himself upon the body of The Masked Marvel.

Now The Angel rises over the fallen Marvel, picks up one foot in both of his hands, and twists the toes downward. It is far beyond the tensile strength of mere ligament, mere cartilage. The Masked Marvel does not hide his agony, but pounds and slaps the floor with his hand, now and then reaching up toward The Angel in an attitude of supplication. I have never seen such suffering. And all the while his black mask rolls from side to side, the mouth pulled to a tight slit through which issues an endless hiss that I can hear from where I sit. All at once, I hear a shouting close by.

"Break it off! Tear off a leg and throw it up here!"

It is Uncle Max. Even in the darkness I can see that he is gray. A band of sweat stands upon his upper lip. He is on his feet now, panting, one fist pressed at his chest, the other raised warlike toward the ring. For the first time I begin to think that something terrible might happen here. Aunt Sarah was right.

"Sit down, Uncle Max," I say. "Take a pill, please."

He reaches for the pillbox, gropes, and swallows without taking his gaze from the wrestlers. I wait for him to sit down.

"That's not fair," I say, "twisting his toes like that."

"It's the toehold," he explains.

"But it's not *fair*," I say again. The whole of the evil is laid open for me to perceive. I am trembling.

And now The Angel does something unspeakable. Holding the foot of The Marvel at full twist with one hand, he bends and grasps the mask where it clings to the back of The Marvel's head. And he pulls. He is going to strip it off! Lay bare an ultimate carnal mystery! Suddenly it is beyond mere physical violence. Now I am on my feet, shouting into the Maple Leaf Gardens.

"Watch out," I scream. "Stop him. Please, somebody, stop him."

Next to me, Uncle Max is chuckling.

Yet The Masked Marvel hears me, I know it. And rallies from his bed of pain. Thrusting with his free heel, he strikes The Angel at the back of the knee. The Angel falls. The Masked Marvel is on top of him, pinning his shoulders to the mat. One! Two! Three! And it is over. Uncle Max is strangely still. I am gasping for breath. All this I remember as I stand at the bedside of Elihu Koontz.

Once again, I am in the operating room. It is two years since I amputated the left leg of Elihu Koontz. Now it is his right leg which is gangrenous. I have already scrubbed. I stand to one side wearing my gown and gloves. And . . . *I am masked.* Upon the table lies Elihu Koontz, pinned in a fierce white light. Spinal anesthesia has been administered. One of his arms is taped to a board placed at a right angle to his body. Into this arm, a needle has been placed. Fluid drips here from a bottle overhead. With his other hand, Elihu Koontz beats feebly at the side of the operating table. His head rolls from side to side. His mouth is pulled into weeping. It seems to me that I have never seen such misery.

An orderly stands at the foot of the table, holding Elihu Koontz's leg aloft by the toes so that the intern can scrub the limb with antiseptic solutions. The intern paints the foot, ankle, leg, and thigh, both front and back, three times. From a corner of the room where I wait, I look down as from an amphitheater. Then I think of Uncle Max yelling, "Tear off a leg. Throw it up here." And I think that forty years later I am making the catch.

"It's not fair," I say aloud. But no one hears me. I step forward to break The Masked Marvel's last toehold.

I Stand Here Writing

Nancy Sommers

I stand in my kitchen, wiping the cardamom, coriander, and cayenne off my fingers. My head is abuzz with words, with bits and pieces of conversation. I hear a phrase I have read recently, something about "a radical loss of certainty." But, I wonder, how did the sentence begin? I search the air for the rest of the sentence, can't find it, shake some more cardamom, and a bit of coriander. Then, by some play of mind, I am back home again in Indiana with my family, sitting around the kitchen table. Two people are talking, and there are three opinions; three people are talking, and there are six opinions. Opinions grow exponentially. I fight my way back to that sentence. Writing, that's how it begins: "Writing is a radical loss of certainty." (Or is it uncertainty?) It isn't so great for the chicken when all these voices start showing up, with all these sentences hanging in mid-air, but the voices keep me company. I am a writer, not a cook, and the truth is I don't care much about the chicken. Stories beget stories. Writing emerges from writing.

The truth. Has truth anything to do with the facts? All I know is that no matter how many facts I might clutter my life with, I am as bound to the primordial drama of my family as the earth is to the sun. This year my father, the son of a severe Prussian matriarch, watched me indulge my daughters, and announced to me that he wished I had been his mother. This year, my thirty-ninth, my last year to be thirty-something, my mother—who has a touch of magic, who can walk into the middle of a field of millions of clovers and find the *one* with four leaves—has begun to think I need help. She sends me cards monthly with four-leaf clovers taped inside. Two words neatly printed in capital letters—GOOD LUCK!! I look at these clovers and hear Reynolds Price's words: "Nobody under forty can believe how nearly everything's inherited." I wonder what my mother knows, what she is trying to tell me about the facts of my life.

When I was in high school studying French, laboring to conjugate verbs, the numerous four-leaf clovers my mother had carefully pressed inside her French dictionary made me imagine her in a field of clovers lyrically conjugating verbs of love. This is the only romantic image I have of my mother, a shy and conservative woman whose own mother died when she was five, whose grandparents were killed by the Nazis, who fled Germany at age thirteen with her father and sister. Despite the sheer facts of her life, despite the accumulation of grim knowable data, the truth is my mother is an optimistic person. She has the curious capacity always to be looking for luck, putting her faith in four-leaf clovers, ladybugs, pennies, and other amulets of fortune. She has a vision different from mine, one the facts alone can't explain. I, her daughter, was left, for a long time, seeing only the ironies; they were my defense against the facts of my life.

In this world of my inheritance in which daughters can become their fathers' mothers and mothers know their daughters are entering into a world where only sheer good luck will guide them, I hear from my own daughters that I am not in tune with their worlds, that I am just like a 50s mom, that they are 90s children, and I should stop acting so primitive. My children laugh uproariously at my autograph book, a 1959 artifact they unearthed in the basement of my parents' home. "Never kiss by the garden gate. Love is blind, but the neighbors ain't," wrote one friend. And my best friend, who introduced herself to me on the first day of first grade, looking me straight in the eye—and whispering through her crooked little teeth "the Jews killed Jesus"—wrote in this autograph book: "Mary had a little lamb. Her father shot it dead. Now she carries it to school between two slices of bread."

My ten-year-old daughter, Rachel, writes notes to me in hieroglyphics and tapes signs on the refrigerator in Urdu. "Salaarn Namma Man Rachaal Ast" reads one sign. Simply translated it means "Hello, my name is Rachel." Alex, my seven-year-old daughter, writes me lists, new lists each month, visibly reminding me of the many things I need to buy or do for her. This month's list includes a little refrigerator filled with Coke and candy; ears pierced; a new toilet; neon nail polish and *real* adult make-up.

How do I look at these facts? How do I embrace these experiences, these texts of my life, and translate them into ideas? How do I make sense of them and the conversations they engender in my head? I look at Alex's list and wonder what kind of feminist daughter I am raising whose deepest desires include neon nail polish and *real* adult make-up. Looking at her lists a different way, I wonder if this second child of mine is asking me for something larger, something more permanent and real than adult make-up. Maybe I got that sentence wrong. Maybe it is that "Love (as well as writing) involves a radical loss of certainty."

Love is blind, but the neighbors ain't. Mary's father shot her little lamb dead, and now she carries it to school between two slices of bread. I hear these rhymes today, and they don't say to me what they say to my daughters. They don't seem so innocent. I hear them and think about the ways in which my neighbors in Indiana could only see my family as Jews from Germany, exotic strangers who ate tongue, outsiders who didn't celebrate Christmas. I wonder if my daughter Rachel needs to tell me her name in Urdu because she thinks we don't share a common language. These sources change meaning when I ask the questions in a different way. They introduce new ironies, new questions.

I want to understand these living, breathing, primary sources all around me. I want to be, in Henry James's words, "a person upon whom nothing is lost." These sources speak to me of love and loss, of memory and desire, of the ways in which we come to understand something through difference and opposition. Two years ago I learned the word *segue* from one of my students. At first the word seemed peculiar. Segue sounded like something you did only on the Los Angeles freeway. Now I hear that word everywhere, and I have begun using it. I want to know how to segue from one idea to the next, from one thought to the fragment lying beside it. But the connections don't always come with four-leaf clovers and the words GOOD LUCK neatly printed beside them.

My academic need to find connections sends me to the library. There are eleven million books in my University's libraries. Certainly these sanctioned voices, these authorities, these published sources can help me find the connections. Someone, probably some three thousand someones, has studied what it is like to be the child of survivors. Someone has written a manual on how the granddaughter of a severe Prussian matriarch and the daughter of a collector of amulets ought to raise feminist daughters. I want to walk into the fields of writing, into those eleven million books, and find the one book that will explain it all. But I've learned to expect less from such sources. They seldom have the answers. And the answers they do have reveal themselves to me at the most unexpected times. I have been led astray more than once while searching books for the truth.

Once I learned a lesson about borrowing someone else's words and losing my own.

I was fourteen, light years away from thirty-something. High school debate teams across the nation were arguing the pros and cons of the United States Military Aid Policy. It all came back to me as I listened to the news of the Persian Gulf War, as I listened to Stormin' Norman giving his morning briefings, an eerie resonance, all our arguments, the millions of combative words—sorties—fired back and forth. In my first practice debate, not having had enough time to assemble my own sources, I borrowed quote cards from my teammates. I attempted to bolster my position that the U.S. should limit its military aid by reading a quote in my best debate style: "W. W. Rostow says: 'We should not give military aid to India because it will exacerbate endemic rivalries.'"

Under cross-examination, my nemesis, Bobby Rosenfeld, the neighbor kid, who always knew the right answers, began firing a series of questions at me without stopping to let me answer:

"Nancy, can you tell me who W. W. Rostow is? And can you tell me why he might say this? Nancy, can you tell me what 'exacerbate' means? Can you tell me what 'endemic rivalries' are? And exactly what does it mean to 'exacerbate endemic rivalries'?"

I didn't know. I simply did not know who W. W. Rostow was, why he might have said that, what "exacerbate" meant, or what an "endemic rivalry" was. Millions of four-leaf clovers couldn't have helped me. I might as well have been speaking Urdu. I didn't know who my source was, the context of the source, nor the literal meaning of the words I had read. Borrowing words from authorities had left me without any words of my own.

My debate partner and I went on that year to win the Indiana state championship and to place third in the nationals. Bobby Rosenfeld never cross-examined me again, but for twenty years he has appeared in my dreams. I am not certain why I would dream so frequently about this scrawny kid whom I despised. I think, though, that he became for me what the Sea Dyak tribe of Borneo calls a *ngarong*, a dream guide, someone guiding me to understanding. In this case, Bobby guided me to understand the endemic rivalries within myself. The last time Bobby appeared in a dream he had become a woman.

I learned a more valuable lesson about sources as a college senior. I was the kind of student who loved words, words out of context, words that swirled around inside my mouth, words like *exacerbate, undulating, lugubrious,* and *zeugma.* "She stained her honour or her new brocade," wrote Alexander Pope. I would try to write zeugmas whenever I could, exacerbating my already lugubrious prose. Within the English department, I was known more for my long hair, untamed and untranslatable, and for my long distance bicycle rides than for my scholarship.

For my senior thesis, I picked Emerson's essay "Eloquence." Harrison Hayford, my advisor, suggested that I might just get off my bicycle, get lost in the library, and read all of Emerson's essays, journals, letters. I had picked one of Emerson's least distinguished essays, an essay that the critics mentioned only in passing, and if I were not entirely on my own, I had at least carved out new territory for myself.

I spent weeks in the library reading Emerson's journals, reading newspaper accounts from Rockford and Peoria, Illinois, where he had first delivered "Eloquence" as a speech. Emerson stood at the podium, the wind blowing his papers hither and yon, calmly picking them up, and proceeding to read page 8 followed by page 3, followed by page 6, followed by page 2. No one seemed to know the difference. Emerson's Midwestern audience was overwhelmed by this strange man from Concord, Massachusetts, this eloquent stranger whose unit of expression was the sentence.

As I sat in the library, wearing my QUESTION AUTHORITY T-shirt, I could admire this man who delivered his Divinity School Address in 1838, speaking words so repugnant to the genteel people of Cambridge that it was almost thirty years before Harvard felt safe having him around again. I could understand the Midwestern audience's awe and adulation as they listened but didn't quite comprehend Emerson's stunning oratory. I had joined the debate team not to argue the U.S. Military Aid Policy, but to learn how to be an orator who could stun audiences, to learn a personal eloquence I could never learn at home. Perhaps only children of immigrant parents can understand the embarrassing moments of inarticulateness, the missed connections that come from learning to speak a language from parents who claim a different mother tongue.

As an undergraduate, I wanted to free myself from that mother tongue. Four-leaf clovers and amulets of oppression weighed heavy on my mind, and I could see no connection whatsoever between those facts of my life and the untranslatable side of myself that set me in opposition to authority. And then along came Emerson. Like his Midwest audience, I didn't care about having him whole. I liked the promise and the rhapsodic freedom I found in his sentences, in his invitation to seize life as our dictionary, to believe that "Life was not something to be learned but to be lived." I loved his insistence that "the one thing of value is the active soul." I read that "Books are for the scholar's idle time," and I knew that he had given me permission to explore the world. Going into Emerson was like walking into a revelation; it was the first time I had gone into the texts not looking for a specific answer, and it was the first time the texts gave me the answers I needed. Never mind that I got only part of what Emerson was telling me. I got inspiration, I got insight, and I began to care deeply about my work.

Today I reread the man who set me off on a new road, and I find a different kind of wisdom. Today I reread "The American Scholar," and I don't underline the sentence "Books are for the scholar's idle time." I continue to the next paragraph, underlining the sentence "One must be an inventor to read well." The second sentence doesn't contradict the one I read twenty years ago, but it means more today. I bring more to it, and I know that I can walk into text after text, source after source, and they will give me insight, but not answers. I have learned too that my sources can surprise me. Like my mother, I find myself sometimes surrounded by a field of four-leaf clovers, there for the picking, waiting to see what I can make of them. But I must be an inventor if I am to read those sources well, if I am to imagine the connections.

As I stand in my kitchen, the voices that come to me come by way of a lifetime of reading, they come on the waves of life, and they seem to be helping me translate the untranslatable. They come, not at my bidding, but when I least expect them, when I am receptive enough to listen to their voices. They come when I am open.

If I could teach my students one lesson about writing it would be to see themselves as sources, as places from which ideas originate, to see themselves as Emerson's transparent eyeball, all that they have read and experienced—the dictionaries of their lives—circulating through them. I want them to learn how sources thicken, complicate, enlarge writing, but I want them to know too how it is always the writer's voice, vision, and argument that create the new source. I want my students to see that nothing reveals itself straight out, especially the sources all around them. But I know enough by now that this Emersonian ideal can't be passed on in one lesson or even a semester of lessons.

Many of the students who come to my classes have been trained to collect facts; they act as if their primary job is to accumulate enough authorities so that there is no doubt about the "truth" of their thesis. They most often disappear behind the weight and permanence of their borrowed words, moving their pens, mouthing the words of others, allowing sources to speak through them unquestioned, unexamined.

At the outset, many of my students think that personal writing is writing about the death of their grandmother. Academic writing is reporting what Elizabeth Kübler-Ross has written about death and dying. Being personal, I want to show my students, does not mean being autobiographical. Being academic does not mean being remote, distant, imponderable. Being personal means bringing their judgments and interpretation to bear on what they read and write, learning that they never leave themselves behind even when they write academic essays.

Last year, David Gray came into my essay class disappointed about everything. He didn't like the time of the class, didn't like the reading list, didn't seem to like me. Nothing pleased him. "If this is a class on the essay," he asked the first day, "why aren't we reading real essayists like Addison, Steele, and Lamb?" On the second day, after being asked to read Annie Dillard's "Living Like Weasels," David complained that a weasel wasn't a fit subject for an essay. "Writers need big subjects. Look at Melville. He needed a whale for *Moby-Dick.* A weasel—that's nothing but a rodent." And so it continued for a few weeks.

I kept my equanimity in class, but at home I'd tell my family about this kid who kept testing me, seizing me like Dillard's weasel, and not letting go. I secretly wanted him out of my class. But then again, I sensed in him a kindred spirit, someone else who needed to question authority.

I wanted my students to write exploratory essays about education, so I asked them to think of a time when they had learned something, and then a time when they had tried to learn something but couldn't. I wanted them to see what ideas and connections they could find between these two very different experiences and the other essays they were reading for the class. I wanted the various sources to work as catalysts. I wanted my students to find a way to talk back to those other writers. The assigned texts were an odd assortment with few apparent connections. I hoped my students would find the common ground, but also the moments of tension, the contradictions, and the ambiguities in those sources.

David used the assigned texts as a catalyst for his thinking, but as was his way, he went beyond the texts I offered and chose his own. He begins his essay, "Dulcis Est Sapientia," with an account of his high school Latin class, suggesting that he once knew declensions, that he had a knack for conjugations, but has forgotten them. He tells us that if his teacher were to appear suddenly today and demand the perfect subjunctive of *venire,* he would stutter hopelessly.

About that Latin class, David asks, "What is going on here? Did I once know Latin and forget it through disuse? Perhaps I never learned Latin at all. What I learned was a bunch of words which, with the aid of various ending sounds, indicated that Gaius was either a good man delivering messages to the lieutenant or a general who struck camp at the seventh hour. I may have known it once, but I never learned it." The class never gave David the gift of language. There was something awry in the method.

What is learning? That's what David explores in his essay as he moves from his Latin lesson to thinking about surrealist paintings, to thinking about barriers we create, to Plato, to an airplane ride in which he observed a mother teaching her child concepts of color and number, all the time taking his readers along with him on his journey, questioning sources, reflecting, expanding, and enriching his growing sense that learning should stress ideas rather than merely accumulating facts and information.

David draws his essay to a close with an analysis of a joke: A man goes to a cocktail party and gets soused. He approaches his host and asks, "Pardon me, but do lemons whistle?"

The host looks at him oddly and answers, "No, lemons don't whistle."

"Oh dear," says the guest, "then I'm afraid I just squeezed your canary into my gin and tonic."

David reflects about the significance of this joke: "One need not be an ornithologist to get the joke, but one must know that canaries are yellow and that they whistle. . . . What constitutes the joke is a connection made between two things . . . which have absolutely nothing in common except for their yellowness. It would never occur to us to make a comparison between the two, let alone to confuse one with the other. But this is the value of the joke, to force into our consciousness the ideas which we held but never actively considered. . . . This knocking down of barriers between ideas is parallel to the process that occurs in all learning. The barriers that we set . . . suddenly crumble; the boundaries . . . are extended to include other modes of thought." Learning, like joking, David argues, gives us pleasure by satisfying our innate capacity to recognize coherence, to discern patterns and connections.

David's essay, like any essay, does not intend to offer the last word on its subject. The civilizing influence of an essay is that it keeps the conversation going, chronicling an intellectual journey, reflecting conversations with sources. I am confident that when David writes for his philosophy course he won't tell a joke anywhere in his essay. But if the joke—if any of his sources—serves him as a catalyst for his thinking, if he makes connections among the sources that circulate within him, between Plato and surrealism, between Latin lessons and mother-child lessons—the dictionaries of *his* life—then he has learned something valuable about writing.

I say to myself that I don't believe in luck. And yet. Not too long ago Rachel came home speaking with some anxiety about an achievement test that she had to take at school. Wanting to comfort her, I urged her to take my rabbit's foot to school the next day. Always alert to life's ironies, Rachel said, "Sure, Mom, a rabbit's foot will really help me find the answers. And even if it did, how would I know the answer the next time when I didn't have that furry little claw?" The next day, proud of her ease in taking the test, she remained perplexed by the one question that seized her and wouldn't let go. She tried it on me: "Here's the question," she said. "Can you figure out which of these sentences cannot be true?"

a. We warmed our hands by the fire.
b. The rain poured in and around the windows.
c. The wind beckoned us to open the door.

Only in the mind of someone who writes achievement tests, and wants to close the door on the imagination, could the one false sentence be "The wind beckoned us to open the door." Probably to this kind of mind, Emerson's sentence "Life is our dictionary" is also not a true sentence.

But life *is* our dictionary, and that's how we know that the wind can beckon us to open the door. Like Emerson, we let the wind blow our pages hither and yon, forcing us to start in the middle, moving from page 8 to page 2, forward to page 7, moving back and forth in time, losing our certainty.

Like Emerson, I love basic units, the words themselves, words like cardamom, coriander, words that play around in my head, swirl around in my mouth. The challenge, of course, is not to be a ventriloquist—not to be a mouther of words—but to be open to other voices, untranslatable as they might be. Being open to the unexpected, we can embrace complexities: canaries and lemons, amulets and autograph books, fathers who want their daughters to be their mothers, and daughters who write notes in Urdu—all those odd, unusual conjunctions can come together and speak through us.

The other day, I called my mother and told her about this essay, told her that I had been thinking about the gold bracelet she took with her as one of her few possessions from Germany—a thin gold chain with three amulets: a mushroom, a lady bug, and, of course, a four-leaf clover. Two other charms fell off years ago— she lost one, I the other. I used to worry over the missing links, thinking only of the loss, of what we could never retrieve. When I look at the bracelet now, I think about the Prussian matriarch, my grandmother, and my whole primordial family drama. I think too of Emerson and the pages that blew in the wind and the gaps that seemed not to matter. The bracelet is but one of many sources that intrigues me. Considering them in whatever order they appear, with whatever gaps, I want to see where they will lead me, what they tell me.

With writing and with teaching, as well as with love, we don't know how the sentence will begin and, rarely ever, how it will end. Having the courage to live with uncertainty, ambiguity, even doubt, we can walk into all of those fields of writing, knowing that we will find volumes upon volumes bidding *us* enter. We need only be inventors, we need only give freely and abundantly to the texts, imagining even as we write that we too will be a source from which other readers can draw sustenance.

Chin Music

Michael Steinberg

I was wrapping up a discussion of *Huck Finn,* and as I began to recite the assignments, my students were already shuffling their feet, packing up books, and grabbing for their coats—the usual cues that it's time for the teacher to quit talking. In the past, I'd often take the hint and end the hour quickly. But lately, I noticed, I'd become less and less patient.

I paused for a second to look at my notes. That's when I spotted Drew—a student I'd already targeted as a trouble maker—moving toward the door. Just as he was about to open it, I said in a tone that was sharper than intended. "Excuse me, but class isn't over yet."

"I thought you were done," he said. Then he murmured under his breath, "You've been lecturing at us for over an hour." Whether it was deliberate or not, he said it loud enough for everyone to hear.

I knew I should let it go, or make light of it somehow. But before I could catch myself, it slipped out. "Drew, you're a fucking piss ant" I said. "Sit your god damned ass down 'til I dismiss the class."

Everyone, including me, was stunned. His eyes blazing, Drew shuffled back to his seat, deliberately kicking the trash can on his way. "Keep it up, pal," I whispered to myself. His coat buttoned to the throat, Drew sat down very slowly and turned his head toward the window.

This wasn't the first time we'd done this little dance. In the first week of the semester, Drew had written an exercise that I liked so much I read it to the class. When I praised the authenticity of the writing, he intervened. "None of that crap was true," he said. "I made the whole thing up."

Students had challenged me before, but never quite this aggressively, and certainly not without some provocation. So, I approached this kid a little more cautiously than I normally do.

"Why did you make it up?" I asked, making certain to keep my tone as neutral as possible.

"Because it was such a Mickey Mouse assignment," he said. So much for being tactful, I thought.

There were some "oohs," followed by a round of nervous giggles. I wanted to lash back, say something nasty or sarcastic. But instead, I took the high ground again. "Fiction or nonfiction," I said, "it's still a good piece of writing." And I left it at that.

Not so tonight, though. Visibly flustered, I stumbled through the litany of assignments. And when the class had filed out, I called Drew up to my desk.

"Look, Drew," I began. "I think you should know why I said wha . . ."

He cut me off in mid-sentence. "You showed me up in front of the whole class," he said. "You owe me an apology."

Then he waited a few seconds while I searched for a reply. Did this kid really believe that he'd done nothing wrong? Just as I was about to respond, he pivoted and headed for the door.

By the time I got home, I was furious—at him, of course—and at myself, for taking the bait. I took a walk around the block to try and calm down. But all I could think about was the anger and resentment that had been building inside me for such a long time.

My patience with freshmen was wearing thin. When students said goofy things like "This sucks. Why can't we read happier books?" my comments were becoming more defensive. I even tossed a few guys out of class when they showed up unprepared or without books. Also a first for me.

Two eye surgeries had given me a chance to step back from teaching for almost two years. Sometimes an enforced absence is just what you need to reinvigorate yourself. But when I got back in the classroom, I could see right away that things had changed.

Or maybe it was it me who'd changed. By mid-semester, I felt like a space invader in my own classroom. Some of my freshmen glided mindlessly into class on skateboards or roller blades. Some wore headphones and others ate snacks and drank soda while I talked. A few even had the chutzpah to take calls on their cell phones.

Conditions outside of class had also changed. For one, I was receiving frequent reports from the counseling center, bureaucratic memos informing me about students who were in alcohol or drug rehab, or who had eating disorders and histories of family abuse. And then there was the student who sent me an email apologizing for not doing her essay on time. She said, without a trace of irony, that she missed the deadline because she'd attempted suicide that weekend. She hoped I'd understand and that I'd give her an extension. Coupled with the effects of over two decades of student papers, mind-numbing faculty meetings, and obligatory committee work, this latest confrontation left me wondering if maybe it wasn't time to move on.

The next day, I was having lunch with a colleague from the Physiology department—someone who I meet with regularly to talk about teaching. She was telling me about two of her colleagues, one of whom she referred to as "an educator," and the other whom she called "a coach."

The word "coach" hit a nerve, and for a moment I drifted away from the conversation. In a sudden flashback, I saw myself at fifteen, standing next to Tom Sullivan, my old V.F.W. baseball coach. My God, I hadn't thought about this guy in almost forty years. Why now?

Just before I fell asleep that night, it all came rushing back. In my second year on Sullivan's team, I'd had a run-in with him, a skirmish that made me think seriously about quitting the game. A game I loved more than anything else in my adolescent world.

The episode came about on a bone-chilling Saturday morning in early March. It was the last day of tryouts and we were down to the final cut. I was on the mound and my best friend, Mike Rubin, was at bat. Last year we'd both made it to the final tryouts. But for some reason, Sullivan cut Rubin and kept me.

I only got to pitch in a few games that summer, so I was apprehensive when right before this year's tryouts began, Sullivan called me into his office. The room was a steam-heated cubbyhole above the St. Francis De Sales gym. Amidst the banging and hissing of the old pipes he told me in no uncertain terms that if I wanted to pitch this season I'd have to convince him that a Belle Harbor "sugar baby" had what it took to play ball for him.

And now, here I was on the mound of the church field staring down at Mike Rubin, who stood sixty feet six inches away nervously taking his practice cuts. Last year's team almost made it to the state finals at Cooperstown. We got eliminated in Westchester County—the final game of the regionals. I'd been thinking about it all winter, and I didn't want to blow my shot at playing summer league ball. But what about Mike? Since we were eight years old, we'd played on every team from Little League through P.A.L. This was his last chance to make the V.F.W. team. Next year we'd move up to American Legion, a tougher, more competitive league.

I knew Rubin couldn't hit the curve ball. If I threw him low breaking balls, my stock-in-trade, he was finished. Kaput. But if I pitched him too fat, Big Tom would know it. Then I'd be history too. While I was trying to figure out what to throw, Sullivan yelled, "Game situation," and ordered Andy Ortiz to be the runner at third. This was not a good sign. Ortiz was a football player from the Arverne projects. And he could hurt you. That's when Sullivan called for a suicide squeeze. It's a risky play, and it's meant to work like this: as soon as I go into my wind-up, Ortiz will head for home and Rubin will square around to bunt. My job is to make certain he doesn't bunt the ball in fair territory.

Instead of tossing me the ball, Sullivan swaggered out to the mound. As he slapped the grass-stained baseball into my glove, he deliberately sprayed black, bitter tobacco juice across the bridge of my nose. Then he motioned Danny Whalen, another football goon, to the mound.

Sullivan and I were inches apart. I could feel his breath on my right cheek. His nose was red and swollen, and slanted to the right. Broken three times in his college football days. Just as Whalen arrived, Coach rasped, "Steinberg, when Ortiz breaks from third, throw it at his head."

He meant the batter, Rubin. Why would I want to throw a baseball at my best friend's head? It wasn't the right strategy. It was another one of Big Tom's stupid tests of courage. I knew that sooner or later he'd be testing me. I just hadn't expected it to happen now.

"At his head, Coach?" I said, stalling for time.

Sullivan gave me his "that's-the-way-it's-done-around-here" look. It wasn't like I didn't know what he was doing. Everyone on the team understood that if you wanted to play ball for Big Tom you did what you were told and you kept your mouth shut. Why was I being such a smart-ass? It wasn't like me. Why was I so willing to risk it all here?

I tried to calm myself down, remind myself what the costs were. I kept telling myself to cool it. Just try and think it through. Pretend to go along with Big Tom's program. The whole time, though, I could feel the knot in my stomach twist and tighten.

Sullivan glared at the third base bleachers where the final eight guys fidgeted nervously, waiting for their chance to bat. Then he looked back at me. With his cap pulled low, the coach's steel-blue pig eyes seemed all the more penetrating. He smiled, but because part of his mouth was distorted from taking too many football hits without a face mask, it came off looking like a mocking leer. The gesture unnerved me even more. I could feel my palms getting clammy and my armpits were drenched with perspiration.

He said loudly for everyone to hear, "Steinberg, you've been with me for two years; let's show this wet-nosed bunch of rookies how we play this game."

Then he grabbed his crotch with his left hand. It was the old comrade routine. He was giving his second-year pitcher a chance to look like a leader by pretending we were buddies. But we weren't. Big Tom and I didn't operate in the same universe. He was a bull-yock Irishman from Hell's Kitchen, a high school stud who learned to fight in the streets. His platoon had fought in the Pacific, and the pride still showed in his eyes. To him, guys like Rubin and me were too privileged. And he resented us for it.

I turned to glance at Rubin. He looked like a Thanksgiving turkey on the block. I was embarrassed for him. Maybe the wind was just blowing at his sweatpants, the stiff ocean breeze we get on the Long Island south shore in early spring. Then again, maybe his knees really were shaking.

"Let's get the god-damned show on the road," Sullivan muttered. I thought about quitting, but our team was good. I had visions of Linda Foreman, our head cheerleader, walking around school wearing my V.F.W. jacket. And there was another incentive. We all knew that our high school coach, Jack Kerchman, scouted his players in the summer—looking to see who was getting better and who was dogging it.

Whalen trotted back behind the plate and Sullivan turned to leave. To him this kind of stuff was routine. I wanted to refuse, but this was my only chance to make it to Cooperstown, to see my dad sitting in the stands watching me pitch at Doubleday Field. I was red-in-the-face pissed, hoping it looked like windburn.

I tried to buy some time, hoping I could reason with Sullivan. Convince him there was another way to do this.

"You want me to stop the bunt, right?" I said meekly.

He turned. What the hell was I saying? Nobody second-guesses the Coach. Sullivan walked back to the mound and spat another wad of chew on the ground, making sure to splatter some on my new spikes. He looked at Whalen, then at Ortiz. Then he turned to me and shook his head from side to side.

"That's right, Steinberg. You stop the bunt. Now, let's please execute the fucking play, shall we?" He muttered to himself through clenched teeth as he trotted back toward the dugout.

It was out of my mouth before I knew it. "Suppose I hit him in the head?" Sullivan's own head swung around like a tetherball making the last tight twist at the top of the pole.

"Don't worry, it's not a vital organ. Pitch."

I think Big Tom knew that he was undermining his credibility by arguing with a piss-ant kid. So he turned and silenced everyone's murmurs with a long glare. As if rehearsed, the eight guys behind me started to grumble, distancing themselves from me and Sullivan's wrath.

"Pitch the fuckin' ball," yelled Whalen from behind the plate.

"Do what Coach tell you, man," spat Ortiz from third.

To those guys, Sullivan was George God. If he told them to take a dump at home plate, they'd get diarrhea. But me? I'm Gary Cooper in *High Noon.* Everyone's watching, no one's volunteering to help.

Then I noticed Mike Rubin, still frozen in his batter's crouch. He looked like a mannequin with bulging eyes. Poor Mike didn't have a prayer. But before I could think, the words slipped out.

"It's the wrong play, Coach."

It was my voice, all right, but it couldn't have been me who said it. I'd never have the guts to say anything like that to Sullivan's face.

Dead silence. You could hear the breeze whistling through the wire mesh of the backstop. At first, Sullivan was too surprised to even curse me out. But after a long moment, he turned and strode up to Rubin, who was still frozen in the box.

It was a considered ploy. I'd seen it before, in the streets. Coach was going to punish me by humiliating my best friend. Like all of us, Rubin was jack-rabbit scared of Sullivan. And just like a rabbit about to be prey, he stood riveted to the ground.

"God damn it," Sullivan ripped off his cap, exposing a jet black crewcut and sunburned forehead. He spoke like rolling thunder, enunciating every word.

"WHAT DID HE SAY, RUBIN?"

My stomach turned over watching Sullivan humiliate my best friend just for the amusement of the guys in the bleachers. And Big Tom knew it. Knew it oh so well.

Rubin managed weakly; "Uh, wrong—wrong play, Coach?"

Louder then, like a Marine D.I.: "NOBODY IN THE STANDS CAN HEAR YOU, RUBIN."

"WRONG PLAY, COACH."

Still advancing, Sullivan took it to the grandstand.

"ALL YOU LADIES, SAY IT!"

The accusing chorus rained down.

"WRONG PLAY, COACH."

"AGAIN."

"WRONG PLAY, COACH."

Then he ran out to the mound yelling, "YOU TOO, STEINBERG, YOU SAY IT."

He was hopping up and down like someone had pranked him with a hot foot. Adrenaline overcame me then, and before Sullivan could order another round, I let the words tumble out in a single breath. "If I throw a pitch-out chest high in the left hand batter's box, all Danny has to do is take two steps to his right and he has a clear shot at Ortiz." I was parroting what Joe Bleutrich, my P.A.L. coach, had taught me two years ago.

By now, my stomach was in knots, Rubin's eyes looked like marbles, and the whole team was hungry to see what would happen next. Sullivan squared himself and casually put his cap back on. He was trying to regain his composure. He'd let a snot-nosed high school kid get to him and now he had to regain control.

Softly now: "That's enough, Steinberg."

Then to Rubin: "Get back in the box. Let's do the play."

And to be sure there was no misunderstanding, he took it right back to me: "My play," he said deliberately. "My play, my way."

He was giving me a second chance. Why didn't I just fake it? I had good control. I'd brushed off plenty of hitters before. Maybe deep down I believed that Sullivan was right about me. Maybe I didn't have what it took to play for him.

I wanted to give in, get it over with. So I said, "I can't do it."

Sullivan slammed his cap to the ground, and in one honest, reckless moment, it came out:

"You Belle Harbor Jews are all alike. No god-damn guts. You're a disgrace to your own people."

Nobody moved. The wind whipped a funnel of dust through the hard clay infield.

So that's what this was all about. Some of the guys, I'm sure, had thought the same thing. But we were teammates and they'd never say it to my face. We all knew that Big Tom didn't favor Jews. But even in my worst moments I believed that this stuff was for the anti-Semites from the sticks, the ones who say "Jew York."

There was no chance Sullivan would apologize. He'd used tactics like this before—to get us mad, to fire us up. If I wanted to be a real putz, I could report him to the league's advisory board. My dad knew most of the officers. But I knew I wouldn't do it. Because if I turned him in, it would confirm what he already thought of me. And I didn't want to give him the satisfaction. Besides, I needed him. And in some odd way, I must have sensed that he needed me. Why else would he be testing me like this? For the moment we were yoked to each other, like Sidney Poitier and Tony Curtis in that movie *The Defiant Ones.*

I think Sullivan believed that somehow I had made him say what he said. He was angry at me for making him look bad. So to cover himself he had to make it seem like it was my fault.

"Get out of my sight, Steinberg," he snapped. "You make me wanna puke."

He motioned toward the bullpen. "Levy, get your butt in here and pitch."

Why Levy? Bert was also a Belle Harbor Jew. And to my mind, he was more timid than anyone else in the neighborhood. On second thought, maybe that was part of Big Tom's design.

Sullivan grunted, the cords of his muscular neck wound tight. He reached to take the ball. Just as he grabbed for it, something snapped inside me; I snatched the baseball back. Then an eerie calm began to wash over me. My stomach stopped churning, my chest didn't feel as if it was about to burst, and my neck wasn't burning. I could tell that Sullivan sensed something was going on, but he wasn't sure what it was. Neither was I. Not yet, anyway.

"I'm not leaving, Coach," I said.

Yeah, he sensed it all right. But he misread it. He waved Levy away. Maybe this was Sullivan's obtuse way of atoning for the Jew remark, by allowing me to stay on *his* pitcher's mound.

"Get back in the box, Rubin," he snapped.

"No, Coach," I said.

"What?"

"You grab a bat, Coach."

A frozen moment. Was I really doing this? I recalled the day at football practice when Stuie Scheneider had knocked Coach Kerchman right on his ass. Kerchman goaded him into it, and Stuie took the bait. Is this what was happening here?

Sullivan looked at me, then he looked at the guys in the bleachers and laughed out loud. We all knew he was going to do it. He ripped off his windbreaker and took a couple of practice cuts, biceps rippling. Sullivan didn't seem to mind when muffled cheers rose up from the third base side. He was wearing that crooked-ass grin of his. The players in the bleachers spilled into foul territory, inching closer to the backstop.

"Okay, Coach," I'm thinking. "You're gonna get just what you asked for."

I was ready to play me some chin music. Chin music, where the ball whistles as it passes under the batter's throat. Before I went into my windup, Whalen took two steps up the first base line. He was sure I was going to throw the pitch-out. Can't blame him. It's what he would have done. It's what anyone in his right mind would have done. Sullivan must have thought so too, that's why he was grinning.

It was the smirk that did it. "Screw chin music, I'll take his goddamn head off."

Then I saw Ortiz streaking from third toward home. In that split second I realized, maybe for the first time, that this really was happening. As Big Tom squared to bunt, I zeroed in on the black line that runs along the inside corner of the plate. "Calm down," I told myself. "Brush him back. Just let him know you're here."

That's what my head was saying, but when I started my motion I lifted my eyes away from the plate and locked them on the bill of Sullivan's cap. Then I pushed hard off the rubber and cut loose. I watched the ball tailing in, in, in, right toward Sullivan's head. But he didn't back off, not even an inch. That shit-eating grin was still on his face. I yelled, "HEADS UP," tucked my chin into my chest and shut my eyes. Then I heard a dull thud. I opened my eyes and watched his cap fly off his head. And as I saw him crumble, feet splayed in the dirt, I felt nauseous.

Stunned players surrounded the fallen Sullivan, not knowing what to do. With leaden strides, I joined them, growing a little more lucid. Rubin shot me a "Man, you are dead meat" look, and I thought about suspension from school. Jail even. But the coach sat up. Jesus, was he lucky. Was I lucky. I must have clipped him right on the bill of the cap. Why was I so surprised? It was the target I was aiming at.

Sighs escaped as one breath. Legs and arms unraveled. Players backed away. Slowly, Big Tom lifted himself up and brushed the dirt off the seat of his pants. He shook his head like a wet cocker spaniel who'd just taken a dip in the ocean. Then he wobbled to the bleachers, looking like a young girl testing out her mother's high-heeled shoes.

Before I could collect my thoughts, Sullivan's voice boomed out: "All right, here we go again. Ortiz, hustle back to third, Rubin, up to bat, Steinberg, get your butt back on the hill. Suicide squeeze, same play as before. This time I know we will get it right, won't we, ladies?"

He'd caught me by surprise again. I should have known that he'd have the last word. But this time I couldn't—wouldn't—jump through his hoops again. So, I took a deep breath, bowed my head, and slowly walked toward the mound—all the time knowing exactly where I was headed. When I got to the rubber, I kept going. At second base, I pushed off the bag with my right foot and began to sprint. I began unbuttoning my shirt, and as I passed our center fielder, Ducky Warshauer, I tossed my cap and uniform jersey right at him. Ducky stared at me like I'd just gone Section Eight. When I stepped onto the walkway outside the locker room, I heard the metallic clack, clack, clack of my spikes on the concrete floor. I opened the door and inhaled the familiar perfume of chlorine, Oil of Wintergreen, and stale sweat socks. For a moment I thought about going back out there; instead I headed straight for the shower and pushed the lever as far to the right as it would go. As the needle spray bit into my shoulders, I watched the steam rise up to surround me.

On the bus ride home, I was thinking about what I'd just done. I did it, I told myself, because he provoked me. It wasn't a conscious decision; it was a knee-jerk response.

All weekend, I thought about the incident. Should I take what was left of my uniform to his office right before the next practice? Nope, all that would do is let him know he'd won. Ok, I'll wait for him to ask for it. But what if he doesn't? Will I lose my nerve and give in?

Sunday night, seven-thirty, he called me at home. Ten minutes later I was back in that stifling office, the steam pipes hissing and banging away. Sullivan was sitting at his desk, head down, shuffling papers. He made me wait for about two minutes. Didn't even look up. When he knew I couldn't take the tension any longer, he said matter-of-factly—as if nothing had ever happened—"I'll see you at practice on Saturday."

Without taking his eyes off his papers, he handed me my cap and jersey and said, "Get your butt out of here, kid. I got work to do."

Of course I went back. That's what you do when you're fifteen and your identity is wrapped up in playing baseball. I had a pretty good season too. And though we didn't win the state title, we did make it to Cooperstown.

While I was on the mound that summer I'd hear Sullivan razzing us from the bench. I always listened closely, curious to see how far he'd push me. But whatever else he yelled, I never heard him shout "sugar baby." And I later found out that Sullivan did indeed invite Coach Kerchman to scout me. He just never took the trouble to tell me about it.

The "incident" happened over four decades ago, and I still couldn't decide whether I won or lost that confrontation. Sometimes I think I got the best of him, and sometimes I think I misread him—that he deliberately goaded me into throwing the ball at his head.

But wondering who won or lost is really to miss the point. Like me, Sullivan was in his early fifties when this happened. Could it be that now in my fifties, I was turning into a version of my old coach?

In the past few years, I noticed that many of my colleagues had turned cynical in the latter stages of their careers. But they stayed on anyway—out of a kind of inertia or fear, perhaps. Or because they needed to put more time in before they could take their benefits or pensions. It was certainly not the way I wanted to end my teaching career.

When I first began to teach, I promised myself I'd never use fear or intimidation to motivate or punish my students. And for the most part, I'd kept that promise. But in the past decade, I'd noticed that there were more and more students like Drew, who, for one reason or another, could push my hot buttons. They could provoke me in the same way that Sullivan had done four decades ago. And the impulsive severity of my retaliation surprised me as much now as it did then. Having crossed that line with Drew, I wanted to make sure it didn't happen again.

The first order of business was to talk privately with him. Yes, he was a mean-spirited kid. But he was also one of the best writers in the class. And despite our run-in, or maybe even because of it, I knew he would expect a high grade—probably a 4.0. I also knew that if he didn't get it, it was within his rights to file a grievance against me.

You walk a fine line with students like that. You don't want to let their insolence pass. Nor do you want to reward them for it. I thought again about the incident with Sullivan. As bigoted as Big Tom was, and as much as I hold him responsible for the Jew remark, I was still the one that hit him in the head with a baseball. And he was the one that put me back on the team. In his own misguided way then, Sullivan had allowed us both to save face and move on. It wasn't pretty, but it was precisely the outcome I wanted to affect with my belligerent student.

Three days later, I called Drew into my office and calmly explained my side of the story—including the earlier scenario that had triggered my outburst. I waited for him to respond, and when it was clear that he was going to hold his ground, I simply apologized.

Naturally, I was disappointed. But, there were two more issues left to resolve. The next night, I apologized to the class for what I'd said to Drew. But I made it clear that I didn't condone or approve of what either of us had done.

For the final month of the semester, Drew and I did not bait one another again. Nor did I single his work out for praise or censure. As if nothing had ever happened, he continued to write with the same insight and imagination—and defiance—as he had before. And when it came time to give the final grade, it was a 3.5, not the 4.0 I knew he was expecting.

Two weeks after the spring semester ended, I applied for early retirement.

At the Buffalo Bill Museum, June 1988

Jane Tompkins

The video at the entrance to the Buffalo Bill Historical Center says that Buffalo Bill was the most famous American of his time, that by 1900 more than a billion words had been written about him, and that he had a progressive vision of the West. Buffalo Bill had worked as a cattle driver, a wagoneer, a Pony Express rider, a buffalo hunter for the railroad, a hunting guide, an army scout and sometime Indian fighter; he wrote dime novels about himself and an autobiography by the age of thirty-four, by which time he was already famous; and then he began another set of careers, first as an actor, performing on the urban stage in wintertime melodramatic representations of what he actually earned a living at in the summer (scouting and leading hunting expeditions), and finally becoming the impresario of his great Wild West show, a form of entertainment he invented and carried on as actor, director, and all-around idea man for thirty years. Toward the end of his life he founded the town of Cody, Wyoming, to which he gave, among other things, two hundred thousand dollars. Strangely enough, it was as a progressive civic leader that Bill Cody wanted to be remembered. "I don't want to die," the video at the entrance quotes him as saying, "and have people say—oh, there goes another old showman. . . . I would like people to say—this is the man who opened Wyoming to the best of civilization."

"The best of civilization." This was the phrase that rang in my head as I moved through the museum, which is one of the most disturbing places I have ever visited. It is also a wonderful place. It is four museums in one: the Whitney Gallery of Western Art, which houses artworks on Western subjects; the Buffalo Bill Museum proper, which memorializes Cody's life; the Plains Indian Museum, which exhibits artifacts of American Indian civilization; and the Winchester Arms Museum, a collection of firearms historically considered.

The whole operation is extremely well designed and well run, from the video program at the entrance that gives an overview of all four museums, to the fresh-faced young attendants wearing badges that say "Ask Me," to the museum shop stacked with books on Western Americana, to the ladies room—a haven of satiny marble, shining mirrors, and flattering light. Among other things, the museum is admirable for its effort to combat prevailing stereotypes about the "winning of the West," a phrase it self-consciously places in quotation marks. There are placards declaring that all history is a matter of interpretation, and that the American West is a source of myth. Everywhere, except perhaps in the Winchester Arms Museum, where the rhetoric is different, you feel the effort of the museum staff to reach out to the public, to be clear, to be accurate, to be fair, not to condescend—in short, to educate in the best sense of the term.

On the day I went, the museum was featuring an exhibition of Frederic Remington's works. Two facts about Remington make his work different from that of artists usually encountered in museums. The first is that Remington's paintings and statues function as a historical record. Their chief attraction has always been that they transcribe scenes and events that have vanished from the earth. The second fact, related to this, is the brutality of their subject matter. Remington's work makes you pay attention to what is happening in the painting or the piece of statuary. When you look at his work you cannot escape from the subject.

Consequently, as I moved through the exhibit, the wild contortions of the bucking broncos, the sinister expression invariably worn by the Indians, and the killing of animals and men made the placards discussing Remington's use of the "lost wax" process seem strangely disconnected. In the face of unusual violence, or implied violence, their message was: what is important here is technique. Except in the case of paintings showing the battle of San Juan Hill, where white Americans were being killed, the material accompanying Remington's works did not refer to the subject matter of the paintings and statues themselves. Nevertheless, an undertone of disquiet ran beneath the explanations; at least I thought I detected one. Someone had taken the trouble to ferret out Remington's statement of horror at the slaughter on San Juan Hill; someone had also excerpted the judgment of art critics commending Remington for the lyricism, interiority, and mystery of his later canvasses—pointing obliquely to the fascination with bloodshed that preoccupied his earlier work.

The uneasiness of the commentary, and my uneasiness with it, were nothing compared to the blatant contradictions in the paintings themselves. A pastel palette, a sunlit stop-action haze, murderous movement arrested under a lazy sky, flattened onto canvas and fixed in azure and ochre—two opposed impulses nestle here momentarily. The tension that keeps them from splitting apart is what holds the viewer's gaze.

The most excruciating example of what I mean occurs in the first painting in the exhibit. Entitled *His First Lesson*, it shows a horse standing saddled but riderless, the white of the horse's eye signaling his fear. A man using an instrument to tighten the horse's girth, at arm's length, backs away from the reaction he clearly anticipates, while the man who holds the horse's halter is doing the same. But what can they be afraid of? For the horse's right rear leg is tied a foot off the ground by a rope that is also tied around his neck. He can't move. That is the whole point.

His First Lesson. Whose? And what lesson, exactly? How to stand still when terrified? How not to break away when they come at you with strange instruments? How to be obedient? How to behave? It is impossible not to imagine that Remington's obsession with physical cruelty had roots somewhere in his own experience. Why else, in statue after statue, is the horse rebelling? The bucking bronco, symbol of the state of Wyoming, on every licence plate, on every sign for every bar, on every belt buckle, mug, and decal—this image Remington cast in bronze over and over again. There is a wild diabolism in the bronzes; the horse and rider seem one thing, not so much rider and ridden as a single bolt of energy gone crazy and caught somehow, complicatedly, in a piece of metal.

In the paintings, it is different—more subtle and bizarre. The cavalry on its way to a massacre, sweetly limned, softly tinted, poetically seized in mid-career, and gently laid on the two-dimensional surface. There is about these paintings of military men in the course of performing their deadly duty an almost maternal tenderness. The idealization of the cavalrymen in their dusty uniforms on their gallant horses has nothing to do with patriotism; it is pure love.

Remington's paintings and statues, as shown in this exhibition, embody everything that was objectionable about his era in American history. They are imperialist and racist; they glorify war and the torture and killing of animals; there are no women in them anywhere. Never the West as garden, never as pastoral, never as home. But in their aestheticization of violent life, Remington's pictures speak (to me, at least) of some other desire. The maternal tenderness is not an accident, nor is the beauty of the afternoons or the warmth of the desert sun. In them Remington plays the part of the preserver, as if by catching the figures in color and line he could save their lives and absorb some of that life into himself.

In one painting that particularly repulsed and drew me, a moose is outlined against the evening sky at the brink of a lake. He looks expectantly into the distance. Behind him and to one side, hidden from his view and only just revealed to ours, for it is dark there, is a hunter poised in the back of a canoe, rifle perfectly aimed. We look closer; the title of the picture is *Coming to the Call*. Ah, now we see. This is a sadistic scene. The hunter has lured the moose to his death. But wait a moment. Isn't the sadism really directed at us? First we see the glory of the animal; Remington has made it as noble as he knows how. Then we see what is going to happen. The hunter is one up on the moose, but Remington is one up on us. He makes us feel the pain of the anticipated killing, and makes us want to hold it off, to preserve the moose, just as he has done. Which way does the painting cut? Does it go against the hunter—who represents us, after all—or does it go against the moose who came to the call? Who came, to what call? Did Remington come to the West in response to it—to whatever the moose represents or to whatever the desire to kill the moose represents? But he hasn't killed it; he has only preserved an image of a white man about to kill it. And what call do we answer when we look at this painting? Who is calling whom? What is being preserved here?

That last question is the one that for me hung over the whole museum.

The Whitney Gallery is an art museum proper. Its allegiance is to art as academic tradition has defined it. In this tradition, we come to understand a painting by having in our possession various bits of information. Something about the technical process used to produce it (pastels, watercolors, woodblock prints, etc.); something about the elements of composition (line and color and movement); something about the artist's life (where born, how educated, by whom influenced, which school belonged to or revolted against); something about the artist's relation to this particular subject, such as how many times the artist painted it or whether it contains a favorite model. Occasionally there will be some philosophizing about the themes or ideas the paintings are said to represent.

The problem is, when you're faced with a painter like Remington, these bits of information, while nice to have, don't explain what is there in front of you. They don't begin to give you an account of why a person should have depicted such things. The experience of a lack of fit between the explanatory material and what is there on the wall is one I've had before in museums, when, standing in front of a painting or a piece of statuary, I've felt a huge gap between the information on the little placard and what it is I'm seeing. I realize that works of art, so-called, all have a subject matter, are all engaged with life, with some piece of life no less significant, no less compelling than Remington's subjects are, if we could only see its force. The idea that art is somehow separate from history, that it somehow occupies a space that is not the same as the space of life, seems out of whack here.

I wandered through the gallery thinking these things because right next to it, indeed all around it, in the Buffalo Bill Museum proper and in the Plains Indian Museum, are artifacts that stand not for someone's expertise or skill in manipulating the elements of an artistic medium, but for life itself, they are the residue of life.

The Buffalo Bill Museum is a wonderful array of textures, colors, shapes, sizes, forms. The fuzzy brown bulk of a buffalo's hump, the sparkling diamonds in a stickpin, the brilliant colors of the posters—the mixture makes you want to walk in and be surrounded by it, as if you were going into a child's adventure story. For a moment you can pretend you're a cowboy too; it's a museum where fantasy can take over. For a while.

As I moved through the exhibition, with the phrase "the best of civilization" ringing in my head, I came upon certain objects displayed in a section that recreates rooms from Cody's house. Ostrich feather fans, peacock feather fans, antler furniture—a chair and a table made entirely of antlers—a bearskin rug. And then I saw the heads on the wall: Alaska Yukon Moose, Wapiti American Elk, Muskox (the "Whitney," the "DeRham"), Mountain Caribou (the "Hyland"), Quebec Labrador Caribou (the "Elbow"), Rocky Mountain Goat (the "Haase," the "Kilto"), Woodland Caribou (world's record, "DeRham"), the "Rogers" freak Wapiti, the "Whitney" bison, the "Lord Rundlesham" bison. The names that appear after the animals are the names of the men who killed them. Each of the animals is scored according to measurements devised by the Boone and Crockett Club, a big-game hunters' organization. The Lord Rundlesham bison, for example, scores 124%, making it number 25 in the world for bison trophies. The "Reed" Alaska Yukon Moose scores 247. The "Witherbee" Canada moose holds the world's record.

Next to the wall of trophies is a small enclosure where jewelry is displayed. A buffalo head stickpin and two buffalo head rings, the heads made entirely of diamonds, with ruby eyes, the gifts of the Russian crown prince. A gold and diamond stickpin from Edward VII; a gold, diamond, and garnet locket from Queen Victoria. The two kinds of trophies—animals and jewels—form an incongruous set; the relationship between them compelling but obscure.

If the rest of the items in the museum—the dime novels with their outrageous covers, the marvelous posters, the furniture, his wife's dress, his daughter's oil painting—have faded from my mind it is because I cannot forget the heads of the animals as they stared down, each with an individual expression on its face. When I think about it I realize that I don't know why these animal heads are there. Buffalo Bill didn't kill them; perhaps they were gifts from the famous people he took on hunts. A different kind of jewelry.

After the heads, I began to notice something about the whole exhibition. In one display, doghide chaps, calfskin chaps, angora goathide chaps, and horsehide chaps. Next to these a rawhide lariat and a horsehair quirt. Behind me, boots and saddles, all of leather. Everywhere I looked there was tooth or bone, skin or fur, hide or hair, or the animal itself entire—two full-size buffalo (a main feature of the exhibition) and a magnificent stone sheep (a mountain sheep with beautiful curving horns). This one was another world's record. The best of civilization.

In the literature about Buffalo Bill you read that he was a conservationist, that if it were not for the buffalo in his Wild West shows the species would probably have become extinct. (In the seventeenth century 40 million buffalo roamed North America; by 1900 all the wild buffalo had been killed except for one herd in northern Alberta.) That the man who gained fame first as a buffalo hunter should have been an advocate for conservation of the buffalo is not an anomaly but typical of the period. The men who did the most to preserve America's natural wilderness and its wildlife were big-game hunters. The Boone and Crockett Club, founded by Theodore Roosevelt, George Bird Grinnell, and Owen Wister, turns out to have been one of the earliest organizations to devote itself to environmental protection in the United States. *The Reader's Encyclopedia of the American West* says that the club "supported the national park and forest reserve movement, helped create a system of national wildlife refuges, and lobbied for the protection of threatened species, such as the buffalo and antelope." At the same time, the prerequisites for membership in the club were "the highest caliber of sportsmanship and the achievement of killing 'in fair chase' trophy specimens [which had to be adult males] from several species of North American big game."

The combination big-game hunter and conservationist suggests that these men had no interest in preserving the animals for the animals' sake but simply wanted to ensure the chance to exercise their sporting pleasure. But I think this view is too simple; something further is involved here. The men who hunted game animals had a kind of love for them and a kind of love for nature that led them to want to preserve the animals they also desired to kill. That is, the desire to kill the animals was in some way related to a desire to see them live. It is not an accident, in this connection, that Roosevelt, Wister, and Remington all went west originally for their health. Their devotion to the West, their connection to it, their love for it are rooted in their need to reanimate their own lives. The preservation of nature, in other words, becomes for them symbolic of their own survival.

In a sense, then, there is a relationship between the Remington exhibition in the Whitney Gallery and the animal memorabilia in the Buffalo Bill Museum. The moose in *Coming to the Call* and the mooseheads on the wall are not so different as they might appear. The heads on the wall serve an aesthetic purpose; they are decorative objects, pleasing to the eye, which call forth certain associations. In this sense they are like visual works of art. The painting, on the other hand, has something of the trophy about it. The moose as Remington painted it is about to become a trophy, yet in another sense it already is one. Remington has simply captured the moose in another form. In both cases the subject matter, the life of a wild animal, symbolizes the life of the observer. It is the preservation of that life that both the painting and the taxidermy serve.

What are museums keeping safe for us, after all? What is it that we wish so much to preserve? The things we put in safekeeping, in our safe-deposit boxes under lock and key, are always in some way intended finally as safeguards of our own existence. The money and jewelry and stock certificates are meant for a time when we can no longer earn a living by the sweat of our brows. Similarly, the objects in museums preserve for us a source of life from which we need to nourish ourselves when the resources that would normally supply us have run dry.

The Buffalo Bill Historical Center, full as it is of dead bones, lets us see more clearly than we normally can what it is that museums are for. It is a kind of charnel house that houses images of living things that have passed away but whose life force still lingers around their remains and so passes itself on to us. We go and look at the objects in the glass cases and at the paintings on the wall, as if by standing there we could absorb into ourselves some of the energy that flowed once through the bodies of the live things represented. A museum, rather than being, as we normally think of it, the most civilized of places, a place most distant from our savage selves, actually caters to the urge to absorb the life of another into one's own life.

If we see the Buffalo Bill Museum in this way, it is no longer possible to separate ourselves from the hunters responsible for the trophies with their wondering eyes or from the curators who put them there. We are not, in essence, different from Roosevelt or Remington or Buffalo Bill, who killed animals when they were abundant in the Wild West of the 1880s. If in doing so those men were practicing the ancient art of absorbing the life of an animal into their own through the act of killing it, realizing themselves through the destruction of another life, then we are not so different from them as visitors to the museum. We stand beside the bones and skins and nails of beings that were once alive, or stare fixedly at their painted images. Indeed our visit is only a safer form of the same enterprise as theirs.

So I did not get out of the Buffalo Bill Museum unscathed, unimplicated in the acts of rapine and carnage that these remains represent. And I did not get out without having had a good time, either, because however many dire thoughts I may have had, the exhibits were interesting and fun to see. I was even able to touch a piece of buffalo hide displayed especially for that purpose (it was coarse and springy). Everyone else had touched it too. The hair was worn down, where people's hands had been, to a fraction of its original length.

After this, the Plains Indian Museum was a terrible letdown. I went from one exhibit to another expecting to become absorbed, but nothing worked. What was the matter? I was interested in Indians, had read about them, taught some Indian literature, felt drawn by accounts of native religions. I had been prepared to enter this museum as if I were going into another children's story, only this time I would be an Indian instead of a cowboy or a cowgirl. But the objects on display, most of them behind glass, seemed paltry and insignificant. They lacked visual presence. The bits of leather and sticks of wood triggered no fantasies in me.

At the same time, I noticed with some discomfort that almost everything in those glass cases was made of feathers and claws and hide, just like the men's chaps and ladies' fans in the Buffalo Bill Museum, only there was no luxury here. Plains Indian culture, it seemed, was made entirely from animals. Their mode of life had been even more completely dedicated to carnage than Buffalo Bill's, dependent as it was on animals for food, clothing, shelter, equipment, everything. In the Buffalo Bill Museum I was able to say to myself, well, if these men had been more sensitive, if they had had a right relation to their environment and to life itself, the atrocities that produced these trophies would never have occurred. They never would have exterminated the Indians and killed off the buffalo. But the spectacle before me made it impossible to say that. I had expected that the Plains Indian Museum would show me how life in nature ought to be lived: not the mindless destruction of nineteenth-century America but an ideal form of communion with animals and the land. What the museum seemed to say instead was that cannibalism was universal. Both colonizer and colonized had had their hands imbrued with blood. The Indians had lived off animals and had made war against one another. Violence was simply a necessary and inevitable part of life. And a person who, like me, was horrified at the extent of the destruction was just the kind of romantic idealist my husband sometimes accused me of being. There was no such thing as the life lived in harmony with nature. It was all bloodshed and killing, an unending cycle, over and over again, and no one could escape.

But perhaps there was a way to understand the violence that made it less terrible. Perhaps if violence was necessary, a part of nature, intended by the universe, then it could be seen as sacramental. Perhaps it was true, what Calvin Martin had said in *Keepers of the Game:* that the Indians had a sacred contract with the animals they killed, that they respected them as equals and treated their remains with honor and punctilio. If so, the remains of animals in the Plains Indian Museum weren't the same as those left by Buffalo Bill and his friends. They certainly didn't look the same. Perhaps. All I knew for certain was that these artifacts, lifeless and shrunken, spoke to me of nothing I could understand. No more did the life-size models of Indians, with strange featureless faces, draped in costumes that didn't look like clothing. The figures, posed awkwardly in front of tepees too white to seem real, carried no sense of a life actually lived, any more than the objects in the glass cases had.

The more I read the placards on the wall, the more disaffected I became. Plains Indian life apparently had been not only bloody but exceedingly tedious. All those porcupine quills painstakingly softened, flattened, dyed, then appliqued through even more laborious methods of stitching or weaving. Four methods of attaching porcupine quills, six design groups, population statistics, patterns of migration. There wasn't any glamour here at all. No glamour in the lives the placards told about, no glamour in the objects themselves, no glamour in the experience of looking at them. Just a lot of shriveled things accompanied by some even drier information.

Could it be, then, that the problem with the exhibitions was that Plains Indian culture, if representable at all, was simply not readable by someone like me? Their stick figures and abstract designs could convey very little to an untrained Euro-American eye. One display in particular illustrated this. It was a piece of cloth, behind glass, depicting a buffalo skin with some marks on it. The placard read: "Winter Count, Sioux ca. 1910, after Lone Dog's, Fort Peck, Montana, 1877." The hide with its markings had been a calendar, each year represented by one image, which showed the most significant event in the life of the tribe. A thick pamphlet to one side of the glass case explained each image year by year: 1800–1801, the attack of the Uncapoo on a Crow Indian Fort; 1802–1803, a total eclipse of the sun. The images, once you knew what they represented, made sense, and seemed poetic interpretations of the experiences they stood for. But without explanation they were incomprehensible.

The Plains Indian Museum stopped me in my tracks. It was written in a language I had never learned. I didn't have the key. Maybe someone did, but I wasn't too sure. For it may not have been just cultural difference that made the text unreadable. I began to suspect that the text itself was corrupt, that the architects of this museum were going through motions whose purpose was, even to themselves, obscure. Knowing what event a figure stands for in the calendar doesn't mean you understand an Indian year. The deeper purpose of the museum began to puzzle me. Wasn't there an air of bad faith about preserving the vestiges of a culture one had effectively extinguished? Did the museum exist to assuage our guilt and not for any real educational reason? I do not have an answer to these questions. All I know is that I felt I was in the presence of something pious and a little insincere. It had the aura of a failed attempt at virtue, as though the curators were trying to present as interesting objects whose purpose and meaning even they could not fully imagine.

In a last-ditch attempt to salvage something, I went up to one of the guards and asked where the movie was showing which the video had advertised, the movie about Plains Indian life. "Oh, the slide show, you mean," he said. "It's been discontinued." When I asked why, he said he didn't know. It occurred to me then that that was the message the museum was sending, if I could read it, that that was the bottom line. Discontinued, no reason given.

The movie in the Winchester Arms Museum, *Lock, Stock, and Barrel,* was going strong. The film began with the introduction of cannon into European warfare in the Middle Ages, and was working its way slowly toward the nineteenth century when I left. I was in a hurry. Soon my husband would be waiting for me in the lobby. I went from room to room, trying to get a quick sense impression of the objects on display. They were all the same: guns. Some large drawings and photographs on the walls tried to give a sense of the context in which the arms had been used, but the effect was nil. It was case after case of rifles and pistols, repeating themselves over and over, and even when some slight variation caught my eye the differences meant nothing to me.

But the statistics did. In a large case of commemorative rifles, I saw the Antlered Game Commemorative Carbine. Date of manufacture: 1978. Number produced: 19,999. I wondered how many antlered animals each carbine had killed. I saw the Canadian Centennial (1962): 90,000; the Legendary Lawman (1978): 19,999; the John Wayne (1980–81): 51,600. Like the titles of the various sections of the museum, these names had a message. The message was: guns are patriotic. Associated with national celebrations, law enforcement, and cultural heroes. The idea that firearms were inseparable from the march of American history came through even more strongly in the titles given to the various exhibits: Firearms in Colonial America; Born in America: The Kentucky Rifle; The Era of Expansion and Invention; The Civil War: Firearms of the Conflict; The Golden Age of Hunting; Winning the West. The guns embodied phases of the history they had helped to make. There were no quotation marks here to indicate that expansion and conquest might not have been all they were cracked up to be. The fact that firearms had had a history seemed to consecrate them; the fact that they had existed at the time when certain famous events had occurred seemed to make them not only worth preserving but worth studying and revering. In addition to the exhibition rooms, the museum housed three "study galleries": one for hand arms, one for shoulder arms, one for U.S. military firearms.

As I think back on the rows and rows of guns, I wonder if I should have looked at them more closely, tried harder to appreciate the workmanship that went into them, the ingenuity, the attention. Awe and admiration are the attitudes the museum invites. You hear the ghostly march of military music in the background; you imagine flags waving and sense the implicit reference to feats of courage in battle and glorious death. The place had the air of an expensive and well-kept reliquary, or of the room off the transept of a cathedral where the vestments are stored. These guns were not there merely to be seen or even studied; they were there to be venerated.

But I did not try to appreciate the guns. They were too technical, too foreign. I didn't have their language, and, besides, I didn't want to learn. I rejoined my husband in the lobby. The Plains Indian Museum had been incomprehensible, but in the Winchester Arms Museum I could hardly see the objects at all, for I did not see the point. Or, rather, I did see it and rejected it. Here in the basement the instruments that had turned live animals into hides and horns, had massacred the Indians and the buffalo, were being lovingly displayed. And we were still making them: 51,600 John Waynes in 1980–81. Arms were going strong.

As I bought my books and postcards in the gift shop, I noticed a sign that read "Rodeo Tickets Sold Here," and something clicked into place. So that was it. *Everything* was still going strong. The whole museum was just another rodeo, only with the riders and their props stuffed, painted, sculpted, immobilized and put under glass. Like the rodeo, the entire museum witnessed a desire to bring back the United States of the 1880s and 1890s. The American people did not want to let go of the winning of the West. They wanted to win it all over again, in imagination. It was the ecstasy of the kill, as much as the life of the hunted, that we fed off here. The Buffalo Bill Historical Center did not repudiate the carnage that had taken place in the nineteenth century. It celebrated it. With its gleaming rest rooms, cute snack bar, opulent museum shop, wooden Indians, thousand rifles, and scores of animal trophies, it helped us all reenact the dream of excitement, adventure, and conquest that was what the Wild West meant to most people in this country.

This is where my visit ended, but it had a sequel. When I left the Buffalo Bill Historical Center, I was full of moral outrage, an indignation so intense it made me almost sick, though it was pleasurable too, as such emotions usually are. But the outrage was undermined by the knowledge that I knew nothing about Buffalo Bill, nothing of his life, nothing of the circumstances that led him to be involved in such violent events. And I began to wonder if my reaction wasn't in some way an image, however small, of the violence I had been objecting to. So when I got home I began to read about Buffalo Bill, and a whole new world opened up. I came to love Buffalo Bill.

"I have seen him the very personification of grace and beauty . . . dashing over the free wild prairie and riding his horse as though he and the noble animal were bounding with one life and one motion." That is the sort of thing people wrote about Buffalo Bill. They said "he was the handsomest man I ever saw." They said "there was never another man lived as popular as he was." They said "there wasn't a man, woman or child that he knew or ever met that he didn't speak to." They said "he was handsome as a god, a good rider and a crack shot." They said "he gave lots of money away. Nobody ever went hungry around him." They said "he was way above the average, physically and every other way."

These are quotes from people who knew Cody, collected by one of his two most responsible biographers, Nellie Snyder Yost. She puts them in the last chapter, and by the time you get there they all ring true. Buffalo Bill was incredibly handsome. He was extremely brave and did things no other scout would do. He would carry messages over rugged territory swarming with hostile Indians, riding all night in bad weather and get through, and then take off again the next day to ride sixty miles through a blizzard. He was not a proud man. He didn't boast of his exploits. But he did do incredible things, not just once in a while but on a fairly regular basis. He had a great deal of courage; he believed in himself, in his abilities, in his strength and endurance and knowledge. He was very skilled at what he did—hunting and scouting—but he wasn't afraid to try other things. He wrote some dime novels, he wrote his autobiography by age thirty-four, without very much schooling; he wasn't afraid to try acting, even though the stage terrified him and he knew so little about it that, according to his wife, he didn't even know you had to memorize lines.

Maybe it was because he grew up on the frontier, maybe it was just the kind of person he was, but he was constantly finding himself in situations that required resourcefulness and courage, quick decisions and decisive action and rising to the occasion. He wasn't afraid to improvise.

He liked people, drank a lot, gave big parties, gave lots of presents, and is reputed to have been a womanizer.[1] When people came to see him in his office tent on the show grounds, to shake his hand or have their pictures taken with him, he never turned anyone away. "He kept a uniformed doorman at the tent opening to announce visitors," writes a biographer. "No matter who was outside, from a mayor to a shabby woman with a baby, the Colonel would smooth his mustache, stand tall and straight, and tell the doorman to 'show 'em in.' He greeted everyone the same."[2]

As a showman, he was a genius. People don't say much about *why* he was so successful; mostly they describe the wonderful goings-on. But I get the feeling that Cody was one of those people who was connected to his time in an uncanny way. He knew what people wanted, he knew how to entertain them, because he *liked* them, was open to them, felt his kinship with them, or was so much in touch with himself at some level that he was thereby in touch with almost everybody else.

He liked to dress up and had a great sense of costume (of humor, too, they say). Once he came to a fancy dress ball, his first, in New York, wearing white tie and tails and a large Stetson. He knew what people wanted. He let his hair grow long and wore a mustache and beard, because, he said, he wouldn't be believable as a scout otherwise. Hence his Indian name, Pahaska, meaning "long hair," which people loved to use. Another kind of costume. He invented the ten-gallon hat, which the Stetson company made to his specifications. Afterward, they made a fortune from it. In the scores of pictures reproduced in the many books about him, he most often wears scout's clothes—usually generously fringed buckskin, sometimes a modified cavalryman's outfit—though often he's impeccably turned out in a natty-looking three-piece business suit (sometimes with overcoat, sometimes not). The photographs show him in a tuxedo, in something called a "Mexican suit" which looks like a cowboy outfit, and once he appears in Indian dress. In almost every case he is wearing some kind of hat, usually the Stetson, at exactly the right angle. He poses deliberately, and with dignity, for the picture. Cody didn't take himself so seriously that he had to pretend to be less than he was.

What made Buffalo Bill so irresistible? Why is he still so appealing, even now, when we've lost, supposedly, all the illusions that once supported his popularity? There's a poster for one of his shows when he was traveling in France that gives a clue to what it is that makes him so profoundly attractive a figure. The poster consists of a huge buffalo galloping across the plains, and against the buffalo's hump, in the center of his hump, is a cutout circle that shows the head of Buffalo Bill, white-mustachioed and bearded now, in his famous hat, and beneath, in large red letters, are the words "Je viens."

Je viens ("I am coming") are the words of a savior. The announcement is an annunciation. Buffalo Bill is a religious figure of a kind who makes sense within a specifically Christian tradition. That is, he comes in the guise of a redeemer, of someone who will save us, who will through his own actions do something for us that we ourselves cannot do. He will lift us above our lives, out of the daily grind, into something larger than we are.

His appeal on the surface is to childish desires, the desire for glamour, fame, bigness, adventure, romance. But these desires are also the sign of something more profound, and it is to something more profound in us that he also appeals. Buffalo Bill comes to the child in us, understood not as that part of ourselves that we have outgrown but as the part that got left behind, of necessity, a long time ago, having been starved, bound, punished, disciplined out of existence. He promises that that part of the self can live again. He has the power to promise these things because he represents the West, that geographical space of the globe that was still the realm of exploration and discovery, that was still open, that had not yet quite been tamed, when he began to play himself on the stage. He not only represented it, he *was* it. He brought the West itself with him when he came. The very Indians, the very buffalo, the very cowboys, the very cattle, the very stagecoach itself which had been memorialized in story. He performed in front of the audience the feats that had made him famous. He shot glass balls and clay pigeons out of the air with amazing rapidity. He rode his watersmooth silver stallion at full gallop. "Jesus he was a handsome man," wrote e. e. cummings in "Buffalo Bill's Defunct."

"I am coming." This appearance of Buffalo Bill, in the flesh, was akin to the apparition of a saint or of the Virgin Mary to believers. He was the incarnation of an ideal. He came to show people that what they had only imagined was really true. The West really did exist. There really were heroes who rode white horses and performed amazing feats. e. e. cummings was right to invoke the name of Jesus in his poem. Buffalo Bill was a secular messiah.

He was a messiah because people believed in him. When he died, he is reputed to have said, "Let my show go on." But he had no show at the time, so he probably didn't say that. Still, the words are prophetic because the desire for what Buffalo Bill had done had not only not died but would call forth the countless reenactments of the Wild West, from the rodeo—a direct descendant of his show—to the thousands of Western novels, movies, and television programs that comprise the Western genre in the twentieth century, a genre that came into existence as a separate category right about the time that Cody died. Don Russell maintains that the way the West exists in our minds today is largely the result of the way Cody presented it in his show. That was where people got their ideas of what the characters looked like. Though many Indian tribes wore no feathers and fought on foot, you will never see a featherless, horseless Indian warrior in the movies, because Bill employed only Sioux and other Plains tribes which had horses and traditionally wore feathered headdresses. "Similarly," he adds, "cowboys wear ten-gallon Stetsons, not because such a hat was worn in early range days, but because it was part of the costume adopted by Buffalo Bill for his show."[3]

But the deeper legacy is elsewhere. Buffalo Bill was a person who inspired other people. What they saw in him was an aspect of themselves. It really doesn't matter whether Cody was as great as people thought him or not, because what they were responding to when he rode into the arena, erect and resplendent on his charger, was something intangible, not the man himself, but a possible way of being. William F. Cody and the Wild West triggered the emotions that had fueled the imaginative lives of people who flocked to see him, especially men and boys, who made up the larger portion of the audience. He and his cowboys played to an inward territory; a Wild West of the psyche that hungered for exercise sprang into activity when the show appeared. *Je viens* was a promise to redeem that territory, momentarily at least, from exile and oblivion. The lost parts of the self symbolized by buffalo and horses and wild men would live again for an hour while the show went on.

People adored it. Queen Victoria, who broke her custom by going to see it at all (she never went to the theater, and on the rare occasions when she wanted to see a play she had it brought to her), is supposed to have been lifted out of a twenty-five-year depression caused by the death of her husband after she saw Buffalo Bill. She liked the show so much that she saw it again, arranging for a command performance to be given at Windsor Castle the day before her Diamond Jubilee. This was the occasion when four kings rode in the Deadwood stagecoach with the Prince of Wales on top next to Buffalo Bill, who drove. No one was proof against the appeal. Ralph Blumenfeld, the London correspondent for the New York *Herald*, wrote in his diary while the show was in London that he'd had two boyhood heroes, Robin Hood and Buffalo Bill, and had delighted in Cody's stories of the Pony Express and Yellow Hand:

> Everything was done to make Cody conceited and unbearable, but he remained the simple, unassuming child of the plains who thought lords and ladies belonged in the picture books and that the story of Little Red Riding Hood was true. I rode in the Deadwood coach. It was a great evening in which I realized a good many of my boyhood dreams, for there was Buffalo Bill on his white rocking horse charger, and Annie Oakley behind him.[4]

Victor Weybright and Henry Blackman Sell, from whose book on the Wild West some of the foregoing information has come, dedicated their book to Buffalo Bill. It was published in 1955. Nellie Snyder Yost, whose 1979 biography is one of the two scholarly accounts of Cody's life, dedicates her book "to all those good people, living or dead, who knew and liked Buffalo Bill." Don Russell's *The Lives and Legends of Buffalo Bill* (1960), the most fact-filled scholarly biography, does not have a dedication, but in the final chapter, where he steps back to assess Cody and his influence, Russell ends by exclaiming, "What more could possibly be asked of a hero? If he was not one, who was?"[5]

Let me now pose a few questions of my own. Must we throw out all the wonderful qualities that Cody had, the spirit of hope and emulation that he aroused in millions of people, because of the terrible judgment history has passed on the epoch of which he was part? The kinds of things he stands for—courage, daring, strength, endurance, generosity, openness to other people, love of drama, love of life, the possibility of living a life that does not deny the body and the desires of the body—are these to be declared dangerous and delusional although he mani-fested some of them while fighting Indians and others while representing his vic-tories to the world? And the feelings he aroused in his audiences, the idealism, the enthusiasm, the excitement, the belief that dreams could become real—must these be declared misguided or a sham because they are associated with the imperialis-tic conquest of a continent, with the wholesale extermination of animals and men?

It is not so much that we cannot learn from history as that we cannot teach history how things should have been. When I set out to discover how Cody had become involved in the killing of Indians and the slaughter of buffalo, I found myself unable to sustain the outrage I had felt on leaving the museum. From his first job as an eleven-year-old herder for an army supply outfit, sole wage earner for his ailing widowed mother who had a new baby and other children to sup-port, to his death in Colorado at the age of seventy-one, there was never a time when it was possible to say, there, there you went wrong, Buffalo Bill, you should not have killed that Indian. You should have held your fire and made your living some other way and quit the army and gone to work in the nineteenth-century equivalent of the Peace Corps. You should have known how it would end. My reading made me see that you cannot prescribe for someone in Buffalo Bill's posi-tion what he should have done, and it made me reflect on how eager I had been to get off on being angry at the museum. The thirst for moral outrage, for self-vindi-cation, lay pretty close to the surface.

I cannot resolve the contradiction between my experience at the Buffalo Bill Historical Center with its celebration of violent conquest and my response to the shining figure of Buffalo Bill as it emerged from the pages of books—on the one hand, a history of shame; on the other, an image of the heart's desire. But I have reached one conclusion that for a while will have to serve.

Major historical events like genocide and major acts of destruction are not simply produced by impersonal historical processes or economic imperatives or ecological blunders; human intentionality is involved and human knowledge of the self. Therefore, if you're really, truly interested in not having any more geno-cide or killing of animals, no matter what else you might do, if you don't first, or also, come to recognize the violence in yourself and your own anger and your own destructiveness, whatever else you do won't work. It isn't that genocide doesn't matter. Genocide matters, and it starts at home.

Notes

1. Iron Eyes Cody, as told to Collin Perry, *Iron Eyes: My Life as a Hollywood Indian* (New York, 1982), 16.

2. Nellie Irene Snyder Yost, *Buffalo Bill: His Family, Friends, Fame, Failures, and Fortunes* (Chicago, 1979), 436.

3. Don Russell, *The Lives and Legends of Buffalo Bill* (Norman, Okla., 1960), 470.

4. Victor Weybright and Henry Blackman Sell, *Buffalo Bill and the Wild West* (New York, 1955), 172.

5. Russell, 480.

Going to the Movies

Susan Allen Toth

I

Aaron takes me only to art films. That's what I call them, anyway: strange movies with vague poetic images I don't understand, long dreamy movies about a distant Technicolor past, even longer black-and-white movies about the general meaninglessness of life. We do not go unless at least one reputable critic has found the cinematography superb. We went to *The Devil's Eye,* and Aaron turned to me in the middle and said, "My God, this is *funny.*" I do not think he was pleased.

When Aaron and I go to the movies, we drive our cars separately and meet by the box office. Inside the theater he sits tentatively in his seat, ready to move if he can't see well, poised to leave if the film is disappointing. He leans away from me, careful not to touch the bare flesh of his arm against the bare flesh of mine. Sometimes he leans so far I am afraid he may be touching the woman on his other side instead. If the movie is very good, he leans forward too, peering between the heads of the couple in front of us. The light from the screen bounces off his glasses; he gleams with intensity, sitting there on the edge of his seat, watching the screen. Once I tapped him on the arm so I could whisper a comment in his ear. He jumped.

After *Belle de Jour,* Aaron said he wanted to ask me if he could stay overnight. "But I can't," he shook his head mournfully before I had a chance to answer, "because I know I never sleep well in strange beds." Then he apologized for asking. "It's just that after a film like that," he said, "I feel the need to assert myself."

II

Bob takes me only to movies that he thinks have a redeeming social conscience. He doesn't call them films. They tend to be about poverty, war, injustice, political corruption, struggling unions in the 1930s, and the military-industrial complex.

209

Bob doesn't like propaganda movies, though, and he doesn't like to be too depressed either. We stayed away from *The Sorrow and the Pity;* it would be, he said, too much. Besides, he assured me, things are never that hopeless. So most of the movies we see are made in Hollywood. Because they are always very topical, these movies offer what Bob calls "food for thought." When we saw *Coming Home,* Bob's jaw set so firmly with the first half that I knew we would end up at Poppin' Fresh Pies afterward.

When Bob and I go to the movies, we take turns driving so no one owes anyone else anything. We park far away from the theater so we don't have to pay for a space. If it's raining or snowing, Bob offers to let me off at the door, but I can tell he'll feel better if I go with him while he parks, so we share the walk too. Inside the theater Bob will hold my hand when I get scared if I ask him. He puts my hand firmly on his knee and covers it completely with his own hand. His knee never twitches. After a while, when the scary part is past, he loosens his hand slightly and I know that is a signal to take mine away. He sits companionably close, letting his jacket just touch my sweater, but he does not infringe. He thinks I ought to know he is there if I need him.

One night after *The China Syndrome* I asked Bob if he wouldn't like to stay for a second drink, even though it was past midnight. He thought awhile about that, considering my offer from all possible angles, but finally he said no. Relationships today, he said, have a tendency to move too quickly.

III

Sam likes movies that are entertaining. By that he means movies that Will Jones of the *Minneapolis Tribune* loved and either *Time* or *Newsweek* rather liked; also movies that do not have sappy love stories, are not musicals, do not have subtitles, and will not force him to think. He does not go to movies to think. He liked *California Suite* and *The Seduction of Joe Tynan,* though the plots, he said, could have been zippier. He saw it all coming too far in advance, and that took the fun out. He doesn't like to know what is going to happen. "I just want my brain to be tickled," he says. It is very hard for me to pick out movies for Sam.

When Sam takes me to the movies, he pays for everything. He thinks that's what a man ought to do. But I buy my own popcorn, because he doesn't approve of it; the grease might smear his flannel slacks. Inside the theater, Sam makes himself comfortable. He takes off his jacket, puts one arm around me, and all during the movie he plays with my hand, stroking my palm, beating a small tattoo on my wrist. Although he watches the movie intently, his body operates on instinct. Once I inclined my head and kissed him lightly just behind his ear. He beat a faster tattoo on my wrist, quick and musical, but he didn't look away from the screen.

When Sam takes me home from the movies, he stands outside my door and kisses me long and hard. He would like to come in, he says regretfully, but his steady girlfriend in Duluth wouldn't like it. When the *Tribune* gives a movie four stars, he has to save it to see with her. Otherwise her feelings might be hurt.

IV

I go to some movies by myself. On rainy Sunday afternoons I often sneak into a revival house or a college auditorium for old Technicolor musicals, *Kiss Me Kate, Seven Brides for Seven Brothers, Calamity Jane,* even, once, *The Sound of Music.* Wearing saggy jeans so I can prop my feet on the seat in front, I sit toward the rear where no one will see me. I eat large handfuls of popcorn with double butter. Once the movie starts, I feel completely at home. Howard Keel and I are old friends; I grin back at him on the screen, admiring all his teeth. I know the sound tracks by heart. Sometimes when I get really carried away I hum along with Kathryn Grayson, remembering how I once thought I would fill out a formal like that. Skirts whirl, feet tap, acrobatic young men perform impossible feats, and then the camera dissolves into a dream sequence I know I can comfortably follow. It is not, thank God, Bergman.

If I can't find an old musical, I settle for Hepburn and Tracy, vintage Grant or Gable, on adventurous days Claudette Colbert or James Stewart. Before I buy my ticket I make sure it will all end happily. If necessary, I ask the girl at the box office. I have never seen *Stella Dallas* or *Intermezzo.* Over the years I have developed other peccadilloes: I will, for example, see anything that is redeemed by Thelma Ritter. At the end of *Daddy Long Legs* I wait happily for the scene where Fred Clark, no longer angry, at last pours Thelma a convivial drink. They smile at each other, I smile at them, I feel they are smiling at me. In the movies I go to by myself, the men and women always like each other.

Six Days

Jesse Wegman

In the classroom where I tutor, a five-year-old boy is fighting with the letter *E*. With knees bent and shoulders cocked, he is poised on his bench as though ready to pounce. His whole being is devoted to this singular, monumental task. I focus on him over the din of the classroom. I see the blunt pencil caught in his grip, and I realize that an entire process is beginning again. Tens of thousands of years of evolution are being re-enacted right in front of me.

E. Look! This simple figure, an outstretched claw. Or three branches, anchored by a trunk as solid and certain as a Joshua tree. It existed in the early Canaanite alphabet, which developed around 1700 B.C. and is the oldest known. At the time, it was a consonant and faced the other way. But within a thousand years it had become a vowel and had taken its current form among the letters of Ancient Greek. Today it is the most common letter in the English language. It has survived this long, and barring a wholesale conversion to binary code, it should see our species to extinction.

I have been mulling over this kind of thing lately because I, too, have been learning an alphabet. I am learning to speak Modern Greek, and to do this I first had to master the Greek alphabet: twenty-four characters, at once as strange as a lemur and as perfectly familiar as a street sign. I remind myself that this new alphabet is the foundation of my own—that without it everything I know about letters and words would be entirely different. Still, I regard these ancient symbols as latecomers.

When you are learning a new language, the sounds guide you. Your energy is devoted to apprehending strange phonetic combinations and barely discernible stresses. But when you are learning a new alphabet, your sensitivity is directed to the minute facts of form. *A* is no longer just *A* but an odd fusion of shapes—lazy slants propped up and apart by a firm crossbar. A triangle with poor boundary control. Or two lovers leaning across a table, kissing. And so it is with the Greek letters. Thanks to the Etruscans, most of the letters that found their way across the sea made it into the Roman alphabet, from which ours is derived. The ones that didn't carry over we still know if we are fraternity or sorority members or students of the classics or of physics. But how carefully do we really look?

There is xi (ξ), a beautiful two-humped sea horse, pronounced—or sneezed—*ksee*, and there is a delicately pierced bowl, psi (ψ), pronounced *psee*. There is theta (Θ), pronounced *theeta*, elegant and timeless, a circle not quite bisected so that top and bottom bleed into each other, and gamma (Γ), a tree struck by lightning. Then there is eta, pronounced *eeta*, a simple-sounding letter that leads us on a wonderful transalphabetic journey. Eta always sounds like our long *e*, but its uppercase looks like our *H*, while its lowercase resembles our *n*. The *n* sound in Greek is represented in lowercase by a character resembling our *v*. One of the *v* sounds in Greek looks like our *u* unless it is uppercase, and then it looks like our *Y*, which can also sound like our long *e*—and we are back at eta.

I am going to all this trouble because I fell in love with a Greek girl during my first year in college. She was a fierce, proud thunderclap of a soul with tightly coiled hair and eyes like Kalamata olives. She had the habit of slipping back and forth between English and Greek mid-sentence, depending on the versatility of the words available to her at the moment. Seeing that I had no choice in the matter, I went out and bought a Greek phrase book, the last few pages of which contained a wonderfully injudicious English-Greek lexicon. Here I was offered the Greek word for "rangefinder" (*apostasiometro*), but a translation for "if" was nowhere to be found. I am still waiting for the chance to say "Excuse me, where is your rangefinder?"

In the face of dire warnings to the contrary, I skipped over the more ponderous sections of my phrase book and came to rest on the alphabet page. I practiced the characters over and over, big and bold across clean sheets of notebook paper, small and studied down the margin of my introductory-psychology textbook. I put the uppercase of each letter next to the lowercase, as on the green banners that wrap around kindergarten classrooms. The final flourish of a lowercase xi, the reverse hook and belly of a small zeta (ζ), carved like a chant into my memory. Forty-eight symbols I would count—and I always counted.

Eventually I committed the alphabet to memory, and could recite it like a pledge, with a fine accent. In the process I became something of a pronunciation snob. I reminded myself of a tourist who has stayed somewhere just long enough to develop a measured disdain for his newly arrived compatriots, cringing when I was invited to a party at *Kye Sye*, or when my statistics professor asked us to calculate the *sigmuh* of voting trends in Dubuque. *Seeghma*, I thought. *Soften the g.* Here was I—a student to whom Achilles was a tendon and Homer a Simpson—suddenly fancying myself one of the last outposts of classical civilization.

This attitude didn't win me many friends. But I did start reading more, and I imagined myself a kindred spirit of Eric Partridge, the distinguished etymologist who, in the introduction to his *Origins: A Short Etymological Dictionary of Modern*

English, wrote of his method, "The transliteration of Greek words, in particular, has been more exact than in several dictionaries one might, but does not, name."

I also discovered that it is less complicated to love a language than to love a person, and so when things with the Greek girl didn't go as planned, I managed instead to fall madly in love with Greek. It is not difficult to do this. Spoken Greek grabs you and wraps you up in its soothing, rapid-fire cadences. No wonder we've looked to Greece for so many of our great oratorical traditions: the language seems built purely to indulge the pleasure of speaking. But it does more than that. I have found that Greeks seem to have an instinctive and deep understanding of the basis of their language. It is as if Greek itself were encoded with the tools to decipher its history; the more you speak, the more you learn. And the more you learn, the more you discover that in a culture that thrives on debate, language is no less debatable than anything else.

Take *aletheia*, for instance. Loosely translated, it is Greek for "truth." Why? The German philosopher Martin Heidegger offered a carefully reasoned—and poetic—etymology. The root *lath* in Greek means "to be concealed," he explained, and the prefix *a-* means "without." So to be truthful in Greek, according to Heidegger, is literally to reveal, to uncover—a better lesson than could ever be learned from our abstract notions of "accuracy" or "authenticity."

Giorgos Patios thinks this is absurd. Giorgos was my waiter at the Taverna Gorgona, a well-kept roadside cafe in Perissa, on the Greek island of Santorini. I had gone to the Gorgona to avoid the sun, drink strong coffee, and stare out at the street—that is, to be like a Greek man. With my practiced accent and command of pleasantries, I thought I fit in nicely. The sun-bleached *Herald Tribune* on my table was a mistake.

Giorgos came over and started talking to me in English. Soon we were on to the subject of language, and I asked him about *aletheia*. He gave me a long, convoluted answer that sounded well rehearsed and had nothing to do with uncovering anything. So Heidegger didn't have it right? I asked. "Of course not," Giorgos replied. But Heidegger was a student of Ancient Greek, I protested. Giorgos smiled a dismissive, chipped-tooth smile at me. "Heidegger was a clown," he said. So there.

Back in the classroom, I hold my gaze on the unnoticing boy. Of course, he doesn't care about any of this; he just wants to write his *E*. But the *E* is fighting back. I am lucky to witness this, I think. In slow, patient steps, the boy is teaching himself movements, groups of movements, that we have never stopped trying to master. In his naiveté the boy draws the branches of the *E* first, and connects them after. No adult would spend enough time on one letter to make this method worthwhile.

But maybe we've forgotten something important. After all, the ability to see things in pieces is at the heart of two of the biggest developments in the history of writing: the alphabet and the movable-type printing press. In our day, of course, it is the basis of the computer. Ones and zeroes—the simplicity permits the complexity.

Today the boy writes in pieces. Branch, branch, branch, trunk. But as he becomes more comfortable fitting together these odd groups of shapes—these trees, fingers, swans, sea horses—he will stop seeing them. Soon, like all the older children, he will be writing just letters.

Maybe that's why I feel this strange connection to him now: we are both following these shapes through their tangled histories, watching them in all their mysterious transformations. We feel the same excitement and wonder that the early Semitic scribes must have felt as they realized that each syllable of their language could be separated into discrete characters. *Aleph-bet*. They saw more than just the shapes too. *Aleph* is ancient Hebrew for "ox"; turn A upside down and see what you get. The alphabet is not just letters; it is alive.

James Ussher, the seventeenth-century Irish archbishop best known for his painstaking calculation of the moment when light was created (at midday on October 23, 4004 B.C.), also understood the necessity of learning piece by piece. Indeed, he considered it divinely ordained. Why should Creation as a whole have happened over six days, rather than in one timeless, inconceivable instant? "To teach us the better to understand their workmanship," Ussher reasoned, "even as a man which will teach a child in the frame of a letter, will first teach him one line of the letter, and not the whole letter together."

Soon the boy will discover all this for himself. But not before going through the necessary steps. First branches, then trunk. First one way, then the other. *E* is as simple, and as complex, as it will ever be.

The Friendship Tarot

Nancy Willard

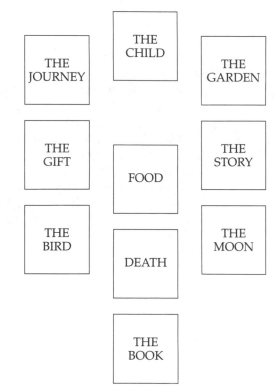

I lay out the cards of our friendship.

The Child

The card shows a child with chocolate on his face wandering through an art gallery in downtown Poughkeepsie devoted—for two weeks—to illustrations from children's books. Ilse Vogel and I have not met, but we both have work in this show. In one room stands the six-foot doll's house I made when I was writing *A Visit to William Blake's Inn.* In the next room hang Ilse's meticulous pen-and-ink drawings for her book *Dodo Every Day.*

What I saw: an elegant woman with white hair, a knitted cloche, and eyes that missed nothing.

What she saw: a woman with a seven-year-old boy whose face was smeared with chocolate.

What I thought: Who is this remarkable person?

What Ilse thought: Her child has a dirty face, but does she worry about it? No. And neither does the child.

The Garden

The card shows two married couples eating dinner in a garden: Eric and me, Howard and Ilse. Four artists: one painter (Howard), one photographer (Eric), one writer (me), and Ilse, who can't be pinned down to one category since she illustrates her own stories. The dinner Ilse has prepared is exquisite. Butter blooms in a little pot; Ilse has sculpted it into the face of a sunflower. Howard helps her carry dishes from the tiny kitchen into the Francesa, a shelter shingled in nasturtiums and morning glories. The front is entirely open to view; over the edge of the second story dangle the tails of four sleeping cats. Once it was a rickety outbuilding for storing tools. Now it is paved with round river stones chosen and put into place years ago by Ilse. Shortly after she'd laid the last stone, she felt chest pains. The day she came home from the hospital, Howard filled the house with anemones.

Ilse heaps seconds on our plates without asking us and tells us they bought this small yellow house in the country because they loved the apple tree blooming outside the kitchen window. The soil is rocky but the garden is full of flowers; Ilse has put out one hundred and four pots of flowers. When a large tabby springs from behind one of them, Ilse explains that they are down to ten cats.

"Ten cats!" exclaims Eric.

"We have only two," I add apologetically.

Is this the first step into friendship? Ilse knows right away she can discuss the excellence of cats without boring me: Velvet Paws, Parsley, Comedy Cat, Mr. Goldie, Chives. Summer and winter the ten cats that live with Howard and Ilse sleep in the garage at night.

Winter and summer the two cats that live with Eric and me sleep at the foot of our bed so they can watch over us.

The Journey

The card shows three people in a car headed for New York. Ilse wears the same knitted cloche she wore at the gallery, and Howard's hat is the identical shade of oatmeal. When I remark on this, Ilse explains that she knitted them both.

We three are traveling to New York to see *The Tin Drum*. On the way, Ilse explains that she lived in Berlin all during the war, so naturally she's curious to see this film.

Of the movie I remember only a few scenes, not because the film was forgettable but because of what happened on the trip back.

The Story

The card shows a woman talking and a woman listening.

I am riding in the back seat of the car and I lean forward and ask, "Ilse, was it really like that in Germany?"

Ilse answers by telling me about the day the Russians marched into Berlin.

"When the Russians came so close to the house, you could hear them talking and shouting. And all the inhabitants of the house were sitting in the bunkers except me, because I hated to be down there with the Nazis. I was in my apartment with a friend of mine. And then we heard shooting and voices, and then we heard a sound as if masses and masses of water would come rushing in, and then my friend said, 'Oh, something has hit the canister of gasoline,' and within seconds I saw the flames and the gasoline floating in under the doorway of my apartment, and everything was in flames. There was just one window where we could get out. We crossed the yard to the door of the bunker and went inside and then the house did burn with tremendous speed. Smoke came and people started to pray and to sing, and others cursed and screamed. I sat with my friend and we held hands and I said, 'This is the end, there's no way out.' And my friend had a little flute with him which he always carried. I'll show it to you tomorrow—I still have it. He pulled it out and played a little Bach sonata for us, to comfort us."

She tells me how she worked in the Resistance against Hitler, hiding Jews in her apartment and printing passports to smuggle them out of Germany. Two hours later we are back in Poughkeepsie.

"Ilse," I say, "have you written this down?"

"It's not a story for children," she says. "And I can't find the right voice to tell it."

"You must tell it," I say, "so people don't forget." Ilse asks to use the bathroom. When she emerges she says with a smile, "I'm so glad your house isn't neat all the time."

The Gift

The card shows a restaurant strung with red and green lights.

The week before Christmas, Ilse and Howard and Eric and I meet for lunch at Dickens. Ilse calls ahead so that we can have the same table we had last year—a table intended for six. She tells the waitress we are expecting another person, a man, and during the meal she laments his bad manners—why couldn't he have phoned? She brings the snapshots we took of each other last year. In the snapshots we are always opening presents. Here I am, opening the present Ilse made for me: a muff, to keep my hands warm. It is made of brown corduroy, lined with synthetic lamb's wool, and decorated in orange and turquoise and lavender: braid, felt hearts, pyramids, and silver beads, each bead no bigger than a mustard seed. It has a corduroy strap and a pocket, into which Ilse has tucked a bright red handkerchief.

Since I ride a bicycle to class and my arms are usually full of books, I seldom have the leisure to use a muff unless I decide to take a muff-walk: a walk with no other purpose than exercise and pleasure. Which is probably why Ilse gave it to me.

This year Howard gives Eric a book of Vuillard's paintings and Ilse gives me a Waring hand-held blender which, she assures me, will make cooking much easier.

Eric gives Howard a photograph he took inside the conservatory of the New York Botanical Gardens and I give Ilse a set of flannel sheets and pillowcases printed with cats.

Food

The card shows dinner tables, side by side.

When we eat dinner at their house, they serve hors d'oeuvres and drinks in the living room or the garden, just for the four of us. Ilse makes the salad dressing. The courses arrive in succession at the proper time.

When they eat dinner at ours, I am famished from having skipped lunch to meet with students, and I rush everything to the table at once. The salad dressing is Paul Newman's finest, the cake is the handiwork of the Aurora Café Bakery. The last time I baked a cake, it collapsed like an old hat and I filled in the holes and cracks with frosting, which made it astonishingly heavy but quite tasty. Howard warned Ilse not to eat it.

"All that chocolate is bad for your heart," he said softly.

She smiled and took another bite.

The Moon

The card shows four people perched on top of the world.

Ilse phones us in great excitement. Tonight, if we stand on a certain hill a mile from their house, we can watch the sun go down and the moon come up, all at the same time. She has checked the weather; the sky will be clear.

The road to the hill runs past stables and pastures broken by white fencing into parcels that give expensive horses enough room to run free by keeping them apart from each other. Howard regrets that the landscape feels so owned.

When we climb out of the car and look east and west from the crest of the windy hill, the valley sweeps broadly around us; could we see the Hudson if we knew where to find it?

As the sun slides into its nest of light behind the Catskills, the moon rises silently, secretly. She is so pale and thin that she might be the shed carapace of some large round animal. As darkness gathers, she grows solider, more golden.

"In German, the moon is masculine," says Ilse. "And the sun is feminine."

I can't think of another language in which those genders are assigned to my old friends in the sky.

Ilse says she is trying to write about those last days before the fall of Berlin, but she is not yet ready to read me what she has written.

The Bird

The card shows an empty cage in a garden.

Ilse phones us—can we come over and see the dove? It seems that the post-mistress in their little town of Bangall runs an animal adoption service on the side, and she has presented Ilse with a dove.

When we arrive, Ilse has put its cage on a pile of stones in the garden, like an altar to flight. The cage is made of the sticks that Ilse gathered in the yard, but it is very small, and when Eric and I approach, the dove beats her wings against the bars. All during dinner she makes endearing noises.

"You can't imagine how we enjoy hearing that wonderful sound," says Ilse. "And the cats don't seem to notice her."

We sit outside and watch the singular stars arrive, one by one, like notes in a music box winding down to silence.

The next day I telephone Joanne, a friend of mine who does excellent carpentry, and ask her to make a catproof cage for Ilse's dove. I tell her it should be made of sticks gathered in a forest and it should be huge. Ilse's birthday is two weeks away—could she possibly have it finished by then?

Two weeks later, Joanne drives up with a cage nearly as tall as herself on her truck. It is a gazebo, a minaret, a chapel, it is the mother of all birdcages. I phone Howard and tell him we want to deliver it as a surprise to Ilse, who likes surprises but does not like unexpected visitors. Howard can tell her whatever he likes; we will arrive with the cage at eleven o'clock on Thursday.

When we appear, the two of them are sitting in the garden, attended by Velvet Paws. Joanne and I carry the cage across the lawn. Ilse is speechless with astonishment. That is just the way I hoped she would be.

"You've given me exactly what I wanted!" she exclaims.

The dove takes to the cage at once. Soon it no longer feels like a cage; Ilse adds branches and leaves and nasturtiums and she removes the bottom so that the dove sits directly on the grass. How good the grass feels on her little coral feet! All night long she enjoys dewfall and moonrise and starshine. When the sun warms the dark world, Howard arrives with her breakfast.

One morning Howard goes to feed the dove and finds a dash of bloody feathers. There is a snake in Eden; nothing but a snake could insinuate itself into so stout a cage.

Ilse mourns her dove. All winter the cage is filled only with cream-colored twigs—and the curious seedpods that catch her eye in the garden. One day the postmistress telephones her. A relative of the slain dove has recently laid a clutch of eggs; two of them hatched. Would Ilse like two doves? Howard snakeproofs the cage. It is spring again and the voices of Ilse's doves are heard in the land.

Death

The card shows a shelf on which Ilse has arranged the skulls of their cats. After their deaths, she digs them up. The skulls are light and beautiful as parchment.

"Some people think it's a strange thing to do," she says, "but see how beautiful their bones are!"

When I cook chicken, I save not only the wishbone but the breastbone. Scrubbed clean and dried, the breastbone looks like a mask or a saddle intended for an animal unaccustomed to carrying passengers. On the apple tree in our back yard hang the shells of half a dozen horseshoe crabs I found on Cape Cod. Anyone passing the tree would take it for the site of a secret ceremony devoted to saving what holds us up but is never seen under the living flesh.

The Book

The card shows pages falling and gathering like snow. Ilse is now seriously at work on her stories about life in Germany under Hitler. Howard is typing them for her. The stories arrive in the mail, one by one, in white envelopes bordered with a green stripe.

Without telling her, I am sending them to my editor at Harcourt Brace.

Velvet Paws has had her kittens behind a canvas of Howard's which he imprudently left leaning against an upstairs wall. Ilse invites us to view the kittens. Eric and I sit in the living room of the little white house and wait for the great moment. We wait and wait. And suddenly here is Ilse, presenting them to us in a basket lined with violets and strawberry leaves, as if she had just picked them in the garden.

Later, as we are leafing through a box of old photographs, I pull out a picture of two blond girls standing side by side: Ilse and her twin sister, Erika, who died of diphtheria when they were nine.

"Which one is you?" I ask.

Ilse is not sure.

"Perhaps that one, with the knees bent a little. Erika was born first and she always was the more courageous one."

Eight years ago, when I published my first novel, *Things Invisible to See,* I dedicated it to Ilse and Howard.

Today I open the book of Ilse's stories, *Bad Times, Good Friends,* and find it is dedicated to Eric and me. Over the dedication is Ilse's pen-and-ink drawing of a dove turning into a woman. She is flying over a bed of pansies, carrying three tulips in one hand and pointing to our names with the other.

"They didn't want a dove-woman on the dedication page," says Ilse. "I had to fight for it."

Part 2

Talking about Creative Nonfiction

One reason we're so enthusiastic about this evolving genre is the role of writers and teachers of creative nonfiction in defining the terms of the conversation. As both teachers and writers we've benefited from that conversation ourselves, and so we believe that writers entering the genre can gain from hearing these writers talk about the making of their own work. After all, in the long tradition of the genre, essayists from Montaigne through Addison, Steele, Lamb, and Hazlitt to E. B. White have not only written the most enduring examples of the essay but also provided the most valuable commentary on the form.

Therefore, in Part Two, Talking about Creative Nonfiction, we've chosen pieces—many of them written by authors whose works are also found in Part One—that reflect these writers' thoughts, opinions, speculations, theories, and critiques of creative nonfiction. They provide a multivoiced discussion of the genre on a wide range of topics related to writing creative nonfiction—from definitions of the form and overviews of some of the subgenres to informal histories of the genre, personal accounts of writing, and hints about strategies and practices. Some writers, such as Bret Lott and Richard Selzer, discuss their personal reasons for writing; others, including Sydney Lea, talk about their composing strategies. Still others offer us insight into the particular forms of creative nonfiction in which they work: Mary Clearman Blew, Annie Dillard, Patricia Hampl, and Fern Kupfer give us different perspectives on the memoir, especially the ways imagination transforms and transposes memory; Phillip Lopate and Scott Russell Sanders talk about the history of the personal essay; Tracy Kidder discusses his views and his experiences in literary journalism; Jane Tompkins explores her motives for anchoring her cultural criticism in the first person singular.

Along with the writers whose work appears in Part One, others offer us insight into the issues surrounding creative nonfiction. Rebecca Blevins Faery and Robert Root explain and illustrate how and why they write disjunctive essays; Peter M. Ives and Mimi Schwartz address the issue of accuracy and honesty; Jocelyn Bartkevicius, Lee Gutkind, and Michael Pearson examine attempts to define and identify creative nonfiction; and Marianna Torgovnick discusses the reasons she practices and promotes experimental critical writing with its use of personal voice in academic discourse (a subject treated by Tompkins as well).

As we've mentioned earlier, many of these selections can be paired with writings in Part One. One glance at the table of contents shows which authors appear in both sections of the book. A cursory look at the titles provides some sense of the specific concerns represented here. For example, if you were to look at Jane Tompkins's Part One essay, "At the Buffalo Bill Museum," you would notice that, although it's a piece of academic cultural criticism, Tompkins has written about her discoveries in an intimate and informal voice. Then if you read "Me and My Shadow" in Part Two, you'd find that in this essay Tompkins is giving herself (and other academic critics) permission to use her own personal presence and voice in her scholarly writing.

Conversely, let's suppose that you want to read some of the Part Two essays to gain a sense of a particular writer's theory of creative nonfiction before you read his or her sample of it in Part One. For example, in his Part Two piece, "What Happened to the Personal Essay?" Phillip Lopate discusses the history of the personal essay and reveals his own particular slant on the kinds of essays he writes. Lopate's Part One essay, "Portrait of My Body," then becomes a model for what he means by "interrogating the self." Similarly, if you first read Scott Russell Sanders's essay on essays in this section, you will then read his personal essay, "Cloud Crossing," with an awareness of what he hopes to accomplish in his writing.

Several of the writers whose works are presented in Part Two are also working teachers in whose courses students often study creative nonfiction. Some of them teach courses expressly focused on creative nonfiction as a subject in itself. As a result, their selections are at least tangentially about the connections between writing and teaching writing, especially writing and teaching creative nonfiction. Like Donald Murray, who first modeled this sensibility in *A Writer Teaches Writing* thirty years ago, each teacher/writer takes a writerly approach to this genre.

Although some of these selections involve critical analysis, they do not present a detached theoretical approach. All of the essays are designed to offer a writerly perspective on the evolving dialogue about creative nonfiction. As a result, the works selected for Part Two ground creative nonfiction in the behaviors and motives of working writers and teachers, reflecting back on the examples of the form in Part One and projecting ahead to essays on composing the fourth genre in Part Three.

The Landscape of Creative Nonfiction

Jocelyn Bartkevicius

> *[I]naccuracy is very often a superior form of truth.*
>
> Virginia Woolf, "Incongruous Memories"

1. The Stranger

I was standing in a garden, tomato plants ripening, chickens dashing about, when I first learned I was a stranger. I was quite young, maybe six or seven, watching my grandmother pick tomatoes and tell stories about her life as a farm girl in Eastern Europe. She had just gotten to the part about hiding in the forest from waves of invading armies—Russians then Prussians then Russians again—when she stopped, stood up, looked me in the eye, and said: "But you are an American; you don't understand."

How can I convey the force of these words? Of course, as a school girl I was familiar with the idea of "being an American." I said the pledge of allegiance, hand on heart like all the other kids. I sang the "Star Spangled Banner" (except for those unreachable glaring red high notes). But this identity had never been pinned upon me so specifically, so singularly, or as an impediment. "Being an American" had never made me an outsider. Standing in my grandmother's garden, among plants and animals raised the old ways, I was the other.

In memory, when she speaks these words, my grandmother is looking me right in the eye. She was a small woman, possibly reaching five feet at her healthiest, before the osteoporosis formed a permanent stoop. And I was a gangly girl who got all her height early. But now that I look at the memory, examine it instead of experiencing it, I must admit that a five-foot-tall six year old is an unlikely creature. Something is wrong with the memory. It is incongruous.

And then there are holes in the memory: I can't remember whether my grandmother continued her story after she stood up and spoke to me. Or whether she returned to her gardening. Or why she began the story at all. It was hard to get her to talk about Lithuania, especially about the years when, as a very young woman, she had to bury food in the forest to survive, had to prepare constantly to flee soldiers and their various hungers, had to watch city people (who could not grow their own food) sicken and die. Perhaps my father stood off to the side prompting her. But he is not in the memory. Maybe I—normally a very shy child and fearful of misunderstanding her difficult Lithuanian accent—had a rare fit of boldness and asked her a question about Europe.

The scene is one that I return to often, for her words fixed the moment as indelibly as a brand. I used to think that the memory drew me in spite of its incongruities and holes. But I am beginning to realize that this memory compels me *because* of the incongruities and holes. The pitted, nearly invisible landscape of the past is a mysterious, inviting place. Each exploration reveals a different topography.

Looking back, I find that my grandmother bequeathed layers of strangeness that day. Her words taught me that I was a stranger in her world. And they taught that, while there had been some unevenness in my life—near poverty, my parents' divorce, and so on—I was nevertheless a stranger to profound suffering and struggle. And now, looking not just at the moment but at the memory itself, at the moment as incongruous memory, I find that my grandmother's words taught me that there is a stranger within. That is, certain moments will not survive unravaged, that going back in time and memory I will discover losses, unreachable territories. Some of the territories remain, buried beneath the surface of daily life and ordinary reminiscence, inaccessible but for accident or imaginative self-interrogation.

In the case of my grandmother's garden, incongruities and obvious gaps drew me back to the memory, signaled its importance. Other moments may disappear without a trace, leaving no path, and the act of writing may be the only way to unearth them.

A few years after I stood with my grandmother in her garden, my father bought a farm—or what I called a farm before I moved from Connecticut to Iowa and saw working farms, counted among my friends actual farmers, and learned that in relation to Iowa farms, my father's place had been not a farm at all but an acreage. There on his land I built a miniature version of my grandmother's garden using compost from the manure pile, sprinkling lime from a stocking to discourage bugs. I followed my father around, riding barely trained horses, acting the cowboy, zipping through forests, sleeping under the stars. And this is how I remember those years, as a little grandma, a little immigrant, a peasant girl in a store-bought peasant blouse (it was the sixties), bringing home-grown organic carrots to high school for lunch. I remember a peaceful Eden punctuated by moments of playing the stereo in my father's hand-built log cabin, Joni Mitchell singing about getting back to the garden, Neil Young loving his country girl.

But recently, I found buried in an old trunk a black and white snapshot of my father and me, pitchfork and all like the pair in Grant Wood's *American Gothic*. Our pitchfork, though, is angled; we both stare at it, and impaled upon one of the tongs is a small bat. In my memory, I am a Romantic peasant girl, gardening as it has been handed down by my Eastern European ancestors, embracing Woodstock, barefoot to Joni and Neil. In the photograph I am a party to the slaughter of a benign and beneficial mammal. Writing about the photograph awakened darker memories from the farm: another child's pointing a loaded pistol at me, my aiming a loaded BB gun at a sleeping bat as it hung from the shed door, and leaving the cabin after an argument to disappear alone into the dark country night.

The self—at least *my* self—is composed of misremembered and unremembered scenes. The path back to that uneven landscape is the path of the mind. Students in my creative nonfiction workshops frequently ask me to define for them, concisely and with directions for construction, "the personal essay." Usually I try to do so by offering a variety of creative nonfiction pieces along with several writers' working definitions of the form. But at times I ask them to define for me, concisely (but without directions for construction), "a person." The definition of "personal essay" is as complicated and various as that of "person," and the personal essay is just one possible manifestation of creative nonfiction.

In writing creative nonfiction, in order to tell the truth, I must let the incongruities be. I was standing in the garden with my grandmother and we were eye to eye although we could not be the same height. I was six while also being ten—perhaps six with shyness and the language barrier and ten chronologically. Or ten in my boldness and six chronologically. Or I was somehow taller for being a stranger and my grandmother was somehow shorter for changing my world. And in order to tell the truth in creative nonfiction I must explore the gaps. I was an earth child on my father's farm and yet I was shooting bats. I focus on the unremembered photograph and dig for more. Memory, the mind's path, enacts wonders, and the creative nonfiction writer's work is not to reason those wonders away with mathematical formulae, but to embrace them, to recreate layer after layer of incongruity.

2. The Terms

The first time I heard the term "nonfiction," I was sitting with twenty other third graders at a veneered table in a grammar school library. I watched the librarian walk from wall to wall tapping books and signs with her pointer. Each book had a hand-typed Dewey decimal system number taped to its spine. Each section had a hand-printed sign fixed above it. She paused at the section labeled "fiction," tapped a row of spines, tapped the sign above, and said: "These books are fiction. They're made up; they aren't true." She stepped to the left, swung her pointer at the next section, labeled "nonfiction," tapped the sign, and said: "These books are not fiction. They aren't made up; they are fact." While the librarian went on with her presentation, my mind went elsewhere. Fiction was not true and nonfiction was not fiction; therefore nonfiction was *not* not true. She was using the forbidden double negative. I sat at the table wondering what made fiction, the not-true, so central that the term "nonfiction" was formed from it.

I probably would have forgotten that moment in the library if similar moments had not recurred throughout my life. The string of assumptions goes like this: Fiction is "made up," and thus crafted, invented, "made." Fiction is art because its creator draws upon imagination. Nonfiction is "not made up," and thus recorded, reported, "unmade." Nonfiction makes itself, the writer is a mere tape recorder or camera. Or, in cases where the material of nonfiction needs some shaping, the writer draws upon reason and logic alone.

Such assumptions are in part an issue of terminology. "Fiction," the root word, comes from "fingere," to form, mold, devise. "Non" simply means "not." Thus we get the implication that nonfiction is not formed, molded, or devised. Although this "non" negates the term "fiction," it is not the strongest available negative prefix. "Dis," which implies expulsion, as in "disfrock" or "disbar," would give us disfiction, a genre deprived of fiction, even, perhaps, expelled from it. "Un," which means "against" or "anti," would give us unfiction, a genre opposed to fiction. Nonfiction, looked at in this context, is not deprived of fiction or opposed to fiction, but simply, like the librarian said, not fiction.

There remains, however, an unsettling nuance to "non." While calling someone non-American does not brand them an enemy (as calling that person un-American would), it still suggests that they are other. A non-American is a foreigner, or, as my grandmother was sometimes called, an alien. Nonfiction is to fiction as non-American is to American. Thus, nonfiction is the stranger, the foreigner (or alien) in the land of fiction. What's more, in both cases, the root word is the point of reference. Many writers and editors add "creative" to "nonfiction" to mollify this sense of being strange and other, and to remind readers that creative nonfiction writers are more than recorders or appliers of reason and objectivity. Certainly many readers and writers of creative nonfiction recognize that the genre can share some elements of fiction; dialogue, place, characters, and plot, for example, might occur in both. When a piece of creative nonfiction resembles fiction, the "non" might suggest not so much "not," as something like "kicking off from." Why else insist that it is not fiction unless it is in danger of being mistaken for fiction?

If "nonfiction" might mean a work that is related to but different from fiction, perhaps works in the genre that are more akin to poetry—sharing with it lyric and image or a structure built on association and repetition rather than on narrative—would benefit from another name. I read some of Virginia Woolf's nonfiction (her lyrical, personal pieces like "Evening Over Sussex," and "The Death of the Moth," for example) for its poetry. Other writers come to mind: Terry Tempest Williams's *Desert Quartet*, for example, a lyrical, concentrated work with gaps and craters, a book written not only from reason, but also from imagination, dreams, and the body. Such works, while not poems per se, use poetry as their inspiration, their model, their "kicking off point." For them, I suggest the term "nonpoetry."

To play with terms and search for definitions can be more than an academic exercise. I'm interested in the genre's possibility, a possibility not just theoretical but practical—that is, involving practice. Rather than map out territory (and thus limit it) I mean to expand it. Rather than build fences, knock them down.

3. The Stars

A few months ago, a formerly estranged cousin gave me a copy of an old home movie. Over antipasto made the old way, we watched ourselves together, children moving in and out of a series of silent, disjointed scenes in black and white. My cousin and I sat together as his father's last birthday party unfolded before us; we watched ourselves celebrate just a few yards from the spot where an accident would later kill his father, shattering our family for decades. But on that night preserved on film, we all sit together on the pool deck of the hotel and nightclub his father and my stepfather ran together, happy beneath the stars. We sit at a long table, laughing and talking silently. Suddenly, my stepfather rises up, grabs a torch-like candle, and begins dancing around our table. While he circles the rest of us, we watch my uncle cut his Italian rum cake from Romano's.

My cousin broke the silence of that old flickering movie. "There must have been bugs," he said, "that's got to be a bug torch and he's spreading the fog around our table." But that's not what I saw. Though I didn't at first remember the scene, I knew my stepfather. He was dancing out his joy, his exuberance, the energy that pored from each cell of his body. "I'd rip the stars out of the sky for you," he used to tell my half sister, the child of his middle age, and there he was, ripping the stars out of the sky, lighting the night for one of our last happy moments together.

The camera recorded the scene for perpetuity. And yet my cousin and I, with similar family experiences, with memories of that moment, and with objective evidence before us, saw it differently. If put alone in separate rooms and interrogated or given blank sheets of paper and told to write that scene, we would come up with different stories. We both sat at the family table that night, and so the party is in our memories, embedded in the very matter of our brains. And we both watched the tape, separately and together, several times in recent months. Nevertheless we tell different stories. Which one is true? Which one imagined?

His story and mine, I believe, contain elements of fact and imagination. Both are true, for they are true to how we remember, how we see, they recreate the topographies of our minds. We can return to the film and we can return to our memories. Either way, each of us returns to a different place.

Recently, I attended another birthday party, for a friend who is a writer. After he blew out the candles, and everyone made the requisite jokes about aging, our conversation turned to writing and memory. "You could never write this scene as nonfiction," one friend, a fiction writer, said. "You couldn't remember the dialogue verbatim; you'd end up remembering words wrong and so you'd have to change them. You'd forget things and leave them out. That would make it fiction." Several others at the table agreed, assuming that without a tape recorder you'd be left with fallible memory and therefore be incapable of creating nonfiction. There were only two ways to write the scene with dialogue, they believed, to write it as fiction (and freely invent and recreate words), or to write it as nonfiction (and record, transcribe, and then report the words exactly as spoken).

One of the guests, a lawyer, objected. "You should read briefs," he said. "Recorded dialogue doesn't make any sense."

"You need the background," another friend, a nonfiction writer, added, "the color of the walls, the smell of the food. How can you understand the dialogue without the scene?"

"What if someone's words trigger a memory?" I asked. "Let's say that as you're speaking, I'm reminded of a scene from my past, like standing in my grandmother's garden. Even if we filmed and taped this party, that wouldn't show up, and yet it changes my experience of the party."

"I was wondering," the literary theorist said, "what I'd do with that moment when I became obsessed with the pattern on this plate, or when I concentrated on the taste of the red beans and rice."

If my birthday party companions read this dialogue, they would no doubt revise it according to their own memories and perceptions. In fact, that same night we suggested—as a joke or perhaps as a challenge—that each of us, two fiction writers, a poet, two creative nonfiction writers, a theorist, a lawyer, and a decorator—should go off immediately and write the scene. By the time we were well into the cake and coffee, we more or less agreed that if we were true to the events as we'd each experienced them, if we didn't write, for example, that the lawyer had stood up, reached across the table, and punched the guest of honor as he blew out his candles (since he had done nothing of the kind), we would be writing creative nonfiction.

We reached common ground in the end, I think, because we shifted both our working notion of genre and our view of "the person." When my friends claimed that nonfiction could work only with the aid of a tape recorder, their concept of the person was external, the person as captured by a machine. They had shared the assumption, arrived at by habit, that nonfiction was restricted to objectivity and reporting, that incongruity must be reasoned away. Fact, as Virginia Woolf points out, is not necessarily the same as truth, and as we talked that night, we explored what it means to be at a birthday party, what it means to participate in a conversation, how much more it is than the sounds we make, the words we speak. What we say and how we move—what machines can pick up—is only the surface of the scene. "Nonfiction" is not a synonym for "recorded surface." It has the range to sweep inward, follow the path of the mind, add layers of contemporaneous imagination, memory, and dream to the observable events of the present moment.

Patricia Hampl, who has said that memory is a place, has also said that the nonfiction writer is homeless.

One such occasion was an informal talk after her reading in the third floor lounge of a certain university's humanities' building. Graduate students used to joke about the symbolism of the building's design: Fiction and poetry were on the top floor. Freshman composition was in the basement. In the middle (just above philosophy) was nonfiction, tucked away in a corner of the literature department. Although Hampl's reading drew a large audience, only a small group of die-hard nonfictionists showed up for the talk.

In our small quarters, nearly invisible in a wing of the literature department, her discussion of the nonfiction writer's homelessness rang true. The department had just changed the name of our program from "expository writing" to "nonfiction writing" and would soon rename it "creative nonfiction." We could see that we were the new kids on the block, that to many, our genre was ill defined and invisible. But there we sat listening to a writer who had made a career of creative nonfiction, who had written two memoirs and many personal essays, and who spoke optimistically about the genre's range and possibility. Many of us felt at home for the first time—not in our lounge, but in her words.

The prospect of literary homelessness drives and limits certain writers to formulae, say, memoir in five parts (action scene followed by predictable summation followed by continuation of the action and so on, like a sitcom or a mini series). They find a "home" and hole up in the corner. And they pass along a favored formula to groups of beginner or intermediate writers, regardless of any particular student writer's emphasis, place of origin, gender, culture, aesthetic, or concept of the self. Handing over a prepackaged piece of creative nonfiction is, in essence, putting the writer into a cell. The bolder explorers, happy not to be enclosed, take advantage of the unsettled terrain of nonfiction, wandering and exploring, allowing themselves to be vulnerable, following the path of the mind even when they enter shadows, pressing on into the territory of the unknown, the mysterious, the incongruous.

Creative nonfiction is at once flourishing and invisible, set and contested. The genre that embraces the often paradoxical nature of the self is itself often paradoxical (in its position in the world of writing and letters). Patricia Hampl provides the metaphor of the creative nonfiction writer as homeless. And she also turns it around. We're lucky, she says, we get to be out under the stars.

The Art of Memoir

Mary Clearman Blew

One of the oldest and loveliest of quilt patterns is the Double Wedding Ring, in which bands of colors lock and interlock in endless circles. If you want to make a Double Wedding Ring quilt, be a saver of fabric. Treasure the smallest scraps, from the maternity dress you have just sewn for your oldest daughter or the Halloween costume you cobbled together for your youngest, from the unfaded inside hems of worn-out clothing or the cotton left over from other quilts. Keep a pair of sharp scissors on hand, and also a pattern, which I like to cut from fine sandpaper, and which will be about an inch wide by two inches long and slightly flared, like a flower petal that has been rounded off at both ends. Whenever you have a scrap of fabric, lay out your pattern on it and snip out a few more blocks.

Save your blocks in a three-pound coffee can. When the can is full, empty the blocks out on the floor and arrange them in the shape of rainbow arcs with a juxtaposition of colors and textures that pleases you. Seven pieces to an arc, seventy-two arcs to a quilt. You can sew the blocks together on a sewing machine, but I like the spell cast by hand sewing. I use a #11 needle, which is an inch-long sliver of steel with an eye so fine that it will barely take the quilter's thread, which measures time by growing infinitesimally shorter with each dip and draw of the needle, and I wear the hundred-year-old thimble of a woman named Amelia Bunn on my finger.

When you have pieced your seventy-two arcs, you must choose a fabric to join your arcs, in a process that is called "setting up" the quilt. Traditionally a Double Wedding Ring quilt is set up on white, but remember that you have all colors to choose from; and while choosing one color means forgoing others, remind yourself that your coffee can of pieces will fill again. There will be another quilt at the back of your mind while you are piecing, quilting, and binding this one, which perhaps you will give to one of your daughters, to trace her childhood through the pieces. Or perhaps you will give it to a friend, to speak the words the pattern spoke to you.

For years I thought of myself as a fiction writer, even during the years in northern Montana when I virtually stopped writing. But in 1987 I came to a divide. My father had died, and my husband was suffering a mental breakdown along with the progressive lung disease that eventually killed him. I was estranged from my older children. Then I lost my job. It was the job that mattered the most. I had a small child to support. And so I looked for another job and found one, teaching in a small college in Idaho, with the northern Rockies between me and the first half of my life.

Far from home and teaching again after years in higher-ed. administration, I felt a hollowness that writing fiction seemed to do nothing to fill. And so I started all over again, writing essays to retrieve the past—in my case, the Montana homestead frontier with its harsh ideals for men and women, its tests and its limitations. The conventions of fiction, its masks and metaphors, came to seem more and more boring to me, like an unnecessary barricade between me and the material I was writing about. But because fiction was what I knew about, I used the techniques of fiction in these essays: plot, characterization, dialogue. What I began to discover was a form that worked for my purpose.

I would select an event out of family legend and retell it in a voice that grew out of my own experience and perceptions. Often the events that beckoned to me the most urgently were the ones that had been preserved in the "secret stories" my grandmothers and my great-aunts told around their Sunday tables after the dishes had been washed, elliptical and pointless and mystifying, in hushed voices that dropped or stopped altogether at the approach of one of the men or an unwise question from an eavesdropping child. Eventually I was trusted with a few of the secret stories, myself. I remember how my aunt's voice fell and her sentences became sparing when she told me a story about her mother, my grandmother. The story was about a time when my grandmother had lived alone on the homestead north of Denton, Montana, for eighteen months without seeing another woman. She had two small children and another baby on the way—her husband was away for weeks on end, trying to sell life insurance to make ends meet—and she had to carry her water in a bucket from a spring a quarter of a mile from the homestead shack, which she did at twilight, when the heat of the sun was not so oppressive. She began to hallucinate. She saw the shapes of women on the other side of the spring, shapes that looked like her dead mother and her dead sister, beckoning to her. She decided she was going crazy. She had her little children to think about. They might not be found for weeks if she broke down. And so she began to go for her water in the heat of the day, when the sun scorched her trail and bleached the color out of the grass and rocks. She never saw the beckoning shapes again.

Unlike my grandmother, I have chosen to follow the beckoning shapes. I don't understand the significance of that story for my grandmother, or why she kept it a secret except for the one time she whispered it to her younger sister in, I presume, those same stark sentences in which her sister whispered it to her niece, my aunt, the same sentences in which my aunt whispered the story just one time to me. But then, I don't fully understand why I continue to wear Amelia Bunn's thimble—it is sterling silver and engraved AB in a fine script—any more than I know what my great-grandmother looked like in life or as she appeared in the dying heat waves of that long-ago Montana twilight.

But sometimes I think I can see the turning points in the lives of dead men and women. For example, my grandmother's decision to return to schoolteaching in 1922, even though it meant breaking up her family, boarding out her oldest daughter, taking the younger children to live with her in a teacherage, leaving her husband alone on the homestead. What did that decision mean to her? I know what it means to me. Or my aunt's mowing machine accident in June of 1942, when a runaway team of sorrel horses spilled her in the path of a sickle bar that nearly cut off her foot. The disaster forced her out of the path of teaching in rural schools that she had been following and into a new life on the Olympic Peninsula. Did she understand the opportunity in the teeth of the sickle bar?

I feel an uneasy balance between writing about my grandmother and my aunt as their lives "really" were and writing about them as a projection of my own experiences. I keep reminding myself that the times when they lived are not my times. Nor do the nuances of their stories necessarily reflect my assumptions about language. And yet I am who I am because of these women and the stories they told; and, as I write about them, they live and breathe again through the umbilical tangle between character and writer.

I've been fortunate in my family's being one of storytellers and private writers who have "documented" their past. Tales, diaries, notebooks, and letters—they saved every scrap. Of course their stories were fictions as much as mine are, told over and over again and given shape and significance. Their connection to literal truth is suspect.

For my part, I struggled for a long time with the conflicting claims of the exact truth of the story and its emotional truth as I perceived it. I restrict myself to what I "know" happened: the concrete details, the objects, the history. When I speculate, I say so.

But any story depends upon its shape. In arranging the scraps that have been passed down to me, which are to be selected, which discarded? The boundaries of creative nonfiction will always be as fluid as water.

Students often ask, what can you decently write about other people? Whose permission do you have to ask? What can you decently reveal about yourself?

I can only speak for myself. I own my past and my present. Only I can decide whether or how to write about it. Also, I know that once I write about the past, I will have changed the past, in a sense set it in concrete, and I will never remember it in quite the same way. The experience itself is lost; like the old Sunday storytellers who told and retold their stories until what they remembered was the tale itself, what I will remember is what I have written.

Certainly, something personal is being sacrificed, for when I write about myself, I transform myself just as I do the past. A side-effect is that while the writing process itself can be painful, I experience a detachment from the finished essay, because I have come to exist in it as a character as separate from myself as any fictional character. I find that I can read my essays to audiences with very little emotion, although once, reading Annick Smith's essay "Homestead" to a creative writing class, I began to cry and thought I would not be able to go on. Her nonfiction character moved me in a way my own could not.

Lately I have been reading my aunt's diaries, which she kept without fail for fifty years. I feel haunted by the parallels between her life and mine. She chose, perhaps with greater self-discipline, perhaps from being closer to the source of the old punishing pressures, to stay all her life on a straight and narrow path I had been perilously near to embarking on. Her diaries reveal her unhappiness, her gradual, unwilling resignation to her lot, and finally, in her old age, her reconciliation with the lone woman she had set out to be. Which has left me with an enormous determination to resist those pressures and to try a new direction: having written my past, I will write the present and transform myself, as she did, in the interstices between fragment and pattern, through the endless interlocking connections between storyteller and story.

We'll see, we'll see. Opportunity lies in the teeth of the sickle bar.

To Fashion a Text

Annie Dillard

I'm here because I'm writing a book called *An American Childhood,* which is a memoir—insofar as a memoir is any account, usually in the first person, of incidents that happened a while ago. It isn't an autobiography, and it isn't "memoirs." I wouldn't dream of writing my memoirs; I'm only forty years old. Or my autobiography; any chronology of my days would make very dull reading—I've spent about thirty years behind either a book or a desk. The book that I'm writing is an account of a childhood in Pittsburgh, Pennsylvania, where I grew up.

The best memoirs, I think, forge their own forms. The writer of any work, and particularly any nonfiction work, must decide two crucial points: what to put in and what to leave out.

So I thought, "What shall I put in?" Well, what is the book about? *An American Childhood* is about the passion of childhood. It's about a child's vigor, and originality, and eagerness, and mastery, and joy.

It's about waking up. A child wakes up over and over again, and notices that she's living. She dreams along, loving the exuberant life of the senses, in love with beauty and power, oblivious of herself—and then suddenly, bingo, she wakes up and feels herself alive. She notices her own awareness. And she notices that she is set down here, mysteriously, in a going world. The world is full of fascinating information that she can collect and enjoy. And the world is public; its issues are moral and historical ones.

So the book is about two things: a child's interior life—vivid, superstitious and timeless—and a child's growing awareness of the world. The structural motion of the book is from the interior landscape—one brain's own idiosyncratic topography—to the American landscape, the vast setting of our common history. The little child pinches the skin on the back of her hand and sees where God made Adam from spit and clay. The older child explores the city on foot and starts to work on her future as a detective, or an epidemiologist, or a painter. Older yet, she runs wild and restless over the city's bridges, and finds in Old Testament poetry and French symbolist poetry some language sounds she loves.

The interior life is in constant vertical motion; consciousness runs up and down the scales every hour like a slide trombone. It dreams down below; it notices up above; and it notices itself, too, and its own alertness. The vertical motion of consciousness, from inside to outside and back, interests me. I've written about it once before, in an essay about a solar eclipse, and I wanted to do more with it.

For a private interior life, I've picked—almost at random—my own. As an aside, this isn't as evident as it may seem. I simply like to write books. About twelve years ago, while I was walking in Acadia National Park in Maine, I decided to write a narrative—a prose narrative, because I wanted to write prose. After a week's thought I decided to write mostly about nature, because I thought I could make it do what I wanted, and I decided to set it all on the coast of Maine. I decided further to write it in the third person, about a man, a sort of metaphysician, in his fifties. A month or so later I decided reluctantly to set the whole shebang in Virginia, because I knew more about Virginia. Then I decided to write it in the first person, as a man. Not until I had written the first chapter and showed it around—this was *Pilgrim at Tinker Creek*—did I give up the pretext of writing in the first person as a man. I wasn't out to deceive people; I just didn't like the idea of writing about myself. I knew I wasn't the subject.

So in this book, for simplicity's sake, I've got my own interior life. It was a lively one. I put in what it was that had me so excited all the time—the sensation of time pelting me as if I were standing under a waterfall. I loved the power of the life in which I found myself. I loved to feel its many things in all their force. I put in what it feels like to play with the skin on your mother's knuckles. I put in what it feels like to throw a baseball—you aim your whole body at the target and watch the ball fly off as if it were your own head. I put in drawing pencil studies of my baseball mitt and collecting insects and fooling around with a microscope.

In my study on Cape Cod, where I write, I've stuck above my desk a big photograph of a little Amazonian boy whose face is sticking out of a waterfall or a rapids. White water is pounding all around his head, in a kind of wreath, but his face is absolutely still, looking up, and his black eyes are open dreamily on the distance. That little boy is completely alive; he's letting the mystery of existence beat on him. He's having his childhood, and I think he knows it. And I think he will come out of the water strong, and ready to do some good. I see this photograph whenever I look up from my computer screen.

So I put in that moment of waking up and noticing that you've been put down in a world that's already under way. The rushing of time wakes you: you play along mindless and eternal on the kitchen floor, and time streams in full flood beside you on the floor. It rages beside you, down its swollen banks, and when it wakes you you're so startled you fall in.

When you wake up, you notice that you're here.

"Here," in my case, was Pittsburgh. I put in the three rivers that meet here. The Allegheny from the north and the Monongahela from the south converge to form the Ohio, the major tributary of the Mississippi, which, in turn, drains the whole continent east of the divide via the Missouri River rising in the Rocky Mountains.

The great chain of the Alleghenies kept pioneers out of Pittsburgh until the 1760s, one hundred and fifty years after Jamestown.

I put in those forested mountains and hills, and the way the three rivers lie flat and moving among them, and the way the low land lies wooded among them, and the way the blunt mountains rise in the darkness from the rivers' banks.

I put in Lake Erie, and summers along its mild shore. I put in New Orleans, the home of Dixieland jazz, where my father was heading when he jumped in his boat one day to go down the river like Huck Finn.

I put in the pioneers who "broke wilderness," and the romance of the French and Indian Wars that centered around Fort Duquesne and Fort Pitt. I put in the brawling rivermen—the flatboatmen and keelboatmen.

I put in the old Scotch-Irish families who dominate Pittsburgh and always have. The Mellons are Scotch-Irish, and so were Andrew Carnegie and Henry Clay Frick. They're all Presbyterians. I grew up in this world—at the lunatic fringe of it—and it fascinates me. I think it's important. I think it's peculiarly American—that mixture of piety and acquisitiveness, that love of work. They're Calvinists, of course—just like the Massachusetts Puritans—and I think I can make a case that their influence on American thought was greater than the Puritans'. There were far more Scotch-Irish Presbyterians, after all, and they settled all over the American colonies and carried their democracy and pragmatism with them.

In Pittsburgh the Scotch-Irish constitute a world of many families whose forebears knew each other, who respect each other's discretion and who admire each other for occupying their slots without fuss. The men are withdrawn, the women are ironic. They believe in their world; they all stay in Pittsburgh, and their children stay there. I alone am escaped to tell thee. I and David McCullough, who grew up a few houses away. And James Laughlin, the publisher. All of us Pittsburgh Scotch-Irish Presbyterians.

My sisters and I grew up in this world, and I put it in *An American Childhood*. I put in our private school and quiet club and hushed neighborhood where the houses were stone and their roofs were slate. I put in dancing with little boys at dancing school, and looking at the backs of their interesting necks at Presbyterian church.

Just to make trouble, I put in money. My grandmother used to tell me never to touch money with my bare hands.

I put in books, for that's where this book started, with an essay I wrote for the *New York Times Magazine* on reading books. Almost all of my many passionate interests, and my many changes of mind, came through books. Books prompted the many vows I made to myself. Nonfiction books lured me away from the world—as I dreamed about working for Scotland Yard, doing field work in freshwater streams, rock collecting in the salt desert, painting in Paris. And novels dragged me back into the world—because I would read whatever was handy, and what was handy in those years were novels about the Second World War. I read so many books about the Second World War that I knew how to man a minesweeper before I knew how to walk in high heels. You couldn't read much about the war without figuring out that the world was a moral arena that required your strength.

I had the notion back then that everything was interesting if you just learned enough about it. Now, writing about it, I have the pleasure of learning it all again and finding that it *is* interesting. I get to inform myself and any readers about such esoterica as rock collecting, which I hadn't thought about in almost thirty years.

When I was twelve a paperboy gave me two grocery bags full of rock and mineral chunks. It took me most of a year to identify them. At a museum shop I bought cards of what they called thumbnail specimens. And I read books about a fairly absurd batch of people who called themselves rockhounds; they spent their evenings in the basement sawing up slabs of travertine into wavy slices suitable, they said, for wall hangings.

Now, in this memoir, I get to recall where the romance of rock collecting had lain: the symbolic sense that underneath the dreary highways, underneath Pittsburgh, were canyons of crystals—that you could find treasure by prying open the landscape. In my reading I learned that people have cracked knobs of granite and laid bare clusters of red garnets and topaz crystals, chrysoberyl, spudomene and emerald. They held in their hands crystals that had hung in a hole in the dark for a billion years unseen. I liked the idea of that. I would lay about me right and left with a hammer and bash the landscape to bits. I would crack the earth's crust like a piñata and spread its vivid prizes in chunks to the light. That's what I wanted to do. So I put that in.

It's also a great pleasure to write about my parents, because they're both great storytellers—comedians, actually—which gives me a chance to tell their wonderful stories. We were all young, at our house, and we enjoyed ourselves.

My father was a dreamer; he lived differently from other men around him. One day he abruptly quit the family firm—when I was ten—and took off down the Ohio River in a boat by himself to search out the roots of jazz in New Orleans. He came back after several months and withdrew from corporate life forever. He knew the world well—all sort of things, which he taught us to take an interest in: how people build bridge pilings in the middle of a river, how jazz came up the river to be educated in Chicago, how the pioneers made their way westward from Pittsburgh, down the Ohio River, sitting on the tops of their barges and singing "Bang Away, My Lulu."

My mother was both a thinker and what one might call a card. If she lay on the beach with friends and found the conversation dull, she would give a little push with her heel and roll away. People were stunned. She rolled deadpan and apparently effortlessly, her arms and legs extended tidily, down the beach to the distant water's edge where she lay at ease just as she had been, but half in the surf, and well out of earshot. She was not only a card but a wild card, a force for disorder.

She regarded even tiny babies as straight men, and liked to step on the drawstring of a crawling baby's gown, so that the baby crawled and crawled and never got anywhere except into a little ball at the top of the gown.

She was interested in language. Once my father and I were in the kitchen listening to a ballgame—the Pirates playing the New York Giants. The Giants had a utility infielder named Wayne Terwilliger. Just as Mother walked through the kitchen, the announcer said, "Terwilliger bunts one." Mother stopped dead and said, "What was that? Was that English?" Father said, "The man's name is Terwilliger. He bunted." Mother thought that was terrific. For the next ten or twelve years she made this surprising string of syllables her own. If she was testing a microphone, or if she was pretending to whisper a secret in my ear, she said, "Terwilliger bunts one." If she had ever had an occasion to create a motto for a coat of arms, as Andrew Carnegie had, her motto would have been "Terwilliger bunts one." Carnegie's was "Death to privilege."

These fine parents taught my sisters and me moral courage, insofar as we have it, and tolerance, and how to dance all night without dragging your arms on your partner, and how to time the telling of a joke.

I've learned a lot by writing this book, not only about writing but about American history. Eastern woodland Indians killed many more settlers than plains Indians did. By the time settlers made it to Sioux and Apache country those Indians had been so weakened by disease and by battles with the army that they didn't have much fight left in them. It was the settlers in the Pennsylvania forests and in Maryland and Virginia who kept getting massacred and burned out and taken captive and tortured. During the four years the French held Pittsburgh at Fort Duquesne they armed the Indians and sent them out from there, raiding and killing English-speaking settlers. These were mostly Scotch-Irish, because the Penn family let them settle in Pennsylvania only if they would serve as a "buffer sect" between Quakers and Indians. When the English held Pittsburgh at Fort Pitt they gave the Indians unwashed blankets from the smallpox hospital.

I put in early industry, because it was unexpectedly interesting. Before there was steel, everything was made out of wrought iron—which I find just amazing. Railroad ties were made out of wrought iron, as if they were candle sconces. Men had to carry wrought iron railroad ties all up and down the country. Wrought iron is made by iron puddlers, who belong to the iron puddlers' union, the Sons of Vulcan. It's a very difficult process: you stir slag back into iron, and it requires skilled labor because carbon monoxide bubbles up. The language is also nice. To sinter, for instance, is to convert flu dust to clinker. And I finally learned what coke is. When I was a child I thought that Coca-Cola was a by-product of steelmaking.

I learned about the heyday of the big industrialists and the endless paradox of Andrew Carnegie, the only one of the great American moguls who not only read books but actually wrote them, including one with a very American title, *The Gospel of Wealth*. He sold U.S. Steel to J. P. Morgan for $492 million, and he said, "A man who dies rich dies disgraced." He gave away ninety percent of his fortune in the few years he had left. While he was giving away money, many people were moved, understandably, to write him letters. He got one such letter from his friend Mark Twain. It said:

You seem to be in prosperity. Could you lend an admirer a dollar & a half to buy a hymn-book with? God will bless you. I feel it. I know it.
P.S. Don't send the hymn-book, send the money.

Carnegie was only five feet three inches tall. He weighed 133 pounds. He built the workers free libraries and museums and an art gallery at the same time that he had them working sixteen hours a day, six days a week, at subhuman wages, and drinking water full of typhoid and cholera because he and the other business owners opposed municipal works like water filtration plants. By 1906 Pittsburgh had the highest death rate in the nation because of wretched living conditions, and yet it was the seat of "wealth beyond computation, wealth beyond imagination." People built stables for their horses with gold mirrors in the stalls. The old Scotch-Irish families were horrified at the new millionaires who popped up around this time because they liked things pretty quiet. One new millionaire went to a barber on Penn Avenue for his first shampoo and the barber reported that the washing brought out "two ounces of fine Mesabi ore and a scattering of slag and cinders."

And what to leave out?

Well, I'm not writing social history. This is not one of those books in which you may read the lyrics or even the titles of popular songs on the radio. Or the names of radio and TV programs, or advertising slogans or product names or clothing fashions. I don't like all that. I want to direct the reader's attention in equal parts to the text—as a formal object—and to the world, as an interesting place in which we find ourselves.

So another thing I left out, as far as I could, was myself. The personal pronoun can be the subject of the verb: "I see this, I did that." But not the object of the verb: "I analyze me, I discuss me, I describe me, I quote me."

In the course of writing this memoir I've learned all sorts of things, quite inadvertently, about myself and various relationships. But these things are not important to the book and I easily leave them out. Since the subject of the book is not me, other omissions naturally follow. I leave out many things that were important to my life but of no concern for the present book, like the summer I spent in Wyoming when I was fifteen. I keep the action in Pittsburgh; I see no reason to drag everybody off to Wyoming just because I want to tell them about my summer vacation. You have to take pains in a memoir not to hang on the reader's arm, like a drunk, and say, "And then I did this and it was so interesting." I don't write for that reason.

On the other hand, I dig deeply into the exuberant heart of a child and the restless, violent heart of an adolescent—and I was that child and I was that adolescent.

I leave out my private involvement with various young men. I didn't want to kiss and tell. I did put in several sections, however, about boys in general and the fascination they exerted. I ran around with one crowd of older boys so decadent, so accustomed to the most glittering of social lives, that one of them carried with him at all times, in his jacket pocket, a canister of dance wax so that he could be ready for anything. Other boys carry Swiss Army knives for those occasions which occur unexpectedly; this boy carried dance wax for the same reason. He could just sprinkle it on the dining room floor and take you in his arms and whirl you away. These were the sort of boys I knew; they had worn ties from the moment their mothers could locate their necks.

I tried to leave out anything that might trouble my family. My parents are quite young. My sisters are watching this book carefully. Everybody I'm writing about is alive and well, in full possession of his faculties, and possibly willing to sue. Things were simpler when I wrote about muskrats.

Writing in the first person can trap the writer into airing grievances. When I taught writing I spent a lot of time trying to convince young writers that, while literature is an art, it's not a martial art—that the pages of a short story or a novel are no place to defend yourself from an attack, real or imagined, and no place from which to launch an attack, particularly an attack against the very people who painstakingly reared you to your present omniscience.

I have no temptation to air grievances; in fact, I have no grievances left. Unfortunately, I seem to have written the story of my impassioned adolescence so convincingly that my parents (after reading that section of my book) think I still feel that way. It's a problem that I have to solve—one of many in this delicate area. My parents and my youngest sister still live in Pittsburgh; I have to handle it with tongs.

As a result of all of this, I've promised my family that each may pass on the book. I've promised to take out anything that anyone objects to—anything at all. When I was growing up I didn't really take to Pittsburgh society, and I was happy to throw myself into any other world I could find. But I guess I can't say so, because my family may think that I confuse them with conventional Pittsburgh society people in the '50s.

I know a writer who cruelly sticks his parents into all his short stories and still pleases them both, because his mother is pleased to see his father look bad and his father is pleased to see his mother look bad. I had, I thought, nothing but good to say about all named people, but I'll make all that better yet. I don't believe in a writer's kicking around people who don't have access to a printing press. They can't defend themselves.

My advice to memoir writers is to embark upon a memoir for the same reason that you would embark on any other book: to fashion a text. Don't hope in a memoir to preserve your memories. If you prize your memories as they are, by all means avoid—eschew—writing a memoir. Because it is a certain way to lose them. You can't put together a memoir without cannibalizing your own life for parts. The work battens on your memories. And it replaces them.

It's a matter of writing's vividness for the writer. If you spend a couple of days writing a tricky paragraph, and if you spend a week or two laying out a scene or describing an event, you've spent more time writing about it than you did living it. The writing time is also much more intense.

After you've written, you can no longer remember anything but the writing. However true you make that writing, you've created a monster. This has happened to me many, many times, because I'm willing to turn events into pieces of paper. After I've written about any experience, my memories—those elusive, fragmentary patches of color and feeling—are gone; they've been replaced by the work. The work is a sort of changeling on the doorstep—not your baby but someone else's baby rather like it, different in some way that you can't pinpoint, and yours has vanished.

Memory is insubstantial. Things keep replacing it. Your batch of snapshots will both fix and ruin your memory of your travels, or your childhood, or your children's childhood. You can't remember anything from your trip except this wretched collection of snapshots. The painting you did of the light on the water will forever alter the way you see the light on the water; so will looking at Flemish paintings. If you describe a dream you'll notice that at the end of the verbal description you've lost the dream but gained a verbal description. You have to like verbal descriptions a lot to keep up this sort of thing. I like verbal descriptions a lot.

Let me put in a word now for a misunderstood genre: literary nonfiction. It's interesting to me because I try to write it and because I respect the art of it very much.

I like to be aware of a book as a piece of writing, and aware of its structure as a product of mind, and yet I want to be able to see the represented world through it. I admire artists who succeed in dividing my attention more or less evenly between the world of their books and the art of their books. In fiction we might say that the masters are Henry James and Herman Melville. In nonfiction the writer usually just points to the world and says, "This is a biography of Abraham Lincoln. This is what Abraham Lincoln was about." But the writer may also make of his work an original object in its own right, so that a reader may study the work with pleasure as well as the world that it describes. That is, works of nonfiction can be coherent and crafted works of literature.

It's not simply that they're carefully written, or vivid and serious and pleasing, like Boswell's *Life of Johnson,* say, or St. Exupéry's wonderful memoir of early aviation, *Wind, Sand, and Stars.* It's not even that they may contain elements of fiction, that their action reveals itself in scenes that use visual descriptions and that often use dialogue. It's not just these things, although these things are important. It's that nonfiction accounts may be literary insofar as the parts of their structures cohere internally, insofar as the things are in them for the sake of the work itself, and insofar as the work itself exists in the service of idea. (It is especially helpful if the writer so fully expresses the idea in materials that only a trained technician can find it. Because the abstract structure of a given text, which is of great interest to the writer and serves to rouse him out of bed in the morning and impel him to the desk, is of little or no interest to the reader, and he'd better not forget it.)

Nonfiction accounts don't ordinarily meet these criteria, but they may. Walden Pond is the linchpin of a metaphysic. In repeated and self-conscious rewritings Thoreau hammered at its unremarkable and rather dreary acres until they fastened eternity in time and stood for the notion that the physical world itself expresses a metaphysical one. He picked up that pond and ran with it. He could just as readily have used something else—a friend, say, or a chestnut. You can do quite a bit with language.

Hemingway in *Green Hills of Africa* wrote a sober narrative account of killing a kudu, the whole of which functions as an elaborate metaphor for internal quests and conquests. Loren Eiseley lays in narrative symbols with a trowel, splashing mortar all over the place, but they hold. In his essay "The Star-Thrower," Eiseley's beachcomber who throws dying starfish back into the surf stands for any hope or mercy that flies in the face of harsh natural law. He stands finally for the extravagant spirit behind creation as a whole; he is a god hurling solar systems into the void.

I only want to remind my writing colleagues that a great deal can be done in nonfiction, especially in first-person accounts where the writer controls the materials absolutely. Because other literary genres are shrinking. Poetry has purified itself right out of the ballpark. Literary fiction is scarcely being published—it's getting to be like conceptual art. All that the unknown writer of fiction can do is to tell his friends about the book he has written, and all that his friends can say is "Good idea." The short story is to some extent going the way of poetry, limiting its subject matter to such narrow surfaces that it can't handle the things that most engage our hearts and minds. But literary nonfiction is all over the map and has been for three hundred years. There's nothing you can't do with it. No subject matter is forbidden, no structure is proscribed. You get to make up your own form every time.

When I gave up writing poetry I was very sad, for I had devoted fifteen years to the study of how the structures of poems carry meaning. But I was delighted to find that nonfiction prose can also carry meaning in its structures and, like poetry, can tolerate all sorts of figurative language, as well as alliteration and even rhyme. The range of rhythms in prose is larger and grander than it is in poetry, and it can handle discursive ideas and plain information as well as character and story. It can do everything. I felt as though I had switched from a single reed instrument to a full orchestra.

Let me close with a word about process. There's a common notion that self-discipline is a freakish peculiarity of writers—that writers differ from other people by possessing enormous and equal portions of talent and willpower. They grit their powerful teeth and go into their little rooms. I think that's a bad misunderstanding of what impels the writer. What impels the writer is a deep love for and respect for language, for literary forms, for books. It's a privilege to muck about in sentences all morning. It's a challenge to bring off a powerful effect, or to tell the truth about something. You don't do it from willpower; you do it from an abiding passion for the field. I'm sure it's the same in every other field.

Writing a book is like rearing children—willpower has very little to do with it. If you have a little baby crying in the middle of the night, and if you depend only on willpower to get you out of bed to feed the baby, that baby will starve. You do it out of love. Willpower is a weak idea; love is strong. You don't have to scourge yourself with a cat-o'-nine-tails to go to the baby. You go to the baby out of love for that particular baby. That's the same way you go to your desk. There's nothing freakish about it. Caring passionately about something isn't against nature, and it isn't against human nature. It's what we're here to do.

On the Possibilities of the Essay: A Meditation

Rebecca Blevins Faery

When one looks from inside at a lighted window, or looks from above at the lake, one sees the image of oneself in a lighted room, the image of oneself among trees and sky— the deception is obvious, but flattering all the same. When one looks from the darkness into the light, however, one sees all the difference between here and there, this and that. Perhaps all unsheltered people are angry in their hearts, and would like to break the roof, spine, and ribs, and smash the windows and flood the floor and spindle the curtains and bloat the couch.

Marilynne Robinson, *Housekeeping*

I

I had, it seemed, to my surprise, terror, and delight, bought a house.

It was high summer, July of 1988, the peak of a season of dazzling heat and soul-wrenching drought. As I drove between Iowa City and Dubuque, where I was teaching a seminar, I watched the corn in fields on either side of the two-lane highway shrivel relentlessly week by week under the baking sun until I heard, or thought I heard, as I drove, a very high-pitched keen or wail, coming from the corn, begging for rain.

Moving day arrived when the seminar ended, according to plan. During the weeks I was away teaching, assorted carpenters and dry-wall workers and plumbers and painters had executed my preliminary plans for turning the house into my own. It was—is—a grand house, old and possessed of great dignity, so I had a lot to work with: high ceilings, wide mahogany pocket doors at once dividing and connecting all the downstairs rooms, multiple tall windows looking out on a wide lawn with room for a terrace, a garden, a grape arbor, a bed of multi-hued lilies. A house full of promise, of possibilities.

The unpacking and settling-in were a strain in the dry heat, well over a hundred degrees day after sizzling day. Indulging a fantasy which my new identity as owner of this grand house allowed me, I adopted in interludes the persona and habits of a woman of leisure and splurged on a Yucatan hammock, which I hung between an old box-elder and a leaning cedar not far from the back porch. I took refuge in their shade when fatigue overtook me, swaying as I read. The novel in my hands, as I recall myself in those moments through the screen of memory, is Marilynne Robinson's *Housekeeping*.

Mornings I rose, made coffee, soothed the cat out of her nervousness at waking in a house whose unfamiliarity she had daily to confront anew, and set to work to establish the cleanliness and order I've been taught to believe is next to godliness. My domestic inclinations I gave full rein: this was my home, my haven, nest, stay against the confusion of impermanence, each room a stanza of the poem to fixity I was trying to make of the enterprise. I had married this house with enthusiasm, and I took up the familiar role and tasks of housewife with an energy made vigorous by commitment. "I was born to live in this house," I said to my friends in the romantic flush of love for my new home; "I intend to stay here forever."

It must be understood, for this tale to make any sense at all, that I have yearned all my adult life for permanence, for "home," for a long commitment to a place, a dwelling that would house me securely and comfortably in return for my love and attention, its walls my fortress against flux and fortune's whims. Yet every home I've had I've lived in only briefly; I've been, despite my longings, a woman forever on the move. Or, more precisely, several women, simultaneously and in succession, and all of them on the move.

In the heat of that summer, I was making another stab at it. I labored in splendid isolation toward splendid order in the arrangement of furniture, pictures on the walls, dishes in the cupboards. This finely articulated distribution of my possessions soothed me into pretending that I was indeed protected from the shifting boundaries of identity, from the fraying and unraveling that are the lot of us all.

The dissonances between my determined housekeeping and the interpolations of lazy late afternoon hours of suspended reading of *Housekeeping* did not escape me. The novel drew me away from my busyness to the still hours in the swaying hammock, drew me with its exquisite sentences, its elegiac tone, its visions that all efforts to stop the flow of time, change, displacement, discomposing are fruitless. It's a vision I share, indeed advocate; the old must be abandoned in pursuit of the new. The difference is that the women in the novel act on that knowledge. I, on the other hand, sometimes at least, act as if I *don't* believe it, though I do. In the novel, Sylvie knows that something means to undo a house, so she opens the doors and windows and lets the undoer in. She underscores the silly futility of housewifely saving and storing by collecting useless things—

empty cans, old newspapers—and arranging them neatly against the walls of all the rooms. Sylvie refuses the bourgeois ideologies of "home" with all their attachments to class privilege, ideologies that confine women within the predictable roles and ordered spaces of domesticity; she embraces the road rather than the cottage beside it. I try to do these things too, in my own way. But I, on the other hand, dweller in contradictions, also batten down, hunker, and hope.

II

In their essay "Feminist Politics: What's Home Got to Do with It?" Biddy Martin and Chandra Talpade Mohanty use their reading of another essay, Minnie Bruce Pratt's "Identity: Skin Blood Heart," to consider the political ideologies of "home": house, family, kin, community in the immediate sense; personal identities grounded in race, class, gender, sexuality, convictions and claimed affinities in the wider sense. And while the following passage from Martin and Mohanty addresses Pratt's remarkable essay alone, I offer it as a perspective on the possibilities of the essay in general:

> [The essay] is a form of writing that not only anticipates and integrates diverse audiences or readers but also positions the narrator as reader. The perspective is multiple and shifting, and the shifts in perspective are enabled by the attempts to define self, home, and community that are at the heart of Pratt's enterprise. The historical grounding of shifts and changes allows for an emphasis on the pleasures and terrors of interminable boundary confusions, but insists, at the same time, on our responsibility for remapping boundaries and renegotiating connections. These are partial in at least two senses of the word: politically partial, and without claims to wholeness or finality.

The essay as a performance of reading. The essayist as reader. The reader of essays as reader. All readings contingent, partial, multiple, shifting. Nothing is fixed, and nobody has a corner on truth.

When Samuel Johnson in his famous *Dictionary* defines the essay as "a loose sally of the mind; an irregular, undigested piece," I at least suspect the privileging of reason over feeling, intellection over intuition. It is the article or treatise which earns from Johnson an implicit description as "a regular, orderly composition," the thing the essay, by his definition, is not. What makes for the difference? The meanderings, for one thing, of the essayist's persona, made precedent by Montaigne. A "composition" requires the writer's subjugation to a monumental discourse. The essay is written by somebody who sallies into a subject loosely, leaving—or making holes that are not knitted up, carrying along and exploring the myriad possible specificities of the writer's experience and identity. The essay rests on perspective, on the position of the essayist within the web of culture. It allows the essayist to say, "This is how the world looks to *me,* from my particular place in it." The essay has, then, the potential for being at least an inroad, if not indeed an attack, on monumental discourse because as a form it negotiates the split between public discourse—formal, ordered, impersonal, knowing, with pretensions to universality and fixity, and private utterance—tentative, personal, questing, provisional. If the "composition" is an edifice, the essay is a nomad's tent. It moves around.

The essay, then, is and has been a form open to the articulation of estrangements and contradictions, a place for expressing the strains, differences, rejections as well as connections experienced by those who feel or have felt particularly marginalized by the discourses which have composed the social text. I am thinking here of writers like James Baldwin, Nancy Mairs, Alice Walker, Audre Lorde, Minnie Bruce Pratt, and many others who have recognized in the essay a potential site for the operations of contesting discourses and have used it to explore and construct in language the multiple perspectives which variant experiences and identities produce.

Virginia Woolf, for instance. Think of all those polite essays she wrote about her reading and published in the *Times Literary Supplement.* Think of how comforting, how comfortable they are, spoken from the privileged position of a woman of means, of well-placed family, of culture. And then think of others, *A Room of One's Own* and *Three Guineas,* in which she speaks from a position as outsider, attempting to undo the cultural stories that have placed her there, on the margins, because of her gender. Such writing from the margins is "guerrilla writing," a term I heard recently and have not been able to forget. In the terrain of monumental discourse, such pieces are eruptions of personal presence based on shifting experiences and identities, eruptions that aim to dis-compose the power relations that reside in textuality. And such moments are accomplished not only *by* particular essays within the field of more orderly forms of writing; they occur also *within* essays, as in Woolf's "Professions for Women," when that-which-cannot-be-said about a woman's experience of her body slips away like a fish escaping a line. Or in "The Moment: Summer's Night," when an imaged scene of domestic violence—"He beats her"—intrudes upon and contrasts with the cultivated civility of the narrator and her companions. Or in "22 Hyde Park Gate," which closes with the astonishing revelation of the sexual abuse Woolf and her sister were subjected to by their half-brother. Is Woolf in these texts violating her own dictum that the purpose of the essay is "to give pleasure"? What sort of pleasure can we get from scenes of wife-beating and forced incest and the taboos against expressing bodily experience? Perhaps the pleasures of heresy—the thing Adorno calls "the law of the innermost form of the essay." And the pleasures of heresy are not small. Carl Klaus has aptly termed the essay an "antigenre, a rogue form of writing in the universe of discourse." I would elaborate only to observe that the essay can be, has been, rogue or heretical not only in form but in effect. As "antigenre," it has the capacity to work against, even to undo, the presumptions that have structured western discourse.

Look, for another example, at what is happening in the realm of conventional academic writing. A couple of years ago, a friend gave me a copy of Jane Tompkins' essay "Me and My Shadow" in an effort to help me out of a difficult period of inability to write. I read about Tompkins' anger at the "straitjacket" of the suppression of the personal voice and personal experience in academic writing, about the "two voices" she felt within her, one of which had been systematically silenced. I read her plea for redressing the damage done by the conventions of intellectual discourse, a plea based on the conviction that readers "want to know about each other":

> Sometimes, when a writer introduces some personal bit of story into an essay, I can hardly contain my pleasure. I love writers who write about their own experience. I feel I'm being nourished by them, that I'm being allowed to enter into a personal relationship with them, that I can match my own experience with theirs, feel cousin to them, and say, yes, that's how it is.

Yes, I said to myself as I read, a seemingly endless stream of tears rolling down my cheeks—whether tears of grief, or joy, or both, I'm still not clear—yes, that's how it is.

Sometimes, though, the voice relating personal perspective and experience in an essay draws me, excites me, because what I read challenges rather than confirms my own experience and thus opens up for me new perspectives on the world. Then my response is not "That's how it is," but "Is that how it is?" If I am to act in the world in a way that attempts to respect and accommodate differences, I need to know what the world is like not only for people who are in some way like me, but also for people who are in some way different. I must be taught as well as teach. Patricia Williams, a Black feminist legal scholar, begins an essay on commercial transactions by telling the story of the rape and impregnation at age twelve of her great-great-grandmother by the girl's white owner. The essay, "On Being the Object of Property," is a dazzling poetic display which inserts the continuing personal pain of such a heritage into the affectless tradition of legal scholarship and thereby unsettles that tradition. It links Williams' meditations on her personal and racial histories, her experiences of race and gender in a hierarchical culture, with legal issues like the "Baby M" case and the forced sterilization of women of color. The essay accommodates passages like this one:

> There are moments in my life when I feel as though a part of me is missing. There are days when I feel so invisible that I can't remember what day of the week it is, when I feel so manipulated that I can't remember my own name, when I feel so lost and angry that I can't speak a civil word to the people who love me best. Those are the times when I catch sight of my reflection in store windows and am surprised to see a whole person looking back. Those are the times when my skin becomes gummy as clay and my nose slides around on my face and my eyes drip down to my chin. I have to close my eyes at such times and remember myself, draw an internal picture that is smooth and whole; when all else fails, I reach for a mirror and stare myself down until the features reassemble themselves like lost sheep.

The passage is a metaphoric description of the dis-composing effect of monolithic racist and sexist discourses on Williams, and of the composing effect of her own writing, in which she reconstructs—*re-members*—a self, however momentary, however *partial* in both senses of the word: invested with self-interest and without claim to finality. Williams' writing simultaneously composes herself and discomposes conventional discourses which in a variety of ways deny her. She makes use of the literary qualities of language, whose task, in their origins in the oral traditions of poetry, was to make memorable the stories of the tribe or culture in order to assure they would be repeated and thus not forgotten. Williams' essay is a frontal attack on the master's house, a stream of words aimed at eroding the rock of oppression at the foundation of culture. Her essay insists that there is never just one story; rather, there are many stories which can and must be told, which must be heard. In this essay Williams, like Sylvie in *Housekeeping,* is an undoer. And that cannot be a futile effort because, as James Baldwin, filled with simultaneous despair and desperate hope, writes in his beautiful essay "Nothing Personal," "For nothing is fixed, forever and forever and forever, it is not fixed; the earth is always shifting, the light is always changing, the sea does not cease to grind down rock."

What the pedagogical implications might be of such a view of the essay I have considered here hardly at all, and then only indirectly. Certainly the form itself has been an outsider in the institution of literary studies, relegated mostly to the composition classroom where, too often, its essential qualities of perspective and personal voice have been masked or even banned. What could happen if we admit the "anti-genre" not only into our polite and scholarly forms of writing, but also into the rigidly generic classrooms and hallways of our educational institutions—what Nancy Mairs calls "the ivory phallus"—I can scarcely imagine. I know I'd like to be around to watch.

III

So. What did I leave out of my story of buying a house, of my attempts to shore up its walls against some imagined ruin? Some of the reasons. I belong, by race and by family tradition, to a propertied class, where owning a house stands in direct equation with respectability. It is my toehold. Also because I am a woman who came of age in an era when "home" was woman's sphere, even when she's also the "head of household." Also because I've been, most of my adult life, relatively rootless, following along after one man, one life plan, in flight from others. Now, my children grown and gone, I become paradoxically even more obsessive about a "nest."

If you wonder why I of all people proved so susceptible to the seductions of "home" with all its attendant ideologies, I can tell you only and simply that I am a woman partially constructed by such ideologies.

But perhaps I've painted an overly romantic picture of the house and my relation to it. It's been almost two years now, after all, since I moved in, two years of mild winters and early springs and one temperate summer. Like all love affairs, this one has lost some of its glow. The house is still grand, I admit; but water pipes burst, the roof leaks, the porches sag. The deep and dark waters of the lake at Fingerbone reach all the way to Iowa and lap at my edges. The house is after all less comfortable, less comforting than I had hoped, and other yearnings have started to surface. I manage to muster, twice a year, the thousand dollars to pay the property tax. But I feed the squirrels that eat holes in the eaves to winter over in the attic, though my more prudent friends urge me to trap them humanely and move them out into the country west of town. And I think I forgot to mention that I share the house—and not just with my cat. In fact I live only in those hardly discrete rooms of the first floor, rooms that flow liquidly one into another. In the upstairs apartment are Karen and Wayne, their black cat and their books. Wayne writes novels, Karen makes poems, so on our good days, all of us are more preoccupied with meanings than with maintenance. In the spare parking place next to the alley, a huge and ancient Buick appears several days a week beside my tenants' Toyota. The Buick is ventilated with rusted-through holes the size of my fist. It belongs to Alex, broad-faced member of the Mesquakie tribe from the settlement over at Tama. He wears a long braid down his back, a feather in his black felt hat; he won a dance competition, he told me, at a pow-wow on the shores of Lake Michigan just a few months ago. Karen and Wayne mentioned casually once that he was "visiting"; instead, I think he lives there with them on the days he needs to be in Iowa City to go to school. They don't tell me that because, I suppose, they think the same impulse that led me to lay a brick terrace and plant lilies would make me exercise a white law and kick him out. But I say nothing. I'm learning to live with, live through contradictions, even learning to love them. I grow weary of defending territory to which I'm not sure I can lay just claim. And I want to be an undoer too, as well as one of the undone. I want this house to be open. Alex, when he sees me in the yard, greets me and calls me "the landlady." The term gives me a start, especially coming from him. Whose home is this, anyway?

I know, I know, it is in some sense mine. But I can give it up. And surely someday, some way or other, I will.

Note

The texts cited in this essay are: T.W. Adorno, "The Essay as Form," in *New German Critique*, 1984; James Baldwin, "Nothing Personal," in *The Price of the Ticket*, 1985; Carl Klaus, "Essayists on the Essay," in *Literary Nonfiction*, ed. Chris Anderson, 1989; Nancy Mairs, *Remembering the Bone House: An Erotics of Place and Space*, 1989; Biddy Martin and Chandra Talpade Mohanty, "Feminist Politics: What's Home Got to Do with It?" in *Feminist Studies/Critical Studies*, ed. Teresa de Lauretis, 1986; Minnie Bruce Pratt, "Identity: Skin Blood Heart," in Bulkin, Pratt, and Smith, *Yours in Struggle*, 1984; Marilynne Robinson, *Housekeeping*, 1981; Jane Tompkins, "Me and My Shadow," in *New Literary History*, 1987; Patricia Williams, "On Being the Object of Property," in *Signs*, 1988; Virginia Woolf, "Professions for Women," in *The Death of the Moth and Other Essays*, 1942; Woolf, "The Moment: Summer's Night," in *The Moment and Other Essays*, 1948; Woolf, "22 Hyde Park Gate," in *Moments of Being*, 1976.

Why I Chose the Creative Nonfiction Way of Life

Lee Gutkind

Deciding to dedicate myself to writing creative nonfiction, and delaying a dream of writing fiction, was a conscious and carefully considered decision. At the time, I was in my middle twenties, and I realized that I didn't know enough about the world to write with the insight and experience necessary to make my novels and short stories culturally and morally significant. To be a better writer (and to be a better and a more well-rounded person) I realized the importance of learning to relate to others and understand the struggles and challenges of people from different walks of life. If the characters I created in my fiction were to be compelling and true, then, I concluded, I had to learn about other lifestyles, other professions and the patchwork of prejudices and kindnesses that make some people different from others. I did not want to become a writer who wrote about the same family, the same high school, the same moral dilemma, nor a writer who wrote about other writers, or other English Departments, exclusively. So I decided to write creative nonfiction, and in that way become more mature by broadening my scope of experiences. At some point, I would gradually return to my literary roots—fiction—and make my impact on the world, I assumed. Perhaps you will think me naive, but I really thought that writers with something to say could affect the world. I still do—and I am still trying.

At that time, in the early 1970s, daring nonfiction writers were rare. By "daring" I mean people who would venture into and experience other lifestyles and then write about it in a literary way. And by "literary," I mean using scenes, dialogue, description, first-person points of view—all the tools available to the fiction writer, while consistently attempting to be truthful and factual. Most people regarded nonfiction as academic (as informal essays about literature, politics, law, etc.) or journalistic (as in news and feature stories and op-ed briefs). A minority of writers, calling themselves "new journalists," were making a statement and caus-ing controversy by writing nonfiction in this dramatic and literary way, however. Some of these writers are still active today, like Norman Mailer, whose coverage of the 1968 and 1972 political conventions in the books *Armies of the Night* and *Miami and the Siege of Chicago* were powerful statements of personal journalism and political and moral activism. Tom Wolfe's out-print-anthology, published in 1973, *The New Journalism*, features Mailer, Rex Reed, Terry Southern, Hunter S. Thompson, etc. as well as a fifty-five-page manifesto boldly defining the roots of this daring new journalism. Lillian Ross, who continues to write for *The New Yorker*, had paved the way for this experimentation in voice and style with her in-depth profiles in which she skillfully recreated vivid and remarkable scenes that captured the charismatic and eccentric personalities of such figures as the film director and actor John Huston and Ernest Hemingway, respectively. The descriptions of Hemingway in his hotel room at the Sherry Netherland in Manhattan, drinking champagne with his wife (Miss Mary) and entertaining visitors in his bathrobe, and subsequently on a shopping outing at Abercrombie and Fitch, illustrated the way in which a writer might discover and reveal character and personality through observation and involvement.

This work inspired me and helped me to recognize the great potential of cre-ative nonfiction. I realized I could exercise most every option available to fiction writers—while experiencing life in an active and involved way, rather than avoiding it or observing it only at the fringes. Some of the best of these daring nonfiction writers were, in fact, also fiction writers and poets. John Updike's es-says about growing up in eastern Pennsylvania and his incredible portrait of Boston Red Sox superstar Ted Williams on his last game in Fenway Park in 1962 (*Hub Fans Bid Kid Adieu*) illustrated the importance of writers taking risks not only by experiencing things they did not know (as in George Plimpton's *Paper Lion*, in which the author scrimmages with the NFL Detroit Lions) but also by crossing genres and reaching beyond the boundaries of their literary comfort zone. Nonfic-tion by E. B. White and George Orwell, both of whom wrote in a variety of forms, also impressed me, as did the poet W.S. Merwin in his memoir *Unframed Originals* and a young Philip Roth in his first collection of essays, *Reading Myself and Others*. I also read some of Hemingway's earliest feature stories from the *Toronto Star*, filed from Paris, Madrid, and other European capitals, in which the roots and in-spirations of his later fictions are easily recognized.

I have yet to mention Gay Talese, who is generally credited for inspiring these literary explorations into nonfiction. In a series of profiles of famous people written in the 1960s for various magazines, and collected under the title *Fame and Obscurity*, Talese demonstrated how extensively a writer could stretch the tradi-tional boundaries of the form by capturing people in scenes and situations that were not only compelling in content and dramatic effect, but at the same time re-flected who they were—a magic moment of action or nugget of personality that captured an essence of their personal or professional life. Wolfe referred to this essence as the "larger truth." Instead of holding forth on Joe Louis's charismatic personality and his slow deterioration in the waning years of his life, Talese treated readers to a visit with Louis's former wife, Rose Morgan, who forced her dinner guests and her current husband, muttering his dissatisfaction, to watch a film of Louis's first Billy Conn fight. Instead of commenting about the pressures of being a Broadway director and the conflicts between high-strung performers, by interviewing actors, directors, and psychiatrists, Talese sat through dozens of rehearsals at the Booth Theatre on 45th Street talking quietly to award-winning director Joshua Logan (*Mister Roberts, South Pacific*), who had been in and out of psychiatric institutions since the beginning of his career, mostly observing and waiting until the day Logan and the actress Claudia McNeil, with whom Talese had observed a mounting tension, clashed. Their arguments were recorded by Talese, word-for-word, in his notebook and subsequently in scenes which anchored his narrative. Their arguments were loud—and ridiculous-sounding, including one shouting match Talese recorded, which captured the tension and the frustration of the experience for both parties:

"CLAUDIA!" Logan yelled, "Don't you give me that actor's vengeance, Claudia."

"Yes, Mr. Logan," she said with a soft, sarcastic edge.

"I've had enough of this today, Claudia."

"Yes, Mr. Logan."

"And stop Yes-Mr.-Logan-ing me."

"Yes, Mr. Logan."

"You're a shockingly rude woman!"

"Yes, Mr. Logan."

"You are being a beast."

"Yes, Mr. Logan."

"Yes, Miss Beast."

"Suddenly Claudia McNeil stopped. It dawned on her that he was calling her a beast; now her face was grey and her eyes were cold, and her voice almost solemn, as she said, "You . . . called . . . me . . . out . . . of . . . my . . . name!" She stood there, rocklike, big and angry, waiting for him to do something. "Oliver," Logan said, turning toward the co-producer, who had lowered his wiry, long body into his chair as if he were in a foxhole. He did not want to be cornered into saying something that might offend Logan, his old friend, but neither did he want Claudia McNeil to come barreling down the aisle and possibly snap his thin frame in half."

The argument continued a while longer, but Logan eventually brokered a truce with McNeil and the show, *Tiger, Tiger Burning Bright*, opened to mixed reviews. Talese received total access not only to the behind the scenes intrigue of the play, but to Logan, who bared his psyche. But it seemed as if Talese could get anyone to talk, or to reveal what they were, or what they were thinking at any given moment, including Floyd Patterson who, while piloting a small plane with Talese and a co-pilot (in *The Loser*), frequently wandered off course while revisiting the moments after he was knocked out for the second time by Sonny Liston:

"How could the same thing happen twice? How? That's all I kept thinking after the knockout . . . Was I fooling these people all these years? Was I ever the champion? . . . And then they lead you out of the ring . . . and up the aisle you go, past those people, and all you want is to get to your dressing room, fast . . . but the trouble was in Las Vegas, they made a wrong turn along the aisle, and when we got to the end, there was no dressing room there . . . and we had to walk all the way back down the aisle, past the same people, and they must have been thinking, 'Patterson's not only knocked out, but he can't even find his dressing room. . . .'" Later, he continued: "I just went into the bathroom, shut the door behind me, and looked at myself in the mirror. I just looked at myself and asked, 'What happened?'"

Talese was a terrific writer, but the root of his skill began with his ability to listen to others and encourage their confidence, and he possessed an abundance of patience and creative confidence. If he could not get behind the scenes of a story in one way, he always found an alternative avenue and angle. Once, when told that he would not be permitted to spend time with Frank Sinatra for a profile for *Esquire* magazine because Sinatra had a cold, Talese decided to follow Sinatra at a distance, talk to every member of his considerable entourage and profile the great man at this time (sick with a cold) when he was most stressed.

"Sinatra with a cold is like Picasso without paint, Ferrari without fuel—only worse. For the common cold robs Sinatra of that uninsurable jewel, his voice, cutting into the core of his confidence, and it affects not only his own psyche, but also seems to cause a kind of psychosomatic nasal drip within dozens of people who work for him, drink with him, love him, depend on him for their own welfare and stability. A Sinatra with a cold can, in a small way, send vibrations through the entertainment industry and beyond, as surely as a president of the United States, suddenly sick, can shake the national economy."

Those sentences to me were nothing less than beautiful music. Here was a man—a mere journalist (he worked as a reporter for the *New York Times*) who could transform concrete material that was not only inherently true, but powerfully poetic. I read the melody of these sentences and others that Talese wrote, and committed them to memory and for years recited excerpts of his prose to myself before I started a new nonfiction writing project, as a reminder of the potential and the freedom of this new nonfiction field.

I continue to refer to this form as the "new" nonfiction or new journalism which is how people were referring to it then more to distinguish between traditional journalism than as a statement or description of a revolutionary and heretofore unheard of development. Of course, everyone who read some of the people I have been naming understood that there was nothing at all new about what these writers were doing. The difference was that Wolfe and a few others were acknowledging—finally—the challenge of the field and potential of it, literally discussing it as an art form (not a craft, like plumbing) as unique and creative and unforgettable as fiction.

These days, the term most often being used is creative nonfiction, which is accurate and means what it says: Essentially nonfiction writers are encouraged to be artful rather than objective or formulaic. Instead of reporting the news, they capture and/or recreate what is behind the news or the forces that generate the news. I define the word news in its broadest context: Something that is happening or has happened, somewhere and somehow and sometime to someone. News includes the death of Princess Di in Paris and the death of someone's Uncle Angus in Peoria. Although some critics like William Zinsser find the term creative nonfiction annoying, most of the best and most popular nonfiction writers like Tracy Kidder, John McPhee and Gay Talese have accepted it as the best way to describe what they and others have attempted to achieve.

It is significant that I am talking about the books that inspired me. Most of my contemporaries have been inspired by books and writers when they were young. This makes sense. Obviously, if you want to be a writer then, first, you will have no doubt been a reader. Even Beethoven, who achieved his best work after he became deaf, was inspired to compose and conduct music by the real thing. Lately I have been astounded to learn that many undergraduate writing majors have not been inspired in that way and, in fact, are not seemingly inspired at all. I don't know exactly when this happened because when I started teaching in the early 1970s, Talese, Wolfe, Jack Kerouac, Lillian Ross, Hemingway, Joseph Mitchell, were student heroes, a mainstay of my students' regular dialogue in class and over beer and some of the other stuff they ingested.

But lately I have been asking my students to name the last good nonfiction book they read or to present the authors who influenced them to choose nonfiction as a career. Not more than perhaps one in ten of my students (we are talking about sophomores, juniors, and sometimes seniors) can usually answer by naming anyone else but Jon Krakauer. Sometimes I name the leading writers in our field. I will say, "Who are these people? Diane Ackerman, Annie Dillard, John McPhee, Tracy Kidder!" The names will be vaguely familiar, but most students won't know. Then why do you want to become writers? Who or what inspired you? I ask. It is not often that a student can provide a reason, I am dismayed to say. Writing seems like an interesting major—a springboard to law school, marketing, sales, etc. I guess it is.

This ambivalence toward literature is certainly not limited to undergraduate students at the University of Pittsburgh where I do most of my teaching. Wherever I travel, giving workshops and readings across the U.S. and abroad, I am always amazed to discover how unfamiliar creative writing students are with creative writers. When people ask for reasons why I think creative writing programs have increased at such a phenomenal rate in this country given the lack of interest in reading, I find it difficult to provide an answer that makes sense from an intellectual perspective. I assume creative writing programs are profitable, which is what must drive the proliferation, but there's surely a limit to the amount of potential income being generated considering that most workshops are limited to fifteen to twenty students. Some of my colleagues in history or philosophy, with the help of a couple grad assistants, lecture to 400+ students in a gigantic auditorium.

While it is true that I have taught in creative writing programs for the last two decades, my best students are almost always students who are not writing majors, exclusively—men and women with a knowledge of and passion for science, for example, or architecture or music in addition to writing, always excel.

Here are people with something to say, which is at the cusp of the best creative nonfiction. All the people I have named above as preeminent leaders in the field have chosen to emphasize the substance of their work over the style of their presentation.

Substance can mean fact, as in the many efforts of John McPhee, and it can mean feeling, as in Diane Ackerman's *Natural History of the Senses,* and it can mean the universal appeal of the human spirit, as proven repeatedly by the work of Talese and many others. This is not to say that style shouldn't be important to writers, but not at the expense of the message and the meaning. Writing programs tend to minimize the intellectual value of the essay or article, while maximizing the presentation. It is interesting and important to note that every writer named in this essay was inspired to a certain degree by other writers and/or by the subjects about which they were writing. Only one of the writers named here (Diane Ackerman) received an M.F.A. degree in creative writing.

Before I decided to be a writer, I thought a lot about what I wanted to accomplish in my life. I admit that I didn't know exactly what that was, but I knew two things: First, I wanted to be understood. That is, I wanted people to be interested in my ideas and feelings generally—and what I knew, specifically. Secondly, I wanted my ideas and experiences to make an impact on other people—to change or influence a small part of the world, in one way or another. In order to achieve those goals, I had to more thoroughly understand myself. And I had to learn a great deal about how other people lived. Of course, I had a passion for writing, and I had been significantly affected by the writers I had been reading. I thought that I would give myself a year to see whether this was the lifestyle and the profession that would help me achieve those objectives. At the time I was a motorcyclist, and I was traveling extensively around the country on my two-wheeled machine. This was the subject of my first book. Since then, I have traveled through a half-dozen different worlds in order to write books—baseball umpires, organ transplantation, veterinary hospitals, psychiatric institutions—with the same ideas and intentions in mind. I'm not exactly certain if I have successfully achieved even an iota of the goals I have described, but I covet the memories and experience of the journeys I have been taking, and although I dreamed of being a novelist, I have never looked back or stopped to rethink my decision or direction. I continue my total involvement in the creative nonfiction experience—an odyssey that has consumed me and monumentally enriched my life.

Memory and Imagination

Patricia Hampl

When I was seven, my father, who played the violin on Sundays with a nicely tortured flair which we considered artistic, led me by the hand down a long, unlit corridor in St. Luke's School basement, a sort of tunnel that ended in a room full of pianos. There many little girls and a single sad boy were playing truly tortured scales and arpeggios in a mash of troubled sound. My father gave me over to Sister Olive Marie, who did look remarkably like an olive.

Her oily face gleamed as if it had just been rolled out of a can and laid on the white plate of her broad, spotless wimple. She was a small, plump woman; her body and the small window of her face seemed to interpret the entire alphabet of olive: her face was a sallow green olive placed upon the jumbo ripe olive of her black habit. I trusted her instantly and smiled, glad to have my hand placed in the hand of a woman who made sense, who provided the satisfaction of being what she was: an Olive who looked like an olive.

My father left me to discover the piano with Sister Olive Marie so that one day I would join him in mutually tortured piano-violin duets for the edification of my mother and brother who sat at the table meditatively spooning in the last of their pineapple sherbet until their part was called for: they put down their spoons and clapped while we bowed, while the sweet ice in their bowls melted, while the music melted, and we all melted a little into each other for a moment.

But first Sister Olive must do her work. I was shown middle C, which Sister seemed to think terribly important. I stared at middle C and then glanced away for a second. When my eye returned, middle C was gone, its slim finger lost in the complicated grasp of the keyboard. Sister Olive struck it again, finding it with laughable ease. She emphasized the importance of middle C, its central position, a sort of North Star of sound. I remember thinking, "Middle C is the belly button of the piano," an insight whose originality and accuracy stunned me with pride. For the first time in my life I was astonished by metaphor. I hesitated to tell the kindly

Olive for some reason; apparently I understood a true metaphor is a risky business, revealing of the self. In fact, I have never, until this moment of writing it down, told my first metaphor to anyone.

Sunlight flooded the room; the pianos, all black, gleamed. Sister Olive, dressed in the colors of the keyboard, gleamed; middle C shimmered with meaning and I resolved never—never—to forget its location: it was the center of the world.

Then Sister Olive, who had had to show me middle C twice but who seemed to have drawn no bad conclusions about me anyway, got up and went to the windows on the opposite wall. She pulled the shades down, one after the other. The sun was too bright, she said. She sneezed as she stood at the windows with the sun shedding its glare over her. She sneezed and sneezed, crazy little convulsive sneezes, one after another, as helpless as if she had the hiccups.

"The sun makes me sneeze," she said when the fit was over and she was back at the piano. This was odd, too odd to grasp in the mind. I associated sneezing with colds, and colds with rain, fog, snow and bad weather. The sun, however, had caused Sister Olive to sneeze in this wild way, Sister Olive who gleamed benignly and who was so certain of the location of the center of the world. The universe wobbled a bit and became unreliable. Things were not, after all, necessarily what they seemed. Appearance deceived: here was the sun acting totally out of character, hurling this woman into sneezes, a woman so mild that she was named, so it seemed, for a bland object on a relish tray.

I was given a red book, the first Thompson book, and told to play the first piece over and over at one of the black pianos where the other children were crashing away. This, I was told, was called practicing. It sounded alluringly adult, practicing. The piece itself consisted mainly of middle C, and I excelled, thrilled by my savvy at being able to locate that central note amidst the cunning camouflage of all the other white keys before me. Thrilled too by the shiny red book that gleamed, as the pianos did, as Sister Olive did, as my eager eyes probably did. I sat at the formidable machine of the piano and got to know middle C intimately, preparing to be as tortured as I could manage one day soon with my father's violin at my side.

But at the moment Mary Katherine Reilly was at my side, playing something at least two or three lessons more sophisticated than my piece. I believe she even struck a chord. I glanced at her from the peasantry of single notes, shy, ready to pay homage. She turned toward me, stopped playing, and sized me up.

Sized me up and found a person ready to be dominated. Without introduction she said, "My grandfather invented the collapsible opera hat."

I nodded, I acquiesced, I was hers. With that little stroke it was decided between us—that she should be the leader, and I the sidekick. My job was admiration. Even when she added, "But he didn't make a penny from it. He didn't have a patent"—even then, I knew and she knew that this was not an admission of powerlessness, but the easy candor of a master, of one who can afford a weakness or two.

With the clairvoyance of all fated relationships based on dominance and submission, it was decided in advance: that when the time came for us to play duets, I should always play second piano, that I should spend my allowance to buy her the Twinkies she craved but was not allowed to have, that finally, I should let her copy from my test paper, and when confronted by our teacher, confess with convincing hysteria that it was I, I who had cheated, who had reached above myself to steal what clearly belonged to the rightful heir of the inventor of the collapsible opera hat. . . .

There must be a reason I remember that little story about my first piano lesson. In fact, it isn't a story, just a moment, the beginning of what could perhaps become a story. For the memoirist, more than for the fiction writer, the story seems already *there,* already accomplished and fully achieved in history ("in reality," as we naively say). For the memoirist, the writing of the story is a matter of transcription.

That, anyway, is the myth. But no memoirist writes for long without experiencing an unsettling disbelief about the reliability of memory, a hunch that memory is not, after all, *just* memory. I don't know why I remembered this fragment about my first piano lesson. I don't, for instance, have a single recollection of my first arithmetic lesson, the first time I studied Latin, the first time my grandmother tried to teach me to knit. Yet these things occurred too, and must have their stories.

It is the piano lesson that has trudged forward, clearing the haze of forgetfulness, showing itself bright with detail more than thirty years after the event. I did not choose to remember the piano lesson. It was simply there, like a book that has always been on the shelf, whether I ever read it or not, the binding and title showing as I skim across the contents of my life. On the day I wrote this fragment I happened to take that memory, not some other, from the shelf and paged through it. I found more detail, more event, perhaps a little more entertainment than I had expected, but the memory itself was there from the start. Waiting for me.

Or was it? When I reread what I had written just after I finished it, I realized that I had told a number of lies. I *think* it was my father who took me the first time for my piano lesson—but maybe he only took me to meet my teacher and there was no actual lesson that day. And did I even know then that he played the violin—didn't he take up his violin again much later, as a result of my piano playing, and not the reverse? And is it even remotely accurate to describe as "tortured" the musicianship of a man who began every day by belting out "Oh What a Beautiful Morning" as he shaved?

More: Sister Olive Marie did sneeze in the sun, but was her name Olive? As for her skin tone—I would have sworn it was olive-like; I would have been willing to spend the better part of an afternoon trying to write the exact description of imported Italian or Greek olive her face suggested: I wanted to get it right. But now, were I to write that passage over, it is her intense black eyebrows I would see, for suddenly they seem the central fact of that face, some indicative mark of her serious and patient nature. But the truth is, I don't remember the woman at all. She's a sneeze in the sun and a finger touching middle C. That, at least, is steady and clear.

Worse: I didn't have the Thompson book as my piano text. I'm sure of that because I remember envying children who did have this wonderful book with its pictures of children and animals printed on the pages of music.

As for Mary Katherine Reilly. She didn't even go to grade school with me (and her name isn't Mary Katherine Reilly—but I made that change on purpose). I met her in Girl Scouts and only went to school with her later, in high school. Our relationship was not really one of leader and follower; I played first piano most of the time in duets. She certainly never copied anything from a test paper of mine: she was a better student, and cheating just wasn't a possibility with her. Though her grandfather (or someone in her family) did invent the collapsible opera hat and I remember that she was proud of that fact, she didn't tell me this news as a deft move in a childish power play.

So, what was I doing in this brief memoir? Is it simply an example of the curious relation a fiction writer has to the material of her own life? Maybe. That may have some value in itself. But to tell the truth (if anyone still believes me capable of telling the truth), I wasn't writing fiction. I was writing memoir—or was trying to. My desire was to be accurate. I wished to embody the myth of memoir: to write as an act of dutiful transcription.

Yet clearly the work of writing narrative caused me to do something very different from transcription. I am forced to admit that memoir is not a matter of transcription, that memory itself is not a warehouse of finished stories, not a static gallery of framed pictures. I must admit that I invented. But why?

Two whys: why did I invent, and then, if a memoirist must inevitably invent rather than transcribe, why do I—why should anybody—write memoir at all?

I must respond to these impertinent questions because they, like the bumper sticker I saw the other day commanding all who read it to QUESTION AUTHORITY, challenge my authority as a memoirist and as a witness.

It still comes as a shock to realize that I don't write about what I know: I write in order to find out what I know. Is it possible to convey to a reader the enormous degree of blankness, confusion, hunch and uncertainty lurking in the act of writing? When I am the reader, not the writer, I too fall into the lovely illusion that the words before me (in a story by Mavis Gallant, an essay by Carol Bly, a memoir by M. F. K. Fisher), which *read* so inevitably, must also have been *written* exactly as they appear, rhythm and cadence, language and syntax, the powerful waves of the sentences laying themselves on the smooth beach of the page one after another faultlessly.

But here I sit before a yellow legal pad, and the long page of the preceding two paragraphs is a jumble of crossed-out lines, false starts, confused order. A mess. The mess of my mind trying to find out what it wants to say. This is a writer's frantic, grabby mind, not the poised mind of a reader ready to be edified or entertained.

I sometimes think of the reader as a cat, endlessly fastidious, capable, by turns, of mordant indifference and riveted attention, luxurious, recumbent, and ever poised. Whereas the writer is absolutely a dog, panting and moping, too eager for an affectionate scratch behind the ears, lunging frantically after any old stick thrown in the distance.

The blankness of a new page never fails to intrigue and terrify me. Sometimes, in fact, I think my habit of writing on long yellow sheets comes from an atavistic fear of the writer's stereotypic "blank white page." At least when I begin writing, my page isn't utterly blank; at least it has a wash of color on it, even if the absence of words must finally be faced on a yellow sheet as truly as on a blank white one. Well, we all have our ways of whistling in the dark.

If I approach writing from memory with the assumption that I know what I wish to say, I assume that intentionality is running the show. Things are not that simple. Or perhaps writing is even more profoundly simple, more telegraphic and immediate in its choices than the grating wheels and chugging engine of logic and rational intention. The heart, the guardian of intuition with its secret, often fearful intentions, is the boss, its commands are what a writer obeys—often without knowing it. Or, I do.

That's why I'm a strong adherent of the first draft. And why it's worth pausing for a moment to consider what a first draft really is. By my lights, the piano lesson memoir is a first draft. That doesn't mean it exists here exactly as I first wrote it. I like to think I've cleaned it up from the first time I put it down on paper. I've cut some adjectives here, toned down the hyperbole there, smoothed a transition, cut a repetition—that sort of housekeeperly tidying-up. But the piece remains a first draft because I haven't yet gotten to know it, haven't given it a chance to tell me anything. For me, writing a first draft is a little like meeting someone for the first time. I come away with a wary acquaintanceship, but the real friendship (if any) and genuine intimacy—that's all down the road. Intimacy with a piece of writing, as with a person, comes from paying attention to the revelations it is capable of giving, not by imposing my own preconceived notions, no matter how well-intentioned they might be.

I try to let pretty much anything happen in a first draft. A careful first draft is a failed first draft. That may be why there are so many inaccuracies in the piano lesson memoir: I didn't censor, I didn't judge. I kept moving. But I would not publish this piece as a memoir on its own in its present state. It isn't the "lies" in the piece that give me pause, though a reader has a right to expect a memoir to be as accurate as the writer's memory can make it. No, it isn't the lies themselves that makes the piano lesson memoir a first draft and therefore "unpublishable."

The real trouble: the piece hasn't yet found its subject; it isn't yet about what it wants to be about. Note: what *it* wants, not what I want. The difference has to do with the relation a memoirist—any writer, in fact—has to unconscious or half-known intentions and impulses in composition.

Now that I have the fragment down on paper, I can read this little piece as a mystery which drops clues to the riddle of my feelings, like a culprit who wishes to be apprehended. My narrative self (the culprit who has invented) wishes to be discovered by my reflective self, the self who wants to understand and make sense of a half-remembered story about a nun sneezing in the sun. . . .

We only store in memory images of value. The value may be lost over the passage of time (I was baffled about why I remembered that sneezing nun, for example), but that's the implacable judgment of feeling: *this,* we say somewhere deep within us, is something I'm hanging on to. And of course, often we cleave to things because they possess heavy negative charges. Pain likes to be vivid.

Over time, the value (the feeling) and the stored memory (the image) may become estranged. Memoir seeks a permanent home for feeling and image, a habitation where they can live together in harmony. Naturally, I've had a lot of experiences since I packed away that one from the basement of St. Luke's School; that piano lesson has been effaced by waves of feeling for other moments and episodes. I persist in believing the event has value—after all, I remember it—but in writing the memoir I did not simply relive the experience. Rather, I explored the mysterious relationship between all the images I could round up and the even more impacted feelings that caused me to store the images safely away in memory. Stalking the relationship, seeking the congruence between stored image and hidden emotion—that's the real job of memoir.

By writing about that first piano lesson, I've come to know things I could not know otherwise. But I only know these things as a result of reading this first draft. While I was writing, I was following the images, letting the details fill the room of the page and use the furniture as they wished. I was their dutiful servant—or thought I was. In fact, I was the faithful retainer of my hidden feelings which were giving the commands.

I really did feel, for instance, that Mary Katherine Reilly was far superior to me. She was smarter, funnier, more wonderful in every way—that's how I saw it. Our friendship (or she herself) did not require that I become her vassal, yet perhaps in my heart that was something I wanted; I wanted a way to express my feeling of admiration. I suppose I waited until this memoir to begin to find the way.

Just as, in the memoir, I finally possess that red Thompson book with the barking dogs and bleating lambs and winsome children. I couldn't (and still can't) remember what my own music book was, so I grabbed the name and image of the one book I could remember. It was only in reviewing the piece after writing it that I saw my inaccuracy. In pondering this "lie," I came to see what I was up to: I was getting what I wanted. At last.

The truth of many circumstances and episodes in the past emerges for the memoirist through details (the red music book, the fascination with a nun's name and gleaming face), but these details are not merely information, not flat facts. Such details are not allowed to lounge. They must work. Their work is the creation of symbol. But it's more accurate to call it the *recognition* of symbol. For meaning is not "attached" to the detail by the memoirist; meaning is revealed.

That's why a first draft is important. Just as the first meeting (good or bad) with someone who later becomes the beloved is important and is often reviewed for signals, meanings, omens, and indications.

Now I can look at that music book and see it not only as "a detail," but for what it is, how it *acts*. See it as the small red door leading straight into the dark room of my childhood longing and disappointment. That red book *becomes* the palpable evidence of that longing. In other words, it becomes symbol. There is no symbol, no life-of-the-spirit in the general or the abstract. Yet a writer wishes—indeed all of us wish—to speak about profound matters that are, like it or not, general and abstract. We wish to talk to each other about life and death, about love, despair, loss, and innocence. We sense that in order to live together we must learn to speak of peace, of history, of meaning and values. Those are a few.

We seek a means of exchange, a language which will renew these ancient concerns and make them wholly and pulsingly ours. Instinctively, we go to our store of private images and associations for our authority to speak of these weighty issues. We find, in our details and broken and obscured images, the language of symbol. Here memory impulsively reaches out its arms and embraces imagination. That is the resort to invention. It isn't a lie, but an act of necessity, as the innate urge to locate personal truth always is.

All right. Invention is inevitable. But why write memoir? Why not call it fiction and be done with all the hashing about, wondering where memory stops and imagination begins? And if memoir seeks to talk about "the big issues," about history and peace, death and love—why not leave these reflections to those with expert and scholarly knowledge? Why let the common or garden variety memoirist into the club? I'm thinking again of that bumper sticker: why Question Authority?

My answer, of course, is a memoirist's answer. Memoir must be written because each of us must have a created version of the past. Created: that is, real, tangible, made of the stuff of a life lived in place and in history. And the down side of any created thing as well: we must live with a version that attaches us to our limitations, to the inevitable subjectivity, of our points of view. We must acquiesce to our experience and our gift to transform experience into meaning and value. You tell me your story, I'll tell you my story.

If we refuse to do the work of creating this personal version of the past, someone else will do it for us. That is a scary political fact. "The struggle of man against power," a character in Milan Kundera's novel *The Book of Laughter and Forgetting* says, "is the struggle of memory against forgetting." He refers to willful political forgetting, the habit of nations and those in power (Question Authority!) to deny the truth of memory in order to disarm moral and ethical power. It's an efficient way of controlling masses of people. It doesn't even require much bloodshed, as long as people are entirely willing to give over their personal memories. Whole histories can be rewritten. As Czeslaw Milosz said in his 1980 Nobel Prize lecture, the number of books published that seek to deny the existence of the Nazi death camps now exceeds one hundred.

What is remembered is what *becomes* reality. If we "forget" Auschwitz, if we "forget" My Lai, what then do we remember? And what is the purpose of our remembering? If we think of memory naively, as a simple story, logged like a documentary in the archive of the mind, we miss its beauty but also its function. The beauty of memory rests in its talent for rendering detail, for paying homage to the senses, its capacity to love the particles of life, the richness and idiosyncrasy of our existence. The function of memory, on the other hand, is intensely personal and surprisingly political.

Our capacity to move forward as developing beings rests on a healthy relation with the past. Psychotherapy, that widespread method of mental health, relies heavily on memory and on the ability to retrieve and organize images and events from the personal past. We carry our wounds and perhaps even worse, our capacity to wound, forward with us. If we learn not only to tell our stories but to listen to what our stories tell us—to write the first draft and then return for the second draft—we are doing the work of memoir.

Memoir is the intersection of narration and reflection, of story-telling and essay-writing. It can present its story *and* reflect and consider the meaning of the story. It is a peculiarly open form, inviting broken and incomplete images, half-recollected fragments, all the mass (and mess) of detail. It offers to shape this confusion—and in shaping, of course it necessarily creates a work of art, not a legal document. But then, even legal documents are only valiant attempts to consign the truth, the whole truth and nothing but the truth to paper. Even they remain versions.

Locating touchstones—the red music book, the olive Olive, my father's violin playing—is deeply satisfying. Who knows why? Perhaps we all sense that we can't grasp the whole truth and nothing but the truth of our experience. Just can't be done. What can be achieved, however, is a version of its swirling, changing wholeness. A memoirist must acquiesce to selectivity, like any artist. The version we dare to write is the only truth, the only relationship we can have with the past. Refuse to write your life and you have no life. At least, that is the stern view of the memoirist.

Personal history, logged in memory, is a sort of slide projector flashing images on the wall of the mind. And there's precious little order to the slides in the rotating carousel. Beyond that confusion, who knows who is running the projector? A memoirist steps into this darkened room of flashing, unorganized images and stands blinking for a while. Maybe for a long while. But eventually, as with any attempt to tell a story, it is necessary to put something first, then something else. And so on, to the end. That's a first draft. Not necessarily the truth, not even *a* truth sometimes, but the first attempt to create a shape.

The first thing I usually notice at this stage of composition is the appalling inaccuracy of the piece. Witness my first piano lesson draft. Invention is screamingly evident in what I intended to be transcription. But here's the further truth: I feel no shame. In fact, it's only now that my interest in the piece truly quickens. For I can see what isn't there, what is shyly hugging the walls, hoping not to be seen. I see the filmy shape of the next draft. I see a more acute version of the episode or—this is more likely—an entirely new piece rising from the ashes of the first attempt.

The next draft of the piece would have to be a true re-vision, a new seeing of the materials of the first draft. Nothing merely cosmetic will do—no rouge buffing up the opening sentence, no glossy adjective to lift a sagging line, nothing to attempt covering a patch of gray writing. None of that. I can't say for sure, but my hunch is the revision would lead me to more writing about my father (why was I so impressed by that ancestral inventor of the collapsible opera hat? Did I feel I had nothing as remarkable in my own background? Did this make me feel inadequate?). I begin to think perhaps Sister Olive is less central to this business than she is in this draft. She is meant to be a moment, not a character.

And so I might proceed, if I were to undertake a new draft of the memoir. I begin to feel a relationship developing between a former self and me.

And, even more compelling, a relationship between an old world and me. Some people think of autobiographical writing as the precious occupation of a particularly self-absorbed person. Maybe, but I don't buy that. True memoir is written in an attempt to find not only a self but a world.

The self-absorption that seems to be the impetus and embarrassment of autobiography turns into (or perhaps always was) a hunger for the world. Actually, it begins as hunger for *a* world, one gone or lost, effaced by time or a more sudden brutality. But in the act of remembering, the personal environment expands, resonates beyond itself, beyond its "subject," into the endless and tragic recollection that is history.

We look at old family photographs in which we stand next to black, boxy Fords and are wearing period costumes, and we do not gaze fascinated because there we are young again, or there we are standing, as we never will again in life, next to our mother. We stare and drift because there we are . . . historical. It is the dress, the black car that dazzle us now and draw us beyond our mother's bright arms which once caught us. We reach into the attractive impersonality of something more significant than ourselves. We write memoir, in other words. We accept the humble position of writing a version rather than "the whole truth."

I suppose I write memoir because of the radiance of the past—it draws me back and back to it. Not that the past is beautiful. In our communal memoir, in history, the death camps *are* back there. In intimate life too, the record is usually pretty mixed. "I could tell you stories . . ." people say and drift off, meaning terrible things have happened to them.

But the past is radiant. It has the light of lived life. A memoirist wishes to touch it. No one owns the past, though typically the first act of new political regimes, whether of the left or the right, is to attempt to re-write history, to grab the past and make it over so the end comes out right. So their power looks inevitable.

No one owns the past, but it is a grave error (another age would have said a grave sin) not to inhabit memory. Sometimes I think it is all we really have. But that may be a trifle melodramatic. At any rate, memory possesses authority for the fearful self in a world where it is necessary to have authority in order to Question Authority.

There may be no more pressing intellectual need in our culture than for people to become sophisticated about the function of memory. The political implications of the loss of memory are obvious. The authority of memory is a personal confirmation of selfhood. To write one's life is to live it twice, and the second living is both spiritual and historical, for a memoir reaches deep within the personality as it seeks its narrative form and also grasps the life-of-the-times as no political treatise can.

Our most ancient metaphor says life is a journey. Memoir is travel writing, then, notes taken along the way, telling how things looked and what thoughts occurred. But I cannot think of the memoirist as a tourist. This is the traveller who goes on foot, living the journey, taking on mountains, enduring deserts, marveling at the lush green places. Moving through it all faithfully, not so much a survivor with a harrowing tale to tell as a pilgrim, seeking, wondering.

The Whole Truth

Peter M. Ives

I

About a year ago, I gave my sister, Kitty, a draft of an essay I'd been working on. Up to that point, I had never shared any of my autobiographical writing with a family member. Part of the essay dealt with the day of our father's death, and I was sincerely interested to see if she could add any details or observations. I spent an anxiety-filled week, second-guessing my decision, before calling her. I was quite surprised by her reaction. It wasn't that she was offended or angry—I had prepared myself for that possibility. No, in fact she was quite generous in her comments about the piece. However, what caught me off guard was the degree to which her memories of that day—April 5, 1969—conflicted substantially with my own recollections.

She remembered the day as being sunny. I remembered a light drizzle with low gray clouds. She remembered being with me in the bedroom when I found my father's body. I remembered only my brother John being there. She remembered the coroner pronouncing my father dead before Father Ramsey came to perform the last rites. I remembered Father Ramsey arriving before the coroner. As we talked, it became clear to me that this event—indisputably the most central instance of my childhood—was subject to conflicting perspectives.

There were other details where our memories conflicted, but in the end it didn't matter whether or not it had been sunny or rainy or whether it was the priest or coroner who arrived first, because one thing has always remained certain: our father died that day, and both of us remembered watching the ambulance attendants carry his body out the front door.

II

Shortly after that revelatory conversation with my sister, I came across an essay written by Anna Quindlen for the *New York Times Book Review*. In her piece, "How Dark? How Stormy? I Can't Recall," Ms. Quindlen questioned the legitimate employment of specific details in memoir. It seems that because the author couldn't remember the name of her kindergarten teacher, she felt compelled to question how Frank McCourt—the author of *Angela's Ashes*—could remember "the raw, itching sore that erupted between his eyes when he was a boy, or the sight of himself in a mirror on his fourteenth birthday." In support of her incredulity, Ms. Quindlen continued: "I can't remember the spread on my parents' bed. If it was quilted satin, I can't remember running my hand over its smooth surface when I was seven or eight years old. If it was chenille, I can't recall feeling the bobbles beneath my palm as I sat and watched in the mirror as my mother braided my long hair." To be fair, Ms. Quindlen reminds readers that she spent most of her life as a reporter, and that the "strictures of her trade run deep." In this regard, it is completely understandable that Ms. Quindlen is, by nature, suspicious of anything as unverifiable as memoir.

As for me, I know very little about quilted satin, and—to the best of my knowledge—my mother never braided my hair. But I do remember the oil stains on my father's callused hands, how his finger nails were bitten down almost to the cuticles; I remember how he used to wear an oversized, fluorescent, orange raincoat to my JV football games—rain or shine—so I could see him as he pranced up and down the sidelines shouting instructions; I remember the doilies my grandmother used to keep on the mahogany dresser in her bedroom, the Jell-O-like flesh that drooped below her upper arms; I remember my mother singing in the kitchen on school mornings; I remember the first time I had the wind knocked out of me; I remember my grandfather on his death bed, rolling imaginary Bull Durham cigarettes and offering them to my grandmother (who'd been dead for eight years); I remember how my mom used to take her boys out to the back fence, line us up, and give crew cuts, washing us off with the hose afterwards so we wouldn't scatter loose hair in the house; I remember faking a stomachache when I was six and winding up having my appendix taken out; I remember playing in a sand pile and almost being eaten by a pig.

These are vivid, honest memories. But I would never swear to them as facts. They are honest and true only in that this is how I remember them, verifying where I can, letting the reader know whenever I step over the line into uncertainty or even imaginative re-recreation. But within each of these memories is a story loaded with details, dialogue, and imagery. And I've told these stories hundreds of times.

III

"The blurring of reality" is a catchy new phrase proclaimed by a self-appointed few out to rescue a gullible reading public from an ontological meltdown. It reminds me of the old "Twilight Zone" episode where a browbeaten author permanently dispatches his wife by burning the tape recording on which he described (dictated) her into being: she feels woozy, puts the back of her hand to her forehead and slowly dissipates into oblivion. Who are these critics? For the most part, I suspect that they are talented writers, columnists, and intellectuals who regard the imminent collapse of the wall separating fiction and nonfiction as having ominous reverberations for literature and for society as a whole. In many ways, I think their concerns are justified. But are they justified in singling out memoir as the prime component of a world slipping into virtual reality?

Turn on the TV and you'll get John Wayne pitching beer commercials or Humphrey Bogart drinking Diet Coke or Fred Astaire dancing with an Electrolux. Watch any broadcast of the national political news then pick up a video of *Wag the Dog* or *Primary Colors*. An article in a recent issue of *Harper's* describes how digital technology calls into question the legitimacy of still photography. Our ability to manipulate images has become so sophisticated that it is now nearly impossible to tell whether an image is a representation of the real world or the product of a hard drive. We are now told that Ansel Adams, the patron saint of nature photography, played around in his dark room "Making little circles with [a] wand over the area he wanted lightened," laughing in "crazy, nasal, Mephistophelean" glee.

Nevertheless, critics continue to blame memoir for a disproportionate share of this blurring of reality. No less a writer than Joyce Carol Oates has jumped into the fray. In a recent article for the *New York Times*, Ms. Oates suggested that "Memoir testifies, perhaps, to our desperate wish that some truth of the spirit be presented to us, though we know it's probably invented. We want to believe! We are a species who clamors to be lied to." I am not going to address, at least directly, what I consider to be the depressingly elitist, cynical, and patronizing tone of Ms. Oates' observations. Rather, I would like to suggest that what people desperately want, what they've always wanted, is not to be lied to, but to be told a story. And if nonfiction is burning up the best seller lists, it's not because memoirists have learned to become better liars than fiction writers; maybe it's because they're just telling a better story.

In a 1997 interview, fiction writer and essayist Bob Shacochis commented upon the underlying hostility within the literary community over the "appropriation" of traditional fiction techniques—dialogue, scene construction, vividly recollected detail—into today's nonfiction. The real issue, he says, is the quality of storytelling, not whether it's invented or remembered, and "beyond that the arguments become uninteresting, and they get precious. If someone tells you that the memoir or essay is this certain thing, they're really not telling you what they know so much as they're telling you what they've read. It doesn't address the magnitude and diversity of what's been done, or being done out there. They try to tell you that 'objectivity' is the rule in nonfiction, where I regard subjectivity as the greater witness."

For all I know, all of my memories could be inaccurate. But as I write, I am not consciously dissembling, creating instances and scenes to fit the awkward angles of a story line. My past is not inhabited by a cast of stick figures awkwardly dramatizing a plodding, unimaginative plot line. And just because I can't remember everything doesn't—or shouldn't—mean I have to let my past evaporate, or say that it wasn't real. I am not ready to surrender my past, my life, to fiction. The world is a strange enough place as it is.

I don't remember what my father wore under his orange raincoat during my JV football games. But if I wrote about it, I'd tell the reader he had on an open collared, red plaid shirt, with black suspenders fastened to dark green cotton trousers—the kind school janitors used to wear. Oh yes! He'd also have on an old, frayed T-shirt, his thick, dark, chest hair curling over the neckband. I'd write all this because it was a standard outfit for my father, because his wearing it beneath his raincoat was both probable and possible. In my mind, when he opens his raincoat, he's not naked. I'm not being "flashed" while my imagination rummages around in wardrobe.

Mary McCarthy, in her memoir *Memories of a Catholic Girlhood*, directly confronted the difficulty of writing from memory. In her foreword, "To the Reader," she wrote: "Many a time, in the course of doing these memoirs, I have wished I were writing fiction. The temptation to invent has been very strong, particularly where recollection is hazy . . . Sometimes I have yielded, as in the case of conversations. My memory is good, but I cannot obviously recall whole passages of dialogue that took place years ago." McCarthy's discussion of the difference between memory and technical reproduction applies not only to dialogue, but to all the other facets of storytelling. A writer must deal honestly with whatever facts he or she has at hand, limited as the facts may be. This requires enormous storytelling skill, because the past is a moving image, requiring almost constant readjustment of the viewing lens. And the images we retrieve arrive in different ways. What transports me back to the past varies greatly: sometimes it's the way my son drops his head when I'm angry; sometimes it's an old Beatles song, a photo album, or a receipt I found in the pocket of a coat I haven't worn in years.

IV

So I would like to challenge the nature of memory, to question the notion that all must be known before an event can be rendered truthfully as story. Indeed, because a large part of our lives can never be retrieved, it is a storyteller's duty to use whatever tools are at hand.

In *How Proust Can Change Your Life*, Alain De Botton discusses Proust's concept of *voluntary* and *involuntary* memory. Voluntary memory is the memory of multiplication tables, bus schedules, and daily agendas—memories that we intellectually attempt to provoke. Involuntary memory, on the other hand, occurs when a recollection is stirred by "a long forgotten smell or an old glove." Something that has remained dormant since childhood and "therefore remains uncorrupted by later associations." These instances of almost epiphanic intensity are also known as *Proustian moments*.

In a letter, the essayist and critic Sven Birkerts elaborates on just such a distinction when he writes: "What we outwardly regard as important—the big events, the key moves, the prominent characters—may have nothing to do with the story that needs to be written. We can banish the idea of telling the story of our life and concentrate on evoking its mystery." He suggests following the patterns of memory, even if that means you "devote six pages to writing about a grandfather's cigar box, then jump to the memory of burning ants with a magnifying glass, and then recall the braid of a girl you sat behind in third grade." Birkerts suggests letting the force of memory, not public concerns, be the measure of an event's importance. As he puts it: "You may leave out entirely—or consign to the margins—the fact that your house was burned down or that your grandfather was George Bush. . . . [W]hat makes this kind of writing stick is the level of absorption. And if in your writer's soul you remember the smell of wool mittens more than you remember climbing Everest with your father, you may have to write the wool mittens." Involuntary memory—what is called up from deep emotional experience and of its own accord—is immensely valuable to writers of any genre. It is far more complicated than fact—the bus schedules of voluntary memory. It is where the heart and soul of our past resides.

V

To Virginia Woolf, the present was a platform for viewing the past, the string of experiences we drag behind us like a bedraggled train. We are not imagined. Our past is real, but it is not static. Like the cosmos, it moves unceasingly away from us, and what a memoirist captures is but a glimpse of its receding illumination, a recollective red shift that can only be adjusted through re-creation. Can we change the past? No. But we can change how it is remembered because we grow, change, and (hopefully) learn from our experiences. Or, as Tomás Eloy Martínez writes in his novel *Santa Evita*: "Every story is by definition, unfaithful. Reality, as I've said, can't be told or repeated. The only thing that can be done with reality is to invent it all over again."

So it comes back to what is real—the rightness of a memory or experience—because in order to make a claim on legitimacy, any story, with the possible exception of parable and allegory, must have a basis in reality. That is, what we read—whether fiction or nonfiction—must in some way correlate to our experience, to our sense of what is real. How many times have you put down a novel or story because the plot or characterizations or details seemed implausible? As Aristotle wrote in his *Poetics*: "It is not the poet's function to describe what actually happened, but the kind of things that might happen, that is, that could happen because they are, in the circumstances, either probable or necessary . . . Even if the poet writes about things that have actually happened, that does not make him any less a poet, for there is nothing to prevent some of the things that have happened from being in accordance with the laws of possibility and probability, and thus he will be a poet in writing about them."

Or, as author Sherwood Anderson put it: "While art is distinct from real life, the imagination must constantly feed upon reality or starve." But sometimes, in order that the real story may be told, the ineluctable passage of time is a necessity. In his magisterial short story "A Death in the Woods," Anderson describes the death of an old woman during a violent Midwestern snowstorm, a story based on an actual event in his childhood. In the following passage, Anderson's narrator, now an adult, reflects: "The whole thing, the story of the old woman's death, was to me, as I grew older, like music heard from far off. The notes had to be picked up slowly one at a time. Something had to be understood. . . ." What is essential, the narrator realizes, is the perspective of distance and age. As children, he and his brother were too young to understand the point of the story. "A thing so complete has its own beauty . . . I shall not try to emphasize the point. I am only explaining why I was dissatisfied then and have been ever since. I speak of that only that you may understand why I have been impelled to try to tell the simple story over again."

This same act of remembering and telling in order to arrive at an understanding is the basic premise of memoir: thinking out loud, retelling a story over and over again, using imagination to understand and reconcile a past where reality served as the background music. We recall it only with the greatest difficulty, following the tune as best we can, using our imaginations to improvise notes where the score goes blank. How many truths are there to an event? How much music have we failed to hear? And when the melody finally comes—a sense of longing, a sudden unexplained feeling of joy or sadness—the best we can do is whistle along, staying as close to the original melody as we can.

William Maxwell's *So Long, See You Tomorrow*, an almost perfect novel, is written in the form of a memoir in which an aging narrator reflects upon his Midwestern childhood. It is an evocative elegy to youth, centered on a fictional murder in a small Illinois farming town around World War I. Like his Midwestern literary predecessor, Sherwood Anderson, Maxwell uses simple and unadorned language that masks an uncompromisingly complex and richly detailed narrative. The genesis for this novel, published in 1980, can be found in another book he wrote nine years earlier: *Ancestors*, a memoir.

It is generally not wise to read a piece of fiction as though it were autobiography. But for anyone who has read both books, the comparisons cannot be avoided: each narrator had an older and younger brother; each lost a mother to the 1919 influenza epidemic; each had a businessman father who ultimately relocated the family to Chicago and remarried a much younger woman. Even some of the scenes are the same: the fictional and nonfictional boy with his arm wrapped around the father's waist as they paced the floor in the days after the mother's death, and the father blowing pipe smoke into the fictional and nonfictional boy's ear to cure an earache. Both books examine the ways in which memory can best interrogate the past. But on this last point they differ. In *Ancestors*, the earlier book, Maxwell writes: "I have to get out an imaginary lens and fiddle with the lens until I see something that interests me, preferably something small and unimportant." But in *So Long, See You Tomorrow*, Maxwell's approach to memory is more circumspect as he repeatedly and directly confronts the complexity and unverifiability of memory: "What we, or at any rate what I, refer to as memory— meaning a moment, a scene, a fact that has been subjected to a fixative and thereby rescued from oblivion—is really a form of storytelling that goes on continually in the mind and often changes with the telling. Too many conflicting emotional interests are involved for life ever to be wholly acceptable, and possibly it is the work of a storyteller to arrange things so that they conform to this end. In any case, in talking about the past, we lie with every breath we draw."

Is Maxwell suggesting that we are incapable of truth? That is not my reading of the passage. Rather, I believe he is speaking in phenomenological terms, suggesting that because of "conflicting emotions" and shifting circumstances everything we witness is but an illusion, representative of a deeper, underlying reality. In this way of thinking, fiction is a play upon illusion, and memoir is the illusion itself. So, in the end, neither is real. Or, put another way, both are equally real.

VI

It has been my experience that we do not perceive or write about things as they are, but, rather, we perceive or write about them as *we* are. What a memoirist describes is often confined to the perspective of an immediate and unfinished circumstance. But between what we remember and what really happened are the shadows from which the truth will ultimately reassert itself.

Vladimir Nabokov, in his memoir *Speak Memory*, addresses one of the most luminous aspects of memory: the conflict that arises when a child's experience is at odds with empirical reality. In one of the early chapters, Nabokov describes a scene in which his aristocratic father is pitched into the air by a group of celebratory villagers. Nabokov writes: "From my place at table I would suddenly see through one of the west windows a marvelous case of levitation. There, for an instant, the figure of my father in his windrippled white summer suit would be displayed, gloriously sprawling in midair, his limbs in a curiously casual attitude, his handsome, imperturbable features turned to the sky . . . and then there he would be, on his last and loftiest night, reclining, as if for good, against the cobalt blue of the summer noon. . . ." The final sentence of this recollection runs for 127 words, during which the child's vision evolves into an extended metaphysical presentiment of his father's death. Could a child have perceived all this? Probably not. But the pristine truth of Nabokov's numinous image serves as the framework for an extended, mature meditation. It is a vision of first things.

VII

There is a story about my father I'd like to write: My father. Forty-five years ago. I have yet to be born. He's flying a single-engine plane above the old house on Franklin Street. My mother is in the back yard hanging out laundry. There are only two children—Holley and John—whom Mom sends in the house when she looks up to see my father swooping low over the neighborhood. It's a beautiful summer evening—a Friday, so she knows that he's already made a quick tour of the city's gin mills.

He's done these fly-bys before, screaming down from above the tree tops in the plane he borrows from Jimmy Durr, a childhood pal. They both earned their wings eight years earlier, flying sub reconnaissance in the South Pacific. But tonight my father has decided to push his fly-by game to the limit. My mother tries to wave him off, but my father thinks she's calling him in closer, and he obliges her, eventually buzzing the whole block. It doesn't take long for Chief of

Police Leo LeBeau and the fire trucks to come barreling in, sirens blaring, lights flashing. From the air it looks like a carnival.

Taking the hint, my father gently rolls the plane and heads north, crossing the mile-wide Saint Lawrence River in order to follow the Ontario shoreline. Every now and then he sweeps down to dip his wings to the ocean freighters, their giant hulls lumbering down the Seaway. The ships flash their running lights in salute as he rolls south, heading back, descending to just above the water as he comes into the mouth of the Oswegatchie, the last light of the day shooting like flames along the fuselage as he hot dogs it home under the Lafayette Street bridge.

I write about my father because there is no one else to write about him. Because he was real and vital and flawed. Because I loved him. Because I want to imagine him as a man close to my own age now. I no longer seek my father's understanding, I seek, through re-creation, to understand him. And so I return to the beginning—April 5, 1969—where, I suppose, the only accurate written history about my father's death can be found in a copy of his obituary. But my hometown newspaper got a couple of the facts wrong. It printed his date of birth as October 25, 1916 when, according to his birth certificate, he was actually born in 1915. The obituary also misrepresented his military service and the ages of two of my siblings. But these are only details.

So much for the first rough draft of history.

Courting the Approval of the Dead

Tracy Kidder

I have never written much about myself, but, like most writers I know, I am interested in the subject. We live in an era surfeited with memoirs. This is my contribution to the excess.

My writing career began at Harvard College about thirty-two years ago, shortly after I enrolled as an undergraduate. I planned to fix the world by becoming a diplomat. I began by studying political science. Thinking I should have a hobby, I also took a course in creative writing. I didn't invest a lot of ego in the enterprise and maybe for that reason the first short stories that I wrote were rather sprightly. I think they contained some dialogue that human beings might have uttered. Anyway, the teacher liked them and, more important, so did some of the young women in the class. My first strong impulse to become a writer sprang from this realization: that writing could be a means of meeting and impressing girls.

The next year I got into a class taught by the poet and great translator Robert Fitzgerald. He admitted only about a dozen students from among dozens of applicants, and I seem to remember that I was the youngest of the anointed group. This mattered to me. In high school I had been addicted to competitive sports, and I conceived of writing in sporting terms. I figured I had won part of the competition already, by being the youngest student admitted to the class. The yearning for distinction is common among writers, and in that sense I had begun to become a writer.

I want to try to summon Mr. Fitzgerald back from the dead. I remember him as a small, elegant man, then in his sixties, I believe. Occasionally during office hours he smoked a cigarette, and did so with great deliberation, making every puff count—I think he'd been warned off tobacco, and had put himself on short rations. He would enter the classroom with a green bookbag slung over his shoulder, and would greet us with a smile and a sigh as he heaved the bag onto the long seminar table. Mr. Fitzgerald's green bag contained our work, *my* work, with his comments upon it. I could not have been more interested in that object if Mr. Fitzgerald had been our adult provider, returning with food he'd found out in the world. But the way he sighed, as he heaved that sack onto the table, insinuated that what lay inside wasn't as valuable as food. Certainly it looked like a heavy load for one professor to carry.

I have always talked too much and listened too little. What is it about certain people that has made me pay attention to everything they say? Their confidence and wit, I guess, but most of all their interest in *me*. Mr. Fitzgerald paid his students the great compliment of taking us seriously. He flattered us, dauntingly. I remember the first day of that class. From his place at the head of the table Mr. Fitzgerald eyed us all. He had a pair of reading glasses, half-glasses, which he often used to great effect. He lowered them and looking at us over the top of them, said something like, "The only reason for writing is to produce something *classic*. And I expect that you will produce *classic* work during this term."

I recall thinking, "You do?"

Of course, none of us did, with the possible exception of one young woman who wrote a poem entitled "The Splendor and the Terror of the Universe as Revealed to Me on Brattle Street." I don't recall the poem, but I still like the title.

Having told us of his expectations, Mr. Fitzgerald offered his first advice for meeting them. He jabbed an index finger at the wastebasket beside him and said, "The greatest repository I know of for writers. And I do hope that it will *precede* me."

After a few weeks of Mr. Fitzgerald, I gave up on political science. I quit right in the middle of a lecture by the then-not-very-famous professor Henry Kissinger. The lecture bored me. Professor Kissinger was only partly to blame. I now described myself as a writer, and I thought a writer shouldn't be interested in politics. I had not yet realized that a writer ought to know about something besides writing, so as to have something to write about. When I left that lecture I went right to the English department office and signed up. I'd already begun to do a lot of reading on my own, mostly fiction, which I was consuming at a rate I've never equaled since. At the same time, I had suddenly acquired an assigned-reading disability and a sleep disorder. I had trouble reading books that appeared on formal course lists, and I often worked all night on stories for Mr. Fitzgerald, then went to sleep around the time when my other classes began.

During the first part of Mr. Fitzgerald's class, he would talk about writing and read aloud to us, very occasionally stuff that a student had written, and more often works by wonderful, famous writers he had known, such as his old friend Flannery O'Connor. He read us one of her stories, and when he finished, he said, "That story unwinds like a Rolex watch." Listening to him read such estimable work made me want to try my hand. I think he aimed for that effect, because in the second half of every class he had us write. He warmed us up, and then made us exercise. It is a testament to those warmups of his that I can't recall ever being unable to write *something* in that room for him. In his presence, even poetry seemed possible. Mr. Fitzgerald insisted I try my hand at a poem now and then. I struggled but complied. Finally, I got one off that he seemed to like. It came back from him with this comment at the bottom: "This is very like a poem."

I prefer other memories, especially this one: I had written a short story, which an undergraduate, literary friend of mine had read and disliked. This was the first and at the time the only literary friend I'd acquired, and I thought him very wise and perspicacious, because he had encouraged me. I guessed that my friend must be right about my story. Once he'd pointed out its flaws, I saw them clearly, too. But I decided to show the thing to Mr. Fitzgerald, just so he'd know that I was working. He opened the next class by saying that he was going to read a student's story, a story that he particularly liked, and I remember sitting there wishing that he would some day single out a story of mine in that way and I recall vividly the moment when I realized that it was my story he was reading. The mellifluous voice that had read to us from the likes of James Agee and Wallace Stevens and Flannery O'Connor was reading something of mine! I felt frightened. Then I felt confused. I don't think it had ever occurred to me that intelligent people could disagree about the quality of a piece of writing. If my literary friend thought the story was lousy, Mr. Fitzgerald surely would, too. I see myself sitting at that table with my mouth hanging open—and closing it fast when I remembered the young women in the room. At first I wanted to ask Mr. Fitzgerald to stop, and then I hoped he never would.

I hoped, indeed expected, to have that experience again. I remember that I had given Mr. Fitzgerald a story I knew to be marvelous, a story I knew he'd want to single out in class. When I came into his office for the private visit all of us periodically received, I said to him, in a voice already exulting at his answer, "How'd you like that story, Mr. Fitzgerald?"

He performed his ritual of the reading glasses, pulling them an inch down his nose and looking at me over the top of them. "Not much," he said.

And then, of course, he told me what was wrong with the story, and I saw at once that he was right. I still have this problem. My judgment of my own work sometimes seems so malleable as not to rate as judgment at all. Any critic, no matter how stupid in praise or transparently spiteful in blame, convinces me—at least for awhile. Generally, harsh criticism tends to make me fear that the critic has an intelligence far superior to mine, and has found out things about my writing that I've been too blind to see myself. A person as easily confused by criticism as I am might well have quit writing after a few rejection slips came in for stories that my girlfriend and my mother thought were really good. Perhaps inadvertently, Mr. Fitzgerald taught me the value of trusting the judgment of just one person above all others—and of getting that judgment as the work is in progress, and a lot of help besides. Which is the role I've inflicted on a single editor, Richard Todd, for more than two decades.

I took Mr. Fitzgerald's course again and again, right up until I graduated. After my first semester with him, I didn't perform very well. It wasn't for lack of trying or, God knows, desire. I had become self-conscious about writing. At one point I started a novel. I wrote twenty pages or so, but the most interesting parts were the comments and little drawings I made in the margins—and created with greater care than anything in the actual text—imagining, as I created these notes in the margins, my biographer's delight in finding them. During this period, almost all of the stories I wrote in my room late at night, and the pastiches I committed in class, came back with such brief comments as "O.K., but no flash," all written in an elegantly penned script, which I can still see in my mind's eye, my heart sinking all over again. Mr. Fitzgerald used to talk about something he called "the luck of the conception," an idea I still believe in, but no longer dream about. I used to have a dream in which I had come upon the perfect story. The dream did not contain the story itself, just the fact that I possessed it. It was a dream suffused with joy, and I'd awake from it with a kind of sorrow that I haven't felt since adolescence. As a reader I felt then as I feel now, that any number of faults in a piece of writing are forgivable if there is life on the page. And there was no life in anything I wrote. Oddly, as the small natural talent I'd had for making up stories began to wane, my ambitions grew immense. Or maybe it was the other way around, and ambition stood in my way.

I can't blame Mr. Fitzgerald. He had only suggested that writing could be a high calling. I alone invented my desire to write for posterity. I am embarrassed to admit to this, but what I really had in mind was immortality. Once as a very young boy at a lecture at the Hayden Planetarium in New York, I learned that the earth would be destroyed in some two and a half billion years, and in spite of all my mother said, I was inconsolable for weeks. Maybe I was born especially susceptible to the fears that attend the fact of human mortality. Maybe I was influenced by certain of the English poets, those whose poems declare that their poems will make them immortal. Or it may be, as my wife suggests, that once a young man has solved the problem of how to meet and impress girls, it just naturally occurs to him that his next job is to figure out how to become immortal.

After college I went to Vietnam as a soldier—not the most likely way of gaining immortality, though I was never in much danger there. I came home with my body and my vaunting literary ambitions still intact and wrote a whole novel about experiences I didn't have in Vietnam. I designed that book for immortality. I borrowed heavily from Conrad, Melville, and Dostoyevsky. About thirty-five editors refused to publish it, thank God. I went to the Iowa Writers Workshop, where it began to seem to me that the well from which I drew for fiction had gone completely dry. (I have written fiction since then, all of it published, but the sum total is three short stories.) I decided to try my hand at nonfiction. That term covers a lot of territory, of course, from weighty treatises on the great problems of the world to diet books—some diet books qualify as nonfiction don't they? I dove into something then labeled The New Journalism. As many people have pointed out, only the term was new. I believe that the form already had a distinguished lineage, which included work by George Orwell and Joseph Mitchell and Mark Twain and Lillian Ross and Edmund Wilson and, my particular favorite, A. J. Liebling. This kind of nonfiction writing, whatever it's called, relies on narrative. Some people describe it by saying that it borrows techniques of fiction, but the fact is that it employs techniques of storytelling that never did belong exclusively to fiction. It is an honorable literary form, not always honorably used, but one can certainly say the same about fiction.

When I first started trying to write in this genre, there was an idea in the air, which for me had the force of a revelation: that all journalism is inevitably subjective. I was in my mid-twenties then, and although my behavior was somewhat worse than it has been recently, I was quite a moralist. I decided that writers of nonfiction had a moral obligation to write in the first person—really write in the first person, making themselves characters on the page. In this way, I would disclose my biases. I would not hide the truth from the reader. I would proclaim that what I wrote was just my own subjective version of events. In retrospect, it seems clear that this prescription for honesty often served instead as a license for self-absorption on the page. But I was still very young, too young and self-absorbed to realize what now seems obvious—that I was less likely to write honestly about myself than about anyone else on earth.

I wrote a book about a murder case, in a swashbuckling first person. It *was* published, I'm sorry to say. On the other hand, it disappeared without a trace; that is, it never got reviewed in the *New York Times*. And I began writing nonfiction articles for the *Atlantic Monthly,* under the tutelage of Richard Todd, then a young editor there. For about five years, during which I didn't dare attempt another book, I worked on creating what many writer friends of mine call "voice." I didn't do this consciously. If I had, I probably wouldn't have gotten anywhere. But gradually, I think, I cultivated a writing voice, the voice of a person who was well-informed, fair-minded, and temperate—the voice, not of the person I was, but of a person I sometimes wanted to be. Then I went back to writing books, and discovered other points of view besides the first person.

Choosing a point of view is a matter of finding the best place to stand from which to tell a story. It shouldn't be determined by theory, but by immersion in the material itself. The choice of point of view, I've come to think, has nothing to do with morality. It's a choice among tools. I think it's true, however, that the wrong choice can lead to dishonesty. Point of view is primary; it affects everything else, including voice. Writing my last four books, I made my choices by instinct sometimes and sometimes by experiment. Most of my memories of time spent writing have merged together in a blur, but I remember vividly my first attempts to find a way to write *Among Schoolchildren,* a book about an inner-city schoolteacher. I had spent a year inside her classroom. I intended, vaguely, to fold into my account of events I'd witnessed in that little place a great deal about the lives of particular schoolchildren and about the problems of education in America. I tried out every point of view that I'd used in previous books, and every page I wrote felt lifeless. Finally, I hit on a restricted third-person narration.

The approach seemed to work. The world of that classroom seemed to come alive when the view of it was restricted mainly to observations of the teacher and to accounts of what the teacher saw and heard and smelled and felt. This choice narrowed my options. I ended up writing something less comprehensive than I'd planned. The book became essentially an account of a year in the emotional life of a schoolteacher. My choice of the restricted third person also obliged me to write parts of the book as if from within the teacher's mind. I felt entitled to describe her thoughts and feelings because she had described them to me, both during class and afterward, and because her descriptions rarely seemed self-serving. Believing in them myself, I thought that I could make them believable on the page.

Belief is an offering that a reader makes to an author, what Coleridge famously called "That willing suspension of disbelief for the moment, which constitutes poetic faith." It is up to the writer to entertain and inform without disappointing the reader into a loss of that faith. In fiction or poetry, of course, believability may have nothing to do with realism or even plausibility. It has everything to do with those things in nonfiction, in my opinion. I think that the nonfiction writer's fundamental job is to make what is true believable. I'm not sure that everyone agrees. Lately the job seems to have been defined differently. Here are some of the ways that some people now seem to define the nonfiction writer's job: to make believable what the writer thinks is true, if the writer wants to be scrupulous; to make believable what the writer wishes were true, if the writer isn't interested in scrupulosity; or to make believable what the writer thinks might be true, if the writer couldn't get the story and had to make it up.

I figure that if I call a piece of my own writing nonfiction it ought to be about real people, with their real names attached whenever possible, who say and do in print nothing that they didn't actually say and do. On the cover page of my last book I put a note that reads, "This is a work of nonfiction," and listed the several names that I was obliged to change in the text. I thought a longer note would be intrusive. I was afraid that it would stand between the reader and the spell that I wanted to create, inviting the reader into the world of a nursing home. But the definition of "nonfiction" has become so slippery that I wonder if I shouldn't have written more. So now I'll take this opportunity to explain that for my last book I spent a year doing research, that the name of the place I wrote about is its real name, that I didn't change the names of any of the major characters, and that I didn't invent dialogue or put any thoughts in characters' minds that the characters themselves didn't confess to.

I no longer care what rules other writers set for themselves. If I don't like what someone has written, I can stop reading, which is, after all, the worst punishment a writer can suffer. (It ought to be the worst punishment. Some critics seem to feel that the creation of a book that displeases them amounts to a felony.) But the expanded definitions of nonfiction have created problems for those writers who define the term narrowly. Many readers now view with suspicion every narrative that claims to be nonfiction, and yet scores of very good nonfiction writers do not make up their stories or the details in them—writers such as John McPhee, Jane Kramer, J. Anthony Lucas. There are also special cases that confound categories and all attempts to lay down rules for writers of narrative. I have in mind Norman Mailer and in particular his *Executioner's Song*, a hybrid of fact and fiction, carefully labeled as such—a book I admire.

Most writers lack Mailer's powers of invention. Some nonfiction writers do not lack his willingness to invent, but the candor to admit it. Some writers proceed by trying to discover the truth about a situation, and then invent or distort the facts as necessary. Even in these suspicious times, writers can get away with this. Often no one will know, and the subjects of the story may not care. They may not notice. But the writer always knows. I believe in immersion in the events of a story. I take it on faith that the truth lies in the events somewhere, and that immersion in those real events will yield glimpses of that truth. I try to hew to what has begun to seem like a narrow definition of nonfiction partly in that faith, and partly out of fear. I'm afraid that if I started making up things in a story that purported to be about real events and people, I'd stop believing it myself. And I imagine that such a loss of conviction would infect every sentence and make each one unbelievable.

I don't mean to imply that all a person has to do to write good narrative nonfiction is to take accurate notes and reproduce them. The kind of nonfiction I like to read is at bottom storytelling, as gracefully accomplished as good fiction. I don't think any technique should be ruled out to achieve it well. For myself, I rule out only invention. But I don't think that honesty and artifice are contradictory. They work together in good writing of every sort. Artfulness and an author's justified belief in a story often combine to produce the most believable nonfiction.

If you write a nonfiction story in the third person and show your face in public afterward, someone is bound to ask, "How did your presence in the scenes you relate affect the people you were observing?" Some readers seem to feel that third-person narration, all by itself, makes a narrative incomplete. The other day I came upon a book about the writing of ethnography. It interested me initially because its bibliography cited a couple of my books and one of its footnotes mentioned me. The author spelled my first name wrong and gave one of my books a slightly different title from the one I chose. I swear I don't hold a grudge on account of that. My first name is a little weird, and the title in question is a long one. But those little mistakes did make me vigilant as I read the following passage:

> Writers of literary tales seldom remark on the significance of their presence on the scenes they represent, and this is in some instances a bothersome problem to field workers in addition to the common concerns for reactivity in any situation. It is, for example, very difficult to imagine that as famous and dandy a writer as Tom Wolfe was merely a fashionable but unobtrusive fly on the wall in the classic uptown parlor scene of *Radical Chic* (1970), or that Tracey [sic] Kidder did not in any way influence the raising of the Souweines' roofbeams in *House* (1985). Since writers of ethnographic tales have begun to break their silence on these matters, it is seemingly time for writers of literary tales to do so too—especially when their accounts so clearly rest on intimacy.

I believe it's possible to learn something from anyone, including ethnographers who have begun to break their silence. But I can't work out the mechanics for calculating the *reactivity* that occurs during *field work.* As I imagine it, field work that is mindful of reactivity would have to proceed in this way: I'd open my notebook in front of a person I planned to write about, and I'd ask, "How did you feel when I opened my notebook just now?" Then I would probably be bound to ask, "How did you feel when I asked you that question about opening my note-book?"

I don't know for sure how my presence has influenced the behavior of any of the people I've written about. I don't believe that I can know, because I wasn't there when I wasn't there. To do the research for a book, I usually hang around with my subjects for a year or more. After a while, most seem to take my presence for granted. Not all do. It worked the other way with one of the carpenters I wrote about in *House.* I remember his saying at one point that he and the other builders ought to put a bell around my neck, so they'd know where I was at all times.

Obviously some readers expect to hear about the story behind the story. But all writing is selective. I think that a narrative should be judged mainly on its own terms, not according to a reader's preexisting expectations. As a reader, I know that I won't always sit still for the story behind the story. As a writer, I have often decided that it isn't worth telling.

I wrote my most recent book, *Old Friends,* which is about some of the residents of a nursing home, in the third person. I hope that I put my own voice in it, but I chose not to write about how I did my research and how I was affected by what I encountered inside the nursing home—never mind how my presence might, arguably, possibly, have affected the inmates' behavior—mainly because what I did—asking questions, listening, taking notes—was much less interesting than what I observed. It is true, however, that my solution to the problem that the book presented did have something to do with my own experience of life inside that place. After writing for a while, I realized that I wanted to reproduce, in a limited sense, the most important part of my experience there.

I entered the nursing home in the late fall of 1990. The place, which is situated in western Massachusetts, is called the Linda Manor Extended Care Facility. I went there with a notebook—I filled ninety notebooks eventually—and prowled around inside almost every day, and many nights, for about a year. And then for another year or so I spent about three days a week there. I chose a decent nursing home, not one of the very best but a clean, well-lighted place where residents weren't tied up and were allowed some of the trappings of their former lives.

I had visited a nursing home only once before in my life, and since then had averted both my eyes and thoughts as I passed by. That was part of the attraction; nursing homes seemed to me like secret places in the landscape. I went to Linda Manor tentatively, though. I was afraid that I might find it dull. I thought I might find myself in a kind of waiting room, a vestibule to eternity, where everything had been resolved or set aside and residents simply lay waiting to die. But waiting was the least of what went on in many of those clean, motel-like rooms. Nearly everyone, it seemed, was working on a project. Some were absurd—one resident kept hounding the office of a U.S. senator to complain about his breakfast eggs. Some were poignant—many of the demented residents roamed the halls searching for exits, asking everyone for directions home. A lot of projects were Quixotic. There was, for instance, one indomitable, wheelchair-bound woman who had set herself the task of raising about $30,000 to buy the nursing home its own chairlift van. She intended to do so through raffles and teacup auctions and by getting other residents to remember the van in their wills. There was also an elderly actress who kept herself and the place somewhat invigorated by putting on plays. Staging those productions took great determination, because Linda Manor had no stage and most of the actors and actresses were confined to wheelchairs and walkers. In between plays, when things got dull, the old actress livened things up by starting fights. There were many residents working doggedly to come to terms with the remorse they felt for past mistakes and offenses. There was also a man in his nineties named Lou Freed who summoned up memories with what seemed like the force of necessity, re-inhabiting his former life with something that resembled joy. And there were, of course, a number who knew their deaths were imminent and struggled to find ways to live in the face of that knowledge.

Even in a decent nursing home, the old often get treated like children. And yet many of the residents refused to become like children. The roommates Lou and Joe, for instance. Let me try to prove this point with a short passage from my book.

> Joe and Lou could not control most of the substance of their life in here, but they had imposed a style on it. The way for instance that Joe and Lou had come, in the past months, to deal with matters of the bathroom. Joe had to go there what seemed to him like a ridiculous number of times each day and night. He and Lou referred to the bathroom as "the library." The mock-daintiness of the term amused Joe. The point was to make a joke out of anything you could around here. Up in the room after breakfast, Joe would say to Lou, "I gotta go to the library. I have to do my, uh, uh, prune evacuation."
>
> This room was now their home. As in any household, people entering were expected to follow local rules. The nursing staff was overwhelmingly female. Lou and Joe referred to all of them as girls, and indeed, next to them, even the middleaged did look like girls. The staff had all, of course, been quite willing to talk frankly about matters of Lou and Joe's biology. Too frankly for Lou. Too frankly for Joe, once Lou had made the point. The aides, "the girls," used to come to the doorway, cradling opened in their arms the large, ledger-like Forest View "BM Book," and they'd call loudly in, "Did either of you gentlemen have a bowel movement today?" It was Lou, some months ago now, who responded to this question by inviting in the girls who asked it, and then telling them gently, "All you have to say is, 'Did you or didn't you.'" The way Lou did that job impressed Joe, Lou did it so diplomatically, so much more diplomatically than Joe would have. Lou, as he liked to say, had trained all the girls by now. Joe took care of reinforcement.
>
> It was a morning in December. Joe had the television news on. He and Lou were listening to the dispatches from the Middle East. Joe wasn't waiting for the aide with the BM Book, but he had a question ready for her. When the aide came to the door, she asked, "For my book. Did you?"
>
> "Yes." Joe tilted his head toward Lou. "And so did he." Then, a little smile blossoming, Joe looked at the aide and asked, "And what about you?"
>
> "None of your business!" The aide looked embarrassed. She laughed.

"Well, you ask me," Joe said.
"But I get paid for it."
"*Good*bye," Joe said pleasantly, and went back to watching the news.

Many residents insisted on preserving their dignity, in spite of the indignities imposed by failing health and institutional confinement. Many people in there were attempting in one way or another to invent new lives for themselves. In the context of that place and of debilitating illnesses, their quests seemed important.

So when I began to write *Old Friends*, I didn't lack for interesting characters or stories. I felt I had an overabundance. I told myself before I started writing that I couldn't fit in everything, and then for about a year I tried to do just that. In the end I had to jettison a lot of portraits and stories that I had written many times and polished up. Among other things, I wrote four or five times and finally discarded what in all modesty I believe to have been the most riveting account of a session of Bingo ever composed. But the plain fact was that about half of what I wrote and rewrote got in the way of the main story that I wanted to tell.

Hundreds of articles and books deal with the big issues that surround aging in late-twentieth-century America. I read some of them. But I didn't want to approach this subject in a general way. It is useful, maybe even necessary, to imagine that a definable group called "the elderly" exists. But all such conceptions inevitably fail. It is accurate only to say that there are many individuals who have lived longer than most of the rest of the population, and that they differ widely among themselves. For various reasons, some can no longer manage what are called the activities of daily living at home, and, for lack of a better solution, some of those people end up living in nursing homes. I chose to write about a few of those people partly because so much well-meaning commentary on old age depicts white-haired folks in tennis clothes—a tendency, it seems to me, that inadvertently denigrates the lives of the many people who haven't been as lucky.

About five percent of Americans over sixty-five—about 1.5 million people—live in nursing homes and, according to one estimate, nearly half of all the people who live past sixty-five will spend some time inside a nursing home. Obviously, they are important places, but nursing homes weren't really the subject I wanted to address. There were already plenty of published exposés of bad nursing homes. I decided to do my research inside a good nursing home on the theory that a good one would be bad enough, inevitably a house of grief and pain, and also because I didn't want to write about the kinds of policy and management issues that would have assumed primary importance in a story set in an evil place. I wanted to write from the inside about the experience of being old and sick and confined to an institution. I wanted to come at the subject of aging, not through statistics, but through elderly people themselves. I wanted to write an interesting, engaging book. The residents of even a decent nursing home are people in a difficult situation, and I think that stories about people in difficult situations are almost always interesting, and often dramatic.

In some ways, research in that place was easy work. In the course of every story I'd done before, I had run into people who hadn't wanted to talk to me. But people in a nursing home never have enough willing listeners. A nursing home like Linda Manor may be the only place on earth where a person with a notebook can hope to receive a universal welcome.

Various sights, smells, and sounds distressed me at first. But gradually, I got used to the externals of the place and people. Almost everyone who has spent some time inside a nursing home begins to look beyond the bodies of the residents. It just happens. But around the time when that happened to me, another problem arose. I remember leaving the room of a dying, despondent resident and stopping in my tracks in a Linda Manor corridor, and hearing myself say to myself, "This is amazing! *Everybody* dies." And, of course, my next thought was, "Including me." I know that sounds silly. One is supposed to have figured that out before pushing fifty. But I hadn't believed it, I think.

I arranged some other troubling moments for myself, during my research. At one point, I decided that I ought to check into Linda Manor for a couple of days and nights, as if I were myself a resident. I hate the kind of story in which a perfectly healthy person decides to ride around in a wheelchair for a day and then proclaims himself an expert in what being wheelchair-bound is like. But I believe in the possibility of imaginatively experiencing what others experience, and I thought I might learn something. With vast amusement, a nurse ushered me into a little room. My roommate, an ancient man who couldn't speak much, terrified me as soon as I climbed into bed. He kept clicking his light on and off. At one point I saw his hand through the filmy, so-called "privacy curtain." His hand reached toward the curtain, grasping at it. He was trying to pull the curtain back, so that he could get a better look at me, and I had to stifle the impulse to yell at him to stop. Then, a little later, I heard a couple of the nurses in the hall outside, saying loudly, speaking of me, "Shall we give him an enema?" An old source of amusement among nurses, the enema.

I didn't learn much that I could use in my book, from my two-night stand at Linda Manor. Except for the fact that a few minutes can seem like eternity in a nursing-home bed and the fact that, from such a perspective, cheerful, attractive, average-sized nurses and nurse's aides can look huge and menacing. Those two nights I kept getting up and looking out the window, to make sure my car was still in the parking lot. I had planned to stay longer, but went home early the third morning in order to get some sleep.

At Linda Manor I got to know a nurse's aide who, when one of her residents had died, insisted on opening up the windows of the room. Asked why she did this, she said she felt she had to let the spirit out. All but a few of the staff were religious, at least in the sense that most believed in an afterlife. I think belief was a great comfort to them. At least I imagined it would be for me. But I possessed only a vague agnosticism. And I couldn't simply manufacture something stronger for the situation.

What troubled me most during my time at Linda Manor wasn't unpleasant sights or smells or even the reawakening of my fears about mortality. It was the problem of apparent meaninglessness. I watched people dying long before life had lost its savor for them or they their usefulness to others. I couldn't imagine any purpose behind the torments that many residents suffered in their last days. Sometimes I'd leave a resident's room feeling that everything, really everything in every life, was pointless. I remember thinking that we all just live awhile and end up dying painfully, or, even worse, bored and inert. What meaning could life have, I'd find myself wondering, if the best of the last things people get to do on earth is to play Bingo? At such times, I'd usually find my way upstairs to the room of the two old men named Lou and Joe. Gradually, I began to notice that a number of the staff did the same thing, even giving up their coffee breaks to go and chat with Lou and Joe. I didn't usually plan to go to their room at these moments of vicarious despair. I'd just find myself wanting to go there. After about ten minutes in their room, I usually felt much better. Lou and Joe had been placed together in one of Linda Manor's little rooms, in what for both would likely be their last place on earth, and they had become great friends. Other residents had formed friendships inside Linda Manor, but none was durable or seemed to run very deep. Out in the wider, youthful world, this accomplishment of Lou and Joe's would have seemed unremarkable but in that place it was profound.

The main thing I wanted to portray was that friendship, surrounded by the nursing home and all its varying forms of claustrophobia. I wanted to infuse the story of that friendship with sentiment, but not in a sentimental way. The difference, as I see it, is the difference between portraying emotion and merely asserting its existence, between capturing the reflection of something real on the page and merely providing handy cues designed to elicit an emotional response. It is, I realize, harder to depict manifestations of human goodness than manifestations of venality and evil. I don't know why that is. I do know that some people think that kindness, for example, is always superficial. That view is the logical equivalent of sentimentality. It's an easy way to feel and it gives some people a lot of pleasure. It has nothing to do with a tragic vision of life. It has about as much to do with an accurate vision of life as a Hallmark card. Anyway, that's how it seems to me. The world seems various to me, and depicting some of the virtue in it seems like a project worth attempting. I do not say that I pulled it off, but that's part of what I had in mind.

After my book was published, I continued to visit Linda Manor about once a week. I went partly because doing so made me feel like a good guy. But I had other reasons. Growing old with dignity calls for many acts of routine heroism, and some of the people I knew at Linda Manor were inspiring, admirable characters. All of them have died now, except for Lou, who has achieved the ripe old age of ninety-six. Joe died last winter. I visit only Lou now, but I used to go mainly in order to visit the two men. I *liked* visiting them. Their room was one place where I knew I was always welcome. They gave me good advice, on such subjects as child-rearing. They were funny, both intentionally and otherwise. Most important, their room was one place in the world where I could count on finding that amity prevailed. That was unusual, in my experience of the world. The crucial thing about Lou and Joe was that they remained *very good* friends, better friends every time I visited. They presented an antidote to despair, which is connectedness, and for me, I learned, it is only the connectedness of the human tribe that can hold despair at bay. Connectedness can, of course, take many different forms. One can find it in religion, or in family, or, as in the case of Lou and Joe, in friendship. Or perhaps in work, maybe even in the act of writing.

Harold Brodkey, who recently died of AIDS, wrote in an essay a couple of years ago, "I think anyone who spends his life working to become eligible for literary immortality is a fool." I agree. But I also think that only a fool would write merely for money or contemporary fame. I imagine that most writers—good, bad and mediocre—write partly for the sake of the private act of writing and partly in order to throw themselves out into the world. Most, I imagine, *endeavor* for connectedness, to create the kind of work that touches other lives and, in that sense at least, leaves something behind. I don't dream of immortality or plant marginalia for my biographers anymore. But I do wonder what Mr. Fitzgerald would think of what I've written and, especially, of what I'm going to write.

A few days after I got back from Vietnam, in June 1969, I traveled to Cambridge and called Mr. Fitzgerald from a pay phone. He invited me to lunch at his house the next afternoon. Of course, I didn't tell him this, but I wanted something from him, something ineffable, like hope. He had prepared sandwiches. I'm not sure that he made them himself, but I like to think that he did, and that he was responsible for cutting the crusts off the bread. I'm not sure why I remember that. It seemed a sweet gesture, a way of making me feel that I was important to him. It also made him seem old, older than I'd remembered him.

I saw Mr. Fitzgerald a few times more over the next year or two, and then he moved away and I moved out west for a while. I fell under other influences. My dreams of writing something classic gave way to my little dreams of writing something publishable, of making a living as a writer, which seemed hard enough. But those early dreams were dormant, not dead. When, almost ten years later, a book of mine, *The Soul of a New Machine,* was awarded the Pulitzer Prize and the American Book Award, my megalomaniacal dreams of literary glory came out of storage. I could tell myself at moments that I'd achieved them all. But I hesitated for a while before sending my book to Mr. Fitzgerald. I was afraid. When I finally worked up the nerve, I wrote an inscription to the effect that I hoped this piece of writing began to approach his expectations. I soon received a letter from him, in which he thanked me, remarked upon the "modesty" of my inscription—no doubt he saw right through that—and apologized for his inability to read the book just now. I wrote right back, proposing that I visit him. He did not reply. I never heard from him again. I don't remember exactly when he died. I think it was a few years later.

His silence has bothered me for a long time, not immoderately but in the way of those embarrassing memories that suddenly appear when you're checking the oil in your car or putting a key in a door. Two summers ago I met one of Mr. Fitzgerald's sons and told him the story. He insisted that his father would never have failed to answer my last letter, if he'd been able to read and write by then. I believed him. And I believe that if Mr. Fitzgerald had been able to read my book, he would have told me what he really thought. It's probably just as well that he never did. I've written other and, I think, better books since then. I'd rather know what he thought of *them.* I've been courting his approval ever since my first day in his class, and I continue to court his approval now, when he's certain to withhold it. That makes me sad sometimes, but not in my better moments. I'll never know if he'd approve of what I've written and am going to write. But I'll never know if he'd disapprove either. He's left me room to go on trying.

Everything But the Truth?

Fern Kupfer

It is the authority of the truth—the idea of truth, anyway—that makes the memoir attractive to readers. "Some story!" we say to survivors of plane crashes and cancer and dysfunctional families after they have written a moving narrative.

We all like good stories, especially those taken from real life. But we also don't like being lied to. Lying—like cheating and stealing—is almost always wrong from an ethical perspective. But *shaping* the truth when writing memoir is an acceptable aspect of the craft. So where are the boundaries here?

Here's a story (and it really *did* happen). A few years ago I had a student in my nonfiction seminar at Iowa State University. Chris was a terrific writer with a real eye for metaphor and a feel for narrative construction. He wrote about his colorful family—the men were all bookies, small-time hoodlums, con-men. I remember in particular one scene where his father had deserted the family, and on the same night a glass chandelier had come down in the dining room. There was a description of his mother, left with children and bad debts, on her hands and knees, picking up shards of glass out of the rug. She turned to her twelve-year-old son: "I'll never get the glass out of this shag. We'll have to wear shoes in this house *forever*."

Well, Chris got his A, graduated, moved on. The next year, I had his girlfriend in a class. One day she was in my office and offhandedly shared that she was going to Chris' parents' home for Thanksgiving.

"Parents?" I raised an eyebrow. "Oh, is his mom remarried?" I asked. I pictured the woman who could not get the glass out of the rug. Well, good for her, I thought.

No. My student shook her head. Same parents. Married for almost thirty years, she told me.

And his father? What does Chris' father do? I pressed on, recalling the stories of seedy apartments in grimy cities, of the police knocking on the door, of a family always on the run.

"Why, he's an English teacher," the girl said, and at the same moment must have seen my jaw drop. "Uh oh," she added.

Suddenly I wasn't just surprised—I was angry. I told her to give a message to Chris that if he were ever back in town to watch out for me. I may have encouraged her to rethink a relationship with someone who was capable of such duplicity. In class we had discussed interpreting and shaping the story. Someone had called this "accessorizing the truth." Sensing that his father's life as an English professor would make for dull reading (he may have been right on that score), Chris did more than our creative judgments could ever have allowed. We had sat in a workshop and carefully talked about a life that Chris had constructed exclusively from his imagination. Chris had lied. And we, his readers, were betrayed.

That afternoon, I went back and read the final that Chris had written for my class. One of the questions had to do with defining what creative nonfiction is. Chris wrote:

> The distinction between the genres is economic, I think. There's money to be made in fiction, money to be made in nonfiction. Publishers like to keep things straight. And readers—some readers at least—they like to keep things straight. Some people want to read true things. Some people don't. Me, I don't give a shit. True, false, fiction, nonfiction, journalism—it all ends up as fiction in the end.

It all ends up as fiction in the end? I don't accept that. But I do acknowledge that the literal truth isn't always the artistic one.

The question of lying comes up all the time in the creative nonfiction classes I teach. Iowa State is a tech-ag-engineering kind of place, and most of my students are fairly literal-minded. "But *that's* how it happened," they sometimes say when I suggest changes that would tighten a narrative and pep up the prose. "Your memoir shouldn't read as slowly as real life," I tell them. We need to give memoir writers permission to lie, but only when the reconstructed version of the story does not deceive the reader in its search for the aesthetic truth.

To my mind, there are three kinds of "lies" that are acceptable—indeed, sometimes even necessary—in memoir writing. The first are the little white lies that are "created" when memory has blurred the details. Was your mother wearing a blue coat or a red coat when she picked you up at school that morning? Your teacher's peculiar habit of drumming her fingers—was it on the desktop? The chalkboard? The point is, you need a brilliant color for the coat as you looked through the window and saw your mother approaching. You need a place for the teacher to drum those fingers, a habit that foreshadows her threat.

Then there are the lies that narrative structure often demands: composite characterization, compression of time, omission of unnecessary detail. When I was writing *Before and After Zachariah*, a book about family life with my severely handicapped child, my editor suggested some changes. I had too many friends' names in the book, she told me. She couldn't keep them all straight—my memoir was beginning to read like a Russian novel. The editor suggested taking out the events which added new people and making composite characters out of some of the others.

So the three friends who drove with me to the hospital, cooked meals, called in the middle of the night, became one person, a sort of paradigmatic friend who was always there for me. Since the use of composites is fairly controversial, I noted in the acknowledgments that for the "sake of privacy and clarity, some characters in this book have been fictionalized and some names and places have been changed." This statement at least protects the reader from feeling duped.

I also compressed time to move the narrative along at a more energetic rate: the events of a week-long hospital stay were told in the frame of an afternoon; test results came with alacrity. I left out the details that clogged the narrative. It wasn't necessary to record all the conversations with all the health-care professionals who came to my home.

The third type of lying—and the most creative—is really a kind of conjecture, what I call "the gift of perhaps." How do we tell what we do not know? How do we reveal what we have not witnessed? Fiction writers make up stories all the time by using conjecture: "What if?" they say, and start spinning a yarn. The idea of a conflict-based hypothesis (what if a man was obsessed with killing a whale to avenge his loss . . . ?) becomes the source for great fiction. Conjecture can serve the same purpose in memoir.

Look in your family album, which probably contains some pictures of generations you have never met. Your grandmother as a laughing young girl in a white dress next to your somber grandfather. Did she love him? Or did she really want to marry a young man from her church, poorer than she, and not considered a good match? In other pictures your grandmother isn't smiling. Did she forever mourn her first child, a baby girl lost to diphtheria before her second birthday? Perhaps.

Here's a memory as I recall it: Me in college—upstate New York on a day in May so beautiful that my breath catches as I walk up the hill from class. I go to my motorcycle parked along the street. My English teacher has just chosen my paper to read to the class as a "sterling example." He has told the class that I am a "real writer"; I look down toward my lap, assuming modesty. Outside, I kickstart the bike and ride—too quickly—down the street. I am twenty years old and wearing tight, white jeans and my long hair, blonde, freshly ironed, blows behind my back. I have this thought: "It will never get any better than this."

Now this is true: I had a motorcycle in college. I used to iron my hair. I did once write an English paper that my professor read to the class. I remember being twenty on a beautiful spring day and thinking, "It will never get any better than this." But did all this happen on the same day? Were the jeans white? Were those the professor's exact words of praise? And does it matter? The truth of the story is the narrator's perception of youth, of fleeting time, of the longing to capture a golden moment. And that's the truth I've told. No lie.

What We Didn't Know We Knew

Sydney Lea

If I begin by stating my unenthusiasm for the designation "creative nonfiction," it's because I lack enthusiasm for the term "creative" as applied to any writing. Is there not more of creativity in the making of a good soup, say, or of a salmon fly than of novel, story, poem or essay? None of these genres brings things into existence, thus "creating" them, so much as it assembles pre-existing things, both public and private. And however free-associative, such assembly of course depends on another pre-existent entity: language.

I admit, though, that "our" kind of essayizing is one I can name only vaguely. And variously: the personal essay, the familiar essay, the impressionistic essay, the informal essay, or—as I've come most often to describe it—the lyrical essay. Be our terms as they may, moreover, reasonable people could argue at length about what actually *characterizes* the work that Annie Dillard or Edward Abbey or Joan Didion or Edward Hoagland or Rick Bass or Terry Tempest Williams or W.D. Wetherell or Geoffrey Wolff or Kathleen Norris have been doing.

Where for example does their sort of essay begin and another leave off? Each of us might make such a division in idiosyncratic fashion. Still, we'd likely agree not only that our sort of essay exists but also that certain generalities apply to it: other kinds of essay veer closer to journalism; in those other kinds, presentation is more dependent on consecutive reasoning and empirical fact than "creative nonfiction's"; thesis is more insistent for Them than for Us, in whose work thesis, properly so called, may not even show.

I am less interested in defining categories than in learning how to do whatever we do with greater energy, greater facility, greater claim on readers' attentions. And yet I'll have to sneak up on such issues of strategy: anarchistic by nature, skeptical of the whole How-To frame of mind, I shy away from precepts, let alone rules, when I discuss writing of whatever variety. After all, whenever I hear precept or rule, no matter how attractive or acceptable to me; whenever I'm given a guideline about How To Do It, I seem automatically to think of literature that contradicts the same stipulation . . . and that wows me anyway.

So let me distinguish the lyrical essay—too simply, too reductively—from the more thesis-bound by asserting that the lyrical makes its point or points in a more indirect way than the reporter, reviewer, speechwriter or scholar makes hers or his.

I think for example of Norman Mailer's booklength essay on the moon landing. Rarely a fan of this author's work, still I recall how taken I was on first reading *Of a Fire on the Moon*. As usual, Mailer's protagonist is himself, but himself in the persona of "Aquarius." Rightfully or otherwise, he mounts his inquiry as a representative of the Love Generation, the Make-Love-Not-War party encountering NASA, whose military ties are historically evident.

Mailer, in short, gives himself an angle, but it is not so much an argumentative angle, a means to thesis, as a quirky point of view which will be important in and of itself. Such distinctive perspective will enable Aquarius to talk about his own sensibility at least as volubly as about the astronauts and their mission. I'll be making much of that aim, not so much in connection with Mailer as with the whole genre under discussion.

In *Of a Fire on the Moon*, Aquarius also finds himself moved, unpremeditatedly (or so the book would suggest), to rely very heavily on his sense of smell in talking about his nominal subject. Once again, the object is specifically not to provide conventional consideration of a highly scientific enterprise but to get at that enterprise in a way that no one, including the author, might have predicted. As it turns out, the sense of smell (or frequently smell-lessness) offers a path to real eloquence, at the same time offering a motif that structurally binds his account. It relieves Mailer/Aquarius, sometimes also called The Nose, of offering coherence by way of dialectical argument.

Of a Fire on the Moon comes to my mind principally as instance of the oblique and peculiar perception that typifies so-called creative nonfiction. Information about the space program's crowning moment does get imparted, but is not primary. And with Mailer as my first exhibit, I'll suggest that the lyrical essay, brief or book-sized, has at its core the way in which the essayist him- or herself, whether as persona or as someone named "I," considers his or her own sensibility.

Or if need be invents that sensibility. For the authorial psyche is as much at the heart of our lyrical essay as it is, say, in a lyrical poem. Both sorts of writer explore the appropriateness or inappropriateness of a personal intellectual-emotional apparatus to a given context or event(s). And each wins either way: if that apparatus is serviceable, then the author has the luxury of a more or less seamless presentation; if it is not, then the clash may become the very subject.

Now in putting the writer's sensibility at the center of the lyrical essay's intentions, I don't mean simply to champion the sort of self-advertisement found in so much of Norman Mailer's work. Though that posture can and often does issue in splendid results, ranging from the book I've just mentioned to the better specimens in Ralph Waldo Emerson's canon, those less inclined to egoism should know there are writers of quite another cast who write brilliantly. I think for example of Ivan Doig, the memoirist of Montana, or of Louise Erdrich, an author of sufficient modesty as at times almost to disappear from her own meditations.

Almost, but never quite entirely. And that is what, I am arguing, constitutes the creative element, to label it so, in our sort of nonfiction.

A few broad statements will govern what follows. To select someone named "I" as the provider of a narrative or a series of impressions (or to select a persona for that I) is simultaneously to select thematic material. If critics sometimes distinguish between technique and content, form and idea, and so on, we writers must not. For us, the choice of first-person delivery, say, cannot be simply a technical one. And more to the point here, we must understand why virtually every lyrical essay makes that very choice: it's again that such an essay's energy is so connected to the identity and the emotional/intellectual makeup of its first person. To begin a narrative by saying even something so simple as "I feel" is automatically to indicate that "I" is an eminent subject in the narrative to come.

In these respects, the protagonist of the so-called American nature essay—from a Thoreau to a Gretel Ehrlich—has far more in common with the prototypical hero of American fiction or poetry than with the conventional magazine essayist, more in common with Melville's Ishmael, Twain's Huck, Whitman's "I" or even the "I" of Emily Dickinson's poetry than with a speaker who means simply to give us the goods, in the directest way possible, on a predetermined subject. We are more poets than journalists, and we must take advantage of our own nature . . . and of *not* having predetermined subjects.

All this is scarcely to say that our essays must begin in a complete vacuum; such a prospect seems impossible on the face of it anyhow. Mailer does mean to write "about" the NASA moon landing, just as Joan Didion, in *Slouching Toward Bethlehem*, means to write about late 20th-century Los Angeles and the great Ryszard Kapucinski means to write about pre-revolutionary Iran in his *Shah of Shahs*. It's just that the treatment of each of these outward subjects is overwhelmingly dependent for its success on presenting, as Wallace Stevens famously said of modern poetry, the mind in the act of finding what will suffice.

I acknowledge that such a presentation may and almost inevitably will be reconsidered, pondered, even much altered in revision. But this will be revision in the originative sense of the term, a "seeing again," an imaginative entry into the world we mean to render.

Instead of erecting an agenda to govern the lyrical essay, therefore, in all my discussion here—including discussion of choosing a subject—I do little more than throw out some suggestions as to how creative nonfiction can become what it wants to become. And in that regard I want right away to stress that we often begin better if we're in doubt, sometimes very considerable doubt, about where we are headed; to stress how important it is to resist any impulse to pre-program our observations; to stress that those observations need the feel of spontaneity, even if that be the result of endless rewriting.

I want in short to emphasize that the very concept of agenda is inimical to our efforts.

Let me turn for example to a writer who's drawn, precisely, to the nature essay, even though I think the gist of my argument (and his, if only implicitly) can apply to all modes of the genre under discussion. The following passage is from Rick Bass's *The Ninemile Wolves*. At the very start, in a marvelously evocative page or so, Bass imagines those Montana wolves pulling down a quarry; and then come some telling afterthoughts:

> They don't have thumbs. All they've got is teeth, long legs, and—I have to say this—great hearts.
>
> I can say what I want to say. I gave up my science badge a long time ago. I've interviewed maybe a hundred people for or against wolves. The ones who are "for" wolves, they have an agenda: wilderness, and freedom for predators, for prey, for everything. The ones who are "against" wolves have an agenda: they've got vested financial interests. It's about money—more and more money—for them. They perceive the wolves to be an obstacle to frictionless cash flow.
>
> The story's so rich. I can begin anywhere.
>
> I can start with prey, which is what controls wolf numbers (not the other way around), or with history, which is rich in sin, cruelty, sensationalism (poisonings, maimings, torture). You can start with biology, or politics, or you can start with family, with loyalty, and even with the mystic-tinged edges of fate, which is where I choose to begin. It's all going to come together anyway. It has to. We're all following the wolf.

Though I scarcely believe good writing in any genre is necessarily, or ever, antirational, in ours there is at least a great deal of *non*-rational energy . . . or, as the quotation above signals, there ought to be. Lest I myself tend too far toward mystic-tinged edges, however, too far toward abstraction, I'll need to root my observations in personal experience.

I've already hinted at one reason that I'm fonder of the term *lyrical essay* than of many other possible names for this sort of writing: namely that my own essays are born and develop much in the manner of my poems. Nor am I speaking here so much of aesthetics or technique as of far more literal matters, like my inclination to hike long distances in the woods alone, seeking not to think up "subjects" but to let my mind float free until, over time, perhaps over a dozen hikes or even years, I find that certain things have lodged themselves in my consciousness and now demand meditation—that *they* have subjected *me*. I surely hadn't imagined myself to be doing "research," but so it seems I was:

> Early June of 1992, below Stonehouse Mountain, Grafton County, New Hampshire—a place and time in which snowsqualls, routine enough just weeks ago, will at last deserve the name freakish. In freshet beds where waters flared and vanished, frail shoots of jewelweed declare themselves; grass bursts the voles' winter tunnels; geese trail the Connecticut northward; the buck deer's antlers

are in velvet; the woodchuck's busy to double in weight; trout sip the ponds' ephemerids; everywhere, the lovesick insistence of birds.

Our family has lived ten years on this foothill's flank, but soon after dawn this morning—beckoned by the full day ahead—I hiked down from its mild summit for perhaps the last time. The ramble, especially under such circumstances, brought back the many I'd made there, in company or alone, one recollection summoning another, and that one still another, till outward prospects opened onto vaster, more labyrinthine inward views.

This is the opening paragraph of "On the Bubble." But in truth it's a paragraph composed late in the construction of that piece, composed well after I happened on what it was "about." The essay actually began in my somehow remembering a brown-phase fisher, who almost stepped across my toes one fall while I was deer-hunting; that, and the fact that, at the time I began feeling an itch to write this chapter of *Hunting the Whole Way Home*, my family was on the point of moving from Stonehouse Mountain, which a so-called developer meant to ruin; that, and the memory of my son blowing bubbles one spring morning at the summit of the same mountain.

These several things were chronologically quite removed from one another; yet they had lodged themselves in my consciousness. My essay was, and is, about *what they all had to do with one another.*

In short, I began in the spirit of Rick Bass: "It's all going to come together anyway. It has to." As I have been arguing, the lyrical essay chiefly concerns the essayist's perception of his or her surroundings, whether natural or otherwise. And since it's concerned with perception, it is ultimately concerned with the essayist's own mind in action.

Perception in the lyrical essay, however, cannot remain static, or so my experience would indicate; it must unfold in the very act of writing, and writing should itself be an act (or acts) of unanticipated discovery. My aim as I sat down to indite "On the Bubble" was simply to see if I could write my way to a connection among a few things, however seemingly disconnected, that had stopped me in my tracks.

The appropriateness of the fragile bubbles my son blew, for example, to the theme of natural fragility that so exercised me when the bulldozers started to chew up the mountain I loved—that appropriateness was something that crept upon me, surprised me, and, however sad the circumstances reflected in my chapter, delighted me as a writer.

What I'm getting at is this: the death knell for any creative writing sounds whenever it knows too accurately where it is going. A novel whose plot has been predetermined will almost inevitably fail to surprise us, say, on the level of characterization, the characters having little to do but walk through their scripts. A poem whose theme has been fore-decided will clank along mechanically, each line illustrating a dominating "idea."

The same hazards can attend the lyrical essay. Indeed, these dangers may apply even more ruinously to such an essay than to the other genres I've referred to, since so often—or so we believe—our plot and setting and characters seem, exactly, to exist in their entirety before we write a word. We know how everything comes out, and who's involved, and where we are: it's simply a matter of recording all that, right?

Wrong. Or wrong, I believe, if you're in the business of writing creative nonfiction, in which, as I've suggested, the creative part must if anything be more important than the nonfiction part. We may too easily be misled by the very concept of nonfictionality; we may be inclined simply to chronicle the facts of a given matter, and to do so is to offer an account, not an essay of the kind most of us want. Ours is, after all, an art form, to which imagination is utterly crucial.

With all this in mind, I'll make some practical observations. At the outset, in grumbling about the word "creative," I pointed out the obvious fact that as writers we work with something that pre-exists, namely language—which I now want to suggest can help us to our "subjects," since language and subject are all but indistinguishably identified, each bound as it is to perception.

The *way* in which we phrase our responses, then, is as much what we are writing about as anything else, and with that in mind, I'll urge that in order to begin we ought to speak with as much particularity as we can. This doesn't mean that we can't muse, reminisce, worry, argue, preach, or even pontificate in our essays. We can. Lord knows, I do. It's only that such rhetorical gestures will always be more effective if they have grounds.

In "On the Bubble," the word "grounds" has a happy double meaning, so much of the essay's concerns having to do, exactly, with grounds, or with their loss. And thus it began with very specific renderings of vivid occurrences upon those grounds, with my effort to recapture the particulars of an encounter with a fisher. I wrote the memory as clearly and accurately as I knew how, and in doing so I was somehow led to other specific experiences in the same locale, notably the time when I took my son to the height of Stonehouse Mountain and watched him blow bubbles.

In the very process of writing out these experiences, in language that was as precise as I could make it, I came gradually to recognize what these two components might have in common: the wonder I felt at beholding that normally elusive weasel at such close distance seemed at least remotely akin to the wonder my five-year-old experienced as he watched his soap bubbles take flight above the granite moraine of Stonehouse Mountain. Each version of wonder was a bit childlike, and each, like childhood itself, was extremely fragile, indeed doomed.

Without setting out to do so, I had hit on the motif of wonder, and on plain facts to serve as its metaphors: weasel and bubble. Soon enough another metaphor presented itself—this one for doom—that seemed so obvious I was puzzled I'd ever missed it: the very sound of the bulldozers and chainsaws on the hillside. Very rapidly now, I came to see the connections among seemingly disparate snatches of memory and present experience.

I had written my way to awareness of those connections. I had written my way not to creativity but to what I prefer to call imagination, as the great poet and theorist Samuel Taylor Coleridge understood the term; he called it "an esemplastic power," which means, roughly, a power that forges unity out of diversity.

My point is that I foisted no metaphors or themes upon my perceptions. Rather, by beginning in particularity, without great regard for what my essay would be "about," I found organic metaphors and thematics coming to *me*. It would have been all too easy just to rant and rave out loud about the developer's greed and the despoliation of wildness; indeed, I had been doing so—eloquently, I hope—for some time. But I had done so in letters to my local paper, which were not by my understanding creative in the way that each of us wants to be in a lyrical essay.

Those letters had a thesis, and I argued it as persuasively and logically as I could. Yet the terms of my letters were for the most part abstract: terms, exactly, like "greed" and "wildness" and "despoliation." In my essay, I'd use the same terms, but now they would be . . . grounded. They'd be grounded in personal observation and unexpected discovery of the kind I've briefly catalogued above.

I was proud of the letters, but they didn't have the same value for me as a writer that the final essay had, and has. "Wildness" became associated with a particular animal, the fisher; the fisher's habitat appeared to be threatened by "despoliation," by a ruinous force associated with the developer's machinery; that machinery perfectly epitomized the brutal effects of "greed." And so the fisher's future, like my son's, perhaps, became as tenuous as the existences of those bubbles I remember my boy making.

With a bunch of specifics in my quiver, I could shoot as many arrows of rhetorical indignation as I wanted, without fear of lapsing from "our" sort of essay into that other sort I spoke of early on. But I repeat: I did not know what my outward subject or my rhetoric would be until I started writing, and I am glad I didn't know, for otherwise I'd merely have written one more letter to the editor. The only agenda I had was that vague poetic one: I sought to connect a number of moments that had stuck in my consciousness, and my only means of doing so was particularized language.

Language led me on, in the most fulfilling way. It permitted me both to learn what was on my mind and to learn how much I had to say about it. The composition of "On the Bubble," then, like the successful composition of any poem, resulted in a better self-understanding. Speaking for myself, this is among the happiest results that an author can experience.

In the famous formulation of a far greater poet than I, Robert Frost, by writing we discover what we didn't know we knew.

Note

See Peter Fritzell's illuminating *Nature Writing and America* (Iowa State University Press: Ames, 1990), whose commentary on the protagonist of American natural-historical literature, along with other keen insights, informs portions of this discussion.

What Happened to the Personal Essay?

Phillip Lopate

The personal or familiar essay is a wonderfully tolerant form, able to accommodate rumination, memoir, anecdote, diatribe, scholarship, fantasy, and moral philosophy. It can follow a rigorously elegant design, or—held together by little more than the author's voice—assume an amoebic shapelessness. Working in it liberates a writer from the structure of the well-made, epiphanous short story and allows one to ramble in a way that more truly reflects the mind at work. At this historical moment the essayist has an added freedom: no one is looking over his or her shoulder. No one much cares. Commercially, essay volumes rank even lower than poetry.

I know; when my first essay collection, *Bachelorhood*, came out, booksellers had trouble figuring out where to stock it. Autobiography? Self-help? Short stories? I felt like saying, "Hey, this category has been around for a long time; what's the big deal?" Yet, realistically, they were right: what had once been a thriving popular tradition had ceased being so. Readers who enjoyed the book often told me so with some surprise, because they hadn't thought they would like "essays." For them, the word conjured up those dreaded weekly compositions they were forced to write on the gasoline tax or the draft.

Essays are usually taught all wrong: they are harnessed to rhetoric and composition, in a two-birds-with-one-stone approach designed to sharpen freshman students' skills at argumentation. While it is true that historically the essay is related to rhetoric, it in fact seeks to persuade more by the delights of literary style than anything else. Elizabeth Hardwick, one of our best essayists, makes this point tellingly when she says: "The mastery of expository prose, the rhythm of sentences, the pacing, the sudden flash of unexpected vocabulary, redeem polemic. . . . The essay . . . is a great meadow of style and personal manner, freed from the need for defense except that provided by an individual intelligence and sparkle. We consent to watch a mind at work, without agreement often, but only for pleasure."

Equally questionable in teaching essays is the anthology approach, which assigns an essay apiece by a dozen writers according to our latest notions of a demographically representative and content-relevant sampling. It would be more instructive to read six pieces each by two writers, since the essay (particularly the familiar essay) is so rich a vehicle for displaying personality in all its willfully changing aspects.

Essays go back at least to classical Greece and Rome, but it was Michel de Montaigne, generally considered the "father of the essay," who first matched the word to the form around 1580. Reading this contemporary of Shakespeare (thought to have influenced the Bard himself), we are reminded of the original, pristine meaning of the word, from the French verb *essayer*: to attempt, to try, to leap experimentally into the unknown. Montaigne understood that, in an essay, the track of a person's thoughts struggling to achieve some understanding of a problem *is* the plot. The essayist must be willing to contradict himself (for which reason an essay is not a legal brief), to digress, even to risk ending up in a terrain very different from the one he embarked on. Particularly in Montaigne's magnificent late essays, free-falls that sometimes go on for a hundred pages or more, it is possible for the reader to lose all contact with the ostensible subject, bearings, top, bottom, until there is nothing to do but surrender to this companionable voice, thinking alone in the dark. Eventually, one begins to share Montaigne's confidence that "all subjects are linked to one another," which makes any topic, however small or far from the center, equally fertile.

It was Montaigne's peculiar project, which he claimed rightly or wrongly was original, to write about the one subject he knew best: himself. As with all succeeding literary self-portraits—or all succeeding stream-of-consciousness, for that matter—success depended on having an interesting consciousness, and Montaigne was blessed with an undulatingly supple, learned, skeptical, deep, sane, and candid one. In point of fact, he frequently strayed to worldly subjects, giving his opinion on everything from cannibals to coaches, but we do learn a large number of intimate and odd details about the man, down to his bowels and kidney stones. "Sometimes there comes to me a feeling that I should not betray the story of my life," he writes. On the other hand: "No pleasure has any meaning for me without communication."

A modern reader may come away thinking that the old fox still kept a good deal of himself to himself. This is partly because we have upped the ante on autobiographical revelation, but also because Montaigne was writing essays, not confessional memoirs, and in an essay it is as permissible, as honest, to chase down a reflection to its source as to admit some past shame. In any case, having decided that "the most barbarous of our maladies is to despise our being," Montaigne did succeed, via the protopsychoanalytic method of the *Essais*, in making friends with his mind.

Having taken the essay form to its very limits at the outset, Montaigne's dauntingly generous example was followed by an inevitable specialization, which included the un-Montaignean split between formal and informal essays. The formal essay derived from Francis Bacon; it is said to be "dogmatic, impersonal, systematic, and expository," written in a "stately" language, while the informal essay is "personal, intimate, relaxed, conversational, and frequently humorous" (*New Columbia Encyclopedia*). Never mind that most of the great essayists were adept at both modes, including Bacon (see, for example, his wonderful "Of Friendship"); it remains a helpful distinction.

Informal, familiar essays tend to seize on the parade and minutiae of daily life: vanities, fashions, oddballs, seasonal rituals, love and disappointment, the pleasures of solitude, reading, going to plays, walking in the street. It is a very urban form, enjoying a spectacular vogue in eighteenth- and early nineteenth-century London, when it enlisted the talents of such stylists as Swift, Dr. Johnson, Addison and Steele, Charles Lamb, William Hazlitt, and a visiting American, Washington Irving. The familiar essay was given a boost by the phenomenal growth of newspapers and magazines, all of which needed smart copy (such as that found in the *Spectator*) to help instruct their largely middle-class, *parvenu* readership on the manners of the class to which it aspired.

Although most of the *feuilletonistes* of this period were cynical hacks, the journalistic situation was still fluid enough to allow original thinkers a platform. The British tolerance for eccentricity seemed to encourage commentators to develop idiosyncratic voices. No one was as cantankerously marginal in his way, or as willing to write against the grain of community feeling, as William Hazlitt. His energetic prose style registered a temperament that passionately, moodily swung between sympathy and scorn. Anyone capable of writing so bracingly frank an essay as "The Pleasures of Hating" could not—as W.C. Fields would say—be all bad. At the same time, Hazlitt's enthusiasms could transform the humblest topic, such as going on a country walk or seeing a prizefight, into a description of visionary wholeness.

What many of the best essayists have had—what Hazlitt had in abundance—was quick access to their blood reactions, so that the merest flash of a prejudice or opinion might be dragged into the open and defended. Hazlitt's readiness to entertain opinions, coupled with his openness to new impressions, made him a fine critic of painting and the theater, but in his contrariness he ended by antagonizing all of his friends, even the benign, forgiving Charles Lamb. Not that Lamb did not have *his* contrary side. He, too, was singled out for a "perverse habit of contradiction," which helped give his "Elia" essays, among the quirkiest and most charming in the English language, their peculiar bite.

How I envy readers of *London* magazine, who might have picked up an issue in 1820 and encountered a new, high-spirited essay by Hazlitt, Lamb, or both! After their deaths, the familiar essay continued to attract brilliant practitioners such as Stevenson, DeQuincey, and Emerson. But subsequently, a little of the vitality seeped out of it. "Though we are mighty fine fellows nowadays, we cannot write like Hazlitt," Stevenson confessed. And by the turn of the century, it seemed rather played out and toothless.

The modernist aesthetic was also not particularly kind to this type of writing, relegating it to a genteel, antiquated nook, *belles lettres*—a phrase increasingly spoken with a sneer, as though implying a sauce without the meat. If "meat" is taken to mean the atrocities of life, it is true that the familiar essay has something obstinately non-apocalyptic about it. The very act of composing such an essay seems to implicate the writer in humanist-individualist assumptions that have come to appear suspect under the modernist critique.

Still, it would be unfair to pin the rap on modernism, which Lord knows gets blamed for everything else. One might as well "blame" the decline of the conversational style of writing. Familiar essays were fundamentally, even self-consciously, conversational: it is no surprise that Swift wrote one of his best short pieces on "Hints Toward an Essay on Conversation"; that Montaigne tackled "Of the Art of Discussion"; that Addison and Steele extensively analyzed true and false wit; that Hazlitt titled his books *Table Talk*, *Plain Speaker*, and *The Round Table*, or that Oliver Wendell Holmes actually cast his familiar essays in the form of mealtime dialogues. Why would a book like Holmes's *The Autocrat of the Breakfast Table*, a celebration of good talk that was so popular in its time, be so unlikely today? I cannot go along with those who say "The art of conversation has died, television killed it," since conversation grows and changes as inevitably as language. No, what has departed is not conversation but conversation-flavored writing, which implies a speaking relationship between writer and reader. How many readers today would sit still for a direct address by the author? To be called "gentle reader" or "*hypocrite lecteur*," to have one's arm pinched while dozing off, to be called to attention, flattered, kidded like a real person instead of a privileged fly on the wall—wouldn't most readers today find such devices archaic, intrusive, even impudent? Oh, you wouldn't? Good, we can go back to the old style, which I much prefer.

Maybe what has collapsed is the very fiction of "the educated reader," whom the old essayists seemed to be addressing in their conversational remarks. From Montaigne onward, essayists until this century have invoked a shared literary culture: the Greek and Latin authors and the best of their national poetry. The whole modern essay tradition sprang from quotation. Montaigne's *Essais* and Burton's *Anatomy of Melancholy* were essentially outgrowths of the "commonplace book," a personal journal in which quotable passages, literary excerpts, and comments were written. Though the early essayists' habit of quotation may seem excessive to a modern taste, it was this display of learning that linked them to their educated reading public and ultimately gave them the authority to speak so personally about themselves. Such a universal literary culture no longer exists; we have only popular culture to fall back on. While it is true that the old high culture was never really "universal"—excluding as it did a good deal of humanity—it is also true that without it, personal discourse has become more hard-pressed. What many modern essayists have tried to do is to replace that shared literary culture with more and more personal experience. It is a brave effort and an intriguing supposition, this notion that individual experience alone can constitute the universal text that all may dip into with enlightenment. But there are pitfalls: on the one hand, it may lead to cannibalizing oneself and one's privacy; on the other hand, much more common (and to my mind, worse) is the assertion of an earnestly honest or "vulnerable" manner without really candid chunks of experience to back it up.

As for popular culture, the essayist's chronic invocation of its latest bandwagon fads, however satirically framed, comes off frequently as a pandering to the audience's short attention span—a kind of literary ambulance chasing. Take the "life-style" pages in today's periodicals, which carry commentaries that are a distant nephew of the familiar essay: there is something so depressing about this desperate mining of things in the air, such a fevered search for a generational *Zeitgeist*, such an unctuously smarmy tone of "we," which assumes that everyone shares the same consumerist-boutique sensibility, that one longs for a Hazlittean shadow of misanthropic mistrust to fall between reader and writer. One longs for any evidence of a distinct human voice—anything but this ubiquitous Everyman/woman pizzazzy drone, listing tips for how to get the most from your dry cleaner's, take care of your butcher block, or bounce back from an unhappy love affair.

The familiar essay has naturally suffered from its parasitic economic dependency on magazines and newspapers. The streamlined telegraphic syntax and homogenized-perky prose that contemporary periodicals have evolved make it all the more difficult for thoughtful, thorny voices to be tolerated within the house style. The average reader of periodicals becomes conditioned to digest pure information, up-to-date, with its ideological viewpoint disguised as objectivity, and is thus ill-equipped to follow the rambling, cat-and-mouse game of perverse contrariety played by the great essayists of the past.

In any event, very few American periodicals today support house essayists to the tune of letting them write regularly and at comfortable length on the topics of their choice. The nearest thing we have are talented columnists like Russell Baker, Ellen Goodman, Leon Hale, and Mike Royko, who are in a sense carrying on the Addison and Steele tradition; they are so good at their professional task of hit-and-run wisdom that I only wish they were sometimes given the space to try out their essayistic wings. The problem with the column format is that it becomes too tight and pat: one idea per piece. Fran Lebowitz, for instance, is a very clever writer, and not afraid of adopting a cranky persona; but her one-liners have a cumulative sameness of affect that inhibits a true essayistic movement. What most column writing does not seem to allow for is self-surprise, the sudden deepening or darkening of tone, so that the writer might say, with Lamb: "I do not know how, upon a subject which I began treating half-seriously, I should have fallen upon a recital so eminently painful. . . ."

From time to time I see hopeful panel discussions offered on "The Resurgence of the Essay." Yes, it would be very nice, and it may come about yet. The fact is, however, that very few American writers today are essayists primarily. Many of the essay collections issued each year are essentially random compilations of book reviews, speeches, journalism, and prefaces by authors who have made a name for themselves in other genres. The existence of these collections attests more to the celebrated authors' desires to see all their words between hardcovers than it does to any real devotion to the essay form. A tired air of grudgingly gracious civic duty hovers over many of these performances.

One recent American writer who did devote himself passionately to the essay was E. B. White. No one has written more consistently graceful, thoughtful essays in twentieth-century American language than White; on the other hand, I can't quite forgive his sedating influence on the form. White's Yankee gentleman-farmer persona is a complex balancing act between Whitmanian democratic and patrician values, best suited for the expression of mildness and tenderness with a resolute tug of elegiac depression underneath. Perhaps this is an unfair comparison, but there is not a single E.B. White essay that compares with the gamy, pungent, dangerous Orwell of "Such, Such Were the Joys . . ." or "Shooting an Elephant." When White does speak out on major issues of the day, his man-in-the-street, folksy humility and studiously plain-Joe air ring false, at least to me. And you would never know that the cute little wife he describes listening to baseball games on the radio was the powerful *New Yorker* editor Katharine White. The suppression or muting of ego as something ungentlemanly has left its mark on *The New Yorker* since, with the result that this magazine, which rightly prides itself on its freedom to publish extended prose, has not been a particularly supportive milieu for the gravelly voice of the personal essayist. The preferred model seems to be the scrupulously fair, sporting, impersonal, fact-gathering style of a John McPhee, which reminds me of nothing so much as a colony of industrious termites capable of patiently reducing any subject matter to a sawdust of detail.

The personal, familiar essay lives on in America today in an interestingly fragmented proliferation of specialized subgenres. The form is very much with us, particularly if you count the many popular nonfiction books that are in fact nothing but groups of personal essays strung together, and whose compelling subject matter makes the reading public overlook its ordinary indifference to this type of writing. Personal essays have also appeared for years under the protective umbrella of New Journalism (Joan Didion being the most substantial and quirky practitioner to emerge from that subsidized training ground, now largely defunct); of autobiographical-political meditations (Richard Rodriguez, Adrienne Rich, Vivian Gornick, Marcelle Clements, Wilfrid Sheed, Alice Walker, Nancy Mairs, Norman Mailer); nature and ecological-regional writing (Wendell Berry, Noel Perrin, John Graves, Edward Hoagland, Gretel Ehrlich, Edward Abbey, Carol Bly, Barry Lopez, Annie Dillard); literary criticism (Susan Sontag, Elizabeth Hardwick, Seymour Krim, Cynthia Ozick, Leslie Fiedler, Joyce Carol Oates); travel writing and mores (Mary McCarthy, V. S. Naipaul, Joseph Epstein, Eleanor Clark, Paul Theroux); humorous pieces (Max Apple, Roy Blount, Jr., Calvin Trillin); food (M. F. K. Fisher). I include this random and unfairly incomplete list merely to indicate the diversity and persistence of the form in American letters today. Against all odds, it continues to attract newcomers.

In Europe, the essay stayed alive largely by taking a turn toward the speculative and philosophical, as practiced by writers like Walter Benjamin, Theodor Adorno, Simone Weil, E. M. Cioran, Albert Camus, Roland Barthes, Czeslaw Milosz, and Nicola Chiaromonte. All, in a sense, are offspring of the epigrammatic style of Nietzsche. This fragmented, aphoristic, critical type of essay-writing became used as a subversive tool of skeptical probing, a critique of ideology in a time when large, synthesizing theories and systems of philosophy are no longer trusted. Adorno saw the essay, in fact, as a valuable countermethod: "The essay does not strive for closed, deductive or inductive construction. It revolts above all against the doctrine—deeply rooted since Plato—that the changing and ephemeral is unworthy of philosophy; against that ancient injustice toward the transitory, by which it is once more anathematized, conceptually. The essay shies away from the violence of dogma. . . . The essay gently defies the ideals of [Descartes'] *clara et distincta perceptio* and of absolute certainty. . . . Discontinuity is essential to the essay . . . as characteristic of the form's groping intention. . . . The slightly yielding quality of the essayist's thought forces him to greater intensity than discursive thought can offer; for the essay, unlike discursive thought, does not proceed blindly, automatically, but at every moment it must reflect on itself. . . . Therefore the law of the innermost form of the essay is heresy. By transgressing the orthodoxy of thought, something becomes visible in the object which it is orthodoxy's secret purpose to keep invisible."

This continental tradition of the self-reflexive, aphoristically subversive essay is only now beginning to have an influence on contemporary American writers. One saw it first, curiously, cropping up in ironic experimental fiction—in Renata Adler, William Gass, Donald Barthelme, John Barth. Their fictive discourse, like Kundera's, often resembles a broken essay, a personal/philosophical essay intermixed with narrative elements. The tendency of many postmodernist storytellers to parody the pedantry of the essay voice speaks both to their intellectual reliance on it and to their uneasiness about adopting the patriarchal stance of the Knower. That difficulty with assumption of authority is one reason why the essay remains "broken" for the time being.

In a penetrating discussion of the essay form, Georg Lukács put it this way: "The essay is a judgment, but the essential, the value-determining thing about it is not the verdict (as is the case with the system), but the process of judging." Uncomfortable words for an age when "judgmental" is a pejorative term. The familiar essayists of the past may have been nonspecialists—indeed, this was part of their attraction—but they knew how to speak with a generalist's easy authority. That is precisely what contemporary essayists have a hard time doing: in our technical age we are too aware of the advantage specialists hold over us. (This may explain the current confidence the public has in the physician-scientist school of essayists like Lewis Thomas, Richard Selzer, Stephen Jay Gould, F. Gonzalez-Crussi, Oliver Sacks: their meditations are embedded in a body of technical information, so that readers are reassured they are "learning" something, not just wasting their time on *belles lettres*.) The last of the old-fashioned generalists, men of letters who seemed able to write comfortably, knowledgeably, opinionatedly on everything under the sun, were Edmund Wilson and Paul Goodman; we may not soon see their like again.

In *The Last Intellectuals*, Russell Jacoby has pointed out the reticence of writers of the so-called generation of the sixties—my generation—to play the role of the public intellectual, as did Lionel Trilling, Harold Rosenberg, C. Wright Mills, Irving Howe, Alfred Kazin, Daniel Bell, Dwight Macdonald, Lionel Abel, etc., who judged cultural and political matters for a large general readership, often diving into the melee with both arms swinging. While Jacoby blames academia for absorbing the energies of my contemporaries, and while others have cited the drying up of print outlets for formal polemical essays, my own feeling is that it is not such a terrible thing to want to be excused from the job of pontificating to the public. Ours was not so much a failure to become our elders as it was a conscious swerving to a different path. The Vietnam War, the central experience of my generation, had a great deal to do with that deflection. As a veteran of the sixties, fooled many times about world politics because I had no firsthand knowledge of circumstances thousands of miles away (the most shameful example that comes to mind was defending, at first, the Khmer Rouge regime in Cambodia), I have grown skeptical of taking righteous public positions based on nothing but simpatico media reports and party feeling. As for matters that I've definitely made up my mind about, it would embarrass me, frankly, to pen an opinion piece deploring the clearly deplorable, like apartheid or invading Central America, without being able to add any new insights to the discussion. One does not want to be reduced to scolding, or to abstract progressive platitudes, well founded as these may be. It isn't that my generation doesn't think politics are important, but our earlier experiences in that storm may have made us a little hesitant about mouthing off in print. We—or I should say I—have not yet been able to develop the proper voice to deal with these large social and political issues, which will at the same time remain true to personal experience and hard-earned doubt.

All this is a way of saying that the present moment offers a remarkable opportunity for emerging essayists who can somehow locate the moral authority, within or outside themselves, to speak to these issues in the grand manner. But there is also room, as ever, for the informal essayist to wrestle with intellectual confusion, to offer feelings, to set down ideas in a particularly direct and exposed format—more so than in fiction, say, where the author's opinions can always be disguised as belonging to characters. The increasing willingness of contemporary writers to try the form, if not necessarily commit themselves to it, augurs well for the survival of the personal essay. And if we do offend, we can always fall back on Papa Montaigne's "*Que sçay-je?*": What do I know?

Toward a Definition of Creative Nonfiction

Bret Lott

The Reverend Francis Kilvert, an English curate in the Welsh Border region, kept a journal of his life—where he went, what he did, what he dreamt, who he knew, and what he thought—from 1870 to 1879. In the journal he wrote, "Why do I keep this voluminous journal! I can hardly tell. Partly because life appears to me such a curious and wonderful thing that it almost seems a pity that even such a humble and uneventful life as mine should pass altogether away without some record such as this." *Kilvert's Diary*, published in 1941 and reprinted in 1960, serves as a beautiful, moving, and genuine glimpse into country life of that time nonetheless. All well and good, but how does it help define what creative nonfiction is?

That passage serves, I hold, to illuminate as best as any passage from any piece of literature I can find the longing each of us carries, or ought to carry, in our hearts as human beings first, and as writers second. Creative nonfiction is, in one form or another, for better and worse, in triumph and failure, the attempt to keep from passing altogether away the lives we have lived.

And though that may sound like a definitive pronouncement on what creative nonfiction is, I mean what I say in giving this essay the title it has: *Toward* a Definition of Creative Nonfiction. We aren't going to arrive anywhere here. We can no more understand what creative nonfiction is by trying to define it than we can learn how to ride a bike by looking at a bicycle tire, a set of handlebars, the bicycle chain itself. Sure, we'll have something of an idea, maybe a glimpse into the importance of finding your balance when we look at how narrow those tires are. But until we get on that thing and try to steer it with this weirdly twisted metal tube and actually try to synchronize pushing down on the pedals and pushing forward at the same time, we won't have a clue.

Any definition of true worth to you as a writer will and must come to you experientially. What creative nonfiction is will reveal itself to you only at the back end of things, once you have written it. Kilvert wrote his journal in the midst of his life, looking back at what had happened that day, trying to piece together the meaning of his life from the shards of it, however exquisitely beautiful or sharply painful they were. It was the piecing together of it that mattered, and that matters to us here, today.

And because we are human beings, as such we are pattern makers, a species desirous of order, no matter how much we as "artists" may masquerade otherwise. Yet looking back at our lives to find that order—and here is the sticky part—must *not* be an effort to reorder our lives as we want them to be seen; rather, we are after, in creative nonfiction, an understanding of what it is that has happened, and in that way to see order, however chaotic it may be.

Frank O'Connor, arguably the most important and influential short story writer of this century, wrote in a letter to a friend, " . . . there are occasions when we all feel guilt and remorse; we all want to turn back time. But even if we were able, things would go in precisely the same way, because the mistakes we make are not in our judgments but in our natures. It is only when we do violence to our natures that we are justified in our regrets . . . We are what we are, and within our limitations we have made our own efforts. They seem puny in the light of eternity, but they didn't at the time, and they weren't."

It is in creative nonfiction we try to divine from what we have done, who we have known, what we have dreamt and how we have failed, an order to our lives. "The test of a first-rate intelligence," F. Scott Fitzgerald wrote in his landmark essay "The Crack-Up," "is the ability to hold two opposed ideas in the mind at the same time, and still retain the ability to function." The two opposed ideas of creative nonfiction are finding order in chaos without reforming chaos into order; retaining the ability to function is the act of writing all this down for someone else to understand.

So let's begin with just that much: a desire not to let slip altogether away our lives as we have known them, and to put an order—again, for better and worse—to our days.

Creative nonfiction can take any form, from the letter to the list, from the biography to the memoir, from the journal to the obituary. When I say we are trying to find order in what has happened, I do *not* mean creative nonfiction is simply writing about what happened to me. Rather, it is writing about oneself *in relation to* the subject at hand. A book review is creative nonfiction in that it is a written record of the reviewer *in relation to* the book in question; John Krakauer's fantastic book *Into the Wild* is a biography of an idealistic young man, Chris McCandless, who upon graduation from college disappeared into the wild, his decomposed body found four months later in an abandoned bus in the Alaskan wilderness. The biography becomes creative nonfiction as the author increasingly identifies himself with the young man, increasingly recognizing in the stupidity of the boy's folly his own reckless self—Krakauer sees himself *in relation to* the subject at hand: the death of Chris McCandless. This essay itself is a form of creative nonfiction in that it is my attempt at defining an abstract through the smallest of apertures: my own experience *in relation to* creative nonfiction. So creative nonfiction is not solely, What happened to me today, and why is it important?

Creative nonfiction can be and often is a euphemism for the personal essay, and my earlier assertion that creative nonfiction's being understood only through its being written is borne out rather handily in the meaning of the word *essay* itself.

The French word *essai* means to attempt something, to give something a trial run, to test. Michel de Montaigne, considered the writer who identified if not invented the form, was the first to use the word *essai* to describe his writings, the first collection of which was entitled strangely enough *Essais*, and which was written between 1572 and 1574. This notion of the attempt, of testing one's words lined up in an order one deems close enough to reveal a personal understanding so that all may have that same understanding is, and will always be, only an attempt. The essay as trial run is inherent to any definition of creative nonfiction; you will only come to know this form by running your own tests.

Montaigne, a landowner and lawyer from a nominally wealthy family in the Perigord region of France, wrote out of his own interests, but wrote convinced that it was his own interest as a human being in a matter or topic at hand that made his attempts universal: "Each man bears the entire form of man's estate," he wrote, and therefore, he reasoned, what he was attempting to render in words might make his attempts of interest to all. Philip Lopate, in his indispensable anthology *The Art of the Personal Essay*, writes, "What Montaigne tells us about himself is peculiarly, charmingly specific and daily: he is on the short side, has a loud, abrasive voice, suffers from painful kidney stones, scratches his ears a lot (the insides itch), loves sauces, is not sure radishes agree with him, does his best thinking on horseback, prefers glass to metal cups, moves his bowels regularly in the morning, and so on. It is as if the self were a new continent, and Montaigne its first explorer."

The self as continent, and you its first explorer: another definition of creative nonfiction. For self, however at the center of what you are writing or however tangential, must inform the heart of the tale you are telling. It is indeed *self* that is the *creative* element of creative nonfiction. Without you and who you are, a piece of writing that tells what happened is simply nonfiction: a police report. But when I begin to incorporate the sad and glorious fact that the way I see it shapes and forms what it is to be seen, I end up with creative nonfiction.

As a kind of sidebar, I'd like to interject here the fact that one doesn't have to have had a bizarre life before that life becomes worthy of writing about. Contrary to popular belief, that belief borne out by even the most cursory look at the lineup of victim-authors on afternoon and morning TV talk shows and evening newsmagazines, one's life needn't have been wracked by incest or murder or poorly executed plastic surgery to be worthy of examination. Which is, of course, not to say that those lives are not worth writing about. They most certainly are. But E. B. White's words from the introduction to his *Letters of E. B. White* speak as eloquently as I have seen to this matter of whether or not one's life has been miserable enough to record: "If an unhappy childhood is indispensable for a writer, I am ill-equipped: I missed out on all that and was neither deprived nor unloved. It would be inaccurate, however, to say that my childhood was untroubled. The normal fears and worries of every child were in me developed to a high degree; every day was an awesome prospect. I was uneasy about practically everything: the uncertainty of the future, the dark of the attic, the panoply and discipline of school, the transitoriness of life, the mystery of the church and of God, the frailty of the body, the sadness of afternoon, the shadow of sex, the distant challenge of love and marriage, the far-off problem of a livelihood."

These normal fears, if we have been paying the least bit of attention to our lives, inform us all; and if E. B. White, who is the greatest American essayist of this century, found in that uneasiness the material for a lifetime, we too have all we need.

But *how* do we look at ourselves in order best to inform our readers that who we are matters, and is worthy of their attention? In the Tyndale commentary on the Book of Proverbs, Derek Kidner writes that the sayings and aphorisms of King Solomon, and to a lesser degree Lemuel and Agur, constitute "not a portrait album of a book of manners: [the Book of Proverbs] offers a key to life. The samples of behavior which it holds up to view are all assessed by one criterion, which could be summed up in the question, 'Is this wisdom, or is this folly?'" I believe that this same criterion is one that helps define creative nonfiction as well. In examining the self as continent, in seeing the way self shades and informs the meaning of what has happened, the writer must be inquiring of himself, Is this wisdom, or is this folly? The self as inquisitor of self is integral to an examination of one's life; it calls for a kind of ruthlessness about seeing oneself in relation to others: Why did I do that? What was I thinking? Who was I trying to kid? What did I hope to achieve? These questions must be asked, and asked with all the candor and courage and objectivity one can muster, though objectivity is an abstract to be hoped for, and not to be achieved; it is, after all, *you* who is writing about you.

Which brings me to another major point on our way toward a definition: creative nonfiction cannot at any time be self-serving. There is no room here for grandstanding of oneself. To my way of thinking—and this is me speaking as a follower of Christ, and therefore one well aware of my transgressions, my iniquities, my falling short of the glory of God—ninety-nine times out of a hundred the answer to the question, Is this wisdom, or is this folly? is, Folly. Hands down.

Phillip Lopate writes, "The enemy of the personal essay is self-righteousness, not just because it is tiresome and ugly in itself, but because it slows down the dialectic of self-questioning . . . The essayist is someone who lives with the guilty knowledge that he is 'prejudiced' (Mencken called his essay collections *Prejudices*) and has a strong predisposition for or against certain everyday phenomena. It then becomes his business to attend to these inner signals, these stomach growls, these seemingly indefensible intuitions, and try to analyze what lies underneath them, the better to judge them."

So, our definition thus far: a desire not to let slip altogether away our lives as we have known them; to put an order, for better and worse, to our days; this is only a test; the self as continent, you its first explorer; is this wisdom, or is this folly?; no self-righteousness.

This last point, however, seems at odds with the entire notion of the personal essay, all this business about me: isn't talk about myself in relation to others by definition egotistical? Wasn't I taught in seventh grade never to include 'I' in an essay? Who cares about what I think in the first place?

Thoreau, in answer to this assertion we have had pounded into our heads most of our lives, wrote in the opening of *Walden*, "In most books the I, or first person, is omitted; in this it will be retained; that, in respect to egotism, is the main difference. We commonly do not remember that it is, after all, always the first person that is speaking." And if one is honestly seeking to understand, circling with a cold eye one's relation to events, places, people—whatever the subject of the essay—then that search's chances of being construed as egotistical will be dismissed. Seventeenth-century English writer Alexander Smith wrote, "The speaking about one self is not necessarily offensive. A modest, truthful man speaks better about himself than about anything else, and on that subject his speech is likely to be most profitable to his hearers . . . If he be without taint of boastfulness, of self-sufficiency, of hungry vanity, the world will not press the charge home."

Another element of any definition of creative nonfiction must include the form's circling bent, its way of looking again and again at itself from all angles in order to see itself most fully. The result is literary triangulation, a finding of the subject in a three-dimensional grid through digression, full-frontal assault, guerrilla tactics and humble servitude, all in an effort, simply, to see. The creative nonfiction form attempts in whatever way it can to grab hold hard and sure its subject in any manner possible. Eudora Welty writes in *One Writer's Beginnings*, "In writing, as in life, the connections of all sorts of relationships and kinds lie in wait of discovery, and give out their signals to the Geiger counter of the charged imagination, once it is drawn into the right field . . . What I do make my stories out of is the whole fund of my feelings, my responses to the real experiences of my own life, to the relationships that formed and changed it, that I have given most of myself to, and so learned my way toward a dramatic counterpart." The dramatic counterpart of which she here writes is, of course, her stories—fiction—but I maintain that this "whole fund" of feelings, the complete range of our responses to our own real experiences, must inform creative nonfiction as well. Only when we use our "whole fund" can we circle our subjects in the most complete way, wringing from our stores of knowledge and wisdom and the attendant recognition of how little we have of both—*the essence of who we are*—then coupling those recognitions with what in fact we do not know altogether, will we find what we have come looking for: ourselves and, by grace and by luck, the larger world perhaps we hadn't seen before.

Lopate writes, "The personal essay is the reverse of that set of Chinese boxes that you keep opening, only to find a smaller one within. Here you start with the small—the package of flaws and limits—and suddenly find a slightly larger container, insulated by the essay's successful articulation and the writer's self-knowledge."

I agree with Lopate in how the essay reveals larger and larger selves in itself, but rather than the Chinese box, the image that comes to my mind is that of the

Russian nesting dolls, one person inside another inside another. But instead of finding smaller selves inside the self, the opposite occurs, as with Lopate's boxes: we find nested inside that smallest of selves a larger self, and a larger inside that, until we come to the whole of humanity within our own hearts.

Now back to our definition: a desire not to let slip altogether away our life as we have known it; to put an order, for better and worse, to our days; this is only a test; the self as continent, you its first explorer; is this wisdom, or is this folly?; no self-righteousness, though it is always the first person talking; circle the subject to see it most whole.

I'm saving perhaps the most conundrum-like element for nearly last. What role, we have to ask once all these prior elements are taken into account, does *truth* have here? If you look at the pieces of our definition thus far, each one contains within it the angle of perception: the fact that it is only me who is seeing. That is, I don't want to let slip away my life as I have seen it, but who is to say I am telling the truth? In my attempt to put order to my days, am I deluding myself, inflicting an order that was and is now nowhere to be seen? If this is only a test, who is to say I pass? If I am the explorer of my self as continent, what does my discovery matter—didn't Leif Erikson set up shop in North America 500 years before Columbus discovered the place? Isn't one man's wisdom another man's folly? How do I know if I'm not being self-righteous unless there's somebody outside myself to cut me down to size? In circling my subject, isn't it me who determines my course, my longitude and latitude, and therefore am I, by definition, being the most subjective of anyone on planet earth when it comes to my subject?

The answer to each and every one of these questions is: continue to question. Only through rigorous and ruthless questioning of the self can we hope to arrive at any kind of truth.

If you wish to understand creative nonfiction, hope to find a definition, then it is up to you to embrace the fact that, as Montaigne saw, "Each man bears the entire form of man's estate." Inherent to that form are the eccentricities, egotism, foolishness, and fraud of all mankind; inherent as well are the wisdom and self-recognition, the worth and value and merit available to mankind, once enough scouring of what we know and do not know has taken place. V. S. Pritchett, in his memoir *Midnight Oil*, wrote, "The true autobiography of this egotist is exposed in all its intimate foliage in his work. But there is a period when a writer has not yet become one, or, just having become one, is struggling to form his talent, and it is from this period that I have selected most of the scenes and people in this book. It *is* a selection, and it is neither a confession nor a volume of literary reminiscences, but as far as I am able I have put in my 'truth.'"

Pritchett puts the word *truth* in quotation marks; he predicates it with the possessive pronoun *my*. We must recognize that this is the deepest truth we can hope to attain on our own: quotation marks, calling it our own. Only when we have scoured as clean as possible by self-inquiry, even interrogation, what we *perceive*, can we approach calling it *truth*; and even then that crutch of the quotation marks and the assignation of who it belongs to—me—must be acknowledged.

Finally, we have to try and further illuminate *why* we write creative nonfiction. Certainly that first element—a desire not to let slip altogether away our lives as we have known them—is a beginning point, but simply trying to capture our lives before they slip away seems more *reactive* than *proactive*. Writing is, I believe, both, and so any definition must encompass both the reactive and the proactive.

Karen Blixen, AKA Isak Dinesen, in a dinner meeting speech she gave in 1959 at the National Institute of Arts and Letters in New York, addressed the subject, "On Mottoes of My Life." In it she said, "The family of Finch Hatton, of England, have on their crest the device *Je responderay*, 'I will answer.' . . . I liked it so much I asked Denys . . . if I might have it for my own. He generously made me a present of it and even had a seal cut for me, with the words carved on it. The device was meaningful and dear to me for many reasons, two in particular. The first . . . was its high evaluation of the idea of the answer in itself. For an answer is a rarer thing than is generally imagined. There are many highly intelligent people who have no answer at all in them. . . . Secondly, I liked the Finch Hatton device for its ethical content. I will answer *for* what I say or do; I will answer *to* the impression I make. I will be responsible."

This is the proactive element of creative nonfiction, and the final element of my *essai* to define creative writing: *our responsibility as human beings to answer for and to our lives.* It is a responsibility that must encompass all the elements laid out in all this talk about definitions; it is a responsibility that must be woven through the recognition of the fleeting nature of this span of days we have been given, woven through our attempt to see order in chaos, through our understanding that we are only attempting this test and through our being the first explorers of the continent of ourselves. This responsibility to answer for and to ourselves must be woven through the interrogation of self as to whether this is folly or wisdom, through the pledge to humility and to avoiding the abyss of self-righteousness, through the recognition that it is always and only me—the first person—talking, and through the relentless circling of the subject to see it most completely. And this responsibility to answer for and to ourselves must be woven through our recognition that the only truth I can hope to approach will finally and always and only be *my truth.*

But if we are rigorous enough, fearless enough, and humble enough to attempt this responsibility, this way of seeing—for creative nonfiction, like fiction, like poetry, is simply and complexly a way of seeing—the rewards we will reap will be great: we will *understand.* To understand, and nothing more, and that is everything.

The Other Creative Writing

Michael Pearson

Creative writing is the art of storytelling, an art as elemental as fire and the circle of civilization. Poetry goes back to our farthest dreams of the past, joining language to our very heartbeat. Writing fiction, or telling lies to find the truth, is as old as Scheherazade and Odysseus, and playwriting is an ancient and respected activity. Our most sacrosanct anthologies include poetry, fiction, and drama, but rarely, and only very recently, do any include nonfiction as literature. If we see a mention of Edward Gibbon or James Boswell, it is most often as historian and biographer, not as literary artists. The Norton anthologies appropriately include modern fiction writers like John Cheever, Joyce Carol Oates, and Ralph Ellison, but where are E. B. White, John Hersey, or Joseph Mitchell? Where are we to place Joseph Mitchell's *The Bottom of the Harbor*, Truman Capote's *In Cold Blood*, Tom Wolfe's *The Electric Kool-Aid Acid Test*, John McPhee's *Coming into the Country*, Joan Didion's *Slouching Toward Bethlehem*, Edward Abbey's *Desert Solitaire*, or Frank McCourt's recent bestseller *Angela's Ashes*? Where do we include *this* literature made not of imagined reality but of verifiable fact, this literature that holds fast to historical truth even as it pursues a truth beyond the facts. Where do we place this "other" creative writing?

The first question to ask might be: does it make a difference if we make our stories out of facts or fictions any more than it matters if a sculptor makes a statue out of marble or clay? One material is more malleable than the other, but either can be used to create a work of art. In the end, everyone who aspires to be a writer makes stories out of the same source—words, the best ones in the best possible order. The essence of language is metaphor, and all metaphor—as Walker Percy said—is a wonderful, illuminating mistake. It's the sort of mistake that lifts the curtain of cliché and dull habit that blinds us, and it permits us to see, to really see ourselves and the world for a moment. That's where language and stories lead us—fiction and nonfiction writers and readers—toward some re-creation of experience, actual or imagined, toward some making of art out of marble or clay. All creative writers work with language, with metaphor, crafting dialogue and description, building character and symbol, using narration and drama. Usually, the progress is crab-like, the writer slowly suggesting, allowing one thing to lead to another, word shaping word until a new world is created. In this respect, all writers—poets, novelists, and nonfiction artists—face the same challenge: how to build something memorable out of something as insubstantial and strangely enduring as language. Nonfiction writers engage in the same activity that all writers are engaged in, attempting to conjure images for the purblind wayfarer, to make stories that by their very nature are ethereal and fundamental, there and not there at the same time.

The best nonfiction bestows a range of pleasures: it offers both information and stories, the specific site and shape of experience and a glimpse of its mysterious soul. In certain circles, actual pleasure in reading is tantamount to an intellectual sin. As David Denby recently wrote, "In some quarters, pleasure in reading has itself become a political error, rather like sex in Orwell's *1984*." Over 30 years ago, Barbara Tuchman objected to the narrowing of the word literature, saying, "I see no reason why the word should always be confined to writers of fiction and poetry while the rest of us are lumped together under the despicable term 'Nonfiction'—as if we were some sort of remainder."

Literature, and that means fiction or nonfiction, is a dreamworld, containing, as Northrop Frye says, both the nightmare and the wish-fulfillment. Similar to dreams, literature has an hallucinatory vividness, a reality that is somehow unreal, what Frye calls a vertical perspective that puts us, alternately, into the darkness and the light. The uniqueness of nonfiction literature is that it also affords a horizontal perspective. It compels our attention outward, toward the Life that it swears to represent accurately. Of course, the obligation to adhere to the known, the reported, the verifiable fact, often limits the depths a piece of nonfiction can discover or the heights it can reach. But, despite the limitations of the form, nonfiction must honor the facts and attempt to get beyond them. Nonfiction writers can use words with the force of poets, they can shape characters syllable by syllable until we feel that we know them better than we know ourselves, they can carve landscapes out of blank space: artistic nonfiction can reach into us as deeply as any literature. And it has the added power of being about actual people and real events.

Literary nonfiction carries a genuine obligation to factual truths. It is a form that has one sacred principle: you can't make it up. Imaginative speculation, based upon the gathered information, is fine as long as the writer tells the reader what he is doing and why. Richard Preston, *The New Yorker* writer, did it fairly and to good effect in *The Hot Zone*; John Demos, the historian, did it in his narrative of early American life *The Unredeemed Captive*. But the nonfiction writer can't just imagine the color of a character's eyes or change the street names to suit the music of the sentence. The dialogue must be accurate, the dates exact, the events real. During the past few years some scholars and writers have put their minds to the task of defining this genre, although there is not yet even consensus on what to call it (creative nonfiction, literary nonfiction, new journalism, personal journalism . . .), and these critics and artists have described many of the characteristics of the form.

Tom Wolfe called it the "new journalism" and with his typical magnification said that it would oust the novel from importance. He felt that it was possible "to write journalism that would . . . read like a novel." It would require, he said, scenic telling, full dialogue, the use of symbolic details, and a point of view that allowed the reader inside characters' minds. Gay Talese talked about the necessity of immersion reporting, of going so deep into the observation of people and scene that the writer attained a semblance of omniscience. The scholar Norman Sims extended the ideas about immersion and accuracy and added to the discussion about the necessary complexity and contradiction that readers should find in such nonfiction narratives. He also focused on the unique voice and the double responsibility of the writer to subject and to truth. Susan Orlean referred to what she called the heart of this kind of nonfiction: a type of writing that chronicles "the dignity of ordinariness," a phrase that reminds me of James Joyce's definition of *epiphany*, "the moment in which the soul of the commonest object . . . seems to us radiant." Although most readers might not see a clear kinship between Joyce and modern writers of nonfiction literature, the relationship exists. Joyce's belief that the artist is charged to find epiphanal moments not among the gods but in the lives of men and women in ordinary, even unpleasant, circumstances could as well be a description of Joseph Mitchell's philosophy in his nonfiction stories about New York.

Classics in the genre like James Agee's *Let Us Now Praise Famous Men* or John Hersey's *Hiroshima* depict the experiences and emotions of common people, not movie stars or politicians or generals. In this respect, as Mark Kramer said, there is something inherently democratic about literary nonfiction. It is "pluralistic, pro-individual, anti-cant, and anti-elite." Such nonfiction achieves creativity not by imagining people or events but by discovering a vision of character or situation, by finding a structure in the facts that will permit the writer to find "truth in the details of real lives." Ultimately, writers of literary nonfiction look to create a story that will endure. "The point," Tracy Kidder once said, "is to write as well as George Eliot in *Middlemarch* and to find a way to do that in nonfiction." The nonfiction writer might be wise to remember Flannery O'Connor's admonition—"to be humble in the face of what-is." Writers, as she suggested, transcend their limitations by staying within them. And probably the surest path to "perdition and melancholy," as Walker Percy reminded us, is to go after the BIG TRUTH. It's always smarter to get all the small details right, and the larger ones will take care of themselves.

Writers of literary nonfiction have been tending to the details for a number of years now. Although many people believe that the genre sprang full grown onto the scene in 1965 with Capote's *In Cold Blood*, the roots of nonfiction literature reach far deeper and were entangled with fiction from the very beginning. Aphra Behn's 17th-century novella *Oronooko* might be considered a highly stylized work of nonfiction, a work of observation and research. Daniel Defoe's *A Journal of a Plague Year*, which appeared in 1722, is a precise description of the

Black Plague from the point of view of a person who experienced it. But the relationship between what is imagined and what is observed or reported is not always clear in either of these books. In 19th-century works by Melville or Twain such as *Typee* or *Roughing It*, the reader is left with the same questions about what is made up and what is verifiably accurate. Writers like Stephen Crane and Ernest Hemingway played with the possibilities of literary nonfiction, but it wasn't until the 1930s that Joseph Mitchell began to write a nonfiction that had the echoes and resonances of literature while at the same time demanding an adherence to the verifiable or observed fact. Mitchell wrote a brand of nonfiction that seemed vital and new. He wrote about the denizens of the Bowery, those who gathered in McSorley's Saloon, the people who spent their days along the wharves and in the fish markets of lower Manhattan. He wrote with great care and patience, a symbolist who looked more to James Joyce than to his fellow journalists for ways to develop his characters and themes. When Mitchell writes about the rats in New York City, their claws rasping on the sidewalks, he is Kafka in nonfiction, and as readers we are haunted by the story, an eerie vision of the facts. There were other writers during the 1930s and '40s who demonstrated the elasticity and power of nonfiction—George Orwell, A. J. Liebling, E.B. White, John Hersey, Lillian Ross—and they opened the doors to the explosion of nonfiction writers in the last 30 years—from Capote's poetic vision of horror to Annie Dillard's clear-eyed view of Tinker Creek. Writers like Bruce Chatwin, Ian Frazier, and William Least Heat-Moon followed paths marked for them by diarists and travel writers in the 16th- and 17th-centuries. Gay Talese and Tracy Kidder must have learned something about immersion reporting from James Boswell's 18th-century account of Samuel Johnson's life. John McPhee could be kin to both Henry David Thoreau and Joseph Mitchell, both artist and reporter.

Most of these writers find a way of making memorable, in stories, the ordinary lives that they encounter. McPhee's description of the inhabitants of New Jersey's Pine Barrens or Didion's depiction of the suburban malaise in the land of golden dreams lingers in our imaginations as all true literature does. Nonfiction literature can appear in many forms: a "comic strip" about the Holocaust by Art Spiegelman or a piece of surrealistic reporting about the Vietnam War by Michael Herr. It can be a memoir by Tobias Wolff or Mary Karr or a satire by Hunter S. Thompson or Terry Southern. It can be seen in the courtroom play and human drama of Jonathan Harr's *A Civil Action*. It can stay with us in the alliterative imagery of Truman Capote's last sentence in *In Cold Blood*: "Then, starting home, he walked toward the trees, and under them, leaving behind him the big sky, the whisper of wind voices in the wind-bent wheat." Or it can reverberate with the power of Joan Didion's opening line to "Slouching Towards Bethlehem"—"The center was not holding"—and her unforgettable chronicling of the drug scene in Haight-Ashbury during the late '60s.

This brings me back to my original question: where do we place this "other" creative writing? For me, the answer is in the work itself: we enjoy it as literature, we place it alongside any other literature, any writing that has found what George Orwell described as a language charged with meaning to the utmost possible degree, whether it is poetry or nonfiction or drama. In his monumental nonfiction narrative about the Civil War, Shelby Foote said that before he began writing about any campaign he had to learn everything he could from all the available sources and then digest it until it was clear in his own mind. Once he had done that he had to try to reproduce it with even more sharpness and clarity than he had seen it before. He described the finished product as "a great wide sea of words with a redoubled necessity for precision." Finally, this may be the best definition of literary nonfiction that we have, a form of writing that Mark Twain might have said sounds like poetry even though it's the petrified truth.

Beyond Linearity:
Writing the Segmented Essay

Robert L. Root, Jr.

i.

Do you know Annie Dillard's essay, "Living Like Weasels"? It's the one that begins, "A weasel is wild. Who knows what he thinks? He sleeps in his underground den, his tail draped over his nose." It's the one that, in the final paragraph, urges you "to grasp your one necessity and not let it go, to dangle from it limp wherever it takes you." The essay gets me caught up in it each time I read it, encourages me to take more risks, to write with more passion, to seize my one necessity. I often give copies to students and friends as a model of a segmented, meditative essay.

In *Teaching a Stone to Talk*, Dillard's essay collection, "Living Like Weasels" is divided into six lyrical, stanza-like sections or segments. The first segment is on the wildness of the weasel, especially its ferocious, tenacious grip—someone found a weasel's skull attached to the neck of an eagle, still biting long after death. The second segment introduces the idea that the narrator has had a very close encounter with a weasel and describes the setting where it took place. The third segment, the longest, recounts the moment during which their gazes locked and her reaction to it. In the fourth segment she tells us that she "would like to learn, or remember, how to live" and speculates about what she might learn from a wild animal. In the fifth segment she imagines exchanging her mind with the weasel's, describes what living like a weasel might be like, and concludes that we "can live any way we want," can even live like the weasel, "yielding at every moment to the perfect freedom of single necessity." In the final segment, she makes the image of the weasel in the beginning of the essay into a metaphor for a way to approach living. She urges us to "grasp your one necessity" and "let it seize you up aloft even, till your eyes burn out and drop; let your musky flesh fall off in shreds, and let your very bones unhinge and scatter, loosened over fields, over fields and woods, lightly, thoughtless, from any height at all, from as high as eagles." It's a heady, risky, powerful essay, full of passion and poetry.

"Living Like Weasels" is often anthologized in composition readers. Not long ago I needed to see it again and quickly found it in a couple of anthologies on my office shelves. But the first textbook I opened, which identified the piece as a "narrative essay," had eliminated all the breaks, the white spaces, that separated the different segments of the essay. It represented the essay as a single, unsegmented piece. The next textbook I examined also reprinted the essay as a single unbroken unit. This anthology, now in its 7th edition, emphasized modal components that the editors found in the essay, especially what seemed to them to be a narrative core. They claimed, "Dillard narrates the story of a chance encounter with a weasel" and invited the reader to notice how "she also makes use of description and comparison and contrast to give a feel for the weasel, the place where they met, and her reactions to the meeting." Nothing was said in either book about the segments of the essay in Dillard's original collection; both texts had eliminated the chief structural devices Dillard uses in the essay.

Leafing through these texts and others I noticed that, when editors advise students about composing, they generally talk about how to write linear, unsegmented articles. This means that, even though composition anthologies usually offer their readings as models for the prose of novice writers, no anthology I ran across advised students how to write a piece like "Living Like Weasels." Moreover, whether through deliberate design or editorial inadvertence, in far too many cases the essay itself was misrepresented by having its actual design obliterated.

ii.

It's a common problem among student writers, starting too far back in the narrative or trying to encompass too much time or too much activity in a single chronology. A paper about high school begins at the moment the writer entered the building for the first time in ninth grade and moves inexorably toward the moment of graduation, growing more perfunctory year by year; a paper about making the team or the cheerleading squad presents a minute by minute account of decision, preparation, and competition that loses more and more energy the longer it goes on.

But it isn't just a novice writer's problem alone. For example, a friend composed an essay about how he came to give up his annual summer stint as manager and player for a fastpitch softball team. He began an early draft with a brief scene in the present, which triggered a flashback to the start of his long involvement. As the draft progressed, from the moment he joined the team to his last game and the end of the draft, chronology prompted his rediscovery of subject matter and determined the order of events. By the end he had covered a lot of ground, much of it labored and protracted. In the associative links of his memory every detail made sense, made connections, but on the page the slow linear march of the chronology dissipated all the emphatic force of his narrative—there's a reason no one is proposing to cash in on the natural disaster film genre ("Twister," "Asteroid") with a movie called "Glacier!".

Any writer can run up against the insidious demands of linear presentation whenever chronology or process is the organizing principle of an essay or article. The connections and associations that arise so readily in the mind often defy easy transitions on a page and impede progress through the text. Such organizational schemes as chronological sequence come easily to us, but they often interfere with issues requiring compression and focus.

In order to overcome the glaciation of linearity in his softball memoir and make his revision more pointed and more dramatic, my friend segmented his essay and cross-cut between scenes in the past and in the present. His revision begins in present tense on the road to the final tournament, then cuts to a scene in past tense recounting his initial involvement with the team, then shifts back to present tense, the immediate circumstance, and a conflict between the tentative tournament and a long-delayed, booked flight to Paris. Throughout the remainder of the essay, past tense vignettes of a softball life alternate with present tense scenes from the decisive summer. The revision is tighter, denser, more focused, and consequently more powerful.

iii.

Works of contemporary creative nonfiction are often segmented, sectioned off by white spaces or rows of asterisks or subheadings in italics or boldface. For example, in a recent essay issue of *Ploughshares*, 14 of the 23 essays are segmented by either paragraph breaks or some more pronounced method of subdividing. In the essay issue of *American Literary Review*, 15 out of 19 essays are segmented. In some, the segmenting is barely noticeable, almost a printer's convention rather than an actual break in the flow of thought or language; in most, however, the segmenting is emphatic, crucial. William Holtz numbers his thirteen sections of "Brother's Keeper: An Elegy" and begins eleven of them with the same sentence, "My brother now is dead," giving the segments the power of incantation or prayer. Lynne Sharon Schwartz, writing about translating a book from Italian to English, begins and constantly interrupts the essay with lists of English words that might be used in the translation. Frederick Smock's "Anonymous: A Brief Memoir" is divided into segments subtitled by locations in his anonymous subject's home: "The Great-Room," "The Landing," "The Dining Room," and so on. Paul Gruchow's "Eight Variations on the Idea of Failure" has eight numbered sections with self-contained vignettes of varying length that thematically explore the subject of failure. These are essays that call attention to their segmentation; they announce to the reader very early on that progress through them will not be linear, although it may be sequential, and that the force of the segments will come from their juxtaposition with one another and their cumulative effect.

The segmented essay has been around a long time and seems to have become the dominant form of the contemporary essay. Peter Elbow called this form the "collage" essay, referring to the technique in visual art of assembling disparate images into an integrated whole; his chapter on cut-and-paste approaches to the collage is a lonely landmark in discussions of the form. The form has also been tagged with the filmmaking term "montage" (the editing of a series of shots and images into an expressive sequence) and with descriptive terms like "disjunctive" (as opposed to the more unified and "conjunctive" linear form) or "paratactic" (a now-obscure grammatical term for "segments of discourse" arranged without connections or transitions). Carl Klaus, who has examined all these terms, now tends to use "discontinuous" to describe the form and distinguish it from the more or less continuous traditional form. None of these terms seems applicable to all segmented essays, especially when the ability to arrange segments allows writers to generate their own unique forms. For example, Mark Rudman has created a series of essays he refers to as "mosaics," composed of little sections, like mosaic tiles, which create a larger picture by an accumulation of associative segments to create mood or attitude. Maybe we should use the term "cumulative essays" or "associative essays."

Segmented essays don't abandon structure—rather, such essays are designed in ways that may be organic with the subject, ways that incrementally explain themselves as the reader progresses through the essay. These are not traditional essays, beginning with some sort of thesis statement, then marching through a linked, linear series of supporting, illustrative paragraphs to a predictable, forceful conclusion. Traditional models of structure that textbooks provide are molds into which to pour the molten thought and language of the essay: comparison/contrast, thesis/support, process—all prefabricated shapes to be selected off the rack to fit the body of the topic—or the five-paragraph theme, the one-size-fits-all product of the rhetorical department store. The segmented essay, on the other hand, attempts a tailor-made design, a structure that may be appropriate only to itself.

iv.

The segmented essay makes demands on both the writer and the reader. It demands that the reader learn to read the structure of the essay as well as its thought. It is a task that the twentieth-century reader is better prepared for than might be expected. The episodic or segmented sequence is a familiar design in many other genres:

- In the interrelated collection of short stories, a concept suggested, for example, by Hemingway with the interludes between stories in *In Our Time* or carried out in Ray Bradbury's *The Martian Chronicles*;
- In cycles of thematically linked poems, each poem separate and independent but enriched by juxtaposition with poems on similar subjects or with similar perspectives;

- In the "concept" album of interlinked songs—the Beatles' *Sgt. Pepper's Lonely Hearts Club Band* or the "suite" on half of *Abbey Road*, Pink Floyd's *The Wall*, or the more loosely thematic *Nebraska* and *Born in the USA* albums of Bruce Springsteen.
- Above all, in sequences of brief scenes in motion pictures. Films like *Pulp Fiction*, *To Die For*, *The English Patient*, and *Shine* all present their stories out of chronological sequence. In none of these is it hard to reconstruct the chronology, but telling the story in strict chronological order would have changed the emphases of these films. But even in strictly chronological films, the film progresses by sequences of shots or scenes, each separated from one another by visual cues as definite as chapter headings or theatrical intermissions.

It might be argued that the modern reader/viewer is more accustomed to disjunctiveness than to strict continuity.

v.

I write this essay in segments. How can I explain what the segmented essay is like, or how it comes about, in an unsegmented essay?

vi.

I teach creative nonfiction and composition classes, talk to friends about their essays, work on essays of my own. I often advise other writers stuck in linearity and chronology, "Why don't you try collaging this?" (I like making a verb of the noun, outraging any grammarians who overhear me.) I insist that my nonfiction students write at least one segmented essay during the term. Here are some ways I prepare their entrance into the segmented essay:

Definitions: Simply by explaining the segmented essay form I call up a range of alternatives: Collage, montage, mosaic, vignette, episode, segment—these are all ways of approaching the form and they suggest alternatives to students immediately.

Models: Segmented essays that students respond to with immediate understanding include Nancy Willard's "The Friendship Tarot," Annie Dillard's "Living Like Weasels," Susan Allen Toth's "Going to Movies," William Holtz's "Brother's Keeper," Naomi Nye's "Three Pokes of a Thistle," Reg Saner's "The Ideal Particle and the Great Unconformity."

Strategies: Segmented essays come together in several ways—

- By juxtaposition, arranging one item alongside another item so that they comment back and forth on one another (Toth's "Going to Movies" is four vignettes, three dates with different men, the fourth a solitary trip to the theater);
- By parallelism, alternating or intertwining one continuous strand with another (a present tense strand with a past tense strand, a domestic strand

with a foreign strand—in "The Ideal Particle and the Great Unconformity" Reg Saner intertwines a hike to the bottom of the Grand Canyon and back with a history of the geological forces that formed the canyon);

- By patterning, choosing an extra-literary design and arranging literary segments accordingly (as Willard does with tarot cards in "The Friendship Tarot" or Smock does with rooms in "Anonymous: A Brief Memoir");
- By accumulation, arranging a series of segments or scenes or episodes so that they add or enrich or alter meaning with each addition, perhaps reinterpreting earlier segments in later ones, up to a final segment (as Holtz does in "Brother's Keeper");
- By journaling, actually writing in episodes or reconstructing the journal experience in drafts (Sydney Lea asks students to write lyrical essays by trying to connect disparate items in their journals; Gretel Ehrlich uses the journal form as a narrative device in many of her works, such as the recent "Cold Comfort").

In the classroom I make students cluster and list and map ideas, all of which encourage segmentation, creating separate items to work from. I let them scribble separate ideas into six or more boxes on a page and then make a flow chart connecting the segments they want to use. Most often, I let them produce partial or full rough drafts in whatever format they choose and then help them find ways of collaging or segmenting appropriate to the piece they're working on. I let others eavesdrop on those conversations since they are more likely to discover their own designs, given what the writer intuits about the meaning of her piece, than to need me to find it for them. Once they are open to the possibility of the segmented essay, there's virtually no limit to the possibilities a roomful of imaginative young writers can bring to the form.

vii.

A student drops by the office to discuss an academic assignment, a report on aspects of her discipline. She wants to know if it would be okay to divide the paper by subheadings and subtopic divisions. It's not only okay but logical—aren't the chapters of her textbook broken up into brief subsections? isn't her spiral-bound, tabbed and color-coded handbook arranged that way? aren't the sections in her disciplinary texts similarly subdivided? We talk about what the divisions of her paper might be like.

After she leaves I rummage the examination copies of textbooks that fill my shelves, looking for a more specific set of guidelines that I can crib and pass on to her. The only place I turn up any useful information of that kind is in my technical writing texts, the site of format-driven composition. Beyond some mention of outlining, the textbooks and handbooks for the general composition courses and the chapters on writing process in course anthologies generally treat all composing as conjunctive, continuous, unified. They all model subdivisions and subtopics in their own presentations; they all use fragmented, segmented discourse as a vehicle to expound advice about linear, conjunctive prose structures. But at no point in my admittedly cursory perusal of those texts do I find any advice that would help students write in the very formats they are reading.

In a library I stumble on two segmented essays in *The Ohio Review*, "In Montaigne's Tower" by Hilary Masters and "Sister Turtle" by Mary Oliver. They are rich, thoughtful essays and I decide that I want others to read them. But as I stand over the photocopier, turning the pages of the journal and lining them up on the glass, I start thinking about their likely future as classroom texts. Oliver's essay is made up of asterisked and numbered segments; it is unlikely to be reprinted in a composition anthology. The segments of Masters's essay are only divided by paragraph breaks; as with "Living Like Weasels" editors would likely ignore the white spaces and run the essay unbroken. To read segmented essays as these authors wrote them, students would have read literary journals or popular magazines.

They don't, of course. And, in spite of all the segmented discourse their magazines, their Internet surfing, their textbooks in every discipline will model, they will likely have to learn the form by intuition or osmosis rather than by overt instruction. In their college composition classes they won't be taught how to read or write segmented essays, won't learn strategies that have produced the most powerful essays of their time, won't be allowed to go beyond linearity.

Works Cited

Ackley, Katherine Anne. *Essays from Contemporary Culture*. 2nd ed. New York: Harcourt, Brace, 1995.

Best American Essays 1991. Ed. Joyce Carol Oates. Series ed. Robert Atwan. Boston: Ticknor & Fields, 1991.

Dillard, Annie. "Living Like Weasels." *Teaching a Stone to Talk: Expeditions and Encounters*. New York: Harper, 1982. 29–34.

Ehrlich, Gretel. "Cold Comfort." *Harper's* 294:1762 (March 1997): 34–44.

Elbow, Peter. *Writing with Power*. New York: Oxford UP, 1981.

Escholz, Paul, and Alfred Rosa. *Subject and Strategy: A Rhetoric Reader*. 7th ed. New York: St. Martin's, 1996.

Gruchow, Paul. "Eight Variations on the Idea of Failure." *Old Friends, New Neighbors: A Celebration of the American Essay, American Literary Review*. Ed. W. Scott Olsen. 5:2 (Fall 1994): 31–38.

Holtz, William. "Brother's Keeper: An Elegy." *Old Friends, New Neighbors: A Celebration of the American Essay, American Literary Review*. Ed. W. Scott Olsen. 5:2 (Fall 1994): 147–63.

Klaus, Carl H. "Excursions of the Mind: Toward a Poetics of Uncertainty in the Disjunctive Essay." *What Do I Know? Reading, Writing, and Teaching the Essay*. Ed. Janis Forman. Portsmouth, N.H.: Boynton/Cook, 1996.

Masters, Hilary. "In Montaigne's Tower." *Ohio Review* 56 (1997): 7–16.

Old Friends, New Neighbors: A Celebration of the American Essay, American Literary Review 5:2 (Fall 1994). Ed. W. Scott Olsen.

Oliver, Mary. "Sister Turtle." *Ohio Review* 56 (1997): 25–31.

Ploughshares. Ed. Rosellen Brown. 20:2–3 (Fall 1994).

Rudman, Mark. "Mosaic on Walking." *The Best American Essays 1991*. Ed. Joyce Carol Oates. Boston: Ticknor & Fields, 1991. 138–153.

Schwartz, Lynne Sharon. "Time Off to Translate." *Old Friends, New Neighbors: A Celebration of the American Essay, American Literary Review*. Ed. W. Scott Olsen. 5:2 (Fall 1994): 15–30.

Smock, Frederick. "Anonymous: A Brief Memoir." *Old Friends, New Neighbors: A Celebration of the American Essay, American Literary Review*. Ed. W. Scott Olsen. 5:2 (Fall 1994): 68–72.

Steinberg, Michael. Unpublished essay ["'I've Got It, No, You Take It': An Aging Ballplayer's Dilemma" and "On the Road Again: A Softball Gypsy's Last Go-Round"].

Steinberg, Michael J., and Robert L. Root, Jr., eds. *The Fourth Genre: Contemporary Writers of/on Creative Nonfiction*. New York: Allyn & Bacon, 1998.

Willard, Nancy. "The Friendship Tarot." *Between Friends*. Ed. Mickey Pearlman. Boston: Houghton Mifflin, 1994. 195–203.

The Singular First Person

Scott Russell Sanders

The first soapbox orator I ever saw was haranguing a crowd beside the Greyhound Station in Providence, Rhode Island, about the evils of fluoridated water. What the man stood on was actually an upturned milk crate, all the genuine soapboxes presumably having been snapped up by antique dealers. He wore an orange plaid sports coat and matching bow tie and held aloft a bottle filled with mossy green liquid. I don't remember the details of his spiel, except his warning that fluoride was an invention of the Communists designed to weaken our bones and thereby make us pushovers for a Red invasion. What amazed me, as a tongue-tied kid of seventeen newly arrived in the city from the boondocks, was not his message but his courage in delivering it to a mob of strangers. I figured it would have been easier for me to jump straight over the Greyhound Station than to stand there on that milk crate and utter my thoughts.

To this day, when I read or when I compose one of those curious monologues we call the personal essay, I often think of that soapbox orator. Nobody had asked him for his two cents' worth, but there he was declaring it with all the eloquence he could muster. The essay, although enacted in private, is no less arrogant a performance. Unlike novelists and playwrights, who lurk behind the scenes while distracting our attention with the puppet show of imaginary characters, unlike scholars and journalists, who quote the opinions of others and shelter behind the hedges of neutrality, the essayist has nowhere to hide. While the poet can lean back on a several-thousand-year-old legacy of ecstatic speech, the essayist inherits a much briefer and skimpier tradition. The poet is allowed to quit after a few lines, but the essayist must hold our attention over pages and pages. It is a brash and foolhardy form, this one-man or one-woman circus, which relies on the tricks of anecdote, conjecture, memory, and wit to enthrall us.

Addressing a monologue to the world seems all the more brazen or preposterous an act when you consider what a tiny fraction of the human chorus any single

329

voice is. At the Boston Museum of Science an electronic meter records with flashing lights the population of the United States. Figuring in the rate of births, deaths, emigrants leaving the country and immigrants arriving, the meter calculates that we add one fellow citizen every twenty-one seconds. When I looked at it recently, the count stood at 249,958,483. As I wrote that figure in my notebook, the final number jumped from three to four. Another mouth, another set of ears and eyes, another brain. A counter for the earth's population would stand somewhere past five billion at the moment, and would be rising in a blur of digits. Amid this avalanche of selves, it is a wonder that anyone finds the gumption to sit down and write one of those naked, lonely, quixotic letters-to-the-world.

A surprising number do find the gumption. In fact, I have the impression there are more essayists at work in America today, and more gifted ones, than at any time in recent decades. Whom do I have in mind? Here is a sampler: Wendell Berry, Carol Bly, Joan Didion, Annie Dillard, Stephen Jay Gould, Elizabeth Hardwick, Edward Hoagland, Phillip Lopate, Barry Lopez, Peter Matthiessen, John McPhee, Cynthia Ozick, Paul Theroux, Lewis Thomas, Tom Wolfe. No doubt you could make up a list of your own—with a greater ethnic range, perhaps, or fewer nature enthusiasts—a list that would provide equally convincing support for the view that we are blessed right now with an abundance of essayists. We do not have anyone to rival Emerson or Thoreau, but in sheer quantity of first-rate work our time stands comparison with any period since the heyday of the form in the mid-nineteenth century.

Why are so many writers taking up this risky form, and why are so many readers—to judge by the statistics of book and magazine publication—seeking it out? In this era of prepackaged thought, the essay is the closest thing we have, on paper, to a record of the individual mind at work and play. It is an amateur's raid in a world of specialists. Feeling overwhelmed by data, random information, the flotsam and jetsam of mass culture, we relish the spectacle of a single consciousness making sense of a portion of the chaos. We are grateful to Lewis Thomas for shining his light into the dark corners of biology, to John McPhee for laying bare the geology beneath our landscape, to Annie Dillard for showing us the universal fire blazing in the branches of a cedar, to Peter Matthiessen for chasing after snow leopards and mystical insights in the Himalayas. No matter if they are sketchy, these maps of meaning are still welcome. As Joan Didion observes in her own collection of essays, *The White Album*, "We live entirely, especially if we are writers, by the imposition of a narrative line upon disparate images, by the 'ideas' with which we have learned to freeze the shifting phantasmagoria which is our actual experience." Dizzy from a dance that seems to accelerate hour by hour, we cling to the narrative line, even though it may be as pure an invention as the shapes drawn by Greeks to identify the constellations.

The essay is a haven for the private, idiosyncratic voice in an era of anonymous babble. Like the bland-burgers served in their millions along our highways, most language served up in public these days is textureless, tasteless mush. On television, over the phone, in the newspaper, wherever humans bandy words about, we encounter more and more abstractions, more empty formulas. Think of the pablum ladled out by politicians. Think of the fluffy white bread of advertising. Think, lord help us, of committee reports. By contrast, the essay remains stubbornly concrete and particular: it confronts you with an oil-smeared toilet at the Sunoco station, a red vinyl purse shaped like a valentine heart, a bowlegged dentist hunting deer with an elephant gun. As Orwell forcefully argued, and as dictators seem to agree, such a bypassing of abstractions, such an insistence on the concrete, is a politically subversive act. Clinging to this door, that child, this grief, following the zigzag motions of an inquisitive mind, the essay renews language and clears trash from the springs of thought. A century and a half ago, in the rousing manifesto entitled *Nature*, Emerson called on a new generation of writers to cast off the hand-me-down rhetoric of the day, to "pierce this rotten diction and fasten words again to visible things." The essayist aspires to do just that.

As if all these virtues were not enough to account for a renaissance of this protean genre, the essay has also taken over some of the territory abdicated by contemporary fiction. Whittled down to the bare bones of plot, camouflaged with irony, muttering in brief sentences and grade-school vocabulary, peopled with characters who stumble like sleepwalkers through numb lives, today's fashionable fiction avoids disclosing where the author stands on anything. In the essay, you had better speak from a region pretty close to the heart or the reader will detect the wind of phoniness whistling through your hollow phrases. In the essay you may be caught with your pants down, your ignorance and sentimentality showing, while you trot recklessly about on one of your hobbyhorses. You cannot stand back from the action, as Joyce instructed us to do, and pare your fingernails. You cannot palm off your cockamamie notions on some hapless character.

To our list of the essay's contemporary attractions we should add the perennial ones of verbal play, mental adventure, and sheer anarchic high spirits. To see how the capricious mind can be led astray, consider the foregoing paragraph, which drags in metaphors from the realms of toys, clothing, weather, and biology, among others. That is bad enough; but it could have been worse. For example, I began to draft a sentence in that paragraph with the following words: "More than once, in sitting down to beaver away at a narrative, felling trees of memory and hauling brush to build a dam that might slow down the waters of time. . . ." I had set out to make some innocent remark, and here I was gnawing down trees and building dams, all because I had let that *beaver* slip in. On this occasion I had the good sense to throw out the unruly word. I don't always, as no doubt you will have noticed. Whatever its more visible subject, an essay is also about the way a mind moves, the links and leaps and jigs of thought. I might as well drag in another metaphor—and another unoffending animal—by saying that each doggy sentence, as it noses forward into the underbrush of thought, scatters a bunch of rabbits that go bounding off in all directions. The essayist can afford to chase more of those rabbits than the fiction writer can, but fewer than the poet. If you refuse to chase any of them, and keep plodding along in a straight line, you and your reader will have a dull outing. If you chase too many, you will soon wind up lost in a thicket of confusion with your tongue hanging out.

The pursuit of mental rabbits was strictly forbidden by the teachers who instructed me in English composition. For that matter, nearly all the qualities of the personal essay, as I have been sketching them, violate the rules that many of us were taught in school. You recall we were supposed to begin with an outline and stick by it faithfully, like a train riding its rails, avoiding sidetracks. Each paragraph was to have a topic sentence pasted near the front, and these orderly paragraphs were to be coupled end-to-end like so many boxcars. Every item in those boxcars was to bear the stamp of some external authority, preferably a footnote referring to a thick book, although appeals to magazines and newspapers would do in a pinch. Our diction was to be formal, dignified, shunning the vernacular. Polysyllabic words derived from Latin were preferable to the blunt lingo of the streets. Metaphors were to be used only in emergencies, and no two of them were to be mixed. And even in emergencies we could not speak in the first person singular.

Already as a schoolboy, I chafed against those rules. Now I break them shamelessly, in particular the taboo against using the lonely capital I. Just look at what I'm doing right now. My speculations about the state of the essay arise, needless to say, from my own practice as reader and writer, and they reflect my own tastes, no matter how I may pretend to gaze dispassionately down on the question from a hot-air balloon. As Thoreau declares in his cocky manner on the opening page of *Walden*: "In most books the *I*, or first person, is omitted; in this it will be retained; that, in respect to egotism, is the main difference. We commonly do not remember that it is, after all, always the first person that is speaking. I should not talk so much about myself if there were anybody else whom I knew as well." True for the personal essay, it is doubly true for an essay about the essay: one speaks always and inescapably in the first person singular.

We could sort out essays along a spectrum according to the degree to which the writer's ego is on display—with John McPhee, perhaps, at the extreme of self-effacement, and Norman Mailer at the opposite extreme of self-dramatization. Brassy or shy, center stage or hanging back in the wings, the author's persona commands our attention. For the length of an essay, or a book of essays, we respond to that persona as we would to a friend caught up in a rapturous monologue. When the monologue is finished, we may not be able to say precisely what it was about, any more than we can draw conclusions from a piece of music. "Essays don't usually boil down to a summary, as articles do," notes Edward Hoagland, one of the least summarizable of companions, "and the style of the writer has a 'nap' to it, a combination of personality and originality and energetic loose ends that stand up like the nap of a piece of wool and can't be brushed flat" ("What I Think, What I Am"). We make assumptions about that speaking voice, assumptions we cannot validly make about the narrators in fiction. Only a sophomore is permitted to ask if Huckleberry Finn ever had any children; but even literary sophisticates wonder in print about Thoreau's love life, Montaigne's domestic arrangements, De Quincey's opium habit, Virginia Woolf's depression.

Montaigne, who not only invented the form but nearly perfected it as well, announced from the start that his true subject was himself. In his note "To the Reader" at the beginning of the *Essays*, he slyly proclaimed:

> I want to be seen here in my simple, natural, ordinary fashion, without straining or artifice; for it is myself that I portray. My defects will here be read to the

life, and also my natural form, as far as respect for the public has allowed. Had I been placed among those nations which are said to live still in the sweet freedom of nature's first laws, I assure you I should very gladly have portrayed myself here entire and wholly naked.

A few pages after this disarming introduction, we are told of the Emperor Maximilian, who was so prudish about exposing his private parts that he would not let a servant dress him or see him in the bath. The Emperor went so far as to give orders that he be buried in his underdrawers. Having let us in on this intimacy about Maximilian, Montaigne then confessed that he himself, although "bold-mouthed," was equally prudish, and that "except under great stress of necessity or voluptuousness," he never allowed anyone to see him naked. Such modesty, he feared, was unbecoming in a soldier. But such honesty is quite becoming in an essayist. The very confession of his prudery is a far more revealing gesture than any doffing of clothes.

A curious reader will soon find out that the word *essay*, as adapted by Montaigne, means a trial or attempt. The Latin root carries the more vivid sense of a weighing out. In the days when that root was alive and green, merchants discovered the value of goods and alchemists discovered the composition of unknown metals by the use of scales. Just so the essay, as Montaigne was the first to show, is a weighing out, an inquiry into the value, meaning, and true nature of experience; it is a private experiment carried out in public. In each of three successive editions, Montaigne inserted new material into his essays without revising the old material. Often the new statements contradicted the original ones, but Montaigne let them stand, since he believed that the only consistent fact about human beings is their inconsistency. In a celebration called "Why Montaigne Is Not a Bore," Lewis Thomas has remarked of him that "He [was] fond of his mind, and affectionately entertained by everything in his head." Whatever Montaigne wrote about—and he wrote about everything under the sun: fears, smells, growing old, the pleasures of scratching—he weighed on the scales of his own character.

It is the *singularity* of the first person—its warts and crotchets and turn of voice—that lures many of us into reading essays, and that lingers with us after we finish. Consider the lonely, melancholy persona of Loren Eiseley, forever wandering, forever brooding on our dim and bestial past, his lips frosty with the chill of the Ice Age. Consider the volatile, Dionysian persona of D. H. Lawrence, with his incandescent gaze, his habit of turning peasants into gods and trees into flames, his quick hatred and quicker love. Consider that philosophical farmer, Wendell Berry, who speaks with a countryman's knowledge and a deacon's severity. Consider E. B. White, with his cheery affection for brown eggs and dachshunds, his unflappable way of herding geese while the radio warns of an approaching hurricane.

E. B. White, that engaging master of the genre, a champion of idiosyncrasy, introduced his own volume of *Essays* by admitting the danger of narcissism:

I think some people find the essay the last resort of the egoist, a much too self-conscious and self-serving form for their taste; they feel that it is presumptuous of a writer to assume that his little excursions or his small observations will interest the reader. There is some justice in their complaint. I have always been aware that I am by nature self-absorbed and egoistical; to write of myself to the extent I have done indicates a too great attention to my own life, not enough to the lives of others.

Yet the self-absorbed Mr. White was in fact a delighted observer of the world, and shared that delight with us. Thus, after describing memorably how a circus girl practiced her bareback riding in the leisure moments between shows ("The Ring of Time"), he confessed: "As a writing man, or secretary, I have always felt charged with the safekeeping of all unexpected items of worldly or unworldly enchantment, as though I might be held personally responsible if even a small one were to be lost." That may still be presumptuous, but it is a presumption turned outward on the creation.

This looking outward helps distinguish the essay from pure autobiography, which dwells more complacently on the self. Mass murderers, movie stars, sports heroes, Wall Street crooks, and defrocked politicians may blather on about whatever high jinks or low jinks made them temporarily famous, may chronicle their exploits, their diets, their hobbies, in perfect confidence that the public is eager to gobble up every least gossipy scrap. And the public, according to sales figures, generally is. On the other hand, I assume the public does not give a hoot about my private life. If I write of hiking up a mountain with my one-year-old boy riding like a papoose on my back, and of what he babbled to me while we gazed down from the summit onto the scudding clouds, it is not because I am deluded into believing that my baby, like the offspring of Prince Charles, matters to the great world. It is because I know the great world produces babies of its own and watches them change cloudfast before its doting eyes. To make that climb up the mountain vividly present for readers is harder work than the climb itself. I choose to write about my experience not because it is mine, but because it seems to me a door through which others might pass.

On that cocky first page of *Walden*, Thoreau justified his own seeming self-absorption by saying that he wrote the book for the sake of his fellow citizens, who kept asking him to account for his peculiar experiment by the pond. There is at least a sliver of truth to this, since Thoreau, a town character, had been invited more than once to speak his mind at the public lectern. Most of us, however, cannot honestly say the townspeople have been clamoring for our words. I suspect that all writers of the essay, even Norman Mailer and Gore Vidal, must occasionally wonder if they are egomaniacs. For the essayist, in other words, the problem of authority is inescapable. By what right does one speak? Why should anyone listen? The traditional sources of authority no longer serve. You cannot justify your words by appealing to the Bible or some other holy text, you cannot merely stitch together a patchwork of quotations from classical authors, you cannot lean on a podium at the Atheneum and deliver your wisdom to a rapt audience.

In searching for your own soapbox, a sturdy platform from which to deliver your opinionated monologues, it helps if you have already distinguished yourself at some other, less fishy form. When Yeats describes his longing for Maud Gonne or muses on Ireland's misty lore, everything he says is charged with the prior strength of his poetry. When Virginia Woolf, in *A Room of One's Own*, reflects on the status of women and the conditions necessary for making art, she speaks as the author of *Mrs. Dalloway* and *To the Lighthouse*. The essayist may also lay claim to our attention by having lived through events or traveled through terrains that already bear a richness of meaning. When James Baldwin writes his *Notes of a Native Son*, he does not have to convince us that racism is a troubling reality. When Barry Lopez takes us on a meditative tour of the far north in *Arctic Dreams*, he can rely on our curiosity about that fabled and forbidding place. When Paul Theroux climbs aboard a train and invites us on a journey to some exotic destination, he can count on the romance of railroads and the allure of remote cities to bear us along.

Most essayists, however, cannot draw on any source of authority from beyond the page to lend force to the page itself. They can only use language to put themselves on display and to gesture at the world. When Annie Dillard tells us in the opening lines of *Pilgrim at Tinker Creek* about the tomcat with bloody paws who jumps through the window onto her chest, why should we listen? Well, because of the voice that goes on to say: "And some mornings I'd wake in daylight to find my body covered with paw prints in blood; I looked as though I'd been painted with roses." Listen to her explaining a few pages later what she is up to in this book, this broody, zestful record of her stay in the Roanoke Valley: "I propose to keep here what Thoreau called 'a meteorological journal of the mind,' telling some tales and describing some of the sights of this rather tamed valley, and exploring, in fear and trembling, some of the unmapped dim reaches and unholy fastnesses to which those tales and sights so dizzyingly lead." The sentence not only describes the method of her literary search, but also exhibits the breathless, often giddy, always eloquent and spiritually hungry soul who will do the searching. If you enjoy her company, you will relish Annie Dillard's essays; if you don't, you won't.

Listen to another voice which readers tend to find either captivating or insufferable:

> That summer I began to see, however dimly, that one of my ambitions, perhaps my governing ambition, was to belong fully to this place, to belong as the thrushes and the herons and the muskrats belonged, to be altogether at home here. That is still my ambition. But now I have come to see that it proposes an enormous labor. It is a spiritual ambition, like goodness. The wild creatures belong to the place by nature, but as a man I can belong to it only by understanding and by virtue. It is an ambition I cannot hope to succeed in wholly, but I have come to believe that it is the most worthy of all.

That is Wendell Berry in "The Long-Legged House" writing about his patch of Kentucky. Once you have heard that stately, moralizing, cherishing voice, laced through with references to the land, you will not mistake it for anyone else's.

Berry's themes are profound and arresting ones. But it is his voice, more than anything he speaks about, that either seizes us or drives us away.

Even so distinct a persona as Wendell Berry's or Annie Dillard's is still only a literary fabrication, of course. The first person singular is too narrow a gate for the whole writer to squeeze through. What we meet on the page is not the flesh-and-blood author, but a simulacrum, a character who wears the label *I*. Introducing the lectures that became *A Room of One's Own*, Virginia Woolf reminded her listeners that "'I' is only a convenient term for somebody who has no real being. Lies will flow from my lips, but there may perhaps be some truth mixed up with them; it is for you to seek out this truth and to decide whether any part of it is worth keeping." Here is a part I consider worth keeping: "Women have served all these centuries as looking-glasses possessing the magic and delicious power of reflecting the figure of man at twice its natural size." It is from such elegant, revelatory sentences that we build up our notion of the "I" who speaks to us under the name of Virginia Woolf.

What the essay tells us may not be true in any sense that would satisfy a court of law. As an example, think of Orwell's brief narrative, "A Hanging," which describes an execution in Burma. Anyone who has read it remembers how the condemned man as he walked to the gallows stepped aside to avoid a puddle. That is the sort of haunting detail only an eyewitness should be able to report. Alas, biographers, those zealous debunkers, have recently claimed that Orwell never saw such a hanging, that he reconstructed it from hearsay. What then do we make of his essay? Or has it become the sort of barefaced lie we prefer to call a story?

Frankly, I don't much care what label we put on "A Hanging"—fiction or nonfiction, it is a powerful statement either way—but Orwell might have cared a great deal. I say this because not long ago I was bemused and then vexed to find one of my own essays treated in a scholarly article as a work of fiction. Here was my earnest report about growing up on a military base, my heartfelt rendering of indelible memories, being confused with the airy figments of novelists! To be sure, in writing the piece I had used dialogue, scenes, settings, character descriptions, the whole fictional bag of tricks; sure, I picked and chose among a thousand beckoning details; sure, I downplayed some facts and highlighted others; but I was writing about the actual, not the invented. I shaped the matter, but I did not make it up.

To explain my vexation, I must break another taboo, which is to speak of the author's intent. My teachers warned me strenuously to avoid the intentional fallacy. They told me to regard poems and plays and stories as objects washed up on the page from some unknown and unknowable shores. Now that I am on the other side of the page, so to speak, I think quite recklessly of intention all the time. I believe that if we allow the question of intent in the case of murder, we should allow it in literature. The essay is distinguished from the short story, not by the presence or absence of literary devices, not by tone or theme or subject, but by the writer's stance toward the material. In composing an essay about what it was like to grow up on that military base, I *meant* something quite different from what I mean when concocting a story. I meant to preserve and record and help give voice to a reality that existed independently of me. I meant to pay my respects to a minor passage of history in an out-of-the-way place. I felt responsible to the truth as known by other people. I wanted to speak directly out of my own life into the lives of others.

You can see I am teetering on the brink of metaphysics. One step farther and I will plunge into the void, wondering as I fall how to prove there is any external truth for the essayist to pay homage to. I draw back from the brink and simply declare that I believe one writes, in essays, with a regard for the actual world, with a respect for the shared substance of history, the autonomy of other lives, the being of nature, the mystery and majesty of a creation we have not made.

When it comes to speculating about the creation, I feel more at ease with physics than with metaphysics. According to certain bold and lyrical cosmologists, there is at the center of black holes a geometrical point, the tiniest conceivable speck, where all the matter of a collapsed star has been concentrated, and where everyday notions of time, space, and force break down. That point is called a singularity. The boldest and most poetic theories suggest that anything sucked into a singularity might be flung back out again, utterly changed, somewhere else in the universe. The lonely first person, the essayist's microcosmic "I," may be thought of as a verbal singularity at the center of the mind's black hole. The raw matter of experience, torn away from the axes of time and space, falls in constantly from all sides, undergoes the mind's inscrutable alchemy, and reemerges in the quirky, unprecedented shape of an essay.

Now it is time for me to step down, before another metaphor seizes hold of me, before you notice that I am standing, not on a soapbox, but on the purest air.

Memoir? Fiction? Where's the Line?

Mimi Schwartz

"It was very cold the night my mother died ..."

Anna Quindlen

I don't remember what my second grade teacher wore! How can I recall the dialogue when my Dad left 10 years ago? All my summers in Maine blur together. That's what my students will say tomorrow when I return their first efforts at turning memories into memoir. They are mostly 21- and 22-year-old college seniors, plus a few retirees and second careerists, all eager to explore their lives on paper for themselves, friends and the world. No one is famous, although one woman said she won the lottery.

The memory worries will come mainly from marine biologists, psychology and history majors who deal in term papers and lab reports, rarely from poets and fiction writers who have taken enough creative writing workshops to understand, as V.S. Pritchett once wrote about memoir, "It's all in the art. You get no credit for living."

Some of these "creative" writers assume such advice excludes their boring lives, and so I have written "Great detail!" in many margins of first essays only to find out that the date rape or house burning down didn't happen. No, no, you can't do that, I say. That's fiction, not memoir. You have to play by the rules; there's a line you can't cross. And where is that? they ask. I don't know, only that if you make up too much, you've crossed it. The murkiness makes writer Anna Quindlen choose fiction over memoir. In "How Dark? How Stormy? I Can't Re-

338

call!" (*New York Times Book Review*), she says that the newspaper reporter in her made her check old weather charts before she could publish the line, "It was very cold the night my mother died." Like my fact-conscious students, she worries: "Was it very cold or was that just the trick memory played on a girl who was sick and shivering, at least metaphorically?" and this worry, combined with a lousy memory, makes Quindlen avoid memoir, "a terrain too murky for me to tread." She says she can't, like Frank McCourt in *Angela's Ashes*, "remember half a century later the raw, itching sore that erupted between his eyebrows when he was a boy." So she writes fiction, preferring to create a world "from the ground up, the imagined minutiae of the lives of characters I invent from my knowledge of characters."

"But what about your *true* stories?" I would ask, if Anna were in my class. Don't you tell your friends, family, especially your children, about who you were, who your family was once upon a time? And do you want those stories to last more than one minute? If we stick only to facts, our past is as skeletal as black-and-white line drawings in a coloring book. We must color it in.

I tell the Annas in my class what I tell myself as memoir writer: Go for the emotional truth, that's what matters. Yes, gather the facts by all means. Look at old photos, return to old places, ask family members what they remember, look up time-line books for the correct songs and fashion styles, read old newspapers, encyclopedias, whatever—and then use the imagination to fill in the remembered experience. You don't need a tape recording of what your parents said to "remember" what they said that day. You don't need a photo of your kindergarten teacher to describe her; the clothes you imagine will match your feeling about her. Maybe you see a red, mini-suited girl; maybe you see a woman in a thick, long black dress with white cuffs. Either way, we see the teacher as you saw her. And who knows? She might even have worn those white cuffs! The subconscious is remembering.

That's also what I told my mother last week when she called to tell me that an essay I'd sent her about my love affair with horses was wrong. "I picked you up that day you fell off that horse, Sultan."

"You did not. I still remember everyone staring because my pants were ripped, my knee all bloody on the bus ride home."

"You were crying in the Pontiac."

"I was not."

It was her memory against mine with no one else to ask, so I wasn't changing my story. It was true for me—the humiliation following my glory riding Sultan—and she could tell her version, I said. That's what Rosemary Wolff threatened when her two sons, Geoffrey and Tobias, wrote separate and conflicting memoirs of their youth. (Or so Geoffrey Wolff said once in a workshop I took in Aspen.)

How subjective can you be in memoir, accidentally or on purpose? That is a central question, and different writers have different solutions. I teach the possibilities. You might start with a disclaimer the way John Irving did in "Trying to Save Piggy Sneed." He warns readers up front to "Please remember that all memoir is fiction," and then tells a wonderful story about how a retarded garbage man started him on his career as a writer. You might hint a disclaimer in your title, as

Mary Carr does in *The Liar's Club*, and leave the reader wondering. You might tip off the reader with phrases such as "I imagine her . . . " or "Perhaps he said . . . ", the way Jane Bernstein does in her retelling of her sister's murder 2,000 miles away and 20 years before. You might use exaggeration as Russell Baker does in *Growing Up*, so that the dialogue of his interview to become a paperboy sounds as if he were being interviewed to head up IBM.

You might even give a lament that you don't remember, as Bret Lott does in his book, *Fathers, Sons, and Brothers*, before he gives a rich description of the morning that his son stopped calling him Mommy:

> The sad thing, though, is that I can't recall the first day he called me Daddy when I went into his room. I could make up a story about it, here and now; I could tell you how it was on a Tuesday—Melanie's morning—and how there seemed something different in his voice as I came up from sleep. . . .

Whatever else, there's always Joan Didion's wonderful permission in "On Reading a Notebook"—that if you remember it, it's true. I use it often.

> Perhaps it never did snow that August in Vermont; perhaps there never were flurries in the night wind, and maybe no one else felt the ground hardening and summer already dead even as we pretended to bask in it, but that was how it felt to me, and it might as well have snowed, could have snowed, did snow.

How it felt to me! What a relief to memoir writers who want to explore the emotional truth of memory. It may be "murky terrain," you may cross the line into fiction and have to step back reluctantly into what really happened—the struggle creates the tension that makes memoir either powerfully true or hopelessly phony. The challenge of this genre is that it hands you characters, plot and setting, and says, "Go figure them out!"—using fact, memory and imagination to recreate the complexity of real moments, big and small, with no invented rapes or houses burning down. If the challenge intrigues you, imaginatively and emotionally, and you find the right voice—one savvy and appealing enough to make the reader say, "Yes. I've been there. I know what you mean!"—you have something good. But if the voice you adopt annoys, embarrasses or bores because of lack of insight, then beware. The reader will say, "So what? I don't care about you!" often in anger.[1]

It's that personal, the judgment. It's YOU, not some anonymous character they are talking about. Like a smile at a cocktail party, the voice of memoir—far

---

[1]James Woolcott's recent article, "Me, Myself and I," in *Vanity Fair* is a good example of that anger. He attacks Anne Roiphe as "the true queen of the daytime soaps," Creative Nonfiction as "civic journalism for the soul," and others like Laurie Stone as "navel gazers"—as if the person, genre and subject ("no detail is too mundane to share") and not the art sinks the "I" of true stories.

more than in fiction—can evoke a quick response. Phony or real. I like this person. I hate this person. Nothing lukewarm or impersonal about it.

That vulnerability—more than a bad memory, I suspect—makes many agree with writer Pam Houston: "I write fiction to tell the truth." The seeming anonymity of fiction, even autobiographical fiction, can be creatively freeing, as Jamaica Kincaid shows in *Annie John*. She makes her real-life, older brothers disappear so that the emotional focus is on a girl and her mother, and she calls the story fiction—even though other basics are true. (Kincaid, like the main character, Annie, grew up on the island of Antigua and left at 17.) But if your story is really about Mom in Iowa, why turn her into a half-sister in New York—unless in the transformation, you, like Kincaid, tap into the real story you need to tell?

One essay, out of the 25 I just finished reading, does hook me with its savvy. This young woman of 22, Nicole Ross, already knows what it has taken me years to figure out: that the ambiguity of memoir, its shifting planes of truth and memory, can take you somewhere important:

> I want to remember a childhood brimming with sunlight, with just enough suffering to make it seem real. Each Christmas becomes bleaker than the last; it always seems as if there are fewer presents under the tree, and less laughter as my grandparents grow older. Ironically, the Christmases of my childhood have become lavish feasts of endless caroling because I don't remember them any more. I think that my collection of memories is nothing more than a soothing deception; many details have been supplied by a fertile imagination. It can't be all bad, though, because my parents still smile at me the way they do in my memories of those early Christmases.

Unlike Anna, Nicole is comfortable with how memory, fact and imagination mix up her Christmases; she trusts the process. I wrote "Great!" in every margin of her six pages. I believed every word, heard the caroling, saw her parents smile.

There *is* one reason not to write memoir, aside from worries about memory and the restraints on creative freedom: Mom may not speak to you again if you write her story, and you care. Frank McCourt waited to publish his memoir until after his mother died because he didn't want to hurt her. Others don't wait and call their story fiction, so they can tell Mom, family, friends, anyone real who appears on the page: "Of course that isn't you. I made that part up." No one is fooled, but you save face, maybe a lawsuit.

A writer does have some fictive leeway even in memoir, I believe—*if* you are cautious (and not too famous). Tomorrow I will tell the student who wrote about her bulimic roommate that her profile could be just as powerful and less hurtful if she moved the girl next door, changed her hair color and did not call her Kimmie.[2] I will tell the class that in a memoir about six months in my marriage, I made a few composite characters of minor characters and wrote this disclaimer in

---

[2]This anonymity is essential if, like me, you have students share their work in progress in class. Why should the roommate's problems become public knowledge?

my introduction: "The story is 90 percent factual; the rest is made up to protect those who didn't ask to be in this book." The problem was not my husband and my children (I was willing to take my chances with them); it was my friends, like the one who was leaving her husband just as I was deciding to stay with mine. In fact, I had three friends who were thinking about divorce, so in the book, I made a composite character and we met for cappuccino.

Depending on the story's focus, you sometimes collapse time and characters as well, I will tell my students, and still are "true" on my truth scale. Writer Jack Connor, in a personal essay about a weekend of watching eagles, collapsed three days into one morning and mentioned only two of the four students who accompanied him on that trip. He wanted to capture how young people reawakened in him the simple pleasure of birding even in a mid-January freeze, and the number of days, the number of people, didn't matter—although in a scientific field report they would. I will show my students how his original journal entry of facts and private observations evolved many drafts later into a published story ("A Lesson from Mott's Creek") with a voice and a point of view.

Journal Entry:

> 1/11/94   —eagle weekend—
> one of the best birding experiences of the last year this weekend—the eagle survey with Jerry Liguori, Brian Sullivan, two folks from Ocean City (mcdermotts?), and on Sunday with Joe Mangion and Bil Seng.
>   . . . both days cold—and windy. temp in teens, with wind chill, probably below 10, maybe even bordering on zero. but blue sky, growing cloudy on saturday around one and then mostly cloudy. Sunday, blue until 2 or so and only partly cloudy after that. . . .

Essay Opening:

> "Binoculars in my fingers, tears in my eyes from the January glare, face stiff from the hard wind, I am standing between Brian Sullivan and Jerry Liguori and wonder, "Why don't I come out here every single day?"

I will also tell my students about a friend who is writing about her aunt who had a lobotomy 50 years ago. My friend visited the mental institution where it happened, looked up records, talked to a nurse and doctor who remembered her aunt and tried writing what her aunt's life was like. But those "facts" weren't enough to recreate the story. She must take an imaginative leap, our writing group told her, imagine herself as her aunt and what would it feel like, maybe write in first person. Draft in hand, my friend can then check with a psychiatrist—"Does this ring true?"—and with relatives, before revising for more accuracy.

The Joan Didions and John Irvings in tomorrow's class will nod their heads in agreement. The Anna Quindlens will not. They want clear-cut boundaries and would side with my writer friend, Andrea Herrmann, who warns me: "If the writer can make a composite character, what prevents her from making up scenes, blending parts of places together, switching historical time frames?" Making up anything, for them, is crossing the line into fiction and should be called that. But I disagree. If the main plot, characters, and setting are true, if the intent is to make honest sense of "how it felt to me" and tell that true story well (with disclaimers as needed), it's memoir to me.

In "Why Memoir Now?" Vivian Gornick writes, "What happened to the writer is not what matters; what matters is the larger sense that the writer is able to make of what happened. For that the power of a writing imagination is required." Use that imagination in memoir, I tell myself and my students, to find the language and complexity of real lives, not imagined ones. It's OK to trust yourself (with a bit of Quindlen's and Herrmann's wariness)—even if you can't remember the temperature on the night Mom died.

The Exact Location of the Soul

Richard Selzer

Someone asked me why a surgeon would write. Why, when the shelves are already too full? They sag under the deadweight of books. To add a single adverb is to risk exceeding the strength of the boards. A surgeon should abstain. A surgeon, whose fingers are more at home in the steamy gullies of the body than they are tapping the dry keys of a typewriter. A surgeon, who feels the slow slide of intestines against the back of his hand and is no more alarmed than were a family of snakes taking their comfort from such an indolent rubbing. A surgeon, who palms the human heart as though it were some captured bird.

Why should he write? Is it vanity that urges him? There is glory enough in the knife. Is it for money? One can make too much money. No. It is to search for some meaning, in the ritual of surgery, which is at once murderous, painful, healing, and full of love. It is a devilish hard thing to transmit—to find, even. Perhaps if one were to cut out a heart, a lobe of the liver, a single convolution of the brain, and paste it to a page, it would speak with more eloquence than all the words of Balzac. Such a piece would need no literary style, no mass of erudition or history, but in its very shape and feel would tell all the frailty and strength, the despair and nobility of man. What? Publish a heart? A little piece of bone? Preposterous. Still I fear that is what it may require to reveal the truth that lies hidden in the body. Not all the undressings of Rabelais, Chekhov, or even William Carlos Williams have wrested it free, although God knows each one of those doctors made a heroic assault upon it.

I have come to believe that it is the flesh alone that counts. The rest is that with which we distract ourselves when we are not hungry or cold, in pain or ecstasy. In the recesses of the body I search for the philosophers' stone. I know it is there, hidden in the deepest, dampest cul-de-sac. It awaits discovery. To find it would be like the harnessing of fire. It would illuminate the world. Such a quest is not without pain. Who can gaze on so much misery and feel no hurt? Emerson has written that the poet is the only true doctor. I believe him, for the poet, lacking the impediment of speech with which the rest of us are afflicted, gazes, records, diagnoses, and prophesies.

I invited a young diabetic woman to the operating room to amputate her leg. She could not see the great shaggy black ulcer upon her foot and ankle that threatened to encroach upon the rest of her body, for she was blind as well. There upon her foot was a Mississippi Delta brimming with corruption, sending its raw tributaries down between her toes. Gone were all the little web spaces that when fresh and whole are such a delight to loving men. She could not see her wound, but she could feel it. There is no pain like that of the bloodless limb turned rotten and festering. There is neither unguent nor anodyne to kill such a pain yet leave intact the body.

For over a year I trimmed away the putrid flesh, cleansed, anointed, and dressed the foot, staving off, delaying. Three times each week, in her darkness, she sat upon my table, rocking back and forth, holding her extended leg by the thigh, gripping it as though it were a rocket that must be steadied lest it explode and scatter her toes about the room. And I would cut away a bit here, a bit there, of the swollen blue leather that was her tissue.

At last we gave up, she and I. We could no longer run ahead of the gangrene. We had not the legs for it. There must be an amputation in order that she might live—and I as well. It was to heal us both that I must take up knife and saw, and cut the leg off. And when I could feel it drop from her body to the table, see the blessed *space* appear between her and that leg, I too would be well.

Now it is the day of the operation. I stand by while the anesthetist administers the drugs, watch as the tense familiar body relaxes into narcosis. I turn then to uncover the leg. There, upon her kneecap, she has drawn, blindly, upside down for me to see, a face; just a circle with two ears, two eyes, a nose, and a smiling upturned mouth. Under it she has printed SMILE, DOCTOR. Minutes later I listen to the sound of the saw, until a little crack at the end tells me it is done.

So, I have learned that man is not ugly, but that he is Beauty itself. There is no other his equal. Are we not all dying, none faster or more slowly than any other? I have become receptive to the possibilities of love (for it is love, this thing that happens in the operating room), and each day I wait, trembling in the busy air. Perhaps today it will come. Perhaps today I will find it, take part in it, this love that blooms in the stoniest desert.

All through literature the doctor is portrayed as a figure of fun. Shaw was splenetic about him; Molière delighted in pricking his pompous medicine men, and well they deserved it. The doctor is ripe for caricature. But I believe that the truly great writing about doctors has not yet been done. I think it must be done *by* a doctor, one who is through with the love affair with his technique, who recognizes that he has played Narcissus, raining kisses on a mirror, and who now, out of the impacted masses of his guilt, has expanded into self-doubt, and finally into the high state of wonderment. Perhaps he will be a nonbeliever who, after a lifetime of grand gestures and mighty deeds, comes upon the knowledge that he has done no more than meddle in the lives of his fellows, and that he has done at least as much harm as good. Yet he may continue to pretend, at least, that there is nothing to fear, that death will not come, so long as people depend on his authority. Later, after his patients have left, he may closet himself in his darkened office, sweating and afraid.

There is a story by Unamuno in which a priest, living in a small Spanish village, is adored by all the people for his piety, kindness, and the majesty with which he celebrates the Mass each Sunday. To them he is already a saint. It is a foregone conclusion, and they speak of him as Saint Immanuel. He helps them with their plowing and planting, tends them when they are sick, confesses them, comforts them in death, and every Sunday, in his rich, thrilling voice, transports them to paradise with his chanting. The fact is that Don Immanuel is not so much a saint as a martyr. Long ago his own faith left him. He is an atheist, a good man doomed to suffer the life of a hypocrite, pretending to a faith he does not have. As he raises the chalice of wine, his hands tremble, and a cold sweat pours from him. He cannot stop for he knows that the people need this of him, that their need is greater than his sacrifice. Still . . . still . . . could it be that Don Immanuel's whole life is a kind of prayer, a paean to God?

A writing doctor would treat men and women with equal reverence, for what is the "liberation" of either sex to him who knows the diagrams, the inner geographies of each? I love the solid heft of men as much as I adore the heated capaciousness of women—women in whose penetralia is found the repository of existence. I would have them glory in that. Women are physics and chemistry. They are matter. It is their bodies that tell of the frailty of men. Men have not their cellular, enzymatic wisdom. Man is albuminoid, proteinaceous, laked pearl; woman is yolky, ovoid, rich. Both are exuberant bloody growths. I would use the defects and deformities of each for my sacred purpose of writing, for I know that it is the marred and scarred and faulty that are subject to grace. I would seek the soul in the facts of animal economy and profligacy. Yes, it is the exact location of the soul that I am after. The smell of it is in my nostrils. I have caught glimpses of it in the body diseased. If only I could tell it. Is there no mathematical equation that can guide me? So much pain and pus equals so much truth? It is elusive as the whippoorwill that one hears calling incessantly from out the night window, but which, nesting as it does low in the brush, no one sees. No one but the poet, for he sees what no one else can. He was born with the eye for it.

Once, I thought I had it: Ten o'clock one night, the end room off a long corridor in a college infirmary, my last patient of the day, degree of exhaustion suitable for the appearance of a vision, some manifestation. The patient is a young man recently returned from Guatemala, from the excavation of Mayan ruins. His left upper arm wears a gauze dressing which, when removed, reveals a clean punched-out hole the size of a dime. The tissues about the opening are swollen and tense. A thin brownish fluid lips the edge, and now and then a lazy drop of the overflow spills down the arm. An abscess, inadequately drained. I will enlarge the opening to allow better egress of the pus. Nurse, will you get me a scalpel and some . . . ?

What happens next is enough to lay Francis Drake avomit in his cabin. No explorer ever stared in wilder surmise than I into that crater from which there now emerges a narrow gray head whose sole distinguishing feature is a pair of black pincers. The head sits atop a longish flexible neck arching now this way, now that, testing the air. Alternately it folds back upon itself, then advances in new boldness. And all the while, with dreadful rhythmicity, the unspeakable pincers open and close. Abscess? Pus? Never. Here is the lair of a beast at whose malignant purpose I could but guess. A Mayan devil, I think, that would soon burst free to fly about the room, with horrid blanket-wings and iridescent scales, raking, pinching, injecting God knows what acid juice. And even now the irony does not escape me, the irony of my patient as excavator excavated.

With all the ritual deliberation of a high priest I advance a surgical clamp toward the hole. The surgeon's heart is become a bat hanging upside down from his rib cage. The rim achieved—now thrust—and the ratchets of the clamp close upon the empty air. The devil has retracted. Evil mocking laughter bangs back and forth in the brain. More stealth. Lying in wait. One must skulk. Minutes pass, perhaps an hour. . . . A faint disturbance in the lake, and once again the thing upraises, farther and farther, hovering. Acrouch, strung, the surgeon is one with his instrument; there is no longer any boundary between its metal and his flesh. They are joined in a single perfect tool of extirpation. It is just for this that he was born. Now—thrust—and clamp—and *yes*. Got him!

Transmitted to the fingers comes the wild thrashing of the creature. Pinned and wriggling, he is mine. I hear the dry brittle scream of the dragon, and a hatred seizes me, but such a detestation as would make of Iago a drooling sucktit. It is the demented hatred of the victor for the vanquished, the warden for his prisoner. It is the hatred of fear. Within the jaws of my hemostat is the whole of the evil of the world, the dark concentrate itself, and I shall kill it. For mankind. And, in so doing, will open the way into a thousand years of perfect peace. Here is Surgeon as Savior indeed.

Tight grip now . . . steady, relentless pull. How it scrabbles to keep its tentacle-hold. With an abrupt moist plop the extraction is complete. There, writhing in the teeth of the clamp, is a dirty gray body, the size and shape of an English walnut. He is hung everywhere with tiny black hooklets. Quickly . . . into the specimen jar of saline . . . the lid screwed tight. Crazily he swims round and round, wiping his slimy head against the glass, then slowly sinks to the bottom, the mass of hooks in frantic agonal wave.

"You are going to be all right," I say to my patient. "We are *all* going to be all right from now on."

The next day I take the jar to the medical school.

"That's the larva of the botfly," says a pathologist. "The fly usually bites a cow and deposits its eggs beneath the skin. There, the egg develops into the larval form which, when ready, burrows its way to the outside through the hide and falls to the ground. In time it matures into a full-grown botfly. This one happened to bite a man. It was about to come out on its own, and, of course, it would have died."

The words *imposter*, *sorehead*, *servant of Satan* spring to my lips. But now he has been joined by other scientists. They nod in agreement. I gaze from one gray eminence to another, and know the mallet-blow of glory pulverized. I tried to save the world, but it didn't work out.

No, it is not the surgeon who is God's darling. He is the victim of vanity. It is the poet who heals with his words, stanches the flow of blood, stills the rattling breath, applies poultice to the scalded flesh.

Did you ask me why a surgeon writes? I think it is because I wish to be a doctor.

Me and My Shadow

Jane Tompkins

I wrote this essay in answer to Ellen Messer-Davidow's "The Philosophical Bases of Feminist Literary Criticisms" which appeared in the Fall 1987 issue of *New Literary History* along with several replies, including a shorter version of this one. As if it weren't distraction enough that my essay depends on someone else's, I want, before you've even read it, to defend it from an accusation. Believing that my reply, which turns its back on theory, constituted a return to the "rhetoric of presence," to an "earlier, naive, untheoretical feminism," someone, whom I'll call the unfriendly reader, complained that I was making the "old patriarchal gesture of representation" whose effect had been to marginalize women, thus "reinforcing the very stereotypes women and minorities have fought so hard to overcome." I want to reply to this objection because I think it is mistaken and because it reproduces exactly the way I used to feel about feminist criticism when it first appeared in the late 1960s.

I wanted nothing to do with it. It was embarrassing to see women, with whom one was necessarily identified, insisting in print on the differences between men's and women's experience, focusing obsessively on women authors, women characters, women's issues. How pathetic, I thought, to have to call attention to yourself in that way. And in such bad taste. It was the worst kind of special pleading, an admission of weakness so blatant it made me ashamed. What I felt then, and what I think my unfriendly reader feels now, is a version of what women who are new to feminism often feel: that if we don't call attention to ourselves *as* women, but just shut up about it and do our work, no one will notice the difference and everything will be OK.

Women who adopt this line are, understandably, afraid. Afraid of being confused with the weaker sex, the sex that goes around whining and talking about itself in an unseemly way, that can't or won't do what the big boys do ("tough it out") and so won't ever be allowed to play in the big boys' games. I am sympathetic with this position. Not long ago, as organizer of an MLA session entitled "Professional Politics: Women and the Institution," I urged a large roomful of women to "get theory" because I thought that doing theory would admit us to the big leagues and enable us at the same time to argue a feminist case in the most unimpeachable terms—those that men had supplied. I busily took my own advice, which was good as far as it went. But I now see that there has been a price for this, at least there has been for me; it is the subject of my reply to Ellen. I now tend to think that theory itself, at least as it is usually practiced, may be one of the patriarchal gestures women *and* men ought to avoid.

There are two voices inside me answering, answering to, Ellen's essay. One is the voice of a critic who wants to correct a mistake in the essay's view of epistemology. The other is the voice of a person who wants to write about her feelings (I have wanted to do this for a long time but have felt too embarrassed). This person feels it is wrong to criticize the essay philosophically and even beside the point: because a critique of the kind the critic has in mind only insulates academic discourse further from the issues that make feminism matter. That make *her* matter. The critic, meanwhile, believes such feelings, and the attitudes that inform them, are soft-minded, self-indulgent, and unprofessional.

    These beings exist separately but not apart. One writes for professional journals, the other in diaries, late at night. One uses words like "context" and "intelligibility," likes to win arguments, see her name in print, and give graduate students hardheaded advice. The other has hardly ever been heard from. She had a short story published once in a university library magazine, but her works exist chiefly in notebooks and manila folders labeled "Journal" and "Private." This person talks on the telephone a lot to her friends, has seen psychiatrists, likes cappuccino, worries about the state of her soul. Her father is ill right now, and one of her friends recently committed suicide.

    The dichotomy drawn here is false—and not false. I mean in reality there's no split. It's the same person who feels and who discourses about epistemology. The problem is that you can't talk about your private life in the course of doing your professional work. You have to pretend that epistemology, or whatever you're writing about, has nothing to do with your life, that it's more exalted, more important, because it (supposedly) *transcends* the merely personal. Well, I'm tired of the conventions that keep discussions of epistemology, or James Joyce, segregated from meditations on what is happening outside my window or inside my heart. The public-private dichotomy, which is to say, the public-private *hierarchy*, is a founding condition of female oppression. I say to hell with it. The reason I feel embarrassed at my own attempts to speak personally in a professional context is that I have been conditioned to feel that way. That's all there is to it.

    I think people are scared to talk about themselves, that they haven't got the guts to do it. I think readers want to know about each other. Sometimes, when a writer introduces some personal bit of story into an essay, I can hardly contain my pleasure. I love writers who write about their own experience. I feel I'm being nourished by them, that I'm being allowed to enter into a personal relationship with them. That I can match my own experience up with theirs, feel cousin to them, and say, yes, that's how it is.

> When he casts his leaves forth upon the wind [said Hawthorne], the author addresses, not the many who will fling aside his volume, or never take it up, but the few who will understand him. . . . As if the printed book, thrown at large on the wide world, were certain to find out the divided segment of the writer's own nature, and complete his circle of existence by bringing him into communion with it. . . . And so as thoughts are frozen and utterance, benumbed unless the speaker stand in some true relation with this audience—it may be pardonable to imagine that a friend, a kind and apprehensive, though not the closest friend, is listening to our talk. (Nathaniel Hawthorne, "The Custom-House," The Scarlet Letter, 5–6)

Hawthorne's sensitivity to the relationship that writing implies is rare in academic prose, even when the subject would seem to make awareness of the reader inevitable. Alison Jaggar gave a lecture recently that crystallized the problem. Western epistemology, she argued, is shaped by the belief that emotion should be excluded from the process of attaining knowledge. Because women in our culture are not simply encouraged but *required* to be the bearers of emotion, which men are culturally conditioned to repress, an epistemology which excludes emotions from the process of attaining knowledge radically undercuts women's epistemic authority. The idea that the conventions defining legitimate sources of knowledge overlapped with the conventions defining appropriate gender behavior (male) came to me as a blinding insight. I saw that I had been socialized from birth to feel and act in ways that automatically excluded me from participating in the culture's most valued activities. No wonder I felt so uncomfortable in the postures academic prose forced me to assume; it was like wearing men's jeans.

Ellen Messer-Davidow's essay participates—as Jaggar's lecture and my précis of it did—in the conventions of Western rationalism. It adopts the impersonal, technical vocabulary of the epistemic ideology it seeks to dislocate. The political problem posed by my need to reply to the essay is this: to adhere to the conventions is to uphold a male standard of rationality that militates against women's being recognized as culturally legitimate sources of knowledge. To break with the convention is to risk not being heard at all.

This is how I would reply to Ellen's essay if I were to do it in the professionally sanctioned way.

The essay provides feminist critics with an overarching framework for thinking about what they do, both in relation to mainstream criticism and in relation to feminist work in other fields. It allows the reader to see women's studies as a whole, furnishing useful categories for organizing a confusing and miscellaneous array of materials. It also provides excellent summaries of a wide variety of books and essays that readers might not otherwise encounter. The enterprise is carried out without pointed attacks on other theorists, without creating a cumbersome new vocabulary, without exhibitionistic displays of intellect or esoteric learning. Its practical aim—to define a field within which debate can take place—is fulfilled by *New Literary History's* decision to publish it, and to do so in a format which includes replies.

(Very nice, Jane. You sound so reasonable and generous. But, as anybody can tell you, this is just the obligatory pat on the back before the stab in the entrails.)

The difficulty with the essay from a philosophical, as opposed to a practical, point of view is that the theory it offers as a basis for future work stems from a confused notion of what an epistemology is. The author says: "An epistemology . . . consists of assumptions that knowers make about the entities and processes in a domain of study, the relations that obtain among them, and the proper methods for investigating them" (p. 87). I want to quarrel with this definition. Epistemology, strictly speaking, is a *theory* about the origins and nature of knowledge. As such, it is a set of ideas explicitly held and consciously elaborated, and thus belongs to the practice of a subcategory of philosophy called epistemology. The fact that there is a branch of philosophy given over to the study of what knowledge is and how it is acquired is important, because it means that such theories are generated not in relation to this or that "domain of study" but in relation to one another: that is, within the context of already existing epistemological theories. They are rarely based upon a study of the practices of investigators within a particular field.

An epistemology does not consist of "assumptions that knowers make" in a particular field; it is a theory about how knowledge is acquired which makes sense, chiefly, in relation to other such theories. What Messer-Davidow offers as the "epistemology" of traditional literary critics is not *their* epistemology, if in fact they have one, but her description of what she assumes their assumptions are, a description which may or may not be correct. Moreover, if literary critics should indeed elaborate a theory of how they got their beliefs, that theory would have no privileged position in relation to their actual assumptions. It would simply be another theory. This distinction—between actual assumptions and an observer's description of them (even when one is observing one's own practice)—is crucial because it points to an all-important fact about the relation of epistemology to what really gets done in a given domain of study, namely this: that epistemology, a theory about how one gets one's knowledge, in no way determines the particular knowledge that one has.

This fact is important because Messer-Davidow assumes that if we change our epistemology, our practice as critics will change, too. Specifically, she wants us to give up the subject-object theory, in which "knowledge is an abstract representation of objective existence," for a theory which says that what counts as knowledge is a function of situation and perspective. She believes that it follows from this latter theory that knowledge will become more equitable, more self-aware, and more humane.

I disagree. Knowing that my knowledge is perspectival, language-based, culturally constructed, or what have you, does not change in the slightest the things I believe to be true. All that it changes is what I think about how we get knowledge. The insight that my ideas are all products of the situation I occupy in the world applies to all of my ideas equally (including the idea that knowledge is culturally based) and to all of everybody else's ideas as well. So where does this get us? Right back to where we were before, mainly. I still believe what I believe and, if you differ with me, think that you are wrong. If I want to change your mind I still have to persuade you that I am right by using evidence, reasons, chains of inference, citations of authority, analogies, illustrations, and so on. Believing that what I believe comes from my being in a particular cultural framework does not change my relation to my beliefs. I still believe them just as much as if I thought they came from God, or the laws of nature, or my autonomous self.

Here endeth the epistle.

But while I think Ellen is wrong in thinking that a change of epistemology can mean a change in the kinds of things we think, I am in sympathy with the ends she has in view. This sympathy prompts me to say that my professionally correct reply is not on target. Because the target, the goal, rather, is not to be fighting over these questions, trying to beat the other person down. (What the goal is, it is harder to say.) Intellectual debate, if it were in the right spirit, would be wonderful. But I don't know how to be in the right spirit, exactly, can't make points without sounding rather superior and smug. Most of all, I don't know how to enter the debate without leaving everything else behind—the birds outside my window, my grief over Janice, just myself as a person sitting here in stockinged feet, a little bit chilly because the windows are open, and thinking about going to the bathroom. But not going yet.

I find that when I try to write in my "other" voice, I am immediately critical of it. It wobbles, vacillates back and forth, is neither this nor that. The voice in which I write about epistemology is familiar, I know how it ought to sound. This voice, though, I hardly know. I don't even know if it has anything to say. But if I never write in it, it never will. So I have to try. (That is why you see, this doesn't sound too good. It isn't a practiced performance, it hasn't got a surface. I'm asking you to bear with me while I try, hoping that this, what I write, will express something you yourself have felt or will help you find a part of yourself that you would like to express.)

The thing I want to say is that I've been hiding a part of myself for a long time. I've known it was there, but I couldn't listen because there was no place for this person in literary criticism. The criticism I would like to write would always take off from personal experience. Would always be in some way a chronicle of my hours and days. Would speak in a voice which can talk about everything, would reach out to a reader like me and touch me where I want to be touched. Susan Griffin's voice in "The Way of All Ideology." I want to speak in what Ursula Le Guin, at the Bryn Mawr College commencement in 1986, called the "mother tongue." This is Le Guin speaking:

The dialect of the father tongue that you and I learned best in college . . . only lectures. . . . Many believe this dialect—the expository and particularly scientific discourse—is the *highest* form of language, the true language, of which all other uses of words are primitive vestiges. . . . And it is indeed a High Language. . . . Newton's *Principia* was written in it in Latin . . . and Kant wrote German in it, and Marx, Darwin, Freud, Boas, Foucault, all the great scientists and social thinkers wrote it. It is the language of thought that seeks objectivity.

. . . The essential gesture of the father tongue is not reasoning, but distancing— making a gap, a space, between the subject or self and the object or other. . . . Everywhere now everybody speaks [this] language in laboratories and government buildings and headquarters and offices of business. . . . The father tongue is spoken from above. It goes one way. No answer is expected, or heard.

. . . The mother tongue, spoken or written, expects an answer. It is conversation, a word the root of which means "turning together." The mother tongue is language not as mere communication, but as relation, relationship. It connects. . . . Its power is not in dividing but in binding. . . . We all know it by heart. John have you got your umbrella I think it's going to rain. Can you come play with me? If I told you once I told you a hundred times. . . . O what am I going to do? . . . Pass the soy sauce please. Oh, shit. . . . You look like what the cat dragged in. (3–4)

Much of what I'm saying elaborates or circles around these quotes from Le Guin. I find that having released myself from the duty to say things I'm not interested in, in a language I resist, I feel free to entertain other people's voices. Quoting them becomes a pleasure of appreciation rather than the obligatory giving of credit, because when I write in a voice that is not struggling to be heard through the screen of a forced language, I no longer feel that it is not I who am speaking, and so there is more room for what others have said.

One sentence in Ellen's essay stuck out for me the first time I read it and the second and the third: "In time we can build a synchronous account of our subject matters as we glissade among them and turn upon ourselves" (p. 79).

What attracted me to the sentence was the "glissade." Fluidity, flexibility, versatility, mobility. Moving from one thing to another without embarrassment. It is a tenet of feminist rhetoric that the personal is political, but who in the academy acts on this where language is concerned? We all speak the father tongue, which is impersonal, while decrying the fathers' ideas. All of what I have written so far is in a kind of watered-down expository prose. Not much imagery. No description of concrete things. Only that one word, "glissade."

> Like black swallows swooping and gliding
>   in a flurry of entangled loops and curves

Two lines of a poem I memorized in high school are what the word "glissade" called to mind. Turning upon ourselves. Turning, weaving, bending, unbending, moving in loops and curves.

I don't believe we can ever turn upon ourselves in the sense Ellen intends. You can't get behind the thing that casts the shadow. *You* cast the shadow. As soon as you turn, the shadow falls in another place. It is still your shadow. You have not got "behind" yourself. That is why self-consciousness is not the way to make ourselves better than we are.

Just me and my shadow, walkin' down the avenue.

It is a beautiful day here in North Carolina. The first day that is both cool and sunny all summer. After a terrible summer, first drought, then heat-wave, then torrential rain, trees down, flooding. Now, finally, beautiful weather. A tree outside my window just brushed by red, with one fully red leaf (This is what I want you to see. A person sitting in stockinged feet looking out of her window—a floor to ceiling rectangle filled with green, with one red leaf. The season poised, sunny and chill, ready to rush down the incline into autumn. But perfect, and still. Not going yet.)

My response to this essay is not a response to something Ellen Messer-Davidow has written; it is a response to something within myself. As I reread the opening pages I feel myself being squeezed into a straitjacket; I wriggle, I will not go in. As I read the list "subject matters, methods of reasoning, and epistemology," the words will not go down. They belong to a debate whose susurrus hardly reaches my ears.

The liberation Ellen promises from the straitjacket of a subject-object epistemology is one I experienced some time ago. Mine didn't take the form she outlines, but it was close enough. I discovered, or thought I discovered, that the poststructuralist way of understanding language and knowledge enabled me to say what I wanted about the world. It enabled me to do this because it pointed out that the world I knew was a construct of ways of thinking about it and, as such, had no privileged claim on the truth. Truth in fact would always be just such a construction, and so one could offer another, competing, description and thus help to change the world that was.

The catch was that anything I might say or imagine was itself the product of an already existing discourse. Not something "I" had made up but a way of constructing things I had absorbed from the intellectual surround. Poststructuralism's proposition about the constructed nature of things held good, but that did not mean that the world could be changed by an act of will. For, as we are looking at this or that phenomenon and re-seeing it, re-thinking it, the rest of the world, that part of it from which we do the seeing, is still there, in place, real, irrefragable as a whole, and making visible what we see, though changed by it, too.

This little lecture pretends to something I no longer want to claim. The pretense is in the tone and level of the language, not in what it says about poststructuralism. The claim being made by the language is analogous to what Barthes calls the "reality effect" of historical writing, whose real message is not that this or that happened but that reality exists. So the claim of this language I've been using (and am using right now) lies in its implicit deification of the speaker. Let's call it the "authority effect." I cannot describe the pretense except to talk about what it ignores: the human frailty of the speaker, his body, his emotions, his history; the moment of intercourse with the reader—acknowledgment of the other person's presence, feelings, needs. This "authoritative" language speaks as though the other person weren't there. Or perhaps more accurately, it doesn't bother to imagine who, as Hawthorne said, is listening to our talk.

How can we speak personally to one another and yet not be self-centered? How can we be part of the great world and yet remain loyal to ourselves?

It seems to me that I am trying to write out of my experience without acknowledging any discontinuity between this and the subject matter of the profession I work in—and at the same time find that I no longer want to write about that subject matter, as it appears in Ellen's essay. I am, on the one hand, demanding a connection between literary theory and my own life and asserting, on the other, that there is no connection.

But here is a connection. I learned what epistemology I know from my husband. I think of it as more his game than mine. It's a game I enjoy playing but which I no longer need or want to play. I want to declare my independence of it, of him. (Part of what is going on here has to do with a need I have to make sure I'm not being absorbed in someone else's personality.) What I am breaking away from is both my conformity to the conventions of a male professional practice and my intellectual dependence on my husband. How can I talk about such things in public? How can I *not.*

Looking for something to read this morning, I took three books down from my literary theory shelf, in order to prove a point. The first book was Félix Guattari's *Molecular Revolution.* I find it difficult to read, and therefore have read very little of it, but according to a student who is a disciple of Deleuze and Guattari, "molecular revolution" has to do with getting away from ideology and enacting revolution within daily life. It is specific, not programmed—that is, it does not have a "method," nor "steps," and is neither psychoanalytic nor Marxist, although its discourse seems shaped by those discourses, antithetically. From this kind of revolution, said I to myself, disingenuously, one would expect some recognition of the personal. A revolution that started with daily life would have to begin, or at least would have sometimes to reside, at home. So I open at a section entitled "Towards a New Vocabulary," looking for something in the mother tongue, and this is what I find:

> The distinction I am proposing between machine and structure is based solely on the way we use the words; we may consider that we are merely dealing with a 'written device' of the kind one has to invent for dealing with a mathematical problem, or with an axiom that may have to be reconsidered at a particular stage of development, or again with the kind of machine we shall be talking about here.
>   I want therefore to make it clear that I am putting into parentheses the fact that, in reality, a machine is inseparable from its structural articulations and conversely, that each contingent structure is dominated (and this is what I want to demonstrate) by a system of machines, or at the very least by one logic machine. (111)

At this point, I start to skip, reading only the first sentence of each paragraph.

> "We may say of structure that it positions its elements . . . "
> "The agent of action, whose definition here does not extend beyond this principle of reciprocal determination . . . "
> "The machine, on the other hand remains essentially remote . . . "
> "The history of technology is dated . . . "
> "Yesterday's machine, today's and tomorrow's, are not related in their structural determinations . . . "

I find this language incredibly alienating. In fact, the paragraph after the one I stopped at begins: "The individual's relation to the machine has been described by sociologists following Friedmann as one of fundamental alienation." I will return to this essay some day and read it. I sense that it will have something interesting to say. But the effort is too great now. What strikes me now is the incredibly distancing effect of this language. It is totally abstract and impersonal. Though the author uses the first person ("The distinction I am proposing," "I want therefore to make it clear"), it quickly became clear to me that he had no interest whatsoever in the personal, or in concrete situations as I understand them—a specific person, at a specific machine, somewhere in time and space, with something on his/her mind, real noises, smells, aches and pains. He has no interest in his own experience of machines or in explaining why he is writing about them, what they mean to him personally. I take down the next book: *Poetry and Repression* by Harold Bloom.

This book should contain some reference to the self, to the author's self, to ourselves, to how people feel, to how the author feels, since its subject is psychological: repression. I open the book at page 1 and read:

> Jacques Derrida asks a central question in his essay on "Freud and the Scene of Writing": "What is a text, and what must the psyche be if it can be represented by a text?" My narrow concern with poetry prompts the contrary question: "What is a psyche, and what must a text be if it can be represented by a psyche?" Both Derrida's question and my own require exploration of three terms: "psyche," "text," "represented."
> "Psyche" is ultimately from the Indo-European root. . . . (1)

—and I stop reading.

The subject of poetry and repression will involve the asking and answering of questions about "a text"—a generalized, nonparticular object that has been the subject of endless discussion for the past twenty years—and about an equally disembodied "psyche" in relation to the thing called "a text"—not, to my mind or rather in view of my desires, a very promising relation in which to consider it. Answering these questions, moreover, will "require" (on whose part, I wonder?) the "exploration" of "three terms." Before we get to the things themselves—psyches, texts—we shall have to spend a lot of time looking at them *as words*. With the beginning of the next paragraph, we get down to the etymology of "psyche." With my agenda, I get off the bus here.

But first I look through the book. Bloom is arguing against canonical readings (of some very canonical poems) and for readings that are not exactly personal, but in which the drama of a self is constantly being played out on a cosmic stage—lots of references to God, kingdom, Paradise, the fall, the eternal—a biblical stage on which, apparently, only men are players (God, Freud, Christ, Nietzsche, and the poets). It is a drama that, although I can see how gripping Bloom can make it, will pall for me because it isn't *my* drama.

Book number three, Michel Foucault's *History of Sexuality*, is more promising. Section One is entitled "We 'other Victorians.'" So Foucault is acknowledging his and our implication in the object of the study. This book will in some way be about "ourselves," which is what I want. It begins:

> For a long time, the story goes, we supported a Victorian regime, and we continue to be dominated by it even today. Thus the image of the imperial prude is emblazoned on our restrained, mute, and hypocritical sexuality. (3)

Who, exactly, are "we"? Foucault is using the convention in which the author establishes common ground with his reader by using the first person plural—a presumptuous, though usually successful, move. Presumptuous because it presumes that we are really like him, and successful because, especially when an author is famous, and even when he isn't, "our" instinct (I criticize the practice and engage in it too) is to want to cooperate, to be included in the circle the author is drawing so cosily around "us." It is chummy, this "we." It feels good, for a little while, until it starts to feel coercive, until "we" are subscribing to things that "I" don't believe.

There is no specific reference to the author's self, no attempt to specify himself. It continues:

> At the beginning of the seventeenth century . . .

I know now where we are going. We are going to history. "At the beginning of the seventeenth century a certain frankness was still common, it would seem." Generalizations about the past, though pleasantly qualified ("a certain frankness," "it would seem"), are nevertheless disappointingly magisterial. Things continue in a generalizing vein—"it was a time of direct gestures, shameless discourse, and open transgressions." It's not so much that I don't believe him as that I am uncomfortable with the level or the mode of discourse. It is everything that, I thought, Foucault was trying to get away from in *The Archaeology of Knowledge*. The primacy of the subject as the point of view from which history could be written, the bland assumption of authority, the taking over of time, of substance, of event, the imperialism of description from a unified perspective. Even though the subject matter interests me—sex, hypocrisy, whether or not our view of Victorianism and of ourselves in relation to it is correct—I am not eager to read on. The point of view is discouraging. It will march along giving orders, barking out commands. I'm not willing to go along for the march, not even on Foucault's say-so (I am, or have been, an extravagant admirer of his).

So I turn to "my" books. To the women's section of my shelves. I take down, unerringly, an anthology called *The Powers of Desire* edited by Christine Stansell, Ann Snitow, and Sharon Thompson. I turn, almost as unerringly, to an essay by Jessica Benjamin entitled "Master and Slave: The Fantasy of Erotic Domination," and begin to read:

> This essay is concerned with the violence of erotic domination. It is about the strange union of rationality and violence that is made in the secret heart of our culture and sometimes enacted in the body. This union has inspired some of the holiest imagery of religious transcendence and now comes to light at the porno newsstands, where women are regularly depicted in the bonds of love. But the slave of love is not always a woman, not always a heterosexual; the fantasy of erotic domination permeates all sexual imagery in our culture. (281)

I am completely hooked, I am going to read this essay from beginning to end and proceed to do so. It gets better, much better, as it goes along. In fact, it gets so good, I find myself putting it down and straying from it because the subject is *so* close to home, and therefore so threatening, that I need relief from it, little breathers, before I can go on. I underline vigorously and often. Think of people I should give it to to read (my husband, this colleague, that colleague).

But wait a minute. There is no personal reference here. The author deals, like Foucault, in generalities. In even bigger ones than his: hers aren't limited to the seventeenth century or the Victorian era. She generalizes about religion, rationality, violence. Why am I not turned off by this as I was in Foucault's case? Why don't I reject this as a grand drama in the style of Bloom? Why don't I bridle at the abstractions as I did when reading Guattari? Well?

The answer is, I see the abstractions as concrete and the issues as personal. They are already personal for me without being personal*ized* because they concern things I've been thinking about for some time, struggling with, trying to figure out for myself. I don't need the author to identify her own involvement, I don't need her to concretize, because these things are already personal and concrete for me. The erotic is already eroticized.

Probably, when Guattari picks up an article whose first sentence has the words "machine," "structure," and "determination," he cathects it immediately. Great stuff. Juicy, terrific. The same would go for Bloom on encountering multiple references to Nietzsche, representation, God the father, and the Sublime. But isn't erotic domination, as a subject, surer to arouse strong feeling than systems of machines or the psyche that can be represented as a text? Clearly, the answer depends on the readership. The people at the convenience store where I stop to get gas and buy milk would find all these passages equally baffling. Though they *might* have uneasy stirrings when they read Jessica Benjamin. "Erotic domination," especially when coupled with "porno newsstands," does call some feelings into play almost no matter who you are in this culture.

But I will concede the point. What is personal is completely a function of what is perceived as personal. And what is perceived as personal by men, or rather, what is gripping, significant, "juicy," is different from what is felt to be that way by women. For what we are really talking about is not the personal as such, what we are talking about is what is important, answers one's needs, strikes one as immediately *interesting*. For women, the personal is such a category.

In literary criticism, we have moved from the New Criticism, which was antipersonal and declared the personal off-limits at every turn—the intentional fallacy, the affective fallacy—to structuralism, which does away with the self altogether—at least as something unique and important to consider—to deconstruction, which subsumes everything in language and makes the self non-self-consistent, ungraspable, a floating signifier, and finally to new historicism which re-institutes the discourse of the object—"In the seventeenth century"—with occasional side glances at how the author's "situatedness" affects his writing.

The female subject par excellence, which is her self and her experiences, has once more been elided by literary criticism.

The question is, why did this happen? One might have imagined a different outcome. The 1960s paves the way for a new personalism in literary discourse by opening literary discussion up to politics, to psychology, to the "reader," to the effects of style. What happened to deflect criticism into the impersonal labyrinths of "language," "discourse," "system," "network," and now, with Guattari, "machine"?

I met Ellen Messer-Davidow last summer at the School of Criticism and Theory where she was the undoubted leader of the women who were there. She organized them, led them (I might as well say us, since, although I was on the faculty as a visiting lecturer, she led me, too). At the end of the summer we put on a symposium, a kind of teach-in on feminist criticism and theory, of which none was being offered that summer. I thought it really worked. Some people, eager to advertise their intellectual superiority, murmured disappointment at the "level" of discussion (code for, "my mind is finer and more rigorous than yours"). One person who spoke out at the closing session said he felt bulldozed: a more honest and useful response. The point is that Ellen's leadership affected the experience of everyone at the School that summer. What she offered was not an intellectual performance calculated to draw attention to the quality of her mind, but a sustained effort of practical courage that changed the situation we were in. I think that the kind of thing Ellen did should be included in our concept of criticism: analysis that is not an end in itself but pressure brought to bear on a situation.

Now it's time to talk about something that's central to everything I've been saying so far, although it doesn't *show*, as we used to say about the slips we used to wear. If I had to bet on it, I would say that Ellen Messer-Davidow was motivated last summer, and probably in her essay, by anger (forgive me, Ellen, if I am wrong), anger at her, our, exclusion from what was being studied at the School, our exclusion from the discourse of "Western man." I interpret her behavior this way because anger is what fuels my engagement with feminist issues; an absolute fury that has never even been tapped, relatively speaking. It's time to talk about this now, because it's so central, at least for me. I hate men for the way they treat women, and pretending that women aren't there is one of the ways I hate most.

Last night I saw a movie called *Gunfight at the OK Corral*, starring Burt Lancaster and Kirk Douglas. The movie is patently about the love-relationship between the characters these men play—Wyatt Earp and Doc Holliday. The women in the movie are merely pawns that serve in various ways to reflect the characters of the men and to advance the story of their relationship to one another. There is a particularly humiliating part, played by Jo Van Fleet, the part of Doc Holliday's mistress—Kate Fisher—whom he treats abominably (everybody in the movie acknowledges this, it's not just me saying so). This woman is degraded over and over again. She is a whore, she is a drunkard, she is a clinging woman, she betrays the life of Wyatt Earp in order to get Doc Holliday back, she is *no longer young* (perhaps this is her chief sin). And her words are always in vain, they are chaff, less than nothing, another sign of her degradation.

Now Doc Holliday is a similarly degraded character. He used to be a dentist and is now a gambler who lives to get other people's money away from them; he is a drunk, and he abuses the woman who loves him. But his weaknesses, in the perspective of the movie, are glamorous. He is irresistible, charming, seductive, handsome, witty, commanding; it's no wonder Wyatt Earp falls for him, who wouldn't? The degradation doesn't stick to Kirk Douglas; it is all absorbed by his female counterpart, the "slut," Jo Van Fleet. We are embarrassed every time she appears on the screen, because every time, she is humiliated further.

What enrages me is the way women are used as extensions of men, mirrors of men, devices for showing men off, devices for helping men get what they want. They are never there in their own right, or rarely. The world of the Western contains no women.

Sometimes I think *the world* contains no women.

Why am I so angry?

My anger is partly the result of having been an only child who caved in to authority very early on. As a result I've built up a huge storehouse of hatred and resentment against people in authority over me (mostly male). Hatred and resentment and attraction.

Why should poor men be made the object of this old pent-up anger? (Old anger is the best anger, the meanest, the truest, the most intense. Old anger is pure because it's been dislocated from its source for so long, has had the chance to ferment, to feed on itself for so many years, so that it is nothing but anger. All cause, all relation to the outside world, long since sloughed off, withered away. The rage I feel inside me now is the distillation of forty-six years. It has had a long time to simmer, to harden, to become adamantine, a black slab that glows in the dark.)

Are all feminists fueled by such rage? Is the molten lava of millennia of hatred boiling below the surface of every essay, every book, every syllabus, every newsletter, every little magazine? I imagine that I can open the front of my stomach like a door, reach in, and pluck from memory the rooted sorrow, pull it out, root and branch. But where, or rather, who, would I be then? I am attached to this rage. It is a source of identity for me. It is a motivator, an explainer, a justifier, a no-need-to-say-more greeter at the door. If I were to eradicate this anger somehow, what would I do? Volunteer work all day long?

A therapist once suggested to me that I blamed on sexism a lot of stuff that really had to do with my own childhood. Her view was basically the one articulated in Alice Miller's *The Drama of the Gifted Child*, in which the good child has been made to develop a false self by parents who cathect the child narcissistically. My therapist meant that if I worked out some of my problems—as she understood them, on a psychological level—my feminist rage would subside.

Maybe it would, but that wouldn't touch the issue of female oppression. Here is what Miller says about this:

> Political action can be fed by the unconscious anger of children who have been . . . mis-used, imprisoned, exploited, cramped, and drilled. . . . If, however, disillusionment and the resultant mourning can be lived through . . ., then social and political disengagement do not usually follow, but the patient's actions are freed from the compulsion to repeat. (101)

According to Miller's theory, the critical voice inside me, the voice I noticed butting in, belittling, doubting, being wise, is "the contemptuous introject."—the introjection of authorities who manipulated me, without necessarily meaning to. I think that if you can come to terms with your "contemptuous introjects," learn to forgive and understand them, your anger will go away.

But if you're not angry, can you still act? Will you still care enough to write the letters, make the phone calls, attend the meetings? You need to find another center within yourself from which to act. A center of outgoing, outflowing, giving feelings. Love instead of anger. I'm embarrassed to say words like these because I've been taught they are mushy and sentimental and smack of cheap popular psychology. I've been taught to look down on people who read M. Scott Peck and Leo Buscaglia and Harold Kushner, because they're people who haven't very much education and because they're mostly women. Or if not women, then people who take responsibility, for learning how to deal with their feelings, who take responsibility for marriages that are going bad, for children who are in trouble, for friends who need help, for themselves. The disdain for popular psychology and for words like "love" and "giving" is part of the police action that academic intellectuals wage ceaselessly against feeling, against women, against what is personal. The ridiculing of the "touchy-feely," of the "Mickey Mouse," of the sentimental (often associated with teaching that takes students' concerns into account), belongs to the tradition Alison Jaggar rightly characterized as founding knowledge in the denial of emotion. It is looking down on women, with whom feelings are associated, and on the activities with which women are identified: mother, nurse, teacher, social worker, volunteer.

So for a while I can't talk about epistemology. I can't deal with the philosophical bases of feminist literary criticisms. I can't strap myself psychically into an apparatus that will produce the right gestures when I begin to move. I have to deal with the trashing of emotion and with my anger against it.

This one time I've taken off the straitjacket, and it feels so good.

References

Benjamin, Jessica. "Master and Slave: The Fantasy of Erotic Domination." *The Powers of Desire: The Politics of Sexuality*. Ed. Ann Snitow, Christine Stansell, and Sharon Thompson. New York: Monthly Review Press, 1983. 280–89.

Bloom, Harold. *Poetry and Repression: Revision from Blake to Stevens*. New Haven, Conn.: Yale UP, 1976.

Foucault, Michel. *The History of Sexuality*, Volume 1: *An Introduction*. Trans. Robert Hurley. New York: Vintage Books, 1980. Copyright 1978 by Random House. [Originally published in French as *La Volonté de Savoir*. Paris: Editions Gallimard, 1976.]

Griffin, Susan. "The Way of All Ideology." *Made from the Earth: An Anthology of Writings*. New York: Harper & Row, 1982. 161–82.

Guattari, Félix. *Molecular Revolution: Psychiatry and Politics*. Trans. Rosemary Sheed, intro. David Cooper. New York: Penguin Books, 1984. [First published as *Psychanalyse et transversalité* (1972), and *La Révolution moléculaire* (1977).]

Hawthorne, Nathaniel. *The Scarlet Letter and Other Tales of the Puritans*. Ed. with an intro. and notes by Harry Levin. Boston: Houghton Mifflin, 1960–61.

Le Guin, Ursula. "The Mother Tongue." *Bryn Mawr Alumnae Bulletin* (Summer 1986): 3–4.

Miller, Alice. *The Drama of the Gifted Child*. New York: Basic Books, 1983.

Experimental Critical Writing

Marianna Torgovnick

At the 1988 MLA Convention I gave a paper called "Malinowski's Body." Since I was afraid to give this paper, I had announced it in the program by the deliberately neutral title "Looking at Anthropologists" so that I could change my mind up to the last minute and substitute something else instead. I was afraid because "Malinowski's Body" does not resemble the usual MLA paper in style or content. I knew that the audience would listen to it and respond to it, and I knew that some members of the audience would not like it and might even walk out—and not because there was another talk they wanted to hear at the same hour.

"Malinowski's Body" did not begin its life in any of the ways I have been taught to consider legitimate. In fact, I wrote it, almost as a dare, after my writing group found the first material I wrote on Malinowski dull. To prove I could do better I went home and wrote several pages that begin this way:

> Malinowski's body looks like Lord Jim's. It's cased rigidly in white or beige trousers and shirt that sometimes becomes stained a muddy brown. When this happens, Malinowski summons his servants and has the clothes washed, immediately. For his clothes somehow seem to him an important part of his body, not just a covering for it.
>
> It's a small body, well fed but not kindly disposed enough toward itself to put on flesh. It has a narrow chest—pale, with just a few hairs and no nipples to speak of. It has thin legs yearning for massive thighs; in fact, if this man does put on weight in later life (and he may) it will show in his thighs first. The buttocks lie flat, unwelcoming, with maybe a stray pimple. The penis is a center of anxiety for him but is in fact no smaller—and no bigger—than anyone else's. It's one of the few points of identification he can settle on between his body and theirs.
>
> Their bodies—almost naked—unnerve him. His body needs its clothes; his head, its hat. He rarely looks at his body—except when washing it. But he has to look at theirs. The dislike he sometimes feels for the natives comes over

him especially when in the presence of their bodies. "Come in and bathe," the
natives say from their ponds and rivers. "No, thanks," says Malinowski, retrieving the pith helmet and camera he momentarily laid aside on the grass.
He looks at their bodies and takes notes about size, ornamentation, haircuts,
and other ethnographic data. He takes photographs. He talks to them about
customs, trade, housing, sex. He feels okay about the customs, trade, and
housing, but the sex makes him uneasy.

The pages are based on an intuition and a hunch about what Malinowski
looked like that were formed before I had found any pictures of him. They begin with an image rather than with the kind of concise generalization that had
been my customary opening. And they were designed to loosen my prose by
giving my imagination free play. Inevitably, I used what I had read by and
about Malinowski—but in an almost unrecognizable way. My premise was
that I would undress the ethnographer for study as Malinowski himself undresses subjects in his ethnographies and undresses, in his diary, the women
he meets in daily life. When I wrote "Malinowski's Body" I did not intend to
use it in the book I was writing. My goals were simply to limber up my style
and to get in touch with what I wanted to say. But "Malinowski's Body" makes
so many points about the ethnographer's scripting of himself according to conventional ideas of what is moral and manly that I decided to include it in my
book. It is a creative piece, risky for the MLA. And yet my audience, or at least
most of its members, seemed delighted. They asked questions about my "intentions" and "effects" that made me feel like a writer, not just a critic—a heady
moment for me and a reception that gave David Laurence reason to invite me
to present my thoughts on experimental critical writing. And it was a moment
that had not come easily.

When I began to write my newest book—called *Gone Primitive* and published in the spring of 1990—I knew that I wanted to write something significantly different in tone and style from my first two books. I had recently been
tenured and then promoted to full professor, and I felt that I was no longer writing for any committees—I was writing for myself. It was not that I would rewrite
the books I had written; I am in fact proud of them. What I wanted was to reach a
larger audience and to go somewhere new. What I discovered was that at first I
did not know how.

The turning point came when I showed an early chapter to the members of
my newly formed writing group. I was writing on an untraditional, uncanonical
topic—Edgar Rice Burroughs' Tarzan novels—but my approach was conventional and scholarly. I began by surveying the critical literature on Tarzan and
protesting (a little uneasily) that earlier critics either had overidentified with Burroughs or had not taken Tarzan seriously with regard to race and gender relations. I tried to pack lots of statistics and facts in the opening paragraphs to prove
that Tarzan was important. In my eagerness to meet accepted standards of academic seriousness, I had succeeded (to borrow a phrase Wayne Booth once used to
describe the freshman essay) in being "boring from within."

The members of my group, from whom I had asked no mercy that day, showed none. The chapter was sluggish, they said; the prose was lifeless and cold. It had no momentum, no narrative. Instinctively, I defended myself; I talked about all the interesting things that happened as I was researching and writing the chapter, telling them how I often found articles on the rebirth of the Tarzan phenomenon in issues of magazines that report the assassination of President Kennedy and reproduce those astonishing pictures we all remember of Jackie and little John-John and of Oswald. I had tried in the chapter to place the Tarzan series in the contexts of the twenties (the decade of its first great popularity) and the sixties (the decade of its rebirth). But I had used a style that censored my own experiences and visceral responses and that hid my writing's source of energy. One member of the group said, cannily, "You know, none of what you've just said comes out in this chapter. And there's a huge difference between the things you say and the things you write. You never write anything funny. You often say funny things." She was right. The other members of the group asked me to say more about La, a barbarian priestess in the Tarzan novels whom I had mentioned in passing. As I warmed to my description of La's importance and La's wrongs, my friend said, "When you start to get dull, pretend you are La—because you *are* La." And she was also right.

For me, "writing like La" became a metaphor for getting to a place where I was not afraid to write in a voice that had passion as well as information—a voice that wanted to be heard. "Writing like La" meant letting myself out of the protective cage of the style I had mastered—a style I now call the thus-and-therefore style because it naturally tends to include distancing words like those. Before I could change my thus-and-therefore style, I had to defamiliarize it; I had to know my cage so that I could open it at will. A fifteen-minute exercise I did with my writing group was a significant breakthrough. In this exercise, I parodied my own dullest style in a description of grocery stores in Durham, North Carolina. I began the description with just the kind of generalization that was one of my primary tics as a writer: "In Durham, one can shop at Food Lion for bargains, or Kroger's for selection. The most interesting shopping of all, however, is done at Harris Teeter." This exercise made me laugh at my own habits and made it impossible for me afterward to write unknowingly in my usual way. But there were still many low points, when I found myself unable to do anything *but* write in my dullest style. In fact, I wrote my excruciatingly bad beginning on Malinowski— the material I replaced with "Malinowski's Body"—roughly eighteen months after I vowed to leave my old style behind.

In preparing this presentation, I discovered in my files my first draft on Malinowski. I would like to share part of its beginning with you as an example of one sort of standard academic prose:

> Implicitly, I have been suggesting that "objectivity" is a delusory principle undergirding both important strands of social scientific and ethnographic thought and aesthetic and artistic-literary theories and methods. Rereading Malinowski, I think I've found a direct and interesting analogy.

Malinowski founded what is called functionalism in anthropology, the theory (and derived method) that explains all elements of a culture in terms of interlocking functions: the ethnographer explicitly "constructs" a model in which all the parts are presumed to contribute to a whole that is organic and unified (though quirkier than a machine). To make his construction, the ethnographer lives inside the culture, inhabits it as a text. He tries to replicate the native's point of view, which is the ground and touchstone of meaning and "accuracy." Functionalism leads, in anthropology, to what is called structural functionalism and then, later, to structuralism.

A point-by-point analogy with New Criticism and other formal approaches exists. Here too the "student" (critic) inhabits the text, assuming the unity of the parts as a whole and constructing an account of that whole in terms of the interlocking functions of its parts. The original ground of meaning is the author's intentions.

What I was doing in these paragraphs was the writerly equivalent of scratching at a scab. I had to say what was closest to the surface of my mind in order to get rid of that content, in order to discover whether it was useful or not, interesting or not. Sometimes, what I write first as a throwaway turns out to contain the intellectual core of my argument; sometimes, as in this real throwaway, it does not. The difference is usually whether I begin with material that I really care about or with material that I think I should care about. In this instance, I began with critical categories and genealogies of influence that I knew, by training, were considered important—and I trotted them out dutifully. Other critics had scratched these scabs; now it was my turn. The paragraphs include a lot of qualifications and distinctions, often inserted in parenthetical remarks, that would be unlikely to interest anyone but me. Sticky academic language coats the whole—"implicitly," "explicitly," "strand of thought." And I explain things in more detail than most people would want to read.

I would be too embarrassed to reproduce this rejected passage if I did not realize that it's representative of the prose that I—and I suspect many of you—habitually write. For this style typifies a great deal of academic writing. How did it come to be a norm? Largely, I think by establishing itself in an era when less criticism was published and the circle of critics was small enough to allow its members to believe they were contributing to the building of a common edifice. In this construction project all the names could and should be named, like those of contributors on a memorial plaque; Professor Z would build on what Professors X and Y had said in their essays; years later, Professors A and B would come along and add some decorative touches or do major renovations.

All of us who write criticism today wrote dissertations yesterday. And our teachers often tried, and succeeded in handing on what they perceived as the correct—that is, the careful, the judicious, the fair—way to write. But the styles we were taught can't work now in the same way as they worked fifty or even fifteen years ago. No one who gets around to writing a book, or even an essay, ever reads everything that has been written about its subject. Yet we cling to the fiction of completeness and coverage that the academic style preserves. This style protects us, we fondly believe, from being careless or subjective or unfair. It prescribes certain moves to ensure that the writer will stay within the boundaries that the academy has drawn.

Like many people who choose an academic life, I have a fundamental need for approval. I needed approval from my graduate advisers, tenure and promotion committees, and reviewers; I need it from my students and colleagues. It has been crucial for me in the last few years to have a writing group that approved of my new writing style: the group provided a different audience from the one I once imagined as my academic superiors, who judged the material I wrote according to more traditional standards. But I have also become aware that I am now not just someone in need of approval but also someone (like many of you) who gives or withholds approval. When we pass on the academic style to our graduate students or newest colleague, we train them to stay within the boundaries, both stylistically and conceptually. When we encourage experimental critical writing, we do not always know what we will get, but we stimulate the profession to grow and to change. We don't control the future of the profession only when we give grades or make hiring or tenure decisions; we control it at the level of the sentence.

At this point I need to back up a bit. It seems pretty clear to me that if all we want to do is to write for professional advancement, to write for a fairly narrow circle of critics who exist within the same disciplinary boundaries as we do, there is nothing really wrong with the traditional academic style. In fact, it's the right style, the inevitable style, because it says, in every superfluous detail and in every familiar move, You don't need to read me except to write your own project; I am the kind of writing that does not want to be heard.

But when critics want to be read, and especially when they want to be read by a large audience, they have to court their readers. And the courtship begins when the critic begins to think of himself or herself as a writer as well, a process that for me, as for some other critics of my generation, means writing as a person with feelings, histories, and desires—as well as information and knowledge. When writers want to be read they have to be more flexible and take more chances than the standard scholarly style allows: often, they have to be more direct and more personal. In a very real way (although my writing includes precious few autobiographical revelations), I could not think of myself as a writer until I risked exposing myself in my writing.

I am not talking here, necessarily, about full-scale autobiographical writing—though I am not ruling it out either. But I am saying that writerly writing is personal writing, whether or not it is autobiographical. Even if it offers no facts from the writer's life, or offers just a hint of them here and there, it makes the reader know some things about the writer—a fundamental condition, it seems to me, of any real act of communication. And real communication is exciting. For me, at any rate, the experience of this new kind of writing—which not only recognizes the pitfalls of the standard academic style but goes out of its way to avoid them—has been exhilarating.

Part 3

Composing Creative Nonfiction

In the earlier sections of this book you've had the chance to pair up what people write when they write creative nonfiction with what people talk about when they talk about creative nonfiction. Many of the writers whose work appears in Part One also talk about the genre in which they work in Part Two. They often also talk about the ways they typically create the work they do in creative nonfiction. In Part Three we take the discussion a little farther by pairing four pieces that could have gone into the first part of this book with four pieces in which their authors describe how they wrote them.

Writers' descriptions of what they did and what they went through as they wrote a particular essay or article often suggest strategies that other writers can use. Even the most experienced writers occasionally find themselves stymied by projects they've been working on, but because they are experienced they have strategies to fall back on that help them to begin writing again. Often their strategies arise not from their own problem solving but by the example of another writer. For example, many writers in many different forms have subscribed to Horace's advice, "Never a day without a line." They try to write every day, even if only for a limited time, because they find there is a creative equivalent of the law of inertia—"A mind in motion tends to stay in motion; a pen at rest tends to stay at rest." To that perhaps they add Hemingway's advice to quit writing for the day before you've exhausted your energy and your ideas and to return to writing the next day knowing where you're going to start up again. There are many sound principles and practices in the creative life, and writers often must rummage among them for the ones that work for them. They also have to be prepared to discard them if they aren't working or if they don't seem to be very useful for a different project. Writers have to be flexible and adaptable in order to be productive, and the best place to find useful strategies and techniques other than those you discover for yourself is in the discoveries that other writers have made for themselves.

Even when writers have been successful in the past and would appear to know a number of moves they might make in their writing, they sometimes need to be reminded of the things they already know about writing. Sometimes the press of a work-in-progress makes it difficult to step back from it and apply alternative approaches, until the writer stumbles on something someone else did and remembers that he or she knew about that approach before. Some writers collect quotes about writing and, to help them remember, tape them to the wall or the word processor—some writers have *a lot* of stuff sticking to their walls, because there's *a lot* of relevant advice out there.

Consider this section, then, as a way to see what other writers have done as they wrote the kind of writing you've been reading in this book. Taken as a whole, the Composing Creative Nonfiction section presents four pairs of essays, arranged alphabetically by author. The first piece in each pair serves as the focus of the second piece, which explains the writer's composing processes on that particular work. Reading all eight pieces together is like sitting in on a writing group where each member reads something she's written and then explains what she went through to get the final draft. The writing is different enough that the responses of the writers and the shifting demands of purpose and form offer a range of strategies and creative decisions. Emily Chase's "Warping Time with Montaigne" is a personal critical essay linking the practices of Montaigne, the original essayist, with those of contemporary writer Richard Rodriguez in his essay "Late Victorians"; her "Notes from a Journey toward 'Warping Time'" explains how this piece of what Marianna Torgovnick calls "experimental critical writing" came about. Simone Poirier-Bures writes a travel memoir in "That Shining Place: Crete, 1966"; her "Afterword: Writing 'The Greece Piece'" traces the course of her attempts to write about the experience more than twenty years later. Mary Elizabeth Pope's "Teacher Training" is an essay running in two parallel strands, one about her first teaching experience, the other about her fourth-grade teacher; "Composing 'Teacher Training'" follows the development of the essay from inception to publication, including changes after the piece was accepted. Maureen Stanton writes a very personal memoir of her fiance's illness in "Zion" and recounts how she composed the essay in "On Writing 'Zion'." Four very different essays, four very different composing processes.

The selections here also connect to pieces in other parts of the book, and they can be read separately, in conjunction with other examples and discussions. Emily Chase's work is related to other pieces demonstrating or discussing personal voice in academic writing, such as those by Jane Tompkins and Marianna Torgovnick. Simone Poirier-Bures's pairing connects to the other writing about time and place in the book, whether in memoir, essay, or literary journalism, including the writing by Mary Clearman Blew, Mimi Schwartz, Pico Iyer, and Patricia Hampl. Mary Elizabeth Pope's writing can handily supplement the segmented essays in the book, especially those that leap lightly across time and space, such as the essays of Mary Clearman Blew, Naomi Shihab Nye, and Nancy Willard. Maureen Stanton's memoir is appropriate to read along with any of the other memory pieces in the book as well as the essays dwelling on the human body and health, such as those by Phillip Lopate, Lucia Perillo, and Richard Selzer. Already in trying to cite a few relevant examples I've begun to repeat references, but that's because the writing in Part Three reverberates in so many other readings throughout the book.

The other connection these selections make is, of course, to your writing. The process pieces here, where the writers describe composing their essays, don't prescribe fail-safe procedures to which you should conform—quite the contrary. As these examples show, writers don't follow a rigid set of universal rules for composing; instead, they rely on general approaches and alternative strategies that they can alter to fit the shape of their individual works-in-progress. The experiences of these writers suggest strategies that you might be able to adapt to your own projects. They would be valuable to consult when you find yourself beginning or developing similar writing projects.

Finally, as you compose your own essays and assignments, you might consider keeping a journal on your own composing processes, to get a handle on what you generally do when you write and what you've done especially for certain projects. Think of Composing Creative Nonfiction as sitting in on a writing group in session, and feel free to enter the conversation with your own writing about your own composing.

Warping Time with Montaigne

Emily D. Chase

I sit bent over the breast beam of my 38 inch LeClerc floor loom pulling individual threads of brilliant, durable yarn through the metal heddles of its six harnesses. The heddles that have already been threaded hang in orderly lines waiting for the command to raise and lower those threads of yarn in the process of creating fabric; the unthreaded heddles hang in unorganized clusters patiently waiting for their turn to take part. This threading process is called "warping the loom" because the yarn that is being threaded onto the loom will become the "warp"—or lengthwise threads—in the fabric that will be woven. This process of reaching through the heddle with the threading hook, catching a strand of yarn, and pulling it back through the heddle does not require a lot of thought, other than that required to make sure the right piece of yarn gets threaded through the right heddle. My mind is free to wander as it will while I prepare my loom. "My style and my mind alike go roaming," Montaigne said (761). Of course I think of Montaigne; I have just spent two weeks reading essays by Montaigne, about Montaigne, and about essayists who have written essays on Montaigne. I have Montaigne on the brain: What sort of essays would Montaigne write if he were still alive? What would he say about the essays being written today? In particular, what would he say about Richard Rodriguez's essay "Late Victorians"? I pull a strand of yarn through a heddle and think of Montaigne and Rodriguez.

Rodriguez's essay uses many of the elements of the genre that Montaigne created. If Montaigne had not spun the first ideas of the essay into a new genre of literature, Rodriguez would not have been able to write "Late Victorians" without first spinning the thread of the genre on his own. I see that Montaigne's thoughts and ideas have been pulled through time to be used as the warp of essays since Montaigne's book *Essais* was first published in 1580. Now I am the one sitting at the loom of time, pulling the thoughts and ideas of Montaigne through the heddles. The full body of Montaigne's essays lies rolled up upon itself on the warp beam of the loom, waiting to be used by anyone with the knowledge and patience to thread it through time and secure it to this side of the past.

I reach through the eyelet of a heddle for a piece of Montaigne and imagine Rodriguez doing the same thing as he created "Late Victorians." For, certainly, he pulled Montaigne's motto through time—"Que scais-je?" (What do I know?). Rodriguez explores this question in "Late Victorians" as he asks himself how he should live his life and how he should *have lived* his life. These are the central questions and themes of his essay. He asks himself if he should have pursued "an earthly paradise charming," like the gay men he has known who have since died of AIDS (131). He considers the possibility of having pursued a career in office buildings which "were hives where money was made, and damn all" (128). At the end of "Late Victorians," he questions his future: Should he remain shifting his "tailbone upon the cold, hard pew," or should he rise to join the volunteers of the local AIDS Support Group (134)?

The genre of the essay offers Rodriguez an opportunity to explore these issues by using Montaigne's question, "What do I know?" Montaigne says:

> This . . . happens to me: that I do not find myself in the place where I look; and I find myself more by chance encounter than by searching my judgment. I will have tossed off some subtle remark as I write. Later I have lost the point so thoroughly that I do not know what I meant; and sometimes a stranger has discovered it before I do. If I erased every passage where this happens to me, there would be nothing left of myself. (26–27)

The form of the essay as Montaigne conceived it allows Rodriguez the freedom to seek answers, or to appear to seek answers, *while* he writes rather than exclusively *before* he writes. For Montaigne, writing was an *essai*, a trial or attempt. The presence of self and the absence of conclusion create a sense of freedom within Montaigne's essays. As he says: "The surest thing, in my opinion, would be to trace our actions to the neighboring circumstances, without getting into any further research and without drawing from them any other conclusions" (241). Like Montaigne, Rodriguez comes to no irrefutable conclusions in "Late Victorians." Instead, his thoughts wander through memories and observations as he seeks an understanding of the world by examining the things which touch his life directly.

As I consider the themes of "Late Victorians," I think of the title of one of Montaigne's essays, "By diverse means we arrive at the same end" (3). It occurs to me that this title describes the realm in which Rodriguez's thoughts wander. For what is Rodriguez writing about but diverse lifestyles and inevitable death? Running across his essay are the threads of gay life and death from AIDS. The texture of the weave is enhanced by Rodriguez's use of details from his own experience; these details form the weft of his essay, the crosswise threads. This weft is beaten into the fabric of "Late Victorians," as the "beater" on a loom locks the warp and weft tightly together by pushing each strand of weft snugly against the preceding strand, creating a cohesive, durable piece of fabric. Rodriguez weaves the fourteen sections of "Late Victorians" in this way, choosing different yarns for the weft of each section to create different textures and density of prose.

The first section is brief and is composed of two conflicting quotes. The first, by St. Augustine, hints at our discontent on earth in our mortal form due to our intuition that we are destined for a better life after death. Life is something to be restlessly passed through. The second quote, by Elizabeth Taylor, speaks of "cerulean" days in this life being undermined by sadness in the knowledge that these days and this life must end. These quotes show that, like Proteus, we are able to change our shape (the shape of our thoughts) as we try to avoid being bound by life. We are free to choose which way we will view life, whether we will suffer life and rejoice the end or embrace life and mourn the end. In "Late Victorians," Rodriguez tries to decide which view is the better view. He weaves these two quotes into his text to prepare us for the creation which is to follow. What is life? What is death? Which one wears the mask covering reality?

Throughout the essay, Rodriguez portrays the paradox of homosexual life in San Francisco. He uses the image of the Victorian house to help him accomplish this. By noting that the "three- or four-story Victorian house, like the Victorian novel, was built to contain several generations and several classes under one roof, behind a single oaken door" (123), he reveals the irony of the housing market whereby "gay men found themselves living with the architectural metaphor for family" (122). From this image, Rodriguez goes exploring through the homosexual landscape of his life and discovers multiple conflicting images. Rodriguez says, "The age-old description of homosexuality is of a sin against nature," yet he observes that as the peaceful, domestic, homosexual community of the Castro district thrived, the perverted "assortment of leather bars . . . outlaw sexuality . . . eroticism of the dark" on heterosexual Folsom street also thrived (124–25). In the Castro district, thanks to gays, "where recently there had been loudmouthed kids, hole-in-the-wall bars, [and] pimps," there were now "tweeds and perambulators, matrons and nannies" (125). The gay men, who have chosen to embrace "the complacencies of the barren house," have made the streets safe once again for the family (127).

This depiction of peaceful homosexual life is strikingly linked to another paradox of gay life as Rodriguez describes two parades in which gay men with AIDS march for gay rights. Rodriguez depicts gay men in one Gay Freedom Day parade as "the blessed in Renaissance paintings," martyrs who cherish "the apparatus of [their] martyrdom" (119). This passage is followed immediately by a description of a parade five years later, which includes "plum-spotted young men." The juxtaposition of the two passages creates the disturbing impression that these people are fighting to choose the way they wish to die rather than the way they wish to live.

How is Rodriguez going to reconcile all of these conflicting images? I pull another strand of Montaigne through time and see that the essay, as a form, allows Rodriguez to go exploring without *having* to reconcile these images. Montaigne says in his essay "Of repentance":

> This is a record of various and changeable occurrences, and of irresolute and, when it so befalls, contradictory ideas: whether I am different myself, or whether I take hold of my subjects in different circumstances and aspects. So, all in all, I may indeed contradict myself now and then; but truth, as Demades said, I do not contradict. If my mind could gain a firm footing, I would not make essays; I would make decisions; but it is always in apprenticeship and on trial. (611)

Montaigne is speaking of his contradictory thoughts and ideas, and yet the passage is equally applicable to Rodriguez's treatment of the paradox of gay life.

Montaigne's passage makes me wonder, as I slowly and steadily thread my way across the loom, if ALL of Montaigne is present in the warp of Rodriguez's essay. Would all of Montaigne's writings have to be threaded through time as an inseparable skein of thought, in order to remain true as a body of writing? Or could a person be selective when choosing which parts she pulled through time? I think of the warp on my loom, and I know that it is not possible to thread just part of a warp through the heddles. ALL of the strands of warp must be threaded, or the warp becomes tangled and knotted on the loom. For this reason, I have to think that all of Montaigne's thoughts are present in the warp of an essay, even when an essay presents an opposing view of that held by Montaigne.

I ponder this question because of the way I have linked Montaigne's quote from his essay "Of repentance" to the image of the AIDS victims in the Gay Freedom Day parades. The quote is pertinent as it applies to the issue of contradictions and paradox, yet Montaigne and Rodriguez do not agree completely on the actual subject of repentance. Both Montaigne and Rodriguez recognize the value of youth and of what is often deemed youth's foolishness. Rodriguez says:

> Though I am alive now, I do not believe that an old man's pessimism is truer than a young man's optimism simply because it comes after. There are things a young man knows that are true and are not yet in the old man's power to recollect. (120)

This is similar to a passage of Montaigne's, in his essay "Of repentance" in which he says:

> I should be ashamed and resentful if the misery and misfortune of my decrepitude were to be thought better than my good, healthy, lively, vigorous years, and if people were to esteem me not for what I have been, but for ceasing to be that. (619)

On the issue of repentance itself, however, Montaigne and Rodriguez differ. While Montaigne declares, "If I had to live over again, I would live as I have lived" (620), Rodriguez says, "It was then I saw that the greater sin against heaven was my unwillingness to embrace life" (132). There is an edge of repentance in Rodriguez's text, which does not exist in Montaigne's writings.

We are never sure, however, of what it is that Rodriguez feels the need to repent. In boldly talking about the gay community in San Francisco, Rodriguez appears to be revealing himself as a gay man, yet Phillip Lopate says, "Richard Rodriguez, for instance, is a master of the confessional tone, yet he tells us that his family calls him 'Mr. Secrets,' and he plays a hide-and-seek game of revealing himself" (xxvii). This is the case in "Late Victorians." Rodriguez describes the gay community of San Francisco from the perspective of a person who has been a part of that community. He has marched in a Gay Freedom Day parade; he has many male friends who are gay; he lives in a Victorian house which has been reclaimed and redecorated by gay men and now contains "four apartments; four single men"; he says, "To grow up homosexual is to live with secrets and within secrets" (122). And yet, on his deathbed, a friend of Rodriguez's, Cesar, says with irony that Rodriguez "would be the only one spared," that he was "too circumspect" (131). Rodriguez never actually says that he is gay. What are we to think?

I continue the process of pulling strands of yarn and thought through the loom: Does it matter if Rodriguez is gay? Does it matter if he tells us he is or isn't gay? What do I, as a reader, think of the authority of voice in the piece if this information appears to be purposefully concealed? Essayist E. B. White declared, "There is one thing the essayist cannot do—he cannot indulge himself in deceit or in concealment, for he will be found out in no time" (xxvi). And yet Alexander Smith wrote of Montaigne, "If you wish to preserve your secret, wrap it up in frankness" (Lopate xxvii). Montaigne said, "We must remove the mask," but he also said that he has "painted [his] inward self with colors clearer than [his] original ones" (504). Clearly, the act of making one's private thoughts public is not as simple as just recording the observations of one's life or even of simply attempting to capture one's mind in the act of thinking, as Montaigne set out to do.

I look back across the loom at the threads I have pulled through the heddles and am reminded that essays consist of explorations, questions, and contradictions. In his essay "Late Victorians," Rodriguez questions his life and lifestyle. Should he embrace life and mourn death, as his gay friends do, or should he withhold himself from life and look forward to death, as he does in his role as a skeptic? "Skepticism became my demeanor toward them—I was the dinner-party skeptic, a firm believer in Original Sin and in the limits of possibility" (Rodriguez 131). Rodriguez does not find the answer to his question in "Late Victorians." In the essay, he remains shifting his "tailbone on the cold, hard pew" while he tries to decide which role to play—which mask to put on or, perhaps, which mask to take off.

It is the *quest* for answers rather than the answers themselves that distinguishes the Montaignian essay. In this respect, "Late Victorians" is a good example of a contemporary essay that has been woven on a warp of Montaigne. In other respects, such as the inclusion of quotations, the essay differs from those of Montaigne. (Montaigne's essays include numerous quotations, Rodriguez's few.) However, when I gaze across the warp threaded through my loom, I am reminded that even this difference is a tribute to Montaigne, for I see Montaigne's strand of thought that advocates rebellion against accepted forms of discourse, including his own.

It is likely that Montaigne's thoughts go warping through most literary nonfiction essays. This is very different from what Montaigne envisioned when he wrote the preface, "To the Reader," for his book *Essais:*

> I have had no thought of serving either you or my own glory. My powers are inadequate for such a purpose. I have dedicated it to the private convenience of my relatives and friends, so that when they have lost me (as soon they must), they may recover here some features of my habits and temperament, and by this means keep the knowledge they have had of me more complete and alive. (2)

I think of this quote as I pull the last strand of warp through its heddle and secure it to the cloth beam on my side of the loom. My loom is now ready to be used to create a piece of individuality. I wonder what I will create. Shall I weave in some of the texture of Rodriguez or of Reg Saner? Emerson or Ehrlich? The possibilities are endless. I step on a treddle to open the warp, throw my shuttle of weft across the threads, and allow "my style and my mind alike" to go roaming. I have warped my loom with Montaigne.

Works Cited

Lopate, Phillip, ed. *The Art of the Personal Essay.* New York: Anchor Books, 1994.

Montaigne, Michel de. *The Complete Works of Montaigne.* Trans. Donald M. Frame. Stanford: Stanford UP, 1957.

Rodriguez, Richard. "Late Victorians." *The Best American Essays 1991.* Ed. Joyce Carol Oates. New York: Ticknor & Fields, 1991. 119–34.

White, E.B. *Essays of E.B. White.* New York: HarperCollins, 1977.

Notes from a Journey Toward "Warping Time"

Emily D. Chase

The path that I took to create the essay "Warping Time with Montaigne" was not a direct path through the writing process. I meandered through personal experiences and through unfamiliar research before I found a thread to connect the two and to help me reach some sort of meaningful understanding of Montaigne and of myself. Since writing that essay, I have noticed that my path through the writing process is almost always indirect and that quite often the meandering path is the most direct way for me to get to insight and understanding. What follows here is essentially a travelogue of my journey toward "Warping Time with Montaigne."

The first time that I heard of Michel de Montaigne was in a course in Graduate Composition. Before that time, the term "essay," to me, was a generic term used by English teachers to refer to short pieces of nonfiction writing. I had no sense of the history of the term or the genre; however, I immediately became interested in Montaigne's writings and therefore decided to write about him for the required research paper in the class. The research paper was written immediately prior to "Warping Time with Montaigne" (the essay included here) and provided me with enough background information to pique my interest and to make me want to have some fun with the information in another piece of writing.

As part of the in-class prewriting for the research paper, I did a cluster/web off of the central term "literary nonfiction." The freewriting that followed the cluster exercise reveals the general direction in which I was drawn:

> Having to research an area of, or a figure in, literary nonfiction, I might like to compare and contrast the original essays everyone quotes—Montaigne, Newman, Emerson, Thoreau—with the modern essayists (especially the nature writers)—Dillard, Ehrlich, Selzer, White—to see if the originals have affected

the moderns. I'd like to find the ties, if any, between personal interaction with nature, religion . . . and the desire to write LNF essays. Part of this study would be taking a look at how each essayist recorded his thoughts (i.e. Thoreau and his journals). Is each day a personal scrutiny of life? an appreciation of being alive? Part of LNF is taking a real daily event and personalizing it by recording your interaction w/it.

But where is this going in terms of research?—Study the masters, study the moderns, draw conclusions. What are people already saying about this link? Has anyone already taken this tack? Is this productive? Is this worthwhile?

I see in this freewrite the idea of not just the original research paper I did on Montaigne but perhaps also the germ of the idea behind "Warping." I never let go of this interest in the correlation between the early essayists and the current essayists.

In just ten days, I discovered a topic and pulled together a reasonable essay about Montaigne and his influence; I used the metaphor of building construction as I discussed the construction of the genre of literary nonfiction upon the foundation of Montaigne's writings. I think better and have more fun writing when I use metaphors to organize and present my thoughts. This fact, no doubt, played a major role in the process that I went through to create the "Warping" essay.

As I was finishing the research paper on Montaigne and just before I began the "Warping" essay, I read Gerald Early's essay "Life with Daughters: Watching the Miss America Pageant" and Jane Tompkins' essay "At the Buffalo Bill Museum." I was overwhelmed by the power of Early's piece, and my original reaction to this essay in my journal reflects this:

> Wow! What an essay! . . . Like a freight train, the fully loaded essay started slowly, exerting effort to overcome inertia, then slowly accumulated speed until it rushed, unstoppably, toward its destination. With Early's final sentence, "My knees had begun to hurt and I realized, painfully, that I was much too old, much too at peace with stiffness and inflexibility, for children's games," the train rushed off the end of the track into the great unknown void of the future. Wow!

By contrast, I did not like Tompkins' essay—or rather I did not understand her essay. My journal reaction to her essay is one long attempt to understand her point; I never do reach that understanding but come to the conclusion that "this is a disturbing piece because I can't see where the author is coming from. I'm not sure a rereading would help." It may seem irrelevant that I read these two essays between writing my two Montaigne essays, yet I think it was crucial that I read as powerful a creative commentary essay as Early's and that I read (and struggled with) Tompkins' essay just as I was directed to write an analysis paper of current literary nonfiction in which I would "explore an individual essay, a series of essays, or a particular author or authors." Both Early and Tompkins use objects and events that they see in their surroundings to launch themselves into realms of contemplation. I must have subconsciously hung onto this technique such that it resurfaced later as I tried to figure out what to do with the analysis assignment.

My initial plans for the analysis paper returned to my interest in the link between Montaigne and the essayists that are writing today. I was still too interested in Montaigne and too convinced of his importance as a crucial element in the genre of literary nonfiction to let go of him. However, we were instructed to comment upon (interpret/analyze) a more current essay. I began to play with possible ways to link Montaigne with current essayists.

On the day that we began working on the analysis paper, I wrote the following prewrite in class:

> Having the chance to write on one element or author in nonfiction, I think I'd like to pursue the elements of Montaigne's essays which can be found in the works of other essayists. Perhaps I could tackle Emerson's essay, "Montaigne," and show how that essay uses Montaignian practices in the process of praising Montaigne. This is a possibility. However, I'd also like to look at Montaigne versus Bacon in terms of voice in the essay and then apply that comparison to critical articles today—(i.e. tackle the 4-woman writers' group who are trying to write "readable" literary criticism [Tompkins, Kaplan, Torgovnik, Davidson]). I'd need to find out if there is much out there in terms of articles/essays on this debate. If *College English* is including these articles now but labeling them as opinion, is anyone reacting to this practice? Is Tompkins? Is Sommers? I think that this could be a much more interesting topic/issue than the piece on Emerson. It would also get me involved in a current intellectual discussion. Having had "Critical Theory" I feel that I have a fairly good base to stand on. Where would Dillard's book, *Living by Fiction*, fit in? or would it? Robert Coles? Who is arguing for Baconian essays in academia? Does Montaigne ever get mentioned in support of personal criticism?—Probably not. But a discussion of Montaigne vs Bacon could be fairly enlightening. I have lots of articles discussing this. I have the background material. I'd just have to dig into the contemporary information. Back to the MLA Bibliography. . . .

I find it interesting as I reread this entry and as I dig through various drafts of the "Warping" essay that one comment I received during a peer editing session of the paper says, "Personally, I think this is better than a lot of the jargon-filled stuff I've read in academic journals." Again, I must have internalized the idea of "readable" criticism such that it resurfaced on its own later in the process.

On the same day that I wrote the above journal entry, as I was beginning work on this final paper, I kept trying to find a way to bring Montaigne into a criticism of a current essay. Because I have watched innumerable episodes of "Star Trek," it did not seem inconceivable to me that one of those hypothetical warps in the space-time continuum could allow Montaigne to suddenly appear in person to comment on the essays being written today. In the preceding research paper, I had already looked at how essayists since Montaigne had used his ideas and examples to help them create their own essays, so it seemed only fair that Montaigne should now have his say about the current essays that are being written.

The word "warp" turned out to be the necessary spark that ignited an inspirational firestorm.

I remember the excitement that I felt when it struck me that the word warp carries a number of different meanings. I had been thinking of the term with a Star Trekian mentality of traveling through time and dimensions of reality, but I am also a weaver, and so as I thought of "warping time," I automatically thought of "warping a loom"—threading a warp onto a loom. After writing the journal entry about Montaigne and Bacon, I jotted down the following notes to myself:

exciting	
Some ^ thoughts-	"Warping Time: Montaigne on _____"
& ideas	sitting at loom, threading warp, thinking about assignments/readings
	critique article in my head by remembering what Montaigne & critics of M.
this	have said.
could	get up to pursue details for more specifics
be	tie in with images of: thread
really	warp/weaving
fun!	distorted/warped time
	structure & patterns & variations of woven cloth
	lay warp on loom, like laying _____ on M.
	or like laying M on _____.

In one moment of inspiration, I made the connection between the elements and process of threading a loom and the elements and process of writing an essay. I couldn't wait to start writing; all I needed was a modern essay to interpret in order to fulfill the requirements of the paper assignment.

It is probably important to note here that I had only one week in which to select and interpret a current essay. The title of Richard Rodriguez's "Late Victorians" drew me to his essay, and then his mix of dry humor and deadly seriousness fascinated me. As I read his essay with the warping idea in mind, I began to see Rodriguez as a weaver of essays and the fourteen sections of "Late Victorians" as variations of weft on the same warp. His essay seemed to be the perfect one for me to work with, and I could barely contain myself as I told my editing group about the ideas for my paper. I can still picture my teacher leaning forward on his chair with keen interest as I explained what I envisioned for my paper.

The writing of both my Montaigne papers was aided in large part by exercises and peer editing that were conducted as part of coursework in the Graduate Composition class. The drafting of each paper was preceded by a number of prewriting exercises to generate and organize ideas, and then once the drafting had begun, several different drafts of each paper were shared with a group of fellow students. I was a part of a four person editing group that provided valuable feedback and suggestions for revisions at every step of the drafting and revising process. The interaction of the editing group also tended to nurture creativity and spontaneity that proved to be crucial in the creation of "Warping Time with Montaigne."

Once I had shared my ideas for the paper with my group and with just two days left before my paper was due in class, I wrote the following journal entries as a way of organizing my thoughts and figuring out what I wanted to do with them in my paper:

> "Warping time" has the potential to be a really interesting essay. I need to list everything I want to be sure to say about Rodriguez's essay, those quotes of Montaigne's which directly apply to the points I want to make, and, then, the precise affiliations I want to assign to each metaphor of time and the loom. I wish I had more time to work on this.
>
> What are the parts to my metaphor? If the loom = time, the warp = Montaigne, and the weft = Rodriguez, then what is the process of "warping the loom"? Is the threading of Montaigne through the hettles of time, the same as Montaigne's transcendence of time? His thoughts have to be durable enough to stand the strain put on the warp by the tension of the loom as well as the wear of the opening and closing of the shed and the friction of the beater as it swings along Montaigne and locks the weft of Rodriguez's ideas into the grasp of Montaigne's warp, while at the same time the interlocking of Rodriguez into Montaigne creates a brand new unique object formed by the interaction of the inter-working parts of time with the materials of Montaigne and Rodriguez.
>
> The ideas of original thinkers get spun into yarn for warp. Rodriguez's end product is a piece of cloth which is available to the reader to use to make other things such as clothing, blankets, or ?.
>
> If Montaigne is the warp, what do the 2 ends signify? The first end is the full body of Montaigne wound around itself in its full potential. The end I am threading is his ideas being taken through time to be used in the creation of new essays. 2 steps to trip through time—hettles and dent. What are they? hettles = individual thoughts and quotes (arranged to create potential of a pattern). dent = combining and spacing of ideas to assure a solid, even weave of the new fabric—literature vs nonliterature? Final step is to tie off Montaigne in the present on the cloth beam in order to hang onto his thoughts in the present to enable the creation of new essays.
>
> My thoughts as I thread the loom consider the process Rodriguez went through in the creation of "Late Victorians." As I tie off the warp on my loom, I have secured Montaigne for use in my own creation and I have examined the creation of an accomplished weaver to glean ideas and techniques. I am ready to write—conceivably the result is essay in the reader's hands. How to do that?
>
> Ending—my thoughts pull Montaigne into the present, now I am ready to weave my thoughts into an essay, I step on the treadles to raise the shed, throw the first pass of the shuttle and create, "I sit bent over the breast beam of my 38 inch LeClerc floor loom . . ."

This last journal entry was written after I had begun drafting my paper but before I had figured out how to conclude the essay. I have quoted the first line of the paper, yet my ideas are still just beginning to take form. I had originally planned to create a circular essay in which the ending leads back to the beginning in a never-ending retelling of this process; however, that idea got too confusing to be adequately developed in the limited amount of time that I had and therefore was changed in favor of the current ending.

I had a number of issues that needed to be sorted out as I tried to create a complete draft of the paper; therefore, as a way of figuring out what ideas I wanted to weave into the paper, I entered in my journal the following lists of what I believed were critical points to be dealt with in my paper:

Individual thoughts of Montaigne:

- Que scais-je?
- I want to be seen in simple, natural . . . it is myself I portray
- essai = trial or attempt
- self-portrait vs autobiography
- to be known not remembered
- to follow wanderings of his mind in process of thinking
- my mind & my thoughts . . .
- find self through writing
- loose disconnected structure—mirrors spontaneous thought
- portrait as friendly gesture
- familiar tone
- rebellion against rigid styles, formal language
- absence of dispositio
- sense of honesty

Points from Rodriguez:

- we choose our lifestyles
- sometimes we choose our deaths
- we all die
- wisdom in youth's foolishness
- R. focused on tragedy   Cesar—you cannot forbid tragedy
- R. full-time skeptic (131)(121)
- jealousy of responsible of irresponsible
- Victorian house as symbol of family—gay reclaim neighborhood
- new residents, new vision of family (Yuppies—birth control)
- masks (123)(131)
- caustic language (124–5) shock value, coarse cloth
- flipping of normal perspectives
- gays vs feminists
- nakedness (129)
- self-questioning in text (129)
- flowing thoughts (131)
- regret, repentance? (132)(134)

I spent successive late nights in the final week of the class working on this paper, as well as on revisions of other papers from that class. On the day before the final draft of the warping essay was due, my eyes felt unnaturally wide open from too much coffee and too little sleep, and yet still every time I thought about my paper, I felt excited about its possibilities. Not only did I not want to sleep, I knew that I couldn't sleep as long as I had the potentials of the warping metaphor at play in my head. It was with enthusiasm and playfulness, not with fatigue or despair, that I wrote the following journal entry:

> I am making progress on my "Warping" essay, but I have so far to go in the 24 hours I have left before I have to hand in the paper. I realize that I cannot get it into a polished state of existence in that time, but I would like to at least have the skeleton of the complete essay put together with some of the shaping musculature before I hand it in to be graded. I can drape it with the appropriate clothing after that. At this point I have 8 1/2 pages written and I feel as if I am 3/4 of the way through the essay. The essay still seems extremely muddy to me, so I am unable to see clearly the points I am trying to make. I need to sort out *exactly* what I want to say about Rodriguez's essay in order to clarify my essay. From there I need to weave my metaphor of the loom more thoroughly and securely into the piece. The entire piece has the substance of gauze, when I want the density of linsey-woolsey. It is also patched together with scraps of yarn, when I want high quality materials. And so I work on it. It is still fun and exciting to play with this essay. The metaphor of the loom and the warp has *many* possibilities. Time. I need a bigger loom for this project.

The final push through those twenty-four hours produced the tenth draft of the essay "Warping Time with Montaigne."

As with the first Montaigne paper, the beginning of this paper appeared in the first draft and remained largely unchanged throughout the remaining drafts. The rest of the essay changed drastically from draft to draft, and it was not until the eighth draft that I found the conclusion to the paper. The middle of the essay continued to grow and take shape, but the ending remained loose and unfinished. I had a loose collection of quotes and comments at the end of the early drafts that I knew I wanted to fit into the paper somewhere. I tend to do this when I write: I cultivate a garden patch of interesting and related thoughts at the end of whatever I am working on as a way of feeding life into my essay (and as a way of keeping me from forgetting insights I may have along the way). There are wonderful passages in that collection that never made it to the final draft. If I were to revise this paper again, I might try harder to fit them into the essay. At the time I was drafting this paper, though, I didn't have time to fit them in, and so after the essay became complete in the eighth draft, I used the ninth and tenth drafts to polish the language and the metaphor. I was forced to be done polishing when the due date arrived and I needed to submit the paper for a grade.

Looking back upon the process I went through to create "Warping Time with Montaigne" makes me realize that I almost always contain a heightened sense of excitement when I am in the process of learning something new or when

I am playing with language. I love every stage of the writing process because I am at play throughout all of it. Even when I am struggling with a concept or with an adequate way to present a concept, I am excited by the infinite possibilities that present themselves to me. I may procrastinate before I start to write, but once I sit down to write, the rest of the world disappears, or becomes a resource at my beck and call. In this sense, the process I went through when I wrote "Warping Time with Montaigne" is not unlike my normal writing process. It was simply heightened by a metaphor that possessed particularly great potential. As part of my response to a journal prompt that was given at the end of the class asking me to "compare the Research and Analysis papers with the earlier papers in the course (my experience)," I wrote the following passage:

> It was very difficult to make the transition from personal essay to academic paper. I felt like I had just gotten the hang of the personal essay and was enjoying the freedom of the collage essay, when suddenly, I had to juggle references, documentation, and other people's arguments. It was not that the research paper was particularly difficult, as the *switch* was difficult. However, having made the switch, I then felt like I was on excellent footing for writing the analysis paper. I had felt the freedom of the personal essay and had plumbed my depths to discover the wealth of details I have within me to use for my writing; I had then felt the rigid demands of the research paper with all of its formality and tradition. Having gone through these two exercises, I was better able to appreciate what literary nonfiction essayists are trying to accomplish. I was able to appreciate Tompkins' "Buffalo Bill" essay in a way that I was incapable of at the beginning of the course. As a result, I felt tremendous excitement about writing the analysis paper. I understood the requirements expected of me in terms of scholasticism, yet I felt the freedom to assert my own voice and technique. What fun!

THIS is the process that led me to "Warping Time with Montaigne." It was a journey of discovery: first of myself and my knowledge, then of different forms of writing available for my use, and finally of the power of freedom, innovation, and inspiration. Fortunately for me, I am now able to start from here as I prepare future journeys through the writing process.

That Shining Place: Crete, 1966

Simone Poirier-Bures

In the photo I remember, Maria looks straight at the camera. A smile flutters at the corners of her mouth, as if she is hesitant to show her ferocious pride, as if she dares not enjoy this moment, surrounded by her children, lest some jealous god yank it away. She rests her hands on the shoulders of Ireni, who barely comes up to her waist. Somber Ireni, whose eyes are large and unsmiling. Smaragdi and Katina stand at their mother's right, their heads reaching just to and just below her shoulders; Katina, distracted by something, looks off to the side. Yannis, at the left, is barely as tall as Smaragdi, though he is older than his sisters. He stands a little apart from the others, as if, as the only male, he feels a need to disassociate himself from the women.

There is something hopeful in their expressions, in the way they are poised there, their faces curious, expectant, as if they are used to standing on the side-lines watching, waiting for things to happen.

Behind them, the stuccoed wall is yellowish brown and peeling. It's the wall of my house, the one I occupied for four months, 31 years ago. Theirs, very much like mine, stands directly across the street. I remember also in this picture the hindquarters of a donkey, a brown shaggy one who carried things for the old man who delivered goods to the small store a few doors down, but perhaps I am confusing this photo with another.

Maria's husband Giorgos is missing from this family portrait, but that is usual. Every morning he would leave his house at dawn, return for the noon meal and a few hours rest, then leave again. He would spend his evenings in one of several *tavernas* along the waterfront. I seldom saw him at home, though I waved to him whenever I saw him along the old harbor, bringing in his catch. And he would wave back, in front of the other fishermen, giving a surprised but pleased smile to this young foreign woman. A friend of his wife's.

The *Yaya*, too, is absent. Maria's mother, all in black, would sit at her chair by the front window watching the goings on. Like all *Yayas*, she knew how to stay in the background, to help when there was work to be done, but otherwise, to remain invisible. I feel her hovering behind the photo, silently moving her toothless mouth.

They are all frozen in that moment—yet as I think of the picture, time softens, moves. Maria stands below my window, yelling "See-moan-ay! See-moan-ay!" It is 10:15 AM, far too late for decent people still to be sleeping, and anyway, she has something to tell me, or she is lonesome and wants some company, or it is the day for making some Greek delicacy, and I must come and watch so I can learn how.

It is 1966 and I am 21. I am in Chania, on the island of Crete, searching for something. Some truth that keeps eluding me. Some peace I long for. I am fleeing old griefs, trying to lose myself, find myself.

I am not completely alone; I am part of a small group of temporary expatriates—Canadians, Americans, Brits. We all live in the old quarter, in ancient three-story houses built by the Venetians in the 14th and 15th centuries. We live there, instead of in the newer parts of the city where there are flush toilets and running water, because the streets in the old quarter are narrow and picturesque, because the rent is cheap, and because none of us cares about flush toilets and running water. We are all there for our own reasons—we do not ask each other such questions—and together we form a community of sorts. We go to the *tavernas* at night, dance with the sailors, drink too much, help each other find the way home.

Much of my day, however, is with Maria. She has "claimed" me. When we walk through the neighborhood she holds my arm and tells the people we meet: "Apo tin Ameriki." I correct her gently: from Canada. She shrugs and laughs. Wherever I am from, it does not matter. She was the first to have me in her house, so now I am known as "Maria's friend."

Come to my house for some *raki*, a woman down the street calls out to me. No, Maria says to her fiercely, she cannot. She is with me. Later, Maria tells me: That woman is not a good woman. But Athena, as she is called, will not give up so easily. When she sees me coming down the street without Maria, she rushes out to speak. She is thirtyish, a few years younger than Maria, but unmarried. She lives with her sister (also unmarried), and with her mother; occasionally she goes out with men from the nearby NATO base, and this makes her vaguely disreputable. I am curious about Athena, this loud, persistent woman who dyes her hair red, who hovers on the edge of respectability, but I do not wish to offend Maria, so I decline her invitations.

In the evenings, when I slip out to dance with the sailors on the waterfront, to drink, to behave in a way that is totally unacceptable for Greek women, I wonder what Maria thinks, at home, alone with her children. The rules are different for me; this is part of my appeal. Come with us, I say to her one Saturday evening when the winds are warm and we can smell spring coming. Giorgos never stays home—why should you? She clicks her tongue and throws her head back. I have proposed something preposterous, impossible. I might as well have proposed that we fly to the moon. She laughs, chides me for being so silly, but she puts on lipstick, and I know she is tempted.

At first I thought I was merely her trophy—something to show off in this city of few westerners. But Maria remained my friend long after it was expedient or prudent.

"See-moan-ay! See-moan-ay!" she yells through the front window. It is unshuttered and open because it is a lovely warm day, even in mid-January. Behind her stands Yannis, ready to supply the appropriate English if I do not understand what his mother tells me. He is 11, small and sturdy, with a curious, intelligent face. He is learning English in school, and eager to try out his new words. When his friends invite him to play kickball down the street, he demurs, telling them he can't right now, that his mother needs his help. I understand enough Greek to catch this, and to know that we could manage without him. He looks at me shyly—I am not like Greek young women—I tease him, and he hides his smiles.

Maria's friend Varvara has invited us for coffee. I must come now. Varvara is one of the band of gypsies who winter over every year in Chania. I know this because I have seen her pull her small cart laden with colorful woven blankets and rugs through the narrow streets of the old quarter. She is short and compact like Maria, with dark fierce eyes like hers. But Varvara has a shrewdness about her. I do not trust her. A few weeks ago, I bought a blanket from her; later I discovered I had paid far too much.

I am surprised to learn that Varvara is Maria's "friend," as the gypsies are not well-liked here. Faces tighten, mouths curl as the gypsies pass. But I do not question this odd alliance. I, too, am an outsider, and I, too, am Maria's friend.

The gypsies are encamped behind the old city wall, a few minutes walk from our street. Yannis may not come, it is only for the women, Maria tells him. Yannis turns away in disappointment. The *Yaya*'s face appears in Maria's front window. She will watch the children. It is a beautiful afternoon and as we walk, I tell Maria about the blanket. She throws her head back and laughs. In Greece, anything is fair in business.

The path to the encampment takes us along the top of the old wall, now crowded with tiny, whitewashed shacks. In the 500 years since the wall was built, the inner face has totally disappeared; the town has sloped up to meet it. Only when you stand at the edge and look down, do you realize that you are on a wall, and how high you are. Maria and I stand there for a moment, looking down. In the clearing below, about two dozen tents form a tiny village, complete with rickety-looking wooden wagons, a motley group of horses and donkeys, a few old cars. A trash fire burns on one side, upwind from the tents. A dog barks. It is eerie to see this scene, like something out of time, something from the Middle Ages. I want to express this observation to Maria, but it is too complicated for my simple Greek vocabulary, so I smile and squeeze her arm, and we follow the path down.

As we approach the camp, we become the focus of attention. I am suddenly aware of my long yellow hair hanging loosely to my waist, my blue eyes. The dark eyes of the men follow me, openly, aggressively. They resemble Greek men in their darkness, in their luxurious mustaches, but their faces are narrower, their cheekbones more pronounced. I hold Maria's arm more tightly. One of them asks us what we want there. Maria tells him in a loud voice that we are looking for Varvara's tent. He points the way. I realize, then, with a sudden twinge of fear, that Maria has never been here before. Is this all some elaborate trap? Has Varvara tricked Maria into bringing me here so that I can be stolen, then sold as a white slave? The youth hostels in Europe were full of such stories.

A man approaches us with a proprietary air. He jerks his head to the right, indicating that we follow him. He spreads his arms out and around us, as if to shield us from the curious eyes of the others. I feel Maria relax a little. Varvara's husband, she tells me.

Their canvas tent, like all the others, is a grayish, stained tan.

Through the partly open front flap we see Varvara, who rises to greet us. We take off our shoes before we enter, leaving them with the others in a neat row outside. The inside is both roomy and cozy. Layers of blankets and rugs in patterns of bright blue, green and red pad the floor. Varvara and her husband exchange a few words in their own language; the husband darts a last look at me, then leaves, pulling the door flap down behind him.

Varvara invites us to sit down on the carpets and we do, forming a circle around a square slab that holds a small stove and a few cooking utensils. I am not sure what to expect from all this, but I suddenly realize that being invited here is a great honor. Maria seems to understand this too, and nods at me solemnly. Varvara lights the stove, a tiny one-burner, fueled by gas. She takes a handful of coffee beans from a burlap bag, puts them in a flat, long-handled copper pan, and shakes them over the fire for a few minutes. The tent fills with a wonderful burnt-brown smell. While the beans cool, she opens a long brass cylinder and begins to assemble what I see now is a coffee grinder. It's a beautiful thing, obviously very old, the elaborate engraving well worn. I wonder for a moment, how many generations of gypsy women have owned this grinder, how many continents it has traveled.

As Varvara grinds the beans, the tent smells more and more aromatic. I wave my hand in front of my nose and say "orea," beautiful, beautiful. Varvara nods at me gravely, but says nothing. She places a few spoonfuls of the powdered coffee with water into a small brass pot, then adds a few large spoonfuls of sugar. When the coffee froths up, she fills three small white cups, paper thin, and hands one each to Maria and me.

Now Varvara smiles. Welcome, my friends, she says. We sip our coffee slowly. Varvara inquires about Maria's family; Maria inquires back. She asks me about my health; I ask back. We are formal, ceremonial. Here, in her own element, Varvara is beautiful. She has loosened her hair and it hangs over her back in a thick mantle of glossy black. She looks softer than before, yet at the same time more powerful. I let the strong, sweet liquid linger on my tongue. Though I have had Greek coffee before, this is the best I have ever tasted. I am in a gypsy camp, I say to myself. A gypsy has called me "friend." I forgive Varvara for the blanket.

You come down through one of the narrow, twisting streets, barely wide enough for a small car, and you come upon it: the old harbor, opening before you like a flower.

A wide paved area separates the buildings from the water, very much like an Italian piazza, which is appropriate, given that this part of Chania was built by the Venetians. At the edge of the piazza, the water is deep, and small fishing boats pull right up to the edge to unload their catches. Mid morning they bring in the octopus. Glossy and silvery gray, raw octopus look like the internal organs of extraterrestrials. There is something vaguely obscene about those thick, slimy appendages; cooked up, however, they are an amazing delicacy. The fishermen throw the octopus by the handfuls on to the pavement, then pick them up and throw them down again, beating them like this to release the dark blue inky substance, and to tenderize them. The octopus are then hung on makeshift racks and lines to dry, and the fishermen wash down the pavement with buckets of sea water.

Sometimes it's sea urchins they bring in, one or two buckets of them, their greenish gray shells bristling with needle-sharp spines. Inside, flesh the color of smoked salmon. I have never tried them—they are food for the wealthy—though I am told they are wonderful. Mostly though, the boats are full of fish and octopus, and all morning the air is briny and aromatic. By noon, all trace of the fishermen is gone.

Everything around the old harbor is a bit shabby. The facades of some of the buildings have begun to crumble. Old paint peels from walls and woodwork like outgrown skin. Some of the buildings are whitewashed, but most are not, unlike the picture postcards one sees of sparkling white Greek villages. Here the buildings are mostly a drab gold—the color of limestone—or light ocher, or the grayish tan of unpainted cement.

Still, there is something enormously pleasing about it all. The crowded buildings face the water like flowers facing the sun. Roofs of red tile and wide doors painted a glossy blue flash patches of color. Old oil cans grow huge red geraniums. The rounded domes of an ancient mosque, a legacy of the Turkish occupation, shimmer in the sun like white hills. A bright green fishing boat moors on the water. Everything seems harmonious, comforting. On fine days, the restaurants spill out into the piazza. Tables and chairs appear on the pavement, inviting. On weekends, the aroma of roasting meat fills the air.

On my way home from the *Instituto,* I stop at one of the sweet shops for a *galato-buriko,* or a bowl of rice custard, or a piece of *baklava,* and look out at the harbor water. Sometimes blue, sometimes black, the water riffles lightly or bristles with foam, depending on its mood. Though the ancient sea wall contains it— a small opening permits the comings and goings of small boats—the harbor water is never totally placid, more like some wild thing, barely domesticated. And it seems emblematic somehow, of all of Crete: Hungers surge up, then subside, waiting for their own good time. A thin layer of order overlays roiling chaos— Apollo and Dionysious held in delicate balance.

At the *Instituto Amerikaniko-Helleniki* I taught three classes: a group of 12- and 13-year-old boys, a co-ed class of about a dozen high school seniors preparing to take the Cambridge proficiency exams, and a group of seven or eight local merchants.

While the other shopkeepers take their meals at home, sleep with their wives, or do whatever they all do between one and four in the afternoon when the shops are closed, these men spend an hour, three afternoons a week, practicing their English with me. They range in age from their late twenties to late forties, and their manner toward me is formal. They call me "Miss," and hold doors open for me, bowing slightly, as if I were a visiting dignitary. I acknowledge their deference with a smile, wondering what their wives would think—their husbands treating a woman this way, while they are expected to obey and please.

We spend about half of our time in general conversation; I gently correct their grammar and pronunciation and supply words when I can guess the intent. We converse mostly about "Amerika"; they are passionately interested in "Amerika." They have heard there is a sexual revolution going on there, and they are eager to learn how it works. "In America, is it true that a girl can go alone at night with a boy who is not her brother, and her parents do not know his parents?" I am careful with my reply, aware of my position, a single woman about whom there is already too much speculation. And in Chania, the old codes still prevail: a boy who dishonors someone's sister is likely to feel a knife in his back.

"It's very different there," I tell them. "Being alone together does not necessarily mean that something shameful will happen." They wrinkle their faces in puzzlement. They would never believe that a man sleeping alone on the third floor of a house would not sometimes wander at night to the bed of a woman, sleeping alone on the second. They would never believe that a woman who dances the *hassapico* with sailors and sometimes sits on their laps, and drinks with them, and sometimes walks home alone with one and lets him kiss her, does not allow him other things as well. But all that is part of my other life, my life in the old quarter. These men never go to the old quarter.

These men live in the better part of the city, in houses with water heaters, small refrigerators, stoves. Their wives do not carry the Sunday roast to the bakery down the street to be cooked in the public oven for a few *drachma* like Maria does. Their wives wear wool and rayon instead of cotton, their coats have fur collars. And at night, when the *tavernas* crackle with music and the scent of grilled *brisoles* wafts through the air—when *retsina, metaxa,* and *ouzo* flow, when feet fly in dance, plates crash on the floor amid cries of "oopa!"—these men are at home with their wives and children.

I know this because I regularly visit such a home. On Saturday mornings I privately tutor the younger sister of one of my 13-year-old boys. There are no English classes for 10-year-old girls, and to send her with the boys would not be proper. The father is not among my businessmen, but he could be; he and they are the same. My pupil's house is relatively new. The surfaces are smooth, the corners of the rooms sharp and well-defined, unlike the rooms of the houses in the old quarter. There are plenty of windows, covered with lace curtains and hung with heavy drapes of velvet and brocade. The chairs and sofas are heavy and ornate.

Solid looking. In this part of town, you never see bedding flung out over the balcony to air like you do in the old quarter.

The mother is attractive in a plump, soft sort of way. She smiles sweetly and greets me graciously in spite of the cheap cotton skirts and shabby tops I wear. She, too, calls me "Miss." I call her *Kyria*—Mrs. Like Maria, she speaks no English and relies on her son to translate. Unlike Maria, she shows no curiosity toward me. Each time I come, she offers me tea in a flowered china cup, then leaves the money for each lesson discreetly on the side-board, near my coat.

One Friday, the boy says to me after class: "My mother, she say no come tomorrow. Come Sunday, for to go on picnic. Three o'clock. We go to country. You come?"

When I arrive, slightly before three, they are all waiting. The children are happy to see me and the mother looks both pleased and relieved, as if she had feared that I wouldn't show. The *Kyrios,* her husband, acknowledges me with a slight nod. This is only the second time I have seen him. On the day of my first lesson with his daughter, he nodded at me on his way out. I suspect he had stayed behind to catch a glimpse of me, to make sure I was "safe," and to give his approval. A *Yaya* appears from one of the back rooms. I have not seen her before and wonder whose widowed mother she is—his or hers. It's impossible to tell. She is dressed all in black with a black wool kerchief pulled over her head like the *Yayas* in the old quarter. She is the one link between these two worlds. She is not introduced.

A big black Mercedes waits out front. The *Yaya* sits in the front with the man and woman, near the door. I sit in the back between the two children. The girl, who is still very much a beginner in English, holds my hand and looks at me adoringly. The boy keeps smiling, as if he can't believe I am really there, his English teacher, on an outing with his family. The adults sit stiffly, silently, in the front. I wonder briefly whose idea it was to invite me. The children's? The mother's?

Kyria says something in Greek to the boy, gesticulating with her head that he should tell me. "My mother she say to tell you that the orchards will be beautiful today." I smile at her: "I'm looking forward to seeing them. I am very happy that you invited me to come." She nods as I speak. She understands more English than she lets on. She translates my words to her husband and returns her eyes to the road. He glances at me through the rearview mirror. He seems aware of me, but not aware; I am part of the women's world with which he need not concern himself.

His wife, however, pulses with awareness. Throughout the ride I feel her controlled attention. Though she speaks mostly to her husband or looks out at the countryside, she is acutely aware of what is going on in the back seat. If we all do not have a wonderful time, she will blame herself. This is my first encounter with upper middle-class Greek life, and I am carefully taking it all in, noting how different this woman is from Maria, how different they all are from the villagers I have met, and from the people in the old quarter. Maria and I would be singing by now. Laughing out loud. Exclaiming over the beauty of the hills. She would be teaching me the Greek names of things.

The girl beside me squeezes my hand. "Is good day, yes?"

There is a tacit understanding that I speak only English, so that makes it difficult to communicate with the adults. The school is total immersion, and we teachers are discouraged from admitting to any knowledge of Greek. I suspect I have been invited along to give the children a chance to practice their English. Why else? *Kyrios* and *Kyria* do not ask me about life in "Amerika," or my life here or what I think about things. And yet I feel they are studying me, discreetly.

The country house is utterly charming—whitewashed stucco and surrounded by a low stone wall. It is grander than any of the houses I saw in my wanderings around the island, though it is still relatively simple. *Kyria* points to the small outhouse, apologizing profusely for the lack of an indoor toilet. This strikes me as very funny, given my own living conditions, but I suppress my smile. Wide windows look out over row upon row of orange trees.

Huge baskets are unloaded from the trunk of the Mercedes and there is a flutter of activity. The women will not let me help and shoo me out of the kitchen. The children hover around me like bees.

"My father say to come and see the orchard," the boy says.

Kyrios stands at the door fingering his worry beads. The children and I follow him out. The day is glorious, the air dazzling in its sweetness, and I want to jump into the air and shout with joy. But I control myself, as seems to be required, and smile demurely. Two donkeys, tied to a stake by a shed, stare at us with comic faces. I have a particular fondness for donkeys, and rush over to stroke their necks and ears. *Kyrios* gestures for me to get on one of them. It's the first time he has addressed me directly. The children shriek with glee when I swing my leg up over the donkey's back. They quickly climb onto the other one.

Their father takes the reins of my donkey and leads us down the rows of the orange grove. The trees are much smaller than I ever imagined they could be, with enormous bright fruit hanging heavily from the branches. *Kyrios* pulls down an orange the size of a cannonball and slices it open with a knife he pulls from his waist. Then he presents it to me with a little bow. I am reminded again how everything in Greece seems fuller, riper, bursting with life. Even the oranges are unrestrained, glorious in their hugeness, their sweetness, their intense color. By now I have lost all reserve and exclaim aloud at the beauty of everything. "It's all so lovely! Lovely!" I tell them. "I feel like a queen!" The children find everything I say and do amusing, and laugh and laugh.

When we get back to the house we find a beautiful meal laid out on a long rectangular table in a shaded area outside—feta cheese, black olives, bread, *dolmathes, taramasalata,* two kinds of beans, several plates of things I don't recognize, and a huge bottle of retsina. We are all more relaxed now, more comfortable with each other. Even the *Yaya* nods and smiles. The sun beats down, waves of fragrance waft in from the orange grove. After a few glasses of retsina, *Kyrios* raises his glass and sings a few lines of a song: "Ego tha kopso to krassi, ya sena agapi mou chrisi . . ." His wife throws him a disapproving glance and mutters something, but too late. I clap my hands, delighted. A drinking song! This is the first sign of passion I've seen in these upper middle-class Greeks.

I insist on learning the song, and sing it over and over, a bit tipsy myself by this time. My pupils and their father sing it with me. *Kyria* sings a few lines herself, though she looks uncomfortable, as if she is doing something vaguely improper.

After the meal, the children and I take a last stroll through the orchard. It's a wonderful afternoon, and I am sorry when it ends.

On the way home we are again subdued, polite. My hosts ask where I live so that they can deliver me to my house. I protest that the streets are too narrow for their car, and ask to be let out by the old harbor, saying that I will walk the rest of the way. I do not want them to see where I live. I do not want them anywhere near my life there.

My class of 12- and 13-year olds was my favorite. A teasing, affectionate relationship existed between us. They found me endlessly amusing, and I was charmed by their small compact bodies, their dark curious eyes. Once when I came into the classroom and turned on the light switch, nothing happened. I flipped it off and on several times while the boys watched me. Nothing. Things often didn't work in Greece, so I shrugged and said, "I guess we'll just have to have class in the dark today." They all burst out laughing. One of the boys climbed up on his desk and turned the light bulb; another flicked on the switch and the room filled with light. We all laughed together. I had enjoyed this trick as much as they had, so when I walked into the classroom the day after my visit to the orange groves and felt an expectant tension in the air, I figured something was up.

One of the boys had just finished writing something in Greek on the blackboard and was hurrying back to his seat. All 16 of them were watching me, suppressing grins.

"Aha," I say, going along with it. "Someone left me a message. Help me translate it." Titters all over the room. "It's nothing," the boy whose sister I tutor says. "I'll erase it for you." He gets up and approaches the board. But something in his face makes me want to know what the words say.

"No, let's figure it out. It'll be good practice. Let's see, the first word is . . ." I squint at the Greek letters and sound out "Ego . . ." Someone from the back row calls out boldly: "Ego tha kopso to krassi."

General laughter. I glance quickly at my friend in the front row who hangs his head sheepishly. Obviously, he has told his friends about our excursion, and they have seized on the part they found most interesting.

"Oh yes, the song I learned yesterday," I say, feeling a little chilled, the private made a bit too public. "I like Greek songs. I'd like to learn a lot of them." The boys are restless, whispering things to each other, their eyes flashing a kind of wildness. One of them calls out something in Greek that I don't understand, and they all laugh again. The laughter has a new, aggressive edge.

"What did you say?" I ask him. He is silent. "Someone tell me what he said." No one answers, and a thick tension hangs in the air. Finally, I look at my friend in the front row. He, after all, started this whole thing. I ask him evenly, "Please tell me what he said."

He swallows hard and says, "He said that perhaps you would like to learn, um . . . *Krevata murmura.*"

"And what, exactly, is that?"

He looks exceedingly uncomfortable, as does the rest of the class. But I persist.

"I don't know how to say in English, but it means the things a man and woman say to each other when they are in bed."

The boys are absolutely still, studying my reaction. The air crackles with danger.

"I see," I say. "Thank you for your translation." Then I turn to the rest of the class. "Take out your homework now, and let's see how well you've done on the exercises for today." I go on with the class as usual, though I smile less and make no joking asides as I usually do. Something between us has changed.

On my way home, I try to figure it out. A single woman drinking wine and singing—did this somehow mean sexual availability in the minds of these 12- and 13-year-old boys? The harbor water is greenish black today; two small boats, moored in the protected area, rock gently in the lapping tongues of water. Beyond the seawall, the water is deep blue; whitecaps surge and break. It's the same water; only the seawall separates it, only the seawall tames it. How easily things can turn, I think, how easily things can careen out of control.

Afterword: Writing "The Greece Piece"

Simone Poirier-Bures

It began, I suppose, in 1982. I was auditing a writing course taught by Ursule Molinaro; she had no car, so after class I drove her home. I was only just beginning to write seriously then, and Ursule was a real writer; alone with her on those rides, I hoped some of her talent would rub off, or I'd learn some secret about how words work.

One afternoon I told her about my backpacking in Europe and the Middle East years before, my stay on the island of Crete. I described a brave young woman traipsing through exotic lands, only half aware of the disturbances her long blond hair created. I spoke of my younger self as I would a colourful ancestor—so removed from my present self did she seem. "That was my life's big adventure," I told Ursule, realizing at that moment that it was.

"You should write about it," Ursule said simply.

I had never thought of this. It had all happened so long ago, back in 1965–66, and my experiences were episodic, they had no centre around which to build a plot. Moreover, I sensed that the real story lay beneath the surface adventures; the real story had to do with friendship, loneliness, the making of a self. I was not quite ready to deal with all that.

Years later, in 1988, after I had finished several writing projects and was looking for another, I remembered Ursule's words and decided to try writing a novel about the four months I had spent in Greece. I would make up a heroine, myself in disguise, and embellish my experiences to make them neater, more story-like. I still occasionally dreamed about my house in Chania, the crumbling cement walls, the dark rooms that became, in those dreams, a labyrinth. Something important had happened there. Something left unfinished.

I was having a hard time getting started, so I began getting up at 5:30 AM and freewriting for an hour. Someone had given me Dorothea Brande's little book, *Becoming a Writer,* and she had suggested this exercise. It wasn't easy. Awakening memory, trying to shape and select its messages, dealing with my own feelings about my younger self—and doing this all at once. I would sit there watching the sky lighten against the window over my desk, my stomach tight, my brow throbbing, an urge to run out of the room rippling through my arms and legs.

Over a period of several weeks, I wrote twenty pages. In the opening scene, a North American woman negotiates with a Greek merchant over the price of a silver and turquoise bracelet. After a good deal of haggling, they settle on a price. Then suddenly they become good friends, in the way this happens in Greece. On the way home, with her new bracelet on her arm, Joanna berates herself: you didn't *need* it. In this way I introduce the theme of material things and Joanna's (my) ambivalence toward them. The day is overcast, damp and chilly, corresponding to Joanna's mood, but also to many days I actually remember in Crete.

Joanna goes home to her Venetian house in the old quarter and is met by her housemate, a bearded British artist (Jack), who is drying his socks by the charcoal brazier, the only source of heat. Relentlessly cheerful, Jack provides a sharp contrast to Joanna's gloominess. Joanna wishes she were in love with him. How much nicer life would be if she loved someone and someone loved her. It rains all night.

The next morning, after a chill, dreary night huddled in her sleeping-bag, Joanna wakes to the sound of her neighbour, Maria, calling her name. When she throws open the shutters, sunlight and warm air rush in. Joanna looks at the brilliant sky, at Maria's short square body, at the long narrow street bustling with activity, and is overtaken with joy.

This is as far as I got. How to develop all the threads? How to tell what happened and make it dramatic without doing injustice to the static-like quality of much of my life there?

I put the twenty pages away and forgot about them.

In 1991 my husband had a sabbatical and between his research trips, we decided to make a quick trip to Greece and Turkey. My husband had spent two years in Turkey in the late sixties helping to set up a land-grant style university, so we each had important memories associated with the two countries.

From the moment we decided on the trip, images of Maria and Chania began trickling steadily up from the past. One afternoon I hunted through an old trunk and found Maria's thin blue airmail letters with the spidery black handwriting. As I read them, I heard Maria's voice, saw her large sad eyes, and was seized with a deep need to see her again. I couldn't remember her last name, and because it was written in Greek script that I could not decipher, I tore off the small piece of envelope with her name and address in case I would have to inquire about her. I remembered that our street was named after El Greco—his Greek name—and though I could still see every detail of the houses and shops, the name eluded me. Fortunately, it was there on the envelope, under Maria's name.

What happened during our visit to Crete is described in the memoir.

After Crete, my husband and I went on to Turkey. In Istanbul, the sister of an old friend, a woman we barely knew, gave us a present—an old brass coffee grinder, almost exactly like the one Varvara had used 25 years before. Such an odd coincidence, I remember thinking. So many wonderful coincidences on this trip. We were busy with visiting and buying gifts, so I forgot about the grinder.

When we returned home, I was once again struck by the need to write about my time in Greece. But how? Months passed. At Christmas, I sent cards and letters to both Maria and Ireni, telling them how much our reunion had meant to me. In mid-January, a Christmas card and letter arrived from Ireni. "You must know," she said, "that always, since I've met you, I've been thinking about you." Her words reminded me piercingly of Maria's letters years ago. As I sat at the kitchen table reading and rereading Ireni's letter, my body felt as if it were literally bursting with memory, with the need *to tell*. The faces of Maria and the children as they had been long ago swam before me. I went up to my study and began writing: "In the photo, Maria looks straight at the camera . . . "

I wrote as far as the dancing scene. Exhilarated and a bit dazed, I went downstairs to make some tea. As I waited for the water to boil, I thought of the day Maria took me to the gypsy camp. I pulled out the coffee grinder the woman in Istanbul had given us and examined it. There was still a little coffee in it, powdered to make Turkish coffee, which is what Greek and gypsy coffee actually is. Suddenly the coffee grinder became like Proust's madeleine: I found myself walking the narrow path down to the gypsy camp; the thin high yelp of camp dogs rang in my ears, the faces of men with high cheekbones and fierce eyes surrounded me, the smell of roasting coffee beans filled the room. I was drowning in memory. The dark lustre of Varvara's hair, the feel of the thick rugs on the floor of the tent—details I had not thought about in decades roiled around me. I rushed upstairs and wrote about Varvara and the coffee.

I was thrilled with what I had written and went over it several times in the next few weeks, polishing the prose. But where to go from there? What was this thing, anyway? It had come from the need to tell; it wasn't trying to *be* anything.

I remembered my old attempt at writing a novel set in Greece, found my old computer file and printed it out. But it was not where I wanted to go anymore. I was fascinated, now, with memory.

I had kept no journal during that year of travel—something I berated myself for now. I hadn't even taken pictures. This had been deliberate. I wanted everything to be *in* me, not *outside*. I wanted memory to be part of my flesh.

I did, however, write letters. Lots of them. To my mother, my sister, and to a whole collection of girlfriends and boyfriends in Canada and the United States. I wrote, now, to my mother and sister and to the few friends from that era I am still close to: "Send my old letters," I begged, "if you still have them."

In the meantime, I wrote another section or two of text, and then stopped. I was stuck, just as I had been with the novel.

After a few months of despair and silence, I began writing down fragments. Whatever I remembered from that time, however small. I had to get it out. I could shape it into something later, I told myself. Often, I found, what started as a tiny memory bloomed into an entire scene. From the memory of stains on the ancient wood floor came the night of the party, the faces of the girls in the protection of their brothers, the near-fight, the persistent rain. It was like yanking at a small string and having a huge fish come up.

Finally, six letters came from my mother. I remember staring at them, the pale-blue airmail envelopes, the tissue paper, the Greek stamps, my handwriting. I was awed by them, and a little afraid. They were like apparitions—my own voice, my own thoughts from the past, a direct line to the person I had been 25 years before. What I remembered of that younger self sometimes embarrassed me, her naïveté, her awkwardness. But her idealism drew me, even as it reproached me. The girl who wanted nothing and the middle-aged woman secure in her comforts—how could they be the same person? With the letters, I would have to confront that old self, uncover her truth, measure the width of my betrayal.

I put the letters in chronological order and read the first one. I was struck by the tone of voice. It was cheerful, happy-go-lucky. A girl on a lark, having a blast, eager to share her adventures. There was none of the sadness, the loneliness, the groping searches I remembered. How could this be? As I read on, I concluded that the person writing was really a persona—one I had consciously developed for my mother and my friends. I was giving them surface. But what a surface it was—full of details and impressions, sights and sounds.

When I read that first letter, I had just finished writing about my arrival in Chania. I hadn't remembered that the youth hostel was a boys' school and that only a shower curtain separated our sleeping quarters from the classroom. I'd remembered being stared at by bunches of schoolboys, but couldn't quite place the circumstances. Reading my younger self telling it made it all come back—and more. I remembered, then, the middle-aged schoolmaster with his patient, wide brow and questioning eyes. But the elderly woman described in the letter, a friend of the schoolmaster, who had written six books of philosophy—who was she? No face emerged.

I went back to my manuscript and added the shower curtain, the staring boys. I did not mention the woman.

I read the letters one at a time, carefully, reverently. Sometimes weeks passed between reading one letter and another. They were rich, heady stuff, and I took them into my present slowly, cautiously. Besides memory, there was that carefree persona to deal with. How reconcile them to each other? How reconcile them to my present, middle-aged self? So many fragments that had to be integrated. Who and what was the real self?

Generally, I tried to write whatever I remembered of a particular period *before* reading the letter I wrote during that period. It was like tuning a guitar string before sounding the pitch pipe. While I was amazed at how much I actually remembered, I was also struck by what I could not recall even with the help of my own words, leaping up from the page. The most important thing that I do not remember has to do with my leave-taking. To my mother I wrote, "We had quite a send-off when we left . . . we had one last dinner with all the 'arty' colony of English-speaking people, and one last wild night at a 'joint' we all go to . . ." I remember nothing of this. I remember only the fear, the sadness. So which is real? Those parties must have occurred, and I am sure I made the most of them, singing and dancing. The persona again.

I have no doubt that if a needle were to be inserted into a part of my brain all those forgotten things would pop to the surface. But they are too far buried, now, ever to call back.

So what does this mean? That those forgotten things are not important? Without the direct link of memory, I cannot know. I chose to leave them out.

In June, 1992, I spent two weeks at the Virginia Centre for the Creative Arts, an artist's colony, where I was determined to finish "My Greece Piece," as I had come to call it. I wrote and wrote, overwhelmed by memory. Even when I lay down to rest on the cot in my studio, waves of images floated over me. Bryan—whose name I hadn't thought of in decades—appearing giddily at my door arm-in-arm with the dark-eyed young sailors. The smell of roasting meat drifting out over the harbour. The way the sea urchins looked in their spiky shells. I was swimming in a deep, rich river, grabbing hold of whatever I could. Sometimes I forgot where I was.

About half of the manuscript was written at VCCA. In those two weeks I wrote as much as I had written in the previous five months. But it was still all fragments. Pieces that had to be fit together into some coherent whole. During my last few days at VCCA I contemplated this. One entire wall of my studio was made out of bulletin board-type white tiles, and a previous occupant had left an assortment of colourful thumbtacks. This gave me an idea. I printed out the whole manuscript and pinned all the pieces up on the wall. Then I began arranging and rearranging. I'd read through the whole thing, then push this piece over here, that piece over there. It seemed as if the pieces could go anywhere—or nowhere. I didn't want a straight chronology; I wanted memory to overtake the present, like it had for me. But the manuscript still needed some kind of order, and that order seemed to escape me. A visual artist friend came by one day to take pictures. On an impulse, I got up and stood against my wall of manuscript, arms outstretched.

I was making a manuscript, but I was also making a self.

My "Greece Piece" still had no real title. Sometimes I called it "Maria" but that didn't seem to be the true focus. One evening I read from the manuscript, including the part about Katzanzakis's grave. A young poet came up to me after and we talked about its lack of a title. "Why don't you use the Katzanzakis quote?" he said. "'I want nothing, I fear nothing, I am free.' That seems to be what the whole thing is about." I went back to my studio and thought about this. He was right. My younger self was looking for freedom, trying to make herself want nothing and fear nothing, in order to find it. The fact that Katzanzakis had found his freedom in death added an additional irony, one that had escaped the notice of my younger self. The title stuck for a while, though I later changed it again.

When my residency at VCCA ended, I found re-entry into normal life extremely difficult. I was still living in Chania in 1966, and memory was more real than anything around me. For days I was unable even to make up a decent grocery list. I'd be on my way to the store and find that I had passed it. I'd have been thinking about the market in Chania, how the olives looked, shining out from huge glass jars. Gradually, painfully, the present asserted itself again.

I spent the rest of the summer shuffling parts, trying to find that elusive order. One afternoon I went looking for the old photos my mother had taken when she visited Maria in Crete. They were not at all as I had remembered them. Yannis was tall, the children were laughing. Their skirts were *short.* How could that be? After I thought about this for a while I realized that my mother's visit was four whole years after I had left. 1970. By then the hemlines had shot up, even in Crete. But why did I remember sombre expressions where the photos clearly showed them all smiling happily? Had I imagined the sadness in their lives? I pulled out Maria's letters again and reread them. No, I had not imagined it. My mother's experience of the family, the one caught by the camera, was not *my* experience of them. And memory had conveniently replaced the celluloid image with its own. I went back to the beginning of my text and changed it: "In a photo I *remember* . . ."

By the end of January the piece was finished, almost exactly a year after I had begun it. In March, I received a package and letter from my sister in Halifax. "I was cleaning out my basement and found these. Do you still want them?" More letters, with postmarks from Greece, Egypt, Lebanon. I was afraid to look at them. What if they were full of things I had not talked about in my memoir? Would I have to open the thing up all over again and integrate yet another layer of truth? I approached them cautiously. To my surprise, the tone of those letters was different from the tone in the letters to my mother. It was more natural, more authentic.

My sister had married at eighteen and was the mother of three by the time I embarked on my adventures. She had married a Lebanese man eleven years older than herself. There was a poignancy about her life that struck me. While I was off galivanting, she kept house, kept children, kept a husband. She was only a year and a half older than I, and her hands were cracked from too many dishes, too many washloads of diapers. I was travelling for her, too, as well as for my mother.

From Greece, I went on, eventually, to Lebanon, to the small village in the mountains where my sister's husband's sisters and their families lived, as well as the whole extended family of cousins and uncles. My sister had never met them. I went there because she couldn't, and described everything in great detail. That was my job.

The letters to my sister from Greece contained no new revelations, but they made me consider the whole matter of personas again. The persona who wrote to my mother was a small part of myself—pushed forward because that's what my mother wanted, that's what would reassure her, please her. The persona who wrote to my sister represented a larger part of myself—more level-headed, less breathy—but still only a part. The real self, I have come to believe, is memory. And that is what I put in my memoir.

Teacher Training

Mary Elizabeth Pope

I stand at the drinking fountain in the hallway outside my classroom. It is the first day of classes, and it is my first day as a graduate teaching assistant. I have no teaching certification to prepare me for this position, and as my qualifications are limited to the grades I earned as an undergraduate in English, I have no idea how I will meet the challenge of teaching Freshman Composition. Earlier, as I passed the classroom, I glanced in to see a number of students sitting in their desks, waiting. I think of all those students now, and wonder about all their different needs—how can I address them collectively, and still address them as individuals? How can I know what they need from me when I have no training or experience with teaching? My watch reads 7:59 am, so I move reluctantly toward the door behind which my students sit. My hands are shaking, and the knot in my stomach is threatening to snap me in half. My heels click on the tiled floor as I enter the classroom and make my way to the podium.

I sat in the new desk on the first day of fifth grade, watching my new teacher pass out textbooks. It was all I could do to sit still for so long; I had been waiting for this day all summer. The new pencils and paper and folders I'd saved my fifty cent allowance for were already arranged in my tray, and I placed each new textbook that Mrs. Crane handed out beside them, feeling very mature. The first day of school was like a clean slate for me; all of the mistakes from fourth grade left safely behind me in Mr. Smith's room and in Mr. Smith's mind. I watched my new teacher as she handed out books; she was a woman of about fifty, and very pretty in a hard sort of pancake makeup way. She walked more purposefully than any woman I had ever known, her posture perfect as she slowly, deliberately put one high-heeled shoe out and placed it carefully in front of her before shifting her weight directly onto it. Her careful, composed walk would be something I would never forget—the way her shoulders moved as she walked, the way her hair didn't, the angle at which she held her chin. I knew instantly that I wanted her to like me, that I wanted to do well in her class, to please this woman whose authority radiated from her every gesture, rang clear in her every word. I rode the bus home that afternoon, bursting with excitement, anxious to tell my mother all about my new teacher.

My students stare at me the first day. Some of them look at me directly; others avert their gaze in case my eyes meet theirs. They are sizing me up. That's okay; I am sizing them up, too. I pass out the syllabus, and discuss classroom policy and course requirements with them. I tell them they must have a C in order to pass my class. They say nothing until I ask them to introduce themselves to the class and say where they are from. After much shifting in their seats, and mumbling out their introduction sentence, they gratefully return their eyes to me. I try hard not to smile too much on the first day, although it is hard. I try to encourage them to understand how my class will help them with all of their classes; I try hard to make them understand that they all have something important to say, that they are all unique and no single other person has the perspective they do. They look at me. I look back at them. I don't know if they believe me or not when it is time to dismiss them, but I watch them file out, and feel hopeful.

I stood in the dime store for maybe thirty minutes, wondering what Mrs. Crane's favorite color was. The folders were there on the shelf—pink, yellow, green, blue, red. On another shelf sat the folders I wished for: clear, plastic binders with front picture slots on the cover. I could just see a collage of Abraham Lincoln underneath those picture slots— Mrs. Crane would like that for sure. But I had only fifty cents, and the clear plastic binders were ninety-nine cents, while the colored cardboard folders were thirty-nine cents. Mrs. Crane wore a lot of blue—navy blue—but since the dime store only carried a corn-flower color of blue—and because it seemed the only color suitable for Abraham Lincoln of the colors available, I took one blue folder to the counter, and watched the lady ring it up. I was sad. What could I do with a plain blue folder that would make Mrs. Crane notice it? I wanted her to know how hard I'd worked on my report, and how much I wanted to do everything right for her. I wanted her to like me.

Holly comes to my office at least once a week. She worries all the time; so much so, that she is terrified to commit anything to paper. She is careful to meet all of the requirements in an assignment, yet she is so careful that it stifles all of the creativity in her expression. She always asks me what I want her to write. Today, her curly brown hair is pulled back in a bun, and above her ruddy cheeks, her eyes are tired and bloodshot, no doubt from staying up all night working, or worrying that she should be working. She is a perfectionist to the point of self-destruction, and although I am pleased with her work, I know she could be more expressive if she were not so afraid of making mistakes.

The assignment I give today is to freewrite about what they want to say in their coming papers. I tell them I won't be grading these and that the only thing that matters is what they discover about their topic. I give them thirty minutes, and I watch Holly hunch over her desk and begin writing. After class, I ask her to stay behind a moment so I can look at her writing. It is thoughtful and original, and much better than what she has been turning in to me on a regular basis. I tell her I want to see her this week, knowing I will anyway. I am hopeful that we can make some progress.

Mrs. Crane stood regally before the class, holding a stack of reports in her hand. I could hardly wait to get mine back and read what she had written. I had worked so hard, and had so carefully and creatively constructed the cover, that I was sure that she would love it. "Class," she began, "why don't we take a look at some of the reports you handed in to me?" I was even more excited—I just knew she would pick mine as a good example for a creative cover, and I could hardly wait to see what she said about it when she held it up. "This is James' report—see how he pasted a mapped picture of Michigan on the cover of his folder for his Michigan report? Very nice. . . .". Next, she held up a crumpled sheet of paper which was half written on in pencil. "This . . ." she paused and her voice fell, as she extended the paper away from her body and pinched it between two fingers, as if it were dirty, or smelled bad, ". . . is Kevin's report." She quickly put Kevin's report on the bottom of the pile, and picked up the next one, commenting favorably on the reports she liked, and giving the same disdainful look and treatment as Kevin's report got to those she did not appreciate. I waited excitedly. I could see the blue edge of my folder sticking out of the pile . . . closer and closer it came to the top . . . and then it was in her hand. "This is Mary Beth's report," she said quickly, and made no comment on it at all, quickly replacing it on the bottom of the pile. I was crushed. My blue folder, with the pennies glued on to form the letters A and L, looked pitiful in the light of Mrs. Crane's disinterest in it. I had been so proud of it, had so carefully selected the shiniest pennies in my father's penny jar to use for the lettering, had handed it in with such confidence; now it seemed a pathetic idea, and I felt embarrassed as my cheeks glowed hotly, wondering how many students were looking at my flushed face, my burning ears.

Jonathan demands a lot of attention. He sits in the front row of my 9:00 class, and has assumed the role and voice of ringleader for the class. He is very entertaining, and I enjoy having him in class most of the time. His constant need to prove that he is the "best" or the most intelligent student in my class, however, is frustrating, because when the class gets into a debate over a particular issue, he cannot let a subject go until he feels he has won. I try to remain a neutral facilitator, although I have at times had to interrupt when Jonathan gets out of hand. I can tell this frustrates him, and I struggle to understand this unfulfilled need he has to be in the spotlight at all times.

Today, I hand back all of the papers except for one that I have saved to read to the class. It is well written, funny, and it meets the assignment's requirements. I choose it because it is a good example, but I have another motive. "I have a paper I'd like to read to you," I tell them. "I enjoyed it and I think all of you will, too." As I read, the class laughs appreciatively, and I do, too. When I am finished, I launch into a description of the next assignment. The students bend over their notes and begin writing, and I casually set Jonathan's paper on his desk. He is smiling, and beads of sweat have formed on his forehead. He is happy, and I am glad. For the rest of the period, things go well.

When Mrs. Crane handed back the folders, I had a second flash of hope: maybe she had only disliked the cover—maybe she had liked the report itself. I watched the other students read her comments, and when my folder was finally in my hands, I flipped through the pages, anxiously looking for her scrawling red script. I couldn't find anything, except for a check mark to signify that she had read it. I looked again, more frantically, and then realized that she had written nothing at all.

Nicole sits in the fifth row, hidden behind Drew, who is tall, and Thomas, who is large. I can just see the top of her blonde head peering at me occasionally as I teach; she is tentative, curious, nervous. Sometimes when class is over and she is on her way out the door, she will glance at me shyly and smile, a blush travelling from her ears to her nose. Nicole works very hard at my assignments; all of her in-class writing is printed, perfectly neat and straight. She is always the last to finish writing. Her papers are very well done, and she is meticulous about meeting every requirement I ask for in each paper. Her writing also reflects the deep thought she puts into the ideas we discuss in class. In Freshman Composition, I could not ask for a better student.

I like to watch her when I hand back papers. On this particular day, what little of her face I can see is lit up, and I am glad for what I have written on the bottom of her paper. "Nicole—this is excellent. Again, I commend you. You meet all of the requirements for this paper, and express your depth of thought on these issues very well. This is the highest grade I have given on this paper, so you should feel proud." I can see all the way from the front of the room that she does.

My name was on the blackboard. Mrs. Crane posted the names of students who had misspelled words in their weekly assignments there until those students could find the correct spelling for the words they had missed. On Monday, my name stood out among the other names simply because it was my name and it had never been on that list before. Then, as the names were gradually erased, those spelling ex-convicts were allowed to join the ranks of the anonymous students who had spelled perfectly that week. Slowly, the list dwindled, and by Thursday, my name was the only one left. I was frustrated. The word was "no one" and it was not one word, as I later learned, but two. I had written "noone," and Mrs. Crane had circled it. I had stared at it for a long time, and then fetched a dictionary from the back shelf of the room. I knew that "someone" and "anyone" and "somebody" and "anybody" and "nobody" were all words. Where was "noone"? I tried "noon," thinking it could be used two ways. Still, it came back marked wrong. I tried "nowan," and again it was marked wrong. On Thursday, I showed Mrs. Crane that it was not in the dictionary. "Well," she had replied frostily, "I can't do anything about that, Mary Beth. The ways you have tried are all wrong." She then dismissed me. I walked back to my desk with heavy heart and burning cheeks, staring at my name on the board. All of the other names were gone, and now everyone knew that I was the stupid girl who couldn't spell. For two long weeks, I stared at my name on the board, the chalky white letters seeming to jump off the blackboard and proclaim to the class my ignorance. Every night, I would hope that some diligent custodian would erase my name by accident. Every morning, my mark of shame would still be there. And every day, Mrs. Crane told me, "It's still wrong."

Darrin sits in the second row of my 9:00 class. I have just returned his paper, and I can see the disappointment that registers on his face. Most mornings, Darrin hides beneath a baseball cap, watching me furtively from beneath it, retreating turtle-like under the visor if my gaze lands momentarily on him. He is a hard worker, and shows up regularly to my office hours to ask for help. I am sorry when I receive his work to have to give it a C+ because of his errors. Darrin has difficulty with spelling and commas, but his work in general is often entertaining and interesting. On the bottom of this particular paper, I have written, "Darrin—this is very funny—I enjoyed reading it. I can see that you are improving the organization and maintenance of focus in your writing. Keep it up (smiley face)! I am still concerned about your use of commas and number of spelling errors that have appeared here. Come see me and we'll talk about it. Good work overall." I know that Darrin will come to my office hours after class. I know what I will say to him. I know how he will respond. And regardless of whether or not he uses the dictionary or spellcheck, regardless of whether the exercises with commas that I will cover with him improve his writing, I know that he will leave my office feeling that he is a good writer who needs a little brushing up, rather than feeling he is a bad writer who is hopeless. He will leave knowing he is capable of doing better, and hopefully this will drive him to improve on his next paper.

On the day before Christmas vacation, we'd made ornaments in Mrs. Crane's class. My ornaments did not look like everyone else's. I had taken the pastry dough and twisted strips together to form candy canes, like the cookies my mother sometimes made at home. I loved art lessons, and I was happy with my ornaments. Mrs. Crane strolled up and down the aisle and paused to compliment those ornaments that she liked. She paused at my desk, and I waited, hopeful that she liked mine. She looked confused for a moment, and then walked quickly up to the front of the room and said, "Now class, let me show you again how to use the cookie cutters. Remember, these ornaments are going to hang on the tree in the big hallway, so we want them to look nice and neat." She searched for a particular cutter. "See," she said with false brightness, as she showed us how to cut the starchy dough, leaving a row of perfectly straight Gingerbread Men in her wake, "they all come out exactly the same if you use a cookie cutter."

Eric is angry. Ever since the first day he walked into my class, it has radiated from him, the aura of anger that surrounds him reminding me of the cloud of dust that follows the *Peanuts* character Pigpen everywhere he goes. With his long, red ponytail and goatee, he sits, withdrawn from the rest of the class, in the back corner, hiding behind his black leather jacket. Eric is brilliant; his forcefully written, anti-establishment, rebellious papers are testimony to this. He is by far the most openly creative student I have, and I handle him carefully because I know he is volatile. However, when he misses several classes in a row, I decide to take action. I stop him on his way out the door and ask him if he will make an appointment with me. He says yes, and we agree on a time. I don't know what I will say to him yet, or whether he will even show up. I only know that I do not want to lose this incredibly bright student, to let him slip through the cracks and disappear, never to return to my class. I am hoping that all he needs is some encouragement.

On the last day of fifth grade, we were allowed to take our brown bag lunches out-side and sit on the lawn in front of the school. I sat with my class and watched Mrs. Crane talk to the students who sat around her. I sat far on the outside of the circle with another girl, and we traded Lifesavers and halves of our sandwiches. When the buses pulled up to take us home that day, Mrs. Crane stood by the door, and hugged each of us. I waited, dreading the hug, but knowing I couldn't get past her. She made a big show out of it, telling the students how much she would miss all of them. When my turn came, she put her mushy arms around me and my cheek burned where it touched her neck. When she fin-ished hugging me, she put her hands on my shoulders and shook me a little. "I'm expect-ing big things from you, Mary Beth." My eyes filled up with tears. I managed good-bye and followed the other students on to the bus. I hated her even more for lying like that in front of all of my friends. As I stood behind the other students in line for my bus, I won-dered why she would say such a thing. The way she had treated me all year told me every-thing I ever wanted to know about what she expected from me.

Mark sits in the back row of my classroom with Walter and Jonathan. All three are football players, and while Walter and Jonathan often doze or talk dis-ruptively, Mark tries to listen closely to what I have to say. He asks questions in class and comes to my office regularly. He is creative and earnest, and usually manages to separate himself, if only in attention span, from his teammates.

I hand his paper back without a grade. While his writing is nearly error free, and might have been an "A" for another assignment, he has not met any of the re-quirements for this paper. Were I to grade it, it would have failed. I know he is a good writer and I do not want to discourage him, so I write on the bottom of his paper, "Mark—your writing, in terms of mechanics and style, is excellent. As a creative piece, this would have received an "A." However, for this assignment, you haven't met the requirements I needed to see. I know you are busy, but I'd like to meet with you and discuss what you need to change here. This is very good writing, Mark, but it doesn't meet the criteria I spelled out in class. You can take your time with it. See me first and we'll talk." Mark reads my comments and looks confused for a moment, but he nods slowly, and I know he understands. I know I haven't crushed him, and I know he will come see me and do better the next time.

Composing "Teacher Training"

Mary Elizabeth Pope

The idea for the "Teacher Training" piece came out of a journal activity assigned in a graduate nonfiction class asking each of us to make a list of all of the topics we would never write about and why. I wrote down "Mrs. Crane" [not her real name] among other things, because even though I was in fifth grade when I had her for a teacher, she was still affecting me in a negative way as a graduate student. The reason, though, that she had made it on the list of things I would never write about was because several months after I'd had her for a teacher, she'd been killed in a car accident. Although I'd never admitted it to anyone but my mother, I had gone home every day in fifth grade praying she would die somehow. I was still harboring a lot of guilt over that, because for years after she was killed, I had nightmares about her; I was convinced that God had answered my prayers and that I was responsible for her death. I still won't ever write about that aspect of my relationship with her, but the exercise got me thinking.

The third paper was to be a personal, non-fiction essay and we were all encouraged to experiment with a format we hadn't used very often. I wasn't sure what to write about, so I went back to my list of things I would never write about, took her name, put it in the middle of a blank page and did some clustering, just to see what would happen. As I clustered, I realized that I had a lot to say about this woman; from the clustering page, I started to freewrite and couldn't believe how angry I was getting just thinking about the things she used to do to me in class. She was the kind of teacher who used humiliation tactics to teach her students, and she really disliked me, even though I tried hard to be a good, hardworking, well-behaved student. I wasn't sure of what aspect of her teaching I wanted to focus on, or if I really wanted to focus more on my reaction to her techniques, but I knew I had a lot to say because I couldn't stop writing.

Another circumstance enters into this topic and my choosing to write about it—at the time I began to write this piece, I was in my second semester teaching freshman composition as a graduate assistant. The whole time I was scribbling about the things she used to do me in class, I was thinking about myself as a teacher and couldn't imagine ever treating my students the way she treated me. My own teaching position had given me a new perspective on the whole Mrs. Crane issue, and it was one I could never have had before then, because I'd never taught. So as I "freewrote," I kept thinking about that aspect of it, although it didn't enter into any of my initial writing.

It actually took me a long time to determine what I wanted to do with this piece, because I knew I had a lot to say about it, and it felt really good getting it on paper. I'd been carrying it around for about thirteen years and had never really discussed it in detail with anyone, except for my mother at the time Mrs. Crane was killed. She had had a profound effect on my confidence as a student. Before I had her for a teacher, my other teachers always made me feel like I was really bright and put me in advanced reading groups and had given me higher level workbooks; I'd always assumed that I was one of the "smart kids," I guess. Before I had her as a teacher, I'd never questioned my abilities or my intelligence; after I had her, I always questioned it, even into graduate school. Getting it out on paper gave me a sense of relief, but at the same time, there was this urgency to do something with it because I needed to make sense of it.

I started with a segmented essay. Although I knew I wanted to use specific episodes from my year in her classroom—I had most of those written—I wasn't sure what to juxtapose with them. I thought of, and actually played around with, a speech I'd been forced to give about her at a tree dedication ceremony. The circumstances were odd—no other student was available to give the speech, and so my sixth grade teacher asked me to do it and gave me about two weeks to prepare. So I had to think about what I could say. No matter what I said about her, if it was nice, it would be a lie. My mother and I worked out a way where I could give the speech without actually saying that I had liked her or that I missed her. And so I played around with juxtaposing the day I gave that speech and the episodes in her classroom. One of the segments went like this:

> "My name is Mary Beth Pope," I began hesitantly, and swallowed out of fear involuntarily. "I was a student in Mrs. Crane's class last year." I paused, thinking of the things I was about to say, and looked at my first notecard. "Mrs. Crane taught us to sing The Grand Old Flag," I said, thinking that all she really taught us was to doubt ourselves, to be afraid, to never put yourself into anything you did lest it be rejected utterly and completely. "She . . . she, uh, liked us to push our . . . uh, chairs in . . ." She also liked to push us until we cried. I looked out at the crowd, and the principal, and at her husband and sisters who sat directly below me. I did not belong here, giving this speech. The wind blew my dress and made me shiver. My voice broke and I began, "She also . . ." I stopped.

It worked okay, but it wasn't really saying what I needed it to say.

After I had done that first freewriting, I prepared for this piece further by visiting the school and classroom where I'd had her for a teacher. The building wasn't being used as an elementary school at the time; it was part of an adult education site, and so there were big desks and bulletin boards with announcements instead of seasonal decorations. But the green shag carpet was still there, and the low chalkboards, and the same heaters where we used to dry our mittens under the window ledges. And the smell was exactly the same. I just stood there and looked. I couldn't breathe very well and the whole thing felt very claustrophobic. I couldn't believe how nothing had changed in terms of my reaction to the room; I instantly felt stupid and ashamed and on guard just by walking through that door at the age of 23, as intensely as I had felt it every morning when I would get off the bus and head for the room when I was ten. It was wild—it really triggered a lot of memories that helped me to remember more specific details in the segments from fifth grade.

After I made that visit to the classroom I talked to my mom about it. We talked about different days that I had come home crying because of something she'd done to me, and Mom even remembered things I had forgotten. The combination of the visit to the classroom and the discussion with Mom helped me to gel some of the ideas that had been brewing or seemed disconnected, and really got me going on the Mrs. Crane segments, although I still was playing around with the "speech" contrast idea and not feeling like it was going in the right direction.

What ultimately happened was that in a peer workshop session, I brought up my concerns about it, and a fellow graduate assistant and I talked about how awful some of our teachers were, and how, now that we were teachers, we couldn't imagine treating our students the way we'd been treated. This was very much an issue for me as I'd been working on the piece, and my friend suggested that maybe I should focus on that aspect of it and drop the whole "speech" thing. Everything fell into place when she said that, and I went home that night after class and just wrote it all out, using different students to compare my teaching style with Mrs. Crane's. I started with a clustering exercise using a few students who struggled with things similar to the issues I struggled with in Mrs. Crane's class, and tried to line up my fifth grade issues with their issues in my class. Then I did a journal entry on how to put it together in the essay, which went like this:

> What I need to do with this paper is show how having been through Mrs. Crane's class, I am much more sensitive to their feelings—I see the defenses, I see the fear, I see the need for approval in them. What I need to do is match one incident from fifth grade with one I've had with my students. For instance, match Darrin with my spelling, Nicole with my need for Mrs. Crane to like me, Mark with the math problems, Jonathan with my need to be admired, Brian with my frustration level, Eric with my need to be understood and accepted, Jason with my need for freedom and creativity within an assignment.
>
> I need to show the little fight I have every day trying to build their confidence while improve their writing skills.
>
> A final paragraph might be me, hunched over a stack of papers late at night. My comments are long—I write at the very least a half a page per student. I am tired. It would be easier to pick out the wrong things and scribble all over their pages, but I cannot.

I still wasn't sure about the exact structure the paper would take—like what student or incident in Mrs. Crane's class to use first, second, etc., but I knew what direction I wanted to go with it, and started writing and rearranging.

Once I had that figured out, the major problem I ran into was how to introduce the piece and how to conclude. I wasn't even sure what exactly I was trying to say, except that having a teacher who made me feel badly about myself helped me to be more sensitive to my own students—I remembered how it felt when she would ignore me or downplay my efforts or tell me I was stupid or wrong. I figured that a logical way to begin would be with the beginning of my first semester teaching, or at the end, looking back on how I had felt at the beginning. I had worried a lot about having had no training in teaching, only in English, and it had bothered me that whole first semester. Over the course of the semester I realized that I had plenty of experience with teaching because I'd been a student my whole life, watching teachers teach. I would think about my favorite English teachers (which was easy because all of my favorite teachers in high school and college taught English) and how they did things, and I'd try and be like them. It never occurred to me that I might have learned the most about how to teach from the worst teacher I'd ever had.

Also, I wanted to conclude by saying that having Mrs. Crane for a teacher made *me* a better teacher—that I had a better understanding of student needs because I'd had experience with my own needs not being met. The problem was how to get it across without making it sound like, "Mrs. Crane was a terrible teacher and I'm a great teacher because I don't do things the way she did," as that wasn't the point. The point was to show that I was able to turn that negative experience into something positive for both my students and myself. I also was hoping that it would be the kind of thing that other teachers could read which would make them think about teachers *they'd* had who'd hurt *them,* and get in touch with their own perspectives as former students. It's kind of a universal experience—I mean, we've all had bad teachers—and I was banking on that so I wouldn't have to do so much explaining.

Actually, I did a lot of explaining anyway in the first draft of the paper—the first paragraph began at the end of the semester of teaching, looking back, and sort of telling what I had learned. This is what it looked like:

> For weeks before my first semester of teaching began, I suffered from severe nausea. My main concern was that I had no experience with teaching—no classes, no training, no nothing. I walked into class on the first day, opened my mouth to speak, and before I knew it the semester was over. I wondered where I had learned to teach, and it was only after that first semester was over, and I had time to think about it, that I realized that I had been a student my whole life. I realized that my real training began in the fifth grade with Mrs. Crane. I have come to believe that only so much of teaching is curriculum; the rest is instinct. For most of my life I have hated this woman who destroyed my self-esteem and all the confidence I'd ever had in myself as a student at the age of eleven. Now, I thank her. Perhaps because of her—or maybe in spite of her—I am too sensitive to my students' needs, and at times I worry that I am too gentle with them. But I am not sorry; in fact, I prefer to be that way, because I

know now that my experiences in her classroom that year have made me a better teacher.

It's awful, when I look at it now, because I manage to sound exactly the way I didn't want to. I concluded the same way, with the teaching evaluations the students wrote at the end of the semester, and I used examples of what they said about me to confirm what I "said" in the body of the paper, comparing my experience with Mrs. Crane to my experience as a teacher. The truth is that when I got back the evaluation sheets that the students had written at the end of that first semester, I sat on the floor of my kitchen and was terrified to open them. When I finally did, and I read the nice things that the students had said about my teaching, I realized that maybe I was a good teacher and that I hadn't done the horrible job that I thought I had. I cried for about two hours that day because the whole semester I'd been afraid I wasn't a good teacher and that my inexperience showed. A lot of them said that they felt like I really cared about them, and that made me think about Mrs. Crane, and how she hadn't cared at all. So when I wrote the conclusion, all that went into it because it was exactly what I was experiencing at the time.

I didn't recognize immediately that both the introduction and conclusion were too self-conscious, and told more than they showed. I didn't really need either—I'd made my point by virtue of the contrast—but I felt obligated to set up some kind of a chronology and demonstrate what I'd learned about my teaching. When my composition instructor handed back the first draft, he said that he liked all of it except the introduction paragraph, which he felt "covered too much ground," and so I took that out and changed it to a scene of me waiting outside my classroom on the first day of class, worried about how I would manage to teach fifty students when I had no experience with teaching at all. Once I did that, I was really happy with it—it gave it the feeling that the reader was going to be there with me, walking into the classroom, scared to death like I was, and it removed that filter of my self-consciousness. I also did some major revisions on what my students said to me in the evaluations—because although I'd taken the quotes right off the evaluations, they were so unbelievably positive and sweet that it made me sound like I was bragging which, again, wasn't the point. What I was trying to do with the evaluations was to give the reader the same sense of "wow" and relief that I'd felt when I read them myself on the floor of the kitchen that day.

That was the point the paper was at when I handed it in for a final grade at the end of the semester, and that was close to the form it was in when I submitted it to the *Language Arts Journal of Michigan.* I did feel at one point that the sections on Mrs. Crane were too wordy, too self-pitying, and that the segments about my teaching were too self-righteous; however, when I was writing it, it felt good to discover something positive had come from that terrible year, and I got really excited about it. Before I submitted it to *LAJM,* I tried to tone it down a little, although after I went back and read it again, I realized I didn't need to make as many changes as I thought.

The draft I sent out ended with the following segments (I had chosen to distinguish past and present by putting the experiences with Mrs. Crane in past tense and italics and my experiences as a teaching assistant in present tense and plain text):

The tears in my eyes blurred the long division problems together until I couldn't see anymore. This was the best day of the month—free morning—and all of the other kids were down in the gym playing games and having fun. Three times I had redone the missed problems, eight of the forty she had given us, and run excitedly down the three flights of stairs to the gym, anxious to join my friends. Three times I had trudged back up the stairs, and been made to sit and rework the problems. I was so frustrated that I couldn't even see the paper, which had been erased so many times that I could see the pattern on my desk through what was left of the paper. Added to this were the tears that now made the page not only wet, but the answers I had gotten right, blurry. I couldn't bring myself to face her again, and I just knew that I could never do it right for her. I hated long division. Mrs. Crane hated me. And I had no idea what to do about it. I couldn't understand why she had singled me out to rework my missed problems—after all, I had worked as hard as all of the other students. And how was it that they all had answered their questions right? Was I the only one who couldn't get the problems right? Maybe it had nothing to do with the work, I thought. Maybe I wasn't pretty enough. She liked Erin and Laurie, who were both pretty. That had to be it—I worked as hard as both of them, but she still didn't like me. Or maybe it really was that I was the only one who didn't know how to do long division exactly right every time. I gave up wondering, and forgot about the gym. It hurt too much to hope that she would let me be like everyone else, so I abandoned my problems and went to look out the window instead.

Mark sits in the back row of my classroom with Walter and Jonathan. All three are football players, and while Walter and Jonathan often doze or talk disruptively, Mark tries to listen closely to what I have to say. He asks questions in class and comes to my office regularly. He is creative and earnest, and usually manages to separate himself, if only in attention span, from his teammates.

I hand his paper back without a grade. While his writing is nearly error free, and might have been an "A" for another assignment, he has not met any of the requirements for this paper. Were I to grade it, it would have failed. I know he is a good writer and I do not want to discourage him, so I write on the bottom of his paper, "Mark—your writing, in terms of mechanics and style, is excellent. As a creative piece, this would have received an "A". However, for this assignment, you haven't met the requirements I needed to see. I know you are busy, but I'd like to meet with you and discuss what you need to change here. This is very good writing, Mark, but it doesn't meet the criteria I spelled out in class. You can take your time with it. See me first and we'll talk." Mark reads my comments and looks confused for a moment, but he nods slowly, and I know he understands. I know I haven't crushed him, and I know he will come see me and do better the next time.

On the last day of fifth grade, we were allowed to take our brown bag lunches outside and sit on the lawn in front of the school. I sat with my class and watched Mrs. Crane talk to the students who sat around her. I sat far on the outside of the circle with another girl, and we traded lifesavers and halves of our sandwiches. When the buses pulled up to take us home that day, Mrs. Crane stood by the door, and hugged each of us. I waited, dreading the hug, but knowing I couldn't get past her. She made a big show out of it, telling the students how much she would miss all of them. When my turn came, she put her mushy arms around me and my cheek burned where it touched her neck. When she finished hugging me, she put her hands on my shoulders and shook me a little. "I'm expecting big things from you, Mary Beth." My eyes filled up with tears. I managed good-bye and followed the other students on to the bus. I hated her even more for lying like that in front of all of my friends. As I stood behind the other students in line for my bus, I wondered why she would say such a thing. The way she had treated me all year told me everything I ever wanted to know about what she expected from me.

I sit on the floor of the living room on the day I receive my student evaluations back. I have no idea what they have said, and I wonder if after reading them I will feel better or worse about my performance this past semester. I open them slowly, afraid of what they could say. I can remember really giving it to some of my teachers; I wonder if anyone has done that to me. I pick up the first one and read what it says: "I really liked this class and teacher. She was always so chipper in the morning." I smile, wondering who wrote it. I pick up the next one: "Miss Pope was a very good teacher. This was a great class, even though it was at 8:00 in the morning. The journals were fun—maybe you could do more of those in your next class." The next one reads: "This is the only class I didn't drop." I laugh, flattered by this student who chose to stick with me, and read another one. "Miss Pope really cares about her students and always has something positive to say about our work, even when we get a low grade." I pick up the next one, and the next. I smile until I come to the one that reads: "Miss Pope's class was my favorite class of all—and the only reason I got up for any of my classes." I don't recognize the writing, but I don't care. It is then that I realize my face is wet from my tears. I think about Mrs. Crane. And I thank her.

When the editors at *LAJM* wrote to me and told me they wanted to publish it, they asked that I make a few changes—essentially, take out two segments: one about the math exercise Mrs. Crane had made me rework instead of letting me play with the other kids in the gym, and the conclusion. I felt kind of funny chopping out the math segment part because I was so angry at her for that—and I think it showed, too, because it was long (probably why they wanted it out). Taking out the conclusion was fine with me, though, because once I realized that it was going to be published and other people besides my composition instructor and classmates would read it, it occurred to me that the conclusion could seem exaggerated or too slanted toward glorifying my teaching success that semester.

The editors also asked me to make the last day of school the final segment for fifth grade, and finish with a segment about my student, Mark. In the passage above, then, I was dropping the first and last segments and reversing the order of the middle two. I was actually really happy with that revision because it gave the piece a nice feeling of continuity, instead of closure, which made it seem as if there had been an end to what I'd learned. And for the purposes of the journal, I could see why they wanted it that way.

When the journal came out, and I saw it in print, and read it again, I realized that I was really happy with the way that it was written. The whole experience of writing it and revising it and then seeing it in print was important for me for a couple of reasons. The first was that I felt like it was okay for me to have really disliked Mrs. Crane as much as I had—I'd never wanted to admit that after she died because it seemed like such an awful thing to say about someone who was dead (especially since I'd wished her that way so often before it happened). Also, it helped me to see that I had left that year in her class with something important—that she really did teach me something significant by not giving me the things that I needed, and that though it was difficult to endure at the ages of ten and eleven, it had become a really significant learning experience for me.

There has been some carryover from writing this piece into the writing I am doing now indirectly. I learned that when I am writing, I need to watch myself think, and not try so hard to make everything go in a particular direction right away. For instance, if I had paid attention to the fact that I kept thinking "I would never treat a student that way" as I was writing the segments about Mrs. Crane, maybe it wouldn't have taken me so long to recognize that *that* was the direction the writing really wanted to go. A lot of times, I will sit down with what seems like a great idea, but then I can't figure out where to go with it. If I just pay attention to what I am thinking, and trust it, and not dismiss it as just an external observation about the work I'm doing, I can get a better perspective on how I really feel about what I am writing. It's hard to do, but I've been trying.

Zion

Maureen Stanton

Sometimes I wake up in the middle of the night and I don't know where I am. My bed is a flying carpet. Flat on my back, I am looking up at the stars, whizzing around in blackness. Then I slow down, the carpet lands. I figure out which direction I am facing and get a map of the room in my head. I recognize the window and the streetlight. The bed, the door, the lamp. I remember where I am, the longitude and latitude of my life. Fixed to locale, nailed to a place, I can begin to make order.

I am dozing in the hospital bed with Steve when he pulls me.

"Mo, something is happening to me. My head is shrinking."

"What do you mean? What does it feel like?"

"It feels like it's the size of a grapefruit." He starts to cry, the first time since all this started. I run to the nurses' station. "Help. Something weird is happening to Steve." Fay and Dora come and give Steve a shot, but this causes his tongue to swell and his eyes to roll back in their sockets. Fay holds his mouth open, while Dora gets a doctor who injects something into Steve's bicep, and after a few seconds he breathes normally.

"It was just a reaction to the new pain medicine," Fay tells us, like it was nothing more than a bee sting. I stand near Steve's head and try not to touch him too much. The feeling that his head is small stays with him the whole night.

We are at the hospital of last resort, a small brick building in Zion, Illinois, an hour north of Chicago. It's a hospital where the bedspreads are worn thin and have holes. A hospital that serves carrot and celery juice, and offers alternative treatments for cancer. One week a month we come here. Steve gets his poison. I bleed.

The doctors here are different than at the hospital Steve checked out of back in Michigan. For one thing, most of them are Filipino. It unnerves Steve's parents who discourage our decision (false hopes, grasping at straws). But here the doctors don't give up as easily. Steve's first oncologist wrote a note on his chart which we read during our flight to Chicago. *It is very sad to see that the patient cannot accept the poor prognosis.* Two months, she predicted for a twenty-nine-year-old man with three small children, then patted his hand and walked out of the room, dry as a desert, tearless, leaving us in the starkness of Steve's future.

Dr. Sanchez and Dr. Melijor give us information, allow us to see Steve's nuclear scans. Married to gray film, Steve's skeleton glows. Small black dots are sprayed from his skull to his kneecaps as if someone plugged him with bird shot. Cranium, sternum, ribs, vertebrae, pelvis, femur. It is a frightening lesson in anatomy. I try not to act shocked, but the black dots are more numerous than I had envisioned when the previous doctors spoke of "widespread metastases" and "multiple tumors." "Multiple" meant six or seven, a six-pack, a touchdown, a number we could beat. I count more than two dozen specks on the little x-ray man that is Steve—malignancies humming inside his flesh. Not to mention his liver, marbleized like a high priced cut of beef, with cancer cells. Now it is real.

I arrive at the hospital at nine in the morning and climb in bed with Steve as if I am joining him in his body, unzipping his skin like it's a space suit, and snuggling in. His roommates, Greg and Chuck, don't seem to mind. Greg is an insect exterminator from South Carolina with testicular cancer. He sleeps most of the time, or reads his Bible. The only noises he makes are vomiting, or buzzing for the nurses. Hand him his urine jug, fix his pillow, bring him a drink. He thinks he is at a resort.

Chuck is in the other bed. He has a clear tube taped inside his nose that pumps oxygen from tanks on the side of his bed into his drowning, malignant lungs. He is an earthbound scuba diver. Chuck breathes loud and heavy, and coughs wet, phlegmy coughs which temporarily paralyze his wife's kinetic fingers as she sits in a chair by his bed and knits violently, like she is weaving Chuck a new set of lungs.

Days pass by slowly. Flowers arrive for Steve from his parents. *When God closes a door, he opens a window.* I put the card on the nightstand, open the curtains and watch activity below, cars and people. Fat, slow winter flies buzz against the sealed glass. They appear out of nowhere, it seems, these retarded creatures, and now they are desperate to get out, as if they know they are trapped, as if they have some power of cognition. That's what I learn when I accompany Steve to the hospital. Empty hours. Time to think.

We walk around the hallways, Steve holding onto his pole like a staff. Bottles are suspended from the pole, clear liquids that feed the catheter in Steve's chest and flow into the big subclavian vein direct to his heart, like a fast underground train. Nitrogen mustard, 5-FU, methotrexate. The names remind me of the defoliants that were dropped on Vietnamese jungles. They cause hair to fall out of Steve's head, off his chest. His underarms and legs are bare. His eyebrows are missing. His pubic hair is gone. He looks like a fetus, a tall, skinny fetus. Still,

he is handsome with his heavy eyelashes and soupy blue eyes, purple hollows below them, like watercolor. His eyes look bigger with his face so thin and his skin
wrapped so tightly over his bones. Delicate bones.

Visitation ends at eight, but the nurses understand that hours matter and allow
me to stay until midnight. Then I walk to the room I have rented from a notice I
saw posted in the hospital cafeteria. Three blocks away and ten dollars a night.
The couple who own the house are up when I arrive.

"Wipe down the shower before you get out. Don't use too much toilet paper. And use the towel more than once." Noma scolds me before I have trans-
gressed. She is a tiny woman with messy gray hair and one sharp, pointy tooth,
like an egg tooth a baby bird uses to peck its way out of a shell.

"Who've ya got in the hospital?" she asks.

"My boyfriend."

"Isn't that a shame." She asks me where I am from, and then says, "Emil's
got a cousin in Detroit."

Emil has filmy blue eyes and hair that is sugar white with bangs cut straight
across his forehead. He looks like an old angel.

"They come from all over to go to that hospital. We've had people from
Florida, Kentucky . . . New Zealand! Staying right in your room," he says, as if I
am privileged.

"We're blessed with good health, thank the Lord," Noma cuts in. "Emil
broke his ankle forty years ago. It was healed by a miracle at our church and it
never bothered him since, right, Em?"

"Still march with the Brothers of Zion band sixty years now. I'm the oldest
clarinet player." Emil opens a closet and pulls out a red, wooly coat and matching
pants with gold braiding up the seams.

"It's no coincidence you're in Zion," he says. "This is a holy town. Miracles
take place all the time."

"That's very nice," I say, and manage to excuse myself. Behind the bedroom
door, I flop onto the lumpy single bed and cry. I do every night. It's part of my
sleep.

Later I am poked awake by noises in the kitchen: a spoon clinking against a dish,
footsteps, cupboards opening and shutting, a toilet flushing. Then the sequence
repeats. I can hear snoring from Noma and Emil's room. They would have had to
pass me to get to the kitchen, but I didn't hear anyone in the hall. I become convinced there is a ghost just outside my door, making that last meal over and over
again, unable to let go. I pull my blankets up around my chin. My heart is pounding, pushing my tired blood, echoing in the small room. I pray. *Please, God, don't
let it come in here.* I lie in stiff fear until gray light when spirits are banished, then
wake up at eleven, groggy. Emil's white toupee is on a styrofoam head on the
kitchen table and his teeth in a jar of water on the bathroom sink. I ask Noma if
she heard noises in the night.

"Just me eating my cereal," she says. "I get up about three every morning and have some cereal."

"What about the flushing?"

"Oh, that's the pump clearing water out of the basement."

In the daytime, I can get along. There are objects, events, people to hold on to, give texture to time, divide up space. But at night, I lose my way, lose my mind. It's easy.

The next month I find a room for $75 a week at the Harbor Hotel. The office is the living room of a small house that smells like curry. A boy is playing on the rug in the fuzzy penumbra of the television. A woman with a red dot on her forehead gives me a key and says there are no refunds, then directs me to their other hotel down the street.

The rooms are in the basement of a small, brick apartment building. There is no front desk, only a broken pay phone, and leaves blowing around the hallway. A disheveled man is loitering near the telephone. As far as I can tell, I am the only guest.

Ramona and Sue and Estherine and Georgia are on the same chemotherapy schedule as Steve, so we see them every month. Steve flirts with them, bald and in their bathrobes. They laugh when he tells them he is going to wear his camouflage hunting shirt and fatigues for his upper G. I. test. He likes the audience, but I don't care to share him much. Of what little he has left, I want it all. I am with him most of the time, in the bathroom even, keeping him company. He sits on the toilet and rests his head on the back of a fold-up chair. I sit on the chair and touch his back lightly. His skin is hot all the time now and I like to put my cold hands on it. We sit there in silence waiting for him to pee.

Steve naps and I read. Mysteries. Cheap little stories that completely absorb me, simple words I can eat, pages I can bend and fold. Perry Mason novels are the main staple of my diet. Perry always finds the killer, always wins his cases. I like the surety of that. There isn't anything in the stories to disturb me, or throw me off balance. They ask nothing of me.

At night I read to Steve, poems, clips about U.F.O.'s from *Omni* magazine, and stories from supermarket tabloids. GIANT FLYING CATS TERRIFY TOWN. WOMAN ABDUCTED BY ALIENS CAN NOW TALK TO ANIMALS. CANCER MAN'S LAST REQUEST: A JAGUAR CAR PARTS CATALOGUE. I envision a man in a leotard and cape with a big "C" on his chest, an action hero defying death. Cancer Man.

This month Cancer Man is undergoing an experimental treatment—whole body hyperthermia. His body temperature will be raised to 108 degrees Fahrenheit. The theory is that abnormal, mutant cancer cells slough off at 107 degrees, while healthy cells, skin, organs, muscle, brain tissue, begin to die at temperatures just above 108. It is a precarious balancing act to reach the right temperature, sustain it long enough to do specific damage, then lower it again. Steve has signed a liability waiver, a disclaimer of some kind that contains the words "result in possible death."

Dr. Kim, the anesthesiologist, brings me into the treatment room to see Steve. He has been stripped naked and wrapped head to toe in gauze like a mummy. To raise his temperature, he is wrapped in a heated plastic blanket filled with water and alcohol. A thermometer in his mouth, one in his rectum, and two others will monitor his fever for the next eight hours.

I spend the day wandering along Lake Michigan, the Illinois side which is not as sandy and beautiful as the Michigan side. Blame it on the wind, I think, noticing this habit I have of searching for culprits. I go to the library and draft a letter to Steve's insurance company pleading with them to pay for the hyperthermia. In the park, a large bird boldly garbed in a blood red hood and black and white tuxedo clings to the bark of a tree, a red-headed woodpecker. It stands out among the muted browns and greens and feels like a gift, blatant beauty. When I return Steve is knocked out, in intensive care, sleeping it off. He wakes later delirious, mumbling like a drunk, lashing out with his hands, yanking at the tubes and bandages. Wild. For two days Steve sleeps fitfully. Finally, he recognizes me. I say, "Tell yourself each day you are going to get better and better." He says, "I'm going to get better and better. I'll be the best."

These treatments—chemicals, radiation, hyperthermia—attempt to murder Steve each time; push him to the brink, lull him back, give him time to fortify then zonk him again. It's a tease, an oxymoron, Orwellian doublespeak. We must kill you to cure you, make you sick to make you better. It's a lie, a trick with fun house mirrors. We don't trust anyone.

The Harbor Hotel is quiet all week. Then late Friday night I hear people yelling and kicking the doors to the rooms, moving towards mine. I click off my lamp so they won't see a sliver of light leaching under my door into the hallway. I'm afraid that if they find me they will kill me. It is my nighttime logic. I practice saying "Who's there?" in a deep, male voice. After a while, they manage to break into a room a couple of doors down and party all night. I make myself small and quiet like the tiny baby cockroaches that scatter whenever I turn on the fluorescent light in the bathroom. I plan my escape out the small casement window above the television, level with the ground. Finally I sleep hard and wake up to the sounds of Big Wheels on pavement.

Outside, I blink at the sunlight. Mothers sit on the brick steps smoking cigarettes. They stare at me like I am an alien, out of my country, away from my land. Timeless, placeless, bodiless.

When I get to the hospital Chuck's bed is empty. He died during the night after a long coughing fit. His wife, Carol, is gone without a trace, not one thread left behind. Steve has gotten scorched from the hyperthermia. Bad wrapping job. The soles of his feet and his scrotum are tender. He's pissed off about this, but when Jane, a volunteer, comes around he forgets for a while. Steve and I stare at her round and bouncy firm flesh encased in stretchy nylon like she is wearing beach balls, at her unruly white hair and huge blurry eyes behind thick glasses. She hands out newspapers and carnations, and speaks in a flat, nasally voice, yogic, like a Sufi chant. "I have five dogs, two cats, a mallard (now in my freezer waiting for the Guinness Book of World Records to verify it as the oldest albino duck—seventeen years, as old as my niece), and a pet starling that barks like a dog and shouts 'thief' every time a stranger comes in my house."

Jane invites me to eat with her in the hospital cafeteria. She talks while she chews, projecting bullets of deviled ham and masticated bread bits. One lands on my cheek and it is all I can focus on, don't know what words she is saying. I avoid her after that. I give Steve enemas, put my fingers in his rectum, mop up his vomit, swab the raw, pink flesh around his catheter site, but none of that fazes me the way having to eat with Jane seems an insurmountable task. Everything seems odd. Off.

This life develops a rhythm: three weeks home, one in Zion. Months go by this way. I dial a number pinned to the hospital bulletin board and a woman named Martha says she has an extra room in her apartment. When I get there Martha is gone and her son, Jeff, is playing chess on a small hand-held computer, smoking a cigarette with a puddle of gray cat on his lap. He explains that Martha was called to take care of someone for the week. She is a home-care aide.

"Bummer," he says, after he asks why I am there. He is in his early twenties with long hair parted in the middle and scruffy sideburns zigging down his jaw line.

"I'm trying to quit drinking," he says. "I haven't had a drink in over two weeks."

"Good." I feel my head bobbing up and down like one of those spring-necked ceramic cats you see on dashboards. I've noticed this: when you tell people your boyfriend has cancer they feel they must ante up their own pain and lay it on the table. At first, I thought it was nice, a kind of offering, but now it just makes me mad. Nobody's pain is equal to ours. I feel self-righteous and chosen. Anointed and doomed at the same time.

When I get up the next day, Jeff is mixing a glass of lemonade, smoking a cigarette and playing chess.

"I guess you like to play chess." I feel obliged to address this man in whose living room I am a stranger.

"Keeps me out of trouble," he replies. "I'm on probation for dealing drugs."

"Good luck," I say. Fucking wingnut, I think. Who cares? It feels good to be mean.

Put your troubles in the hands of the Lord and he will help you. Steve flings this month's card from his parents across the room. I pick it up and set it on the night-stand. I can't stomach the tension of a thing being where it doesn't belong, throwing off order, tempting chaos. I fill a plastic urine jug with water for the flowers and arrange them. I check selections on Steve's menu card, cut his toenails, get ice from the machine down the hall for his pitcher, try to keep busy before succumbing, inevitably, to watching television. Nothing airs in the morning except for talk shows, game shows, and odd sports, like curling, a bizarre contest involving a puck and a broom, a tight little silly game. Lunch arrives. Steve looks at it and puts the metal lid back on. I walk across the street and pick up some Kentucky Fried Chicken.

Later Steve unhooks himself from the tubes and we escape from the hospital. Outside it is cold and gray. We walk around holding hands. I like Steve's hands, his long, slender fingers, nails brittle and yellowed, his palms still rough and callused though he has not worked in over a year. He has two warts on his left hand, stubborn, rubbery bumps that I like to bite. They're large, these hands, but deft as he glues a part on a model car with his son, or takes an eyelash out of my eye. Steve used to stand behind me and press my nipples between his fingers while I stirred spaghetti sauce, and when we slept, his leg draped over mine, clinging like sweaty children, he cupped my breast in his palm like it was a dove. Now touching hurts him, so the only kisses I give are little brush strokes.

Steve makes it one block to a park near the hospital before he tires. We sit on a bench and watch a mother absentmindedly hand bread to her daughter. The little girl stuffs fistfuls of the bread into her mouth, every now and then flinging a crust at the ducks. Steve laughs, and I kiss his knuckles as the girl fills her cheeks and her mother stares at something else across the pond.

Friday night Jeff is playing chess with the television shouting in the background. I crawl into bed and stare at squares of light on the wall. Street lights, window panes, simple inanimate objects make me feel sad.

Hours later I am awakened by a cat screeching, then Jeff laughing loudly. The sound is distorted, like in a tunnel. Too loud for laughing alone, I think. My eyes are wide open, sucking in the dim light. I hear Jeff's maniacal laugh again and the cat yelps painfully. I envision Jeff screwed up on hallucinogens, torturing the cat. Greenish street light burnishes the door knob, which I expect to rotate at any moment, Jeff entering my room to rape me and carve me up with a knife, laughing that wild, enormous laugh the whole time. I stuff the corner of the pillow in my mouth to muffle sobs.

Nights can be like this—scenes from frightening horror films. Disaster is no longer an abstract concept. Anything is possible and danger is everywhere. I have a hard time differentiating the real from the imagined. Steve used to scare me, curling his index finger and growling, "redrum redrum redrum" like the little boy in *The Shining,* amused by how I had to skulk from light switch to light switch to pee in the middle of the night. I have asked him not to come back and haunt me, even if it is just a joke. He has asked me not to write about him, wants to disappear. I am terrified of his leaving, waking up next to a stiff corpse. I think about it every night when I lie down beside him, of being left alone, abandoned.

I wake up at seven stiff-necked, and for a second surprised to be alive and okay. Lines pressed into my face from the wrinkled sheets make a map, look like a place. I gather my stuff, don't stop to wash. Downstairs, Jeff is gone. I leave the key on the table and walk to the hospital. The nurses break the rules and let me sleep in Chuck's old bed for one night. In the morning, the long black hospital limousine delivers Steve and me to the airport. People in cars pass us on the highway and stare into our opaque windows like we are celebrities. We can see them, but they can't see us, as if we are ghosts. We exist in a parallel life: we can see our peers (getting married, having babies, buying houses), but we can't touch them anymore. We are headed somewhere else.

On Writing "Zion"

Maureen Stanton

"Zion" began as journal entries made in 1986 when the events in the essay were taking place. I wasn't thinking then that in the future this might be a story or an essay, but was writing for the same reason I record anything in my journal—to understand what is happening in my life. (This isn't always the case. There are other experiences that I know I will want to turn into an essay, so I keep specific notes, though they are mostly facts, ideas, and observations rather than the "talking to myself" of journal writing.)

I didn't look at the journal until probably two years after the experience. Grief over the death of Steve, the subject of this essay, consumed me, and I was busy trying to figure out how to fill up my life, which had revolved around Steve's cancer for eighteen months. Also, Steve had asked me not to write about him and I was struggling with this issue. When I started to write Zion as a "piece," I talked with a counselor who had helped me through this period about whether I could write about Steve. She was blunt and logical. Steve was dead, and this was my story too so I had a right to tell it.

After the fogginess of grief started to lift I began to remember interesting details of the experience, interactions and events I couldn't seem to recall when I was engulfed by emotions. The lifting of the veil of grief brought a flurry of raw material forward and I jotted notes everywhere, often waking up at night to write down a sentence that would later trigger a whole episode.

This has become my modus operandi for writing. I get very excited about an idea and become preoccupied with it. My mind is constantly tugged back to that subject whenever it is not engaged (usually when I am trying to sleep, but I will always sacrifice sleep for inspiration, even when it means arriving at work the next day a bit exhausted).

These scribbled thoughts, observations, words, and memories are stashed in a file because they seem somehow related. The file thickens and at some point reaches a critical mass. Visually, I think of it as a bunch of free-floating atoms and molecules ranging around in their own individual orbits, then something like the Big Bang happens, a tiny pop perhaps, and these particles react to one another and begin to attract and repel, combine and multiply to create a cluster of raw material. This is accompanied by an almost physical restlessness to write the piece, and suddenly (it often seems) I begin to work on it in earnest (leaving other pieces I am working on half-finished).

For this piece, which at various times was titled, "Cancer Man," "The Rooms I Stayed In" (thankfully that one didn't last long), then "Dreaming in Zion," the critical mass occurred about three years after Steve died. I pulled the piece together and brought it to a fiction workshop at the Iowa Summer Writing Program. I had been writing short stories exclusively, largely because that is what I focused on in creative writing classes in college. No one ever mentioned anything about essays. In fact, in four undergraduate and one graduate creative writing classes, I never heard the word essay mentioned, nor was it offered as a course on its own. Even in the writing groups I joined everyone seemed to be writing fiction.

The version of "Zion" I took to the workshop was only slightly different than this final version, yet I was naively trying to pass it off as a short story. That version was straight narrative, factual recitation with detailed description but little reflection. The workshop attendants wanted to see more of "me" in the piece, and they thought that, although it was moving, it was not complete and was not a successful short story. As with nearly all of my writing at that time, I didn't know what it was or what to do with it. I wasn't really writing short stories but I kept trying to squash my pieces into that mold.

I tried to put more "me" into the story but what came out, I see now, was not poignant reflection but raw emotion, untempered anger and resentment mostly. The piece took on a maudlin and self-pitying tone. I did not know what to do with Zion at this point, so I did nothing. It sat for a while before I decided to bring it to a living room writing group I participated in (after removing the added "me"). Two of the members of the writing group were professors of English and accomplished writers, and the others were professionals of all ages, all good writers and critics. This group felt the piece was flat, and although the writing was good, it lacked something. I still did not know what to do with the piece, so it landed back in hibernation, this time for about three years. But it was in that living room group that I first heard the term creative nonfiction from Mike Steinberg. I didn't grasp immediately what he was talking about, but as I slowly began to open up to this genre, I felt like I was finding my way home. This was the type of writing I naturally tended to and I was excited about it, but I still didn't know what made good creative nonfiction.

Having been somewhat liberated from my fixation with short stories and the constraints of trying to fit my personal experiences into that format (and feeling like a liar and a fraud doing so), I began to write about whatever stirred me without trying to set up dialogue, point of view and develop characters. (Although I think what I learned in fiction workshops helped me with pacing, tone, freshness of language, and precision.) I wrote two more essays, both about Steve, who managed to work himself into nearly everything I was writing regardless of how remotely related he seemed to be to the subject at hand. Both of these essays were published, but I felt that it was dumb luck, that I had stumbled into something that I couldn't sustain or duplicate as I was unaware of how I did it or why people liked the essays.

At this time, I began to get increasingly frustrated with my demanding job, which was eclipsing my free time and energy to write. (Writing had always been my umbilical cord to a meaningful existence.) I saved money for over a year, quit my job, and moved to the homes of friends and family members where I could live inexpensively. (Although this was frightening financially, as soon as I did this part-time and consulting opportunities began to fall into my lap. It was uncanny.) This is significant because if I had not done this, I feel strongly that "Zion" and many other pieces would never have been resurrected at all. (More importantly, continuing to live an artless, passionless existence and working a thankless, dull job would have caused my soul to wither on the vine, the marrow in my bones to dry up.) With the luxury of time I could put my heart and soul into creating more finished works that gave me a greater sense of satisfaction.

Having bought myself time to write (I envisioned a big parking meter into which I deposited my hard-won savings that now registered one year of time, ticking, ticking . . .), I began to work on my essays and to read other essayists in literary journals, collections, and magazines. It was this reading that helped to bring me along. Who knows how long it would have taken for me to discover truths about writing creative nonfiction on my own? Although I did not retrieve "Zion" to work on right away, in this incubation period I was beginning to get a sense of what makes a good essay, and why people bother to write essays after all. (I do think that it was good, though, to write creative nonfiction without formally studying it at first. There was a terrific freedom about not knowing what I was trying to do, to let the writing range freely. I think it allowed my voice to emerge.)

I attended a creative nonfiction workshop at the Stonecoast Writers' Conference in 1996, encouraged by Mike Steinberg, the man who had first introduced me to the term "creative nonfiction." This was the first time I had ever taken a workshop in this genre. The workshop was excellent. It reminded me of a trip I took to Brazil where I was immersed in the Portuguese language, yet could only pick up a word or two from each exchange. Then, after three weeks there, something happened, some leap of understanding, where I began to be able to interpret whole sentences and chunks of conversation. I liken that experience to Stonecoast because afterwards, instead of moving towards the writing blindfolded, occasionally glimpsing into some secret chamber of knowledge, I began to comprehend holistically the concept of creative nonfiction so that I could now purposefully sculpt the subconscious or "blind" part of my writing.

After the workshop, I pulled "Zion" from its entombment. It had been one of my favorite subjects, the surrealness of the experience, and I wanted to perfect it as much as I could. I didn't want it to sit in my file drawer forever. I wanted people to read it, like most anything I write. I wanted to create a thing of beauty, a story that intrigued and moved people. A decade had passed since the actual experiences in Zion, but writing it in the present tense returned me to the scene, placed me squarely back in the hospital and those seedy rooms where I slept. I cried every time I read each revision. It was biologically ordained, this weeping, from a deep, forgotten place inside me.

My process is to work on a computer draft, then to rearrange paragraphs, edit, and mark up the text by hand, then back to the computer, only to repeat the process. I revised the manuscript probably two dozen times over the course of a month or so, sometimes setting the piece aside for a day or two and working on something else, or gardening, which is my form of meditation. I originally intended to change the piece from present to past tense after getting it all down. I was only using the present to make the experience come alive for me again, to sharpen details, but as the writing progressed, I began to grow attached to the piece the way it was. I liked the immediacy of the story, the sense of being transported into the hospital or hotel room. And I had a strong desire to preserve the authenticity of that section of my life, to keep it intact, like a clipping from a film reel. I wanted to keep the memory pure, not to muddy the events with thoughts that represent how I feel now rather than how I felt then.

I can become obsessed with a piece, and lately I am fortunate enough to have time for obsessions. With Zion, the prose seemed sparse, pared down (compared to all that happened in real life and compared to earlier drafts). Every word mattered so I often spent a half-hour on one word, going back and forth, changing my mind then changing it back to the way it was originally. I realized I needed to be exact about Steve's chemotherapy instead of relying on my memory. Staring at the names of cancer drugs in the library released waves of memories about this experience. Sometimes I would go in search of metaphors, once sitting in the library all afternoon reading the Biblical references to Zion (which I didn't import into the essay after all since they felt forced). Sometimes I think I was trying too hard to create a "thing" instead of letting the "thing" create itself, but I usually recognized the artificial passages after a few days time and removed them (no matter how fond I was of the phrase or image I wanted to push into the piece).

I dug back into my original journals of a decade before, reread my old letters from Steve and listened to a tape of his voice. In the end, I added little to the factual bulk of the piece. I reviewed earlier drafts with comments made by my peers at the Iowa Workshop and in my writers' group. My typed out questions to the living room group at the bottom of the essay demonstrate my confusion about what I was attempting. These "questions for the group" were: what tense should the story be told in? Should this be a short story or an essay? Is there such a thing as true fiction? It seems I was still leaning towards writing fiction.

I found the copy of the manuscript from Mike Steinberg. His comments, thoughtfully offered four years prior to this rewrite, were exactly what the piece needed. He liked a lot of the external description, but said, "I'd like to see you get more reflective about the experience . . . and yes, we'll talk about your questions regarding autobiographical essay/fiction." He pointed out places where the piece could be "opened up." It appears I wasn't ready for his comments when he gave them to me years ago, but after the Stonecoast workshop, I finally understood what he was getting at. (I have saved all the manuscripts from workshop reviewers over the years because I value their comments, but interestingly, Mike Steinberg was the only one who referred to Zion as an "essay" and treated it as such when critiquing it.)

When it was obvious that I was doing nothing more than fiddling with prepositions and articles, the tiniest bits of text, I decided the piece was done. In any event, I simply didn't know where else to go with it and called it done. I may someday rewrite this piece in past tense, as I have been encouraged to do, and maybe this will strengthen the story and give it more weight and relevance. But more time will have to pass. When I work on something as intensely as I did this, I get weary of it. I start to feel ridiculous about the amount of time I am spending on it (which feels disproportionate to things taking place in the larger world around me). This happens often with my writing. I tire of pieces (they wear me out), so I put them away, which usually turns out to be a good thing. When I return to them later, what is missing, what is false or contrived, what is sloppy or sophomoric becomes more obvious. And I, for the distance passed (often years), am wiser in my approach to the piece. Unfortunately, this does not make me a prolific writer, only a careful one.

Overall "Zion" has not changed dramatically since its original incarnation nearly a decade ago and many, many hours of labor later. The format turned out to be the same, and the opening and ending paragraphs are similar. Some passages are verbatim from the original draft. But the difference lies in telling phrases, observations, and reflections, which give the narrative facts a luminescence that only distance and learning can yield. It seems that finally, after a decade, I could look with relative detachment at this experience and see it for what it really was, and in subtle ways, infuse these small epiphanies into the essay.

In looking back, I see four stages that this, and most of my other essays, passed through. The first is the molecular stage, that early collection of bits of information, what I find fascinating, unusual, funny or poignant at the time it occurs, whether I retain it in memory or in a physical form on pieces of paper. The critical mass stage is next. The particles are vibrating on their own in proximity to one another until they reach a critical mass and a reaction occurs. The writing begins in a fury, raw data, raw memory, stream of consciousness writing.

Incubation happens throughout the writing when I walk away from the piece and it sits inside me, silently arranging itself, so that when I next visit it, I have made important connections. Then I edit and rewrite. The placement of events and observations creates irony, mood, pathos, humor. Events are taken out of the chronological or random order and purposefully placed, refined, commented on. With Zion, incubation occurred over ten years as I intermittently resuscitated the piece, but also during the active writing periods, each night when I turned off my computer and went to bed with the essay on my mind. This seems important, that the essay was written only partially at the desk. Much of it was written while I gardened or walked or lay in bed mulling it over.

Insight is the last thing to come, what the story is really about. I often don't know until very late in the process, and the story is frequently about something other than I intended, if I let the piece take the path it wants (which I did not do when I was forcing it to be a short story). The sensation I get when taking a train from Grand Central station, sitting in a seat facing where you just came from (not being able to see where you are headed) is the same one I feel when I read Zion. Distance. Perspective. It took me ten years to learn how that experience sculpted me, to tell the story, to locate its pulsing heart.

Alternative Contents

Approaches to Writing and Discussing Creative Nonfiction

Memoir

Writers on Their Work

Further Examples of the Form

Further Discussion of the Form

Personal Essay

Writers on Their Work

Further Examples of the Form

Personal Literary and Cultural Criticism

Writers on Their Work

Further Examples of the Form

Further Discussion of the Form

Literary Journalism

Writers on Their Work

Examples of the Form

On Composing Processes

On Form and Genre in Nonfiction

Credits

Index